World Trade Regulation

Eun Sup Lee

World Trade Regulation

International Trade under the WTO Mechanism

Springer

Eun Sup Lee
Division of International Trade
Pusan National University
Pusan
Republic of South Korea

ISBN 978-3-642-31142-0 ISBN 978-3-642-31143-7 (eBook)
DOI 10.1007/978-3-642-31143-7
Springer Heidelberg New York Dordrecht London

Library of Congress Control Number: 2012952998

Printed on acid-free paper

Springer is part of Springer Science+Business Media (www.springer.com)

To my family: My mother in my hometown, my wife Kee Hyang Son, my three children Suh Yeon, Sung A and Seung Woon, and my teacher Young Sook Kim, for their sacrificed dedication to me while I have worked.

Preface

Toward the end of World War II, a number of international negotiations were set in motion in order to create institutional structures for the conduct of international relations in the post-war world. One of the most important negotiating processes at the time was the United Nations Conference on Trade and Employment, held in Havana, Cuba, in 1947, after lengthy preparatory stages in New York, London, and Geneva. At the end of this Conference, the Havana Charter for the International Trade Organization was adopted. The proposed ITO was an ambitious undertaking, covering not only trade, but also employment, commodity agreements, economic development, and restrictive business practice. However, for various reasons including the failure of the United States to ratify it, the Havana Charter never entered into force. As part of the negotiations on the Havana Charter, a group of countries engaged in tariff negotiations and in 1947 agreed on substantial tariff reductions.

Pending the entry into force of the Havana Charter, a mechanism was needed to implement and protect the tariff concessions negotiated in 1947. To do so, it was decided to take the Chapter on Commercial Policy of the Havana Charter and convert it, with certain additions, into the General Agreement on Tariffs and Trade. To bring GATT into force quickly, a Protocol of Provisional Application was developed and entered into force in 1948. Thus, GATT was born, as a provisional agreement until such time as the Havana Charter would be ratified. The Protocol of Provisional Application, however, stated that provisions on non-tariff barriers would apply only to the fullest extent "not inconsistent with existing legislation."

Throughout its 48-year history, GATT provided the structure for a global process of steady trade liberalization through eight "rounds" of multilateral trade negotiations sponsored by its Contracting Parties, covering progressively larger volumes of international trade. This process evolved with its own dynamics, through the initial years of the Cold War, the emergence to independence of many developing countries, the creation of the European Communities, the rise of new and important trading countries, the transition of many nonmarket countries to market economies, the increasing globalization of the world economy, and the consolidation of the multilateral trading system through the establishment of the World Trade Organization.

This process of trade liberalization achieved the reduction of tariff rates on industrial products in developed countries from an average of around 40 % to less than 4 %; the practical elimination of quantitative restrictions; the development and strengthening of clear rules for the administration of different trade policy measures such as safeguards, subsidies, anti-dumping duties, and technical barriers to trade; and development of procedures to resolve disputes. The eighth GATT round, the Uruguay Round, carried this liberalization forward.

After the Ministerial meeting of GATT Contracting Parties in 1982, which could be regarded as the seeds of the Uruguay Round, and the Ministerial meeting at Punta del Este in 1986, on December 15, 1993, every issue for negotiations was resolved, including market access for goods and services.

On April 15, 1994, the Final Act Embodying the Results of the Uruguay Round of Multilateral Trade Negotiations was signed by Ministers from most of the 155 governments participating in the Uruguay Round at a meeting in Marrakesh, Morocco.

The World Trade Organization is the institutional framework of the multilateral trading system. The Marrakesh Agreement, establishing the World Trade Organization, is included in the Final Act Embodying the Results of the Uruguay Round of Multilateral Trade Negotiations. It constitutes the principal result of the Uruguay Round and incorporates, in its Annexes, the multilateral agreements on trade in goods including the General Agreement on Tariffs and Trade, the General Agreement on Trade in Services, the Agreement on Trade-Related Aspects of Intellectual Property Rights, the Understanding on Rules and Procedures Governing the Settlement of Disputes, the Trade Policy Review Mechanism, and, for those countries having accepted them, the plurilateral trade agreements.

The Uruguay Round was the most ambitious negotiating exercise ever undertaken multilaterally. The negotiations made improvements on GATT provisions through understandings of GATT Articles; strengthened the institutions of the multilateral trading system through the creation of the WTO and the adoption of the integrated dispute settlement system; gave a more precise focus to disciplines on contingent remedy action, such as safeguards, anti-dumping, and countervailing measures; modernized border regimes through agreements on customs valuation, rules of origin, import licensing procedures, pre-shipment inspection, etc.; integrated trade in agricultural products and in textiles and clothing into the mainstream of GATT rules; adapted to the process of globalization of the world economy through the adoption of multilateral rules on trade in services and intellectual property rights protection; and further liberalized world markets through market access negotiations on all products, including agricultural products and tropical products, and trade in services.

Besides, substantial improvement in market access conditions was achieved through an average reduction in tariffs for industrial products of about 38 %.

One hundred and twenty-five countries participated in the Uruguay Round. This is another indication of the global scope and coverage of these negotiations. Unlike the Tokyo Round of 1973–1979, in which developing countries, whether members or not of GATT, were invited to participate fully in the negotiations with no preset conditions, participation in the Uruguay Round was open only to those countries declaring their intention to accede to GATT through the negotiations.

The creation of the WTO and the adoption of the integrated dispute settlement mechanism provide a solid legal basis for the multilateral trading system and for international cooperation and consultation on international trade relations.

The results of the Uruguay Round constitute a global, integrated, and interrelated package, which covers the interests of all trading partners, large and small. The new institutional and legal status of the WTO, with its integrated dispute settlement system, provides a framework for certainty, security, and stability of market access conditions, not only for trade in industrial products but also for trade in agriculture, in textiles and clothing, in services, as well as a new, coherent system of protection of intellectual property rights. The overall results of the Uruguay Round are contained in more than 500 pages of legal texts, plus over 26,000 pages of schedules of concessions and commitments in market access for goods and schedules of specific commitments on trade in services. These schedules are an integral part of the WTO Agreement.

Particularity, for the first time in history, a multilateral framework of rules was adopted for international trade in services. It consists of the General Agreement on Trade in Services (GATS), based on general rules and principles, negotiated specific commitments, and commitment to progressive liberalization through future rounds of negotiations on trade in services. Protection of intellectual property rights at the international level was systematically restructured on the basis of existing conventions; the adoption of new disciplines on the availability, scope, coverage, and use of intellectual property rights; and clear rules for their enforcement. It consists of the Agreement on Trade-Related Aspects of Intellectual Property Right (TRIPs). An important work program was also adopted on the relationship between international trade and the protection of the environment, and other issues such as investment and competition policies were clearly indicated as potential subjects for future negotiations.

In publishing this text book, I have benefited very much from the valuable materials of the WTO Homepage (http://www.wto.org/english/info_e/cont_e.htm) and its official documents. Without such materials and documents, I could not attempt to publish this book.

Particularly, I would like to thank the WTO Secretariat for the permission to use such materials in publishing this book, as well as Mr. Bernard Kuiten, Head of External Relations, for his kind and deep consideration extended to me. Special appreciation should be expressed to Mr. Eki Kim, Counselor, Market Access Division of the WTO, for his valuable comments and advice in bringing about this book.

Contents

Part I

Introduction

1 Outline of the WTO

Learning Objectives

This chapter aims to help students understand:

1. The legal structure of the WTO Agreement compared with that of GATT;
2. The operating system of the WTO compared with other international organizations such as World Bank and International Monetary Fund;
3. The contractual nature of the WTO Agreements;
4. Distinguishing factors of the WTO system from the GATT system, from the viewpoints of a legal nature, multilateral agreements and single undertaking and dispute settlement system;
5. The main functions of the WTO Agreement, particularly in relation with the member countries;
6. The main principles of the multilateral trading system as embodied in the WTO Agreement.

1.1 Structure of the WTO Agreement

1.1.1 Final Act

The Final Act[1] is the legal instrument by virtue of which participants in the Uruguay Round of Multilateral Trade Negotiations certify that the annexed agreements, including the legal texts, the schedules of concessions and commitments in trade in goods, and the schedules of specific commitments in trade in services, are the result of their negotiations. Their commitment to bring these results for consideration by their domestic authorities, and to seek their ratification, is also set out in the

[1] Final Act Embodying the Results of the Uruguay Round of Multilateral Trade Negotiation, Apr. 15, 1994, 33. I.L.M. 1125.

E.S. Lee, *World Trade Regulation*,
DOI 10.1007/978-3-642-31143-7_1,

Final Act. The Final Act embodying the results of the Uruguay Round of Multilateral Trade Negotiations was signed by Ministers in Marrakesh on April 15, 1994.[2]

1.1.2 The WTO Agreement

The agreement establishing the World Trade Organization (the WTO Agreement)[3] is the legal instrument through which all countries participating in the Uruguay Round decided to create the WTO. The WTO Agreement includes provisions on establishment, scope, functions and structure, relations with other organizations, secretariat, budget and contributions, legal status, decision-making procedures, including special voting procedures, amendment, definition of original Members,[4] accession, non-application, acceptance, entry into force and deposit, denunciation and final provisions. Since all the other agreements are annexed to the agreement establishing the World Trade Organization, the expression "the WTO Agreement" is understood to cover the totality of all the agreements.[5]

1.1.3 Annexes

The Annexes to the agreement establishing the World Trade Organization include:

Annex 1A: Multilateral Agreements on Trade in Goods: GATT 1994; Agriculture; Sanitary and Phytosanitary Measures; Textiles and Clothing; Technical Barriers to Trade; Trade-Related Investment Measures; Application of Article VI of GATT 1994 (Anti-dumping); Application of Article VII of GATT 1994 (Customs Valuation); Pre-shipment Inspection; Rules of Origin, Import Licensing Procedures; Subsidies and Countervailing Measures; and Safeguards.

Annex 1B: General Agreement on Trade in Services.

Annex 1 C: Trade-Related Aspects of Intellectual Property Rights.

Annex 2: Understanding on Rules and Procedures for the Settlement of Disputes.

Annex 3: Trade Policy Review Mechanism.

Annex 4: Plurilateral Trade Agreements: Civil Aircraft; and Government Procurement.[6]

[2] Ray et al. (2009, pp. 336–337).

[3] Marrakesh Agreement Establishing the World Trade Organization, Apr. 15, 1994, 33 I.L.M. 1125 (1994) (WTO Agreement).

[4] Hereforth, "Members" in its capitalized form refers to member nations of the WTO/GATT.

[5] WTO Agreement. *Id.* List of Annexes.

[6] Matsushita et al. (2006, pp. 7–8).

1.1.4 Ministerial Declarations and Decisions

A certain number of technical and political issues had to be covered through Ministerial Decisions and Declarations. The declarations were adopted by Ministers: the first related to the contribution of the WTO to greater coherence in the formulation of global economic policy; the second to the relationship of the WTO to the International Monetary Fund; and the third to the application of the dispute settlement system in the area of anti-dumping and subsidies and countervailing duties.

More than 20 decisions were adopted, covering three major areas: questions relating to least-developed and net food-importing countries; technical questions such as notification procedures and other questions related to the application of some of the agreements (such as on textiles and clothing, on technical barriers to trade, and on customs valuation); and pending negotiations and other issues under GATS (trade in services and the environment, movement of natural persons, basic telecommunications, etc.). Finally, a Decision was adopted on the application and review of the Understanding on Dispute Settlement. The Decisions and Declarations are not "covered agreements" and are not directly subject to dispute settlement. Some of them, however, covered are relevant to the interpretation of a covered agreement.[7]

DOHA WTO MINISTERIAL 2001

Ministerial declaration

1. The multilateral trading system embodied in the World Trade Organization has contributed significantly to economic growth, development and employment throughout the past fifty years. We are determined, particularly in the light of the global economic slowdown, to maintain the process of reform and liberalization of trade policies, thus ensuring that the system plays its full part in promoting recovery, growth and development. We therefore strongly reaffirm the principles and objectives set out in the Marrakesh Agreement Establishing the World Trade Organization, and pledge to reject the use of protectionism.
2. International trade can play a major role in the promotion of economic development and the alleviation of poverty. We recognize the need for all our peoples to benefit from the increased opportunities and welfare gains that the multilateral trading system generates. The majority of the WTO Members are developing countries. We seek to place their needs and interests at the heart of the Work Program adopted in this Declaration. Recalling the Preamble to the Marrakesh Agreement, we shall continue to make positive efforts designed to ensure that developing countries, and

(continued)

[7] Palmeter (2000, p. 466).

especially the least-developed among them, secure a share in the growth of world trade commensurate with the needs of their economic development. In this context, enhanced market access, balanced rules, and well targeted, sustainably financed technical assistance and capacity-building programs have important roles to play.

3. We recognize the particular vulnerability of the least-developed countries and the special structural difficulties they face in the global economy. We are committed to addressing the marginalization of least-developed countries in international trade and to improving their effective participation in the multilateral trading system. We recall the commitments made by ministers at our meetings in Marrakesh, Singapore and Geneva, and by the international community at the Third UN Conference on Least-Developed Countries in Brussels, to help least-developed countries secure beneficial and meaningful integration into the multilateral trading system and the global economy. We are determined that the WTO will play its part in building effectively on these commitments under the Work Program we are establishing.
4. We stress our commitment to the WTO as the unique forum for global trade rule-making and liberalization, while also recognizing that regional trade agreements can play an important role in promoting the liberalization and expansion of trade and in fostering development.
5. We are aware that the challenges Members face in a rapidly changing international environment cannot be addressed through measures taken in the trade field alone. We shall continue to work with the Bretton Woods institutions for greater coherence in global economic policy-making.

. . .. . .

11. In view of these considerations, we hereby agree to undertake the broad and balanced Work Program set out below. This incorporates both an expanded negotiating agenda and other important decisions and activities necessary to address the challenges facing the multilateral trading system.

Source: DOHA WTO MINISTERIAL 2001. November 20, 2001. WT/MIN(01)/DEC/1. http://www.wto.org

1.2 Operation of the WTO System

The WTO is run by its Member governments. All major decisions are made by the membership as a whole, either by ministers (who meet every two years) or by officials (who meet regularly in Geneva). Decisions are normally taken by consensus.[8] In this respect, the WTO is not like some other international organizations such as the World Bank and International Monetary Fund. In the WTO, power is not delegated to a board of directors, and the bureaucracy has no influence over individual countries' policies (although some analytical comments are made in the regular trade policy reviews).[9]

When the WTO rules impose disciplines on countries' policies, that is, the outcome of negotiations among the WTO Members, the rules are enforced by the Members themselves under agreed procedures that they negotiated. Sometimes enforcement includes the threat of trade sanctions. But, those sanctions are imposed by Member countries, not by the organization. This is quite different from other agencies, which can, for example, withhold credit from a country.[10]

Reaching decisions by consensus among 140 or more Members can be difficult. Its main advantage is that decisions made this way are more acceptable to all Members. And despite the difficulty, some remarkable agreements have been reached. Nevertheless, proposals for the creation of a smaller executive body, perhaps like a board of directors each representing different groups of countries, have been made periodically. But for now, the WTO is a Member-driven, consensus-based organization.[11]

1.2.1 Ministerial Conference

The WTO belongs to its Members. The countries make their decisions through various councils and committees, whose membership consists of all the WTO Members. Topmost is the ministerial conference which has to meet at least once every two years (ministers met for the first time in Singapore in December 1996). The ministerial conference can take decisions on all matters under any of the multilateral trade agreements.[12]

The WTO Ministerial Conference

The First WTO Ministerial Conference

Trade, foreign, finance and agriculture ministers from more than 120 World Trade Organization Member governments and from those in the process of

(continued)

[8] WTO Agreement. *Supra* note 3. Art. 9.1.

[9] August 2009, *supra* note 2, at 343.

[10] WTO, Understanding the WTO: The Organization (Whose WTO is it anyway?), *available at* http://www.wto.org/english/thewto_e/whatis_e/tif_e/org1_e.htm. Accessed Oct. 19, 2012.

[11] *Id.*

[12] WTO, Understanding the WTO: The Organization (Whose WTO is it Anyway?), *available at* http://www.wto.org/english/thewto_e/whatis_e/tif_e/org1_e.htm. Accessed Oct. 19, 2012.

acceding to the WTO participated in a Ministerial Conference in Singapore from December 9 to 13, 1996. The conference was the first since the WTO entered into force on January 1, 1995. It included plenary meetings and various multilateral, plurilateral and bilateral business sessions. The examined issues related to the work of the WTO's first two years of activity and the implementation of the Uruguay Round Agreements. The Singaporean Government was the official host of the Ministerial.

The Second WTO Ministerial Conference

This Second Session of the Ministerial Conference of the WTO took place at a particularly significant time for the multilateral trading system, when the fiftieth anniversary of the WTO establishment was being commemorated. On the occasion ministers paid tribute to the system's important contribution over the past half-century to growth, employment and stability by promoting the liberalization and expansion of trade and providing a framework for the conduct of international trade relations, in accordance with the objectives embodied in the Preambles to the General Agreement on Tariffs and Trade and the World Trade Organization Agreement. At the conference, they recognized the importance of enhancing public understanding of the benefits of the multilateral trading system in order to build support for it and agreed to work towards this end. Particularly, they agreed to consider how to improve the transparency of WTO operations, and to continue to improve efforts towards the objectives of sustained economic growth and sustainable development.

The Third WTO Ministerial Conference

The WTO Ministerial Conference of 1999 was a meeting of the World Trade Organization, convened at the Washington State Convention and Trade Center in Seattle, Washington, USA, over the course of three days, beginning November 30, 1999. A week before the meeting, delegates admitted failure to agree on the agenda and the presence of deep disagreements with developing countries. Intended as the launch of a new round of trade negotiations that would have been called "The Millennial Round", the negotiations were marred by poor organization and controversial management of large street protests. Developing country representatives became resentful and uncooperative on being excluded from talks as the United States and the European Union attempted to cement a mutual deal on agriculture. The negotiations collapsed and were reconvened at Doha, Qatar, in November 2001. The Doha venue enabled on-site public protests to be excluded. Necessary agenda concessions were made to include the interests of developing countries, which were learning how to form their own powerful negotiating blocs. Thus, the current round is called the Doha Development Round.

The Fourth WTO Ministerial Conference

The ministers agreed that the multilateral trading system embodied in the World Trade Organization has contributed significantly to economic growth, development and employment throughout the past fifty years. They determined, particularly in the light of the global economic slowdown, to maintain the process of reform and liberalization of trade policies, thus ensuring that the system plays its full part in promoting recovery, growth and development. They strongly reaffirmed the principles and objectives set out in the Marrakesh Agreement Establishing the World Trade Organization, and pledged to reject the use of protectionism.

The Fifth WTO Ministerial Conference

In this conference, the ministers affirmed their declarations and decisions made in Doha. They took note of the progress that had been made towards carrying out the Work Program agreed on in Doha, and recommitted that efforts be made to complete it fully. They also renewed their determination to conclude the negotiations launched in Doha successfully by the agreed date of January 1, 2005. In pursuance of the objectives, they agreed to mandate on several issues including TRIPs, public health, agriculture negotiations, services negotiation, etc.

The Sixth WTO Ministerial Conference

Here, the ministers reaffirmed the declarations and decisions adopted in Doha, as well as the decision adopted by the General Council on August 1, 2004, and their full commitment to give effect to them. They renewed their resolve to complete the Doha Work Program fully and to conclude the negotiations launched in Doha successfully in 2006.

Moreover, they emphasized the central importance of the development dimension in every aspect of the Doha Work Program and recommitted themselves to making it a meaningful reality, in terms both of the results of the negotiations on market access and rule-making and of the specific development-related issues, including agricultural negotiations, NAMA negotiations, balance between agriculture and NAMA, service negotiations, etc.

The Seventh WTO Ministerial Conference

In his report to the General Council on November 17, 2009, the WTO Director-General Pascal Lamy said that while the Ministerial Conference would not be a negotiating session, it would be "a platform for ministers to review the functioning of this house", including the Doha Round, and an occasion "to send a number of strong signals to the world with respect to the

(continued)

entire WTO waterfront of issues – from monitoring and surveillance to disputes, accessions, Aid for Trade, technical assistance and international governance". The conference took place exactly ten years after the 1999 Ministerial Conference in Seattle, a turning point in the struggle of the anti-globalization movement.

The atmosphere in Geneva just prior to the conference was soured by a demonstration which got out of hand. Genuine protestors were infiltrated by extremists who took the opportunity to shatter the tranquil surroundings by breaking some shop windows and burning a few cars. As the WTO Director-General Pascal Lamy said, it was really sad to see that demonstrators – who have the right to make their views known in a peaceful way – should have their event hijacked by a small group of people who preach violence for its own sake.

Source: Ministerial Conferences. http://www.wto.org/english/thewto_e/minist_e/minist_e.htm.

1.2.2 General Council in Three Guises

Day-to-day work in between the ministerial conferences is handled by three bodies: The General Council; The Dispute Settlement Body; and The Trade Policy Review Body. All three are in fact the same and come under a single title. The Agreement establishing the WTO states they are all the General Council, although they meet under different terms of reference. All three consist of all the WTO Members, and they report to the Ministerial Conference. The General Council acts on behalf of the ministerial conference on all WTO affairs. It meets as the Dispute Settlement Body and the Trade Policy Review Body to oversee procedures for settling disputes between Members and to analyze Members' trade policies.[13]

1.2.3 Councils for Each Broad Area of Trade

Three more councils, each handling a different broad area of trade, report to the General Council: The Council for Trade in Goods (Goods Council); The Council for Trade in Services (Services Council); and The Council for Trade-Related Aspects of Intellectual Property (TRIPs Council). As their names indicate, the three are responsible for the workings of the WTO agreements dealing with their

[13] WTO, Understanding the WTO: The Organization (Whose WTO is it Anyway?). http://www.wto.org/english/thewto_e/whatis_e/tif_e/org1_e.htm. Accessed Oct. 19, 2012.

respective areas of trade. Again they consist of all the WTO Members. The three also have subsidiary bodies.[14]

Six other bodies report to the General Council. The scope of their coverage is smaller, so they are "committees". But they still consist of all the WTO Members. They cover issues such as trade and development, the environment, regional trading arrangements, and administrative issues. The Singapore Ministerial Conference in December 1996 decided to create new working groups to look at investment and competition policy, transparency in government procurement, and trade facilitation.[15] Four more subsidiary bodies dealing with the plurilateral agreements (which are not signed by all the WTO Members) keep the General Council informed of their activities regularly.[16]

Each of the higher level councils has subsidiary bodies.[17] The Goods Council has 11 committees dealing with specific subjects (such as agriculture, market access, subsidies, anti-dumping measures and so on). Again, these consist of all Member countries. Also reporting to the Goods Council is the Textiles Monitoring Body, which consists of a chairman and 10 Members acting in their personal capacities, and groups dealing with notifications (governments informing the WTO about current and new policies or measures) and state trading enterprises.[18]

The Services Council has seen some changes in its subsidiary bodies. The completion of the basic telecommunications negotiations in February 1997 meant the end of the negotiating group, at least until the new services negotiating round, which started in 2000. In theory, the negotiating group on maritime services still exists, but with the talks suspended since 2000, the group is unlikely to be active. Other subsidiaries deal with professional services, GATS rules and specific commitments.[19]

At the General Council level, the Dispute Settlement Body also has two subsidiaries: the dispute settlement "panels" of experts appointed to adjudicate on unresolved disputes, and the Appellate Body that deals with appeals.[20]

1.2.4 Informal Meetings

It could be said that important breakthroughs are rarely made in any of these formal bodies, least of all in the higher level councils. With consensus and without voting,

[14] *Id.*

[15] *Id.*

[16] *Id.*

[17] *Id.*

[18] *Id.*

[19] *Id.*

[20] *Id.*

informal consultations within the WTO – and even outside – play a vital role in bringing a vastly diverse membership round to an agreement.[21]

One step away from the formal meetings is informal meetings that still include the full membership, such as those of the Heads of Delegations. More difficult issues have to be thrashed out in smaller groups. For much of the Uruguay Round, a system of so-called Green Room meetings was established, involving perhaps as many as 40 countries most interested in the particular issue under discussion.

Occasionally a deadlock can only be broken in a small group of two, three or four countries; sometimes at meetings they have organized themselves in their own countries. In a market access negotiation, where the final outcome is a multilateral package of individual countries' commitments, those commitments are the result of numerous bilateral, informal bargaining sessions. (Examples include the traditional tariff negotiations, and the recently concluded talks on basic telecommunications in services and on information technology products.)[22]

To this day, informal consultations in various forms play a vital role in allowing consensus to be reached, but they never appear in organization charts. They are not separate from the formal meetings, however. They are necessary for making formal decisions in the councils and committees. Nor are the formal meetings unimportant. They are the forums for exchanging views, putting countries' positions on the record, and ultimately for confirming decisions. The art of achieving agreement among all the WTO Members is to strike an appropriate balance, so that a breakthrough achieved among only a few countries can be acceptable to the rest of the membership.[23]

1.3 Nature and Function

1.3.1 Nature

The World Trade Organization, as GATT before it, is the cornerstone of the multilateral trading system. The WTO provides the institutional framework for a unique system of rights and obligations for trade in goods and services and for certain aspects of intellectual property underpinned by rules and procedures for the settlement of disputes.[24]

The multilateral agreements on trade in goods, including the country-specific schedules of tariff concessions and commitments on non-tariff barriers, are an integral part of the WTO Agreement. They provide detailed rules on how the

[21] *Id.*

[22] *Id.*

[23] *Id.*

[24] WTO Agreement. *Supra* note 3. Art. 2.1.

WTO Members may regulate access to their markets or give support to their own traders.

International trade in services is, for the first time, covered by a multilateral negotiated agreement, the General Agreement on Trade in Services (called GATS).[25] Commitments negotiated in the Uruguay Round and included in the country-specific schedules of specific commitments annexed to GATS by the WTO Members cover a wide range of domestic regulations affecting services sectors. They provide a basis on which international trade in services should develop further and provide the WTO Members with new opportunities for the export of services and for access to efficient, internationally traded services.[26]

The Agreement on Trade-Related Aspects of Intellectual Property Rights (called the TRIPs Agreement)[27] provides a new international system for the protection and enforcement of intellectual property rights. It is in part based on not only the existing international agreements and conventions administered through the World Intellectual Property Organization, but also the basic GATT principles of non-discrimination and transparency and requires Members to provide effective means for enforcing trade-related intellectual property rights.[28]

Members of the WTO recognize the contractual nature of the WTO Agreement, wherein they have made and received numerous specific concessions and commitments. The contractual nature of the WTO Agreement is reflected in its structure of rights and obligations. Every Member of the WTO has entered into commitments related to its trade policy regime and measures, including trade in goods and services and protection for intellectual property rights. Every commitment adopted by a WTO Member constitutes a right for its trading partners. Rights and obligations of WTO Members are enforced through the dispute settlement system. The WTO Members recognize the dispute settlement system as a central element in providing security and predictability to the multilateral trading system, serving to preserve their rights and obligations.[29]

Although the WTO is not, formally and legally speaking, a successor agreement to GATT 1947 in the sense of the international law of treaties, the WTO multilateral

[25] General Agreement on Trade in Services. 1994. Marrakesh Agreement Establishing the World Trade Organization, Annex 1B, Legal Instruments-Results of the Uruguay Round, 33 I.L.M. 1125 (Apr. 15, 1994). (GATS Agreement).

[26] WTO, Understanding the WTO: The Agreements-Service (rules for growth and investment). http://www.wto.org/english/thewto_e/whatis_e/tif_e/agrm6_e.htm. Accessed 15 Oct. 2003.

[27] Agreement on Trade-Related Aspects of Intellectual Property Rights. 1994. Marrakesh Agreement Establishing the World Trade Organization, Annex 1B, Legal Instruments-Results of the Uruguay Round, 33 I.L.M. 1125 (Apr. 15, 1994). (TRIPs Agreement).

[28] WTO, Understanding the WTO: The Agreements-Intellectual Property (protection and enforcement). http://www.wto.org/english/thewto_e/whatis_e/tif_e/agrm7_e.htm. Accessed Oct. 19, 2012.

[29] WTO, Dispute Settlement System Training Module: Chapter 1 (Introduction to the WTO dispute settlement system). http://www.wto.org/english/tratop_e/dispu_e/disp_settlement_cbt_e/c1s3p1_e.htm. Accessed Oct. 19, 2012.

system as such can be considered the successor to the former GATT system. Wider coverage and a genuine thrust for universal participation, however, make the WTO system clearly distinct from the old GATT system.

The WTO system has the fallowing differences from GATT system:

While GATT[30] was a set of rules, with no institutional foundation, applied on a provisional basis, the WTO is a permanent institution with a permanent framework and its own secretariat. While the GATT rules applied to trade in goods, the WTO Agreement covers trade in goods, trade in services and trade-related aspects of intellectual property rights.[31]

While GATT was a multilateral instrument, a series of new agreements were adopted during the Tokyo Round on a plurilateral – that is, selective – basis, causing a fragmentation of the multilateral trading system, the WTO has been adopted, and accepted by its Members, as a single undertaking: the agreements which constitute the WTO are all multilateral, and therefore involve commitments for the entire membership of the organization.[32]

The WTO dispute settlement system has specific time limits and is therefore faster than the GATT system; it operates more automatically, thus ensuring fewer blockages than in the old GATT[33]; and it has a permanent appellate body to review findings by dispute settlement panels. There are also more detailed rules on the process of the implementation of findings.[34]

[30] General Agreement on Tariffs and Trade.1947. 61 Stat. A-11, 55 U.N.T.S. (Oct. 30, 1947). (GATT).

[31] The GATT did not have a formal organizational constitution but functioned wholly through the customary practice and "decisions" of the Contracting Parties under Article XXV. *See* Hudec (1993, p. 261, *cited by* Chua 1998, pp. 175–176).

[32] Gupta (2008, p. 260–262).

[33] For the inefficient operation of dispute settlement procedures under GATT system. Leebron (1995, pp. 14–15). ". . . at every stage of the dispute settlement process, one of the disputants could block that process. . .the respondent. . .could block. . .to establish a panel. . .the losing party could block the adoption of the report. . .that prevailing party could take no action in the event of the failure of the other party to implement the report. . .in only one instance has the GATT ever authorized the only punishment available to parties who fail to comply with obligations. . . ."

[34] The most frequently recurring complaints about dispute settlement under GATT 1947 are indicated to include the following: GATT lacked a single dispute settlement procedure, with the Tokyo Round Code containing separate dispute settlement mechanisms, GATT dispute were sometimes resolved through the grant of waives; small countries were handicapped on achieving effective results against large countries; the GATT panel process was lengthy and subject to delaying tactics. GATT contained no provision for the automatic establishment of a panel; inadequate staff and experts often hamstrung panels on their fact finding; the insistence on approval of panel reports by consensus permitted the losing country to block adoption of reports; effective enforcement and sanctions were almost nonexistent, with the exception of bilateral retaliation, GATT did not require notification of the implementation of a panel recommendation. *See* Kennedy (1998, pp. 511–512).

Tokyo Round (1973–1979)

The Tokyo Round was the seventh trade negotiating round which was predominantly concerned with non-tariff measures. The Tokyo Round results included, in addition to tariff reduction protocols, nine special agreements, and four "understandings," dealing with subjects as follows:

- Agreements on:
  1) Technical Barriers to Trade
  2) Government Procurement
  3) Interpretation and Application of Articles VI, XVI & XXIII (Subsidies)
  4) Arrangement Regarding Bovine Meat
  5) International Dairy Arrangement
  6) Implementation of Article VII (Custom Valuation)
  7) Import Licensing Procedures
  8) Trade in Civil Aircraft
  9) Implementation of Article VI (Anti-Dumping duties)
- Understandings on:
  1) Differential and More Favorable Treatment, Reciprocity and Fuller Participation of Developing Countries
  2) Declaration on Trade Measures Taken for Balance-of-Payments Purposes
  3) Safeguard Action for Development Purposes
  4) Understanding Regarding Notification, Consultation, Dispute Settlement and Surveillance

Source: John H. Jackson, William J. Davey, and Alan O. Sykes, Jr. 2002. Legal Problems of International Economic Relations. West Publishing 5th ed. 235–237.

1.3.2 Function

Preambles of the WTO Agreement state that the objectives of the WTO are: to raise standards of living; to ensure full employment; growing volume of real income and effective demand, expanding the production of and trade in goods and services; keeping sustainable development and environmental protection; and making consideration of developing countries.[35]

Relations among Members of the WTO in the field of trade and economic endeavors should be conducted with a common underlying set of objectives: to raise the standards of living of their populations; to ensure full employment of their economies; to promote the steady growth of real income and effective demand in their markets; to expand the production of and trade in goods and services, while

[35] WTO Agreement Preambles.

allowing for the optimal use of the world's reserves in accordance with the objective of sustainable development and protecting and preserving the environment; and in a manner consistent with the respective needs and concerns of Members at different levels of development.[36]

The main functions of the WTO are summarized as: implementation,[37] administration and operation of the covered agreements; providing forums for negotiations; overseeing dispute settlements; reviewing national trade policies; and achieving coherence in global economic policy-making.[38] The WTO facilitates the implementation, administration and operation of the WTO Agreement and the Multilateral Trade Agreements, and furthers their objectives. It also provides the framework, for those of its Members that have accepted them, for the implementation, administration and operation of the Plurilateral Trade Agreements.[39]

The WTO provides the forum for negotiations on multilateral trade relations in matters covered by its various agreements. It may also, on decision by the Ministerial Conference, provide a forum for further negotiations, and a framework for the implementation of their results, on other issues arising in the multilateral trade relations among its Members.[40]

The WTO administers an integrated dispute settlement system, which is a central element in providing security and predictability to the multilateral trading system, serving to preserve the rights and obligations of the Members of the WTO.[41]

The WTO administers the Trade Policy Review Mechanism, which is designed to contribute to greater transparency and understanding of the trade policies and practices of WTO Members, to their improved adherence to the rules, disciplines and commitments of the multilateral trading system, and hence to the smoother functioning of the system.[42]

A Ministerial Declaration adopted at the Marrakesh Ministerial Meeting recognizes the role of trade liberalization in achieving greater coherence in global economic policy-making. For this purpose, the WTO cooperates, as appropriate, with the International Monetary Fund and with the World Bank.[43]

[36] WTO Agreement Preambles.

[37] There are two distinct but interactive levels for implementing the WTO Agreements: (i) by the WTO as an international institution that enforces the implementation mechanisms and methods embedded in the WTO Agreements; (ii) by each member at its national level through legislative, administrative and judicial actions that entrench the WTO Agreements into the domestic legal system. *See* Zhang (2003, p. 383).

[38] WTO Agreement, *supra* note 3. Art. 3.

[39] WTO Agreement, *supra* note 3. Art. 3.1.

[40] WTO Agreement, *supra* note 3. Art. 3.2.

[41] WTO Agreement, *supra* note 3. Art. 3:3.

[42] WTO Agreement, *supra* note 3. Art. 3.4;

[43] WTO Agreement, *supra* note 3. Art. 3.5.

TRADE POLICY REVIEW

Report by China

I. Introduction

1. China is at a critical development stage of building a moderately prosperous society. Guided by the strategic concept of scientific development and putting the interests of the people first, the Chinese Government is reconsidering its thinking on development, introducing new development pattern and improving development quality so that the socio-economic development will be accelerated on a more comprehensive, balanced and sustainable track.

……

II. General Economic Environment and Policy Direction

(1) Economic Environment

(i) Severe impact of the global financial crisis

1. In the latter half of 2008, the global financial crisis triggered by the subprime mortgage problem in the United States began to inflict an increasing impact on China's economy and development. The crisis brought the world economy into deep recession. External demand contracted drastically, resulting in a sharp decline in China's foreign trade, in particular in its exports. A lot of enterprises encountered difficulties; some even suspended production or closed down. Unemployed people increased significantly and many migrant workers had to return to their home villages. The global financial crisis not only brought greater downward pressure on China's economic growth in the short term, but also posed serious challenges to the Chinese Government in its long-term efforts to develop the economy in a more balanced way.
2. The fourth quarter of 2008 saw China's total value of imports and exports reverse to a negative growth of 1.6 % year on year, compared with the increases of 24.7 %, 26.9 % and 24.3 % registered respectively in the previous three quarters. In the fourth quarter, the first decline came in November, with a rate of 9.3 %. This was the first monthly decline year on year in China's total value of imports and exports since March 2002. In December, the figure continued to decline by 11.2 %. In the first quarter of 2009, China's total imports and exports dropped further by 24.9 %. After that the figure was not as big but still reached 22.0 % and 16.6 % in the second and third quarter of the year.

……

(continued)

3. With respect to employment, an estimate based on a sample survey suggested that among the 130 million migrant workers in China, 15.3 % or as many as 20 million either might have lost their jobs or could not find any at the time around the 2009 Chinese New Year (late January to early February) due to the fact that under the shadow of the global financial crisis many enterprises were not able to operate at full capacity.

Source: TRADE POLICY REVIEW. April 26, 2010. 2WT/TPR/G/230. www.wto.org/english/tratop_e/tpr_e/g230_e.doc

1.4 Principles

1.4.1 General Principles: Non-Discrimination

The basic principles of the multilateral trading system, as embodied in the WTO Agreement, derive mostly from the principles that constituted the foundations of GATT. Trade without discrimination is one of these basic principles, guaranteed through the operation of various clauses included in the multilateral agreements on trade in goods, in GATS, and in the TRIPs Agreement.[44]

The non-discrimination principles embedded in the WTO Agreement are most-favored-nation treatment, national treatment and transparency principles.[45]

The most-favored-nation clause[46] has been the pillar of the system since the inception of GATT in 1947.[47] The Contracting Parties to GATT 1947 were bound to grant to the products of other contracting parties treatment no less favorable than that accorded to products of any other country. Members of the WTO have entered into similar commitments, under GATT 1994 for trade in goods, under the GATS

---

[44] WTO, Basic Principles of WTO. http://big5.ec.com.cn/gate/big5/tradeinservices.mofcom.gov.cn/en/h/2007-10-24/7836.shtml. Accessed Oct. 19, 2012.

[45] *Id.*

[46] GATT, *supra* note 29. Art. 1.1. (With respect to customs duties and charges of any kind imposed on or in connection with importation or exportation or imposed on the international transfer of payments for imports or exports, and with respect to the method of levying such duties and charges, and with respect to all rules and formalities in connection with importation and exportation, and with respect to all matters referred to in paragraphs 2 and 4 of Article III,* any advantage, favor, privilege or immunity granted by any contracting party to any product originating in or destined for any other country shall be accorded immediately and unconditionally to the like product originating in or destined for the territories of all other contracting parties.).

[47] For a few fundamental principles of substantive GATT law that have historically been litigated extensively under the GATT dispute settlement mechanism, *see* Reitz (1996, pp. 573–575). "Articles I, II, III, XI and XXIII of the GATT have been cited most frequently. The numerous references to article XXIII as because that article is the framework for the GATT 1947 dispute resolution system. . . .The case distribution reveals that other important-and controversial-areas of GATT law have not been the subject of significant panel consideration. . . ."

Agreement in relation to treatment of service suppliers and trade in services, and under the TRIPs Agreement in regard to the protection of intellectual property.[48]

– Trade Disputes in Relation with **Most-Favored-Nation Treatment**
Panel Report, *Colombia-Indicative Prices and Restrictions on Ports of Entry*, WT/DS366/R (Apr. 27, 2009).

INTRODUCTION

1.1 On July 12, 2007, Panama requested consultations with Colombia pursuant to Article 4 of the Understanding on Rules and Procedures Governing the Settlement of Disputes ("DSU"), Article XXII:1 of the General Agreement on Tariffs and Trade 1994 ("*GATT 1994*") and Article 19.1 and 19.2 of the Agreement on Implementation of Article VII of GATT *1994* ("*Customs Valuation Agreement*") with respect to enacted Colombian customs regulations on the importation of certain textiles, apparel and footwear classifiable under HS Chapters 50–64 of Colombia's Tariff Schedule and arriving from Panama. Panama and Colombia held consultations on the measures on July 31, 2007. However, no mutually agreed solution was found.

1.2 On September 14, 2007, Panama requested the establishment of a panel pursuant to Article 19.1 of the *Customs Valuation Agreement*, and Article 6.2 of the DSU.

1.3 China, Ecuador, the European Communities, Guatemala, Honduras, India, Chinese Taipei, Turkey and the United States reserved their rights to participate in the Panel proceedings as third parties.

2. Main arguments of the parties:

Panama requested the Panel to find that the ports of entry measure violates Article I:1 of GATT *1994*. In Panama's view, if the discriminatory aspects of the measure could not be found to be inconsistent with Article XIII, there would need to be recourse to Article I:1 of GATT *1994*. Panama justifies this late claim on the grounds that "[i]n its first written submission, [it] did not elaborate on its Article I:1 claim because it seemed indisputable that the port of entry restrictions fall under Articles XI and XIII." Panama notes, however, in its request for establishment, that it claimed the ports of entry measure to be inconsistent with Article I:1 in addition to Article XI:1 and Article XIII:1.

Panama considers the ports of entry measure discriminatory and thus, inconsistent with Article I:1, as textiles, apparel and footwear of non-

(continued)

[48] WTO, Basic Principles of WTO, *supra* note 43.

Panamanian origin may enter at any of 11 ports, as long as the goods do not transit through Panama, while identical goods arriving from Panama may only enter at two ports. Panama considers the right to enter products at Colombian ports is a rule in connection with importation. Moreover, Panama argues that access to additional ports is an advantage that is not immediately and unconditionally extended to imports from Panama.

Colombia objects to the inclusion of what it considers a new claim and argues that the failure to develop any legal and factual arguments in respect of such claim implies that Panama failed to make a prima facie case of violation under GATT Article I:1. While Colombia acknowledges that Article I:1 of GATT *1994* is mentioned in Panama's request for establishment, Colombia submits that this claim was not part of Panama's request for establishment and is therefore not part of the Panel's terms of reference. As such, Colombia has not presented any substantive rebuttal arguments at this stage as it has decided there simply is no case to answer at the moment in the absence of any development of the claim by Panama. Nevertheless, Colombia notes that the ports of entry measure is not origin-based and does not fail to extend "immediately" and "unconditionally" an "advantage" to products originating from Panama.

CONCLUSIONS AND RECOMMENDATIONS

3. The Panel *upholds* Panama's claims that the ports of entry measure is inconsistent with Article I:1, the first and second sentences of Article V:2, the first sentence of Article V:6, and Article XI:1 of GATT *1994*.
4. The Panel *declines to rule* separately on Panama's claims that the port of entry measure is inconsistent with Articles I:1 and XIII:1 of GATT *1994*.
5. The Panel further *rejects* Colombia's defense that the ports of entry measure is justified under Article XX(d) of GATT *1994*.

Source: Panel Report. Colombia-Indicative Prices and Restrictions on Ports of Entry. 27 April 2009. WT/DS366/R. http://www.worldtradelaw.net/reports/wtopanels/colombia-portsofentry(panel).pdf

The national treatment principle[49] condemns discrimination between foreign and national goods or services and service suppliers or between foreign and national

[49] GATT, *supra* note 29. Art. 3.2 (The products of the territory of any contracting party imported into the territory of any other contracting party shall not be subject, directly or indirectly, to internal taxes or other internal charges of any kind in excess of those applied, directly or indirectly, to like domestic products. Moreover, no contracting party shall otherwise apply internal taxes or other internal charges to imported or domestic products in a manner contrary to the principles set forth in paragraph 1.).

holders of intellectual property rights. GATT 1994 and the TRIPs Agreement provide for national treatment as one of the main commitments of WTO Members. Imported goods, once duties have been paid, must be given the same treatment as domestic products in relation to any charges, taxes, or administrative or other regulations.

With regard to the protection of intellectual property rights, and subject to exceptions in existing international conventions, Members of the WTO are committed to grant to nationals of other Members treatment no less favorable than that accorded to their own nationals.[50] GATS, however, due to the special nature of trade in services, deals with national treatment under its Part III, Specific Commitments, where national treatment becomes a negotiated concession and may be subject to conditions or qualifications that Members have inscribed in their schedules on specific commitments in trade in services.[51]

Regarding the transparency principle,[52] provisions on notification requirements and the Trade Policy Review Mechanism are set out in the WTO Agreement and its Annexes, with the objective of guaranteeing the fullest transparency possible in the trade policies of its Members in goods, services and the protection of intellectual property rights: GATT 1994 deals with the publication and administration of trade regulations; GATS sets out provisions on transparency as one of the general obligations and disciplines[53]; The TRIPs Agreement establishes transparency rules.[54]

[50] TRIPs Agreement, *supra* note 26. Art. 3.

[51] GATS Agreement, *supra* note 24. Art. 17.

[52] GATT, supra note 29. Art. 10 (Laws, regulations, judicial decisions and administrative rulings of general application, made effective by any contracting party, pertaining to the classification or the valuation of products for customs purposes, or to rates of duty, taxes or other charges, or to requirements, restrictions or prohibitions on imports or exports or on the transfer of payments therefore, or affecting their sale, distribution, transportation, insurance, warehousing inspection, exhibition, processing, mixing or other use, shall be published promptly in such a manner as to enable governments and traders to become acquainted with them. Agreements affecting international trade policy which are in force between the government or a governmental agency of any contracting party and the government or governmental agency of any other contracting party shall also be published. The provisions of this paragraph shall not require any contracting party to disclose confidential information which would impede law enforcement or otherwise be contrary to the public interest or would prejudice the legitimate commercial interests of particular enterprises, public or private.).

[53] GATS Agreement, *supra* note 24. Art. 3.

[54] TRIPs Agreement, *supra* note 26. Art. 63.

– Trade Disputes in Relation with **National Treatment**

Appellate Body Report, *Dominican Republic-Measures Affecting the Importation and Internal Sale of Cigarettes*, WT/DS302/AB/R (Apr. 25, 2005).

Introduction

1. The Dominican Republic and Honduras each appeals certain issues of law and legal interpretations developed in the Panel Report, *Dominican Republic – Measures Affecting the Importation and Internal Sale of Cigarettes*. The Panel was established on January 9, 2004 to consider claims by Honduras in respect of five measures taken by the Dominican Republic in connection with the importation and internal sale of cigarettes. Honduras made claims in respect of these measures under various provisions of Articles II, III (National Treatment on Internal Taxation and Regulation), X, and XI of the *General Agreement on Tariffs and Trade 1994*.
2. The Panel Report was circulated to Members of the World Trade Organization (the "WTO") on November 26, 2004. The Panel found that: the requirement of the Dominican Republic that a tax stamp be affixed to all cigarette packets in its territory and under the supervision of the local tax authorities is inconsistent with Article III:4 of GATT 1994, which cannot be justified under Article XX(d) of GATT 1994. The Panel recommended that the Dispute Settlement Body (the "DSB") request the Dominican Republic to bring these measures into conformity with its obligations under GATT 1994.
3. The Panel found that Honduras had failed to establish that the requirement by the Dominican Republic that importers and domestic producers post a bond of five million pesos (RD$5 million) is inconsistent with Article XI:1 or, alternatively, with Article III:4, of GATT 1994.

Findings and Conclusions

4. The Appellate Body: (a) *upholds* the Panel's finding, in paragraphs 7.311, 7.316, and 8.1(f) of the Panel Report, that Honduras failed to establish that the bond requirement accords less favorable treatment to imported cigarettes than that accorded to like domestic products, in a manner inconsistent with Article III:4 of GATT 1994;
5. At the oral hearing, the participants agreed that the tax stamp regime as a whole had been altered by a new decree in October 2004. Both participants nevertheless requested the Appellate Body to rule on the WTO-consistency of the original measure. In view of the above, the Appellate Body *recommends* that the Dispute Settlement Body request the

Dominican Republic to bring the tax stamp requirement, found in this Report and in the Panel Report as modified by this Report to be inconsistent with GATT 1994, into conformity with its obligations under that Agreement if, and to the extent that, they said modifications to the tax stamp regime have not already done so.

6. The Appellate Body also *recommends* that the Dispute Settlement Body request the Dominican Republic to bring its other measures, found in the Panel Report as modified by this Report, to be inconsistent with GATT 1994, into conformity with its obligations under that Agreement.

Source: Appellate Body Report. *Dominican Republic-Measures Affecting the importation and Internal Sale of Cigarettes.* Apr. 25, 2005. WT/DS302/AB/R. http://www.wto.org/english/tratop_e/dispu_e/302abr_e.pdf

1.4.2 Market Access

Predictable and growing access to markets for goods and services is an essential principle of the WTO. This principle is fulfilled through various provisions so as to guarantee security, predictability and continued liberalization of trade. In the case of goods, a basic GATT postulate is that tariffs should normally be the only instrument used to protect domestic industry. Furthermore, tariffs should be predictable and stable.[55]

In the past, tariff negotiations were launched periodically under the auspices of GATT. These negotiations served to reduce progressively the level of tariff protection in many countries now Members of the WTO. Tariff negotiations will remain important in the future, particularly in relation to agricultural products, where all non-tariff barriers have been eliminated and substituted by tariffs, in many cases at very high levels.[56]

Security and predictability in trade in goods are achieved through the commitments embodied in the "binding of tariffs". A "bound" tariff is a tariff in respect of which there is a legal commitment not to raise it beyond the bound level. The binding of a tariff at a level higher than the tariff actually applied is considered a legitimate concession. In this case, the concession is the binding itself, that is, the commitment not to raise the tariff beyond that level.

Developed countries have normally bound their tariffs at the applied levels. By contrast, and consistently with open market policies, developing countries have adopted commitments on "ceiling bindings", that is, bindings at levels higher than the applied rates. This has allowed developing countries to substantially increase

[55] WTO, Trade Policy Courses-Chapter 3 Market Access (goods) 3.3. ictplgeorgia.ge/uploads/pages/8be2ac5bd32fdcc41810be42245bdc8e.doc. Accessed Oct. 15, 2003.

[56] *Id.*

their binding commitments, thus underpinning their open markets policies, while keeping a certain margin for protection in case of need.[57]

The contractual nature of a bound tariff concession lies in the fact that the tariff rate cannot be increased beyond the bound level.[58] However, countries would not enter into this kind of commitment without the possibility of revision when the situation of a domestic industry so requires. A Member desiring to withdraw or modify tariff bindings has to renegotiate them with other interested Members and provide compensation, that is, substantially equivalent tariff concessions on other products.[59]

GATT Rounds

One of the more important roles that GATT has played during the last four decades has been its sponsorship of a series of major multinational trade negotiations. So far there have been eight such trade negotiating "rounds."

The first five of these rounds focused on negotiations for the reduction of tariffs. As it turned out, the sixth round also focused on tariffs, although one of the expressed goals for the round was to deal significantly with non-tariff barriers. The seventh round was predominantly concerned with non-tariff measures, although considerable attention was still given to tariff reductions. Finally, the Uruguay Round continued detailed work on many non-tariff measures, but greatly expanded the scope of the trading system by adding services and intellectual property subjects, and, as previously indicated, created a significant new institution. Preliminary estimates of the trade

---

[57] *Id.*

[58] For the devices to prevent circumvention of tariff bindings under GATT/WTO system, *see* Kennedy (1998, *supra* note 33, pp. 429–430) (stating "In order to prevent circumvention of tariff bindings, GATT employs a number of devices, including (1) rules on valuation that prevent . . . from overvaluing imported items and thereby wiping out the benefit of any tariff concession, (2) rules on national treatment that require imported items and the like domestic product to be treated equally for purposes of internal taxes and regulations, and (3) rules on government subsidies to local industries where such subsidies can have the effect do lowering the price of domestically produced goods to the competitive disadvantage of the imported like product. A fourth innovation to prevent circumvention of tariff bindings was introduced in 1994. Prior to 1994, a contracting party was not required under GATT 1947 to record with GATT its "other duties or charges" under Article II. This lack of transparency made it difficult for other contracting parties to determine if a contracting party was in violation of its Article II obligations regarding such duties and charges. However, the Uruguay Round Understanding . . . required Members to record in their schedule of concessions all such "other duties or charges" levied on bound tariff items. . . . The 1994 Understanding further required Members to record in their schedule of concessions the nature and level of all other duties or charges, regardless of whether those duties and charges are imposed on bound items or on imports generally. Such recordation is without prejudice to the right of other WTO Members to challenge at any time the GATT-consistency of such other duties or charges.").

[59] WTO, *supra* note 54.

affected by the Uruguay Round include $2.7 trillion for goods, plus approximately $1 trillion for services.

From the time that the new WTO organization came into being (Jan. 1, 1995), this organization has endeavored to launch and complete a new round of negotiations (the ninth of the ongoing system, or the first under the WTO), but success has been difficult, as will be discussed at the end of this section.

Source: John H. Jackson, William J. Davey, and Alan O. Sykes, Jr. 2002. Legal Problems of International Economic Relations. West Publishing 5th ed. 234–235.

1.5 Consideration of Developing Countries

The developed Members of the WTO have committed themselves to accord high priority to the reduction and elimination of barriers to products currently or potentially of particular export interest to developing countries, including customs duties and other restrictions which differentiate unreasonably between such products in their primary and in their processed forms.[60]

There are also provisions to safeguard the interests of developing countries as follows. GATS stipulates that the increasing participation of developing country Members in world trade shall be facilitated through the negotiation of specific commitments, relating to the strengthening of their domestic service capacity and its efficiency and competitiveness through access to technology on a commercial basis; the improvement of their access to distribution channels and information networks; and the liberalization of market access in sectors and modes of supply of export interest to them.[61]

The Anti-Dumping Agreement provides that special regard must be given by the developed country Members to the special situation of developing country Members when considering the application of anti-dumping measures. The Agreement also stipulates that constructive remedies provided for by the Agreement must be explored before applying anti-dumping duties where they would affect the essential interests of developing country Members.[62]

---

[60] GATT, *supra* note 29. Art. 37(a) (. . . recalling that the basic objectives of this Agreement include the raising of standards of living and the progressive development of the economies of all contracting parties, and considering that the attainment of these objectives is particularly urgent for less-developed contracting parties.).

[61] GATS Agreement, *supra* note 24. Art. 4.

[62] Agreement on Implementation of Article VI of the General Agreement on Tariffs and Trade 1994. 1994. Marrakesh Agreement Establishing the World Trade Organization, Annex 1B, Legal Instruments-Results of the Uruguay Round, 33 I.L.M. 1125, Art. 15 (Apr. 15, 1994).

The Agreement on Subsidies and Countervailing Measures[63] calls for any countervailing duty investigation of a product originating in a developing country Member to be terminated as soon as the authorities concerned have determined that: (a) the overall level of subsidies granted upon the product in question does not exceed 2 percent of its value calculated on a per unit basis; or (b) the volume of subsidized imports represents less than 4 percent of the total imports of the like product in the importing Member, unless imports from developing country Members whose individual shares of total imports represent less than 4 percent collectively account for more than 9 percent of the total imports of the like product of the importing Member.[64]

The Agreement on Safeguards[65] provides that safeguard measures shall not be applied against a product originating in a developing country Member as long as its share of imports of the product concerned in the importing Member nation does not exceed 3 percent, provided that developing country Members with less than 3 percent import share collectively account for not more than 9 percent of total imports of the product concerned.[66]

The TBT Agreement[67] provides that in the preparation and application of technical regulations, standards and conformity assessment procedures, Members must take into account the special development, financial and trade needs of developing country Members.[68]

The SPS Agreement[69] similarly provides that in the preparation and application of sanitary or phytosanitary measures, Members must take into account the special needs of developing country Members, and, in particular, the least-developed country Members.[70]

Aside from these, there are ministerial declarations to make special consideration for the least-developed countries: At the time of the establishment of the WTO in Marrakesh, Ministers made a number of decisions in favor of the least-developed countries. Ministers decided that least-developed countries will only be required to

---

[63] Agreement on Subsidies and Countervailing Measures. 1994. Marrakesh Agreement Establishing the World Trade Organization, Annex 1B, Legal Instruments-Results of the Uruguay Round, 33 I.L.M. 1125, art. 15 (Apr. 15, 1994). (SCM Agreement).

[64] SCM Agreement. *Id.* Art. 27.10.

[65] Agreement on Safeguards. 1994. Marrakesh Agreement Establishing the World Trade Organization, Annex 1B, Legal Instruments-Results of the Uruguay Round, 33 I.L.M. 1125, art. 15 (Apr. 15, 1994). (SG Agreement).

[66] SG Agreement. *Id.* Art. 9.

[67] Agreement on Technical Barriers to Trade. 1994. Marrakesh Agreement Establishing the World Trade Organization, Annex 1B, Legal Instruments-Results of the Uruguay Round, 33 I.L.M. 1125, art. 15 (Apr. 15, 1994). (TBT Agreement).

[68] TBT Agreement. *Id.* Art. 12.

[69] Agreement on the Application of Sanitary and Phytosanitary Measures. 1994. Marrakesh Agreement Establishing the World Trade Organization, Annex 1B, Legal Instruments-Results of the Uruguay Round, 33 I.L.M. 1125, art. 15 (Apr. 15, 1994). (SPS Agreement).

[70] SPS Agreement. *Id.* Art.10.

undertake commitments and concessions to the extent consistent with their individual development, financial and trade needs, or their administrative and institutional capabilities. They furthermore decided that MFN (most-favored nation) concessions on tariff and non-tariff measures agreed upon in the Uruguay Round for products of export interest to the least-developed countries may be implemented autonomously, in advance and without staging.[71]

Assignment

To ensure students become equipped with the capability to apply knowledge from the classroom to the field, students are, in this chapter, required to write a report, deliver a presentation and participate in a discussion on the following issues:

The legislative history of the WTO Agreement, focusing on the concessions and conflicts among the Member countries, particularly stressing the conflicts between developing Member countries and developed Member countries.

References

Books

Hudec R (1993) Enforcing international trade law: the evolution of the modern GATT legal system. Lexis Law Pub

Matsushita M, Schoenbaum T, Mavroidis P(2006) The world trade organization: law, practice, and policy, 2nd edn. Oxford University Press, Oxford

Articles

Adrian TL Chua (1998) Precedent and principles of WTO panel jurisprudence. Berkeley J Int'l L 16:175

August R, Mayer D, Bixby M (2009) International business law: text, cases, and readings, 5th edn. Pearson, Upper Saddle River

Gupta S (2008) Changing faces of international trade: multilateralism to regionalism. J Int'l Com L & Tech 3

Kennedy KC (1998) The GATT-WTO system at Fitty. Wis Int'l L J 16

Leebron DW (1995) An overview of the Uruguay round results, column. J Transnat'l L 34

Palmeter D (2000) The WTO as a legal system. Fordham Int'l L J 24

Reitz C (1996) Enforcement of the general agreement on tariffs and trade. U Pa J Int'l Econ L 17

Zhang X (2003) Implementation of the WTO agreements: framework and reform. Nw J Int'l L & Bus 23

[71] Uruguay Round Agreement: Marrakesh Declaration of April 15, 1994. http://www.wto.org/english/docs_e/legal_e/marrakesh_decl_e.pdf. Accessed Oct. 15, 2003.

WTO Agreements

Agreement on the Application of Sanitary and Phytosanitary Measures, Apr. 15, 1994, Marrakesh Agreement Establishing the World Trade Organization, Annex 1B, Legal Instruments-Results of the Uruguay Round, 33 I.L.M. 1125, art. 15 (1994)

Agreement on Implementation of Article VI of the General Agreement on Tariffs and Trade 1994, Apr. 15, 1994, Marrakesh Agreement Establishing the World Trade Organization, Annex 1B, Legal Instruments-Results of the Uruguay Round, 33 I.L.M. 1125, art. 15 (1994).

Agreement on Safeguards, Apr. 15, 1994, Marrakesh Agreement Establishing the World Trade Organization, Annex 1B, Legal Instruments-Results of the Uruguay Round, 33 I.L.M. 1125, art. 15 (1994)

Agreement on Subsidies and Countervailing Measures, Apr. 15, 1994, Marrakesh Agreement Establishing the World Trade Organization, Annex 1B, Legal Instruments-Results of the Uruguay Round, 33 I.L.M. 1125, art. 15 (1994)

Agreement on Technical Barriers to Trade, Apr. 15, 1994, Marrakesh Agreement Establishing the World Trade Organization, Annex 1B, Legal Instruments-Results of the Uruguay Round, 33 I. L.M. 1125, art. 15 (1994)

Agreement on Trade-Related Aspects of Intellectual Property Rights, Apr. 15, 1994, Marrakesh Agreement Establishing the World Trade Organization, Annex 1B, Legal Instruments-Results of the Uruguay Round, 33 I.L.M. 1125 (1994).

Final Act Embodying the Results of the Uruguay Round of Multilateral Trade Negotiation, Apr. 15, 1994, 33. I.L.M. 1125 (1994).

General Agreement on Tariffs and Trade, Oct. 30, 1947, 61 Stat. A-11, 55 U.N.T.S. 194.

General Agreement on Trade in Services, Apr. 15, 1994, Marrakesh Agreement Establishing the World Trade Organization, Annex 1B, Legal Instruments-Results of the Uruguay Round, 33 I. L.M. 1125 (1994).

Part II

Regulation on Trade in Goods

2 GATT 1994

Learning Objectives

This chapter is to help students understand:

1. Legal distinctions between GATT 1994 and GATT 1947;
2. Legal status of GATT 1994 in WTO Agreements;
3. Legal instruments incorporated into the WTO Agreement;
4. Main features of GATT 1994;
5. Authority to adopt interpretation of the WTO Agreement;
6. Structure of GATT 1994;

2.1 Introduction

2.1.1 Background

The original General Agreement on Tariffs and Trade,[1] now referred to as GATT 1947, provided the basic rules of the multilateral trading system from 1948 until the World Trade Organization entered into force in 1995. These rules, which dealt only with trade in goods, were supplemented and modified by many further legal instruments adopted over the 47 years between 1948 and 1995, as a result of multilateral negotiations, protocols of accession, waivers and other decisions. Provisions of GATT 1947 dealing with such matters as accession, joint action by the Contracting Parties (the signatories of the agreement) and consultations and complaints allowed GATT to function effectively as an international organization.

[1] General Agreement on Tariffs and Trade. Oct. 30, 1947. 61 Stat. A-11, U.N.T.S. 55: 194. (GATT).

E.S. Lee, *World Trade Regulation*,
DOI 10.1007/978-3-642-31143-7_2, © Springer-Verlag Berlin Heidelberg 2012

A further important feature of GATT 1947, however, was its "grandfather clause", included in the Protocol of Provisional Application.[2] This provided that the rules in Part II of GATT 1947, which essentially dealt with non-tariff trade measures, need be applied only to the extent that they were not inconsistent with legislation in effect when a country acceded to GATT. GATT 1947 is no longer in force having been superseded by GATT 1994.[3]

GATT 1994, which sets out the main WTO rules that bear specifically on trade in goods, is legally distinct from GATT 1947. Many of its key elements, including post-1948 legal instruments, have been carried over without change from GATT 1947. Examples are the most-favored-nation rule[4] and the provisions on trade and development.[5] Other Articles carried over into GATT 1994 have effectively been modified, sometimes substantially, by individual agreements negotiated in the Uruguay Round. Some Articles are no longer valid, having been replaced by provisions of the WTO Agreement. The Protocol of Provisional Application is specifically excluded from GATT 1994.[6] GATT 1994 is defined by a short Uruguay Round agreement entitled "General Agreement on Tariffs and Trade 1994". This does not provide a new physical text for GATT 1994, but indicates the relationship between it and GATT 1947.[7]

2.1.2 Status of GATT 1994

The Marrakesh Agreement Establishing the World Trade Organization states that the General Agreement on Tariffs and Trade 1994 (GATT 1994) is an instrument legally distinct from the General Agreement on Tariffs and Trade dated October 30, 1947, annexed to the Final Act of the United Nations Conference on Trade and Employment (Havana Conference), and referred to as GATT 1947.[8]

GATT 1994, as set out in Annex 1A to the WTO Agreement, consists of: (a) the provisions of GATT 1947; (b) the provisions of legal instruments which entered into force under GATT 1947 before the date of entry into force of the WTO Agreement; (c) the Understandings on the interpretation of a number of GATT Articles, adopted at the end of the Uruguay Round; and (d) the Marrakesh Protocol to GATT 1994. The provisions of GATT 1947 incorporated into GATT 1994 include the rectifications, amendments or modifications introduced through the

[2] Protocol of Provisional Application of the General Agreement on Tariffs and Trade. Oct. 30, 1947. Stat. pts. 61: 5–6. TIAS N. 1700, UNTS 55: 308.

[3] Jackson et al. (2008, pp. 214–224).

[4] GATT, *supra* note 1. Art. 1.

[5] GATT, *supra* note 1. Art. 4.

[6] Matsushita et al. (2006, p. 9).

[7] August et al. (2009, p. 347).

[8] *Id.*, at 336–337.

terms of pre-Uruguay Round legal instruments – i.e., instruments which entered into force before the date of entry into force of the WTO Agreement.[9]

The legal instruments incorporated into GATT 1994 include: (i) protocols and certifications relating to tariff concessions; (ii) protocols of accession; (iii) waivers granted under Article XXV of GATT 1947 and still in force on the date of entry into force of the WTO Agreement; and (iv) other decisions of the contracting parties (CONTRACTING PARTIES)[10] to GATT 1947. These instruments maintain their prior status under GATT 1994. In respect of the protocols of accession, GATT 1994 excludes the provisions concerning provisional application and withdrawal of provisional application and providing that Part II of GATT 1947 shall be applied provisionally to the fullest extent not inconsistent with legislation existing on the date of the Protocol. The Uruguay Round Understandings incorporated into GATT 1994 include those on: (i) interpretation of Article II:1(b); (ii) interpretation of Article XVII; (iii) balance-of-payments provisions; (iv) interpretation of Article XXIV; (v) waivers of obligations; and (vi) interpretation of Article XXVIII.[11]

The Marrakesh Protocol to GATT 1994 is the legal instrument that incorporates the schedules of concessions and commitments on goods negotiated under the Uruguay Round into GATT 1994, and establishes their authenticity and the modalities for their implementation.[12]

2.1.3 Main Features

The scope and coverage of the provisions of GATT 1994 have been fully clarified, and have been given a firm legal basis by incorporation into a full-fledged international treaty, accepted by governments and ratified by national parliaments. Whereas GATT 1947 was based on an interim instrument under provisional application, GATT 1994 is one of the Multilateral Agreements attached to the WTO Agreement.[13]

---

[9] *Id.*, at 338.

[10] Contracting parties are "those governments which [apply] the provisions of (the GATT) under Article 26, or pursuant to the (PPA)." GATT art. 32(1), *cited by* Reitz (1996, p. 556, fn. 4); Article 25 uses "CONTRACTING PARTIES," in all capital letters, to mean "the contracting parties distinction and will utilize all capital letters to indicate those instances where the contracting parties act jointly". In the GATT 1994 agreement, the 12 European Community ("EC") nations are listed individually and as a collective. Most contracting parties are nations, but the GATT system is open to entities not recognized by the international community as sovereign nations. A "government acting on behalf of a separate customs territory possessing full autonomy in the conduct of its external commercial relations and of the other matters provided for in this Agreement may accede to (the GATT system)." For example, Hong Kong and Macau are listed as contracting parties. *See* GATT, *supra* note 1, Art. 33, *cited by id.*

[11] Agreement Establishing the WTO, Apr. 15, 1994, Marrakesh Agreement Establishing the World Trade Organization, legal Instruments-Results of the Uruguay Round, 33 I.L.M. 1125, art.2.4 & Annex 1A (1994) (WTO Agreement); *See* Matsushita et al. (2006, pp. 5–9).

[12] Jackson et al. (2008, *supra* note 3, at 216).

[13] *Id.*, at 224.

Regarding the interpretation of the WTO Agreement, in accordance with Article IX of the WTO Agreement, the authority to adopt interpretations of that Agreement and the Multilateral Trade Agreements rests exclusively on the Ministerial Conference and the General Council. However, before the entry into force of the WTO Agreement, a number of understandings on the interpretation of GATT provisions were negotiated under the Uruguay Round. These understandings are an integral part of GATT 1994. Any further interpretations will be subject to the provisions of Article IX of the WTO Agreement.[14]

Regarding the schedules on trade in goods, for every Member of the WTO there is a Schedule of Concessions on Goods which forms an integral part of GATT 1994. Each schedule incorporates all the concessions made by the Member concerned in the Uruguay Round or in earlier negotiations. Under Article II of GATT 1994 Members are obliged to accord to the trade of other Members treatment "no less favorable than that provided for in the appropriate part of the appropriate schedule". Modalities for the modification or withdrawal of a concession (or "binding") inscribed in a schedule are described in Article XXVIII of GATT 1994.[15]

In the event of a conflict between a provision of that agreement and a provision of any of the multilateral trade agreements (of which GATT 1994 is one), the provision of the WTO Agreement shall prevail to the extent of the conflict.[16] A general interpretative note to Annex 1A to the WTO Agreement, which includes all the multilateral agreements related to trade in goods, provides that, in the event of conflict between a provision of GATT 1994 and a provision of another agreement in Annex 1A, the provision of the other agreement shall prevail to the extent of the conflict.[17]

2.1.4 Structure

GATT 1994 is constituted with Parts I, II, III and IV:[18]

[14] WTO Agreement, *supra* note 11. Art. 9.

[15] GATT, *supra* note 1. Art. 2.

[16] WTO Agreement, *supra* note 11. Art. 16.3.

[17] WTO Agreement Annex 1A (In the event of conflict between a provision of the General Agreement on Tariffs and Trade 1994 and a provision of another agreement in Annex 1A to the Agreement Establishing the World Trade Organization (referred to in the agreements in Annex 1A as the "WTO Agreement"), the provision of the other agreement shall prevail to the extent of the conflict.).

[18] Jackson et al. (2008, *supra* note 3, at 216).

Part I of GATT 1994 is made up of Articles I and II. Article I, the Most Favored Nation Clause,[19] sets forth the concept of non-discrimination. Article II states the obligations applicable to the schedules of concessions of each WTO Member.[20]

Part II covers Articles III through XXIII of the General Agreement. Article III deals with the concept of National Treatment.[21] Articles IV to XIX cover a wide variety of subjects which can all broadly be regarded as non-tariff measures. Provisions in this group cover unfair trade practices such as dumping and export subsidies, quantitative restrictions, restrictions for balance-of-payments reasons (and related cooperation with the International Monetary Fund), state-trading enterprises, government assistance to economic development, and emergency safeguard measures, as well as a number of technical issues related to the application of border measures (screen quotas for cinema films, freedom of transit, customs valuation, fees and formalities, marks of origin and transparency of trade regulations).

General and national security exceptions are provided for in Articles XX and XXI, respectively. Provisions on consultations and dispute settlement in Articles XXII and XXIII are elaborated in the WTO dispute settlement rules.[22]

Part III comprises Articles XXIV through XXXV. Article XXIV deals with customs unions and free trade areas, as well as with territorial application, frontier traffic, and the responsibilities of Members for actions by their regional and local governments.[23] Articles XXVIII and XXVIII cover the negotiation and

[19] GATT, *supra* note 1. Art. 1.1 (With respect to customs duties and charges of any kind imposed on or in connection with importation or exportation or imposed on the international transfer of payments for imports or exports, and with respect to the method of levying such duties and charges, and with respect to all rules and formalities in connection with importation and exportation, and with respect to all matters referred to in paragraphs 2 and 4 of Article III,* any advantage, favor, privilege or immunity granted by any contracting party to any product originating in or destined for any other country shall be accorded immediately and unconditionally to the like product originating in or destined for the territories of all other contracting parties.); Qureshi (1996).

[20] GATT, *supra* note 1. Art. 2.1(a) (Each contracting party shall accord to the commerce of the other contracting parties treatment no less favorable than that provided for in the appropriate Part of the appropriate Schedule annexed to this Agreement.).

[21] GATT, *supra* note 1. Art. 3.1 (The contracting parties recognize that internal taxes and other internal charges, and laws, regulations and requirements affecting the internal sale, offering for sale, purchase, transportation, distribution or use of products, and internal quantitative regulations requiring the mixture, processing or use of products in specified amounts or proportions, should not be applied to imported or domestic products so as to afford protection to domestic production.).

[22] GATT, *supra* note 1. Arts. 4–23.

[23] GATT, *supra* note 1. Art. 24.1 (The provisions of this Agreement shall apply to the metropolitan customs territories of the contracting parties and to any other customs territories in respect of which this Agreement has been accepted under Article XXVI or is being applied under Article XXXIII or pursuant to the Protocol of Provisional Application. Each such customs territory shall, exclusively for the purposes of the territorial application of this Agreement, be treated as though it were a contracting party; provided that the provisions of this paragraph shall not be construed to create any rights or obligations as between two or more customs territories in respect of which this Agreement has been accepted under Article XXVI or is being applied under Article XXXIII or pursuant to the Protocol of Provisional Application by a single contracting party.).

renegotiation of tariffs. Article XXIX spells out the relationship between GATT 1994 and the Havana Charter, and Article XXXIV makes the annexes an integral part of GATT 1994. Other articles dealing with joint action, entry into force, accession, amendments, withdrawal, non-application, etc., are no longer valid as they have been overridden by corresponding provisions in the WTO Agreement.[24]

Three articles were added to the General Agreement in 1965 in the form of Part IV, Trade and Development, providing special rules and benefits for developing countries. Article XXXVI stipulates specifics about contributions to the advancement of developing countries. Article XXXVII (Commitments) outlines measures that developed country Members might, on a best endeavor basis, undertake in the trade area to promote development. Article XXXVIII (Joint action) provides for joint collaboration of the Members to further the objectives set out in Article XXXVI.

2.2 GATT 1994: Part I

2.2.1 The Most-Favored Nation Clause

The Most-Favored Nation (MFN) clause embodied in Article I[25] was the cornerstone of the GATT 1947 system, and is equally the cornerstone of the new WTO multilateral trading system. The commitment that "...any advantage, favor, privilege or immunity granted by any contracting party [now Member] to any product originating in or destined for any other country shall be accorded immediately and unconditionally to the like product originating in or destined for the territories of all other contracting parties [Members]" is the starting-point of the WTO system of rights and obligations. It is fundamental to all the multilateral trade agreements annexed to the WTO Agreements.[26]

[24] GATT, *supra* note 1. Arts. 24–35.

[25] GATT, *supra* note 1. Art. 1.1 (With respect to customs duties and charges of any kind imposed on or in connection with importation or exportation or imposed on the international transfer of payments for imports or exports, and with respect to the method of levying such duties and charges, and with respect to all rules and formalities in connection with importation and exportation, and with respect to all matters referred to in paragraphs 2 and 4 of Article III,* any advantage, favor, privilege or immunity granted by any contracting party to any product originating in or destined for any other country shall be accorded immediately and unconditionally to the like product originating in or destined for the territories of all other contracting parties.).

[26] Steger (2002). (The core principles of MFN and national treatment under GATT/WTO are evaluated to be "negative" integration rules rather than "positive" integration rules from the viewpoints that they do met tell governments what policies to adopt and that they are not positive obligations that require governments to harmonize their policies to international standards.).

2.2.2 Schedules of Concessions

Article II provides that products from one Member, upon importation into the market of another Member shall "... be exempt from ordinary customs duties in excess of those set forth and provided therein [in the Schedule of the importing Member]", thus establishing a ceiling on the level of customs duties that can be applied on a product whose tariff is bound. These products must also be exempt from all other duties and charges on or in connection with importation in excess of those imposed on the date "of this Agreement" or those directly and mandatorily required to be imposed thereafter by legislation in force in the importing Member on that date.[27]

An Understanding on this Article was negotiated in the Uruguay Round and is legally incorporated into GATT 1994. It provides, for the purposes of transparency, that the level, as of April 15, 1994, of these "other duties and charges" on tariff items included in the schedules be also registered therein and thus be subject to binding.

Current Status of Schedules of WTO Members

It was agreed at the Market Access Committee meeting of June 22, 1999 that Annex II of this document, setting out the status of schedules of the WTO Members, would be updated periodically. In this connection, the attached table is an update of the status of Members' schedules incorporating information up to March 17, 2009. The introductory text contained in Annex II of the original document has been updated to take into account developments since the last revision.

I. Introduction

All of the WTO Members have a schedule of tariff concessions which is either annexed to the Marrakesh Protocol to GATT 1994 or to a Protocol of Accession. Some Members also have schedules pre-dating the Uruguay Round which reflect concessions granted previously.

The attached table reflecting the current status of schedules of the WTO Members has been prepared for information purposes in order to assist, inter alia, the project team in the Secretariat updating the CTS files into HS2002 and into HS2007. The pending work on the schedules of concessions derives from obligations related to the introduction of the Harmonized System and its subsequent amendments, the results of the Uruguay Round, technical modifications or rectifications to the schedules, as well as renegotiations under GATT Article XXVIII. Some background information on these issues has been provided for ease of reference.

(continued)

[27] GATT, *supra* note 1. Art. 2.19(c).

The table consists of the following columns:

Column 1: Lists the WTO Members in alphabetical order. It also indicates whether or not the Member is a party to the Harmonized System Convention.

Column 2: Indicates the Roman numeral assigned to the Member's schedule. Its equivalent Arabic numeral is included in parenthesis for ease of reference.

Column 3: Indicates the situation of the Pre-Uruguay Round schedule, if any.

Column 4: Indicates whether the schedule is annexed to the Marrakesh Protocol or to a Protocol of Accession. The date of accession and references to the relevant documentation is included for the latter.

Column 5: Provides information on the transposition of Uruguay Round schedules into the Harmonized System and its subsequent amendments. In the case of Members having acceded after January 1, 1995, it also indicates the tariff nomenclature used in the schedule annexed to its protocol of accession.

Column 6: Provides information on the rectifications/modifications requested by the Member, if any.

Column 7: Provides information on the renegotiations under GATT Article XXVIII initiated by the Member, if any.

II. Harmonized System and its amendments

Introduction of Harmonized System

Following the entry into force of the Harmonized System (HS) on January 1, 1988 (HS88), the pre-UR schedules of those GATT Contracting Parties which were also contracting parties to the HS Convention were required to be transposed into the HS nomenclature. The GATT Committee on Tariff Concessions developed procedures for this purpose. A number of schedules were transposed, certified and annexed to protocols. Some Members undertook to renegotiate their schedules in connection with the implementation of the HS. The situation surrounding pre-UR schedules is set out in column 3 of the table. The term "None" is used for those Members that had no GATT schedule of concessions. It should, however, be noted that these Members did submit a schedule either during the Uruguay Round or at the time of their accession.

Source: Current Situation of Schedules of WTO Members. G/MA/W/23/Rev.7. http://www.wto.org/english/tratop_e/schedules_e/goods_schedules_table_e.htm

2.3 GATT 1994: Part II

2.3.1 Non-Tariff Measures

A number of non-tariff measures fall under provisions in Part II of GATT 1994.[28] These articles cover, successively, measures related to national treatment with regard to internal taxation and regulations,[29] screen quotas for cinema films,[30] freedom of transit,[31] anti-dumping and countervailing duties,[32] valuation for customs purposes,[33] fees and formalities,[34] marks of origin,[35] quantitative restrictions,[36] subsidies,[37]restrictions imposed for balance-of payments reasons and government assistance to economic development.[38] Further provisions in Part II deal with general and security exceptions, and consultations and complaints.[39]

2.3.2 National Treatment

Article III of GATT deals with the principle of national treatment on imported goods.[40] Paragraph 1 establishes the principle that internal taxes and other internal charges, laws, regulations and requirements, and internal quantitative regulations, should not be applied so as to afford protection to domestic production.[41]

The main obligations of national treatment refer to (i) internal taxes or other internal charges of any kind, which should not be imposed on imported products in excess of those applied to like domestic products or in a manner dissimilar to directly competitive or substitutable domestic products, and (ii) treatment in respect

[28] Jackson et al. (2008, *supra* note 3, at 216).

[29] GATT, *supra* note 1. Art. 3.

[30] GATT, *supra* note 1. Art. 4.

[31] GATT, *supra* note 1. Art. 5.

[32] GATT, *supra* note 1. Art. 6.

[33] GATT, *supra* note 1. Art. 7.

[34] GATT, *supra* note 1. Art. 8.

[35] GATT, *supra* note 1. Art. 9.

[36] GATT, *supra* note 1. Art. 11.

[37] GATT, *supra* note 1. Art. 16.

[38] GATT, *supra* note 1. Art. 12.

[39] GATT, *supra* note 1. Art. 14.

[40] The national treatment obligation in Article III of the GATT applies to de facts as well as de jure discrimination since the first affirmative ruling relating to a claim of de facto discrimination in the panel report on Japan-Customs Duties, Taxes and Labeling Practices on Imported Wines and Alcoholic Beverages, Nov. 10, 1987, GATT B.I.S.D. (34th Supp.) at 83 (1988). Steger (2002), *supra* note 26, at 141–142.

[41] GATT, *supra* note 1. Art. 3.1.

of all laws, regulations and requirements affecting[42] the internal sale, offering for sale, purchase, transportation, distribution or use of products, which should be accorded to imported products no less favorably than that accorded to like products of national origin.[43]

Local content requirements are also dealt with through provisions on internal quantitative regulations, which indicate that no Member shall require that any specified amount or proportion of any product which is the subject of the regulation must be supplied from domestic sources, or in such a manner as to allocate any such amount or proportion among external sources of supply.[44]

2.3.3 Unfair Trade Practices

Articles VI (Anti-dumping and Countervailing Duties) and XVI (Subsidies), dealing with what are sometimes known as "unfair trade practices", provide the basis for the much more detailed, and generally more constraining, rules developed in subsequent multilateral trade negotiations and now incorporated in the separate WTO Agreements dealing with anti-dumping, subsidies and countervailing duties, and agriculture.[45]

Dumping is defined as the introduction of a product into the commerce of an importing country at less than its normal value, that is, less than the comparable price, in the ordinary course of trade, for the like product when destined for consumption in the exporting Member. Anti-dumping duties may be applied in order to offset or prevent dumping, and countervailing duties for the purpose of offsetting any subsidy on the manufacture, production or export of any merchandise. In both cases, such duties may only be imposed if imports of dumped or subsidized products cause or threaten to cause material injury to an established industry in the importing country or materially restrict the establishment of a domestic industry.[46]

On subsidies in general, there is a requirement for the notification of all subsidy programs maintained by the contracting parties, and for the opportunity of consultations on limiting the subsidization whenever serious prejudice to the

[42] The operative word "affecting" is a broad term that includes internal regulations that not only govern the sale, purchase, or distribution of imported products but also those which have a negative effect on the competitive opportunities enjoyed by imports vis-à-vis the domestic like product in the importing Member is home market. *See* Report of the Panel. 1959. Italy – Discrimination against Imported Agricultural Machinery. L/833-7 S/60 (Jul. 15, 1958). GATT B.I.S.D. (7th Supp.) 60–64, *cited* by Kennedy (1998, p. 432).

[43] GATT, *supra* note 1. Arts. 3.2, 3.4.

[44] GATT, *supra* note 1. Arts. 3.5, 3.7.

[45] Qureshi (1996, *supra* note 19, at 78–81).

[46] *Id.*, at 29.

interests of a contracting party may be caused or threatened.[47] On export subsidies, it is recognized that they may have harmful effects, possibly causing undue disturbances on commercial interests, which in turn may hinder the achievement of the objectives of GATT.[48]

2.3.4 Quantitative Restrictions

Quantitative restrictions (QRs) are generally prohibited from being imposed, whether on imports or exports.[49] The only restrictions on trade allowed are duties, taxes or other charges, and not prohibitions, quotas or licensing (quantitative restrictions).[50] The provisions for the prohibition of quantitative restrictions do not apply to restrictions temporarily applied to prevent critical shortages of foodstuffs, to restrictions necessary to apply standards for commodities or to any agricultural or fisheries products.[51]

There are a number of exceptions to this general rule. Several of the WTO Agreements contain their own provisions governing the use of QRs in their own particular areas of concern. For example, the WTO Agreement on Agriculture has rules for the phase-out of QRs in this sector. In addition, some provisions contain exceptions for reasons specified in these Articles, i.e. for balance of payments reasons, in emergency safeguard action, or for reasons such as protection of public health or national security. Notification of all QRs is required by all Members.[52]

Prohibitions and quantitative restrictions, when applied, should be administered on a non-discriminatory basis;[53] that is, to all trading partners equally. In applying

---

[47] GATT, *supra* note 1. Art. 14.

[48] Qureshi (1996, *supra* note 19, at 27–29).

[49] Article 11 prohibits quantitative restrictions for two reasons: First, quotas lack the transparency of customs duties. Second, by creating an artificial short supply, quotas prevent the laws of supply and demand from determining the price at which domestic and imported goods should be sold. Kennedy (1998, *supra* note 42, at 433).

[50] For the widespread and continued use of quotas during the GATT period, *see id.*, at 433–434 (1998) (stating "When GATT 1947 entered into force, the use of quotas was widespread. Despite the Article XI commitment the use of quotas continues relatively unabated in several key economic sectors over the next five 434 decades. In some instances, import and export quotas were formalized through legal agreement between exporting and importing countries, the most notorious of these being the Multitier Arrangement on textiles and clothing that was in effect continuously from 1947 through 1994. In other instances, export quotas were put in place through legal instruments labeled "voluntary export restraints" ("VERs"). The most noteworthy of these VERs are the 1981 agreement between the United States and Japan limiting exports of Japanese automobiles to the United States, and the VERs of the 1970s and 1980s on exports of steel products. Although VERs were passed off to the public as beneficial and harmless, there is little doubt that their sting was felt in the form of higher prices to consumers.").

[51] GATT, *supra* note 1. Art.11.2.

[52] GATT, *supra* note 1. Arts 12, 18, 19, 20 & 21.

[53] GATT, *supra* note 1. Art. 18.

import restrictions, Members should aim at a distribution of trade approaching as closely as possible to the shares which various supplying countries would have obtained in the absence of the restrictions. Furthermore, when quotas are allocated among supplying countries, these should be allotted based upon the proportions supplied by the various supplying countries during a previous representative period.[54]

Import Quotas

Import quotas are limitations on the quantity of goods that can be imported into the country during a specified period of time. An import quota is typically set below the free trade level of imports. In this case it is called a *binding quota*. If a quota is set at or above the free trade level of imports then it is referred to as a *non-binding quota*. Goods that are illegal within a country effectively have a quota set equal to zero. Thus many countries have a zero quota on narcotics and other illicit drugs.

There are two basic types of quotas: absolute quotas and tariff-rate quotas. Absolute quotas limit the quantity of imports to a specified level during a specified period of time. Sometimes these quotas are set globally and thus affect all imports while sometimes they are set only against specified countries. Absolute quotas are generally administered on a first-come first-serve basis. For this reason, many quotas are filled shortly after the opening of the quota period. Tariff-rate quotas allow a specified quantity of goods to be imported at a reduced tariff rate during the specified quota period.

In the US in 1996, milk, cream, brooms, ethyl alcohol, anchovies, tuna, olives and durum wheat were subject to tariff-rate quotas. Other quotas exist on peanuts, cotton, sugar and syrup.

In the US most quotas are administered by the US Customs Service. The exceptions include dairy products, administered by the Department of Agriculture, and watches and watch movements, administered by the Department of the Interior and the Commerce Department.

Source: *International Trade Theory and Policy – Chapter 10–2. Last Updated on 6/13/06.* http://internationalecon.com/Trade/Tch10/T10-2.php

2.3.5 Emergency Safeguard Action

Emergency safeguard action is provided for instances where emergency action on imports of particular products is needed, and for the basic principles upon which the

[54] Qureshi (*supra* note 19, at 38–39).

WTO Agreement on Safeguards[55] was negotiated during the Uruguay Round. It is intended to address a situation where, as a result of unforeseen developments and the effect of obligations under GATT, including tariff concessions, a product is being imported into a country in such increased quantities and under such conditions as to cause or threaten serious injury to domestic producers of like or directly competitive products. In these circumstances, the importing Member will be free to suspend the obligation or withdraw or modify the concession, provided it fulfills certain requirements.[56]

2.3.6 Application of Border Measures

A number of other principles and provisions set out in Part II of GATT 1994 relate to border measures, including screen quotas for cinema films, freedom of transit, customs valuation, fees and formalities, marks of origin, and transparency of trade regulations.[57]

Issue of environmental border trade measures raised at Copenhagen

The WTO director-general Pascal Lamy described the outcome of the Copenhagen conference as "a step forward." The Kyoto Protocol addresses about 30 % of global carbon emissions. In contrast, the framework accord hammered out in Copenhagen may encompass the majority of world emissions. "But much work remains to be done so that we can accelerate the pace of emissions reduction and make commitments taken in Copenhagen more binding," he added. "Some have criticized the process of this meeting as cumbersome. But procedural difficulties are inevitable when leaders confront problems, which are global while remaining accountable largely to domestic politics. We are familiar with this in the WTO," he further stated.

Multilateral processes involve a great many actors and this makes reaching consensus complicated. But in the end, it is only through a multilateral process that we can achieve results, which are legitimate and credible, Lamy said. "Border measures are a hotly debated policy tool that may be applied to imported products based on their carbon footprint. The details of how that footprint would be calculated in an increasingly globalized market, where products are manufactured in a number of different countries, has itself been part of the debate," the organization said.

(continued)

[55] Agreement on Safeguards, Apr. 15, 1994, Marrakesh Agreement Establishing the World Trade Organization, Annex 1, Legal Instruments-Results of the Uruguay Round, 33 I.L.M. 1125. (Safeguards Agreement).

[56] Qureshi (1996, *supra* note 19, at 38–39; 88–92).

[57] GATT, *supra* note 1. Part. II.

The conclusion of a global climate change agreement that determines what each country must do to reduce emissions based on the environmental principle of "common but differentiated responsibility" could alleviate some of the concerns linked to trade.

As part of the Doha mandate, the WTO Members agreed to negotiate greater market opening in environmental goods and services, the relationship between the WTO rules and trade obligations set out in multilateral environmental agreements (MEAs) and on the exchange of information between those institutions. The WTO added that agreement in these areas would help address climate change by outlining: a more open market for environmental goods and services; more coherence between trade and environment rules; better cooperation between the WTO and MEAs; and by reducing fisheries subsidies, which was also part of the Doha mandate.

Source: Issue of environmental border trade measures raised at Copenhagen. January 5, 2012. http://www.engineeringnews.co.za/article/issue-of-environmental-border-trade-measures-raised-at-copenhagen-2010-01-05

2.3.7 Freedom of Transit

Regarding freedom of transit, goods, and their means of transport, are defined as being in transit when their passage across a territory is only a portion of a complete journey beginning and terminating beyond the frontiers of the country through whose territory the traffic passes. Other principles applicable to this traffic are non-discrimination and reasonableness in relation to all charges, regulations and formalities in connection with transit.[58]

2.3.8 Fees and Formalities

The principle is established that all fees and charges (other than duties) imposed on or in connection with import or export shall be limited to the approximate cost of services rendered, and shall not constitute indirect protection to domestic products or taxation for fiscal purposes. This principle applies to all fees, charges, formalities and requirements including those relating to consular transactions, quantitative restrictions, licensing, exchange control, and statistical services, as well as to documents, documentation and certification, to analysis and inspection, and to quarantine, sanitation and fumigation.[59]

[58] GATT, *supra* note 1. Art. 5.

[59] GATT, *supra* note 1. Art. 8.

2.3.9 Exceptions

Article XX (General Exceptions) and Article XXI (Security Exceptions) recognize that governments may need to apply and enforce measures necessary[60] for general purposes, such as protection of public morals, human, animal or plant life and health, protection of national treasures, etc., and for security purposes. Nothing in GATT 1994 prevents governments from adopting and enforcing such measures. In the case of general exceptions, the measures adopted are subject to the requirements that they do not constitute a means of arbitrary or unjustifiable discrimination, and that they do not represent disguised restrictions on international trade.[61]

2.4 GATT 1994: Part III

2.4.1 Territorial Application

Among international agreements, a feature unique to GATT 1994 and the WTO Agreement, as it was to GATT 1947, is the concept of a customs territory, which is the territory to which the agreement applies. This concept derives from the existence in 1947, at the end of World War II, of metropolitan and dependent territories,

[60] GATT, *supra* note 1. Art. 20(b) authorizes measures "necessary to protect human, animal or plant life or health." This provision allows Members to give priority to health over trade liberalization, provided a measure is "necessary." In US-Gasoline case, the panel examined whether U.S. Clean Air Act regulations that discriminated against imported gasoline were "necessary," within the meaning of Article 20(b). The panel agreed with the United States that "a policy to reduce air pollution resulting from the consumption of gasoline was a policy within the range of those concerning the protection of human, animal and plant life or health." The panel asked whether alternative measures were reasonably available that were either GATT-consistent or less inconsistent with it than the existing U.S. regulations. The panel concluded that a regulatory scheme that permitted importers to use individual baselines similar to those available to U.S. refiners was one such alternative, in contrast to the statutorily mandated baselines that included penalties for submission of false foreign data. In the panel's view, "the United States had not demonstrated that data available from foreign refiners was [sic] inherently less susceptible to established techniques of checking, verification, assessment and enforcement than data for other trade in goods subject to US regulation [e.g., under the antidumping or countervailing duty laws]." Panel Report. United States-Standards for Reformulated and Conventional Gasoline. WT/DS2/R. (Jan. 29, 1996), *cited by* Kennedy (1998, *supra* note 42, at 437–438).

[61] GATT, *supra* note 1. Art. 20; The Appellate Body has prescribed a sequential analysis to determine whether measures meet the requirements of one of the Article 20 exceptions: In order that the justifying protection of article 20 may be extended to it, the measure at issue must not only come under one or another of the particular exceptions-paragraphs (a) to (j) – listed under Article 20; it must also satisfy the requirements imposed by the opening clauses of Article 20. The analysis is, in other words, two-tiered: first, provisional justification by reason of characterization of the measure under the introductory clauses of Article 20. Appellate Body Report, United Stated-Standards for Reformulated and Conventional Gasoline, at 21–22, WT/DS2/AB/R (Apr. 29, 1996) (establishing the series of steps to be used by Panels in interpreting whether a measure falls under an Article XX exception).

and of customs regimes applied in the dependencies that might not be the same as in the metropolitan territory. This is the concept that has allowed not only sovereign countries but also territories such as Hong Kong, China, and Macao to be full Members (previously contracting parties under GATT 1947) of the WTO.[62]

2.4.2 Customs Territory

A customs territory is defined, as any territory with respect to which separate tariffs or other regulations of commerce are maintained for a substantial part of its trade with other territories.[63] Any state or separate customs territory with full autonomy in the conduct of its external commercial relations may be the Member of the WTO.[64]

2.4.3 Tariff Negotiations

It is common that periodically Members will engage in rounds of multilateral trade negotiations for reduction of tariffs on a reciprocal and mutually advantageous basis.[65] Members are allowed to modify or withdraw tariff concessions included in their schedules. Such action can be taken only by negotiation and agreement of Members with whom the concession was initially negotiated and with any other Member having a principal supplying interest. Consultations have to be held also with any other Member which has a "substantial interest" in the concession.

The main principle is that in these negotiations compensatory adjustment should be made so as to retain the pre-existing level of reciprocal concessions. If the Member concerned is unable to give compensation through alternative concessions the affected Members get the right to withdraw equivalent concessions that they made to that Member.[66] The Understanding on the Interpretation of Article XXVIII of GATT 1994, inter alia, extends negotiating rights in favor of small and medium-sized exporting Members, through the definition of a "principal supplying interest" as that of a Member having "the highest ratio of exports affected by the concession to its total exports".[67]

---

[62] GATT, *supra* note 1. Art. 24.

[63] *Id.*

[64] GATT, *supra* note 1. Art. 22.

[65] GATT, *supra* note 1. Art. 28.

[66] *Id.*

[67] *Id.*

Renegotiations under GATT Article XXVIII

Members are allowed to modify or withdraw concessions from their schedule through negotiation and agreement with other Members. Article XXVIII entitled "Modification of Schedules" is the main GATT 1994 provision dealing with the renegotiation of a tariff concession.

A 1957 note by the GATT Secretariat, concerning arrangements for negotiations under Article XXVIII, set out the procedural guidelines that were used until November 1980 when the current guidelines for procedures were adopted. Although the early practice makes it difficult to determine the exact number of renegotiations that took place under GATT, the Secretariat's records show that at least 42 GATT Contracting Parties initiated roughly 300 renegotiations between 1951 and 1994.

The 1980 procedures provide for a Member undertaking GATT Article XXVIII negotiations to submit to the Secretariat: (i) a report and a joint letter upon completion of each bilateral negotiation and (ii) a final report upon completion of all its bilateral negotiations. In practice, however, only 19 final reports were received by the Secretariat for the 79 renegotiations initiated between 1981 and 1994. The status recorded by the Secretariat for renegotiations lacking a final report is diverse. While in a few cases the Contracting Parties withdrew the invocation of Article XXVIII, in others they only submitted partial information regarding the bilateral agreements reached. No further information has been received by the Secretariat after the initiation of these renegotiations and only a few of them were formally carried-over into the WTO.

It remains unclear for the majority of these Pre-UR renegotiations whether they were: (i) concluded with the relevant Contracting Parties and their results incorporated into the Schedule annexed to the Marrakesh Protocol to GATT 1994 (MP) during the Uruguay Round, (ii) concluded, but its results overridden by the Schedule annexed to the MP, (iii) concluded with all the relevant Contracting Parties, but never reported or included in a schedule, or (iv) are still ongoing.

There have been 34 requests to enter into renegotiations under GATT Article XXVIII since the establishment of the WTO in 1995, 4 of which have been withdrawn, 8 have been concluded and formally certified, and 5 have been concluded but have not been certified for various reasons. Although the remaining 17 are in principle still ongoing, it should be noted that 2 of them relate to schedules which were withdrawn in the context of an enlargement of the European Communities (i.e. Hungary and Bulgaria).

Column 7 reflects the status recorded by the Secretariat for all renegotiations invoked from 1 January 1981 when the current procedures

(continued)

started being implemented. The table also includes renegotiations related to GATT Article XXIV:6. The term "unclear" has been used for all those GATT renegotiations initiated between 1981 and 1994 in which there is no final report or any other formal document indicating the conclusion of such negotiations. It should finally be noted that 19 Article XXVIII renegotiations invoked before the end of the UR by the EEC-9 and some of the EC-15 member states are not reflected therein.

Source: Renegotiations under GATT Article XXVIII. http://www.wto.org/english/tratop_e/schedules_e/goods_schedules_table_e.htm

2.5 GATT 1994: Part IV

Principles and objectives on trade and development set out in Article XXXVI of GATT 1994 refer to: rapid and sustained expansion of export earnings of developing countries; ensuring that less developed countries secure a share in the growth in international trade commensurate with the needs of their economic development (reflected in the Preamble of the WTO Agreement); improved market access conditions both for primary products and manufactures and semi-manufactures; increased collaboration with the financial institutions and United Nations organizations; and joint action by Members in the pursuit of these principles and objectives.[68]

It is provided that developed countries do not expect reciprocity for commitments made by them in trade negotiations to reduce or remove tariffs and other barriers to the trade of developing countries. An interpretative note clarifies that the sentence "do not expect reciprocity" means that developed countries do not expect developing countries, in the course of trade negotiations, to make contributions which are inconsistent with their individual development, financial and trade needs.[69]

Three main commitments are established to be given effect "to the fullest extent possible" by developed countries: priority to the reduction and elimination of tariff and non-tariff barriers to products of export interest to developing countries; restraint in introducing or increasing tariff or non-tariff barriers on these products; and restraint on imposing new fiscal measures, and consideration to their reduction and elimination in the framework of fiscal policy adjustments, on primary products wholly or mainly produced in the territories of developing countries.[70]

[68] GATT, *supra* note 1. Art. 36.

[69] GATT, *supra* note 1. Art. 36.8

[70] GATT, *supra* note 1. Art. 37.

Assignment

To ensure students become equipped with the capability to apply knowledge from the classroom to the field, students are, in this chapter, required to write a report, deliver a presentation and participate in a discussion on the following issues:

1. The difference between GATT 1947 and GATT 1994, focusing on legal status as multilateral agreements and the structure of the agreements.
2. The historical review on the conflicts and harmonization between developed countries and developing countries, focusing on the tariff-related trade measures.
3. The GATT/WTO's cooperation with other multilateral organizations including World Bank and International Monetary Bank in relation with world economic development.

Regulation on Non-tariff Measures 3

Learning Objectives

This chapter is to help students understand:

1. Importance of technical regulations from the viewpoints of the harmonization between the pursuit of member countries' policy objectives and the free trade promotion of the member countries as a whole;
2. Main objectives to implement the technical regulation from the viewpoints of member countries' domestic policy objectives;
3. Necessity to avoid the unnecessary technical obstacles to trade from the viewpoints of the multilateral trading world;
4. Necessity to extent flexibility in implementing technical regulations;
5. International harmonization of standards to reduce or eliminate technical barriers to international trade;
6. Background to establish the separate agreement on the Application of Sanitary and Phytosanitary Measures in parallel to the major agricultural trade negotiations during the Uruguay Round Negotiations;
7. Scope and coverage of the SPS Agreement in comparison with the TBT Agreement;
8. Necessity and main principles to harmonize the systems of customs valuation among WTO member countries;
9. Legislative history to establish the WTO Agreement on Rules of Origin;
10. Main reasons justifying the fact that the WTO Agreement on Rules of Origin has not yet been established;
11. Barriers to international trade arising from the implementation of pre-shipment inspection;
12. Barriers to international trade arising from the implementation of import licensing systems;

E.S. Lee, *World Trade Regulation*,
DOI 10.1007/978-3-642-31143-7_3,

3.1 Technical Barriers to Trade

3.1.1 Introduction

3.1.1.1 Importance of Technical Regulations

In recent years, the number of technical regulations and standards adopted by countries has grown significantly as a result of higher standards of living worldwide, which have boosted consumers' demand for safe and high-quality products, and of growing problems of water, air and soil pollution, which have encouraged modern societies to explore environmentally-friendly products.

Although it is difficult to give a precise estimate of the impact on international trade of the need to comply with different foreign technical regulations and standards, it certainly involves significant costs for producers and exporters. In general, these costs arise from the translation of foreign regulations, hiring of technical experts to explain foreign regulations, and adjustment of production facilities to comply with the requirements. In addition, there is the need to prove that the exported product meets the foreign regulations. The high costs involved may discourage manufacturers from trying to sell abroad. In the absence of international disciplines, a risk exists that technical regulations and standards could be adopted and applied solely to protect domestic industries.[1]

The provisions of GATT 1947 contained only a general reference to technical regulations and standards.[2] A GATT working group, set up to evaluate the impact of non-tariff barriers in international trade, has concluded that technical barriers were the largest category of non-tariff measures faced by exporters. After years of negotiations at the end of the Tokyo Round in 1979, the plurilateral Agreement on Technical Barriers to Trade (TBT) was established. The Standards Code, as the agreement was called, laid down the rules for preparation, adoption and application

[1] For the product standards (including technical regulation) as the impediments to the flow of international trade, see Kennedy (1998, *supra* note 42, at 457–458): "The elimination of tariffs as a significant barrier to trade is cold comfort to manufacturers whose products cannot enter a foreign market . . . because of nonconformity with local product standards. The cost of having products modified, tested, and approved . . . can effectively cancels the benefit of reduced tariffs. In the arsenal of weapons at a country's disposal to block the free flow of goods across national borders, one of the most insidious and effective NTBs is product standards. What makes product standards insidious is that the same standard can simultaneously be a legitimate health and safety regulation and a disguised restriction on trade. For example, a country may decide to set the bar high . . . out of a legitimate concern for the health and welfare of its citizens, but perhaps also in part to protect local manufacturers from import competition. Even when national product standards are not consciously used to block imports, standards often differ from one country to another, impeding the free flow of goods. Because of such differences, minor but costly modifications must often be made to a product destined for foreign markets."

[2] GATT, *supra* note 1. Arts. 3, 11 and 20.

of technical regulations, standard[3] and conformity assessment procedure.[4] The WTO Agreement on Technical Barriers to Trade, or TBT Agreement,[5] has strengthened and clarified the provisions of the Tokyo Round Standards Code. The TBT Agreement, negotiated during the Uruguay Round, is an integral part of the WTO Agreement.[6]

3.1.1.2 Technical Regulations, Standards and Conformity Assessment Procedures

Technical regulations and standards set out specific characteristics of a product – such as its size, shape, design, functions and performance, or the way it is labeled or packaged before it is put up for sale. In certain cases, the way a product is produced can affect these characteristics, and it may then prove more appropriate to draft technical regulations and standards in terms of a product's process and production methods rather than its characteristics per se. The TBT Agreement makes allowance for both approaches in the way it defines technical regulations and standards.[7]

The difference between a standard and a technical regulation lies in compliance.[8] While conformity with standards is voluntary, technical regulations are by nature mandatory. They have different implications for international trade. If an imported product does not fulfill the requirements of a technical regulation, it will not be allowed to be put up for sale. In case of standards, non-complying imported products will be allowed on the market, but then their market share may be affected if consumers prefer products that meet local standards such as quality or color standards for textiles and clothing.[9]

Conformity assessment procedures are technical procedures – such as testing, verification, inspection and certification – which confirm that products fulfill the requirements laid down in regulations and standards. Generally, exporters bear the cost, if any, of these procedures. Non-transparent and discriminatory conformity assessment procedures can become effective protectionist tools.[10]

---

[3] Herewith, technical regulations and standards set out specific characteristics of a product including a product's process and production methods. The difference between a standard and a technical regulation is that while conformity with standards is voluntary, technical regulations are by nature mandatory, which has different implications for international trade (*id.*, at 333).

[4] Conformity assessment procedures are technical procedures-such as testing, verification, inspection and certification-which confirm that products meet the requirements imposed by the regulations and standards. Non-transparent and discriminatory operation of such procedures may affect adversely the international trade. See (*id.*, at 334–335).

[5] Agreement on Technical Barriers to Trade. 1994. Marrakesh Agreement Establishing the World Trade Organization, Annex 1, Legal Instruments-Results of the Uruguay Round, I.L.M. 33: 1125. (Apr. 15, 1994). (TBT Agreement).

[6] Wolfrum et al. (2007, pp. 169–170).

[7] TBT Agreement, *supra* note 75. Annex 1.1.

[8] Wolfrum et al. (2007, *supra* note 76, at 187–193).

[9] *Id.*, at 197–193; TBT Agreement, *supra* note 75. Annex 1.2.

[10] *Id.*, at 197–193; TBT Agreement, *supra* note 75. Annex 1.3.

3.1.1.3 Objective of Regulation

The vast majority of technical regulations and standards are adopted to aim at protecting human safety or health. Numerous examples can be given. National regulations that require that motor vehicles be equipped with seat belts to minimize injury in the event of road accidents, or that sockets be manufactured in a way to protect users from electric shocks, fall under the first category. A common example of regulations whose objective is the protection of human health is labeling of cigarettes to indicate that they are harmful to health.[11]

Regulations that protect animal and plant life or health are very common. They include regulations intended to ensure that animal or plant species endangered by water, air and soil pollution do not become extinct. Some countries, for example, require that endangered species of fish reach a certain length before they can be caught, and soil pollution problems have led many governments to adopt regulations aimed at protecting the environment. Regulations of this type cover for example, the re-cycling of paper and plastic products, and levels of motor vehicle emissions.[12]

With regard to prevention of deceptive practices, most of these regulations aim to protect consumers through information, mainly in the form of labeling requirements.[13] Other regulations include classification and definition, packaging requirements, and measurements (size, weight, etc.), so as to avoid deceptive practices. Other objectives of regulations are quality, technical harmonization, or simply trade facilitation.[14] Quality regulations – e.g. those requiring that vegetables and fruits reach a certain size to be marketable – are very common in certain developed countries. Regulations aimed at harmonizing certain sectors, for example that of telecommunications and terminal equipment, are widespread in economically integrated areas such as the European Union and EFTA.[15]

3.1.1.4 Avoidance of Unnecessary Obstacles to Trade

Technical barriers to trade generally result from the preparation, adoption and application of different technical regulations and conformity assessment procedures. If a producer in country A wants to export to country B, he will be obliged to satisfy the technical requirements that apply in country B, with all the financial consequences this entails. Differences between one country and another in their technical regulations and conformity assessment procedures may have

---

[11] *Id.*, at 170–171.

[12] Wolfrum et al. (2007, *supra* note 76, at 170–171).

[13] For the defining labels and labeling programs, see Emslie (2005, pp. 488–493). "... Labels are not basic standard requirements for product. Instead, basic standards are the minimum requirements for a product being commercialized in a given country. Conversely, labeling programs do not pose "internal requirements" on the product ... but rather impose an 'external requirement' ...".

[14] TBT Agreement, *supra* note 75. Art. 2.2.

[15] Wolfrum et al. (2007, *supra* note 76, at 172–173).

legitimate origins such as differences in local tastes or levels of income, as well as geographical or other factors.[16]

For a government, avoiding unnecessary obstacles to trade means that when it is preparing a technical regulation to achieve a certain policy objective – whether protection of human health, safety, the environment, etc. – regulations shall not be more trade-restrictive than necessary to fulfill the legitimate objective. According to the TBT Agreement, specifying, whenever appropriate, product regulations in terms of performance rather than design or descriptive characteristics will also help in avoiding unnecessary obstacles to international trade.[17] Avoidance of trade obstacles means also that if the circumstances that led a country to adopt technical regulations no longer exist or have changed, or the policy objective pursued can be achieved by an alternative less trade-restrictive measure, they should not be maintained.[18]

Unnecessary obstacles to trade can result when (i) a regulation is more restrictive than necessary to achieve a given policy objective, or (ii) when it does not fulfill a legitimate objective. A regulation is more restrictive than necessary when the objective pursued can be achieved through alternative measures which have less trade-restricting effects, taking account of the risks non-fulfillment of the objective would create. Elements that Members can use for risk assessment are: available technical and scientific information, technology or end-uses of the products. Article 2.2 of the agreement specifies that legitimate objectives include inter alia: national security requirements, prevention of deceptive practices, protection of human health or safety, protection of animal and plant life or health or the environment.[19]

China steps up technical barrier research

In February of 2000, confronting the impact that might be brought by foreign goods after China's prospective entry into the World Trade Organization (WTO), Chinese specialists called for a study of technological barriers in accordance with common international practices and strengthening inspection and quarantine of imported and exported commodities.

(continued)

---

[16] Regarding the reasons for complication and inhibition of international trade in relation with technical regulation, see Jackson et al. (2008, *supra* note 3, at 538–539); For example, countries with areas prone to earthquakes might have stricter requirements for building products; others, facing serious air-pollution problems might want to impose lower tolerable levels of automobile emissions. High levels of per capita income in relatively rich countries result in higher demand for high-quality and safe products.

[17] Art. 2.8; For example, a technical regulation on fire-resistant doors should require that the door passes successfully all the necessary tests on fire resistance. Thus it could specify that "the door must be fire resistant with a 30-minute burn through time"; it should not specify how the product must be made, e.g., that "the door must be made of steel, one inch thick".

[18] Wolfrum et al. (2007, *supra* note 76, at 173–175).

[19] *Id.*, at 170–171.

In recent years, Chinese exported commodities had frequently encountered technical, environment-protection and green barriers. Unlike tariffs, quotas and other non-tariff measures, technical barriers are protective means conforming to the WTO rules, and had already been widely adopted by many countries, especially developed countries. Nevertheless, China was lagging far behind the developed countries in this respect.

At a national exit and entry inspection and quarantine working conference, State Counsellor Wu Yi said that in the face of the new situation regarding China's accession to the WTO, it was necessary to give further play to the role of the inspection and quarantine department. In line with the common international practices, it would become essential to appropriately adjust the inspection and quarantine supervision and management method and to properly manage staple, important commodities that affect the national economy and people's livelihood; and properly handle the important inspection and quarantine problems that affect people's health and the security of industry and agriculture, and to safeguard national interests according to law. With regard to commodities and animals and plants concerning safety, sanitation, and environmental protection, it would become necessary to set down a standard and conduct strict inspection and quarantine in accordance with common international trading practice.

The State Administration for Inspection and Quarantine of Imported and Exported Commodities vowed to step up planning and take measures for research on inspection and quarantine technical barriers immediately.

Source: China Steps Up Technical Barrier Research February 18, 2000. http://english.peopledaily.com.cn/english/200002/18/eng20000218X210.html

3.1.1.5 Provisions on Technical Regulations

The TBT Agreement takes into account the existence of legitimate divergences of taste, income, geographical and other factors between countries. For these reasons, the Agreement accords to Members a high degree of flexibility in the preparation, adoption and application of their national technical regulations. The Preamble to the Agreement states that "no country should be prevented from taking measures necessary to ensure the quality of its exports, or for the protection of human, animal, and plant life or health, of the environment, or for the prevention of deceptive practices, at the levels it considers appropriate". However, Members' regulatory flexibility is limited by the requirement that technical regulations "are not prepared, adopted or applied with a view to, or with the effect of, creating unnecessary obstacles to trade".[20]

[20] TBT Agreement, *supra* note 75. Art. 2.2.

3.1.1.6 Conformity Assessment Procedures

The obligation to avoid unnecessary obstacles to trade applies also to conformity assessment procedures. An unnecessary obstacle to trade could result from stricter or more time-consuming procedures than are necessary to assess that a product complies with the domestic laws and regulations of the importing country.[21] For instance, information requirements should be no greater than needed, and the construction of facilities to carry out conformity assessment, and the selection of samples should not create unnecessary inconvenience to the agents.[22]

Like many other WTO agreements, the TBT Agreement includes GATT's most favored nation (MFN) and national treatment obligations: In respect of their technical regulations, products imported from the territory of any Member should be accorded treatment "no less favorable than that accorded to like products of national origin and to like products originating in any other country".[23] The MFN and national treatment provisions also apply to conformity assessment procedures.

Procedures for conformity assessment shall be applied to products imported from other WTO Members "in a manner no less favorable than that accorded to like products of national origin and to like products originating in any other country".[24] This means that imported products must be treated equally with respect to any fees charged to assess their conformity with regulations. Similarly, Members must respect the confidentiality of information about the results of conformity assessment procedures for imported products in the same way as for domestic products so that commercial interests are protected.[25]

3.1.2 Harmonization

3.1.2.1 International Harmonization of Standards

Harmonization of technical regulations is necessary for the connection and compatibility of parts of products, i.e. telecommunications equipment or car parts. Lack of technical compatibility might otherwise generate barriers to international trade. For example, television sets suitable for the US market would be unsalable in Europe due to divergences in color broadcasting formats (NTSC vs. PAL or SECAM). Similarly, in order to be marketable in the United Kingdom, French or German motor vehicles need to be adjusted to right-hand drive.

---

[21] They include information requirements, setting of facilities to carry out conformity assessment, and the selection of samples. TBT Agreement, *supra* note 75. Arts. 5.2.3 and 5.2.6.

[22] TBT Agreement, *supra* note 75. Arts. 5.2.3 and 5.2.6.

[23] TBT Agreement, *supra* note 75. Art. 2.1.

[24] TBT Agreement, *supra* note 75. Art. 5.1.1.

[25] TBT Agreement, *supra* note 75. Arts. 5.2.4 and 5.2.5; Wolfrum et al. (2007, *supra* note76, at 214–217).

History of right and left hand drive

About a quarter of the world drives on the left, and the countries that do are mostly old British colonies. This strange quirk perplexes the rest of the world; but there is a perfectly good reason.

In the past, almost everybody traveled on the left side of the road because that was the most sensible option for feudal, violent societies. Since most people are right-handed, swordsmen preferred to keep to the left in order to have their right arm nearer to an opponent and their scabbard further from him. Moreover, it reduced the chance of the scabbard (worn on the left) hitting other people.

Furthermore, a right-handed person finds it easier to mount a horse from the left side of the horse, and it would be very difficult to do otherwise if wearing a sword (which would be worn on the left). It is safer to mount and dismount towards the side of the road, rather than in the middle of traffic, so if one mounts on the left, then the horse should be ridden on the left side of the road.

In the late 1700s, however, teamsters in France and the United States began hauling farm products in big wagons pulled by several pairs of horses. These wagons had no driver's seat; instead the driver sat on the left rear horse, so he could keep his right arm free to lash the team. Since he was sitting on the left, he naturally wanted everybody to pass on the left so he could look down and make sure he kept clear of the oncoming wagon's wheels. Therefore he kept to the right side of the road.

In addition, the French Revolution of 1789 gave a huge impetus to right-hand travel in Europe. The fact is, before the Revolution, the aristocracy traveled on the left of the road, forcing the peasantry over to the right, but after the storming of the Bastille and the subsequent events, aristocrats preferred to keep a low profile and joined the peasants on the right. An official keep-right rule was introduced in Paris in 1794, more or less parallel to Denmark, where driving on the right had been made compulsory in 1793.

Later, Napoleon's conquests spread the new rightism to the Low Countries (Belgium, the Netherlands and Luxembourg), Switzerland, Germany, Poland, Russia and many parts of Spain and Italy. The states that had resisted Napoleon kept left – Britain, the Austro-Hungarian Empire and Portugal. This European division, between the left- and right-hand nations would remain fixed for more than 100 years, until after the First World War.

Although left-driving Sweden ceded Finland to right-driving Russia after the Russo-Swedish War (1808–1809), Swedish law – including traffic regulations – remained valid in Finland for another 50 years. It wasn't until 1858 that an Imperial Russian decree made Finland swap sides.

The trend among nations over the years has been toward driving on the right, but Britain has done its best to stave off global homogenization. With the expansion of travel and road building in the 1800 s, traffic regulations were made in every country. Left-hand driving was made mandatory in Britain in 1835. Countries which were part of the British Empire followed suit. This is why to this very day, India, Australasia and the former British colonies in Africa go left. An exception to the rule, however, is Egypt, which had been conquered by Napoleon before becoming a British dependency.

Although Japan was never part of the British Empire, its traffic also goes to the left. Although the origin of this habit goes back to the Edo period (1603–1867) when Samurai ruled the country, it wasn't until 1872 that this unwritten rule became more or less official. That was the year when Japan's first railway was introduced, built with technical aid from the British. Gradually, a massive network of railways and tram tracks was built, and of course all trains and trams drove on the left-hand side. Still, it took another half century till in 1924 left-side driving was clearly written in a law.

When the Dutch arrived in Indonesia in 1596, they brought along their habit of driving on the left. It wasn't until Napoleon conquered the Netherlands that the Dutch started driving on the right. Most of their colonies, however, remained on the left as did Indonesia and Suriname.

In the early years of English colonization of North America, English driving customs were followed and the colonies drove on the left. After gaining independence from England, however, they were anxious to cast off all remaining links with their British colonial past and gradually changed to right-hand driving. (Incidentally, the influence of other European countries' nationals should not be underestimated.) The first law requiring drivers to keep right was passed in Pennsylvania in 1792, and similar laws were passed in New York in 1804 and New Jersey in 1813.

Despite the developments in the US, some parts of Canada continued to drive on the left until shortly after the Second World War. The territory controlled by the French (from Quebec to Louisiana) drove on the right, but the territory occupied by the English (British Columbia, New Brunswick, Nova Scotia, Prince Edward Island and Newfoundland) kept left. British Columbia and the Atlantic provinces switched to the right in the 1920s in order to conform to the rest of Canada and the USA. Newfoundland drove on the left until 1947, and joined Canada in 1949.

In Europe, the remaining left-driving countries switched one by one to driving on the right. Portugal changed in 1920s. The change took place on the same day in the whole country, including the colonies. Territories, however, which bordered other left-driving countries, were exempted. That is why Macau, Goa (now part of India) and Portuguese East Africa kept the old system. East Timor, which borders left-driving Indonesia, did change to the right though, but left-hand traffic was reintroduced by the Indonesians in 1975.

(continued)

In Italy the practice of driving on the right first began in the late 1890 s. The first Italian Highway Code, issued on the 30th of June 1912, stated that all vehicles had to drive on the right. Cities with a tram network, however, could retain left-hand driving if they placed warning signs at their city borders. The 1923 decree is a bit stricter, but Rome and the northern cities of Milan, Turin and Genoa could still keep left until further orders from the Ministry of Public Works. By the mid-1920s, right-hand driving became finally standard throughout the country. Rome made the change on the 1 of March 1925 and Milan on the 3rd of August 1926.

Up till the 1930s Spain lacked national traffic regulations. Some parts of the country drove on the right (e.g. Barcelona) and other parts drove on the left (e.g. Madrid). On the 1st of October 1924 Madrid switched to driving on the right.

The break-up of the Austro-Hungarian Empire caused no change: Czechoslovakia, Yugoslavia and Hungary continued to drive on the left. Austria itself was something of a curiosity. Half the country drove on the left and half on the right. The dividing line was precisely the area affected by Napoleon's conquests in 1805.

When Germany annexed Austria in 1938, Hitler ordered that the traffic should change from the left to the right side of the road, overnight. The change threw the driving public into turmoil, because motorists were unable to see most road signs. In Vienna it proved impossible to change the trams overnight, so while all other traffic took to the right-hand side of the road, the trams continued to run on the left for several weeks. Czechoslovakia and Hungary, one of the last states on the mainland of Europe to keep left, changed to the right after being invaded by Germany in 1939.

Meanwhile, the power of the right kept growing steadily. American cars were designed to be driven on the right by locating the drivers' controls on the vehicle's left side. With the mass production of reliable and economical cars in the United States, initial exports used the same design, and out of necessity many countries changed their rule of the road.

Gibraltar changed to right-hand traffic in 1929 and China in 1946. Korea now drives right, but only because it passed directly from Japanese colonial rule to American and Russian influence at the end of the Second World War. Pakistan also considered changing to the right in the 1960s, but ultimately decided not to do it. The main argument against the shift was that camel trains often drove through the night while their drivers were dozing. The difficulty in teaching old camels new tricks was decisive in forcing Pakistan to reject the change. Nigeria, a former British colony, had traditionally been driving on the left with British imported right-hand-drive cars, but when it gained independence, it tried to throw off its colonial past as quick as possible and shifted to driving on the right.

After the Second World War, left-driving Sweden, the odd one out in mainland Europe, felt increasing pressure to change sides in order to conform with the rest of the continent. The problem was that all their neighbors already drove on the right side and since there are a lot of small roads without border guards leading into Norway and Finland, one had to remember in which country one was.

In 1955, the Swedish government held a referendum on the introduction of right-hand driving. Although no less than 82.9 % voted "no" to the plebiscite, the Swedish parliament passed a law on the conversion to right-hand driving in 1963. Finally, the change took place on Sunday, the 3rd of September 1967, at 5 o'clock in the morning.

All traffic with private motor-driven vehicles was prohibited four hours before and one hour after the conversion, in order to be able to rearrange all traffic signs. Even the army was called in to help. Also a very low speed limit was applied, which was raised in a number of steps. The whole process took about a month. After Sweden's successful changeover, Iceland changed the following year, in 1968.

In the 1960s, Great Britain also considered changing, but the country's conservative powers did everything they could to nip the proposal in the bud. Furthermore, the fact that it would cost billions of pounds to change everything round wasn't much of an incentive... Eventually, Britain dropped the idea. Today, only four European countries still drive on the left: the United Kingdom, Ireland, Cyprus and Malta.

Source: Left Hand Drive Car Specialist. http://www.lhdspecialist.com/history_of_lhd_and_rhd.php.

In consequence, the involved costs of designing, manufacturing, and delivering the same product in various configurations may be high.

For many years, technical experts have worked towards the international harmonization of standards. An important role in these efforts is played by the International Standardization Organization (ISO),[26] the International

[26] The ISO is currently developing two series of standards directly bearing on the TBT Agreement. One series is known as the ISO 14000 series for environmental management systems, environmental auditing systems, life-cycle analysis, and environmental labeling. See generally Clements (1996); Sayre (1996); Tibor and Feldman (1996); Murray (1997, p. 577), cited by Kennedy (1998, *supra* note 42, at 461). These standards will have a far-ranging impact on environmental management programs of firms located in Members that these standards. Information on the ISO 14000 series is available at http://www.iso14000.com. Accessed Oct. 15, 2001. See generally Peterson (1997, p. 613). Information on the work by the U.S. member of the ISO on ISO 14000, the American National Standards Institute ("ANSI"), http://www.ansi.org/home.html. Accessed Oct. 15, 2001. The second series is known as ISO 9000 series of quality standards. These standards

Electrotechnical Commission (IEC) and the International Telecommunication Union (ITU). Their activities have had major impact on trade, especially in industrial products.

International Electrotechnical Commission (IEC)

The International Electrotechnical Commission (IEC) is an organization that prepares and publishes international standards for all electrical, electronic and related technologies. These serve as a basis for national standardization and as references when drafting international tenders and contracts. The IEC came into being on June 26–27, 1906 in London, UK, and ever since has been giving the very best global standards to the world's electrotechnical industries.

IEC's international standards facilitate world trade by removing technical barriers to trade, leading to new markets and economic growth. Put simply, a component or system manufactured to IEC standards and manufactured in country A can be sold and used in countries B through to Z. IEC's standards represent the core of the World Trade Organization's Agreement on Technical Barriers to Trade (TBT), whose 100-plus central government members explicitly recognize that international standards play a critical role in improving industrial efficiency and developing world trade.

IEC standards provide industry and users with the framework for economies of design, greater product and service quality, more interoperability, and better production and delivery efficiency. At the same time, IEC's standards also encourage an improved quality of life by contributing to safety, human health and the protection of the environment.

For more details, see http://www.iec.ch.

International Telecommunication Union (ITU)

International Telecommunication Union (ITU) is an agency for information and communication technology issues, and the global focal point for governments and the private sector in developing networks and services.

cover five areas in the production and manufacturing process: (1) design, development, production, installation, and servicing; (2) build-to-print, installation, and servicing without design; (3) assembly and test; (4) implementation and control; and (5) implementation of ISO 9000 (audits, certification, and registration). See Bandyopadhyay (1996); Rabbit and Bergh (1993), Hutchins (1994), Craig 1994; Thompson and Thompson (1997, p. 155). Information on ISO 9000 is available at <http://www.iso9000.com> cited by Kennedy (1998, *id.*, at 461–462). A typical use of ISO 9000 standards is in the automobile industry. In the United States, for example, the Big Tree (General Motors, Ford, and Chrysler) require that suppliers of raw materials, component parts, subassemblies, and service parts meet ISO 9000 quality standards. See Bandyopadhyay (1996, *id.*, at 4) cited by Kennedy (1998, *id.*, at 462).

ITU was founded in 1865 making it the oldest international organization in the UN family. For nearly 145 years, ITU has coordinated the shared global use of the radio spectrum, promoted international cooperation in assigning satellite orbits, worked to improve telecommunication infrastructure in the developing world, established the worldwide standards that foster seamless interconnection of a vast range of communications systems and addressed the global challenges of our times, such as mitigating climate change and strengthening cybersecurity.

For more details, see http://www.itu.int.

The agreement encourages Members to use existing international standards for their national regulations, or for parts of them, unless "their use would be ineffective or inappropriate" to fulfill a given policy objective. This may be the case, for example, "because of fundamental climatic and geographical factors or fundamental technological problems".[27] Technical regulations in accordance with relevant international standards are reputably presumed "not to create an unnecessary obstacle to international trade".

Similar provisions apply to conformity assessment procedures: international guides or recommendations issued by international standardizing bodies, or the relevant parts of them, are to be used for national procedures for conformity assessment unless they are "inappropriate for the Members concerned for, certain reasons".[28]

3.1.2.2 Equivalence

The process leading to the preparation of an international standard can be lengthy and costly. Reaching consensus on technical details can take several years. The time gap between the adoption of an international standard and its implementation by national regulators can also be significant. For these reasons, negotiators introduced in the TBT Agreement a complementary approach to technical harmonization, known as equivalence.[29] Technical barriers to international trade may be eliminated if Members accept that technical regulations different from their own fulfill the same policy objectives even if through different means.[30]

[27] TBT Agreement, *supra* note 75. Art. 2.4.

[28] They are such reasons as national security requirements, prevention of deceptive practices, protection of human health or safety, animal or plant life or health, or protection of the environment; fundamental climatic or other geographical factors; fundamental technological or infrastructural problems. TBT Agreement, *supra* note 75. Art. 5.4.

[29] This approach, based on the European Community's 1985 "new approach" to standardization, is contained in Art. 2.7 of the TBT Agreement.

[30] TBT Agreement, *supra* note 75. Art. 2.7.

Let us assume that country A, wishing to protect its environment from high auto emission levels, requires that cars be equipped with a catalytic converter. In country B, the same objective is achieved through the use of diesel engines in motor vehicles. Since environmental concerns are common in the two countries – to reduce the level of pollutant in the air – they can agree that their technical regulations are essentially equivalent. Thus, if car manufacturers in country A want to export to B, they will not be obliged to satisfy country B's requirement to fit diesel engines, and vice versa. This will eliminate the costs of adjusting production facilities to fulfill foreign regulations.[31]

3.1.2.3 Mutual Recognition

As explained in the previous section, demonstrating compliance with technical regulations may impede international trade. In particular, if products are to be exported to multiple markets, multiple testing may be required. Manufacturers can have difficulties in securing approval for their products on foreign markets, for instance, because testing experts disagree on optimal testing procedures, from bureaucratic inertia, or even from manipulation of the testing process by protectionist groups. Whatever the reason might be, such diversity of procedures and methods significantly increases the costs of producers who sell in multiple markets.

One of the main difficulties exporters face is costly multiple testing or certification of products. These costs would be drastically reduced if a product could be tested once and the testing results be accepted in all markets. In practice, countries would agree to accept the results of one another's conformity assessment procedures, although these procedures might be different. WTO Members are strongly encouraged to enter into negotiations with other Members for the mutual acceptance of conformity assessment results.

3.1.3 Transparency

3.1.3.1 Notifications

Members must notify when two conditions apply: (1) whenever a relevant international standard or guide or recommendation does not exist, or the technical content of a proposed or adopted technical regulation or procedure is not in accordance with the technical content of relevant international standards or guides of recommendations; and (2) if the technical regulation or conformity assessment procedure may have a significant effect on the trade of other Members.[32]

Each WTO Member must, promptly after the agreement enters into force for it, notify Members of the measures in existence or taken to ensure the implementation

[31] Wolfrum et al. (2007, *supra* note 76, at 228–229).

[32] TBT Agreement, *supra* note 75. Arts. 2.9–2.12.

and administration of the agreement and of any subsequent changes to them.[33] This written statement has to include, inter alia, all relevant laws, regulations, administrative orders, etc., to ensure that the provisions of the agreement are applied; the names of the publications where draft and final technical regulations, standards and conformity assessment procedures are published; the expected length of time for the presentation of written comments on technical regulations, standards or conformity assessment procedures; and the name and address of the enquiry points established under Article 10.

A Member who has reached an agreement with any other country or countries on issues related to technical regulations, standards or conformity assessment procedures which may have a significant effect on trade must notify other Members through the WTO Secretariat of the products to be covered by the agreement, and provide a brief description of the agreement.[34]

3.1.3.2 Enquiry Points

As a complement to the obligation to notify, each WTO Member must set up a national enquiry point. This acts as a focal point where other WTO Members can request and obtain information and documentation on a Member's technical regulations, standards and test procedures, whether impending or adopted, as well as on participation in bilateral or plurilateral standard-related agreements, regional standardizing bodies and conformity assessment systems.[35] Enquiry points are generally governmental agencies, but the relevant functions can also be assigned to private agencies.[36]

3.1.4 Code of Good Practice

Product standards can be prepared by governmental or non-governmental standardizing bodies. The Code of Good Practice, contained in Annex 3 of the WTO TBT Agreement provides disciplines, including those related to transparency, for the preparation, adoption and application of standards by all central governments, local governmental, non-governmental and regional standardizing bodies.[37]

The Code is open for acceptance to any standardizing bodies, whether central government, local government or non-governmental and regional standardizing bodies. The Code of Good Practice contained in Annex 3 of the WTO TBT

[33] TBT Agreement, *supra* note 75. Art. 15.2.

[34] TBT Agreement, *supra* note 75. Art. 2.9.

[35] TBT Agreement, *supra* note 75. Art. 10; Wolfrum et al. (2007, *supra* note 76, at 310–311).

[36] Wolfrum et al. (2007, *supra* note 76, at 310–311).

[37] TBT Agreement, *supra* note 75. Annex 3; TBT Agreement, *supra* note 5. Art. 10; Wolfrum et al. (2007, *supra* note 76, at 247).

Agreement seeks to bring all standards within its purview and provides for [and gives] transparency in the preparation, adoption and application of standards.[38]

Members of the TBT Agreement are responsible for the acceptance and compliance with the Code of Good Practice by their central government standardizing bodies. Furthermore, they are required to take such reasonable measures as may be available to them to ensure also that local government and non-governmental standardizing bodies within their territories, and regional standardizing bodies of which they are members, accept and comply with the code.[39]

– Trade Disputes in Relation with **TBT Agreement**

Appellate Body Report, *European Communities Measure Affecting Asbestos and Asbestos-containing product*, para. 1, WT/DS135/AB/R (Mar. 12, 2001) (EC-Asbestos AB Report).

Facts and Overview

Canada was disappointed with the Panel's findings and appealed the decision to the Appellate Body. The reexamination of the French Decree No. 961133 concerning asbestos and asbestos containing products and the Canadian claim against the decree began on January 1, 1997.

Canada claims the decree was inconsistent with Article 2 of the Agreement on Technical Barriers to Trade (the TBT Agreement), Articles III & XI of the General Agreement on Tariffs and Trade 1994 (GATT 1994) and the decree nullified or impaired advantages Canada had accrued directly or indirectly from the Marrakesh Agreement Establishing the World Trade Organization (the WTO Agreement) when that agreement is examined under Article XXIII: 1 (b) of GATT 1994. The Panel Report given to the WTO Members on 18 September 2000 concluded that:

a) The "prohibition" part of the Decree does not fall within the scope of the TBT Agreement. The part of the Decree relating to the "exceptions" does fall within the scope of the TBT Agreement. However, as Canada has not made any claim concerning the compatibility with the TBT Agreement of the part of the Decree relating to exceptions, the Panel refrains from reaching any conclusion with regard to the latter.
b) Chrysotile asbestos fibers as such and fibers that can be substituted for them as such are like products within the meaning of Article III: 4 of GATT 1994. Similarly, the Panel concludes that the asbestos-cement

[38] TBT Agreement, *supra* note 75. Annex 3, sub-Annex B.

[39] TBT Agreement, *supra* note 75. Annex 3, sub Annex A–C.

products and the fibro-cement products for which sufficient information has been submitted to the Panel are like products with the meaning of Article III: 4 of GATT 1994.

c) With respect to the products found to be like, the Panel concludes that the decree violates Article III: 4 of GATT 1994.
d) However, the decree, insofar as it introduces a treatment of these products that is discriminatory under Article III: 4, is justified as such and in its implementation by the provisions of paragraph (b) and the introductory clause of Article XX of GATT 1994.
e) Finally, Canada has not established that it suffered non-violation nullification or impairment of a benefit within the meaning of Article XXIII: 1(b) of GATT 1994.

The Panel did not find it necessary to consider the claims of Canada under Article XI of GATT 1994.

Unsatisfied with the Panel's conclusions, Canada appealed specific aspects of the Panel's Report to the Dispute Settlement Body pursuant to Article 16.4 of the Understanding on Rules and Procedures Governing the Settlement of Disputes (the DSU), Canada filed an appellant's submission on 16 November 2000. The next month involved appellant submissions, appellate submissions and third participant submission by all parties connected to the case.

The Appellate Body decided that the Panel's finding in paragraph 8.72(a) of the Panel's Report that the TBT Agreement does not apply to the part of the decree relating to the ban on imports of asbestos and asbestos containing products because that part does not constitute a "technical regulation" within the meaning of Annex 1.1 to the TBT Agreement should be reversed. In the Appellate Body's view the measure is a "technical regulation" under the TBT Agreement. The exception clause does not make sense unless considered as a part of a whole. Consequently the Appellate Body reverses the Panel's 2-stage examination. When considered as a whole, the Decree becomes a technical regulation because it

a) affects more than one product;
b) specifies technical characteristics (in the exception clause);
c) compliance is mandatory.

Additionally, the Appellate Body considers it necessary to examine the health risks associated with chrysotile asbestos fibers under likeness under Article III: 4. Consequently the Appellate Body reverse the Panel's findings on paragraphs 8.132 and 8.149 of the Panel Report. The Appellate body also disagree that chrysotile asbestos fibers and PCG fibers are like product; nor does the Appellate body consider Canada to have satisfied the burden of proof that these fibers are like. Since the Chrysotile fibers and PCG fibers are not like products under Article III: 4 of GATT 1994. This will also mean that paragraph 8.158 of the Panel Report is inconsistent with Article III: 4 of GATT 1994.

(continued)

The Appellate agrees that paragraphs 8.194, 8.222, 8.223 of the Panel Report is "necessary to protect human . . . life or health" under Article XX (b) of GATT 1994 and supports the Panel's action as consistent with Article 11 of the DSU. Additionally, the Panel's finding, in paragraphs 8.265 and 8.274 of the Panel Report may encourage a cause of action under Article XXIII: 1 (b) of GATT 1994.

Canada's bid to appeal the Panel's decision was unsuccessful and Canada is considered to have not provided evidence that the measure is not consistent with various obligations of the European Communities under the current agreements.

Source: Appellate Body Report. *European Communities Measure Affecting Asbestos and Asbestos-containing product*, para. 1. 12 March 2001. WT/DS135/AB/R. http://www.wto.org/english/tratop_e/dispu_e/135abr_e.pdf

3.2 Sanitary and Phytosanitary Measures

3.2.1 Introduction

During the Uruguay Round, agricultural negotiations strove to lower barriers that countries used to protect their domestic markets. Some countries feared, however, that the elimination of agriculture-specific non-tariff measures and the tariff reductions would be circumvented by disguised protectionist measures in the form of sanitary or phytosanitary regulations.[40] This concern provided a major driving force which led negotiators to create a separate Agreement on the Application of Sanitary and Phytosanitary Measures (the "SPS Agreement"),[41] in parallel to the major agricultural trade negotiations.[42]

[40] As the importance of traditional trade barriers diminished, the world trading regime turned its attention to other issues such as licensing requirements, safety and health standards, and other domestic measures that restricted the importation of foreign goods and services, or disproportionately disadvantaged such goods and services once they entered the country. Such measures are, of course, much harder to identify and even harder to remove than simple tariffs and quotas (Young 2001, pp. 753, 769).

[41] Agreement on the Application of Sanitary and Phytosanitary Measures. 1994. Marrakesh Agreement Establishing the World Trade Organization, Annex 1, Legal Instruments-Results of the Uruguay Round, 33 I.L.M. 1125 (Apr. 15, 1994). (SPS Agreement).

[42] The SPS Agreement applies, inter alia, to measures to protect human life from risks arising from additives, contaminants, toxins or disease-carrying organisms in foods and beverages (Jackson et al. 2008, *supra* note 3, at 539).

The SPS and Agriculture Agreements are complementary,[43] but they differ in their design. While the Agreement on Agriculture contains not only rule-based commitments, but also detailed, specific quantitative commitments to reduce protection and support over a well-defined implementation period,[44] the SPS Agreement does not impose any quantitative and legally-binding schedules of concessions. It is a set of rules, principles and benchmarks for the WTO Members to ensure, among other things, that sanitary and phytosanitary trade measures are justified and do not constitute disguised restrictions on international trade.[45]

Prior to the negotiation of the SPS Agreement, many food safety, animal and plant health regulations fell within the scope of the plurilateral 1979 Agreement on Technical Barriers to Trade (TBT). The "TBT Agreement", also called the "Standards Code", resulted from the Tokyo Round of multilateral negotiations.[46] In light of the reforms resulting from the agricultural trade negotiations, it was felt that the relationship between health protection and trade measures required more specific and in-depth coverage than the Standards Code provided.

Another potential loophole existed in GATT 1947, under Article XX, General Exceptions, point (b). Under this clause, a measure could be exempt from other

[43] For the problem of misuse of SPS measures in connection with imports of agricultural products, see Kennedy (1998, p. 456–457). "There was a concern in some quarters that as the provisions of the Uruguay Round Agreement on Agriculture eliminate or substantially reduce tariff and quota barriers to agricultural trade, a new set of SPS measures would be introduced as contingent protection, … . To counter such a development preemptively, the SPS Agreement was negotiated … to ensure that the benefits of liberalized agricultural trade are not diluted. Indeed, Art. 14 of the Agreement on Agriculture underscore the importance of not allowing unjustified SPS measures to undermine the gains of the Agriculture Agreement. It provides that 'Member agree to give effect to the Agreement on the Application of Sanitary and Phytosanitary Measure.' As illustrated by the long-brewing dispute between the United States and the EU over the 1987 EU ban on U.S. beef from cattle fed with growth-inducing hormones, the problem of SPS measures used to block trade in agricultural products is a real one. The United States claimed the ban lacked any scientific justification, a position with which the EU took strong issue. The issue finally was resolved by the Appellate Body in 1998 in favor of the United Stated."

[44] The Agreement on Agriculture is part of a package of Uruguay Round Agreement that addresses agricultural trade issues. The Agreement has three main features: (1) increased market access for agricultural products; (2) commitments to reduce domestic subsidies on agricultural products; and (3) commitments to reduce export subsidies on agricultural products. The long-term objective of the WTO Members is to establish a fair and market-oriented agricultural trading system that includes substantial in agricultural support and protection. See Agreement on Agriculture, preamble, para. 2, cited by Kennedy (1998, *supra* note 42, at 463). The Agreement on Agriculture initiates this reform process in the areas of market access, domestic subsidies, and export subsidies (Kennedy 1998, *id*).

[45] SPS Agreement, *supra* note 111. Art. 2.3.

[46] This Code permitted its limited number of signatories to introduce potentially trade-restrictive technical or sanitary and phytosanitary regulations in the pursuit of a "legitimate" objective, by invoking for example the protection of human, animal or plant health, the protection of the environment, animal welfare, religious considerations, and national security motives.

GATT provisions if it was "necessary[47] to protect human, animal or plant life or health". There was some concern that in the absence of clearer and more detailed rules on the scope of measures permitted in this regard governments would be pressured to resort to sanitary barriers as a device to shield domestic industries from competition and to frustrate measures to liberalize trade in agriculture. This added further weight to the view that a self-contained agreement was needed in order to provide an expanded and clearer set of rules and principles[48] regulating the application of sanitary and phytosanitary measures.[49]

Considering the concern about possible disguised restrictions on international trade under TBT Agreement and Article XX of GATT, the SPS Agreement provides an expanded and clearer set of rules and principles[50] regulating the application of sanitary and phytosanitary measures.[51] The SPS and TBT Agreement are complementary[52] formally but different in their design.[53] Thus, the TBT

---

[47] For the meaning of "necessary to" in Art. XX(b) language, see Rogers and Withlock (2002, pp. 488–489). "The Appellate Body in the Reformulated Gasoline case stressed the importance of differentiating among measures 'essential' n105 or 'necessary,' as opposed to measures merely 'relating to,' 'in pursuance of,' 'for the protection of,' or 'involving'. Such distinctions must be because 'an interpreter is not free to adopt a reading that would result in reducing whole clauses . . . to redundancy or inutility.' The Appellate Body argued that a measure that is 'necessary' or 'essential' to some state interest would require a greater 'degree of connection' with the state interest than a measure that is merely 'relation to' a given state interest. Similarly, because 'necessary' does neo imply as close and imperative a relationship as 'essential' n113 measures 'necessary' to a state interest permit greater flexibility in design than measures 'essential' to a state interest. Thus, trade restrictive measures under Art. XX range from 'essential' measures to measure 'involving' a state interest: an 'essential' measure must be the least trade-restrictive alternative, while a measure 'involving' a state interest may be any one of many alternatives. Measures 'necessary' to the attainment of a given state interest are closer to the middle of the spectrum than 'essential' measures, so a country instituting a 'necessary' measure would not be limited to the single least trade-restrictive measure conceivable."

[48] The Agreement on Agriculture contains not only rule-based commitments, but also quantitative commitments to reduce protection while the SPS Agreement does not impose any quantitative and legally binding schedules of concessions.

[49] Herewith, sanitary measures are those related to human or animal health, and phytosanitary measures deal with plant health. WTO, SPS Agreement. http://www.wto.org/english/thewto_e/whatis_e/eol/e/world.htm. Accessed Oct.15, 2003.

[50] The Agreement on Agriculture contains not only rule-based commitments, but also quantitative commitments to reduce protection while the SPS Agreement does not impose any quantitative and legally binding schedules of concessions.

[51] Herewith, sanitary measures are those related to human or animal health, and phytosanitary measures deal with plant health. WTO, SPS Agreement. http://www.wto.org/english/thewto_e/eol/e/world.htm. Accessed June 15, 2003.

[52] For example, the TBT agreement defines its scope in part through reference to the SPS Agreement. TBT Agreement, *supra* note 75. Art. 1.5.

[53] The differences between them are: "First, while the SPS Agreement provides an affirmative defense explaining the general exceptions in GATT, the TBT Agreement explains the obligations contained on the GATT, . . . Second the scope if the SPS Agreement is well defined and relatively narrow, . . . , the scope of the TBT Agreement is extremely broad and diverse. Consequently, the

Agreement excludes from its scope of coverage sanitary and phytosanitary measures as defined SPS Agreement.[54] The SPS Agreement similarly provides that it does not affect Members' rights under the TBT Agreement with respect to measures outside the scope of the SPS Agreement.[55] The SPS Agreement contains rules, principles and benchmarks for the WTO Members to ensure and to justify sanitary and phytosanitary measures not constituting disguised restrictions on international trade.[56]

The SPS Agreement explicitly recognizes Members' sovereign rights to take measures which may restrict trade in order to implement national laws protecting human, animal or plant life or health. In line with the national treatment and MFN principles of GATT, such measures should apply to domestically-produced food or to local animal and plant diseases requirements, as well as to products coming from other countries, without unjustified discrimination among foreign sources of supply.[57] The SPS Agreement recognizes, however, that the animal and plant disease status may differ among supplying countries, and this must be taken into consideration in the trade measures applied.

The basic right of Members under the SPS Agreement is the ability to take SPS measures necessary for the protection of human, animal, or plat life or health. This right is qualified by three provisos. Such measures must be (1) applied only to the extent necessary, (2) based on scientific principles, and (3) maintained with

TBT Agreement contains mainly procedural requirements with few substantive obligations, ... Agreement's principal and not in significant contribution to the international trading system has been assessed to promote transparency and information exchange" (Thorm and Carlson 2000, p. 841).

[54] TBT Agreement, *supra* note 75. Art. 1.5.

[55] SPS Agreement, *supra* note 111. Art. 1.4, For more details, see Kennedy (1998, *supra* note 42, at 461). "Despite their mutual exclusivity, the substantive provisions of the two agreements mirror each other in most respects. A significant difference between the SPS and TBT Agreements, however, of the test used to determine whether a measure is impermissibly protectionist in nature. Whereas the TBT Agreement relies on a nondiscrimination test, the inquiry under the SPS Agreement is based in scientific justification and risk assessment. A strict requirement if nondiscrimination would not be practicable for SPS measures that discriminate against imported goods based on their origin. Goods may pose a risk of disease precisely because the goods come form a member where such disease is prevalent. The same situation might not be true for similar goods coming from another member. Discrimination is, therefore, tolerated under the SPS Agreement, so long as it is not arbitrary or unjustifiable".

[56] SPS Agreement, *supra* note 111. Art. 2.3.

[57] For a means of unjustifiable discrimination between countries in Art. XX chapeau language, *see* Rogers and Whitlock (2002, *supra* note 117, at 490–491). "The Appellate Body Report on Shrimp contains a discussion of 'unjustifiable discrimination between countries where the same conditions prevail.' The Appellate Body ultimately found that the application of the U.S. import ban constituted 'unjustifiable discrimination.' It faulted the United States for failing to consider conditions in other country and for failing to negotiate with other WTO Members on the issue of endangered sea turtles. The general rule appears to be that a WTO Member who wishes to advance a state interest by means of a de facto discriminatory measure must be careful not to do so unilaterally and without taking into account conditions in other WTO Member territories."

sufficient scientific evidence, except that such measures may be imposed temporarily, when evidence is insufficient, pending receipt of additional information necessary for a more objective assessment of risk.[58]

A major purpose of this Agreement is to reduce the possible arbitrariness[59] of governments' decisions in the field of sanitary and phytosanitary measures by clarifying which factors should be taken into account when imposing health protection measures. In particular, measures taken to ensure food safety and animal and plant health should be based on the analysis and assessment of objective and accurate scientific data. At the same time, the SPS Agreement encourages consistent and transparent decision-making in determining an appropriate level of health protection. It requires that potentially trade-restrictive measures be applied for no other purpose than that of ensuring food safety and animal and plant health, and do not result in unjustified barriers to trade.[60]

Trade Disputes in Relation with **Scientific Evidence**

Appellate Body Report, *Japan-Measures Affecting Agricultural Products*, WT/DS76/AB/R (Feb. 22, 1999) (Japan-Agricultural Products AB Report).

Introduction:

Apples, cherries, peach (this includes nectarines), walnuts, apricots, pears, plums and quince sound more like a fruit vendor's inventory than cause for a case before the World Trade Organization Appellate Body. However, these innocuous fruits are at the heart of a conflict between the United States and Japan concerning a Japanese requirement for each variety of these products ("the varietal testing requirement"). If an exporting country provides a quarantine treatment alternative that achieves the same level of protection as the import prohibition, then the import prohibition may be lifted.

[58] SPS Agreement, *supra* note 111. Arts. 2.3, 5.7, cited by Kennedy (1998, *supra* note 42, at 45).

[59] For a means of arbitrary discrimination in Art. XX of the GATT chapeau language, see Rogers and Whitlock (2002, *supra* note 117, at 490). "Arbitrary discrimination is akin to a procedural due process concept. The Appellate Body in the Shrimp case said the rigid application of a U.S. statute resulted in arbitrary discrimination. It based this determination on the statute's lack of transparency, lack of a 'formal opportunity for an applicant country to be heard, or to respond to any arguments that may be made against it,' and the lack of 'formal written reasoned decisions.' N116 because the statute was applied in a 'singularly informal and caused' manner, which could lead to the 'negation of rights of Members,' the Appellate Body held the statute to constitute 'arbitrary discrimination.'"

[60] Wolfrum et al. (2007, *supra* note 76, at 396–398).

Facts and Overview

The 1950 Plant Protection Law as well as the 1950 Plant Protection Law Enforcement Regulation specifies that eight agricultural products, all originating from the United States, be prohibited on the grounds that each of these products could potentially be a host to the codling moth. The codling moth is a pest, which fruit must be quarantined for in Japan.

The *Experiment Guideline for Lifting Import Ban-Fumigation, and the Experimental Guide for Cultivar Comparison Test on Insect Mortality-Fumigation (the "Experimental Guide")*, have been developed as guidelines for the model test procedures of any alternative quarantine treatment. The Experimental Guide deals with varietal testing requirements that the United States believes to be inconsistent with Japan's obligations according to the Agreement on the Application of Sanitary and Phytosanitary Measures (the "SPS Agreement"). The Panel determined that Japan had not been consistent with its obligations according to the SPS Agreement and found specifically that Japan was unfair in maintaining the varietal test requirement in regards to apples, cherries, nectarines, and walnuts, had been more trade-restrictive than necessary, as well as not provided published version of the variety testing requirement. Japan received a recommendation to bring the measure into conformity. In November, 1998, Japan appealed the case.

Principal Issues on Appeal

One of the principal issues raised in the appeal was: If the Panel's decision to find that the variety testing requirement has been maintained without enough scientific evidence within the scope of Article 2.2 of the SPS Agreement;

Arguments of Parties

Japan

Article 2.2 of the SPS Agreement

The term "sufficient scientific evidence" from Article 2.2 of the SPS Agreement has been inaccurately interpreted and this misinterpretation of the term is the reason why Japan would like to see Panel decision concerning Article 2.2 to be reversed. If the essential rights and obligations of scientific evidence from Article 2.2 of the SPS Agreement are substantiated with Articles 5.1 and 5.2 of the SPS Agreement, the Panel will have little decision than to overturn its previous decision.

The idea that Article 2.2 requires measures to be "based on" scientific evidence is not supported by the language in Article 2.2. Japan also finds the notion that an "actual causal link" being necessary when precaution is the guiding principle to be equally unsupported by the SPS Agreement. The precautionary principle recognized in *EC-Measures Concerning Meat and*

(continued)

Meat Products (Hormones) ("European Communities-Hormones") and *Australia–Measures Affecting Importation of Salmon ("Australia-Salmon")* has not been given its due measure from the Panel in evaluating this case.

United States

Article 2.2 of the SPS Agreement

The United States agrees with the Panel that Japan's varietal testing requirement has been maintained without the correct scientific evidence and that Article 2.2 of the SPS Agreement supports this opinion. Article 2.2 of the SPS Agreement does not have any "objective and rational" relationship except in the eyes of the Japanese. According to the United States, the criticism of Japan over the Panel's finding disregards the Appellate Body's injunction to consider Articles 2.2 and 5.1 of the SPS Agreement together.

The scope of the Appellate Body's conclusion in *European Communities-Hormones*

Article 5.7 of the SPS Agreement has been exaggerated; exactly what the Appellate Body feared might happen. Without sufficient scientific evidence, Japan can only hypothesize about any differences in varieties of treatment efficacy.

The relationship between Articles 2.2 and 5.1 does not support Japan's decision that applying Article 2.2 should only pertain to situations that are inconsistent with the sufficiency requirement. Finally, the United States cannot agree with Japan that varietal testing is merely information requirement that must be met regardless of Annex C of the SPS Agreement. If it were an information requirement, more information would be provided by the requests, but this, in effect, limits information.

Rationale and Holdings

Article 2.2 of the SPS Agreement

According to Article 2.2 of the SPS Agreement, all phytosanitary and sanitary measure are expected to be maintained with "sufficient scientific evidence." The question becomes what is sufficient. If 'sufficient' is taken as a relationship concept between the SPS Agreement and the scientific evidence, then the Appellate Body supports the decision of the Panel to find that the variety testing requirement specifically aimed at apples, cherries, nectarines and walnuts is without the proper sufficient scientific evidence within the scope of Article 2.2 of the SPS Agreement.

Commentary

Whether "testing by product" or "varietal testing" is required when a country tries to export fruit to another, the standards must be clear. In the case, the lack of transparency is at the core of the problem. To require Members to provide information for standards that have not been published is a way to discriminate against Members.

Additionally, when examining this case, one must look at the goals of Japan in requiring varietal testing and the reaction of the United States. Japan has the right to require Members to obtain sanitary and phytosanitary high standards and if testing by product, as suggested by the United States in lieu of varietal testing, does not meet those standards than the Member must strive to reach a higher goal.

Both Japan and the United States are known for the lack of transparency in their governmental standards, this case should be a good example of why transparency is necessary in international trade. In addition to greater transparency, more attention should be brought to the concept of alternative testing and what means are appropriate. If a Member country rejects standard testing, does that Member country have the right to choose the method of alternative testing, or would a far better solution be a host of testing alternatives from which an exporting Member country would choose? Is it possible to ever determine if the every form of testing is equal to another?

Source: Appellate Body Report. Japan-Measures Affecting Agricultural Products. 22 February 1999. WT/DS76/AB/R. http://www.worldtradelaw.net/reports/wtoab/japan-agproducts(ab).pdf

3.2.2 SPS Agreement

3.2.2.1 Scope and Coverage

The Agreement defines its scope as a function or the objective of the measure, i.e. food safety and animal and plant health protection,[61] as opposed to the type of measure. Consequently, products, processes and production methods are equally covered by its provisions.[62] Sanitary and phytosanitary measures apply to domestically-produced food or to local animal and plant diseases, as well as to products coming from other countries. Any discrimination among foreign suppliers must be justified on the basis of their animal and plant health conditions.[63]

Sanitary measures are those related to human or animal health, and phytosanitary measures deal with plant health.[64] The protection of fish and wild fauna, forests and wild flora are included in this definition while the protection, for

---

[61] Preamble of the SPS Agreement, *supra* note 111. Art. 1. of Annex, A, SPS Agreement.

[62] Art. 1. of Annex A, SPS Agreement, *supra* note 111. For example, slaughterhouses must comply with strict sanitary standards if the end-users are to receive safe meat products.

[63] SPS Agreement, *supra* note 111. Annex A. para. 1; Wolfrum et al. (2007, *supra* note 76, at 379–384).

[64] SPS Agreement, *supra* note 111. Annex A. para. 1.

example of the environment per se and animal welfare, is excluded. The SPS Agreement further narrows this broad definition to a limited range of situations.

The scopes or the objectives of the SPS measures are as follows:

(i) Protection of human or animal life or health from risks arising from additives, contaminants, toxins or disease-causing organisms in their food.[65] Other human health risks, such as nutrition concerns, medical treatments, or car safety risks, do not fall within this category[66]; (ii) Protection of human life from plant- or animal-carried diseases[67]; (iii) Protection of animal or plant life from the introduction of pests, diseases or disease-causing organisms[68]; (iv) Protection of a country from damage caused by the entry, establishment or spread of pests. The undesired importation of certain weeds can cause major damage in terms of crowding out domestic animal and plant species without necessarily causing a disease.[69]

The SPS Agreement applies to any kind of measure which has one of the objectives identified above. Some kinds of measures, like processing requirements or certification, may take place in the exporting country and not upon arrival in the importing country. However, although the measure may be imposed outside the territory of the importing country, its purpose must be to protect health within the territory of the importing country.[70]

3.2.2.2 Main Features

The SPS Agreement aims to overcome health-related impediments to market access by encouraging the "establishment, recognition and application of common sanitary and phytosanitary measures by different Members".[71] The establishment of national sanitary and phytosanitary regulations that are consistent with international standards, guidelines and recommendations is referred to as "harmonization". The

---

[65] *Id.*

[66] Restrictions on imports of oranges containing a certain level of pesticide residues, or regulations applied to imports of poultry products containing salmonella, are examples of typical SPS measures. Veterinary drugs given to farm animals are also covered in so far as they may pose a threat to humans later consuming the meat.

[67] SPS Agreement, *supra* note 111. Annex A. para. 1. The threat of plant- or animal-carried diseases can be illustrated by measures taken to prevent, for example the spread of rabies or the banning of imports of meat and meat products originating from foot-and-mouth disease regions.

[68] SPS Agreement, *supra* note 111. Annex A. para. 1. An import ban on live cattle originating from herds infected by Bovine tuberculosis would be one example of an SPS measure taken with the objective of avoiding the introduction and spread of the disease to domestic cattle. Another example might be restrictions on certain fruit from areas plagued by the fruit fly.

[69] SPS Agreement, *supra* note 111. Annex A. para. 1. A measure taken to protect a country from damage caused by the spread of such weeds would fall under this fourth category.

[70] Sanitary measures can take many forms, such as imposing specific product or process criteria, requiring products to come from disease-free areas, quarantine regulations, certification or inspection procedures, sampling and testing requirements, health-related labeling measures, setting of permissible maximum levels of pesticide residues, or permitted use of only certain additives in food.

[71] SPS Agreement, *supra* note 111. Annex A. para. 2.

primary incentive for the use of common international norms is that these provide the necessary health protection based on scientific evidence and improve trade flows at the same time.[72]

The SPS Agreement explicitly refers to three standard-setting international organizations whose activities are considered to be particularly relevant to its objectives: the FAO/WHO Codex Alimentarius Commission,[73] the Office International des Epizooties,[74] and the international and regional organizations operating within the framework of the FAO International Plant Protection Convention (IPPC).[75] These organizations are often referred to as the "Three Sisters". They are observers and important contributors to SPS Committee meetings. They can also be called in as experts to give advice to the WTO dispute settlement panels.[76]

Food and Agriculture Organization of United Nations (FAO)

Food and Agriculture Organization (FAO) is a specialized agency of the United Nations that leads international efforts to defeat hunger. FAO serves both developed and developing countries to achieve food security to make

(continued)

[72] SPS Agreement, *supra* note 111. Annex A. para. 2.

[73] The Codex Alimentations Commission, based in Rome, is a subsidiary organ of the Food and Agriculture Organization of the United Nations (FAO) and the World Health Organization (WHO). The SPS Agreement designates Codex as the authority for all matters related to international food safety evaluation and harmonization. Several Codex activities relate to the evaluation of food-borne hazards, although Codex also develops non-health related technical food standards, like nutrition, composition, and quality standards. Codex develops scientific methodologies, concepts and standards to be used worldwide for food additives, microbiological contaminants, and veterinary drug and pesticide residues to be used worldwide. It has also developed useful references like the "General Principles on Food Hygiene" and the "General Principles on Meat Hygiene".

[74] The Office International des Epizooties (OIE) is the world animal health organization, based in Paris. The OIE's "International Animal Health Code" and "Aquatic Animal Health Code" offer international animal health standards and procedures that are periodically amended to take into account the latest scientific research. The OIE develops manuals on: animal diseases; standards for diagnosis, vaccination, epidemiological surveillance, disease control and eradication; procedures such as disinfection and certification; and laboratory equipment. It shares scientific information with its member countries and identifies countries that are free of a particular disease.

[75] The International Plant Protection Convention (IPPC), based in Rome, is a subsidiary body of the FAO. Its main objectives are to take specific actions to prevent the introduction and spread of plant pests, and to promote measures for pest control, including information exchange. It has developed region-specific lists of plant pests. The IPPC develops international plant import health standards, principally on quarantine pests, a "Glossary of Phytosanitary Terms", basic principles governing phytosanitary laws and regulations, and harmonized plant quarantine procedures. The IPPC guidelines for pest risk assessment provide a scientific means for evaluating risks before governments determine the appropriate level of plant protection.

[76] Wolfrum et al. (2007, *supra* note 76, at 379–384).

sure people have regular access to enough high-quality food to lead active, healthy lives. FAO provides the kind of behind-the-scenes assistance that helps people and nations help themselves. If a community wants to increase crop yields but lacks the technical skills, FAO introduce simple, sustainable tools and techniques. When a country shifts from state to private land ownership, FAO provide the legal advice to smooth the way. When a drought pushes already vulnerable groups to the point of famine, FAO mobilize action. And in a complex world of competing needs, FAO provide a neutral meeting place and the background knowledge needed to reach consensus.

For more details, see http://www.fao.org.

3.2.3 International Harmonization

3.2.3.1 Equivalence

The SPS Agreement recognizes that there may be varied ways of ensuring food safety or animal and plant health protection in different countries, but provides that the WTO Members should accept each other's regulations as equivalent whenever the same level of human, animal or plant health protection is achieved.[77] Thus, mutual recognition agreements acknowledging the equivalence of health protection measures enforced by different approaches are negotiated on a bilateral or regional basis, and can help, for example, overcome any lack of international standards.[78]

The concept of equivalence requires countries to develop confidence in their trading partners' health and safety standards without compromising their own health objectives. Bilateral consultations and the sharing of information are essential to the successful negotiation of equivalence agreements. For example, if Country A is concerned with foot-and-mouth disease in Country B, the latter must cooperate by letting experts from Country A visit its farm operations and inspect its meat processing facilities.

3.2.3.2 Risk Assessment

Members must establish SPS measures on the basis of an evaluation of the actual risks involved.[79] The parameters used in such risk analyses commonly include substantial safety margins as a precautionary measure.

[77] SPS Agreement, *supra* note 111. Art. 4.1.

[78] SPS Agreement, *supra* note 111. Art. 4.2.

[79] SPS Agreement, *supra* note 111. Art. 5.1.

– Trade Disputes in Relation to **Precautionary Measures**
Appellate Body Report, *EC-Measures Concerning Meat and Meat Products (Hormones)*, WT/DS26/AB/R, WT/DS48/AB/R (Jan. 16, 1998) (EC-Hormones AB Report).

Facts and Overview

The Panel Report, *EC-Measures Concerning Meat and Meat Products (Hormones)*, managed to attract appeals from the European Communities, the United States and Canada. The original Panel report focused on a complaint against the European Communities on the EC prohibition of imported meat and meat products from cattle that had been given oestradiol-17β, progesterone or testosterone, all natural hormones, or synthetic hormones, such as trenbolone acetate, zeranol or melengestrol acetate ("MGA") These hormones are normally given to cattle to encourage growth. The import prohibition was announced through a series of directives.

The first directive, Directive 81/602 disallowed giving farm animals anything that would create a thyrostatic action. Imported meat and meat products from farm animals exposed to these substances was prohibition with the exceptions of substances that cause an oestrogenic, androgenic or gestagenic reaction if use by a veterinarian or under the veterinarian's care when used for therapeutic or zootechnical reasons, as well as three natural hormones (oestradiol-17β, progesterone or testosterone) and two synthetic hormones (trenbolone acetate and zeranol) if the purpose was growth promotion as permitted in the regulations of the member states of the European Economic Community (EEC) until further notice could be given.

Experiencing a regulatory 7-year itch, Directive 88/146 rescinded the previous directives powers and prohibited trenbolone acetate and zeranol for all purposes and disallowed using natural hormones (oestradiol-17β, progesterone or testosterone) for growth promotion or fattening reasons. Some exceptions were allowed if the Member States of the EEC authorized the use. Directive 88/146 specifically prohibited meat and meat products for all intra EEC trade and third country from animals which had been given substances that creates an oestrogenic, androgenic, gestagenic, or thyrostatic action.

Directives 81/602, 88/146/ and 88/209 were replaced with Council Directive 96/22/EC in 1996. This Directive prohibits giving farm animals any substances that create a hormonal or thyrostatic action. The main difference between this last directive and the first directives was the possibility of placing meat and meat products from animals which has received these substances in certain situations.

(continued)

In September of 1997, the European Communities notified the DSB that the European Communities would appeal. In October of 1997, the United States and Canada filled appellants' submissions and appellee submissions. The very same day, Australia, New Zealand and Norway filed third party participants' submissions.

Principal Issues on Appeal

One of the principal issues raised in the appeal was: If the precautionary principle applies to this interpretation of the SPS Agreement and to what extent;

Arguments of Parties

The Precautionary Principle

According to the European Communities, the precautionary principle can be interpreted as a general custom of adherence to standard international law, which may be applied to risk management and risk assessment. Articles 5.1, 5.2 and Annex 1.4 of the SPS Agreement are not intended to specify risk assessments but identify factors to be considered in a risk assessment. As such, there is not any conflict that would prevent Members from setting health standards that may exceed conflicting scientific information.

However, the United States cannot agree with the European Communities understanding that international law is synonymous with the term, precautionary principle. The SPS Agreement acknowledges the rights of Members to choose their level of sanitary and phytosanitary protection. Nonetheless, the right of the Member to chose a level of sanitary and phytosanitary protection does not preclude the right to neglect correct risk assessment. Canada sees the concept of "precautionary principle" as being included in other SPS Agreement provisions. Consequently, Canada would like some further clarification as to the definition of precautionary principle used by the European Communities.

Objective Assessment of the Facts

The European Communities does not believe that the Panel objectively assessed the facts, which means that the Panel did not correctly comply with its obligations under Article 11 of the DSU. Further indiscretions committed by the Panel including ignoring expert advice, distorting scientific evidence presented by the European Communities.

The European Communities suspects the Panel of creating an unnecessary distinction between general studies and specific studies to the Monographs of the International Agency for Research on Cancer (IARC) as irrelevant. Six reasons given by the European Communities were ignored or given only a cursory glance. This in itself is evidence of the Panel neglecting the obligation to consider all the evidence before it.

The United States finds the European Communities request to review information to be based on inadequate or prejudice requests. Even if the Panel were inclined to honor the European Communities requests, Article 17 of the DSU put the factual findings beyond review. Additionally, the United States cannot see how the European Communities has proven improper influence.

Temporal Application of the SPS Agreement

As the European Communities sees the situation, to apply the SPS Agreements to all measure before and after the date is overreaching the intended powers of the agreement. Since Article 5.1 to 5.5 focuses on the preparatory actions needed before a measure is enacted. Considering this fact, the SPS Agreement does not apply to this situation.

As the United States sees the situation, the European Communities has not read the SPS Agreement correctly. Contrary to the European Communities claims, Articles 5.1 to 5.5 still applies to measure adopted before the SPS Agreement. Both the United States and Canada agree that it is unreasonable to ask for a risk assessment for each substance. Canada suggests that starting with chemical families is a good way to provide maximum risk assessment coverage in a reasonable manner.

The Precautionary Principle

The precautionary principle, whether it is a general principle of international law as well as how often it is observed by Members is the center of much controversy. The Appellate Body chooses not to answer the debate, but focus on how it applies to this situation. While the Appellate Body agrees with the European Communities that Article 5.7 is not the definitive source of the precautionary principle, and that the combination of Article 5.7, the sixth paragraph of the preamble, and Article 3.3 recognize the rights of Members to determine the appropriate level of sanitary protection, the precautionary principle does not at any point allow a Panel to ignore customary international law principles. Consequently, we agree with the Panel that the precautionary principles do not take precedence of the provisions of Articles 5.1 and 5.2 of the SPS Agreement.

Temporal Application of the SPS Agreement

The SPS Agreement was applied to EC measures that were enacted before 1 January 1995 because these measures continued to exist after 1 January 1995. The SPS Agreement does not the use of this agreement to any measures after starting date. Although the requirement of the SPS measure to provide a risk assessment may be burdensome to some Member, flexibility for this situation

(continued)

has been provided in Article 5.1. The Appellate Body cannot find a reason to grant the European Communities its wish. The Panel's findings are upheld.

Commentary

Hormones, meat, and how the countries decision to handle such problems is becoming more important on a daily basis. Much of this case revolves around the linguistic differences between "based on" and "conform to" and was a point of difference between the Panel and the Appellate Body. This type of linguistic difference is likely to cause problems in the future. The Appellate Body *utilized in dubio mitius* to determine which definition of the possible interpretation was most appropriate to the situation, and the least onerous to the involved parties.

The interaction between the precautionary principle and the general customary law was also an issue in this case. The fact that the precautionary principle was given so much attention as well as used so specifically should have observable reactions in the future. When does precautionary principle become the general customary law? One must question if the aims of the precautionary principle and the general customary law are the same.

Another aspect of important in this case is the use of SPS measures themselves. The Panel and the Appellate Body examined the question of the possible retroactive application of SPS measures and came to the conclusion that SPS measures do apply to decision made before the enacting of the measure and to measures to follow. The logic following the fact that any decision made before the SPS measures will still be current under a new SPS measure. In other words, previous decisions cannot rely on being Grandfathered into a SPS measure.

A final key point in this case and its effect on future cases is the notion that discrimination in international trade will be based on the intent of the party instituting a measure. This will be very difficult to determine, but it is only slightly less difficult to determine discrimination based on the effect of legislation. The SPS Agreement is supposed to minimize conflicts between Members, promote the most favored nation clause, and encourage international trade. The idea that only the intent of the instigating party is proof of discrimination will be difficult to prove.

Source: Appellate Body Report. *EC-Measures Concerning Meat and Meat Products (Hormones)*. 16 January 1998. WT/DS26/AB/R, WT/DS48/AB/R. http://www.worldtradelaw.net/reports/wtoab/ec-hormones(ab).pdf

The SPS Agreement encourages the use of a systematic approach to risk assessment. All factors considered, as well as the procedures and decisions used by a Member in evaluating the food-borne risks or threats to animal or plant health, must be made available to other Members upon request. Risk assessments may be qualitative or quantitative. Quantitative risk assessment in particular can be a costly process requiring expertise, and an adequate sanitary infrastructure, and this may not always be within the reach of countries with budget constraints and scarce resources. This implies that there are significant advantages in adopting established international standards.[80]

The WTO Members have the right to determine what they consider to be an appropriate level of health protection, including a "zero risk" level if it so chooses.[81] However, this level should be a reflection of health protection, not a means to protect domestic producers from competition. In particular, where the health risks are similar, the acceptable level of protection should normally be similar, if any distinction would result in discrimination or a disguised restriction on international trade.[82]

An acceptable level of risk can often be ensured in alternative ways. Once the government has determined its appropriate level of sanitary and phytosanitary protection, it should not choose a measure that is more stringent and trade-restrictive than necessary.[83]

The SPS Agreement allows Members to take precautionary measures in cases of emergency and when sufficient scientific evidence does not yet exist to support definitive measures.[84] However, these emergency measures should only be provisional. Within a reasonable period of time, governments must seek the additional information needed to carry out a more objective assessment of the risks involved, and review their measures accordingly.[85]

– Trade Disputes in Relation to **Risk Assessment**
Appellate Body Report, *Australia-Measures Affecting Importation of Salmon*, WT/DS18/AB/R (Oct. 20, 1998) (Australia-Salmon AB Report).

(continued)

[80] Wolfrum et al. (2007, *supra* note 76, at 379–384; 447–449).

[81] Kennedy (1998, *supra* note 42, at 387–388).

[82] SPS Agreement, *supra* note 111. Art. 5.5.

[83] A complete ban on imports of wheat may be one way to limit pesticide residue levels causing certain health risks to consumers. However, the importing country's obligation under the SPS Agreement is to consider alternative measures to the ban, bearing in mind not only its health protection objectives but the potential trade effects of the measures as well. Random testing for maximum residue levels at the port of entry may be a less trade-restrictive measure than a complete ban of wheat imports, and wheat complying with the relevant residue requirements could safely be distributed on the domestic market.

[84] SPS Agreement, *supra* note 111. Art. 4.1.

[85] SPS Agreement, *supra* note 111. Art. 5.7.

Background

Before June 30, 1975 and the beginning of QP86A, Australia did not have any restrictions on salmonid products. QP86A was the beginning of restrictions on imported salmonid products. After Canada requested the rights to send fresh, chilled, frozen, or uncooked salmon to the Australian market, Australia undertook an import risk analysis for said product, specifically ocean-caught Pacific salmon. The final analysis delivered a recommendation that present quarantine policies for uncooked salmon products remain in place.

The Panel found that Australia's actions have been inconsistent with Article 5.1, 5.1 and 5.6 of the *Agreement on the Application of Sanitary and Phytosanitary Measures* ("SPS Agreement") as well as indirectly inconsistent with Article 2.2 and 2.3 of the SPS Agreement. Criticisms of Australia were that Australia had not conducted a proper risk assessment, had applied arbitrary levels of sanitary protection and been more trade-restrictive than necessary. It was recommended that Australia bring its measures in line with the SPS Agreement. On 22 July 1998, Australia began the appeal process following with an appellant's submission on 3 August 1998. Later in the month, both Australia and Canada filed an appellant's submission and appellee's submissions. The European Communities, Indian, Norway and the United States joined in as separate third participant's submissions.

Principal Issues on Appeal

Both appellants, Australia and Canada, raised the following issues:
Australia

a) If the Panel interpreted the terms of reference in relation to the measure and product at issue incorrectly;
b) Whether the Panel went outside the boundaries of reference by increasing the scope of its examination of Article 5 by subsuming Article 6 into Article 5 of the SPS Agreement;
c) If the Panel was incorrect is assessing that the measure, when applied to ocean-caught Pacific salmon, does not fit the definition of risk assessment, and, as a result, that Australia has acted inconsistently with Article 5.1 and Article 2.2 of the SPS Agreement;
d) If the Panel's decision that Australia actions were inconsistent with Article 5.5 and Article 2.3 of the SPS Agreement;
e) If the Panel incorrectly decided that Australia acted inconsistently with Article 5.6 of the SPS Agreement; and
f) Whether or not the Panel's allocation of the burden proof was correct as well as if the assessment was objective, were errors made concerning evidence related to written submissions.

Canada

a) If the Panel incorrectly applied the principle of judicial economy and failed to appropriately extend the assessment of Canada's claims under Articles 5.5 and 5.6 of the SPS Agreement of other Canadian salmon; and
b) If the Panel was incorrect in not finding a violation of Article 2.3 in the first sentence, separately from the inconsistency of Australia in relation to Article 5.5 of the SPS Agreement.

Arguments of Parties

Terms of References

To begin with, Australia sees this litigation as being far too general considering that QP86A covers all salmonid products. More substantially, the Panel's terms of reference are so vast that they are not useful. In extending the terms of reference to include fresh, chilled or frozen salmon including heat treatment, which is applied only to smoke salmon, the Panel has shows "Sharply flawed logic." Australia cannot see how the same measures can be applied to fresh, chilled or frozen salmon as well as smoked salmon. Additionally, the Panel has not given enough consideration that these products come under different tariffs at different times. By exceeding the terms of reference, the Panel has also been faulty in including Article 6 of the SPS Agreement in the scope of the examination.

Canada, on the other hand, does not see how it would have been possible for the 1996 Decision of the Director of Quarantine to hold everything connected to this issue since it only applies to ocean-caught Pacific salmon. The most important document in connection to this issue is the QP86A. These problems concerning salmon have been in discussion and endless rounds of negotiation with Australia since 1975. The problem at the table in this measure is the prohibition of fresh, chilled or frozen salmon. Australia is playing semantical games by throwing smoked salmon into the mess. Heat-treated salmon is allowed entry into Australia and there is not any dispute about the product. Finally, Canada does not how Australia can blow a reference the Panel made to Article 6 into subsuming Article 5 into Article 6.

Burden of Proof

Whether or not Canada has supported its claims but fulfilling the burden of proof connected to Articles 5.1, 5.5 and 5.6 of the SPS Agreement is the responsibility of the Panel, but the Panel did not properly merit the evidence before it in the opinion of Australia. Australia also believes that Canada did not prove a *prima facie*. The Panel did not adequately insist upon scientific data strong enough to support Canadian argument. The Panel claimed to have taken the interpretative approach of the Appellate Body in EC Measures Concerning Meat and Meat Products (Hormones) ("European Communities

(continued)

Hormones") but Australia finds this claim in doubt. In spite of the assertion that it would follow the interpretive approach of the above case, the Appellate Body actually followed the SPS Agreement in a fashion similar to Article III and Article XX of GATT 1994 specifically concerned with Articles 5.1, 5.5 and 5.6 as well as Articles 2.2 and 2.3 in regard to the allocation of the burden of proof.

Objective Assessment of the Matter

Australia is unsatisfied with the Panel's inability to give the proper accord to the evidence provided by Australia. This inability to examine evidence appropriately manifested itself by ignoring Australia's appropriate level of protection, Australia's view of the legal status and application of SPS measures, as well as ignoring Australia's domestic practices for risk assessments. Canada, of course, completely disagrees with Australia's perception of the Panel's actions and supports the Panel's findings.

Article 5.1 of the SPS Agreement

Australia disagrees with the violation of Article 5.1 that the Panel gave due to the missing risk assessment for heat treatment. The heat treatment is not applicable to the heart of the complaint. The Panel's interpretation of risk assessment and risk should have been interpreted in the spirit of Annex A of the SPS Agreement as done so by the Appellate Body in *European Communities-Hormones*. Among the misinterpretations on the Panel's part are the obligations of Article 5.1, 5.2 and 2.2 of the SPS Agreement. As Australia sees it, the process method if only important when used for producing any product to be imported in either fresh, chilled, or frozen form. Consequently, Australia cannot see any reason why there should be a discussion of a risk assessment for the heated method when it is irrelevant to the discussion. Canada, however, fully supports the Panel's findings and believes the correct legal standard was applied.

Article 5.5 of the SPS Agreement

The Panel's interpretation of "risk" was not clear enough for the situations to which the word was applied as well as the term "different situations." As Australia sees the situation, the correct interpretation of "risk" would have come from Annex A of the SPS Agreement in which risk focuses on the context of the risk of entry or spread of disease as well as any biological or economic consequences. Another example of misinterpretation, different situations, was misapplied by the Panel, according to Australia. Australia suggests that the proper application of Article 5.5 would show that it is not necessary to have a risk assessment for all 24 diseases in common.

The Panel's determination that Australia must limit its protection levels to the disease agents positively detected limits Australia's ability to govern its level of protection. Consequently, the Panel has not observed Articles 3.2 and 19.2 of the DSU. Additionally the Panel inappropriately used the statement in paragraph 215 of the Appellate Body Report in *European Communities-Hormones* to create artificial distinctions between protection levels. Australia also does not agree with the Panel that an adverse finding under Article 5.1 is a finding of disguised trade restriction as well.

According to Canada, the question is not whether different products have the same risks but if the levels of protection maintain by Australia are appropriate or are the protection barriers simply forms of trade discrimination. The main point the Panel focused on, in Canada's opinion, was that the lack of evidence that salmon for human consumption has introduced disease to human. Although Australia believes that the Panel denied Australia the right to determine protection levels, Canada believes that the Panel only compared measures imposes by Australia on non-salmonids and salmonids.

Article 5.6 of the SPS Agreement

Australia's dissatisfaction with the Panel on Article 5.6 of the SPS Agreements stems from the application of the three-pronged test to determine inconsistency. Although the 1996 Final Report holds four alternative quarantine policy options, Australia believes that no evidence was presented to this effect. Additionally, heat treatment protection levels cannot be considered as a possible protection level factor for fresh or chilled salmon.

Canada does not see how the other quarantine policy options identified in the 1996 Final Report could meet Australia's protection levels. Nor can Canada understand how Australia sees prohibition as the only acceptable level of protection.

Article 5.1 of the SPS Agreement

The Panel decided that the 1996 Final Report fit the needs of a risk assessment that the heat-treatment requirement is the focus of the 1996 Final Report. Since the Panel has previously found in this report that the focus of the measure, the Panel's finding in paragraph 8.99 is reversed. In spite of Article 17 of the DSU, the Panel does not make any ruling on the import prohibition on fresh, chilled or frozen salmon and whether it is based on a risk assessment.

To begin examining this section of the report, it was mentioned as a concern that the Appellate Body may decide that "zero risk" would be deemed an inappropriate risk level of protection. The European Communities may rest assures that the Appellate Body also aggress that "zero risk" is a possible level of protection that a Member may choose. The Panel does not see any reason to interfere on that point.

To determine if the 1996 Final Report qualifies as a risk assessment, it must first identify potential diseases which may spread to an area, secondly

(continued)

evaluate the odds of entry and the spread of these diseases as well as any economic consequences, and finally consider the likelihood of the entry of spread of these diseases in connection to SPS measures that might be applied. Although the 1996 Final Report meets the first requirement, it does not meet the second or third requirement of risk assessment. The 1996 Final Report is not an appropriate risk assessment under Article 5.1 of the SPS Agreement. Since the 1996 Final Report is not appropriate to determine risk assessment and it is the only risk assessment put forth by Australia, the import prohibition on fresh, chilled or frozen salmon is not based on a risk assessment required in the SPS Agreement and Australia has acted inconsistently with that measure. By extension, the Appellate Body agrees with the Panel that Australia's actions have also been inconsistent with Article 2.2 of the SPS Agreement.

Article 5.5 of the SPS Agreement

Concerning Article 5.5 of the SPS Agreement, the Panel considered whether there were different levels of protection, any differences in the levels and if the differences were justifiable, and if this resulted in "discrimination or disguised restriction on international trade". The Panel determined that all three were present and that Australia was inconsistent with Article 5.5. Australia craftily responded by stating the Panel had made a variety of mistakes but not without directly challenging the ruling. The Appellate Body finds that the Panel was correct in finding the situations were comparable to either risk of entry or associated economic and biological potential consequence. As a result, the Appellate Body upholds the Panel's ruling that the import prohibition on fresh, chilled or frozen salmon and the admission of other fish are different under Article 5.5 of the SPS.

The presence of unjustifiable distinctions in different situations hinges on whether the Panel erred in limiting the disease agents to ocean-caught Pacific salmon. The Appellate Body disagrees with Australia and upholds paragraph 8.141 that the second element of the report is also present. As to the Panel's decision that Australia also exhibited disguised restrictions on international trade, the Appellate Body reverses one small portion, but agrees with the rest of the Panel report on this issue. Therefore, the Panel's finding that Australia's actions were inconsistent with Article 5.5 and, by implication; Article 2.3 of the SPS Agreement is upheld.

Article 5.6 of the SPS Agreement

The next question on the table is whether the SPS measure is more restrictive to trade than necessary to achieve the level of protection desired by Australia. If Australia has been more trade-restrictive than necessary, Australia will have acted inconsistently with Article 5.6 of the SPS Agreement. A measure is deemed trade restrictive if there is another measure that is

a) "reasonably available taking into account technical and economic feasibility";
b) "achieves [Australia's] appropriate level of sanitary ... protection"; and
c) is "significantly less restrictive to trade than other sanitary measure."

The Panel found all three elements present under Article 5.6 and the Appellate Body agrees with the presence of the first and third elements, but not with the second element.

Australia states that it seeks very low levels of exposure but not zero risk. However, because the Panel erred in examining heat-treatment rather than the import prohibition, the Appellate Body cannot appropriately determine if the second element is present or not. The Appellate Body reverse the Panel's finding on Article 5.6 but does not make any comment about whether Australia has violated Article 5.5.

Commentary

One of the main issues in this measure and many other measures is how to determine if a country is trying to determine the appropriate level of protection or simply using the cover of self-protection to cleverly discriminate against trade partners. This measure goes no further than any other in clearing up the matter, either. As Canada pointed out, Australia was quick to advocate a total ban on importing fresh, chilled or frozen salmon from other countries due to alleged disease concerns, but at the same time did not keep any kind of internal regulations on Australian salmon, which may have been no different than Canadian salmon when considering the impact of transporting salmon from one area to the next.

The European Communities also voiced a concern that the Panel and Appellate Body might look at this as an opportunity to declare a "zero risk" policy as being overly trade-restrictive. At some point, the World Trade Organization will have to come up with clearer rules about trade discrimination and a finer eye for the possibilities of trade discrimination against trade partners sullying the benefit of allowing Members to determine their own protection levels.

Another difficult issue in this measure is the inability of the Panel to clearly separate heat-treated salmonid products from fresh, chilled or frozen salmon. There were some measures the Appellate Body was unable to rule upon because of the Panel's error. This was also the case of judicial economy. While the Panel hoped to employ judicial economy by limiting the categories of salmon examined, the judicial economy was anything but economical since the Appellate Body was unable to determine many of the questions based on this concept.

Source: Appellate Body Report, Australia-Measures Affecting Importation of Salmon, Oct. 20, 1998. WT/DS18/AB/R. http://www.worldtradelaw.net/reports/wtoab/australia-salmon(ab).pdf

3.2.3.3 Disease-Free Areas

Governments should recognize disease- or pest-free areas which may not correspond to political boundaries, that is, areas which might be only part of a country or might cover parts of several countries.[86] Product requirements should be adapted to suit those regions. For example, animal diseases such as foot-and-mouth disease may be limited only to a geographical area in a country. In the past, importing countries often required the whole exporting country to be free from a disease before it could be granted access. Today, products coming from disease-free areas within a given country should be considered on the basis of their disease status, not that of the rest of the country.[87]

The burden rests on the exporting Member (as with the principle of equivalence above) to demonstrate that given areas within an exporting country are free from a disease. The exporting country must allow experts from the importing country to inspect the area concerned and the controls in place to check the disease from spreading.[88]

3.2.3.4 Transparency

Each WTO Member must designate a national central government authority as responsible for the implementation of the notification procedures. Whenever a government intends to put into effect a new sanitary or phytosanitary regulation, or modify an existing law that may restrict trade and differs from an international standard, it must notify the WTO Secretariat.[89] A list of national notification authorities and their addresses is regularly circulated by the WTO Secretariat.

Governments must also set up enquiry points, whose task is to provide to their trading partners any information requested on the application of food safety and animal and plant health regulations, the existence of equivalence agreements, or information on risk assessment procedures and decisions. The enquiry point should be able to answer any reasonable question regarding SPS measures, and should be able to provide the texts of the new or modified regulations that were notified to the WTO, as well as other relevant documents.[90]

3.2.4 Consideration of Developing Countries

The agreement calls for assistance to developing country Members to enable them to strengthen their food safety and animal and plant health protection. These countries may ask for technical assistance during SPS Committee meetings.

[86] SPS Agreement, *supra* note 111. Art. 6.1.

[87] SPS Agreement, *supra* note 111. Art. 6.1; Wolfrum et al. (2007, *supra* note 76, at 470–471).

[88] Wolfrum et al. (2007, *supra* note 76, at 379–384; 447–449).

[89] SPS Agreement, *supra* note 111. Art. 7, Annex B:3–4.

[90] Wolfrum et al. (2007, *supra* note 76, at 379–384; 447–449).

Members are encouraged to provide technical assistance on a bilateral basis or through other international organizations.[91] Such assistance can be in the area of processing technology, research or infrastructure development, and may take the form of technical advice, expertise, financial assistance or procurement of adequate equipment.[92] OIE technical assistance activities include development of animal health and epidemiology networks, programs for eradication of foot-and-mouth disease, and information exchange.

Several FAO programs focus on food safety and Codex standards, as well as the assessment of food control systems. Other FAO programs address needs in establishing plant protection structures.[93] Technical assistance is also provided at an informal level when governments seek additional information or legal advice directly from the WTO Secretariat. The Secretariat regularly assists Members in developing an effective understanding of SPS provisions, including the notification procedures, and helps them to appreciate their roles, responsibilities, rights and obligations in the context of this agreement.[94]

3.2.5 Institutions

The SPS Committee is the forum for discussion, information exchange and, where appropriate, resolution of sanitary and phytosanitary issues.[95] It is open to all the WTO Members, who often send capital-based food safety and animal and plant health experts to attend the meeting. Observer status has been granted not only to the Office International des Epizooties (OIE), the joint FAO/WHO Codex Alimentarius Commission (Codex), and the International Plant Protection Convention (IPPC), but also to other intergovernmental organizations active in this area, including World Health Organization (WHO), Food and Agriculture Organization of the United Nations (FAO), United Nations Conference on Trade and Development (UNCTAD), International Trade Centre (ITC) and the International Standards Organization (ISO).[96]

[91] SPS Agreement, *supra* note 111. Art. 9.1.

[92] SPS Agreement, *supra* note 111. Art. 9.1.

[93] Wolfrum et al. (2007, *supra* note 76, at 500).

[94] *Id.*, at 499–500.

[95] SPS Agreement, *supra* note 111. Art. 12.1.

[96] SPS Agreement, *supra* note 111. Art. 12.3.

United Nations Conference on Trade and Development (UNCTAD)

Established in 1964, the United Nations Conference on Trade and Development (UNCTAD), promotes the development-friendly integration of developing countries into the world economy. UNCTAD has progressively evolved into an authoritative knowledge-based institution whose work aims to help shape current policy debates and thinking on development, with a particular focus on ensuring that domestic policies and international action are mutually supportive in bringing about sustainable development.

UNCTAD works to fulfill the mandate by carrying out three key functions:

- It functions as a forum for intergovernmental deliberations, supported by discussions with experts and exchanges of experience, aimed at consensus building.
- It undertakes research, policy analysis and data collection for the debates of government representatives and experts.
- It provides technical assistance tailored to the specific requirements of developing countries, with special attention to the needs of the least developed countries and of economies in transition. When appropriate, UNCTAD cooperates with other organizations and donor countries in the delivery of technical assistance.

For more details, see http://www.unctad.org.

International Trade Center (ITC)

The International Trade Center (ITC) is the joint agency of the World Trade Organization and the United Nations. Since 1964, ITC has helped to enable small business export success in developing countries by providing trade development programs to the private sector, trade support institutions and policymakers.

ITC works in partnership with the World Trade Organization (WTO) and the United Nations Conference on Trade and Development (UNCTAD), supporting their regulatory, research and policy strategies and helping to turn them into practical projects.

ITC's overarching goal is to help developing countries to achieve sustainable development through exports; activating, supporting and delivering projects with an emphasis on competitiveness.

To achieve our mandate, we work with national, regional and international bodies. However, it is our daily contact with business people and policymakers that gives us the unique perspective and the experience to deliver tangible results.

For more details, see http://www.intracen.org.

– Trade Disputes in Relation with **SPS Agreement**

Appellate Body Report, Japan – Measures Affecting the Importation of Apples, WT/DS245/AB/R (Nov. 26, 2003) (Japan-Apples AB Report).

Introduction

Fire blight, caused by Erwinia amylovora, is "a destructive bacterial disease of apples and pears that kills blossoms, shoots, limbs, and, sometimes, entire trees" (Steiner, van der Zwet, and Biggs). Fire blight, although considered indigenous to North America, has a recorded and uncontested history of traveling to new lands via oceanic travels. A cure for fire blight has not been found. Current practices to restrict the growth of fire blight, which has already infected most of the mid-Atlantic region, are to treat the apples with chlorine, keep the treated apples away from other fruits, and follow other standard procedures. Japan has not had a recorded case of fire blight.

Japan determined that the United States was not doing enough to prevent the spread of fire blight into Japan and consequently imposed additional restrictions that the United States did not accept. The Panel found that the additional restrictions that Japan had imposed on the United States to be too restrictive.

Japan was unsatisfied with the results of the Panel, while the United States did not believe that the Panel had the authority to make judgments about fruit other than the mature fruit listed in the initial action. Both Japan and the United States appealed specific areas and legal interpretations of the Panel Report, Japan-Measures Affecting the Importation of Apples (the "Panel Report").

Issues Raised:

The principal issues raised on appeal were:

a) whether or not the Panel has the right under Article 2.2 of the SPS Agreement to make rulings on infected apples as well as mature symptomless apples and if the measure is maintained without scientific evidence.
b) if, under Article 5.7 of the SPS Agreement, the Panel has too narrowly interpreted Article 5.7 of the SPS Agreement because this Article 5.7 is to address situations in which not enough information and evidence exists while there is a wealth of information about fire blight.
c) if the Panel's interpretation of Article 5.1 of the SPS Agreement is erroneous when considering risk assessment.
d) if the use of Article 11 of the DSU on the pathways of fire blight transmission is incorrect.
e) if the claim of "Authority" of the Panel was inappropriate.

(continued)

Rationale and Holdings

Japan's largest area of contention with the Panel Report was the assertion that Japan applied and maintained these measures to infected apples and symptomless, mature apples "without sufficient scientific evidence," a point that the United States also agrees was considered incorrectly by the Panel. Both countries agree that the measures should be limited to mature, symptomless apples.

Japan considered the 200-year recorded history of the transmission of fire blight to be considered scientific evidence and argued that the Panel erroneously concluded that Japan had the burden of proof while Japan stated that the United States' had not established a *prima facie* case, and consequently, the United States was responsible for the burden of proof. Subsequently, the Panel should have determined that Japan had acted in accordance to its obligations under Article 2.2.

According to Japan, the United States had the responsibility to establish a prima facie case about either all infected apples or mature, symptomless apples. Since the U.S. has failed to establish such a case, Japan argues that Article 2.2 of the SPS Agreement should not have been examined, or that the Panel did not correctly establish the burden of proof.

In order to establish a prima facie case under Article 2.2 concerning the transmission of fire blight in infected fruit the United States needed to prove "(i) that the pathway would not be completed even if infected apple fruit were exported to Japan, or (ii) that Japan's scientific evidence on this risk would nonetheless be insufficient for the measure in question." The limited evidence the United States presented on the transmission pathways of fire blight for mature, symptomless fruit is considered by Japan to be insufficient. In fact, Japan suggested that the United States did not promote any factual claim or evidence about infected apple fruit.

The burden of proof, according to the Panel, was mainly shouldered by Japan regardless of the absent United States prima facie case. Without an established prima facie case, the United States did not deserve to have a measure maintained without sufficient scientific evidence. Japan suggests that perhaps the Panel unduly weighed some evidence as more important than other pertinent evidence and neglected to notice the United States lack of proof. Additionally Japan sees the Appellate Body as having "implicitly rejected this sort of arbitrary distillation of arguments" by not conforming to the panel finding under Article 5.6 of the SPS Agreement in *Japan-Agriculture Products II*. Japan also considers that the Panel's conclusion about infected apple fruit is understandable only if this were considered a "defensive plea"; however, Article 2.2 does not involve defensive pleas. As such, Japan believes that the Panel erred on this point.

The United States believes that that the re-weighing of evidence as Japan suggests is needed is a challenge to the Panel's fact finding. A challenge to the findings could be raised under Article 11 of the DSU, but since Japan has not found a violation of Article 11, the Panel's findings with Article 2.2 should be upheld.

The Panel's conclusion that Japan has not presented sufficient scientific evident with the meaning of Article 2.2 of the SPS Agreement is based the lack of evidence that mature, symptomless apples can be carriers of fire blight and fire blight disease-causing organisms. Japan argues that the United States should make a prima facie case, but since the United States is presenting evidence only about mature, symptomless apples the burden of proof rests on Japan. In regard to mature, symptomless apples, the Panel has the right to chose the type of methodology used based on the circumstances and the Appellate Body does not find any fault with the methodology chosen.

Article 5.7 of the SPS Agreement

While the United States agreed with the Panel interpretation and asked that the Appellate Body uphold the Panel's findings, Japan found the Panel's "narrow" understanding of Article 5.7 of the SPS Agreement undesirable. Article 5.6, according to Japan, is appropriate for situations where reliable evidence is not available, which is not the case of fire blight. While Japan based its actions on 200 years of historical evidence, Japan does not believe that the Panel should use this evidence since the United States has not objected to the evidence used by Japan.

Japan sees it as the right of every Member to decide the level of protection each importing Member feels necessary and that the Panel should not be swayed by the ease of other Members feel with the threat of fire blight.

Article 5.1 of the SPS Agreement

Article 5.1 has also been assessed incorrectly according to Japan. The Panel considered the risk assessment to be limited to apple fruit when in fact it applies to all fruits susceptible to fire blight. Additionally Article 5.1 does not indicate how risk assessment should be done, only that it should be done. Therefore, Japan's method of risk assessment looking at historical evidence in addition to the scientific evidence is a legitimate means of inquiry.

The alternative phytosanitary measures that Japan is suggesting should be considered a part of "methodology" of risk assessment which is not addressed in Article 5.1 the Panel's evaluation of risk assessment Japan also believes that the distinction between compliance to Article 5.1 during initial risk assessment and continuing compliance should be clearer. Since some of the information the Panel used to make the decision became available after initial investigation and due to that new information Japan was unfairly required to do a full risk assessment.

(continued)

As for the subsequent information, Japan believes the importing Member should have the right to evaluate any new information and it importance to the situation. Japan does not agree that a Member should complete a new risk assessment every time a new piece of information becomes available. Due to cost and time such risk assessment would be inefficient.

The United States agreed with the Panel's decisions and asked that the findings be upheld by the Appellate Court as well.

The Appellate Body finds that the Panel's decisions were correctly formed. Japan would like to base the risk assessment on vague possible transmissions rather than specific transmission methods. The Panel also only used information based on the 1999 risk assessment.

Panel's objective assessment under Article 5.1

The presentation of facts to the Panel's fact-finding was an area of dispute. The United States claims that during presentation of the facts in discussion of Article 5.1 was not done appropriately. Because the facts were not presented properly, the United States would like the Appellate Body to ignore this aspect of the appeal.

Claim of "Authority" of the Panel

The United States questions whether the Panel has any authority to make decision about "immature apples" because immature apples were not raised in any claim. The case in questions is about exported apple fruit to Japan and only mature, symptomless apples are harvested and sent to Japan. The addition of immature apples adds an unnecessary dimension to the proceeding. The actual wording of the document states "measures restriction the importation of US apples in connection with fire blight or the fire blight disease-causing organism, Erwinia amylovora." Since it is possible for immature apples exported to Japan due to human errors and the specific wording of the measure does not specific mature apples, the Appellate finds the Panel was correct to assume a broader scope of authority.

Commentary:

One aspect of this case shines through clearer than others; that Japan was arguing about the theoretical, and unproven, transmission pathways of fire blight in mature, symptomless imported apples, from the United States, that the United States was talking about mature, symptomless exported apples to Japan, and that the Panel was discussing immature/mature, symptomatic, and symptomless apples that would end up in Japan. This is an apple laden example of the apples and oranges argument, but one that with a decision that pleased neither Japan nor the United States. The Appellate ruled that the Panel had the authority to come to conclusion about all apple fruit from the United States, including immature apples.

Does Japan have the right to enforce additional measures to protect its land from fire blight to the extent that trade obligations may be set aside? According to the Panel and the Appellate, the answer is no. The Appellate Body upheld all the Panel's findings. The Appellate Body found that the Panel not only had the authority to make a decision about apple fruit, the Appellate Body also found that the Panel acted consistently in regard to paragraphs. 8.199 and 9.1(a) of the Panel Report. Japan's phytosanitary measure does not have the appropriate scientific evidence with the scope of Article 2.2 of the SPS Agreement and is not a justifiable provision measure under Article 5.7 of the SPS Agreement.

The Appellate Body also finds that Japan's 1999 Pest Risk Analysis does not meet the "risk assessment" definition in paragraph 4 of Annex A of the SPS Agreement. The Appellate Body supports the Panel's actions under Article 11 of the DSU in regards to the Unites States' claim under Article 2.2 of the SPS Agreement. Finally the Appellate Body agrees that the Panel complied with Article 11 of the DSU when consider the United States' claim under Article 5.1 of the SPS Agreement. The Appellate Body does not comment as to the Notice of Appeal because the Notice of Appeal was not correctly raised before the Panel.

The Panel and the Appellate agreed that the measure Japan was trying to create was inconsistent with its obligations under the SPS Agreement and that the measure should be amended to meet the obligations or the measure should be dropped.

Source: Appellate Body Report. Japan – Measures Affecting the Importation of Apples. Nov. 6, 2003. WT/DS245/AB/R. http://www.wto.org/english/tratop_e/dispu_e/245_abr_e.pdf

3.3 Customs Valuation

3.3.1 Introduction

Customs valuation is a customs procedure applied to determine the customs value of imported goods. If the rate of duty is ad valorem, the customs value is essential to determine the duty to be paid on an imported good. Article VII of the General Agreement on Tariffs and Trade laid down the general principles for an international system of valuation.

The value for customs purposes of imported merchandise should be based on the actual value of the imported merchandise on which duty is assessed, or of like merchandise, and should not be based on the value of merchandise of national origin or on arbitrary or fictitious values.[97] Although Article VII also contains a definition of "actual value", it still permitted the use of widely differing methods of valuing goods. In addition, 'grandfather clauses' permitted continuation of old standards which did not even meet the very general new standard.[98] It was clear that a more flexible and uniform valuation method was needed which would harmonize the systems of all countries.

The Tokyo Round Valuation Code, or the Agreement on Implementation of Article VII of GATT, concluded in 1979, established a positive system of Customs Valuation based on the price actually paid or payable for the imported goods. Based on the "transaction value", it was intended to provide a fair, uniform and neutral system for the valuation of goods for customs purposes, conforming to commercial realities. This differs from the "notional" value used in the Brussels Definition of Value (BVD).[99] As a stand-alone agreement, the Tokyo Round Valuation Code was signed by more than 40 contracting parties.

3.3.2 Customs Valuation Agreement

3.3.2.1 Background

The Tokyo Round Code was replaced by the WTO Agreement on Implementation of Article VII of GATT 1994[100] following conclusion of the Uruguay Round. This Agreement is essentially the same as the Tokyo Round Valuation Code and applies only to the valuation of imported goods for the purpose of levying ad valorem duties on such goods. It does not contain obligations concerning valuation for purposes of determining export duties or quota administration based on the value of goods, nor does it lay down conditions for the valuation of goods for internal taxation or foreign exchange control.[101]

---

[97] GATT, *supra* note 1. Art. 7.

[98] GATT, *supra* note 1. Art. 7.1.

[99] Starting in the 1950s, customs duties were assessed by many countries according to the Brussels Definition of Value (BVD). Under this method, a normal market price, defined as "the price that a good would fetch in an open market between a buyer and seller independent of each other," was determined for each product, according to which the duty was assessed. Factual deviations from this price were only fully taken into account where the declared value was higher than the listed value. Downward variations were only taken into account up to 10 percent. This method caused widespread dissatisfaction among traders, as price changes and competitive advantages of firms were not reflected until the notional price was adjusted by the customs office after certain periods of time. New and rare products were often not captured in the lists, which made determination of the "normal price" difficult.

[100] Agreement on Implementation of Art. VII of the General Agreement on Tariffs and Trade 1994 (customs valuation). 1994. Marrakesh Agreement Establishing the World Trade Organization, Annex 1, Legal Instruments-Results of the Uruguay Round. 33 I.L.M. 1125 (Apr. 15, 1994). (Customs Valuation Agreement).

[101] WTO, Customs Valuation-Technical Information on Customs Valuation (The New Agreement), http://www.wto.org/english/tratop_e/cusval_e/cusval_info_e.htm. Accessed Oct. 28, 2011.

The Agreement stipulates that customs valuation shall, except in specified circumstances, be based on the actual price of the goods to be valued, which is generally shown on the invoice. This price, plus adjustments for certain elements listed in Article 8, equals the transaction value, which constitutes the first and most important method of valuation referred to in the Agreement.

For cases in which there is no transaction value, or where the transaction value is not acceptable as the customs value because the price has been distorted as a result of certain conditions, the Agreement lays down five other methods of customs valuation, to be applied in the prescribed hierarchical order. Overall the following six methods are considered in the Agreement: that is, transaction value, transaction value of identical goods, transaction value of similar goods, deductive method, computed method, and fall-back method.[102]

3.3.2.2 Method 1: Transaction Value

The price actually paid or payable is the total payment made or to be made by the buyer to or for the benefit of the seller for the imported goods, and includes all payments made as a condition of sale of the imported goods by the buyer to the seller, or by the buyer to a third party to satisfy an obligation of the seller.[103] Customs valuation based on the transaction value method is largely based on documentary input from the importer. Customs administrations have the right to "satisfy themselves as to the truth or accuracy of any statement, document or declaration."[104]

3.3.2.3 Method 2: Transaction Value of Identical Goods

The transaction value is calculated in the same manner on identical goods if the goods are: the same in all respects including physical characteristics, quality, and reputation; produced in the same country as the goods being valued; and produced by the producer of the goods being valued. For this method to be used, the goods must be sold for export to the same country of importation as the goods being

[102] WTO, Customs Valuation-Technical Information on Customs Valuation (Basic principle: Transaction value). http://www.wto.org/english/tratop_e/cusval_e/cusval_info_e.htm. Accessed Oct. 19, 2012.

[103] Customs Valuation Agreement, *supra* note 170. Annex 3:7.

[104] GATT, *supra* note 1. Art. 17; A "Decision Regarding Cases Where Customs Administrations Have Reasons To Doubt The Truth Or Accuracy Of The Declared Value" taken by the Committee on Customs Valuation pursuant to a Ministerial Decision at Marrakesh spells out the procedures to be observed in such cases. As a first step, customs may ask the importer to provide further explanation that the declared value represents the total amount actually paid or payable for the imported goods. If the reasonable doubt still exists after reception of further information (or in absence of a response), customs may decide that the value cannot be determined according to the transaction value method. Before a final decision is taken, customs must communicate its reasoning to the importer, who, in turn, must be given reasonable time to respond. In addition, the reasoning of the final decision must be communicated to the importer in writing. WTO, Customs Valuation-Technical Information on Customs Valuation (Method 1: Transaction value). http://www.wto.org/english/tratop_e/cusval_e/cusval_info_e.htm. Accessed Oct. 19, 2012.

valued. The goods must also be exported at or about the same time as the goods being valued.[105]

3.3.2.4 Method 3: Transaction Value of Similar Goods

The transaction value is calculated in the same manner on similar goods if they are: goods closely resembling the goods being valued in terms of component materials and characteristics; goods which are capable of performing the same functions and are commercially interchangeable with the goods being valued; goods which are produced in the same country and by the producer of the goods being valued. For this method to be used, the goods must be sold to the same country of importation as the goods being valued. The goods must be exported at or about the same time as the goods being valued.[106]

3.3.2.5 Method 4: Deductive Value

The Agreement provides that when customs value cannot be determined on the basis of the transaction value of the imported goods or identical or similar goods, it will be determined on the basis of the unit price at which the imported goods or identical or similar goods are sold to an unrelated buyer in the greatest aggregate quantity in the country of importation. The buyer and the seller in the importing country must not be related and the sale must take place at or about the time of importation of the goods being valued.[107]

The unit price at which the imported goods or identical or similar imported goods are sold in the greatest aggregate quantity is to be the basis for establishing the customs value.[108] The greatest aggregate quantity is the price at which the greatest number of units is sold to unrelated persons at the first commercial level after importation at which such sales take place.[109]

3.3.2.6 Method 5: Computed Value

Computed value, the most difficult and rarely used method, determines the customs value on the basis of the cost of production of the goods being valued, plus an amount for profit and general expenses usually reflected in sales from the country of

[105] WTO, Customs Valuation-Technical Information on Customs Valuation (Method 2: Transaction value of identical goods (Art. 2)). http://www.wto.org/english/tratop_e/cusval_e/cusval_info_e.htm. Accessed Oct. 19, 2012.

[106] WTO, Customs Valuation-Technical Information on Customs Valuation (Method 3: Transaction value of similar goods (Art. 3)). http://www.wto.org/english/tratop_e/cusval_e/cusval_info_e.htm. Accessed Oct. 19, 2012.

[107] WTO, Customs Valuation-Technical Information on Customs Valuation (Method 4: Deductive value). http://www.wto.org/english/tratop_e/cusval_e/cusval_info_e.htm. Accessed Oct. 19, 2012.

[108] GATT, *supra* note 1. Art. 5.1.

[109] Interpretative Note to Art. 5.1; To determine the greatest aggregate quantity all sales at a given price are taken together and the sum of all the units of goods sold at that price is compared to the sum of all the units of goods sold at any other price. The greatest number of units sold at one price represents the greatest aggregate quantity.

exportation to the country of importation of goods of the same class or kind. Computed value is the sum of the following elements:

The cost or value of materials and fabrication or other processing employed in producing the imported goods. Materials would include, for example, raw materials, such as lumber, steel, lead, clay textiles, etc.; costs to get the raw materials to the place of production; subassemblies, such as integrated circuits; and prefabricated components which will eventually be assembled. Fabrication would include the costs for labor, any costs for assembly when there is an assembly operation instead of a manufacturing process, and indirect costs such as factory supervision, plant maintenance, overtime, etc. Cost or value is to be determined on the basis of information relating to the production of the goods being valued, supplied by or on behalf of the producer. If not included above, packing costs and charges, assists, engineering work, artwork, etc. undertaken in the country of importation would be added.[110]

3.3.2.7 Method 6: Fall-back Method

When the customs value cannot be determined under any of the previous methods, it may be determined using reasonable means consistent with the principles and general provisions of the Agreement, and on the basis of data available in the country of importation. To the greatest extent possible, this method should be based on previously determined values and methods with a reasonable degree of flexibility in their application.[111]

3.3.2.8 Institutions

The Agreement establishes a Committee on Customs Valuation composed of representatives from each of the Members for the purpose of affording Members the opportunity to consult on matters relating to the administration of the customs valuation system by any Member or the furtherance of the objectives of the Agreement.[112] The Agreement also establishes a Technical Committee on Customs Valuation under the auspices of the World Customs Organization with a view to ensuring, at the technical level, uniformity in interpretation and application of the Agreement. The responsibilities of the Technical Committee include advising on specific technical matters as requested by Members or by a panel in a dispute.[113]

[110] WTO, Customs Valuation-Technical Information on Customs Valuation (Method 5: Computed value). http://www.wto.org/english/tratop_e/cusval_e/cusval_info_e.htm. Accessed Feb. 28, 2012.

[111] WTO, Customs Valuation-Technical Information on Customs Valuation (Method 6: Fall-back method). http://www.wto.org/english/tratop_e/cusval_e/cusval_info_e.htm. Accessed Feb. 28, 2012.

[112] Customs Valuation Agreement, *supra* note 170. Art. 18:1.

[113] Customs Valuation Agreement, *supra* note 170. Art. 18:2.

3.4 Rules of Origin

3.4.1 Introduction

Rules of origin are the criteria needed to determine the national source of a product. Their importance is derived from the fact that duties and restrictions in several cases depend upon the source of imports. There is wide variation in the practice of governments with regard to the rules of origin. While the requirement of substantial transformation is universally recognized, some governments apply the criterion of change of tariff classification, others the ad valorem percentage criterion and yet others the criterion of manufacturing or processing operation. In a globalizing world it has become even more important that a degree of harmonization is achieved in these practices of Members in implementing such a requirement.[114]

GATT had no specific rules governing the determination of the country of origin of goods in international commerce. Each contracting party was free to determine its own origin rules, and could even maintain several different rules of origin depending on the purpose of the particular regulation.[115] It is accepted by all countries that harmonization of rules of origin i.e., the definition of rules of origin that will be applied by all countries and that will be the same whatever the purpose for which they are applied – would facilitate the flow of international trade. In fact, misuse of rules of origin may transform them into a trade policy instrument per se instead of just acting as a device to support a trade policy instrument.[116]

Since, the GATT Secretariat prepared a note on rules of origin and, in 1982, Ministers agreed to study the rules of origin used by GATT Contracting Parties, not much more work was done on rules of origin until well into the Uruguay Round negotiations.[117]

---

[114] Rules of origin are used : to implement measures and instruments of commercial policy such as anti-dumping duties and safeguard measures; to determine whether imported products shall receive most-favored-nation (MFN) treatment or preferential treatment; for the purpose of trade statistics; for the application of labeling and marking requirements; and for government procurement. WTO, Rules of Origin-Technical Information on Rules of Origin (Definition). http://www.wto.org/english/tratop_e/roi_e/roi_info_e.htm. Accessed Feb. 28, 2012.

[115] The draftsmen of the General Agreement stated that the rules of origin should be left: "...within the province of each importing country to determine, in accordance with the provisions of its law, for the purpose of applying the most-favored-nation provisions (and for other GATT purposes), whether goods do in fact originate in a particular country". WTO, Rules of Origin-Technical Information on Rules of Origin (No specific provision in GATT). http://www.wto.org/english/tratop_e/roi_e/roi_info_e.htm. Accessed Feb. 28, 2012.

[116] *Id.*

[117] In the late 1980s developments in three important areas served to focus more attention on the problems posed by rules of origin: First, an increased use of preferential trading arrangements, including regional arrangements, with their various rules of origin; Second, an increased number of origin disputes growing out of quota arrangements such as the Multifibre Arrangement and the "voluntary" steel export restraints; and Lastly, an increased use of anti-dumping laws, and subsequent claims of circumvention of anti-dumping duties through the use of third country

3.4.2 Agreement on Rules of Origin

3.4.2.1 Introduction

The increased number and importance of rules of origin led the Uruguay Round negotiators to tackle the issue during the negotiations. The Agreement on Rules of Origin[118] aims at harmonization of non-preferential rules of origin, and to ensure that such rules do not themselves create unnecessary obstacles to trade. The Agreement sets out a work program for the harmonization of rules of origin to be undertaken after the entry into force of the World Trade Organization (WTO), in conjunction with the World Customs Organization (WCO). Until the completion of the harmonization work program, Members are expected to ensure that their rules or origin are transparent; that they are administered in a consistent, uniform, impartial and reasonable manner; and that they are based on a positive standard.[119]

Rules of origin are defined as those laws, regulations and administrative determinations of general application applied to determine the country of origin of goods except those related to the granting of tariff preferences.[120] Thus, the Agreement covers only rules of origin used in non-preferential commercial policy instruments, such as MFN treatment, anti-dumping and countervailing duties, safeguard measures, origin marking requirements and any non-discriminatory quantitative restrictions or tariff quotas, as well as those used for trade statistics and government procurement. It is, however, provided that the determinations made for purposes of defining domestic industry or "like products of domestic industry" shall not be affected by the Agreement.[121]

The Agreement establishes a Committee on Rules of Origin within the framework of the WTO, open to all WTO Members. It is to meet at least once a year and is to review the implementation and operation of the Agreements.[122] A Technical Committee on Rules of Origin is created under the auspices of the World Customs Organization (formerly the Customs Cooperation Council). Its main functions are (a) to carry out the harmonization work; and (b) to deal with any matter concerning technical problems related to rules of origin. It is to meet at least once a year. Membership is open to all the WTO Members; other WCO members and the WTO Secretariat may attend as observers.[123]

---

facilities. WTO, Rules of Origin-Technical Information on Rules of Origin (Interest in the harmonization of rules of origin) http://www.wto.org/english/tratop_e/roi_e/roi_info_e.htm. Accessed Feb. 28, 2012.

[118] Agreement on Rules of Origin, Apr. 15, 1994, Marrakesh Agreement Establishing the World Trade Organization, Annex 2, Legal Instruments-Results of the Uruguay Round, 33 I.L.M. 1125 (1994) (Origin Agreement).

[119] WTO, Rules of Origin-Technical Information on Rules of Origin (Aims of the Agreement). http://www.wto.org/english/tratop_e/roi_e/roi_info_e.htm. Accessed Feb. 28, 2012.

[120] Origin Agreement, *supra* note 188. Art. 1.1.

[121] Origin Agreement, *supra* note 188. Art. 1.2.

[122] Origin Agreement, *supra* note 188. Art. 4:1.

[123] Origin Agreement, *supra* note 188. Arts. 4:2 and Annex I.

World Customs Organization (WCO)

The World Customs Organization (WCO) is the only intergovernmental organization exclusively focused on customs matters. With its worldwide membership, the WCO is now recognized as the voice of the global customs community.

It is particularly noted for its work in areas covering the development of global standards, the simplification and harmonization of customs procedures, trade supply chain security, the facilitation of international trade, the enhancement of Customs enforcement and compliance activities, anti-counterfeiting and piracy initiatives, public-private partnerships, integrity promotion, and sustainable global Customs capacity building programs. The WCO also maintains the international Harmonized System goods nomenclature, and administers the technical aspects of the WTO Agreements on Customs Valuation and Rules of Origin.

For more details, see http://www.wcoomd.org.

3.4.2.2 Disciplines During Transition Period

During the transition period (i.e. until the entry into force of the new harmonized rules) Members are required to ensure that: (a) rules of origin, including the specifications related to the substantial transformation test, are clearly defined; (b) rules of origin are not used as a trade policy instrument; (c) rules of origin do not themselves create restrictive, distorting or disruptive effects on international trade and do not require the fulfillment of conditions not related to manufacturing or processing of the product in question; (d) rules of origin applied to trade are not more stringent than those applied to determine whether a good is domestic, and do not discriminate between Members (the GATT MFN principle).

However, with respect to rules of origin applied for government procurement, Members are not be obliged to assume additional obligations other than those already assumed under GATT 1994 (the national treatment exception for government procurement contained in GATT Article III:8); (e) rules of origin are administered in a consistent, uniform, impartial and reasonable manner; (f) rules of origin are based on a positive standard. Negative standards are permissible either as part of a clarification of a positive standard or in individual cases where a positive determination or origin is not necessary; (g) rules of origin are published promptly; (h) upon request, assessments of origin are issued as soon as possible but no later than 150 days after such request, they are to be made publicly available; confidential information is not to be disclosed except if required in the context of judicial proceedings.

Assessments of origin remain valid for three years provided the facts and conditions remain comparable, unless a decision contrary to such assessment is made in a review referred to in (j). This advance information on origin is considered as a great innovation of the Agreement; (i) new rules of origin or modifications thereof do not apply retroactively; (j) any administrative action in relation to the determination of origin is reviewable promptly by judicial, arbitral or administrative tribunals or procedures independent of the authority issuing the determination; such findings can modify or even reverse the determination; (k) confidential information is not disclosed without the specific permission of the person providing such information, except to the extent that this may be required in the context of judicial proceedings.[124]

As from the conclusion of the harmonization work program, non-preferential rules of origin will be harmonized and Members will be bound to apply only one rule of origin for all purposes covered by Article 1. The principles contained in (d) through (k) above will continue to apply – i.e. transparency, non-discrimination (also including rules of origin applied for government procurement), and the possibility of reviewing any administrative actions concerning determination of origin.[125]

3.5 Pre-shipment Inspection

3.5.1 Introduction

Since the second half of the last century, private-sector buyers and sellers have resorted to pre-shipment inspection (PSI) to ensure that the quantity and quality of the goods to be traded conform to the specifications of the sales contract. However, government-contracted, comprehensive PSI service is a recent phenomenon, with the first of such contracts signed only in the 1960s. Beginning in the 1980s, it became common for a number of countries primarily developing countries to hire commercial inspection firms to verity the customs classification and value of goods destined for their markets.

These companies usually operate at seaports and airports in developed countries where they examine export claims concerning the quality, quantity, price and financing terms of the goods for export.[126] In response to a growing concern that the use of inspection firms was impeding the flow of trade, the Uruguay Round negotiators included the Agreement on Pre-shipment Inspection (PSI Agreement).[127] The PSI Agreement requires WTO Members employing inspection

[124] Origin Agreement, *supra* note 188. Art. 2.

[125] Origin Agreement, *supra* note 188. Art. 3.

[126] Stewart (1996, pp. 738—739) cited by Kennedy (1998, *supra* note 42, at 472).

[127] Agreement of Pre-shipment Inspection, Apr. 15, 1994, Marrakesh Agreement Establishing the World Trade Organization, Annex 1, Legal Instruments-Results of the Uruguay Round, I.L.M. 33: 1125 (1994) (PSI Agreement). See Kennedy (1998, *id*).

companies (user Members) to ensure that pre-shipment inspections are conducted in a reasonable manner so as not to unnecessarily interfere with legitimate trade.[128]

The PSI Agreement applies to all government-mandated pre-shipment inspection activities carried out inside the territory of the Members (i.e. in the country of export prior to exportation). PSI activities have been defined as any government or government body contracting for or mandating the use of PSI activities.[129] The preamble of the Agreement recognizes the need for developing countries to have recourse to pre-shipment inspection as long and in so far as it is necessary to verify the quality, quantity or price of imported goods. But it also recognizes the need for the programs to be carried out without giving rise to unnecessary delays or unequal treatment. Equal emphasis is laid on the objective of transparency of the operation of pre-shipment inspection entities and of laws and regulations relating to pre-shipment inspection.[130]

3.5.2 Obligations of User Members

Pre-shipment inspection activities are to be carried out in a non-discriminatory manner and procedures and criteria used in carrying out these activities should be objective and applied on an equal basis to all exporters affected by such activities.[131] User Members are to ensure that national treatment obligations are respected to the extent they are relevant. In other words, Members using PSI services should not apply national regulations which result in less favorable treatment to the inspected goods as compared to like domestic products.[132]

Pre-shipment inspection should take place in the customs territory from which the goods are exported or, if that is not possible, the customs territory in which the goods are manufactured.[133] Pre-shipment inspection activities are to be conducted in a transparent manner.[134] There is an obligation for the user Members to publish all applicable laws and regulations relating to pre-shipment inspection activities in order to enable other governments and traders to become acquainted with them.[135]

User Members are to ensure that PSI entities treat all information received in the course of the pre-shipment inspection as business confidential in so far as such

[128] Kennedy (1998, *id*).

[129] PSI Agreement, *supra* note 197. Art. 1.

[130] PSI Agreement, *supra* note 197. Preamble.

[131] PSI Agreement, *supra* note 197. Art. 2.1.

[132] PSI Agreement, *supra* note 197. Art. 2.2.

[133] PSI Agreement, *supra* note 197. Art. 2.3.

[134] For example, PSI companies are to provide to exporters on request a list of information necessary for exporters to comply with inspection requirements, such as a reference to procedures and criteria used for inspection and for price verification purposes, exporters' rights vis-a-vis the inspection authorities, and the appeals procedures.

[135] PSI Agreement, *supra* note 197. Arts. 2.5–2.8.

information is not already published, generally available to third parties, or otherwise in the public domain. Information is also to be provided by user Members as to how they are giving effect to this obligation of confidentiality.

Additionally, user Members are to ensure the PSI entities do not request exporters to provide information on inter alia manufacturing data related to patented, licensed or undisclosed processes, internal pricing, and profit levels. PSI entities may share confidential business information with government entities that have contracted or mandated them only to the extent that such information is required for letters of credit or other forms of payment or for customs, import licensing or exchange control purposes.[136]

User Members are to ensure that PSI entities maintain procedures to avoid conflicts of interest between: (1) PSI entities and any of their related entities including any entities which have a financial interest in the PSI entity in question and whose shipments the PSI entity is to inspect; and (2) between PSI entities and any other entities, including those subject to pre-shipment inspection, with the exception of the government entities contracting or mandating inspections.[137]

User Members are to ensure that PSI entities establish procedures to receive, consider, and render decisions concerning grievances raised by exporters. Information has to be made available to exporters. These procedures are the first step towards the resolution of a dispute. If this step has been taken, but no mutually acceptable solution has been found, it is possible for the parties concerned to refer the matter for an independent review. The possibility also exists for the governments concerned to raise the matter through the dispute settlement process in the WTO.[138]

3.5.3 Obligations of Exporter Members

Exporter Members are to ensure that their laws and regulations relating to PSI activities are applied in a non-discriminatory manner.[139] All applicable laws and regulations relating to PSI activities are to be published promptly and in such a manner as to enable other governments and traders to become acquainted with them.[140] In order to achieve the objectives of this agreement, technical assistance is to be offered by exporter Members to user Members.[141]

[136] PSI Agreement, *supra* note 197. Arts. 2.9–2.13.

[137] PSI Agreement, *supra* note 197. Art. 2.14.

[138] PSI Agreement, *supra* note 197. Art. 2.21.

[139] PSI Agreement, *supra* note 197. Art. 3.1.

[140] PSI Agreement, *supra* note 197. Art. 3.2.

[141] PSI Agreement, *supra* note 197. Art. 3.3.

3.5.4 Independent Review Procedures

The object of the independent review shall be to establish whether, in the course of the inspection in dispute, the parties to the dispute have complied with the provisions of this agreement. The procedures shall be expeditious and provide the opportunity for both parties to present their views in person or writing.[142]

The Independent Entity is to be constituted jointly by an organization representing exporters and an organization representing pre-shipment inspection entities: The General Council decided that the former would be represented by the International Chamber of Commerce (ICC) and the latter by the International Federation of Inspection Agencies (IFIA). The ICC and IFIA entrusted the WTO with the task of setting up the Independent Entity.

The Independent Entity was established as a subsidiary body of the Council for Trade in Goods and to be serviced by the WTO Secretariat.[143] The independent review procedures to be conducted by the IE are unprecedented in the WTO terms, because both parties to the dispute are private entities.[144]

International Chamber of Commerce (ICC)

International Chamber of Commerce (ICC), founded in 1919, is the largest, most representative business organization in the world. Its hundreds of thousands of member companies in over 130 countries have interests spanning every sector of private enterprise.

ICC activities cover a broad spectrum, from arbitration and dispute resolution to making the case for open trade and the market economy system, business self-regulation, fighting corruption or combating commercial crime.

ICC has direct access to national governments all over the world through its national committees. The organization's Paris-based international secretariat feeds business views into intergovernmental organizations on issues that directly affect business operations.

ICC carries out following functions:

- **Setting rules and standards**
  - Arbitration under the rules of the ICC International Court of Arbitration is on the increase. Since 1999, the Court has received new cases at a rate of more than 500 a year.

[142] PSI Agreement, *supra* note 197. Art. 3.3.

[143] WTO-Trade Policy Courses, Chapter 9: Pre-shipment Inspection (PSI) 9.6, *available at* ictplgeorgia.ge/uploads/pages/6aadd428ffb2d7b1db98523ff46dc273.doc. Accessed Oct. 15, 2012.

[144] Thus, the obligation on governments under the Independent Review Procedures is to take "such reasonable measures as may be available to them to ensure fulfillment of the provisions and objectives" (G/PSI/WP/W/1); WTO-Trade Policy Courses, Chapter 9:Pre-shipment Inspection (PSI) 9.6, *id.*

  - ICC's Uniform Customs and Practice for Documentary Credits (UCP 500) are the rules that banks apply to finance billions of dollars worth of world trade every year.
  - ICC Incoterms are standard international trade definitions used every day in countless thousands of contracts. ICC model contracts make life easier for small companies that cannot afford big legal departments.
  - ICC is a pioneer in business self-regulation of e-commerce. ICC codes on advertising and marketing are frequently reflected in national legislation and the codes of professional associations.
- **Promoting growth and prosperity**
  - ICC supports government efforts to make a success of the Doha trade round. ICC provides world business recommendations to the World Trade Organization.
  - ICC speaks for world business when governments take up such issues as intellectual property rights, transport policy, trade law or the environment.
  - Signed articles by ICC leaders in major newspapers and radio and TV interviews reinforce the ICC stance on trade, investment and other business topics.
  - Every year, the ICC Presidency meets with the leader of the G8 host country to provide business input to the summit.
  - ICC is the main business partner of the United Nations and its agencies.
- **Spread business expertise**
  - At UN summits on sustainable development, financing for development and the information society, ICC spearheads the business contribution.
  - Together with the United Nations Conference on Trade and Development (UNCTAD), ICC helps some of the world's poorest countries to attract foreign direct investment.
  - In partnership with UNCTAD, ICC has set up an Investment Advisory Council for the least-developed countries.
  - ICC mobilizes business support for the New Partnership for Africa's Development. At ICC World Congresses every two years, business executives tackle the most urgent international economic issues.
  - The World Chambers Congress, also biennial, provides a global forum for chambers of commerce.
  - Regular ICC regional conferences focus on the concerns of business in Africa, Asia, the Arab World and Latin America.

For more details, see http://www.iccwbo.org.

International Federation of Inspection Agencies (IFIA)

IFIA is the trade association for inspection agencies and other organizations that provide inspection, testing and certification services internationally. The promotion of integrity is one of the federation's top priorities.

(continued)

IFIA was founded in 1982 and members and associate members include the leading international inspection companies from around the world. They cover every field of inspection and related testing making IFIA's work and views truly representative of the profession.

IFIA is a nonprofit making organization. Its objectives are to review and, where possible, to improve the methods, standards, safety procedures and rules used and observed by members for the benefit of members and their clients.

IFIA promotes cooperation between inspection agencies, laboratories and allied businesses throughout the world in order to:

- Develop and coordinate technical and professional standards, methods of inspection and testing, and codes of practice
- Improve efficiency and establish standard procedures
- Develop methods of technical education and training
- Represent the profession to government authorities and trade associations
- Promote uniform interpretation of international conventions on safety and cooperate in their implementation

For more details, see http://www.ifia-federation.org.

3.6 Import Licensing

3.6.1 Introduction

Import licensing can be defined as administrative procedures requiring the submission of an application or other documentation (other than those required for customs purposes) to the relevant administrative body as a prior condition for importation of goods.[145]

GATT documentation – entitled Fees and Formalities Connected with Importation and Exportation – deals with import licensing procedures in a non-specific manner[146]: general obligation is established concerning formalities whereby Members recognize the need for minimizing the incidence and complexity of

[145] Agreement on Import Licensing Procedures, Apr. 15, 1994, Marrakesh Agreement Establishing the World Trade Organization, Annex 1, Legal Instruments-Results of the Uruguay Round, 33 I.L. M. 1125, Art. 1 (1994) (Import Licensing Agreement).

[146] Import licensing means administrative procedures requiring the submission of an application or other documentation to the relevant authority as a prior condition for importation. WTO Agreement on Import Licensing. http://www.wto.org/english/tratop_e/implic_e/implic_e.htm. Accessed Feb. 28, 2012; GATT, *supra* note 1. Art. 8.

import and export formalities and for decreasing and simplifying import and export documentation requirements[147]; each Member is required "to review the operation of its laws and regulations in the light of the provisions of this Article" upon request by another Member[148]; and Members are prohibited from imposing "substantial penalties for minor breaches of customs regulations or procedural requirements."[149]

Members are required to publish promptly laws, regulations, judicial decisions and administrative rulings of general application, including those pertaining to requirements on imports or exports and to administer them in a uniform, impartial and reasonable manner. The Tokyo Round Import Licensing Code[150] was one of the agreements covering non-tariff measures, with the objective of preventing import licensing procedures from unnecessarily hindering international trade. During the Uruguay Round, this indenture, as a stand-alone agreement, was revised to strengthen the disciplines on transparency and notifications.[151]

3.6.2 Principles

The main objectives of the Agreement are to simplify, and bring transparency to, import licensing procedures, to ensure their fair and equitable application and administration, and to prevent procedures applied for granting import licenses having in themselves, restrictive or distortive effects on imports.[152]

Members are to apply import licensing procedures neutrally, and administer them in a fair and equitable manner.[153] Applications are not to be refused for minor documentation errors, nor to be penalized heavily for any omissions or mistakes in documentation or procedures obviously made without fraudulent intent or gross negligence.[154] Licensed imports are not to be refused for minor variations in value, quantity or weight from the amount shown on the license for reasons consistent with normal commercial practices.[155]

Rules and all information concerning procedures for the submission of applications, including the eligibility criteria for applicants, the administrative

[147] GATT, *supra* note 1. Art. 8:1(c).

[148] GATT, *supra* note 1. Art. 8:2.

[149] GATT, *supra* note 1. Art. 8:3.

[150] GATT, *supra* note 1. 26th Supp. BISD 154 (1980) cited by Jackson et al. (2008, *supra* note 3, at 431, n4).

[151] WTO, Import Licensing: Technical Information on Import Licensing (From the Tokyo Round Code to the Uruguay Round Agreement). http://www.wto.org/english/tratop_e/implic_e/implic_info_e.htm. Accessed Feb. 28, 2012.

[152] Import Licensing Agreement, *supra* note 215. Preamble.

[153] Import Licensing Agreement, *supra* note 215. Art. 1.3.

[154] Import Licensing Agreement, *supra* note 215. Art. 1.7.

[155] Import Licensing Agreement, *supra* note 215. Art. 1.8.

bodies to be approached and lists of products subject to import licensing are to be published.[156] Application form procedures and renewal form procedures are to be simple.[157] Applicants are to be allowed a reasonable period to submit license applications. The number of administrative bodies which an applicant has to approach in connection with an application is not to exceed to a maximum of three.[158]

3.6.3 Automatic Import Licensing

Automatic import licensing (licensing maintained to collect statistical and other factual information on imports) is defined as import licensing where the approval of the application is granted in all cases.[159] Automatic licensing procedures are not to be administered in such a way as to have restrictive effects on imports[160]; there should be no discrimination among those applying for automatic licenses. Any person or entity fulfilling the legal requirements should be equally eligible to apply for and obtain import licenses.[161]

3.6.4 Non-Automatic Import Licensing

Non-automatic import licensing is defined as licensing not falling within the definition of automatic import licensing.[162] Non-automatic licensing is used to administer trade restrictions such as quantitative restrictions which are justified within the WTO legal framework: under the non-automatic licensing system, only a limited number of licenses are issued.[163] Non-automatic import licensing must not have restrictive or distorting effects on imports additional to those caused by the imposition of restriction, and is to correspond in scope and duration to the measure it is used to implement.[164]

Members are to publish all relevant information, including purposes other than the implementation of quantitative restrictions, exceptions or derogations, quota amounts, opening and closing dates of quotas and country-specific quota allocations. There may be no discrimination among applicants. If a license is

[156] Import Licensing Agreement, *supra* note 215. Art. 1.4(a).

[157] Import Licensing Agreement, *supra* note 215. Art. 1.5.

[158] Import Licensing Agreement, *supra* note 215. Art. 1.6.

[159] Import Licensing Agreement, *supra* note 215. Art. 2.1.

[160] An automatic licensing system is used to monitor, but not to regulate, the importation of goods (Kennedy 1998, *supra* note 42, at 472–473).

[161] Import Licensing Agreement, *supra* note 215. Art. 2.2.

[162] Import Licensing Agreement, *supra* note 215. Art. 3.1.

[163] Kennedy (1998, *supra* note 42, at 473).

[164] Import Licensing Agreement, *supra* note 215. Art. 3.2.

refused, the applicant, on request, shall be given the reason for refusal, and shall have a right of appeal or review of the decision.[165]

The validity of a license is to be of reasonable duration and not be so short as to preclude imports, including those from distant sources.[166] Full utilization of quotas is not to be discouraged.[167] Licenses are to be issued in economic quantities.[168] The Committee on Import Licensing, open to all Members, meets as necessary to consult on matters relating to the operation of the Agreement or the furtherance of its objectives.[169]

Assignment

To ensure students become equipped with the capability to apply knowledge from the classroom to the field, students are, in this chapter, required to write a report, deliver a presentation and participate in a discussion on the following issues:

1. Devices to eliminate or reduce the technical and sanitary/phytosanitary barriers to international trade under the SPS and TBT agreements.
2. EC-Hormones case focusing on the friction and harmonization between free trade promotion and environmental protection.
3. Importance of the pre-shipment inspection from the viewpoints of developing countries.
4. The US-textile Rules of Origin case focusing on the possibility of the rules of origin to be used as the instruments for the member countries' policy objectives

[165] Import Licensing Agreement, *supra* note 215. Art. 3.5(e).

[166] Import Licensing Agreement, *supra* note 215. Art. 3.5(g).

[167] Import Licensing Agreement, *supra* note 215. Art. 3.5(h).

[168] Import Licensing Agreement, *supra* note 215. Art. 3.5(i).

[169] Import Licensing Agreement, *supra* note 215. Art. 4.

4 Regulation on Trade Measures

Learning Objectives

This chapter is to help students understand:

1. Basic purpose of regulating dumping activities under the WTO Anti-dumping agreement;
2. Complicated issues in making objective anti-dumping investigations;
3. Importance of definition of domestic industry in determining injury to domestic industry caused by dumped imports;
4. Factors to be considered for proper anti-dumping investigations;
5. Requirements for challenging government subsidies under the multilateral trading system or to be countervailed by importing countries;
6. Requirements for imposing safeguards by damaged member countries.

There are provisions in GATT 1994 on "unfair trade practices" providing the framework for the detailed and constraining rules developed in multilateral trade negotiations and incorporated in the separate WTO Agreements dealing with anti-dumping, subsidies and countervailing duties. These are also provided for emergency action on imports of particular products, and for the basic principles upon which the WTO Agreement was negotiated during the Uruguay Round.[1]

[1] WTO-Trade Policy Courses, Chapter 1: Basic Principle 1.6. http://www.wto.org/english/thewto_e/whatis_e/tif_e/understanding_e.pdf. Accessed Oct. 19, 2012.

E.S. Lee, *World Trade Regulation*,
DOI 10.1007/978-3-642-31143-7_4,

4.1 Dumping

4.1.1 Introduction

Dumping is, in general, a situation of international price discrimination, where the price of a product when sold in the importing country is less than the price of that product in the market of the exporting country.[2] Thus, in the simplest of cases, one identifies dumping simply by comparing prices in two markets. However, the situation is rarely, if ever, that simple, and in most cases it is necessary to undertake a series of complex analytical steps in order to determine the appropriate price in the market of the exporting country (known as the "normal value") and the appropriate price in the market of the importing country (known as the "export price") so as to be able to undertake an appropriate comparison.[3]

GATT 1994 sets forth a number of basic principles applicable in trade between Members of the WTO, including the most favored nation principle. It also requires that imported products not be subject to internal taxes or other changes in excess of those imposed on domestic goods, that imported goods be accorded treatment no less favorable than domestic goods under domestic laws and regulations, and that Members establish rules regarding quantitative restrictions, fees and formalities related to importation and customs valuation. Members of the WTO also agreed to the establishment of schedules of bound tariff rates. Article VI of GATT 1994, on the other hand, explicitly authorizes the imposition of a specific anti-dumping duty on imports from a particular source, in excess of bound rates, in cases where dumping causes or threatens injury to a domestic industry, or materially retards the establishment of a domestic industry.[4]

The Agreement on Implementation of Article VI of GATT 1994,[5] commonly known as the Anti-Dumping Agreement, provides further elaboration on the basic principles set forth in Article VI itself, to govern the investigation, determination, and application, of anti-dumping duties. As tariff rates were lowered over time following the original GATT agreement, anti-dumping duties were increasingly

[2] For instance, Art. VI requires a determination of material injury, but does not contain any guidance as to criteria for determining whether such injury exists, and addresses the methodology for establishing the existence of dumping in only the most general fashion.

[3] WTO, Anti-Dumping: Technical Information on Anti-dumping (Dumping in the GATT/WTO). http://www.wto.org/english/tratop_e/adp_e/adp_info_e.htm. Accessed Feb. 28, 2012.

[4] WTO, Anti-Dumping: Technical Information on Anti-dumping (Art. VI of GATT and the Anti-Dumping Agreement). http://www.wto.org/english/tratop_e/adp_e/adp_info_e.htm. Accessed Feb. 28, 2012.

[5] Agreement on Implementation of Art. VI of the General Agreement on Tariffs and Trade 1994 (Antidumping), Apr. 15, 1994, Marrakesh Agreement Establishing the World Trade Organization, Annex 1, Legal Instruments-Results of the Uruguay Round, I.L.M. 33: 1125, Art. 2.1 (1994). (Anti-dumping Agreement).

imposed as the inadequacy of Article VI to govern their imposition became ever more apparent.[6]

The Tokyo Round Code, which entered into force in 1980, provided greater guidance about the determination of dumping and of injury than did Article VI. Equally important, it set out in substantial detail certain procedural and due process requirements that must be fulfilled in the conduct of investigations. Nevertheless, the code still represented no more than a general framework for countries to follow in conducting investigations and imposing duties.[7]

4.1.2 Anti-dumping Agreement

Dumping is defined in the Agreement on Implementation of Article VI of GATT 1994 (Anti-Dumping Agreement) as the introduction of a product into the commerce of another country at less than its normal value.[8] Under Article VI of GATT 1994, and the Anti-Dumping Agreement, the WTO Members can impose anti-dumping measures,[9] if, after investigation in accordance with the Agreement, a determination is made (a) that dumping is occurring, (b) that the domestic industry producing the like product in the importing country is suffering material injury, and (c) that there is a causal link between the two.[10] In addition to substantive rules governing the determination of dumping, injury, and causal link, the Agreement

[6] Anti-dumping Agreement, *id.* Art. 1.1; For the ambiguous provisions about the various potential antidumping law, see Reitz (1996, p. 599). "... when, following imposition of on antidumping duty, an exporter physically changes the product in some way. Is the imposing authority required to institute a new set of proceedings to consider whether the goods, as changed, are being dumped? Strategic moves to avoid duties are referred to as circumvention, and the corresponding response is termed anti-circumvention. The validity, under GATT law, of various potential anti-circumvention measures is unclear".

[7] WTO, Anti-Dumping: Technical Information on Anti-dumping (Previous Agreements). http://www.wto.org/english/tratop_e/adp_e/adp_info_e.htm. Accessed Feb. 28, 2012.

[8] Anti-dumping Agreement, *supra* note 244. Art. 2.1.

[9] Thus, the Anti-Dumping Agreement does not qualify dumping as an unfair trade practice per se and does not discipline dumping, but rather anti-dumping. This is in contrast to WTO member countries domestic legislation. For example, the U.S. legislation still refers to dumping as unfair practice, Tariff Act of 1930, Title VII, § 701–783 (codified at U.S.C. §1671–1677 2000), the EC Practice, of then referring to dumping as unfair trade practice, for example, in the Regulation of the European Commission, Commission Regulation No. 2720/93, O.J.L 246/12 (1993), *cited* by Adamantopoulos and De Notaris (2000, pp. 32–33).

[10] Here it should be stressed that the Anti-Dumping Agreement is an instrument to restrain the use of anti-dumping. Anti-dumping practices cause WTO members to deviate from the general principles of tariff binding/predictability and non-discrimination and should therefore be restrained. Applying the principle of restriction of anti-dumping practices to the interpretation of the agreement, the agreement should be interpreted in a restrictive way. In the presence of more than one possible interpretation, the interpretation most restrictive of the use of anti-dumping should prevail (Adamantopoulos and De Notaris 2000, *id.*, at 33).

sets forth detailed procedural rules for the initiation and conduct of investigations, the imposition of measures, and the duration and review of measures.[11]

The Committee, which meets at least twice a year, provides Members of the WTO the opportunity to discuss any matters relating to the Anti-Dumping Agreement.[12] The Committee has undertaken the review of national legislations notified to the WTO.[13] Members may challenge the imposition of anti-dumping measures, in some cases may challenge the imposition of preliminary anti-dumping measures, and can raise all issues of compliance with the requirements of the agreement, before a panel established under the DSU.

In disputes under the Anti-Dumping Agreement, a special standard of review is applicable to a panel's review of the determination of the national authorities imposing the measure. The standard provides for a certain amount of deference to national authorities in their establishment of facts and interpretation of law, and is intended to prevent dispute settlement panels from making decisions based purely on their own views.[14]

4.1.3 Comparison of Normal Value and Export Price

4.1.3.1 Determination of Normal Value

The normal value is generally the price of the product at issue, in the ordinary course of trade, when destined for consumption in the exporting country market.[15] In certain circumstances, for example when there are no sales in the domestic market, it may not be possible to determine normal value on this basis. The agreement provides alternative methods for the determination of normal value in such cases.[16]

---

[11] For the imposition of "anti-circumvention" duties as one question that the Uruguay Round negotiations were unable to resolve, see Leebron (1995). "...This matter has been referred to the Committee...but in the interim, many countries will unilaterally adopt anti-circumvention measures".

[12] Anti-dumping Agreement, *supra* note 244. Art. 16.

[13] Anti-dumping Agreement, *supra* note 244. Art. 18.6.

[14] Anti-dumping Agreement, *supra* note 244. Art. 17.6.

[15] Anti-dumping Agreement, *supra* note 244. Art. 2.1.

[16] According to Adamantopoulos and De Notaris (2000), there are tour kinds of situations which are particularly penalizing in the calculation of the dumping margin and leave much discretion to administering authorities with regard to the determination to dumping : "First, the situation in which the exporter does not sell sufficient quantities domestically to permit a comparison between normal value and export price ... In such cases, it would appear more reasonable ... to calculate normal value on the basis of the price to the largest export market, ... Second, a situation under which the amount of domestic sales ... are below cost and considered too large to permit comparison between domestic and export price. ... In fact, the exporting company ... does not earn a monopolistic surplus on its domestic market, and therefore cannot cross-subsidize its exports to the export market concerned. ... A third situation regards exports operating in 'non-market' economy countries, in relation to which many administering authorities often use

One of the most complicated questions in anti-dumping investigations is the determination whether sales in the exporting country's market are made in the "ordinary course of trade" or not. One of the bases on which countries may determine that sales are not made in the ordinary course of trade is if sales in the domestic market of the exporter are made below cost. The Agreement defines the specific circumstances in which home market sales at prices below the cost of production may be considered as not made in the "ordinary course of trade", and thus may be disregarded in the determination of normal value.[17]

Those sales must be made at prices that are below per unit fixed and variable costs plus administrative, selling and general costs, they must be made within an extended period of time (normally one year, but in no case less than six months), and they must be made in substantial quantities.[18] Those sales made below costs may only be disregarded in the determination of normal value where they do not allow for recovery of costs within a reasonable period of time. If sales are below cost when made but are above the weighted average cost over the period of the investigation, the Agreement provides that they allow for recovery of costs within a reasonable period of time.[19]

If there are sales below cost that meet the criteria set out in the Agreement, they can simply be ignored in the calculation of normal value, and normal value will be determined based on the remaining sales. However, exclusion of these below-cost sales may result in a level of sales insufficient to determine normal value based on home market prices. In the case where there are no sales in the exporting country of the product under investigation, it is not possible to base normal value on such sales, yet it is possible that, while there are some sales in the exporting country's market, the level of such sales is so low that its significance is questionable.[20]

Regarding alternative bases for calculating normal value, two alternatives are provided for the determination of normal value if sales in the exporting country market are not an appropriate basis. These are (a) the price at which the product is sold to a third country; and (b) the "constructed value" of the product, which is

constructed normal values, after a superficial investigation of their particular situation. . . . Finally, very high standards of burden of proof for duty drawback allowances applied by certain administrative authorities render Art. 2.4 of little use to exporters wanting to benefit from duty drawback allowances. . . ." (Adamantopoulos and De Notaris 2000, *supra* note 248, at 48–50).

[17] Anti-dumping Agreement, *supra* note 244. Art. 2.

[18] Sales are made in substantial quantities when (a) the weighted average selling price is below the weighted average cost; of (b) 20 % of the sales by volume were below cost.

[19] Anti-dumping Agreement, *supra* note 244. Arts. 2.1 and 2.2.

[20] WTO, Anti-Dumping: Technical Information on Anti-dumping (Determination of normal value – Insufficient volume of sales), *available at* http://www.wto.org/english/tratop_e/adp_e/adp_info_e.htm. Accessed Oct. 19, 2012. Thus, the Agreement recognizes that in some cases sales in the home market may be so low in volume that they do not permit a proper comparison of home market and export prices. It provides that the level of home market sales is sufficient if home market sales constitute 5 percent or more of the export sales in the country conducting the investigation, provided that a lower ratio "should" be accepted if the volume of domestic sales nevertheless is "of sufficient magnitude" to provide for a fair comparison.

calculated on the basis of the cost of production, plus selling, general, and administrative expenses, and profits.[21]

In the situation where products are not imported directly from the country of manufacture, but are exported from an intermediate country, the Agreement provides that the normal value shall be determined on the basis of sales in the market of the exporting country. However, the Agreement recognizes that this may result in an inappropriate or impossible comparison, for instance if the product is not produced in the exporting country, there is no comparable price for the product in the exporting country, or the product is merely transshipped through the exporting country. In such cases, the normal value may be determined on the basis of the price of the product in the country of origin, and not the price in the exporting country.[22]

4.1.3.2 Determination of Export Price

The export price will normally be based on the transaction price at which the foreign producer sells the product to an importer in the importing country. However, as is the case with normal value, the Agreement recognizes that this transaction price may not be appropriate for purposes of comparison.[23] There may be no export price for a given product, for instance, if the export transaction is an internal transfer, or if the product is exchanged in a barter transaction.

In addition, the transaction price at which the exporter sells the product to the importing country may be unreliable because of an association or a compensatory arrangement between the exporter and the importer or a third party. In such a case, the transaction price may not be an arms-length market price, but may be manipulated, for instance for tax purposes. The Agreement recognizes that, in such cases, an alternative method of determining an appropriate export price for comparison is needed.[24]

The Agreement provides that in circumstances where there is no export price, or where the export price is unreliable due to an association or compensatory arrangement between the exporter and the importer or a third party, an alternative method may be used to determine the export price. This results in a "constructed export price", and is calculated on the basis of the price at which the imported products are first resold to an independent buyer.[25] If the imported product is not resold to an independent buyer, or is not resold as imported, the authorities may determine a reasonable basis on which to calculate the export price.[26]

[21] Anti-dumping Agreement, *supra* note 244. Art. 5.2.

[22] Anti-dumping Agreement, *supra* note 244. Art. 2.5.

[23] *Id.*

[24] *Id.*

[25] Anti-dumping Agreement, *supra* note 244. Art. 2.3.

[26] WTO, Anti-Dumping: Technical Information on Anti-dumping (Determination of export price – Alternative method of calculation). http://www.wto.org/english/tratop_e/adp_e/adp_info_e.htm Accessed Feb. 28, 2012.

4.1.3.3 Fair Comparison

The Agreement requires that a fair comparison of the export price and the normal value be made. The basic requirements for a fair comparison are that the prices being compared are those of sales made at the same level of trade, normally the ex-factory level, and of sales made at as nearly as possible the same time.[27] As part of the Agreement's requirements regarding transparency and participation, the investigating authorities are required to inform parties of the information needed to ensure a fair comparison, for instance, information regarding adjustments, allowances, and currency conversion, and may not impose an "unreasonable burden of proof" on parties.[28]

To ensure that prices are comparable, the Agreement requires that adjustments be made to either the normal value, or the export price, or both, to account for differences in the product, or in the circumstances of sale, in the importing and exporting markets. These allowances must be made for differences in conditions and terms of sale, taxation, quantities, physical characteristics, and other differences demonstrated to affect price comparability.[29]

4.1.3.4 Calculation of Dumping Margins and Duty Assessment

In the usual case, the Agreement requires either the comparison of the weighted average normal value to the weighted average of all comparable export prices, or a transaction-to-transaction comparison of the normal value and export price.[30] A different basis of comparison can be used if there is "targeted dumping": that is, if a pattern exists of export prices differing significantly among different purchasers, regions or time periods. In this situation, if the investigating authorities provide an explanation as to why such differences cannot be taken into account in weighted average-to-weighted average or transaction-to-transaction comparisons, the weighted average normal value can be compared to the export prices on individual transactions.[31]

Members are required to collect duties on a non-discriminatory basis on imports from all sources found to be dumped and causing injury, except with respect to sources from which a price undertaking has been accepted.[32] Moreover, the amount of the duty collected may not exceed the dumping margin, although it may be a

---

[27] Anti-dumping Agreement, *supra* note 244. Art. 2.4.

[28] WTO, Anti-Dumping: Technical Information on Anti-dumping (Fair comparison of normal value and export price-Basic requirements). http://www.wto.org/english/tratop_e/adp_e/adp_info_e.htm. Accessed Feb. 28, 2012.

[29] Anti-dumping Agreement, *supra* note 244. Art. 2.4.

[30] Anti-dumping Agreement, *supra* note 244. Art. 2.4.2.

[31] WTO, Anti-Dumping: Technical Information on Anti-dumping (Calculation of dumping margins and duty assessment – Calculation of dumping margins). http://www.wto.org/english/tratop_e/adp_e/adp_info_e.htm. Accessed Feb. 28, 2012.

[32] Anti-dumping Agreement, *supra* note 244. Art. 9.2.

lesser amount.[33] The Agreement specifies two mechanisms to ensure that excessive duties are not collected. The choice of mechanism depends on the nature of the duty collection process. If a Member allows importation and collects an estimated anti-dumping duty, and only later calculates the specific amount of anti-dumping duty to be paid, the Agreement requires that the final determination of the amount must take place as soon as possible, upon request for a final assessment.[34]

The Agreement requires that, when anti-dumping duties are imposed, a dumping margin be calculated for each exporter. However, it is recognized that this may not be possible in all cases, and thus the Agreement allows investigating authorities to limit the number of exporters, importers, or products individually considered, and impose an anti-dumping duties on uninvestigated sources on the basis of the weighted average dumping margin actually established for the exporters or producers actually examined.[35]

4.1.4 Determination of Injury

4.1.4.1 Like Products

An important decision must be made early in each investigation to determine the domestic "like product". A like product is defined as "a product which is identical, i.e. alike in all respects to the product under consideration or, in the absence of such a product, another product which, although not alike in all respects, has characteristics closely resembling those of the product under consideration".[36]

The determination involves first examining the imported product or products that are alleged to be dumped, and then establishing what domestically produced product or products are the appropriate "like product". The decision regarding the like product is important because it is the basis of determining which companies constitute the domestic industry, and that determination in turn governs the scope of the investigation and determination of injury and causal link.[37]

---

[33] Anti-dumping Agreement, *supra* note 244. Art. 9.3.

[34] Anti-dumping Agreement, *supra* note 244. Art. 9.3.1.

[35] WTO, Anti-Dumping: Technical Information on Anti-dumping (Calculation of dumping margins and duty assessment-Individual exporter dumping margins) http://www.wto.org/english/tratop_e/adp_e/adp_info_e.htm. Accessed Feb. 28, 2012.

[36] Anti-dumping Agreement, *supra* note 244. Art. 2.6.

[37] For the ambiguities of the definition of "like product" in the anti-dumping context, see Adamantopoulos and De Notaris (2000, *supra* note 248, at 36–41). (Stating " ... since the definition of 'like product' has not been settled in the anti-dumping the product scope of anti-dumping investigations. ... while the Commission ... hold that all PSF types are one 'like product', the Department of Commence initiated ... on antidumping proceeding concerning PSF ... specifically excluding from the scope of the investigation PSF use ..."; WTO, Anti-Dumping: Technical Information on Anti-dumping (Like product-Definition)) http://www.wto.org/english/tratop_e/adp_e/adp_info_e.htm. Accessed Feb. 28, 2012.

4.1.4.2 Domestic Industry

The term "domestic industry" is defined to mean "the domestic producers as a whole of the like products or those of them whose collective output of the products constitutes a major proportion of the total domestic production of those products".[38] In certain circumstances, it may not be appropriate to include all producers of the like product in the domestic industry. Thus, Members are permitted to exclude from the domestic industry producers related to the exporters or importers under investigation, and producers who are themselves importers of the allegedly dumped product.

A producer can be deemed "related" to an exporter or importer of the allegedly dumped product if there is a relationship of control between them, and if there is reason to believe that the relationship causes the domestic producer to behave differently from non-related producers.[39] In exceptional circumstances, consideration of injury to producers comprising a "regional industry" is allowed. A regional industry may be found to exist in a separate competitive market if producers within that market sell all or almost all of their production of the like product in that market, and demand for the like product in that market is not to any substantial degree supplied by producers of the like product located outside that market.

If this is the case, investigating authorities may find that injury exists, even if a major proportion of the entire domestic industry, including producers outside the region, is not materially injured. However, a finding of injury to the regional industry is only allowed if (1) there is a concentration of dumped imports into the market served by the regional industry, and (2) dumped imports are causing injury to the producers of all or almost all of the production within that market.[40]

4.1.4.3 Injury

In order to impose anti-dumping measures, the investigating authorities of the importing Member must make a determination of injury. The term "injury" is defined to mean either (i) material injury to a domestic industry, (ii) threat of material injury to a domestic industry, or (iii) material retardation of the establishment of a domestic industry, but is silent on the evaluation of material retardation of the establishment of a domestic industry.[41]

The notion of "material" is not defined. However, it is required that a determination of injury must be based on positive evidence and involve an objective examination of (i) the volume of dumped imports and the effect of the dumped imports on prices in the domestic market for like products, and (ii) the consequent impact of the dumped imports on domestic producers of the like product.[42]

---

[38] Anti-dumping Agreement, *supra* note 244. Art. 4.

[39] Anti-dumping Agreement, *supra* note 244. Art. 4.

[40] Anti-dumping Agreement, *supra* note 244. Art. 4.

[41] Anti-dumping Agreement, *supra* note 244. fn. 9.

[42] Art. 3 contains some specific additional factors to be considered in the evaluation of these two basic elements, but does not provide detailed guidance on how these factors are to be evaluated or weighed, or on how the determination of causal link is to be made. Anti-dumping Agreement, *supra* note 244. Art. 3.1.

The Agreement sets forth factors to be considered in the evaluation of threat of material injury. These include the rate of increase of dumped imports, the capacity of the exporter(s), and the likely effects of prices of dumped imports, and inventories. There is no further elaboration on these factors, or on how they are to be evaluated. The Agreement does, however, specify that a determination of threat of material injury shall be based on facts, and not merely on allegation, conjecture, or remote possibility, and moreover, that the change in circumstances which would create a situation where dumped imports caused material injury must be clearly foreseen and imminent.[43]

4.1.5 Elements of Analysis

4.1.5.1 Volume and Price of Dumped Imports

Investigating authorities are required to consider whether there has been a significant increase in the dumped imports, either in absolute terms or relative to production or consumption in the domestic industry.[44]

Investigating authorities are also required to consider whether there has been significant price undercutting by the dumped imports as compared with the price of a like product of the importing Member. Investigating authorities are, besides, required to consider whether the effect of dumped imports is "otherwise" to depress prices to a significant degree, or to prevent price increases, which otherwise would have occurred, to a significant degree.[45]

4.1.5.2 Volume and Price Effects of Dumped Imports

The Agreement does not specify how the investigating authorities are to evaluate the volume and price effects of dumped imports: merely that consideration of these effects is required. Thus, investigating authorities have to develop analytical methods for undertaking the consideration of these factors. Moreover, since no single factor or combination of factors will necessarily result in either an affirmative or negative determination, in each case investigating authorities have to evaluate which factors are relevant, and which are important, in light of the circumstances of the particular case at issue.[46]

4.1.5.3 Impact of Dumped Imports on Domestic Industry

In examining the impact of dumped imports on the domestic industry, the authorities are to evaluate all relevant economic factors bearing upon the state of

---

[43] Anti-dumping Agreement, *supra* note 244. Art. 3.7.

[44] Anti-dumping Agreement, *supra* note 244. Art. 3.2.

[45] Anti-dumping Agreement, *supra* note 244. Art. 3.2.

[46] WTO, Anti-Dumping: Technical Information on Anti-dumping (Elements of analysis-Evaluation of volume and price effects of dumped imports), *available at* http://www.wto.org/english/tratop_e/adp_e/adp_info_e.htm. Accessed Oct. 19, 2012.

the domestic industry. The Agreement lists a number of factors which must be considered, including actual or potential declines in sales, profits, output, market share, productivity, return on investments, utilization of capacity, actual or potential effects on cash flow, inventories, employment, wages, growth, ability to raise capital or investments, and the magnitude of the margin of dumping. However, the list is not exhaustive, and other factors may be deemed relevant.[47]

4.1.5.4 Demonstration of Causal Link

Demonstration of a causal relationship between the dumped imports and the injury to the domestic industry is required. This demonstration must be based on an examination of all relevant evidence. The Agreement does not specify particular factors or give guidance in how relevant evidence is to be evaluated.[48] Thus, the investigating authorities must develop analytical methods for determining what evidence is or may be relevant in a particular case, and for evaluating that evidence, taking account of other factors which may be causing injury.[49]

4.1.5.5 Cumulative Analysis

Cumulative analysis refers to the consideration of dumped imports from more than one country on a combined basis in assessing whether dumped imports cause injury to the domestic industry. Obviously, since such analysis will increase the volume of imports whose impact is being considered, there is a greater possibility of an affirmative determination in a case involving cumulative analysis. The practice of cumulative analysis was the subject of much controversy under the Tokyo Round Code, and in the negotiations for the Agreement.

The authorities must determine that the margin of dumping from each country is not de minimis, that the volume of imports from each country is not negligible, and that a cumulative assessment is appropriate in light of the conditions of competition among the imports and between the imports and the domestic like product.[50] De minimis dumping margins and negligible import volumes are defined in the Agreement.[51]

---

[47] Anti-dumping Agreement, *supra* note 244. Art. 3.4.

[48] Anti-dumping Agreement, *supra* note 244. Art. 3.5 does require, however, that known factors other than dumped imports which may be causing injury must be examined, gives examples of factors (such as changes in the pattern of demand, and developments in technology) which may be relevant, and specifies that injury caused by such "other factors" must not be attributed to dumped imports.

[49] Anti-dumping Agreement, *supra* note 244. Art. 3.5.

[50] Anti-dumping Agreement, *supra* note 244. Art. 3.3.

[51] Anti-dumping Agreement, *supra* note 244. Art. 5.8.

4.1.6 Investigation

Regarding the initiation of investigations, it is specified that investigations should generally be initiated on the basis of written request submitted "by or on behalf of" a domestic industry. This "standing" requirement includes numerical limits for determining whether there is sufficient support by domestic producers to conclude that the request is made by or on behalf of the domestic industry, and thereby warrants initiation. The Agreement establishes requirements for evidence of dumping, injury, and causality, as well as other information regarding the product, industry, importers, exporters, and other matters, in written applications for anti-dumping relief, and specifies that, in special circumstances when authorities initiate without a written application from a domestic industry, they shall proceed only if they have sufficient evidence of dumping, injury, and causality.[52]

In order to ensure that investigations without merit are not continued, potentially disrupting legitimate trade, it is provided immediate termination of investigations in the event the volume of imports is negligible or the margin of dumping is de minimis, and numeric thresholds for these determinations. Authorities are required to guarantee the confidentiality of sensitive information and verify the information on which determinations are based.[53]

In addition, to ensure the transparency of proceedings, authorities are required to disclose the information on which determinations are to be based to interested parties and provide them with adequate opportunity to comment. The Agreement establishes the rights of parties to participate in the investigation, including the right to meet with parties with adverse interests, for instance in a public hearing. Further guidance on the conduct of investigations, including rules for the on-the-spot investigations as well as rules for the use of best information available, is contained in two annexes to the Agreement.[54]

---

[52] Anti-dumping Agreement, *supra* note 244. Art. 244; As far as the quality of evidence required for initiation of an investigation is concerned, WTO panels do not interpret the Agreement very strictly. It is established WTO case law that the evidence required to initiate a case need not be of the same quality as the evidence required for a decision on imposition of duties. While WTO panels do not interpret the provisions regarding initiation of an investigation in the narrowest way, important consequences follow from procedural infringements in the initiation of an anti-dumping investigation. For example, the initiation of an anti-dumping investigation, or even rumors of possible initiation, often onerously impact an exporting country's industry (Adamantopoulos and De Notaris 2000, *supra* note 248, at 43).

[53] Anti-dumping Agreement, *supra* note 244. Art. 5.

[54] Anti-dumping Agreement, *supra* note 244. Art. 6. For the application of the general principle of restriction of anti-dumping and possible reforms, see Adamantopoulos and De Notaris (2000, *supra* note 248, at 44–46). (stating "First, the principle of restriction of anti-dumping should lead us to consider that only anti- dumping petitions with serious grounds should be considered worth for the purpose of initiating a complex and burdensome proceeding .... Second, the principle of enhancing fair competition suggests that the domestic industry's use of anti-dumping petitions to commercially harass exporters should be prohibited, or at least limited. Third, the legal certainty principle requests that the standards of review for the information provided in the petition should not allow the administering authorities to excessively permissive interpretations ...").

4.1.7 Provisional Measures and Price Undertakings

Authorities are required to make a preliminary affirmative determination of dumping, injury, and causality before applying provisional measures, and no provisional measures may be applied sooner than 60 days after initiation of an investigation. Provisional measures may take the form of a provisional duty or, preferably, a security by cash deposit or bond equal to the amount of the preliminarily determined margin of dumping. The Agreement also contains time limits for the imposition of provisional measures – generally four months, with a possible extension to six months at the request of exporters. If a Member, in its administration of anti-dumping duties, imposes duties lower than the margin of dumping when these are sufficient to remove injury, the period of provisional measures is generally six months, with a possible extension to nine months at the request of exporters.[55]

Price undertakings may be offered and accepted in lieu of the imposition of anti-dumping duties. The Agreement establishes the principle that undertakings between any exporter and the importing Member, to revise prices, or cease exports at dumped prices, may be entered into to settle an investigation, but only after a preliminary affirmative determination of dumping, injury and causality has been made. It also establishes that undertakings are voluntary on the part of both exporters and investigating authorities. In addition, an exporter may request that the investigation be continued after an undertaking has been accepted, and if a final determination of no dumping, no injury, or no causality results, the undertaking shall automatically lapse.[56]

4.1.8 Collection of Duties

It is the general principle that imposition of anti-dumping duties is optional, even if all the requirements for imposition have been met. It is also desirable to apply a "lesser duty" rule. Under a lesser duty rule, authorities impose duties at a level lower than the margin of dumping if this level is adequate to remove injury. In any case, duties in excess of the dumping margin shall not be collected.[57]

As a general rule, both provisional and final anti-dumping duties may be applied only as of the date on which the determinations of dumping, injury and causality have been made. However, it is recognized that injury may have occurred during the period of investigation, or that exporters may have taken actions to avoid the imposition of an anti-dumping duty: the retroactive imposition of dumping duties may be possible in specified circumstances.[58]

[55] Anti-dumping Agreement, *supra* note 244. Art. 7.

[56] Anti-dumping Agreement, *supra* note 244. Art. 8.

[57] Anti-dumping Agreement, *supra* note 244. Art. 9.

[58] Anti-dumping Agreement, *supra* note 244. Art. 10.

If the imposition of anti-dumping duties is based on a finding of material injury, as opposed to threat of material injury or material retardation of the establishment of a domestic industry, anti-dumping duties may be collected as of the date provisional measures were imposed. If provisional duties were collected in an amount greater than the amount of the final duty, or if the imposition of duties is based on a finding of threat of material injury or material retardation, a refund of provisional duties is required. The application of final duties may be made retroactively to a date not more than 90 days prior to the application of provisional measures in certain exceptional circumstances involving a history of dumping, massive dumped imports, and potential undermining of the remedial effects of the final duty.[59]

With relation to the duration of anti-dumping duties, the "sunset" requirement establishes that dumping duties shall normally terminate no later than five years after first being applied, unless a review investigation prior to that date establishes that expiry of the duty would be likely to lead to continuation or recurrence of dumping and injury. This five year "sunset" provision also applies to price undertakings. The Agreement requires authorities to review the need for the continued imposition of a duty upon request of an interested party.[60]

Public notice is required to be made by investigating authorities about the initiation of investigations, preliminary and final determinations, and undertakings. The public notice must disclose non-confidential information concerning the parties, the product, the margins of dumping, the facts revealed during the investigation, and the reasons for the determinations made by the authorities, including the reasons for accepting and rejecting relevant arguments or claims made by exporters or importers. These public notice requirements are intended to increase the transparency of determinations, with the hope that this will increase the extent to which determinations are based on fact and solid reasoning.[61]

– Trade Disputes in Relation with **Anti-Dumping Agreement**

Panel Report, *United States-Continued Dumping and Subsidy Offset Act of 2000*, WT/DS217/R/, WT/DS234/R (Jan. 16, 2003) (U.S.-Offset Act Panel Report).

[59] Anti-dumping Agreement, *supra* note 244. Art. 10.6.

[60] Anti-dumping Agreement, *supra* note 244. Art. 11.

[61] Anti-dumping Agreement, *supra* note 244. Art. 12.

Facts and Overview

The United States Continued Dumping and Subsidy Offset Act of 2000 (hereinafter known as CDSOA) was enacted on October 28, 2000 as part of the Agriculture, Rural Development, Food and Drug Administration and Related Agencies Appropriations Act, 2001. The CDSOA went into effect on September 21, 2001. The CDSOA takes money from foreign companies for dumping and countervailing and disperses the money to the domestic producers of the same products. The foreign company is twice penalized; first, by the initial duty, and again when the money is given to a domestic competitor. The money may be used for any of the following categories:

A. Manufacturing facilities; B. Equipment; C. Research and development; D. Personnel training; E. Acquisition of technology; F. Health care benefits to employees paid for by the employer; G. Pension benefits to employees paid for by the employer; H. Environmental equipment, training or technology; I. Acquisition of raw material and other inputs; J. Working capital or other funds needed to maintain production.

The money from the CDSOA is distributed 60 days after the beginning of the year after the money was collected and any money left over after the distributions have been made is deposited into the U.S. Treasury.

On December 21, 2000, Australia, Brazil, Chile, the European Communities, India, Indonesia, Japan, Korea and Thailand jointly requested a consultation with the United States of America under Article 4 of the Understanding on Rules and Procedures governing the Settlement of Dispute (the DSU), Article XXII: 1 of GATT, Articles 17.2 and 17.3 of the Anti-Dumping Agreement, and Articles 7.1 and 30 of the Subsidies and Countervailing Measures Agreement (the SCM Agreement) regarding an amendment to the Tariff Act of 1930 signed on October 20, 2000 by the President under the title "*Continued Dumping and Subsidy Offset Act of 2000*"(WT/DS217/1). Consultations held in Geneva about this matter failed to find a solution.

On May 21, 2001, Canada and Mexico requested consultations with the United States to discuss Article 4 of the DSU, Article XXII: 1 of GATT 1994, Articles 7.1 and 30 of the SCM Agreement and Article 17 of the Anti-Dumping Agreement of WS/DS234/l.

On July 12, 2001, Australia, Brazil, Chile, the European Communities, India, Indonesia, Japan, Korea and Thailand requested that a panel be establish in regards to Articles 4.7 and 6 of the DSU, Article XXIII of GATT 1994, Article 17 of the Anti-Dumping Agreement and Article 30 of the SCM Agreement, using the standard terms of reference provided for in Article 7.1 of the DSU (WT/DS217/13). The need for a panel was established for these requests on August 23, 2001 (WT/DS/234/14).

On October 25, 2001 the Director-General announced that the panel was established. Argentina, Canada, Costa Rica, Hong Kong, China, Israel,

(continued)

Mexico and Norway reserved their third party right to DS 217 and the Panel considered them to be third parties. Australia, Brazil, Canada (with special regard to Mexico's complaint) the European Communities, Indian, Indonesia, Japan, Korea, Mexico (with special regard to Canada's complaint) and Thailand reserved their third party rights in DS234.

Principal Issues on Appeal

The principal issues raised in the appeal were: A. Whether the United States has not conformed to AD Article 18.1, B. Whether the United States has not conformed to SCM Article 32.1; C. Whether the United States has not conformed to paragraph 2 of GATT Article VI; D. Whether the United States has not conformed to paragraph 3 of GATT Article VI.

Rationale and Holdings

AD Article 18.1

The United States used a two-pronged approach to AD Article 18.1. Firstly the United States believed the Appellate Body would enforce that AD Article 18.1 only applies to dumping. The United States stated that the CDSOA payments were not based on the dumping specifically, and consequently not subject to the AD Article 18.1. Secondly, AD Article 18.1 is restricted to specific actions "against" dumping. CDSOA payments are not payments against dumping, but rather "in response to" dumping.

The Panel determined that a measure can be considered a "specific action against dumping" when "(1) it acts specifically in response to dumping, in the sense that it may be taken only in situations presenting the constituent elements of dumping, and (2) it acts "against" dumping, in the sense that it has an adverse bearing on dumping." The United States CDSOA goes into effect when the constituent elements of dumping are present.

The discussion of whether the payments affect the product or simply offset the gains made by the imported product is splitting hairs that do not need to be split. AD Article 18.1 refers to the practice of "dumping." There is not any specification that the action must be specifically against the imported product. AD Article 18.1 applies both directly and indirectly against dumping. The CDSOA has a negative impact on dumping.

SCM Article 32.1

CDSOA is a specific action taken against situations that hold the constituent elements of dumping and this has an adverse impact on dumping. The Panel concludes that CDSOA is non-permissible under SCM Article 32.1. There are conflicts between CDSOA and AD Article 18.1 as well as SCM Article 32.1. Finally the CDSOA violates paragraphs 2 and 3 of Article VI of GATT 1994.

AD Articles 5.4/ SCM Article 11.4/Standing

The claim that the CDSOA violates AD Article 5.4 and SCM Article 11.4 cannot be sufficiently investigated. The text states that a certain amount of support before an application before a Member can begin an investigation. The CDOSA will then handle the distribution of duties and the conditions of eligibility. The CDSOA does not amend any of the United States' statutory provision under Article 5.4 AD and 11.4 SCM Agreement. The real question is whether the CDSOA runs in a manner that the US investigating authorities will be unable to conduct an objective and impartial examination of an application and its documentation and whether the CDSOA has undermined the provisions of AD Article 5.4 and SCM Article 11.4.

According to the panel, there is a strong incentive for producers in a particular industry to petition and to support the petitions of other domestic producers to obtain compensation. This incentive will have a snowball effect of producers petitioning the CDSOA to allege dumping by foreign companies. It is impossible to deny the impact on the industry.

There are several consequences to this situation. The quantitative tests required by CDSOA as support are in the panel' words "irrelevant" and take away the opportunity for the investigated parties of a CDSOA claim a means to determine the validity of the investigation. The United States is not considered to have worked in good faith with its trading partners. Requiring support for a petition as a prerequisite for an investigation is a way of insuring that investigate parties are forced to pay exorbitant duties to CDSOA that will in turn be given to the "affected domestic partner." CDSOA is inconsistent with Article 5.4 and SMS Article 11.4.

AD Article 8.3/ SCMS Article 18.3

Although the complaining parties argue that CDSOA is inconsistent with AD Article 8.3 and SCM Article 18.3. AD Article 8.3 provides that an undertaking may be rejected for many reasons. If the CDSOA mandated an explicit violation of the provisions in question, then the CDSOA would be considered as in violation of AD Article 8.3 and SCMS Article 18.3. As it stands, the CDSOA does not mandate an explicit violation, but allow the potential for violation indirectly.

The complainants' argument revolves around the role of the domestic industry in the United States AD/CVD system in whether price undertakings are accepted. It is the interaction between the CDSOA and the domestic producers as to whether or not an undertaking is accepted and that, according to the complaining parties, violates AD Article 8.3 and SCM Article 18.3.

As a matter of general policy the United States does not always reject undertakings. The power of the petitioners' objections need not be given so much weight by the complaining parties. While the objections of the petitioners are some of the items considered in an investigation, they are

(continued)

not the only things considered in an investigation. According to the Panel, the United States investigating authority retains the power to accept an undertaking without concern for the views of the petitioners.

While the CDSOA may affect domestic industry in regards to undertakings, there is no reason to conclude that the CDSOA mandates a violation of AD Article 8.3 and SCM Article 18.3. CDSOA is not considered to be inconsistent with AD Article 8.3 and SCM Article 18.3.

Developing Country Issue-AD Article 15

Although AD Article 15 would not normally fall within the terms of reference for the Panel, DSU Article 12.11 requires the panel to "explicitly indicate the form in which account has been taken of relevant provisions on differential and more-favorable treatment for developing country Members that form part of the covered agreements which have been raised by the developing country Member in the course of the dispute settlements procedures." In view of the above passage, considering AD Article 15 is relevant to the situation. The true concern of Indonesia and India on this case is that under US Law, the domestic industry has the power to veto any price undertakings by the USDOC. Although this is a concern, there is not any factual evidence that the USDOC does not undertake price undertakings simply because of the veto power of the US domestic industry. Therefore, this is considered unsubstantiated. No further action will be taken on this point.

AD Articles 18.1, 5.4, 8.3/ SCM Article 32.5/ WTO Article XVI: 4 – Necessary steps to ensure conformity

Because all parties agree that a violation of AD Articles 18.1, 5.4, 8.2 or a violation of SCM 32.1, 11.4 and 18.3 would also be a violation of AD Article 18.4, SCM Article 32.5, WTO Article XVI: 4, we find that the CDSOA is inconsistent with AD Article 18.4, SCM Article 32.5 and, consequently, WTO Article XVI: 4.

Adverse Effects of SCM Article 5

The real question is whether the CDSOA is an actionable subsidy since whether the CDSOA qualifies as a subsidy is uncontested. Even more specifically, it is Article 2.1 (a) that Mexico uses for de jure specificity. De facto specificity is not an issue. If the CDSOA specifically limits access to offset payments to certain enterprises, the de jure specificity is in play. The U.S. states that CDSOA payments are not limited to individual enterprises or industries that have been affected by dumping and that the diversity within the group of affected domestic producers renders it impossible to define a set group. Mexico does not argue that the CDSOA per se limits access as much as it causes adverse effects, such as "non-violation." However the panel's final decision is that DSU Article 3.8 has not been proven. Mexico has not shown that the use of a subsidy cause nullification or impairment.

As for "non-violation" both Mexico and the United States suggested viewpoints that the panel rejected. In order to apply GATT Article XXIII: 1 (b) a WTO Member must be applying a particular measure, a benefit accrued under the agreement must have existed, and a nullification or impairment must have resulted from the application of the measure. Under the precedent set in Japan- film, regardless of whether money has been dispersed the first condition has been met. Neither Mexico nor the United States dispute that benefits exist for Mexico under Articles II and VI of GATT 1994 and the second condition is considered to have been met. However, GATT Articles II and VI do not state that Members must promise other Members "total predictability," and without that assumption, there is not enough evidence to support the nullification claim. The CDSOA is considered to be consistent with Article 5 (b) of the SCM Agreement.

GATT Article X: 3(a)

For the panel, the main question was whether or not the CDSOA was administrative in nature or not. The panel agrees with the United States that the CDSOA is not administrative by nature. Therefore, the complaining parties claim that Article X: 3(a) is rejected.

Commentary

The United States has been criticized on several occasions for both its anti-dumping laws and its inability to stick to agreements. The Continued Dumping and Subsidy Offset Act of 2000 is a continuation of the type of behavior that has alienated trade partners. According to the Cato Institute, the negativity generated by this act boils down to two main claims: first, reimbursement of expenses means expanding, or ignoring the scope of the Antidumping Agreement and the ASCM, and secondly, that the CDSOA both encourages affected domestic producers to file and support claims because of the financial compensation the affected domestic partners stand to receive.

Additionally, considering the wording of what qualifies as expenses, the money collected and distributed from foreign exporters and given to affected domestic producers could be used in such a loose fashion that the possibility for this money to be used against the very people the money was taken from. Furthermore the lack of any governing body within the United States to monitor how the money is spent concerns trading partners. In other words, rather a simple 'rob Peter to pay Paul' scenario, the CDSOA encourages Peter to claim Paul owes Peter money because Paul's products are cheaper and then Peter using that very money to give himself a competitive edge over Paul without anyone but Peter knowing for sure.

(continued)

Another problem mentioned but within the scope of the WTO consideration was the limited range of companies who benefited from the action. While the United States state that companies from all industries are able to file a complaint if they meet the criteria, about 50 % of the payments went to only five companies in 2004 fiscal year. Four of the five companies are the Timken Company, Torrington Company, 5 % MPB Corporation, and the Zenith Electronics Corporation. Since the United States has rejected the WTO suggestion to repeal the CDSOA, affected countries, specifically Canada, the European Union, Mexico, and Japan, are fighting back by imposing more tariffs on the U.S. and four other countries are considering the same action. One must question if the more prudent overall plan for the United States would not be to repeal the CDSOA since it mainly benefits only five benefits, but the tariffs that may be imposed as an international response to the U.S. not repealing the CDSOA could be much more financially destructive to the overall U.S. economy.

Within the United States, this case has caused controversy about the amount of power the WTO Dispute Settlement Panel and Appellate Bodies has to change rules negotiated by the WTO trade partners. Some people would like to see a return to negotiations rather than the judicial-like system currently in practice. Regardless of a return to more negotiation or more judicial investigations, the problem remains of the friction caused between the United States and trade partners.

Source: Panel Report. *United States-Continued Dumping and Subsidy Offset Act of 2000. January 16, 2003*. WT/DS217/R/, and WT/DS234/R. http://www.sice.oas.org/dispute/wto/ds217_234/ds217a1e.asp

– Trade Disputes in Relation with **Anti-dumping Agreement**
Appellate Body Report, United States-Measures Relating to Zeroing and Sunset Review (Recourse to Article 21.5 of the DSU by Japan, WT/DS322/AB/RW (Aug. 18, 2009)).

Introduction

1. The United States appeals certain issues of law and legal interpretations developed in the Panel Report, *United States – Measures Relating to Zeroing and Sunset Reviews – Recourse to Article 21.5 of the DSU by Japan* (the "Panel Report"). The Panel was established pursuant to Article 21.5 of the *Understanding on Rules and Procedures Governing the*

Settlement of Disputes (the "DSU") to consider a complaint by Japan concerning the existence and consistency with the *Agreement on Implementation of Article VI of the General Agreement on Tariffs and Trade 1994* (the "*Anti-Dumping Agreement*") and the *General Agreement on Tariffs and Trade 1994* ("GATT 1994") of measures taken by the United States to comply with the recommendations and rulings of the Dispute Settlement Body (the "DSB") in *US – Zeroing (Japan).*

2. This dispute concerns the use of the so-called "zeroing" methodology by the United States Department of Commerce (the "USDOC") when calculating margins of dumping. In the original proceedings, the Appellate Body upheld the panel's finding that the United States' zeroing procedures constituted a measure that can be challenged "as such" in dispute settlement proceedings in the World Trade Organization (the "WTO"). The original panel found that, by maintaining model zeroing procedures in the context of original investigations, the United States acts inconsistently with Article 2.4.2 of the *Anti-Dumping Agreement.* The Appellate Body also found that: (a) the United States acts inconsistently with Articles 2.4 and 2.4.2 of the *Anti-Dumping Agreement* by maintaining zeroing procedures when calculating margins of dumping on the basis of transaction-to-transaction comparisons in original investigations; (b) the United States acts inconsistently with Articles 2.4 and 9.3 of the *Anti-Dumping Agreement* and Article VI:2 of GATT 1994 by maintaining zeroing procedures in periodic reviews; and (c) the United States acts inconsistently with Articles 2.4 and 9.5 of the *Anti-Dumping Agreement* by maintaining zeroing procedures in new shipper reviews.
3. As regards Japan's "as applied" claims, the original panel held that, by using model zeroing in the anti-dumping investigation regarding imports of cut-to-length carbon quality steel products from Japan, the United States acted inconsistently with Article 2.4.2 of the *Anti-Dumping Agreement.* This finding of the original panel was not appealed. The Appellate Body additionally found that: (a) the United States acted inconsistently with Articles 2.4 and 9.3 of the *Anti-Dumping Agreement* and Article VI:2 of GATT 1994 by applying zeroing procedures in the 11 periodic reviews at issue in that appeal; and (b) the United States acted inconsistently with Article 11.3 of the *Anti-Dumping Agreement* by relying, in two sunset review determinations, on margins of dumping calculated in previous proceedings through the use of zeroing.
4. The Appellate Body recommended that the DSB request the United States to bring its measures into conformity with its obligations under the *Anti-Dumping Agreement* and GATT 1994.

(continued)

5. Japan did not consider that the United States had brought itself into compliance with the DSB's recommendations and rulings. Consequently, on April 7, 2008, Japan requested that the matter be referred to the original panel pursuant to Article 21.5 of the DSU, and this occurred on April 18, 2008.
6. The United States contended that the zeroing procedures challenged "as such" by Japan in the original proceedings no longer existed because the United States had ceased to apply the zeroing procedures in weighted average-to-weighted average comparisons in original investigations.
7. The panel concluded that, to the extent that the United States has failed to comply with the DSB's recommendations and rulings in the original proceedings, these recommendations and rulings remain operative. The panel also recommended that the DSB request the United States to bring Reviews 4, 5, 6, and 9, and the relevant liquidation actions, into conformity with the *Anti-Dumping Agreement* and GATT 1994.

Findings and Conclusions

8. The Appellate Body: (a) upholds the panel's findings, in paragraphs 7.107, 7.114, and 7.116 of the Panel Report, that Review 9 was properly within the panel's terms of reference; (b) and also upholds the panel's finding, in paragraphs 7.154 and 8.1(a)(i) of the Panel Report, that the United States is in continued violation of its obligations under Articles 2.4 and 9.3 of the *Anti-Dumping Agreement* and Article VI:2 of GATT 1994; (c) upholds the panel's finding, in paragraphs 7.168 and 8.1(b) of the Panel Report, that the United States has acted inconsistently with Articles 2.4 and 9.3 of the *Anti-Dumping Agreement* and Article VI:2 of GATT 1994 by applying zeroing in the context of Reviews 4, 5, 6, and 9; and
9. To the extent that the United States has failed to comply with the recommendations and rulings of the DSB in the original dispute, the recommendations and rulings remain operative. The Appellate Body recommends that the DSB request the United States to bring into conformity with its obligations under the *Anti-Dumping Agreement* and GATT 1994 the measures found in this Report and in the Panel Report to be inconsistent with those Agreements.

Source: Appellate Body Report. United States-Measures Relating to Zeroing and Sunset Review. Aug. 18, 2009. WT/DS322/AB/RW. http://www.wto.org/english/tratop_e/dispu_e/322abrw_e.pdf

4.2 Subsidies and Countervailing Measures

4.2.1 Introduction

4.2.1.1 Applicability

The Agreement on Subsidies and Countervailing Measures (SCM Agreement)[62] addresses two separate but closely related topics: multilateral disciplines regulating the provision of subsidies, and the use of countervailing measures to remove the injury caused by subsidized imports. Multilateral disciplines are the rules regarding whether or not a subsidy may be provided by a Member. They are enforced through invocation of the WTO dispute settlement mechanism. More concretely, certain subsidies are prohibited, and most other specific subsidies may be challenged if they cause adverse effects to the interests of other Members. Three categories of subsidies are non-actionable and cannot be challenged. Thus all specific subsidies are grouped into three kinds: prohibited, actionable, and non-actionable [63]

Countervailing measures[64] are a unilateral remedy but may only be applied by a Member after an investigation by that Member and a determination that the criteria set forth in the SCM Agreement are satisfied. The substantive criteria require that a Member not impose a countervailing measure unless it determines that there are

---

[62] Agreement on Subsidies and Countervailing Measures, Apr. 15, 1994, Marrakesh Agreement Establishing the World Trade Organization, Annex 1. 1994. Legal Instruments-Results of the Uruguay Round. I.L.M. 33: 1125. [hereinafter SCM Agreement]; The main changes resulting from the Uruguay Round are the addition of the two mechanisms used to limit the use of countervailing duties (the specificity and financial contributions requirements), and the traffic-eight framework, which are complex changes, and have the potential to have both protectionist and anti-protectionist consequences (Wilcox 1998, p. 151).

[63] Pritchard and MacPherson (2003, p. 6).

[64] CYDs, when used to offset subsidies by foreign governments to foreign producers, can be an effective means of reducing market distortions and restoring "fair trade," see Southwick (1988, pp. 1173–1175), and can also be positive for the world economy as a whole, as well as for each country that avoid using a subsidy. For the unlikeliness of the indemnification of such positive effect made on a cost-effective basis. See Sykes (1989, pp. 199, 200–201). However CVDs can also be used to protect domestic industries. Certainly, businesses will attempt to use them for that purpose, regardless of any injury that could result to foreign competition. For the protectionist manipulation of CVDs, see Horlick (1993, p. 1202). In fact, the potential for gains from manipulation of government programs has grown to such an extent that it is now being taught to MBA students as one of the top five methods of "earning excess returns in the long run" (Shapiro 1992). "By creating such advantages, a firm can impose barriers to entry by potential competitors, resulting in a less-than-perfectly competitive market and the possibility of positive net present value project" (*id*). "Investments in projects protected from competition by government regulation can lead to extraordinary profitability" (*id*., at 64). When subsidy laws are ambiguous and avoid defining which subsidies are permissible and which are countervailable, as has been the case with U.S. law throughout this century, the result can lead to more protectionism and more distortion than there would have been with no law at all. For the entire prohibition of CVD as the best CVD policy, see Sykes (1989, *id*., at 201, 263). (Stating "Because the need for any countervailing duty policy is questionable, abolition of the countervailing duty laws might best serve the national economic interest.")

subsidized imports, injury to a domestic industry, and a causal link between the subsidized imports and the injury. In-depth procedural requirements regulate the conduct of countervailing investigations and the imposition and maintenance in place of countervailing measures. A failure to respect either the substantive or procedural requirements can be taken to dispute settlement and may be basis for invalidation of the measure.[65]

4.2.1.2 Definition of Subsidy

Unlike the earlier Tokyo Round SCM Agreement, which it replaces, the WTO SCM Agreement contains a definition of the term "subsidy".[66] The definition contains three basic elements: (i) a financial contribution (ii) by a government or any public body within the territory of a Member (iii) which confers a benefit. All three of these elements must be satisfied in order for a subsidy to exist.[67]

Under the SCM Agreement, only measures that take the form of a "financial contribution", or where there is any form of income or price support in the sense of the Agreement, can constitute a subsidy. The Agreement contains an exhaustive list of the type of measures that represent a financial contribution. These include direct transfers of funds (e.g. grants, loans, and equity infusion) and potential direct transfers of funds or liabilities (e.g. loan guarantees). A financial contribution also exists where government revenue that is otherwise due is foregone or not collected (e.g. fiscal incentives such as tax credits); where a government provides goods or services other than general infrastructure, or purchases goods; or where a government entrusts or directs a private body to carry out these functions.[68]

In order for a financial contribution to be a subsidy, it must be made by a government or any public body within the territory of a Member. Thus, the SCM Agreement applies not only to measures of national governments, but also to

[65] Pritchard and MacPherson (2003, *supra* note 302, at. 7).

[66] Defining the scope and characteristics of the definition of a subsidy is important as the General Agreement in Tariffs and Trade (GATT) allows contracting parties to use countervailing duties under certain circumstances when other countries use subsidies. See Agreement on Subsidies and Countervailing Measures, Dec. 15, 1993, GATT Doc. MTN/FA 11–12, reprinted in Office of the U.S. Trade Representative Final Act Embodying the Result of the Uruguay Round of Multilateral Trade Negotiations (1993) [hereinafter Subsidies Agreement]. When formed and applied correctly, multilateral countervailing duty (hereafter CVD) laws allow countries to protect their domestic industries against the market distortions caused by subsidizing countries. See Sykes (1989, *supra* note 303, at 200–201). Inappropriate CVD laws allow countries to practice protectionism by using CVDs in response to legitimate internal policies of other countries, if those policies can be construed as subsides. See (*id.*, at 214). This can result in countries outwardly declaring their CVD to be merely a correction of a market distortion, when in reality these CVDs may be much more distorting and damaging than the original subsidy. See (*id.*, at 257–258). If this is allowed by an inappropriate GATT definition of a subsidy, this will not only counter the success of the GATT, but will also diminish its credibility. Cited by Wilcox (1998, *supra* note 301, fn. 1).

[67] WTO-Trade Policy Courses, Chapter 14: Subsidies & Countervailing Measures 14.2. http://www.wto.org/english/tratop_e/scm_e/subs_e.htm. Accessed Feb. 28, 2012.

[68] SCM Agreement, *supra* note 301. Art. 1.1.

measures by sub-national governments and to such public bodies as state-owned companies.[69]

A financial contribution by a government is not a subsidy unless it confers a "benefit". In certain cases, as in the case of a cash grant, the existence of a benefit and its valuation will be clear. In most cases, however, the issue of benefit will be more complex. For example, when does a loan, an equity infusion or the purchase by a government of a good confer a benefit?

Although the concept of benefit was much discussed during the Uruguay Round (a basic issue was whether the amount of a benefit should be assessed with reference to a commercial benchmark or with reference to the cost to the government), the Agreement provides only partial guidance with respect to the concept of "benefit". It is provided that, in a countervailing duty context, the existence of a benefit may be assessed by reference to commercial benchmarks, and provides some guidance for determining the amount of the benefit with respect to certain types of measures.[70]

The government provision of equity capital is considered as conferring a benefit only if the investment decision can be regarded as inconsistent with the usual investment practice of private investors.[71] A government loan is not considered as conferring a benefit unless there is a difference between the amount that the firm receiving the loan pays on the government loan and the amount the firm would pay on a comparable commercial loan. A government loan guarantee would not be considered as conferring a benefit unless there is a difference between the amount that the firm receiving the guarantee pays and the amount that the firm would pay on a comparable commercial loan absent the government guarantee.

The provision of goods or services or purchase of goods by a government is not considered as conferring a benefit unless the provision is made for less than adequate remuneration, or the purchase is made for more than adequate remuneration. The adequacy of remuneration is to be determined in relation to prevailing market conditions for the good or service (including price, quality, availability, marketability transportation and other conditions of purchase).[72]

4.2.1.3 Specificity

Assuming that a measure is a subsidy within the meaning of the SCM Agreement, it nevertheless is not subject to SCM Agreement disciplines unless it has been specifically provided to an enterprise or industry or group of enterprises or industries.[73] The basic principle is that a subsidy that distorts the allocation of resources within an economy should be subject to discipline. Where a subsidy is

---

[69] *Id.*

[70] SCM Agreement, *supra* note 301. Art. 14.

[71] *Id.*

[72] *Id.*; Cameron May. 2002. WTO Disputes: Anti-Dumping, Subsidies and Safeguards. 955.

[73] Specificity has been made a requirement under the GATT for the first time, after the Uruguay Round (Cobb 1995 cited by Wilcox 1998, *supra* note 301, at 153).

widely available within an economy, such a distortion in the allocation of resources is presumed not to occur. Thus, only "specific" subsidies[74] are subject to the SCM Agreement disciplines.[75]

There are four types of "specificity" within the meaning of the SCM Agreement: a government targets a particular enterpriser or enterprisers for subsidization; a government targets a particular industry or industries for subsidization; a government targets producers in specified parts of its territory for subsidization; a government targets export goods or goods using domestic inputs for subsidization.[76]

If, notwithstanding any appearance of "de jure" non-specificity resulting from the application of the stated principles, there are reasons to believe that the subsidy may in fact be specific, other factors may be considered. Such factors are: use of a subsidy program by a limited number of certain enterprises, predominant use by certain enterprises, the granting of disproportionately large amounts of subsidy to certain enterprises, and the manner in which discretion has been exercised by the granting authority in the decision to grant a subsidy.

In this regard, information on the frequency with which applications for a subsidy are refused or approved and the reasons for such decisions are also considered. The extent of diversification of economic activities within the jurisdiction of the granting authority as well as the length of time during which the subsidy program has been in operation are taken into account. Consideration of such factors may lead to a "de facto" finding of specificity.[77]

4.2.1.4 Prohibited Subsidies

Subsidies contingent upon export performance, or upon the use of domestic over imported goods, are prohibited ("red").[78] These two categories of subsidies are prohibited because they are designed to affect trade and thus are most likely to cause adverse effects to the interests of other Members.[79]

---

[74] For the, at least, two possible complaints about the use of specificity and contribution for the limitation of countervailing duties under the WTO Agreement, see Wilcox (1998, *supra* note 301, at 160–161): " The first . . . it . . . allow legitimate internal decisions to be countervailed. . . . The second . . . it . . . allow no recourse to contracting parties against subsidies that are used for protection of domestic industry . . .".

[75] SCM Agreement, *supra* note 301. Art. 2.1.

[76] SCM Agreement, *supra* note 301. Arts. 2.1(a), 2.1(b).

[77] SCM Agreement, *supra* note 301. Art. 2.1(c).

[78] SCM Agreement, *supra* note 301. Art. 3; The only function of export subsidies is to give domestic produces an unfair advantage in the international market, regardless of any financial contribution or specificity test, which are almost inherently inefficient and are therefore prohibited. See generally Andoh (1992, p. 1515). (discussing economic efficiency and resource allocation in conjunction with export and other type of subsidies). Cited by Wilcox (1998, *supra* note 301, at 152).

[79] WTO-Trade Policy Courses, Chapter 14: Subsidies & Countervailing Measures 14.5 http://www.wto.org/english/tratop_e/scm_e/subs_e.htm. Accessed Feb. 28, 2012.

Regardless of being in law or in fact, or, being wholly or as one of other several requirements, subsidies contingent upon export performance, that is, "export subsidies", are prohibited.[80]

Among the government measures that may represent export subsidies are currency retention schemes which involve a bonus on exports; provision of goods or services for use in the production of exported goods on terms more favorable than those for the production of goods for domestic consumption; export-related exemption, remission or deferral of direct taxes and social welfare charges; excess exemption, remission, or deferral of indirect taxes or import duties; export credits extended at rates below the government's cost of funds; and provision of export credit guarantee or insurance programs at premium rates which are inadequate to cover the operating costs and losses of the programs.[81]

The second prohibited category comprises subsidies contingent, whether solely or as one of several other conditions, upon the use of domestic over imported goods – the so-called import substitution subsidies. Article 3.1(b) enshrines the prohibition on subsidization that is contingent upon a domestic content requirement. As such the provision reflects Article III of GATT 1947, i.e. the principle of national treatment. While the provision of subsidies exclusively to domestic producers,[82] as such, does not constitute a violation of the national treatment requirement, the provision of subsidies contingent on use of domestic over imported goods does violate that requirement.[83] The TRIMs Agreement also prohibits a variety of measures contingent upon either an export performance requirement or a domestic content requirement.[84]

Prohibited subsidies may be challenged through the panel process in the WTO. The very fact that a subsidy is an export or import substitution subsidy, and thus designed to affect trade, means that it is most likely to cause adverse effects; there is therefore no need for the complaining Member to show trade effects. Prohibited subsidies may also be subject to countervailing action. Agricultural export subsidies that are fully consistent with the provisions of the Agreement on Agriculture are not prohibited under the SCM Agreement, but instead are subject to the disciplines of the Agreement on Agriculture.[85]

[80] A detailed illustrative list of export subsidies is annexed to the SCM Agreement (Annex 1).

[81] Creskoff and Walkenhorst (2009, p. 3).

[82] GATT, *supra* note 1. Art. 3.8(b).

[83] Canada-Administration of the Foreign Investment Review Act (Panel Report) (LI5504), 30th supp. GATT, BISD140 (1984) (FIRA Panel Report).

[84] SCM Agreement, *supra* note 301. Art. 11.

[85] WTO-Trade Policy Courses, Chapter 14: Subsidies & Countervailing Measures 14.6. http://www.wto.org/english/tratop_e/scm_e/subs_e.htm. Accessed Feb. 28, 2012.

4.2.2 Actionable Subsidies

4.2.2.1 Introduction

Most specific subsidies, such as production subsidies, fall in the "actionable" category ("yellow").[86] Actionable subsidies are not prohibited. However, they are subject to challenge, either through multilateral dispute settlement or through countervailing action, in the event that they cause adverse effects to the interests of another Member.[87]

There are three possible types of adverse effects, that is, injury, serious prejudice and nullification or impairment: First, there is injury to a domestic industry caused by subsidized imports in the complaining Member's customs territory. This type of adverse effect can be challenged either multilaterally or through application of a countervailing duty. However, only one form of relief (either countervailing duty or an authorized countermeasure) is applicable.

Second, there is serious prejudice. Serious prejudice can arise where a subsidy causes (1) displacement or impedance of the complaining Member's imports or exports, either in the market of the subsidizing Member or in a third country market; (2) significant price undercutting, price suppression or depression, or lost sales, of the complaining Member's product in a given market; or (3) an increase in the subsidizing Member's world market share in a subsidized primary product or commodity. Thus, serious prejudice can serve as the basis for a complaint related to harm to a Member's exporting interests. Finally, there is nullification or impairment of benefits. Nullification or impairment arises most typically where the improved access to a market that is presumed to flow from a bound tariff reduction is undercut by subsidization in that market.

Thus, like serious prejudice, nullification or impairment can serve as the basis for a complaint related to harm to a Member's exporting interests.[88]

4.2.2.2 Injury

As mentioned earlier, there are three types of adverse effects a complaining Member can cite. Injury, one of these effects, is the negative effect of subsidized imports on the position of a domestic industry. There are three types of injury, which are, current material injury, threat of material injury and material retardation of the establishment of a domestic industry. A determination of current material injury to a domestic industry is to be based on positive evidence and involves an objective examination of both the volume of the subsidized imports and the effect

[86] WTO-Trade Policy Courses, Chapter 14: Subsidies & Countervailing Measures 14.7. http://www.wto.org/english/tratop_e/scm_e/subs_e.htm. Accessed Feb.28, 2012; Yellow-light subsidies must be examined in light of the specificity and financial contribution requirements. The specificity requirement is most important for tallow-light subsidies (Cobb 1995, cited by Wilcox 1998, *supra* note 301, at 153).

[87] WTO-Trade Policy Courses, Chapter 14: Subsidies & Countervailing Measures 14.7, *id.*

[88] SCM Agreement, *supra* note 301. Art. 15.6.

of these imports on prices in the domestic market for like products and the consequent impact of these imports on the domestic producers of such products.[89]

A determination of a threat of material injury to a domestic industry must be based on facts and not merely on possibility. The change in circumstances, which would create a situation in which the subsidy would cause injury, must be clearly foreseen and imminent. Factors to be considered are: nature of subsidy and trade effects likely to arise therefrom; significant rate or increase of subsidized imports; and sufficient freely disposable capacity or an imminent substantial increase in capacity of the exporter, indicating the likelihood of substantially increased subsidized exports to the importing Member's market.[90]

While the Agreement contains details on the consideration of material injury and threat of material injury, it is silent on the evaluation of material retardation of the establishment of a domestic industry.[91] Subsidization that causes injury can be challenged both at a unilateral level through countervailing action as well as at a multilateral level through the WTO's Dispute Settlement Mechanism. Injury is the sole basis for countervailing action. Serious prejudice (which may be demonstrated or arise as a presumption) and nullification or impairment can give rise to the challenge at the multilateral level only.[92]

4.2.2.3 Serious Prejudice

Serious prejudice may arise in any case where the effect of the subsidy is to displace or impede exports to the subsidizing country Member; displace or impede exports to a third country; cause significant undercutting, suppression, or depression of prices, or loss of sales; or result in an increase in the subsidizing Member's world market share for a primary commodity.[93]

The Agreement sets out situations where factors other than the subsidization appear to explain the displacement or impeding of a complaining Member's exports and where serious prejudice therefore should not be found to exist. These include cases where there are export restrictions in the complaining country, there are import restrictions in the third country, or the complaining country's goods do not conform to standards and other regulatory requirements in the importing country. Annex V sets out procedures for developing information concerning serious prejudice in a dispute. In making its determination, the panel may draw adverse inferences from instances of non-cooperation by any party involved in the information-gathering process.[94]

---

[89] SCM Agreement, *supra* note 301. Art. 15.7.

[90] *Id.*

[91] WTO-Trade Policy Courses, Chapter 14: Subsidies & Countervailing Measures 14.8. http://www.wto.org/english/tratop_e/scm_e/subs_e.htm. Accessed Feb. 28, 2012.

[92] WTO-Trade Policy Courses, Chapter 14: Subsidies & Countervailing Measures 14.9. http://www.wto.org/english/tratop_e/scm_e/subs_e.htm. Accessed Feb. 28, 2012.

[93] SCM Agreement, *supra* note 301. Art. 6.3.

[94] SCM Agreement, *supra* note 301. Art. 6.6.

The creation under the SCM Agreement of a system of remedies that allows Members to challenge subsidies which give rise to adverse effects represents a major advance over the GATT regime. The difficulty, however, remains the need in most cases for a complaining Member to demonstrate the adverse trade effects arising from subsidization, through a complex and fact-intensive analysis.[95]

4.2.3 Non-actionable Subsides

The SCM Agreement creates three narrowly-defined categories of subsidies which are non-actionable ("green"),[96] i.e. which cannot be challenged multilaterally or be subject to countervailing action.[97] These subsidies presumably are protected either because they are considered extremely unlikely to cause adverse effects or because they are considered to be of particular value and not to be discouraged. These subsidies include research and development subsidies, assistance to disadvantaged regions, and environmental subsidies.[98]

Regarding research subsidies, these subsidies cannot exceed a designated proportion of project costs – up to 75 percent of industrial research and up to 50 percent of pre-competitive development activity up to the first non-saleable prototype – and can only be used for certain expenditures in order to be non-actionable. Research and development subsidies in the civil aircraft sector do not benefit from non-actionable status.[99]

Regarding assistance to disadvantaged regions, regional aids are non-actionable provided that they are not limited to specific enterprises or industries within the region, that they are given pursuant to a general scheme of regional development, and that the region is disadvantaged by comparison with the Member as a whole in terms of objective criteria such as GDP per capita or unemployment. The GDP per capita must not be greater than 85 percent of the average for the territory of the

[95] SCM Agreement, *supra* note 301. Art. 6.1.

[96] For the for concern of the specific domestic subsidies to escape the imposition of countervailing duties because of such subsidies to be nominally categorized as green-lighted subsidies see Wilcox (1998, *supra* note 301, at 152–153): "Many manufacturers ... are constantly in the process of developing new products, and therefore always be eligible for green-light government assistance ... there may always be a recipient for market distorting disadvantage-based subsidies".

[97] For the possible two ways of legitimizing its actions for a country to give a subsidy with or distorted effect on the world market through the yellow-light approach and green-light approach, see Wilcox (1998, *supra* note 301, at 162): " ... could take the yellow-light approach and disguise the subsidy ... the green-light approach would be easier ...".

[98] For the negative potential effect of the green-light subsidies in the world market, see Wilcox (1998, *supra* note 301, at 161–162): "... the green-light exceptions may be contrary to the essence of GATT itself. ... The green-light provisions for regional development and industrial research are directly contrary to the goal of efficiency ... The essence of these policies is that of eliminating or neutralizing comparative disadvantage, or of creating artificial comparative advantage ...".

[99] SCM Agreement, *supra* note 301. Art. 8.2.

Member concerned, or the unemployment rate must be at least 110 percent of the average for that territory.[100]

Regarding environmental subsidies, such assistance must be given for the purpose of adaptation of existing facilities to new environmental requirements, on a one-time basis, be limited to 20 percent of adaptation costs, and be available to all firms which can adopt the new equipment and processes.[101]

4.2.4 Countervailing Measures

There are provided detailed rules regarding the initiation and conduct of countervailing investigations, the imposition of preliminary and final measures, the use of undertakings, and the duration of measures. A key objective of these rules is to ensure that investigations are conducted in a transparent manner, that all interested parties have a full opportunity to defend their interests, and that investigating authorities adequately explain the bases for their determinations. Most of the procedural rules that apply in the case of the Anti-Dumping Agreement apply also to the SCM Agreement.[102]

A Member may not impose a countervailing measure unless it has determined the existence of subsidized imports, injury to a domestic industry, and a causal link between the subsidized imports and the injury. The SCM Agreement contains an important provision that authorizes the accumulation of the effects of subsidized imports from several Members provided that the specific criteria are met.[103]

4.2.5 Institutions

The Committee on SCM is composed of representatives from each of the Members. It affords Members the opportunity of consulting on any matter relating to the operation of the Agreement or the furtherance of its objectives.[104]

The Committee has established a Permanent Group of Experts (PGE) composed of five independent persons, highly qualified in the fields of subsidies and trade

[100] *Id.*

[101] WTO-Trade Policy Courses, Chapter 14: Subsidies & Countervailing Measures 14.10. http://www.wto.org/english/tratop_e/scm_e/subs_e.htm. Accessed Feb. 28, 2012.

[102] SCM Agreement, *supra* note 301. part 5; Some notable differences particular to the SCM Agreement include: the period of time preliminary measures may remain in force; the circumstances under which domestic producers related to importers of the product subject to investigation may be excluded from the domestic industry; the provisions relating to review of the rates of subsidization for exporters not investigated for reasons other than non-cooperation; and the types of undertakings that may be entered into.

[103] SCM Agreement, *supra* note 301. Art. 11.2.

[104] SCM Agreement, *supra* note 301. Art. 24.1.

relations. These experts are elected by the Committee to five year terms and one of them is replaced every year. The PGE is assigned three functions by the Agreement. First, it may be requested to assist a panel with regard to whether a measure is a prohibited subsidy. The PGE's conclusions on the issue must be accepted by the panel without modification. Second, the PGE may be requested by the Committee to provide an advisory opinion on the existence and nature of any subsidy. Finally, the PGE may be consulted by any Member and give a confidential advisory opinion on the nature of any subsidy proposed or maintained by the Member.[105]

4.2.6 Dispute Settlement

In the context of the SCM Agreement, the dispute settlement mechanism provides a forum for Members to challenge other Members prohibited or actionable subsidies, as well as the application by other Members of countervailing measures. Although the provisions of the Dispute Settlement Understanding generally apply to disputes under the SCM Agreement, the SCM Agreement contains a significant number of special or additional rules and procedures that supplement and in some cases replace those of the DSU. These rules are somewhat different between prohibited subsidies and actionable subsidies.[106]

With respect to prohibited subsidies, the SCM Agreement[107] supplements or modifies in a number of respects the rules of the DSU. One significant difference between dispute settlement under the SCM Agreement[108] and other dispute settlement is its expedited nature. As a general rule, time periods under the SCM Agreement are half those of the DSU. For example, the panel report must be circulated to all Members within 90 days of its composition and establishment of its terms of reference, rather than the usual 6 months. Further, the defending Member has no opportunity to delay establishment until the second meeting of the DSB; rather, the panel must be established immediately.

A panel established under the SCM Agreement may request the assistance of the Permanent Group of Experts, whose conclusion on whether or not a subsidy is prohibited must be accepted by a panel without modification. A panel under the SCM Agreement which finds the existence of a prohibited subsidy shall recommend that the Member withdraw the subsidy without delay, and shall specify the time-period within which it must be withdrawn. Should the Member fail to implement the recommendation within the time allowed, the DSB must authorize the complaining Member to take "appropriate countermeasures".[109]

---

[105] SCM Agreement, *supra* note 301. Arts. 24.3–24.4.

[106] SCM Agreement, *supra* note 301. part. 10.

[107] SCM Agreement, *supra* note 301. Art. 4.

[108] *Id.*

[109] WTO-Trade Policy Courses, Chapter 14: Subsidies & Countervailing Measures 14.12. http://www.wto.org/english/tratop_e/scm_e/subs_e.htm. Accessed Feb. 28, 2012.

Actionable subsidy cases under the SCM Agreement also are expedited by comparison with other WTO dispute settlements. Thus, a panel must circulate its report to all Members within 120 days of its composition and establishment of its terms of reference. Where the complainant alleges serious prejudice, the SCM Agreement sets forth specific and detailed procedures to facilitate information gathering.[110] In the event a panel finds that a subsidy has caused adverse effects, it must recommend that the subsidizing Member take appropriate steps to remove the adverse effects or that it withdraw the subsidy. If the subsidizing Member fails to implement the recommendation within six months of the date that the DSB adopts the panel or Appellate Body report, the DSB must authorize the complaining Member to take countermeasures commensurate with the degree and nature of the adverse effects found to exist.[111]

– Trade Disputes in Relation with **SCM Agreement**

Panel Report, European Communities and Certain Member States-Measures Affecting Trade in Large Civil Aircraft, WT/DS316/R (Jun. 30, 2010).

INTRODUCTION

A. COMPLAINT OF THE UNITED STATES

1.1 On October 6, 2004, the United States requested consultations with the European Communities and certain EC member states (Germany, France, the United Kingdom, and Spain) pursuant to Articles 1 and 4 of the *Understanding on Rules and Procedures Governing the Settlement of Disputes* ("DSU"), Article XXIII:1 of the *General Agreement on Tariffs and Trade 1994* ("GATT 1994") and Articles 4, 7 and 30 of the *Agreement on Subsidies and Countervailing Measures* ("SCM Agreement")(to the extent that Article 30 incorporates Article XXIII of GATT 1994), with regard to measures affecting trade in large civil aircraft.2 Consultations were held on November 4, 2004, but the parties failed to resolve the dispute.

1.2 On May 31, 2005, the United States requested the establishment of a panel pursuant to Article 6 of the DSU, Article XXIII:2 of GATT 1994, and Articles 4, 7 and 30 of the SCM Agreement (to the extent that Article 30 incorporates Article XXIII of GATT 1994). In its request for establishment of a panel, the United States requested that the Dispute Settlement Body

(continued)

[110] SCM Agreement, *supra* note 301. Annex V.

[111] WTO-Trade Policy Courses, Chapter 14: Subsidies & Countervailing Measures 14.12-14.13. http://www.wto.org/english/tratop_e/scm_e/subs_e.htm. Accessed Feb. 28, 2012.

(the "DSB") initiate the procedures provided in Annex V of the SCM Agreement pursuant to paragraph 2 of that Annex.

CONCLUSIONS AND RECOMMENDATION

A. CONCLUSIONS

2. In light of the findings set out in the foregoing sections of our Report, we conclude that the United States ***has established*** the following concerning the existence of subsidies:

(a) concerning the provision of LA/MSF;

(i) that each of the challenged LA/MSF measures constitutes a specific subsidy within the meaning of Articles 1 and 2 of the SCM Agreement, and

(ii) that the German, Spanish and UK A380 LA/MSF measures are subsidies contingent in fact upon anticipated export performance, and therefore prohibited export subsidies within the meaning of Article 3.1(a) and footnote 4 of the SCM Agreement.

(b) concerning the provision of infrastructure and infrastructure-related grants;

(i) that the provision of the Mühlenberger Loch site constitutes a specific subsidy within the meaning of Articles 1 and 2 of the SCM Agreement,

(ii) that the provision of the lengthened Bremen Airport Runway constitutes a specific subsidy within the meaning of Articles 1 and 2 of the SCM Agreement,

(iii) that the provision of the ZAC Aéroconstellation site and associated EIG facilities constitutes a specific subsidy within the meaning of Articles 1 and 2 of the SCM Agreement, and

(iv) that challenged grants provided by authorities in Germany and Spain for the construction of manufacturing and assembly facilities in Nordenham, Germany, and Sevilla, La Rinconada, Toledo, Puerto de Santa Maria and Puerto Real, Spain, and by the governments of Andalusia and Castilla-La Mancha to Airbus in Puerto Real, Sevilla, and Illescas (Toledo) are specific subsidies within the meaning of Articles 1 and 2 of the SCM Agreement.

(c) concerning the German government's transfer of its ownership share in Deutsche Airbus to the Daimler Group;

(i) that the 1989 acquisition by KfW of a 20 percent equity interest in Deutsche Airbus is a specific subsidy within the meaning of Articles 1 and 2 of the SCM Agreement, and

(ii) that the 1992 transfer by KfW of its 20 percent equity interest in Deutsche Airbus to MBB is a specific subsidy within the meaning of Articles 1 and 2 of the SCM Agreement.

(d) concerning the equity infusions that the French government and Crédit Lyonnais provided to Aérospatiale;

(i) that the 1987, 1988, 1992 and 1994 equity infusions to Aérospatiale are specific subsidies within the meaning of Articles 1 and 2 of the SCM Agreement, and

(ii) that the 1998 transfer by the French government of its 45.76 percent interest in Dassault Aviation to Aérospatiale is a specific subsidy within the meaning of Articles 1 and 2 of the SCM Agreement.

(e) concerning the research and technological development funding provided by the European Communities and certain EC member states;

(i) that grants under the Second, Third, Fourth, Fifth and Sixth EC Framework Programs identified in Annexes I.1, I.2, I.3, I.4 and I.5 are specific subsidies within the meaning of Articles 1 and 2 of the SCM Agreement,

(ii) that French government grants amounting to a maximum of EUR 391 million between 1986 and 1993 and EUR [***] between 1994 and 2005 are specific subsidies within the meaning of Articles 1 and 2 of the SCM Agreement,

(iii) that German Federal government grants under the LuFo I, LuFo II and LuFo III programs amounting to EUR [***] are specific subsidies within the meaning of Articles 1 and 2 of the SCM Agreement,

(iv) that German sub-Federal government grants amounting to EUR [***] from the Bavarian authorities under the OZB and Bayerisches Luftfahrtforschungsprogramm, EUR 11 million from the Bremen authorities under the AMST programs, and EUR [***] from the Hamburg authorities under the Luftfahrtforschungsprogramm are specific subsidies within the meaning of Articles 1 and 2 of the SCM Agreement,

(v) that loans under the Spanish government PROFIT and PTA programs amounting to, respectively, EUR 62.2 million and EUR [***], are specific subsidies within the meaning of Articles 1 and 2 of the SCM Agreement, and

(vi) that UK government grants under the CARAD and ARP programs amounting to GBP [***] are specific subsidies within the meaning of Articles 1 and 2 of the SCM Agreement.

3. Furthermore, in light of the findings set out in the foregoing sections of our report, we conclude that the United States ***has established*** the following with respect to adverse effects:

(a) that the effect of the subsidies is to displace the imports of a like product of the United States into the European market within the meaning of Article 6.3(a) of the SCM Agreement, constituting serious prejudice to the interests of the United States within the meaning of Article 5(c) of the SCM Agreement,

(b) that the effect of the subsidies is to displace the exports of a like product of the United States from the markets of Australia, Brazil, China, Chinese Taipei, Korea, Mexico, and Singapore within the meaning of Article 6.3(b) of the SCM Agreement, constituting serious prejudice to the interests

(continued)

of the United States within the meaning of Article 5(c) of the SCM Agreement,

(c) that the effect of the subsidies is likely displacement of exports of a like product of the United States from the market of India within the meaning of Article 6.3(b) of the SCM Agreement, constituting a threat of serious prejudice to the interests of the United States within the meaning of Article 5(c) of the SCM Agreement, and

(d) that the effect of the subsidies is significant lost sales in the same market within the meaning of Article 6.3(c) of the SCM Agreement, constituting serious prejudice to the interests of the United States within the meaning of Article 5(c) of the SCM Agreement.

Source: Panel Report. European Communities and Certain Member States-Measures Affecting Trade in Large Civil Aircraft. 30 June 2012. WT/DS316/R. http://www.wto.org/english/tratop_e/dispu_e/316r_e.pdf

– Trade Disputes in Relation with **SCM Agreement**

Appellate Body Report, *United States-Final Countervailing Duty Determination with Respect to Certain Softwood Lumber from Canada*, WT/DS257/AB/R (Jan. 19, 2004) (U.S.-Softwood Lumber AB Report).

Introduction and Background Information

About 90 % of Canadian softwood lumber industry is obtained from cutting down trees on government-owned property. To gain the right to cut down trees on government property is done by paying a "stumpage" fee which is determined province by province in Canada. The United States wanted to see the low "stumpage" fees in some province to be considered a subsidy and as such as the WTO to allow the United States to impose countervailing duties. The WTO Panel agreed that the stumpage program was a form of a subsidy but that United States had acted inappropriately in regards to specific provisions of the SCM Agreement, to the extent that any benefits Canadian companies may have accrued under the SCM Agreement were nullified or impaired. The Panel recommended that the Dispute Settlement Body (the "DSB") inform the United States that its measure needed to conform to the obligations state under the SCM Agreement and GATT 1994. By October 27, 2003, Canada and the United States filed appellant and appellee submissions. The European Communities and Japan joined as third party participants. India announced it would make a statement, but not join as a third party participant.

Principal Issues on Appeal

The principal issues raised in this appeal were:

a) Whether the panel mistakenly found that the Canadian provincial stumpage program "provide goods" which end in making a financial contribution in accordance with Article 1.1(a)(1)(iii) of the SCM Agreement.
b) If, when considering paragraphs 7.64 and 7.65 of the Panel Report, the panel erred in finding that the USDOC did not determine benefit using methods consistent with Articles 14 and 14(d) of the SCM Agreement. Subsequently, the USDOC's [United States Department of Commerce] countervailing measures are inconsistent with the United States' obligations under Articles 10, 15, 14(d) and 32.1 of the SCM Agreement.
c) Whether or not the Panel erred in deciding that the USDOC's "pass-through" analysis consideration of arm's length sales of logs and lumber from tenure-holding timber harvesters including those who own sawmills and produce lumber as well as unrelated sawmills and lumber remanufacturers, does not comply with Articles 10 and 32.1 of the SCM Agreement and Article VI: 3 of GATT 1994.

Rationale and Holdings:

Does a subsidy exist?

Whether or not a subsidy exists depends on two factors: a financial contribution from a government or price support; and the financial contribution must confer some form of benefit. Canada argues that the issues of financial contribution and benefit must be separated under SCM Agreement Article 1.1(a)(1)(iii) which address the possibility of the government both raising and lowering a price artificially. Canada does not find that "standing timber" meets the definition of "goods" arguing that the term, "goods," is limited to "tradable items with an actual or potential tariff classification," nor does the term fit the definition of "personal property." Canada also takes issue with the idea that the government "provides" the right to harvest the timber when the right to harvest timber is intangible.

All parties agree that cut timber fits the definition of "goods" and the Appellate Body finds that standing timber fits Black's Law Dictionary, which further defines the term "goods" as "growing crops, and other identified things to be severed from real property." Consequently "standing timber" will be considered as a "good."

Canada's disapproval of the interpretation of the word "provides" is noted, but the Appellate Body finds that the manner in which the word "provides" has been correctly interpreted by the Panel in relation to Article 1.1(a)(1)(iii) of the SCM Agreement. The Appellate Body also disagrees with Canada that there is an intangible right to harvest timber, that allowing companies to

(continued)

obtain special permission to harvest timber through "stumpage" programs does not mean supplying timber, and that this does constitute providing good.

Consequently the Appellate Body upholds the panel's finding in paragraph 7.30 of the Panel Report.

Have the benefits been calculated correctly?

The USDOC used benchmark prices of stumpage prices from bordering states in the United States to make adjustments between those states and the Canadian provinces. Canada declares that this is inconsistent with Articles 10, 14, 14(d), 19.1, 19.4, and 32.1 of the SCM Agreement and Article VI:3 of GATT 1994. As raised by Japan, why did the United States think that only the northern U.S. states could reflect a fair standard for standing timber in Canada? Article 14(d) of the SCM Agreement states that "[t]he adequacy of remuneration shall be determined in relation to prevailing market conditions for the goods or service in the country of provision or purchase(including price, quality, availability, marketability, transportation and other conditions of purchase or sale)".

Although this portion of 14(d) does not permit the United States to use information from outside Canada, no matter that the northern states uses for comparison butt against the provinces in question, the Appellate Body agrees with the United States that paragraphs (a) through (d) of Article 14 that a little more latitude should be given rather assuming the paragraphs must be interpreted strictly. If the paragraphs are taken literally and the government's role is providing a financial contribution so widespread that it controls the prices at which private suppliers conduct business, then a comparison of other prices in the country of provision will be useless. However while the panel and Appellate Body agree that are some problems of "economic logic" in the interpretation of Article 14(d), nothing states the country in dispute should be the country used to determine if the country of provision has affected the market prices beyond usability in determining the calculation of benefit. The guideline requires that a different method may be selected, but there must be some connection to the prevailing market conditions of the country of provision.

Is it possible to use another country rather than the country of provision as a benchmark?

Since the prices of the country of provision are the first, but not the only possible, benchmark for calculating benefit, when is it possible for prices of another country to be used in calculating benefits? The United States would like the Appellate Body to overturn what the United States sees as the Panel's error in not acknowledging that Article 14(d) allow other benchmarks than private prices in the country of provision when the prices have been substantially influence by the benefits conferred by the government. Consequently the

Panel's decision as stated in paragraph 7.64 of the Panel Report concerning the interpretation of Article 14(d) of the SCM Agreement is reversed.

However in looking at the method of determining benefit, the United States opted for using the prevailing prices of northern states adjacent to the Canadian provinces adjusted to reflect Canadian market conditions rather than the market conditions of the United States. The method that the USDOC used to determine the market benefits the Canadian provincial governments give to timber companies does not meet the definition of consistency according to Articles 14 and 14(d) of the SCM Agreement and that it was inconsistent with Articles 10 and 32.1 of the same Agreement. If the Appellate Body is to decide if the USDOC's benefit determination is a fair benefit determination, a legal analysis must be completed. A legal analysis of the USDOC's benefit determination has not been completed.

The Panel made a decision on two points concerning the USDOC and benefit determination: (i) that "the USDOC acknowledged the existence of a private market for stumpage in Canada"; and (ii) that "the USDOC had before it private stumpage prices for four of the most important [Canadian] provinces". The panel did not tackle the problem of sufficient evidence of price supports or the lack of a proper analysis of the government presence in the market. While the USDOC may have been justified under Article 14(d) to bring in a benchmark from outside of Canada, there is simply not enough evidence for a decision to be made. Even if another benchmark could fairly be used by the USDOC, the question as to why the northern bordering states of the United States should be used rather than another country would need to be justified and it has not been justified correctly, nor has why Canada claims that the United States has acted inconsistently with Article 14(d) of the SCM Agreement. Consequently the Appellate Body decides to reverse the panel's finding about paragraph 7.64 of the Panel Report that an alternative benchmark may be used in a country of provision when the prices have been so heavily influenced by the government that an accurate price cannot be determined. Subsequent to the decision to reverse the panel's finding about paragraph 7.64, the Appellate Body also reverses the finding that the United States acted inconsistently with Articles 10, 14, 14(d), and 32.1 of the SCM Agreement.

Did the USDOC fail to conduct a "pass-through" analysis?

The scope of the "pass-through" analysis is limited to situations in which a tenured timber harvester harvests softwood lumber to sell for itself as well as selling arm's length logs to other sawmills for processing, and when the a tenured timber harvester sells arm's length logs to lumber remanufacturers for further processing. The United States agrees that a pass-through analysis is required for indirect subsidy. However, a pass-through analysis is not necessary for arm's length sales of logs by tenured timber harvesters who sell to unrelated sawmills. According to the United States the fact that primary

(continued)

lumber and remanufactured lumber are both investigated should excuse primary lumber and remanufactured lumber from pass-through analysis. Canada submits that the United States in accepting indirect subsidization and not conducting pass-through analysis on the necessary category has countervailed subsidies based on presumptions rather than factual determination.

The Appellate Body finds that it is impossible to determine if countervailing duties on processed products are in excess if the subsidies conferred on the products. Additionally, the investigating authority must determine the benefits that have been transmitted from the producers of logs to the producers of softwood lumber and remanufactured lumber if the purpose of countervailing is to offset any financial contributions.

Is an aggregate basis acceptable?

According to United States, Article 19.3 allows exporters who have not been investigated individuals to be subject to countervailing duties on an aggregate basis. The Appellate Body agrees with the United States that Article 19.3 allows aggregate basis. However, Article 19 does not permit a Member to neglect the obligation to determine the subsidy amount and countervailing duty rate according to the SCM Agreement and Article VI of GATT 1994. It must be decided that a financial benefit exists and has been given directly through the input producer, according to Article 1.1. The Appellate Body rejects the United States' opinion that pass-through analysis need not be done.

What happens when a tenured timber harvester/sawmill sells arms' length logs to unrelated lumber producers?

In the situation that harvesters owning sawmills sell to unrelated sawmills for additional processing, the Appellate Body is not convinced by the United States argument that the fact that some of those logs are turned into softwood lumber is relevant to determining pass-through analysis. While the United States accepts that a pass-through analysis is required for a tenured "independent harvester" without a sawmill that sells logs at arm's length to unrelated sawmills, the Appellate Body does not see why that should there should be a distinction of with or without a sawmill. Consequently, the Appellate Body upholds paragraph 7.99 of the Panel Report.

What if the arm's length lumber is sold to unrelated lumber remanufacturers? Is a pass-through analysis required?

The USDOC does this type of investigation on an aggregate basis and Canada accepts the aggregate investigation taking issue only with how the USDOC calculates the subsidy amount and the countervailing duty date. The Appellate Body does not make any comment on this aspect of the report beyond observing that the calculation issues are not within the purpose of this appeal.

However, the Appellate Body does reverse the panel's finding in paragraph 7.99 that the USDOC's failure to do pass-through analysis concerning arm's length sales of lumber by tenured harvesters/ sawmills to unrelated remanufactures is inconsistent with Articles 10 and 32.1 of the SCM Agreement and Article VI:3 of GATT 1994.

Conclusions:

The Appellate Body:

A) Upholds the panel's finding of paragraph 7.30 that the USDOC's determination that the stumpage programs are providing a financial contribution and that there is not any inconsistency with Article 1.1(a)(1)(iii) of the SCM Agreement.

B) Reverses the panel's finding in paragraph 7.64 of the Panel Report and determines that another benchmark than the private prices in the country of provision may be used by an investigating authority if the following two conditions have been met:

   It has been determined that the private prices of the goods under discussion in the country of provision are distorted because of governmental influence.

   The alternative benchmark is connected to the market conditions of the country of provision, such as price, quality, availability, marketability, transportation and other market conditions.

C) Reverses the decision that the United States acted inconsistently in Articles of 10, 14, 14(d) and 32.1 of the SCM Agreement concerning the USDOC's benefit determination in countervailing duty investigation.

D) Has decided that there is not enough evidence to complete the analysis of the benchmark, namely the conditions in the northern bordering states of the United States, that the USDOC used under Article 14(d) of the SCM Agreement, and, hence, no findings can be made whether the USDOC's benefit determination is consistent with Articles 14, 14(d), 10, 32.1 of the SCM Agreement.

E) Upholds paragraph 7.99 of the Panel Report that a pass-through analysis of arm's length sales of logs by tenured harvesters/sawmills to unrelated sawmills must be conducted and, since these pass-through analysis has not been done, it is not consistent with Articles 10 and 32.1 of the SCM Agreement and Article VI: 3 of GATT 1994.

In conclusion, the Appellate Body has recommended that the United States bring its measure into alignment with the SCM Agreement and GATT 1994.

Commentary:

The difficulties between Canada and the United States concerning softwood have been ongoing for two decades and look to continue into a third decade.

(continued)

In the December 17th, 2005 meeting of the DSB, the United States informed the DSB that it had complied with the recommendations made by the WTO but the problems of Canadian government subsidies to the softwood industry have not changed from the United States viewpoint. The countervailing and anti-dumping duties were reduced from a total of 20.15 percent (16.37 percent for countervailing duties and 3.78 percent for anti-dumping duties) down to 10.8 percent, 8.7 percent for countervailing and 2.11 percent for anti-dumping. Additionally, some years of the higher countervailing duties will be partially refunded to avoid more legal complications.

Will this be enough to cease the squabbling over softwood between Canada and the United States? Most likely, it will not. An argument that has endured between the neighboring countries for more than 20 years will not go away easily, especially when an underlying issue is the relationship between Canada and the United States and how the countries organize labor. The United States timber industry is run by independent timber harvesters while the Canadian government has a strong hand in the organization of the Canadian timber harvesting industry.

A conflict over government assistance, or government interference depending on the viewpoint, evolve between two countries that share connected resources, such as forests, is a natural conclusion. The American Coalition for Fair Lumber Imports sees this as a conflict of labor rather than resources, and they claim that the American lumber industry can compete against other lumber industries, but that the Canadian government support of the lumber industry is too much competition. There may not be any solution to make both countries happy, only a legislative decision made by the countries to quit spending so much time and money in courts over a sensitive issue.

Source: Appellate Body Report. United States-Final Countervailing Duty Determination with Respect to Certain Softwood Lumber from Canada. 19 January 2004. WT/DS257/AB/R. http://www.sice.oas.org/dispute/wto/ds257/ds257a1e.asp

4.3 Safeguards

4.3.1 Introduction

The Agreement on Safeguards ("SG Agreement")[112] sets forth the rules for application of safeguard measures pursuant to Article XIX of GATT 1994. Safeguard measures are defined as "emergency" actions with respect to increased imports of

[112] Agreement on Safeguards, Apr. 15, 1994, Marrakesh Agreement Establishing the World Trade Organization, Annex 1, Legal Instruments-Results of the Uruguay Round, I.L.M. 33: 1125 (1994). (SG Agreement).

particular products, where such imports have caused or threaten to cause serious injury to the importing Member's domestic industry.[113] Such measures, which in broad terms take the form of suspension of concessions or obligations, can consist of quantitative import restrictions or of duty increases to higher than bound rates. They are one of three types of contingent trade protection measures, along with anti-dumping and countervailing measures, available to the WTO Members.[114]

The guiding principles of the Agreement with respect to safeguard measures are that such measures must be temporary; that they may be imposed only when imports are found to cause or threaten serious injury to a competing domestic industry; that they (generally) be applied on a non-selective (i.e. most-favored-nation, or "MFN") basis; that they be progressively liberalized while in effect; and that the Member imposing them generally must pay compensation to the Members whose trade is affected. Thus, safeguard measures, unlike anti-dumping and countervailing measures, do not require a finding of an "unfair" practice, generally must be applied on an MFN basis,[115] and generally must be "paid for" by the Member applying them.[116]

Under GATT 1947, safeguards were regulated only by Article XIX. The SG Agreement was negotiated in large part because GATT Contracting Parties had been increasingly applying a variety of so-called "grey area" measures (bilateral voluntary export restraints, orderly marketing agreements, and similar measures) to limit imports of certain products. These measures were not imposed pursuant to Article XIX, and thus were not subject to multilateral discipline through GATT, and the legality of such measures under GATT was doubtful.[117] The Agreement now clearly prohibits such measures, and has specific provisions for eliminating those that were in place at the time the WTO Agreement entered into force.

In its own words, the SG Agreement, which explicitly applies equally to all Members, aims to: (i) clarify and reinforce GATT disciplines, particularly those of Article XIX; (ii) re-establish multilateral control over safeguards and eliminate measures that escape such control; and (iii) encourage structural adjustment on the part of the industries adversely affected by increased imports, thereby enhancing competition in international markets.[118]

---

[113] SG Agreement, *id.*, Art. 2.

[114] WTO, Safeguard Measures: Technical Information on Safeguard Measures (General principle). http://www.wto.org/english/tratop_e/safeg_e/safeg_info_e.htm. Accessed Feb. 28, 2012.

[115] SG Agreement, *supra* note 351. Art. 9.

[116] SG Agreement, *supra* note 351. Art. 5.

[117] For the abuse of the "grey area" measures under the GATT system, see Kennedy (1998, *supra* note 42, at 434–435):"A de facto . . . exception to both the Article XI proscription on quantitative and the Article XIII requirement of nondiscrimination in the allocation of quotas is the VRA or VER. Under the terms of a VRA, exporting countries of a product agree to limit the volume of their exports to an importing country. The proliferation of these grey-area measures (a neologism for "GATT-inconsistent") was becoming a serious threat to the continued relevance of GATT both as an institution and as a legal instrument for regulating international trade."

[118] SG Agreement, *supra* note 351. Preamble.

4.3.2 Safeguard Agreement

In general terms, the Safeguard Agreement has four main components: (1) general provisions[119]; (2) rules governing Members' application of new safeguard measures (i.e., those applied after entry into force of the WTO Agreement)[120]; (3) rules pertaining to pre-existing measures that were applied before the WTO entry into force[121]; and (4) multilateral obligations and institutions regarding application of safeguard measures.[122]

The SG Agreement is the vehicle through which measures may be applied pursuant to Article XIX of GATT 1994. That is, any measure for which the coverage of Article XIX (which allows suspension of GATT concessions and obligations under the defined "emergency" circumstances) is invoked, must be taken in accordance with the provisions of the SG Agreement.[123] There are provided the conditions under which safeguard measures may be applied.[124] These conditions are: (i) increased imports and (ii) serious injury or threat thereof caused by such increased imports. Such safeguard measures should be applied on an MFN basis.[125]

4.3.3 Substantial Requirements

4.3.3.1 Increased Quantity of Imports

The determination of increased quantity of imports that a Member must make before it may apply a safeguard measure can be of either an absolute increase or an increase relative to domestic production.[126]

4.3.3.2 Injury

Two possibilities of injury are grouped into serious injury and threat of serious injury. The Agreement defines "serious injury" as a significant overall impairment in the position of a domestic industry.[127] In determining whether serious injury is present, investigating authorities are to evaluate all relevant factors having a bearing on the condition of the industry.

---

[119] SG Agreement, *supra* note 351. Art. 1.2.

[120] SG Agreement, *supra* note 351. Art. 3.9.

[121] SG Agreement, *supra* note 351. Arts. 10–11.

[122] SG Agreement, *supra* note 351. Arts. 12–14.

[123] SG Agreement, *supra* note 351. Art. 1.

[124] SG Agreement, *supra* note 351. Art. 2.

[125] *Id.*

[126] *Id.*

[127] SG Agreement, *supra* note 112. Art. 4.1.

Factors that must be analyzed are the absolute and relative rate and amount of increase in imports, the market share taken by the increased imports, as well as changes in level of sales, production, productivity, capacity, utilization, profits and losses, and employment of the domestic industry.[128] "Threat of serious injury" refers to threat that is clearly imminent as shown by facts, and not based on mere allegation, conjecture or remote possibility.[129] If present serious injury is not found, a safeguard measure nevertheless can be applied if a threat of serious injury is found.[130]

4.3.3.3 Domestic Industry

A "domestic industry" is defined as the producers as a whole of the like or directly competitive products operating within the territory of a Member, or producers who collectively account for a major proportion of the total domestic production of those products. This definition allows a broader consideration of effects than in anti-dumping or countervailing cases.[131]

4.3.3.4 Causation

A determination of serious injury cannot be made unless there is objective evidence of the existence of a causal link between increased imports of the product concerned and serious injury. Further, when factors other than increased imports are causing injury to the domestic industry at the same time, such injury must not be attributed to increased imports. The criterion of a causal link falls short, however, of proposals made during the Uruguay Round that would have required imports to be the "principal cause" of injury.[132]

4.3.4 Investigation

The WTO Agreement on Safeguards provides the need for investigation, procedural transparency, participation by interested parties and confidential information as follows. New safeguard measures may be applied only following an investigation conducted by competent authorities in accordance with established procedures.[133]

Investigation procedures must be established and published prior to being used. Although the Agreement does not contain detailed procedural requirements, it does

[128] SG Agreement, *supra* note 112. Art. 4.2.

[129] SG Agreement, *supra* note 351. Art. 4.1.

[130] SG Agreement, *supra* note 351. Art. 4.2.

[131] WTO, Safeguard Measures: Technical Information on Safeguard Measures (Domestic industry). http://www.wto.org/english/tratop_e/safeg_e/safeg_info_e.htm. Accessed Feb. 28, 2012.

[132] WTO, Safeguard Measures: Technical Information on Safeguard Measures (Causation). http://www.wto.org/english/tratop_e/safeg_e/safeg_info_e.htm. Accessed Feb. 28, 2012.

[133] WTO, Safeguard Measures: Technical Information on Safeguard Measures (Need for investigation). http://www.wto.org/english/tratop_e/safeg_e/safeg_info_e.htm. Accessed Feb. 28, 2012.

require reasonable public notice of the investigation. The relevant authorities are obligated to publish a detailed analysis of the case in the form of a report presenting and explaining their findings on all pertinent issues, including a demonstration of the relevance of the factors examined.[134] Investigating authorities are required to hold public hearings or provide other appropriate means for interested parties (importer, exporters, producers, etc.) to present their views and to respond to the views of others with respect to the matters being investigated. Among the topics on which parties' views are required to be sought is whether or not a safeguard measure would be in the public interest.[135]

The Agreement also contains specific rules for the handling of confidential information in the context of an investigation. In general, information for which confidential treatment is requested must be accompanied by a public summary thereof, or an explanation why no such summary is possible. If confidentiality is found not to be warranted, and the party submitting the information is unwilling to summarize it or authorize its disclosure, the authorities may disregard the information, unless through other sources it is demonstrated that the information is correct.[136]

4.3.5 Safeguard Measures

The WTO Agreement on Safeguards provides tariff measures, quotas and quota modulation, and duration of measures as definite measures and provisional measures. Other than the general requirement that safeguard measures be applied only to the extent necessary to remedy or prevent serious injury and to facilitate adjustment, the Agreement provides no guidance as to how the level of a safeguard measure in the form of an increase in the tariff above the bound rate should be set.[137]

If the measure takes the form of a quantitative restriction, the level must not be below the actual import level of the most recent three representative years, unless there is clear justification for setting a different, lower, level. Rules also govern how quota shares are to be allocated among supplier countries based on past market

[134] WTO, Safeguard Measures: Technical Information on Safeguard Measures (Procedural transparency). http://www.wto.org/english/tratop_e/safeg_e/safeg_info_e.htm. Accessed Feb. 28, 2012.

[135] WTO, Safeguard Measures: Technical Information on Safeguard Measures (Participation by interested parties). http://www.wto.org/english/tratop_e/safeg_e/safeg_info_e.htm. Accessed Feb. 28, 2012.

[136] WTO, Safeguard Measures: Technical Information on Safeguard Measures (Confidential information). http://www.wto.org/english/tratop_e/safeg_e/safeg_info_e.htm. Accessed Feb. 28, 2012.

[137] WTO, Safeguard Measures: Technical Information on Safeguard Measures (Definitive safeguard measures- Tariff measures). http://www.wto.org/english/tratop_e/safeg_e/safeg_info_e.htm. Accessed Feb. 28, 2012.

shares. These levels may be departed from (i.e. the quota levels may be modulated) if (i) the percentage increase in imports from certain Members has been disproportionate to the overall increase in imports, (ii) the reasons for departure from the general rule are justified, and (iii) the conditions of such a departure are equitable to all suppliers of the product concerned.[138]

The maximum duration of any safeguard measure is four years, unless it is extended consistent with the Agreement's provisions. In particular, a measure may be extended only if it is found, through a new investigation, that its continuation is necessary to prevent or remedy serious injury, and only if evidence shows that the industry is adjusting. The initial period of application plus any extension generally cannot exceed eight years (see special and differential treatment). In addition, safeguard measures in place for longer than one year must be progressively liberalized at regular intervals during the period of application. If a measure is extended beyond the initial period, and it should continue to be liberalized, any measure of more than three years duration must be reviewed at mid-term. If appropriate, based on that review, the Member applying the measure must withdraw it or increase the pace of its liberalization.[139]

Members applying safeguard measures generally must "pay" for them through payment of compensation. A Member applying a safeguard measure must maintain a substantially equivalent level of concessions and other obligations with respect to affected exporting Members. To do so, any adequate means of trade compensation may be agreed among the affected Members through consultation.

If no such agreement on compensation is made within 30 days, the affected exporting Members individually may suspend substantially equivalent concessions and other obligations (i.e., "retaliate") unless the Council for Trade in Goods disapproves.[140] The right to retaliate, if compensation is not agreed on, cannot be exercised during the first three years of application of a safeguard measure if the measure is taken based on an absolute increase in imports, and otherwise conforms to the provisions of the Agreement.[141]

Under critical circumstances, defined as circumstances where delay would cause damage that would be difficult to repair, provisional measures may be imposed, on the basis of a preliminary determination that there is clear evidence that increased

[138] WTO, Safeguard Measures: Technical Information on Safeguard Measures (Definitive safeguard measures- Level of quotas and quota modulation). http://www.wto.org/english/tratop_e/safeg_e/safeg_info_e.htm. Accessed Feb. 28, 2012.

[139] WTO, Safeguard Measures: Technical Information on Safeguard Measures (Definitive safeguard measures- Duration and review of measures). http://www.wto.org/english/tratop_e/safeg_e/safeg_info_e.htm. Accessed Feb. 28, 2012.

[140] WTO, Safeguard Measures: Technical Information on Safeguard Measures (Level of concessions and other obligations – General rule). http://www.wto.org/english/tratop_e/safeg_e/safeg_info_e.htm. Accessed Feb. 28, 2012.

[141] WTO, Safeguard Measures: Technical Information on Safeguard Measures (Level of concessions and other obligations – Partial exception). http://www.wto.org/english/tratop_e/safeg_e/safeg_info_e.htm. Accessed Feb. 28, 2012.

imports have caused or threaten to cause serious injury. Such measures should be in the form of refundable tariff increases, and may be kept in place for a maximum of 200 days. The period of application of any provisional measure must be included in the total period of application of a safeguard measure.[142]

4.3.6 Special and Differential Treatment

Developing country Members receive special and differential treatment with respect to other Members' safeguard measures, in the form of a de minimis import volume exemption. As users of safeguards, developing country Members receive special and differential treatment with respect to applying their own such measures, with regard to permitted duration of extensions, and with respect to re-application of measures.[143]

A safeguard measure shall not be applied to low volume from developing country Members. That is, where imports from a single developing country Member account for no more than 3 percent of the total imports of the product concerned, and provided developing country Members below this threshold on an individual basis do not collectively account for more than 9 percent of those imports, such imports shall be excluded from the measure.[144]

4.3.7 Surveillance and Notifications

Multilateral discipline on the use of safeguard measures is established through notification requirements, as well as through the creation of a Committee on Safeguards charged with reviewing safeguard notifications, among other duties.[145]

The Committee's role generally is to monitor (and report and make recommendations to the Council for Trade in Goods on) the implementation and operation of the Agreement, to review Members' notifications, and to make findings as to Members' compliance with respect to the procedural provisions of the Agreement for the application of safeguard measures, to assist with consultations,

[142] WTO, Safeguard Measures: Technical Information on Safeguard Measures (Reapplication of measures to a product). http://www.wto.org/english/tratop_e/safeg_e/safeg_info_e.htm. Accessed Feb. 28, 2012.

[143] WTO, Safeguard Measures: Technical Information on Safeguard Measures (Special and differential treatment-Introduction). http://www.wto.org/english/tratop_e/safeg_e/safeg_info_e.htm. Accessed Feb. 28, 2012.

[144] WTO, Safeguard Measures: Technical Information on Safeguard Measures (Special and differential treatment- De minimis import exemption). http://www.wto.org/english/tratop_e/safeg_e/safeg_info_e.htm. Accessed Feb. 28, 2012.

[145] WTO, Safeguard Measures: Technical Information on Safeguard Measures (Surveillance and notifications- Introduction). http://www.wto.org/english/tratop_e/safeg_e/safeg_info_e.htm. Accessed Feb. 28, 2012.

to monitor the phase-out of pre-existing measures, to review proposed retaliation, and to perform any other functions determined by the Council for Trade in Goods.[146]

Members are required to notify their own laws, regulations and administrative procedures, and any changes thereto, to the Committee.[147] Members are required to notify the Committee of initiations of investigations into the existence of serious injury or threat and the reasons therefore; findings of serious injury or threat caused by increased imports; and decisions to apply or extend safeguard measures. Such notifications must contain the relevant information on which the decisions are based. Members are not obliged to disclose confidential information in their notifications.[148]

Members are required, before applying or extending a safeguard measure, to provide an adequate opportunity for consultations with Members who have substantial interests as exporters of the product. The aims of such consultations shall include review of information as to the facts of the situation, the exchange of views on the proposed measures, and the reaching of understandings as to maintaining substantially equivalent levels of concessions and obligations. The results of such consultations must be properly notified.[149]

Provisional measures must be notified before being applied, and consultations must be initiated immediately after such measures are applied. The results of consultations, of mid-term reviews of measures taken, any form of concession, and/or proposed suspension of concessions, must be notified immediately to the Council for Trade in Goods through the Safeguards Committee by the Member concerned.[150]

[146] WTO, Safeguard Measures: Technical Information on Safeguard Measures (Surveillance and notifications- Committee on Safeguards). http://www.wto.org/english/tratop_e/safeg_e/safeg_info_e.htm. Accessed Feb. 28, 2012.

[147] WTO, Safeguard Measures: Technical Information on Safeguard Measures (Surveillance and notifications- Extensive notification requirements (Notification of legislative framework)). http://www.wto.org/english/tratop_e/safeg_e/safeg_info_e.htm. Accessed Feb. 28, 2012.

[148] WTO, Safeguard Measures: Technical Information on Safeguard Measures (Surveillance and notifications- Extensive notification requirements (Notification of investigations and application of measures)). http://www.wto.org/english/tratop_e/safeg_e/safeg_info_e.htm. Accessed Feb. 28, 2012.

[149] WTO, Safeguard Measures: Technical Information on Safeguard Measures (Surveillance and notifications- Extensive notification requirements (Notification of investigations and application of measures)). http://www.wto.org/english/tratop_e/safeg_e/safeg_info_e.htm. Accessed Feb. 28, 2012.

[150] WTO, Safeguard Measures: Technical Information on Safeguard Measures (Surveillance and notifications- Extensive notification requirements (Notification of investigations and application of measures)). http://www.wto.org/english/tratop_e/safeg_e/safeg_info_e.htm. Accessed Feb. 28, 2012.

– Trade Disputes in Relation with **Safeguard Agreement**

Appellate Body Report, *United States-Definitive Safeguard Measures on Imports of Certain Steel Products*, WT/DS248/AB/R, WT/DS249/AB/R, WT/DS251/AB/R, WT/DS252/AB/R, WT/DS253/AB/R, WT/DS254/AB/R, WT/DS258/AB/R, WT/DS259/AB/R (Nov. 10, 2003).

Introduction

1. The United States appeals certain issues of law and legal interpretations developed in the Panel Reports, *United States – Definitive Safeguard Measures on Imports of Certain Steel Products* (the "Panel Reports").
2. In their requests for the establishment of a panel, the Complaining Parties claimed that the ten safeguard measures applied by the United States on imports of certain steel products were inconsistent with the obligations of the United States contained in Articles 2, 3, 4, 5, 7, 8, 9, and 12 of the *Agreement on Safeguards*.
3. The panel found that:
   (a) the application of safeguard measures by the United States on imports of CCFRS, hot-rolled bar, and stainless steel rod was inconsistent with Articles 2.1 and 3.1 of the *Agreement on Safeguards*, because "the United States failed to provide a reasoned and adequate explanation of how the facts supported its determination with respect to 'increased imports" ;
   (b) the application of safeguard measures by the United States on imports of CCFRS, hot-rolled bar, cold-finished bar, rebar, welded pipe, FFTJ, and stainless steel bar was inconsistent with Articles 2.1, 3.1, and 4.2 (b) of the *Agreement on Safeguards*, because "the United States failed to provide a reasoned and adequate explanation that a 'causal link' existed between any increased imports and serious injury to the relevant domestic producers" ;
   (c) the application of safeguard measures by the United States on imports of tin mill products and stainless steel wire was inconsistent with Articles 2.1, 3.1, and 4.2(b) of the *Agreement on Safeguards*, because "the United States failed to provide a reasoned and adequate explanation of how the facts supported its determinations with respect to 'increased imports" and the existence of a "causal link" between any increased imports and serious injury, "since the explanation given consisted of alternative explanations partly departing from each other, which given the different product bases, cannot be reconciled as a matter of substance" ; and

(d) the application of safeguard measures by the United States on imports of CCFRS, tin mill products, hot-rolled bar, cold-finished bar, rebar, welded pipe, FFTJ, stainless steel bar, stainless steel rod, and stainless steel wire was inconsistent with Articles 2.1 and 4.2 of the *Agreement on Safeguards*, because "the United States failed to comply with the requirement of 'parallelism' between the products for which the conditions for safeguard measures had been established, and the products which were subjected to the safeguard measure".

4. In addition, the Panel concluded, in the Panel Reports concerning the complaints of China, the European Communities, New Zealand, Norway, and Switzerland, that:
the application of safeguard measures by the United States on imports of CCFRS, tin mill products, hot-rolled bar, cold-finished bar, rebar, welded pipe, FFTJ, stainless steel bar, stainless steel rod, and stainless steel wire was inconsistent with Article XIX:1(a) of GATT 1994 and Article 3.1 of the *Agreement on Safeguards*, because "the United States failed to provide a reasoned and adequate explanation demonstrating that 'unforeseen developments' had resulted in increased imports causing serious injury to the relevant domestic producers".
5. The panel concluded that, to the extent that the United States had acted inconsistently with the provisions of the *Agreement on Safeguards* and GATT 1994 set out above, it had nullified or impaired the benefits accruing to the Complaining Parties under the *Agreement on Safeguards* and GATT 1994. The panel recommended that the DSB request the United States to bring all the safeguard measures into conformity with its obligations under the *Agreement on Safeguards* and GATT 1994.

Findings and Conclusions

6. The Appellate Body :
(a) upholds the panel's conclusions, that the application of all safeguard measures at issue in this dispute is inconsistent with the *Agreement on Safeguards* because "the United States failed to provide a reasoned and adequate explanation demonstrating that 'unforeseen developments' had resulted in increased imports causing serious injury to the relevant domestic producers";
(b) upholds the panel's conclusions, that the application of the safeguard measures on imports of CCFRS, stainless steel rod and hot-rolled bar is inconsistent with the requirements of Articles 2.1 and 3.1 of the *Agreement on Safeguards* because "the United States failed to provide a reasoned and adequate explanation of how the facts supported its determination with respect to 'increased imports'";
(c) reverses the panel's conclusions, that the application of the safeguard measures on imports of tin mill products and stainless steel wire is

(continued)

inconsistent with Articles 2.1 and 3.1 of the *Agreement on Safeguards* because "the United States failed to provide a reasoned and adequate explanation of how the facts supported its determination with respect to 'increased imports', since the explanation given consisted of alternative explanations partly departing from each other, which given the different product bases, cannot be reconciled as a matter of substance"; and finds it unnecessary to complete the analysis to decide whether the determination with respect to "increased imports" for tin mill products and stainless steel wire is consistent with Articles 2.1 and 3.1 of the *Agreement on Safeguards*;

(d) reverses the panel's conclusions, that the application of the safeguard measures on imports of tin mill products and stainless steel wire is inconsistent with Articles 2.1, 4.2(b), and 3.1 of the *Agreement on Safeguards* because "the United States failed to provide a reasoned and adequate explanation of how the facts supported its determination of a 'causal link' between any increased imports and serious injury, since the explanation given consisted of alternative explanations partly departing from each other, which given the different product bases, cannot be reconciled as a matter of substance"; and finds it unnecessary to complete the analysis to decide whether the determination with respect to a "causal link" for tin mill products and stainless steel wire is consistent with Articles 2.1, 4.2(b), and 3.1 of the *Agreement on Safeguards*;

(e) upholds the panel's conclusions, in the relevant sections of paragraph 11.2 of the Panel Reports, that the application of all safeguard measures at issue in this dispute is inconsistent with Articles 2.1 and 4.2 of the *Agreement on Safeguards* because "the United States failed to comply with the requirement of 'parallelism' between the products for which the conditions for safeguard measures had been established, and the products which were subjected to the safeguard measure";

Source: Appellate Body Report. United States-Definitive Safeguard Measures on Imports of Certain Steel Products. 10 November 2003. WT/DS248/AB/R, WT/DS249/AB/R, WT/DS251/AB/R, WT/DS252/AB/R, WT/DS253/AB/R, WT/DS254/AB/R, WT/DS258/AB/R, and WT/DS259/AB/R. http://www.worldtradelaw.net/reports/wtoab/us-steelsafeguards(ab).pdf

Assignment

To ensure students become equipped with the capability to apply knowledge from the classroom to the field, students are, in this chapter, required to write a report, deliver a presentation and participate in a discussion on the following issues:

1. Devices to prevent unfair trade practices from being used and their countervailing actions from being abused by the Member countries under the WTO Agreement.
2. The US-DRAMs CVD case (United States – Countervailing Duty Investigation on Dynamic Random Access Memory Semiconductors from Korea) focusing on the explicit and affirmative measures imposed on the non-governmental institutes made by the government.
3. The stricter requirements of the safeguards to be imposed by the damaged Member countries compared with those of the trade measures under the Anti-dumping on Subsidy/Countervailing Agreements.

Other Regulation on Trade in Goods

5

Learning Objectives

This chapter is to help students understand:

1. Trade-related measures not in compliance with the Agreement on Trade-related Investment Measures;
2. State trading systems found in developed countries with significant agricultural trading interests;
3. Trade practices of state trading enterprises which are not consistent with WTO provisions, particularly, in cases where they are used as a vehicle for implementing a number of trade policy measures;
4. Allowing WTO members to enter into regional trade agreements even though the intrinsic preferential nature of regional agreements contrasts with a major principle underlying the WTO framework of rules;
5. The legitimacy of regional trade agreements under GATS.

E.S. Lee, *World Trade Regulation*,
DOI 10.1007/978-3-642-31143-7_5,

5.1 Trade-Related Investment Measures

5.1.1 Introduction

The primary catalyst for the proliferation of trade-related investment measures (TRIMs)[1] has been the massive increase in the flow of foreign investment.[2] As foreign direct investment (FDI) has grown, so has the use of TRIMs, because host countries have increasingly employed TRIMs, to extract greater economic benefit from foreign investment.[3]

Since founding visions from the Charter for an International Trade Organization (1948) containing provisions on commercial policy were incorporated into GATT,[4] the linkage between trade and investment received little attention in the framework of GATT[5] until the Uruguay Round negotiations, resulting in their seeming

[1] TRIMs are government measures that require or encourage specific behavior by private investors (Edwards and Lester 1997, p. 109). Despite the growing multilateral concern about the increased use of TRIMs, there is no exact formula for identifying them, in part because the term itself reflects a political judgment that a certain measure reduces economic welfare and should therefore be prohibited (Edwards and Lester 1997, *id.*, at 172). The United Nations has devised four categories of TRIMs: performance requirements, investment incentives, corporate measures (restrictive business practices), and home-country measures. See the United Nations, The Impacts of Trade-related Investment Measures on Trade and by Edwards and Lester (1997, *id.*, at 172).

[2] The growth of multinational enterprises has resulted in a tremendous increase in the volume of foreign direct investment (Kennedy 1998, *supra* note 42, at 519). $203 billion of that figure to developed countries see Worked Investment Report 1996, cited by Kennedy (1998, at 519). The inflow of foreign direct investment into developing countries increased from $13 billion in 1981 to nearly $100 billion in 1995. See World Investment Report 1996 (*id.*). Total worldwide FDI in 1995 increased 40 percent from $225 billion in 1994 (*id.*). Five countries received two-thirds of total FDI, with the four Leading host countries for FDI inflows during the decade 1985–98 being the United States ($478 billion), the UK ($200 billion), France ($138 billion), and China ($130 billion) see Trade and Foreign Direct Investment 1996, cited by Kennedy (1998, *id.*).

[3] See Edwards and Lester (1997, *supra* note 390, at 170).

[4] While the idea of negotiating a Multilateral Investment Treaty has been appeared, see Salacuse (1994, pp. 1005–1009) (Arguing for a general agreement on direct investment), cited by Shenkin (1994, p. 593). The international consensus that now exists in at least four key investment areas I knew: "i) the WTO TRIPs proves that both developed and developing nations are willing to grant national treatment or specific treatment with respect to some investment establishment performance requirements; ii) with respect to investment maintenance or conduct in host countries, most investment treaties guarantee national treatment and every treaty guarantees at least MFN treatment; iii) every investment treaty, except for the Organization of the Islamic Conference, guarantees at least full compensation with reference to international law in the event of the nationalization; iv) every investment treaty, except for the Organization of the Islamic Conference, permits foreign investors to challenge directly sovereign conduct that injures them, usually through International Centre for Settlement of Investment Disputes" (Shenkin 1994, *id.*, at 593–594).

[5] During the period through 1960–1981, FDI was seen as only one component of the balance of payments problem traced by many nations, and was not considered a crucial component of industrialization as a result of which no specific guidelines were created Edward and Lester (1997, *supra* note 390, at 188).

incompatibility with the globalization of the modern economy.[6] The Charter for an International Trade Organization (1948) contained provisions on the treatment of foreign investment as part of a chapter on economic development. This Charter was never ratified and only its provisions on commercial policy were incorporated into the General Agreement on Tariffs and Trade (GATT).[7]

International Trade Organization (ITO)

Immediately after World War II, several initiatives converged into a proposal to establish an International Trade Organization (ITO). After years of international negotiations, the 1948 draft Havana Charter was completed. This charter would have established an ITO to become the framework for international rules designed to prevent the kind of destructive national government "beggar-thy-neighbor" policies many thought had contributed to the causes of the war. Despite these elaborate preparations, the effort to create an ITO ultimately failed (although an earlier effort to create monetary rules and a monetary fund – the IMF – had succeeded). The ITO effort failed largely because of the domestic constitutional and political structure of the country then economically preeminent – the United States. It failed despite the fact that the major leadership for the effort to create it had come from the United States itself. But this leadership was that of the executive branch or presidency in the United States. Under the US constitutional and legal requirements, for the government to formally accept the ITO charter, the executive branch had to get the approval of the US Congress, and this the Congress refused to give. In 1950 it was clear that it would be futile to continue trying to obtain this approval, and the ITO was stillborn.

Source: John H. Jackson, William J. Davey, and Alan O. Sykes, Jr. 2002. Legal Problems of International Economic Relations. West Publishing 5th ed. 61–62.

Perhaps the most significant development with respect to investment in the period before the Uruguay Round was a ruling by a panel in a dispute settlement

---

[6] The modern economy may be global, but the international commercial system is not synchronized, for which private party rights should be expanded within the WTO and a multilateral investment treaty must be negotiated (Shenkin 1994, *supra* note 393, at 579).

[7] In 1955, the GATT CONTRACTING PARTIES adopted a resolution on International Investment for Economic Development in which they, inter alia, urged countries to conclude bilateral agreement to provide protection and security for foreign investment. TRIMs first came up as a distinct issue in 1981, in the context of GATT discussions on structural adjustment and trade policy (Stewart 1996, pp. 2056–2057, cited by Edwards and Lester 1997, *supra* note 390, at fn. 117). The Consultative Group of 18 concluded that TRIMs produced trade-distorting economic effects, but reached no conclusions, but elected to keep the matter on the agenda for further discussion (Stewart 1996, *supra* note 196, at 2062, n. 242, cited by Edward and Lester 1997, *supra* note 390, at 120).

proceeding between the United States and Canada. In Canada – administration of the Foreign Investment Review Act ("FIRA"),[8] which was an example of a statutory scheme that provided for the negotiation of particularized requirements on a case-by-case basis,[9] a GATT dispute settlement panel considered a complaint by the United States regarding certain types of undertakings which were required from foreign investors by the Canadian authorities as conditions for the approval of investment projects.

These undertakings pertained to the purchase of certain products from domestic sources (local content requirements) and to the export of a certain amount or percentage of output (export performance requirements). The panel concluded that the local content requirements were inconsistent with the national treatment obligation but that the export performance requirements,[10] which were among the most trade-distorting TRIMs, were not inconsistent with GATT obligations.[11]

[8] Canada's FIRA provided that the acquisition or establishment of individual business by foreigners would be allowed in Canada only if the Canada government determined that such operations would be a "significant benefit to Canada". Act of Dec. 12, 1973 (Foreign Investment Review Act), ch. 46, 1973–74 Can. Stat. 619, amended by ch. 52, 1976–77 Can Stat. 1193 (FIRA), 2(1), cited by Shenkin (1994, *supra* note 393, at 561). In section 2(2), the FIRA provided five sectors to be considered when determining whether a particular foreign investment would provided a significant benefit to Canada – "(a) effect of the acquisition or establishment on the level and nature of economic activity . . .; (b) degree and significant of participation by Canadians in the business enterprises . . .; (c) effect of the acquisition or establishment on productivity . . .; (d) effect of the acquisition or establishment on competition. . .; (e) compatibility of the acquisition or establishment with national industrial and economic policies . . .". FIRA, (*id.*, 2(2)) cited by Shenkin (1994, *id*). The FIRA also provided that foreign investors could submit their own "written understandings" to be considered in eight of the five factors. Canada-Administration of the Foreign Investment Review Act (Panel Report) (LI5504), 30th supp. GATT, BISD140 (1984) (FIRA Panel Report, 143–146), cited by Shenkin (1994, *id*). They took the form of local content and export performance requirements, FIRA Panel Report, (*id.*, at 143–144), cited by Shenkin (1994, *id.*, at 561–562). In theory, the performance requirements were optional under the SIRA, but in practice, they became mandatory in order for a foreign invest to obtain the Canadian Government's approval. They can therefore be classified as performance requirements that were both an investment establishment condition and a legally binding investment maintenance condition (Shenkin 1994, *id.*, at 562).

[9] Edwards and Lester (1997, *supra* note 390, at 186).

[10] These requirements require products sold within their borders to contain a certain percentage of domestic content (value produced within the country, or materials coming from within the country). One such rule, considered in the United States in 1982, would have required automakers selling cars in the United Sates to meet increasingly higher domestic content minimums as their U.S. sales increased (e.g., U.S. sales of 100,000:25 domestic content required; sales of 150,000:50 percent; sales of 200,000:75 percent; sales of 500,000:90 percent) or suffer penalties. The penalties. The penalties would require that the offender's next year's sales be reduced 25 percent. While there had been the disputes over the question whether the proposed legislation consistent with the GATT provision and the United States-Japan FCN Treaty, the House of Representatives passed the bill described in 1982, followed by the failure in the Senate to act upon it (Jackson et al. 2008, *supra* note 3, at 521).

[11] Besides, export performance is one of the concerns high o the priority list of the industrialized countries, as these TRIMs may promote dumping in their home markets and disrupt trade flows to third country markets. (Edwards and Lester 1997, *supra* note 390, at 191–192).

The panel decision in the FIRA case was evaluated to ensure that existing obligations under GATT were applicable to performance requirements imposed by governments in context of investment so far as such requirements involve trade-distorting measures.[12] At the same time, the panel's conclusion that export performance requirements were not covered by GATT also underscored the limited scope of existing GATT disciplines with respect to such trade-related performance requirements.[13] The Punta del Este Ministerial Declaration which launched the Uruguay Round included the subject of trade-related investment measures as a subject for the new round.[14]

During the debatable Uruguay Round negotiations on trade-related investment measures,[15] strong disagreement among participants over the coverage and nature

[12] Shenkin (1994, *supra* note 393 at 564).

[13] There are various forms of TRIMs such as: local content requirement affecting ownership; foreign exchange restrictions; export or trade-balancing requirements; foreign exchange balancing requirements; manufacturing limitations; technology transfer requirements, remittance restrictions, licensing requirements and product mandating requirements. See Curtiss and Atkinson (1995, p. 127), and Low and Subramania (1995, p. 5), cited by Civello (1999, p. 99). Out of such measures, beside the local content requirements, the issue of trade-balancing did not arise in the FIRA controversy, and the FIRA Panel declined to hold that Canada's purchase undertakings violated GATT Art. XI, FIRA Panel Report, at 162–163, cited by Civello (1999, *id.*), but its refusal to do so may not mean that Art. XI does not protect against trade-balancing regulations. Indeed the reason for such Panel's decision should be ascribed to the drafters of the United States' complaint rather than to the FIRA Panel: The United States only alleged that the purchase and manufacturing undertakings violated Art. XI (general prohibition against quantitative restrictions); the export undertakings were only alleged to violate GATT Art. XVII: 1(c). *See* FIRA Panel Report, at 154–155, cited by Civello (1999, *id.*, at 114).

[14] Since the investment and competition policies were clearly indicated as potential subjects for further negotiations, at the Ministerial Conference held at Singapore in 1996, http://www.wto.org/ehglish/thewto_e/whatis_e/eol/e/wto01/wto1_32.htm. Accessed April 9, 2004; Ministers decided to, inter alia, establish a working group to examine the relationship between trade and investment. http://www.wto.org/ehglish/thewto_e/whatis_e/eol/e/wto01/wto1_26.htm. Accessed April 9, 2004 and at the Ministerial Conference held at Geneva in 1998, it was mandated for the General Council to treat with this matter continuously. http://www.wto.org/ehglish/thewto_e/whatis_e/eol/e/wto01/wto1_27.htm. Accessed April 9, 2004.

[15] Authors categorized TRIMs for the new agreement by fitting TRIMs into the traffic light categories, considering the fact that TRIMs have similar purposes with subsidies, that is, to promote economic growth and to further other social and economic objectives: "a. Prohibited (red light) TRIMs... Because these TRIMs are inherently trade distorting, ... they should therefore be eliminated... export performance requirements, product-mandating requirements, trade-balancing requirements, local content requirements, and manufacturing requirements and limitations, b. Actionable (yellow light) TRIMs... If actionable TRIMs impose adverse effects on investors, the measure will be prohibited... equity requirements, licensing requirements, and technology transfer requirements. c. Permitted (green light) TRIMs... they must be used to enhance economic development in specific region. ...as is true in the Subsidies Agreement, TRIMs that fall into the red light category ... is prohibited regardless of their purpose" (Edwards and Lester 1997, *supra* note 390, at 210–211). This categorization is similar to Swiss government's proposal, made during the Uruguay Round negotiations, which divided TRIMs into the same three categories: Prohibited, permitted, and actionable (*id.*, at 211).

of possible new disciplines arose.[16] While some developed countries proposed provisions that would prohibit a wide range of measures[17] in addition to the local content requirements found to be inconsistent with Article III in the FIRA panel case, many developing countries opposed this.[18] The resulting WTO Agreement on Trade-Related Investment Measures is a compromise.[19] The Agreement is essentially limited to the application of trade-related investment measures of GATT provisions to national treatment of imported goods[20] and to quantitative restrictions

[16] Two issues were central to the TRIMs negotiations: "First, ... under the Uruguay Round, TRIMs were to some extent acknowledged to be covered by existing GATT articles. ... The industrialized countries took the position that a separate agreement or TRIMs was within the scope of the Negotiating Groups Mandate. In contrast, ... mostly developing countries, felt the inquiry should be limited to an examination of how existing articles applied to TRIMs" (Stewart 1996, *supra* note 396, at 194). "The second issue was whether the targeted TRIMs should be prohibited outright, or to be actionable ..., taking into account the actual economic effects of the measure .... The developing countries felt strongly ... to look only at the direct effect of the measures, not at the measures themselves." See Stewart (1996, *supra* note 396, at 2081–2082), cited by (*id.*, at 194). As a Result, the Agreement specifies that certain TRIMs are prohibited only in the context of existing GATT articles. Thus, other trade-distorting TRIMs are still permitted (Edwards and Lester 1997, *supra* note 390, at 196). The data from GATT showed that nineteen developing countries maintained local content requirements in various industries between 1991 and 1994 (Edwards and Lester 1997, *supra* note 390, at 178).

[17] For the most common restrictions to foreign investment, particularly, in the member countries of OECD, see Kennedy (1998, *supra* note 42, at 519–520): "Despite the benefits of FDI and the tremendous growth worldwide in FDI, many barriers still exist. The most common restrictions include investment notification, approval, or authorization requirements that are sometimes contingent upon satisfying criteria that are highly subjective and, therefore, subject to political manipulation; limitations on the acquisition of real estate; and conditions requiring nationality or residency of senior managers or members of the board of directors. One study of the investment policies of the members of the Organization of Economic Cooperation and Development ("OECD"), whose investment policies should in theory be the most liberal in the world, reveals that they collectively maintain over 400 investment restrictions, accounting for 54 percent of all restrictions identified for OECD members. The United States has the second largest number of restrictions, accounting for 17 percent of the OECD total, followed by Canada, Mexico, and Australia, with 14 percent, 7 percent, and 6 percent, respectively."

[18] Three major TRIMs negotiation positions were represented in the Uruguay MTN Round, that is, positions espoused by both the United States and Japan, the EEC and developing countries (Shenkin 1994, *supra* note 393, at 564). The United States and Japan, however, both wanted the TRIMs negotiations to result in an agreement that specifically detailed the treatment of TRIMs in the GATT (Knaw 1991, p. 327, cited by Shenkin 1994, *id*). The EEC took a moderate view toward TRIMs in the GATT (Shenkin 1994, *id*). The EEC, proposed to limit the GATT's scope only to investment measures directly related to trade in goods, such as local content, manufacturing, and export requirement (*id.*). Similar to the EEC, developing countries argued for the exclusion of non-trade related investment measures, such as local equity requirements and investment incentives (Knaw 1991, *id.*, at 84–85, cited by Shenkin 1994, *id*).

[19] Agreement on Trade Related Investment Measures, Apr. 15, 1994, Marrakesh Agreement Establishing the World Trade Organization, Annex 1A, reprinted in the Results of the Uruguay Round of Multilateral Trade Negotiations-The Legal Texts, 163 (1994) (TRIMs Agreement).

[20] TRIMs Agreement, *id.* Art. III.

of imports or exports.[21] Thus, the TRIMs Agreement does not cover many of the other relevant issues such as export performance and transfer of technology requirements.[22]

---

[21] TRIMs Agreement, *id.* Art. XI.

[22] Insufficient coverage of the TRIMs Agreement has been criticized: (*id.*), Art. XI. The TRIMs Agreement's failure has been described: "it does nothing new. . . . the Agreement merely reiterates what was already in GATT, providing no new protections or remedies for foreign investors, . . . the Agreement contains no plan or procedural framework for moving forward investment liberalization and shies away from innovation or experimentation . . . the TRIMs Agreement is at best a transitional arrangement that may serve, at least, as a sign that future trade negotiations have to address FDI. . . ." (Civello 1999, *supra* note 402, at 97); The multilateral Agreement on Investment proposed by Organization for Economic Co-operation and Development, as an alternative to inefficient TRIMs, focuses directly on Foreign Direct Investment, and includes the two provisions that the TRIMs Agreement sorely lacks: a MFN obligation and an national treatment obligation for investment, as well as, the explicit prohibitions on performance requirements and regulations on investment incentives, which, if approved, would provide a blueprint for future arrangements that may eventually include the developing countries. See the MAI Negotiating Text http://www.oecd.ord/dat.cmis/mai/negtext.htm. Accessed Feb. 28, 2004, cited by Civello (1999, *supra* note 402, at 123); Regarding the automobile trade and investment policies of Brazil and Indonesia, against which the United States launched a Section 301 to WTO Dispute Settlement Body, 1997; Parry and Taylor (Mar. 18, 1997) cited by Civello (1999, *supra* note 402, at 111), the numerous complaints those policies elicited, and their resolutions expose the ineffectiveness of the TRIMs Agreement and the need for new directions in international investment policy: (Civello 1999, *id.*, at 111). Brazil has taken a series of measures in recent years that have provoked sharp criticism from developed nations containing two TRIMs: a local content requirement and a trade-balancing regulation. See Kleinfeld and Wengel (1991, p. 406), cited by Civello (1999, *id.*, at 111). Against Brazil complaints have been made to WTO by Japan, the United States and European Union respectively. However, they preferred to try to resolve the conflict through negotiations instead of requesting (Civello 1999, *id.*, at 112–113). "The Brazilian controversy reveals several reasons for the TRIMs Agreement's ineffectiveness in preventing and remedying TRIMs. All stem from the Agreement's glaring unoriginality, its refusal to confront issues regarding investment measures which have not previously been faced" (Civello 1999, *id.*, at 113). "Redundancy is not the TRIMs Agreement's only flaw. The Agreement does nothing beyond recapitulating Arts. III, XI, and the dispute settlement process of GATT. . . . Yet the Brazilian controversy cries out for new, innovative approaches to the problem of TRIMs and FDI, and the Agreement offers no response. . . ."; (Civello 1999, *id.*, at 115). The Indonesian "Pioneer Auto Program" contained two features that violated the Agreement: a local content requirement and an important preference. European Union submitted the complaint to the WTO in 1996 (Civello 1999, *id.*, at 118). Due to the Asian economic crisis, until now, Indonesia's "Pioneer Auto Program" is moribund, if not dead. Like the Brazilian controversy, the Indonesian debacle demonstrates the inefficacy of the TRIMs Agreement (*id.*, at 120–121). The Agreement's effectiveness against Brazil's local content requirement holds true in the Indonesian case (Civello 1999, *id.*, at 121), but the Indonesian controversy adds two new features about which the TRIMs Agreement is silent: an import preference and equity requirement. The import preference like the local content requirement, being sufficiently covered by GATT, equity requirements, however, are not prohibited by the GATT or the Uruguay Round Agreements, and the TRIMs Agreement's failure to do so is perhaps its biggest shortcoming (Civello 1999, *id.*, at 121–122).

5.1.2 Principles

The TRIMs Agreement is the first successful attempt made within the GATT-WTO system to facilitate foreign investment by eliminating nontariff barriers to trade in goods associated with foreign investment. The agreement is designed to ensure that governments do not apply measures to foreign investments that create restrictions or distortions for trade in goods. It gives investors the assurance that they may freely buy, sell, import, and export goods that are produced in countries outside the country in which their investment is located.[23]

The objectives of the Agreement are to promote the liberalization of world trade and to facilitate investment across international frontiers so as to increase economic growth while ensuring free competition.[24] The Agreement applies to investment measures related to trade in goods only. Thus, the TRIMs Agreement does not apply to services.[25]

As an agreement that is based on existing GATT disciplines on trade in goods, the Agreement is not concerned with the regulation of foreign investment. The disciplines of the TRIMs Agreement focus on discriminatory treatment of imported and exported products and do not govern the issue of entry and treatment of foreign investment. For example, a local content requirement imposed in a non-discriminatory manner on domestic and foreign enterprises is inconsistent with the TRIMs Agreement because it involves discriminatory treatment of imported products in favor of domestic products.[26] The fact that there is no discrimination between domestic and foreign investors in the imposition of the requirement is irrelevant under the TRIMs Agreement.[27]

Members are required not to apply any TRIM that is inconsistent with the provisions of Article III (national treatment of imported products) or Article XI (prohibition of quantitative restrictions on imports or exports) of GATT 1994. Measures in the annexed Illustrative List that are inconsistent with these provisions include those where Members' obligations cover TRIMs which are mandatory or

---

[23] Kennedy (1998, *supra* note 42, at 523).

[24] TRIMs Agreement, *supra* note 408. Preamble.

[25] The term "trade-related investment measures" ("TRIMs") is not defined in the Agreement. However, the Agreement contains in an annex an Illustrative List of measures that are inconsistent with GATT Art. III:4 or Art. XI:1 of GATT 1994. Art. 2.1 of TRIMs Agreement, *supra* note 408.

[26] FIRA Panel Report, Canada-Administration of the Foreign Investment Review Act (Panel Report) (LI5504), 30th supp. GATT, BISD140 (1984) (FIRA Panel Report) 160, cited by Shenkin (1994, *supra* note 393, at 565).

[27] Even though the TRIMs Decision would incidentally and indirectly affect foreign investors, it would not provide foreign investors with a right or a remedy within GATT. After claim espousal from injured goods producers or exporters, dispute provisions, Arts. XXII and XXIII, which is improved and substituted by the WTO Dispute Settlement Understandings (Shenkin 1994, *supra* note 393, at 566). The impact of this on foreign investors is that although their investments, they have no legal recourse under the TRIMs Agreement; only goods producers do (*id*).

enforceable under domestic law or under administrative rulings, as well as TRIMs with which compliance is necessary to obtain an advantage.[28]

5.1.3 Measures Inconsistent

TRIMs identified in paragraph 1 of the Illustrative List as being inconsistent with the national treatment principle (art.III:4) concern the purchase or use of products by an enterprise, while the TRIMs listed in paragraph 2 as inconsistent with prohibition of quantitative restrictions (art.XI:1) concern the importation or exportation of products by an enterprise.

Paragraph 1(a) of the Illustrative List covers local content TRIMs, which require the purchase or use by an enterprise of products of domestic origin or domestic source (local content requirements) while paragraph 1(b) covers trade-balancing TRIMs, which limit the purchase or use of imported products by an enterprise to an amount related to the volume or value of local products that it exports. In both cases, the inconsistency with prohibition of quantitative restrictions results from the fact that the measure subjects the purchase or use by an enterprise of imported products to less favorable conditions than the purchase or use of domestic products.[29]

Paragraph 2(a) of the Illustrative List covers measures which limit the importation by an enterprise of products used in its local production in general terms or to an amount related to the volume or value of local production exported by the enterprise.[30] Measures identified in paragraph 2(b) of the list involve a restriction of imports in the form of a foreign exchange balancing requirement, whereby the ability to import products used in or related to local production is limited by restricting the enterprise's access to foreign exchange to an amount related to the foreign exchange inflows attributable to the enterprise.[31]

Finally, paragraph 2(c) covers measures involving restrictions on the exportation of or sale for export by an enterprise, whether specified in terms of particular products, volume or value of products or in terms of a proportion of volume or value of its local production. Other measures relating to exports, such as export incentives and export performance requirements, are therefore not covered by the TRIMs Agreement.[32]

---

[28] TRIMs Agreement, *supra* note 408. Annex: Illustrative List.

[29] TRIMs Agreement, *supra* note 408. Art. 2.

[30] There is a conceptual similarity between this paragraph and paragraph 1(b) in that they both cover trade-balancing measures. The difference is that paragraph 1(b) deals with internal measures affecting the purchase or use of products after they have been imported, while paragraph 2(a) deals with border measures affecting the importation of products.

[31] TRIMs Agreement, *supra* note 408. Art. 2.

[32] *Id.*

5.2 State Trading

5.2.1 Introduction

In the sphere of international trade, there is a general presumption that trading enterprises will act on the basis of commercial considerations, and that based on the theories of comparative advantage, they will expand their international trade in order to reap the benefits. However, a private firm, if it has significant power in a given market, may exercise this power in a way that distorts trade and thus causes economic detriment, rather than benefit. Furthermore, governments can act in indirect ways to influence world trade in an uneconomic direction; for example, acting through firms or enterprises to provide protection against imports or to advance exports, to the detriment of foreign producers.

Thus, the drafters of the General Agreement sought to place state trading enterprises in the same competitive position – with regard to governmental support or protection – as private firms. In other words, they sought to make state traders behave as private competitive traders, and, thus, to remove the potential for trade distortion offered by government involvement in an enterprise's decisions and activities.[33]

State trading is a common feature of many economies where agriculture is an important sector of trade. For this reason, state trading enterprises are found in developed countries with significant agricultural trading interests, as well as in agriculturally-based developing countries. The heavy emphasis on agriculture in state trading activities would seem to indicate governments' belief that state trading is an appropriate means of implementing agriculture-related policy objectives, such as providing price support for important agricultural products or ensuring food security. In the area of industrial goods, state trading may arise as a by-product of the nationalization of an ailing industry or as a means of pursuing government policies on products or industries considered to have strategic importance.[34]

State trading enterprises may be used as a vehicle for implementing a number of trade policy measures which are not consistent with the WTO provisions. The most common is a violation of market access obligations. For example, an STE might be used to provide protection for the domestic market in a given product by setting resale prices of imports at very high levels, thus negating tariff concessions bound in the WTO Schedules. The provision of subsidies to STEs which are mainly involved in exporting may run afoul of export subsidy disciplines.

Even in cases where the objective of the government acting through the STE is not intentionally trade-distorting, the STE's operations may nevertheless distort trade. For example, the protection of public health, which is a frequently stated

[33] WTO, Technical Information on State Trading Enterprises. http://www.wto.org/english/tratop_e/statra_e/statra_info_e.htm. Accessed Feb. 28, 2012.

[34] *Id.*

rationale for the maintenance of monopolies on alcohol and alcoholic beverages, may seriously distort trade in those products. It is only when the activities of state trading enterprises can be examined that their impact on trade can be analyzed and, ultimately, more effective rules developed.[35]

5.2.2 State Trading Enterprises

5.2.2.1 Definition

Throughout the history of GATT many attempts were made at a definition of a state trading enterprise, but all of them failed to express a comprehensive designation of this entity.

Article XVII itself provides the basic idea of what a state trading enterprise is, without attempting an actual definition. It refers to three types of enterprises: (i) "state enterprises" (that is, owned by the state); (ii) enterprises granted special privileges by the state (for example a subsidy or subsidy equivalent); and (iii) enterprises granted exclusive privileges (i.e. a monopoly in the production, consumption or trade of certain goods).[36]

Thus, a private corporation or enterprise that receives some special rights or privileges from the state (that is, rights or privileges not generally available to other private sector entities in the same area and thus giving the enterprise an advantage over those firms) and as a result of these rights or privileges is in a position to influence the level or direction of trade, could be considered to be a state trading enterprise. It is important to note that the special right or privilege granted need not give the enterprise a monopoly position.[37]

The results of the Uruguay Round of multilateral trade negotiations include the Understanding on the Interpretation of Article XVII of GATT 1994. One of the main features of the understanding is the "working definition of the state trading enterprise", which reads: "governmental and non-governmental enterprises, including marketing boards, which have been granted exclusive or special rights or privileges, including statutory or constitutional powers, in the exercise of which they influence through their purchases or sales the level or direction of imports or exports".[38] Three fundamental elements are identified in this "working definition": (i) a governmental or non-governmental entity, including marketing boards; (ii) the granting to the enterprise of exclusive or special rights or privileges; and (iii) a resulting influence, through the enterprise's purchases or sales, on the level or direction of imports or exports.[39]

---

[35] *Id.*

[36] *Id.*

[37] *Id.*

[38] GATT, *supra* note 1, Art. XVII.2

[39] WTO, Technical Information on State Trading Enterprises, *supra* note 422.

Particularly important in this definition is the phrase: "in the exercise of which they influence through their purchases or sales the level or direction of imports or exports", because this goes to the heart of what the regulation of state trading in the WTO is aimed at: that is, the potentially distorting effects of the operations of STEs on trade. However, although this text provides considerable clarification of Article XVII, it still leaves room for differing interpretations of what is intended. Once again, it must be emphasized that an enterprise need not be state owned, nor need it have a monopoly position, in order to be covered by Article XVII and subject to the WTO rules on STEs. The important criteria for STEs are that they enjoy exclusive or special rights or privileges, and that in the exercise of these rights and privileges they influence imports or exports by their buying and selling activities.

5.2.2.2 Types of State Trading Enterprises

There are several typical types of state trading enterprises including statutory marketing boards, regulatory marketing boards, fiscal monopolies, foreign trade enterprise, and etc.

Statutory marketing boards, also referred to as "statutory marketing authorities" and "control boards", appear to be the most common type of state trading enterprise in the agricultural sector. They often combine a monopoly on foreign trade with responsibility for management of domestic production and distribution. Export marketing boards could largely be classified as a form of statutory marketing board, with their defining feature being that they deal only with exports. They generally are producer-controlled bodies that pursue export promotion and advantageous terms of sales on foreign markets.

Regulatory marketing boards have functions similar to statutory marketing boards, with one distinctive feature: they do not themselves engage in foreign trade operations, but rather contract out the actual trading operations to private entities. Fiscal monopolies are a type of STE typically established to cover trade in goods for which domestic demand is relatively price-inelastic and foreign demand is relatively price-elastic, and with respect to which the government may have a policy of protecting public health. Ethyl alcohol, alcoholic beverages, tobacco, salt, and matches and related inflammables are products frequently covered by such monopolies. Canalizing agency is the term used by a number of developing countries to describe the STEs they maintain.

The term refers to the channeling, or "canalizing", of imports and/or exports through a designated product-specific enterprise. Such STEs aim to provide some degree of price stabilization, particularly for producers, as well as to ensure availability of supplies for domestic consumers.[40] Foreign trade enterprise is the term used for the State trading enterprises of some current and former non-market economies. Such STEs are also known as foreign trade organizations. In some cases STEs have been chosen by governments to assume responsibility for nationalized

[40] *Id.*

industries. In developed countries, this is typically done to minimize social disruption, i.e. unemployment due to an industry's decline.[41]

5.2.3 Regulation

The rules on state trading essentially try to ensure that STEs: operate on the basis of commercial considerations and in a non-discriminatory manner; do not erode or nullify the value of negotiated tariff concessions; do not serve to implement otherwise WTO-inconsistent measures, such as quantitative restrictions or subsidies; and are fully notified to the WTO on a regular basis.[42]

Given that so little is known of state trading operations world-wide, the transparency obligation is perhaps one of the most important rules at present. As more becomes known and understood of the functions and operations of STEs, there are likely to be efforts to further tighten the rules governing them. However, it should be stressed that the WTO does not seek to prohibit or even discourage the establishment of maintenance of STEs, but rather to ensure that they are used and operated in a manner consistent with the WTO principles and rules.[43]

Members undertake that any state trading enterprise shall, in its purchases or sales involving imports or exports, act in a manner consistent with the general principles of non-discriminatory treatment set out in the General Agreement for governmental measures affecting imports or exports by private traders.[44]

It should be noted that a strict MFN (most-favored nation) treatment was not intended: A state trading enterprise is allowed to charge different prices for its sales of a product in different markets, provided this is done for commercial reasons, to meet conditions of supply and demand in export markets. Also, a country's receipt of a "tied loan" (whereby country "A" receives a loan from country "B" in order to buy goods from country "B") falls in the category of "commercial considerations".[45]

---

[41] *Id.*

[42] Understanding on the interpretation of Art. XVII of the General Agreement on Tariffs and Trade 1994, Preamble.

[43] Understanding on the interpretation of Art. XVII of the General Agreement on Tariffs and Trade 1994, Preamble.

[44] GATT, *supra* note 1, Art. XVII:I(a), This standard of conduct is further explained in paragraph 1 (b): "... such enterprises shall... make any such purchases or sales solely in accordance with commercial considerations including price, quality, availability, marketability, transportation and other conditions of purchase or sale, and shall afford... other contracting parties adequate opportunity... to compete for participation in such purchases or sales."

[45] Interpretative Note to Art. XVII:1.

5.3 Restrictions for Balance of Payments

5.3.1 Introduction

Under the rules of the WTO, any trade restriction taken by a Member must be consistent, or in compliance, with the rules of the international trading system. Under the provisions of Article XII, XVIII:B and the "Understanding of the Balance-of-Payments Provisions of GATT 1994", a Member may apply import restrictions for balance-of-payments reasons.[46]

Article XII and XVIII:B in their current form were redrafted in 1957 by the Working Party on Quantitative Restrictions. At that time, balance-of-payments measures referred to quantitative restrictions and were an exception to Article XI which prohibits the use of quantitative restrictions. Article XII can be invoked by all Members and Article XVIII:B by the developing country Members (defined as those in the early stages of development and with a low standard of living).[47]

The basic condition for invoking Article XII is to "safeguard the [Member's] external financial position and its balance-of-payments"; Article XVIII:B mentions the need to "safeguard the [Member's] external financial position and ensure a level of reserves adequate for the implementation of its program of economic development". Both articles refer to the need to "restore equilibrium on a sound and lasting basis". While Article XII mentions the objective of "avoiding the uneconomic employment of resources", Article XVIII:B refers to "assuring an economic employment of production resources".[48]

In the Understanding, Members confirm their commitment to: (i) "announce publicly, as soon as possible, time-schedules for the removal of restrictive import measures taken for balance-of-payments purposes" and to explain why if they choose not to do so; (ii) "give preference to those measures which have the least disruptive effect on trade"; (iii) justify why price-based measures are not adequate if they have chosen to impose quantitative restrictions; (iv) not apply more than one type of restrictive trade measure to the same product.[49]

It has been clarified that price-based measures have the least disruptive effect on trade and such measures are understood to include import surcharges, import deposit requirements or other equivalent trade measures with an impact on the price of imported goods. It is expressly provided that, notwithstanding the provisions of Article II, price-based measures taken for balance-of-payments purposes may be applied by a Member in excess of the duties inscribed in the Schedule of that Member.[50]

---

[46] Understanding of the Balance-of-Payments Provisions of the GATT 1994, Preamble; GATT Art. 12, 18(b).

[47] *Id.*

[48] *Id.*

[49] Understanding of the Balance-of-Payments Provisions of the GATT 1994, Art. 1.

[50] Understanding of the Balance-of-Payments Provisions of the GATT 1994, Art. 2.

The Understanding also confirms that restrictive import measures taken for balance-of-payments purposes may only be applied to control the general level of imports and may not exceed what is necessary to address the balance-of-payments situation. In order to minimize any incidental protective effects, restrictions have to be administered in a transparent manner.[51]

In sum, measures taken for balance-of-payments purposes have to be temporary, preferably price-based, administered in a transparent manner, and apply to the general level of imports (i.e. avoid sectoral specificity).[52]

5.3.2 Consultation

A Member applying new restrictions or substantially intensifying existing ones is obliged to consult with the Committee on Balance-of-Payments Restrictions immediately after taking action or before doing so if prior consultation is practicable.[53] A Member maintaining such restrictions is required to consult annually[54] or biennially.[55] A third type of consultation may be initiated on the basis of a complaint by a Member adversely affected by restrictions maintained by another, if these are inconsistent with the relevant provisions relating to these restrictions.[56]

Article XV of GATT 1994 requires that in all cases in which the WTO is called upon to consider or deal with problems concerning monetary reserves, balance-of-payments or foreign exchange arrangements, they shall consult fully with the International Monetary Fund. In all such consultations the bodies are required to accept all findings of statistical and other facts presented by the Fund relating to foreign exchange, monetary reserves and balance-of-payments. Accordingly the Fund participates in the consultations in the Committee on Balance-of-Payments Restrictions, provides documentation and makes a formal statement.[57]

5.3.3 Work of Committee

Consultations under Articles XII:4 and XVIII:12 cover the nature of the balance-of-payment difficulties of the Member in question, alternative measures which may be available, and the possible effect of the restrictions on the economies of other Members. They are intended to provide an opportunity for a free exchange of

---

[51] Understanding of the Balance-of-Payments Provisions of the GATT 1994, Art. 2.

[52] Understanding of the Balance-of-Payments Provisions of the GATT 1994, Arts. 1–4.

[53] Art. XII:4(a) and XVIII:12(a).

[54] Art. XII:4(b); Understanding of the Balance-of-Payments Provisions of the GATT 1994, Art. 5.

[55] Art. XVIII:12(b).

[56] Art. XII:4(d) and XVIII:12(d); Understanding of the Balance-of-Payments Provisions of the GATT 1994, Art. 6.

[57] GATT Agreement, Art. 15

views, contributing to a better understanding of the problems facing the consulting countries, of the various measures taken by them to deal with these problems, and of the possibilities of further progress in the direction of freer, multilateral trade.[58]

The balance-of-payments provisions of GATT have traditionally emphasized that import restrictions are but a temporary relief and not the optimal form of restoring equilibrium to the balance-of-payments position. Members should undertake to pay due regard to the need for maintaining or restoring equilibrium in their balance-of-payments on a sound and lasting basis and to the desirability of avoiding an uneconomic employment of productive resources.[59] Thus, the Committee addresses the issue, when discussing alternative measures, of the appropriate fiscal and monetary policies, other measures aimed at structural reform, including liberalization of the trade and investment regimes, and a correctly valued exchange rate. The IMF Articles of Agreement expressly prohibit currency depreciation for competitive purposes.[60]

The Committee may come to a consensus that the balance-of-payments situation warrants the measures imposed, and that the application of the measures is consistent with the balance-of-payments provisions. If the Committee finds that the measures are not being applied consistent with the accepted criteria, it will request the consulting Member to make the necessary adjustments, e.g. convert quantitative restrictions to price-based measures, or to disinvoke the balance-of-payments provisions.

If agreement cannot be reached by the Committee, e.g. Members find the measures inconsistent but the consulting Member is not in a position to withdraw its balance-of-payments measures or bring them into conformity with the provisions, consultations may terminate without agreed conclusions. Members may also "reserve their rights", if they consider that the consulting country is not applying the balance-of-payments provisions consistent with its obligations, to invoke the consultation and dispute settlement under the DSU.[61]

5.4 Regional Trade Agreement

5.4.1 Introduction

By definition, parties to regional trade agreement (RTA) offer to each other more favorable treatment in trade matters than to the rest of the world (including the WTO Members). The depth of such preferential treatment varies from one RTA to

[58] Arts. XII:4 and XVIII:12.

[59] Art. XII, XVIII; Understanding of the Balance-of-Payments Provisions of the GATT 1994, Art. 6.

[60] Arts. XII:4 and XVIII:12.

[61] Arts. XII:4 and XVIII:12.

another. It may involve only a few products/sectors, or it may apply to the whole range of trade-related relations among parties. Barriers may be completely abolished in intra-RTA trade, or merely reduced.[62]

The intrinsic preferential (i.e. discriminatory) nature of RTAs contrasts with a major principle underlying the WTO framework of rules: the most-favored nations (MFN) treatment among Members. Nevertheless, the WTO allows Members, as did its predecessor GATT, to enter into RTAs, albeit under the terms stipulated in some specific provisions. The number of RTAs involving GATT/WTO Members has increased significantly in recent years. Up to the conclusion of the Uruguay Round, rules concerning customs unions and free-trade areas were spelled out only in Article XXIV.[63]

This unsatisfactory situation placed Article XXIV on the Uruguay Round agenda and some progress was made in the adoption of the Understanding on the Interpretation of Article XXIV of GATT 1994. Thus, the Understanding on the Interpretation of Article XXIV of GATT 1994 (the Understanding) complements Article XXIV of GATT 1994. Disciplines on economic integration agreements liberalizing trade in services have also been included in the General Agreement on Trade in Services (GATS).[64]

5.4.2 Regional Trade Agreement Under GATT 1994

Article XXIV of GATT 1994 and its Understanding contain rules and disciplines applicable to customs unions and free-trade areas, as well as interim agreements which lead to a customs union or a free-trade area.[65] The rules and disciplines of Article XXIV aim to ensure that such RTAs facilitate trade between the parties while minimizing any adverse effect to their trade with the WTO Members that are not parties to such agreements.

Article XXIV provides for the examination of RTAs by the WTO Members. This examination serves two purposes: ensuring the transparency of RTAs and evaluating whether the agreement concerned is consistent with the WTO rules. In the case of customs unions, there is a third element – the renegotiation of tariff bindings in cases where the adoption of the customs union's common external tariff leads a party to the union to apply higher tariffs than those recorded in its WTO Schedule of concessions.[66]

---

[62] WTO, Trade Policy Courses, Chapter 24: Regionalism, at. 24.2. http://www.wto.org/english/thewto_e/whatis_e/tif_e/understanding_e.pdf. Accessed Oct. 19, 2012.

[63] *Id.*

[64] *Id.*

[65] GATT Agreement, *supra* note 1. Art. 24.

[66] GATT Agreement, *supra* note 1. Art. 24.

Customs unions, free-trade areas or interim agreements should aim to facilitate trade between the parties and not to raise barriers to the trade of third parties.[67] Apart from a few exceptions permitted under the terms of certain other GATT Articles,[68] the duties and other restrictive regulations of commerce are to be eliminated with respect to "substantially all the trade" between the parties of a customs union or free-trade area.[69]

To qualify as a customs union its members shall apply "substantially the same duties and other regulations of commerce" to trade with non-members. In practice, this condition implies a common external tariff and trade policy.[70] In the case of a free-trade area, or an interim agreement leading to a free-trade area, the duties and other regulations of commerce imposed on the trade of third parties at the formation of the free-trade area or adoption of the interim agreement shall not be higher or more restrictive than those existing prior to its formation.[71] In the case of a customs union or an interim agreement leading to a customs union, the requirement is that "the duties and other regulations of commerce shall not on the whole be higher or more restrictive than that of the general incidence of the duties and other regulations of commerce" applied prior to its formation.[72]

5.4.3 Examination Process

RTAs falling under Article XXIV are notified to the Council for Trade in Goods (CTG). The CTG adopts the terms of reference for the examination of an agreement and transfers the examination itself to the CRTA. Once the CRTA has finished the examination and approved the report, it submits it to the CTG, which has then to take appropriate action – i.e. adopt the report and make any appropriate recommendations. The examination is based on information provided by the parties to the RTA. This information may be provided through a "Standard Format for Submission of Information on RTAs" developed by the CRTA, through written replies to written questions posed by Members or through oral replied to questions posed at the meetings of the CRTA where the agreement is examined.[73]

Throughout the history of GATT, practically no RTA was formally approved by the GATT Contracting Parties. The situation reflected the absence of agreed conclusions in the reports of the examinations. As a result, the legal status of these RTAs in relation to the GATT system, and in particular the question of

[67] GATT 1994, Art. 24:4.

[68] Understanding of the Balance-of-Payments Provisions of the GATT 1994, Art. XI, XII, XIII, XIV, XV, XX.

[69] GATT Agreement, *supra* note 1. Art. 24:8.

[70] GATT Agreement, *supra* note 1. Art. 24:8.

[71] GATT Agreement, *supra* note 1. Art. 24:5(b).

[72] GATT Agreement, *supra* note 1. Art. 24:5(a).

[73] WTO, Trade Policy Courses, Chapter 24: Regionalism, at. 24.5, *supra* note 451.

whether they could be challenged under dispute settlement procedures, was unclear. The Uruguay Round Understanding has clarified the issue of dispute settlement: It provides that the provisions regarding dispute settlement “may be invoked with respect to any matters arising from the application of these provisions of Article XXIV relating to customs union, free-trade areas or interim agreements”.[74]

5.4.4 Regional Trade Agreement Under GATS

Under GATS,[75] like in the case of GATT,[76] acknowledgement is made for Members’ freedom to enter into regional economic integration agreements liberalizing trade in services.[77] Besides a requirement for prompt notification and supply of relevant information, it also lays down the conditions that such agreements must fulfill in order to be compatible with GATS.[78]

These are: a regional economic integration agreement should provide for a substantial sectoral coverage in terms of number of sectors, volume of trade and modes of supply. In particular, there should be no prior exclusion of any mode of supply; any such agreement should provide for the absence or elimination of all discrimination among its parties in the sectors it covers, by eliminating existing measures and or preventing the introduction of new discrimination; any such agreement must be designed to facilitate trade between parties; and it should not lead to the erection of new external barriers around the regional economic zone, making trade between this zone and the rest of the world more difficult. In other words, it should not have “fortress” effects.[79]

Some flexibility is allowed when examining whether all its conditions are met by a given economic integration agreement, in order to take into account the global context in which it is inscribed. This should particularly be the case when developing countries are parties to the integration agreement. The Council for Trade in Services (CTS) may establish a working party to examine any such economic integration agreement, or enlargement or modification of it, in order to review its consistency with the provisions of GATS.[80]

[74] *Id.*

[75] General Agreement on Trade in Service, Apr. 15, 1994, Marrakesh Agreement Establishing the World Trade Organization, Annex 1B, Legal Instruments-Results of the Uruguay Round, 33 I.L.M. 1125 (1994). (GATS).

[76] Understanding of the Balance-of-Payments Provisions of the GATT 1994, Art. XXIV.

[77] GATS, *supra* note 464. Art. V.

[78] *Id.*

[79] *Id.*

[80] *Id.*

Article V of GATS deals with a special category of integration agreements, which is provided to cover labor markets – that is, agreements that provide a right of free entry into the employment market of the parties, and include measures concerning conditions of pay, other conditions of employment and social benefits. In order to be compatible with GATS, such agreements must exempt citizens of the parties to the agreement from requirements concerning residency and work permits.[81]

5.4.5 Enabling Clause

An Enabling Clause allows developing countries to establish regional or global preferential arrangements for the mutual reduction or elimination of tariffs and, in accordance with criteria and conditions that may be prescribed by the WTO Members, for the mutual reduction or elimination of non-tariff measures.[82] Two substantive requirements applicable to these arrangements are: (1) such arrangements "shall be designed to facilitate and promote the trade of developing countries and not to raise barriers to or create undue difficulties" for the trade of any other Member; (2) they "shall not constitute an impediment to the reduction or elimination of tariffs and other restrictions to trade on a most-favored-nation basis".[83]

Assignment

To ensure students become equipped with the capability to apply knowledge from the classroom to the field, students are, in this chapter, required to write a report, deliver a presentation and participate in a discussion on the following issues:

1. Newly developed regional free trade agreements since the WTO was launched in 1995 compared with the previous GATT multilateral trading system, focusing on the reason why the regional agreements have been so increased under the WTO system as the multilateral-regulating organization.
2. Argentina-Footwear Safeguards case focusing on "parallelism", to consider the Member countries of the regional agreements in relation with the determination of domestic industries' injury and the imposing of safeguards measures.

---

[81] *Id.*

[82] Paragraph 2(c) of the Enabling Clause.

[83] Paragraph 3 of the Enabling Clause.

References

Articles

Adamantopoulos K, De Notaris D (2000) The future of the WTO and the reform of the anti-dumping agreement : a legal perspective. Fordham Int'l L J 24
Andoh EK (1992) Countervailing duties in a not quite perfect world: an economic analysis. Stan L Rev 44:1515
August R, Mayer D, Bixby M (2009) International business law: text, cases, and readings, 5th edn. Pearson, p. 347
Bandyopadhyay JK (1996) QS-9000 handbook: a guide to registration and audit, Taylor & Francis
Clements RB (1996) Complete guide to ISO 14000, Prentice Hall, Inc., Englewood Crffs. WJ
Craig RT (1994) The no-nonsense guide to achieving ISO 9000 registration, american society of mechanical engineers
Creskoff S, Walkenhorst P (2009) Achieving WTO compliance for special economic zones in developing countries. The Poverty Reduction and Economic Management Network 134:1, 3
Cobb J (1995) A guide to the new GATT agreement. Heritage Foundation Pep
Edwards Jr. RH, Lester SN (1997) Towards a more comprehensive world trade organization agreement on trade. Stan. J. Int'l L. 109
Emslie JJ (2005) Labeling programs as a reasonably available least restrictive trade measure under Article XX's nexus requirement. Brook J Int'l L 30
Horlick G (1993) Avoiding international economic interdependence: the E.C. and U.S. try to turn protectionist in the Uruguay round. L & Pol'y Int'l Bus 24
Hutchins G (1994) The ISO 9000 implementation manual: Ten steps to ISO 9000 registration
Jackson JH, Davey WJ, Sykes Jr. AO (2008), Legal problems of international economic relations: case, materials and text, 5th edn. Thomson West, pp. 214–224
Kennedy KC (1998) The GATT-WTO system at fifty. Wis Int'l L J 16:432
Leebron DW (1995) An overview of the Uruguay round results. Colum J Transnat'l L 34:20
Matsushita M, Schoenbaum T, Mavroidis P (2006) The world trade organization: law, practice, and policy, 2nd edn. Oxford University Press, p. 9
Murray PC (1997) The international environmental management standard, ISO 14000: a non-tariff barrier or a step to an emerging environmental policy? UPA J Int'l Econ L 18:577
Petersen R (1997) ISO 14000. Internet databases. Envtl Law 3:613
Pritchard D, MacPherson A (2003) The trade and employment implications of a new aircraft launch: the case of the Boeing 7E7. Canada–United States trade center occasional paper 28:1, 6
Qureshi AH (1996) The world trade organization: implementing international trade norms,1st edn. Manchester University Press, p. 15
Rabbit JT, Bergh PA (1993) The ISO 9000: A global competitor's guide to compliance and certification
Reitz C (1996) Enforcing the general agreement on tariffs and trade. U Pa J Int'l Econ L 17, fn. 4
Rogers JW, Whitlock JP (2002) Is section 337 consistent with the GATT and the TRIPs agreement? Am U Int'l L Rev 17:490–491
Sayre D (1996) Inside ISO 14000: The competitive advantage of environmental management (St Lucie), CRC Press
Shapiro AC (1992) In Stern JM, Chew DH (eds) The revolution in corporate finance. Blackwell, Malden
Southwick JD (1988) Note, the lingering problem with the specificity test in United States countervailing duty law. Minn L Rev 72:1159,1173–1175
Steger DP (2002) The boundaries to the WTO: afterword : the "Trade and" conundrum – a commentary. A J I L 96:141
Stewart FP (1996) The GATT Uruguay round: a negotiating history (1986–1992), pp. 738–739
Sykes AO (1989) Countervailing duty law: an economic perspective. Colum L Rev 89 (199):200–201

Thompson LC, Thompson WJ (1997) The ISO 9000 quality standards: will they constitute a technical barrier to free trade under the NAFTA and the WTO? Ariz. J Int'l & Comp L 14:155
Thorm C, Carlson M (2000) Agreement on technical barriers to trade and agreement on the application of sanitary and phytosanitary measures (SPS). Law & Pol'y Int'l Bus 31:841
Tibor T, Feldman I (1996) Implementing ISO 14000: a guide to the new environmental management, McGraw-Hill
Wilcox WK (1998) GATT-based protection and the definition of a subsidy. B U Int'l L J 16:151
Wolfrum R, Stoll P-T, Seibert-Fohr A (2007) WTO-technical barriers and SPS measures, 1st. edn. Leiden, Boston, pp. 169–170
Young MK (2001) Lessons from the battle front: US – Japan trade wars and their impact on the multilateral trading system. George Washington Int'l L Rev 33:753,769

WTO Agreement

Agreement on the Application of Sanitary and Phytosanitary Measures, Apr. 15, 1994 Marrakesh Agreement Establishing the World Trade Organization, Annex 1, Legal Instruments-Results of the Uruguay Round, 33 I.L.M. 1125 (1994).
Agreement on Implementation of Article VII of the General Agreement on Tariffs and Trade 1994 (customs valuation), Apr. 15, 1994, Marrakesh Agreement Establishing the World Trade Organization, Annex 1, Legal Instruments-Results of the Uruguay Round, 33 I.L.M. 1125 (1994).
Agreement on Implementation of Article VI of the General Agreement on Tariffs and Trade 1994 (Antidumping), Apr. 15, 1994, Marrakesh Agreement Establishing the World Trade Organization, Annex 1, Legal Instruments-Results of the Uruguay Round, 33 I.L.M. 1125, art. 2.1 (1994).
Agreement on Import Licensing Procedures, Apr. 15, 1994, Marrakesh Agreement Establishing the World Trade Organization, Annex 1, Legal Instruments-Results of the Uruguay Round, 33 I.L. M. 1125, art. 1 (1994).
Agreement on Pre-shipment Inspection, Apr. 15, 1994, Marrakesh Agreement Establishing the World Trade Organization, Annex 1, Legal Instruments-Results of the Uruguay Round, 33 I.L. M. 1125 (1994).
Agreement on Rules of Origin, Apr. 15, 1994, Marrakesh Agreement Establishing the World Trade Organization, Annex 2, Legal Instruments-Results of the Uruguay Round, 33 I.L.M. 1125 (1994).
Agreement on Safeguards, Apr. 15, 1994, Marrakesh Agreement Establishing the World Trade Organization, Annex 1, Legal Instruments-Results of the Uruguay Round, 33 I.L.M. 1125 (1994).
Agreement on Subsidies and Countervailing Measures, Apr. 15, 1994, Marrakesh Agreement Establishing the World Trade Organization, Annex 1, Legal Instruments-Results of the Uruguay Round, 33 I.L.M. 1125 (1994).
Agreement on Technical Barriers to Trade, Apr. 15, 1994, Marrakesh Agreement Establishing the World Trade Organization, Annex 1, Legal Instruments-Results of the Uruguay Round, 33 I.L. M. 1125 (1994).
GATT Dispute Panel Report on Italy – Discrimination against Imported Agricultural Machinery, Oct. 23, 1958, GATT B.I.S.D. (7th Supp.) (1959)
Protocol of Provisional Application of the General Agreement on Tariffs and Trade, Oct. 30, 1947, 61 Stat. pts. 5, 6, TIAS N. 1700, 55 UNTS 308 (1947).

Homepage

WTO, Anti-Dumping: Technical Information on Anti-dumping (Dumping in the GATT/WTO), *available at* http://www.wto.org/english/tratop_e/adp_e/adp_info_e.htm.

WTO, Customs Valuation-Technical Information on Customs Valuation (The New Agreement), *available at* http://www.wto.org/english/tratop_e/cusval_e/cusval_info_e.htm.
WTO, Customs Valuation-Technical Information on Customs Valuation (Basic principle: Transaction value), *available at* http://www.wto.org/english/tratop_e/cusval_e/cusval_info_e.htm.
WTO, Import Licensing: Technical Information on Import Licensing (From the Tokyo Round Code to the Uruguay Round Agreement), *available at* http://www.wto.org/english/tratop_e/implic_e/implic_info_e.htm.
WTO, Rules of Origin-Technical Information on Rules of Origin (Definition), *available at* http://www.wto.org/english/tratop_e/roi_e/roi_info_e.htm.
WTO, Safeguard Measures: Technical Information on Safeguard Measures (General principle), *available at* http://www.wto.org/english/tratop_e/safeg_e/safeg_info_e.htm.
WTO-Trade Policy Courses, Chapter 9:Pre-shipment Inspection (PSI) 9.6, *available at* http://www.wto.org/english/thewto_e/whatis_e/tif_e/understanding_e.pdf. Accessed Oct. 19, 2012.

Part III

Regulation on Trade in Services

Outline of GATS

6

Learning Objectives

This chapter is to help students understand:

1. Importance of trade in services for WTO member countries;
2. Importance of regulations on trade in services compared with those for trade in goods;
3. Distinctions between regulation on trade barriers to distort competition or restrict market access and regulation on requirements from the legitimate policy objectives to be pursued by the government;
4. Legal characteristics of GATS compared with GATT;
5. Definition of service in trade by the supplying modes;
6. Extremely wide scope of application of GATS compared with GATT.

6.1 Introduction

Services production is a core economic activity in virtually all countries, developing and developed alike.

In a number of countries, services have been very important for employment and employment growth, because many traditional services, including distribution, education and social services, are labor intensive. In many service sectors it has also proved more difficult to substitute capital for labor than in manufacturing. The expansion of services[1] has been driven in particular by income-related demand

[1] For more details, *see* Kennedy (1998, p. 484). "The service sector has overtaken manufacturing as the most import part of developed country's economies. Service industries account for 61 percent of gross domestic product ("GDP") and over one-half of employment in developed countries. The ratio of world merchandise trade to services trade was four to one in 1995. The WTO estimates that world trade in services $4 trillion annually. Jobs in the service sector provide nearly 80 percent of U.S. employment. That figure is expected to increase to 88 by 2005. The service sector generated 75 percent of GDP in the United States in 1996. Services trade represents more than one quarter of total U.S. exports. In 1995, total U.S. exports of services was over $210

E.S. Lee, *World Trade Regulation*,
DOI 10.1007/978-3-642-31143-7_6, © Springer-Verlag Berlin Heidelberg 2012

shifts, benefiting for example the hotel and tourist industry; the economic stimulus results from new information and communication technologies; and the growing importance of basic infrastructural services, including transport, communication and finance, for a wide range of user industries.[2]

New transmission technologies have overturned traditional concepts of distance – banking, education and medical services may now be provided over the Internet – and many governments have sought to open long-entrenched monopolies so as to promote efficiency and mobilize new capital and expertise.[3]

As the share of services in international trade has steadily increased, international efforts to deal with international trade in services also have increased.[4] This has culminated in the adoption of the General Agreement on Trade in Services (GATS).[5] GATT 1947 was concerned almost exclusively with rules on trade in goods. The Uruguay Round's banner achievements were in expanding the scope of the GATT-WTO system to include non-goods sectors, liberalizing trade in several advanced sectors, and setting the WTO Members on a course to further liberalization agreements on advanced-sector trade. With the successful conclusion of the General Agreement on Trade in Services and the TRIPs Agreement, the negotiators broke new ground by introducing core GATT disciplines to trade in services and

billion, which grew in 1996 to nearly $224 billion. This figure compares with surplus in services of $68 billion in 1995, and of $73 billion in 1996. It enjoys a services trade surplus with Canada, the EU, and Japan."

[2] WTO-Trade Policy Course, Chapter 19: Service, at 19.2. http://www.wto.org/english/thewto_e/whatis_e/tif_e/understanding_e.pdf. Accessed Oct. 19, 2012.

[3] *Id.*

[4] GATS, as the result of the first step to internationally regulate the trade in services, would raise the interpretation public agreements like GATS, except the attempts by the Vienna Convention of the Law of International Treaties, Jan. 27, 1980, 1155, U.N.T.S. 331 (Art. 3.2 of the Dispute Settlement Understandings brings the Vienna Convention into the interpretative sphere of the WTO, because the Convention is clearly recognized as incorporating customary rules of interpreting public international law). Regarding the interpretation of GATS, it was analyzed: "GATS, . . . and Lists of Art. II Exemptions are, . . . unique instrument. The WTO . . . is comprised of nations with various legal systems and economic policies, diverse historical and cultural backgrounds, and vastly different economic strengths and populations. These considerations, . . . must be appreciated when interpreting GATS. . .". *See* Jarreau (1999). It is reasonable to read the drafters' intention interpreting the agreements. Remembering the WTO does not have legislative histories, in the domestic sense, reference to the achievement of respected trade periodicals may be a beneficial, secondary source of authority (*id.*, at 71). The Preamble offers interpretative insight into GATS (*id*). The Dispute Settlement Panel in Brazil-Measures Affecting Desiccated Coconuts held that "central objects and purposes" of the WTO Agreements are reflected in the preambles to the Agreements. Brazil-Measures Affecting Desiccated Coconuts held that "central objects and purposes" of the WTO Agreements are reflected in the preambles to the Agreements. *See also* Abu-Akeel (1999, p.189).

[5] General Agreement on Trade in Service, Apr. 15, 1994, Marrakesh Agreement Establishing the World Trade Organization, Annex 1B, Legal Instruments-Results of the Uruguay Round, 33 I.L. M. 1125 (1994) [hereinafter GATS]; Final Act Embodying the Results of the Uruguay Round of Multilateral Trade Negotiations. Apr. 15, 1994. Legal Instruments – results of the Uruguay Round 1(1994). *I.L.M. 33:* 1125.

providing effective protection of intellectual property rights. Follow-on the WTO negotiations also have produced agreements on trade in information technology products, telecommunications, and financial services.[6]

Even though GATS originated from GATT with the same spirit,[7] the particular characteristics of trade in services produces deviations under GATS regulations, in certain key respects, from the concepts and rules incorporated in GATT.[8] Considering that many service industries are required to remain carefully regulated to protect public interest, GATS regulates trade barriers that distort competition or restrict access to markets on the one hand, and distinctively, requires legitimate policy objectives to be pursued and ensures the orderly functioning of markets on the other hand.[9]

Thus, restrictions on service suppliers in specified fields or discrimination against foreign suppliers are considered as barriers to service trade, however, regulations requiring compliance with technical standards or qualification requirements to ensure the quality of services and the protection of public interest are considered necessary. Multilateral negotiations have progressively liberalized GATS regulations by removing trade barriers in service markets, while not restricting the individual governments' authority to maintain and develop necessary regulation to pursue their national policy objectives.[10]

6.2 Characteristics

GATS is designed to secure progressively higher levels of liberalization of trade in services through successive rounds of negotiations, which should aim at promoting the interests of all Members of the WTO and at achieving an overall balance of rights and obligations. Through liberalization of trade in services GATS will promote economic growth and the development of developing countries, as GATT does through the liberalization of trade in goods.[11]

Liberalization of services trade should not be confused with deregulation. Many service industries must and will remain carefully regulated in the public interest. GATS therefore makes a distinction between trade barriers that distort competition and restricts access to markets on the one hand, and regulations which are necessary to pursue legitimate policy objectives and ensure the orderly functioning of markets

[6] Kennedy (1998, *supra* note 1, at 483).

[7] They are improving trade and investment conditions through multilaterally agreed disciplines; stabilizing trade relations through policy bindings on an MFN basis; and achieving progressive liberalization through subsequent rounds of negotiations.

[8] Abu-Akeel (1999, *supra* note 4, at 189).

[9] Trachtman (1995, fn. 34, p. 27).

[10] Lee (2004, pp. 117, 125).

[11] GATS, *supra* note 5. Preamble.

on the other hand.[12] For example, restrictions on the number of suppliers of a certain service or discrimination against foreign suppliers are considered barriers to trade in services and are in principle subject to liberalization in negotiations.

On the other hand, requiring compliance with technical standards or qualification requirements which aim at ensuring the quality of the service and the protection of public interest are considered necessary forms of regulation. Through the process of progressive liberalization, GATS aims to reduce and eventually eliminate trade barriers while not restricting the ability of governments to maintain and develop necessary regulation to meet national policy objectives. It also recognizes the particular need of developing countries to develop appropriate regimes to regulate services.[13]

International trade has normally been understood as involving only the movement of goods and services across national borders.[14] Because the delivery of services very often requires the physical presence of the person or company supplying the service in the export market, the definition of trade in GATS has to be much more comprehensive. It covers not only the supply of services across national borders but also transactions that involve the cross-border movement of factors of production (capital and labor). Thus, the sale of an insurance policy in country A by a local branch of a company owned in country B is under the GATS definition a service exported from B to A. Services supplied by an individual service supplier in a foreign country are also regarded as exports from that person's country of origin.[15]

The expanded definition of international trade under GATS, to encompass cross-border movement of factors of production, means that GATS have an impact on a far wider range of domestic policy and regulation than GATT. For example, the

---

[12] The most intractable barriers in services are indicated to arise from government regulation, instead of tariff and non-tariff barriers as like in the case of goods, which, sometimes, have explicit protectionist rationales, even if they are justified by "infant industry" arguments, and may constitute barriers even when they are non-discriminatory in application. Considering these, the real question is not the actual existence of the barrier but the willingness to dismantle it. *See* Trachtman (1995, *supra* note 9, fn. 27).

[13] GATS, *supra* note 5. Preamble.

[14] In general, the differences between trade in goods and trade in services are indicated to exist at four levels. "First, services are intangible and perishable. Second, there are numerous modes for trade in services. In contrast to the exclusively cross-border mode for trade in goods, services can be provided at the location of the service supplier, at the location of the service consumer, or at neither of these two locations. Third, international trade in services usually requires movement of one or more factors of production, such as the movement of capital or the movement of labor. Fourth, the national regulation level of trade in services is more extensive and diverse than trade in goods." *See* Abu-Akeel (1999, *supra* note 4, at 189).

[15] WTO, *supra* note 2, at 19.3–19.4.

national treatment obligation in GATS concerns not only the treatment of the service (the product) but also the treatment of the business or person supplying the service.[16] Therefore, domestic regulations relating to the treatment of foreign investment and foreign personnel in their service-supplying activities are directly relevant to the obligations of Members under GATS. GATS is the first multilateral agreement containing obligations on the treatment of foreign investors. It does not cover investment policies per se but does so to the extent that they relate to the supply of services.[17]

6.3 Structure

Like GATT, GATS is structured into two parts. The first part is the text of the Agreement – its Articles and Annexes. The second part is the schedules of specific commitments undertaken by the WTO Members.[18] The schedules are an integral part of the Agreement, as tariff schedules are an integral part of GATT. While the text of the Agreement applies uniformly to all Members of the WTO, the scheduling of commitments is decided by the Member concerned, subject to negotiation and agreement with other Members. Each Member may undertake specific commitments in a manner commensurate with its level of development; Thus, developing countries are likely to accept a narrower range of commitments than their industrialized partners.[19]

[16] The GATT provides little protection against discriminatory enforcement for imported goods and incidentally, provides no protection for foreign investors who manufacture goods abroad. GATS provides greater protection, and even protects the foreign investor's "commercial presence", but only for trade in services, and only for services in which specific commitments have been undertaken.

[17] GATS, *supra* note 5. Part I.

[18] The two parts are further divided into six parts: (i) Scope and Definition; (ii) General Obligations and Disciplines; (iii) Specific Commitments; (iv) Progressive Liberalization; (v) Institutional Provisions; and (vi) Final Provisions. The six parts are further divided into thirty-two articles, reflecting the influence of WTO members with civil law traditions. The articles, which reflect the influence of common law statutory drafting techniques, are more encompassing than customary civil law legislation. *See* Jarreau (1999, *supra* note 4, at 32).

[19] WTO, *supra* note 2, at 19.4.

Schedule of Specific Commitments

REPUBLIC OF KOREA – REVISED SCHEDULE OF SPECIFIC COMMITMENTS IN FINANCIAL SERVICES

Modes of supply:	(1) Cross-border supply (2) Consumption abroad	(3) Commercial presence	(4) Presence of natural persons
Sector or subsector	**Limitations on market access**	**Limitations on national treatment**	**Additional commitments**
7. FINANCIAL SERVICES[20] As described in paragraph 2(a) of the Annex on Financial Services, Korea shall not be prevented from taking prudential measures including requirements related to parent companies, the minimum capital requirement, or minimum operating funds requirement. In those cases where the establishment of commercial presence by foreign companies in the financial sector is allowed, approval by the relevant authorities is required in accordance with related laws and regulations unless otherwise specified in any of subsectors below.			
All financial services covered by this schedule including Insurance	(1),(2),(3) Korea undertakes a standstill commitment for limitations on market access, where specific commitments are undertaken, in financial services listed in this schedule as of 31 August 1997. Cross-border supply of financial services and supply through consumer movement may not be settled in Korean currency. After the establishment of a commercial presence, financial institutions may handle only transactions, denominated and settled in Korean currency, with residents. Approval is required for transactions denominated or settled in foreign currency or transactions with non-residents. The management and operation of assets of a financial institution are restricted. A financial institution may not own non-business real estate. Assets owned by branches must be kept within the territory of Korea. The capital of the head office is not recognized as the basis for determining the extent of funding and lending activities of branches.	(1),(2),(3) Korea undertakes a standstill commitment for limitations on national treatment, where specific commitments are undertaken, in financial services listed in this schedule as of 31 August 1997.	

(continued)

[20] Subsectors in financial services are classified based on the unit of business establishment. A financial institution must be established for only one business defined in subsectors (1) through (14), and thus cannot engage in business activities in other subsectors.

Modes of supply:	(1) Cross-border supply	(2) Consumption abroad	(3) Commercial presence	(4) Presence of natural persons
	- Demand deposit interest rates are regulated. Some new financial products, including derivatives, are subject to approval. - With interest rate and foreign exchange liberalization, such products will be more widely allowed, subject to relevant laws and regulations.			
BANKING AND OTHER FINANCIAL SERVICES (1) BANKING BUSINESSES Following banking services:				
(i) Deposit and related services[21] [81115*, 81116*] (ii) Loan and related services[22] [81131*, 81132*]	(1) Unbound (2) Unbound (3) <Horizontal limitations on banking services>	(1) Unbound (2) Unbound (3) None		

6.4 Scope and Definition

Regarding scope of application of the Agreement, the Agreement has an extremely wide scope of application. It applies to any measure by a Member of the WTO affecting trade in services. The term "measure" (defined in Article XXVIII of GATS) covers any action taken by any level of government as well as by non-governmental bodies to which regulatory powers have been delegated. A "measure" could take any form; a law, regulation, administrative decision or guideline or even an unwritten practice. Also, the use of the term "affecting",[23] rather than other

[21] Activities in which banks obtain funds from the public by receiving deposits or issuing transferable instruments or other securities.

[22] Activities, such as loans and bill discounts, in which banks provide funds to the public in order to receive interest.

[23] The WTO Dispute Settlement Panel interpreted the meaning of the term "affecting" in Appellate Body Report, *EC-Regime for the Importation, Sale and* Distribution of Bananas, at 370, WT/DS27/AB/R (Sep. 9, 1997). Relying on Art. 31 of the Vienna Convention, the panel noted that GATS, like GATT, is an "umbrella agreement" applicable to all section of trade in service and all types of resolutions. In its efforts to determine the ordinary meaning of the term "affecting", the panel stated that Art. I(1) of the GATS does "not convey any notion of limiting the scope of GATS to certain types of measures or to a certain regulatory domain" The panel concluded that the term "affecting" should be "interpreted broadly", *cited by* Jarreau (1999, *supra* note 4, at 51–52).

terms such as "governing", means that the scope of the Agreement encompasses not only measures designed to regulate trade in services directly but also any other measures that might be designed to regulate other matters but which incidentally affect the supply of a service.[24]

With relation to the definition of "trade in services", GATS does not define "services" but does define "trade in services". The definition covers not only the cross-border supply of services but also transactions involving the cross-border movement of capital and labor. This is necessary because services must very often be supplied through a commercial presence in the export market or through the presence of an individual service supplier. There are also many situations, as in tourism, where the consumer purchases the service abroad.[25]

Trade in services is defined as the supply of a service through any of four modes of supply:

(1) Cross-border supply of a service from the territory of one Member into the territory of another. This is the type of transaction analogous to trade in goods; (2) Consumption abroad of a service. This happens when the consumer moves to the territory of another country and buys services there. It may also happen when the property of the consumer is sent abroad for servicing, as in the case of ship repair; (3) Supply through commercial presence.[26] This involves direct investment in the export market through the establishment of a business there for the purpose of supplying a service; (4) Supply through the presence of natural persons.[27] This means the temporary presence in the export market of an individual (not a legal person as in the case of commercial presence) for the purpose of supplying a service. This person could be the service supplier himself or an employee of the service supplier. In both cases, the GATS definition covers only the temporary stay

[24] GATS, *supra* note 5. Art. 28.

[25] GATS, *supra* note 5. Art. 1:2.

[26] Many WTO members have placed limitations on market access and national treatment in connection with the commercial presence mode of supply. Typical limitations that member countries list in their schedules of commitments relating to commercial presence are restrictions on the types of legal entity through which a service supplier many supply a service, and limitations on the participation in foreign capital in terms of the maximum percentage of foreign shareholding or aggregate foreign investment permitted. *See* GATS, *supra* note 5. Art. 16.2(e)–(f), *cited by* Kennedy (1998, *supra* note 1, at 525).

[27] GATS, *supra* note 5. Art. 1.2.

of such persons. It does not cover situations where a person is seeking citizenship, residency or employment on a permanent basis.[28,29,30]

The first, second, and fourth modes of supply involve the cross-border delivery of services. The third mode of supply involves the sale of services through an affiliate, i.e., the delivery of services by a foreign-owned firm within the territory of another Member through facilities or other commercial presence.[31]

This wide definition of trade in services[32] makes the GATS directly relevant to many areas of regulation[33] which traditionally have not been touched upon by multilateral trade rules.[34,35] The domestic regulation of professional activities is the

---

[28] Influenced by the economic literature and analysis preceding GATS negotiations, the drafters of GATS appear to have reached two conclusions in their attempt to define the scope of service activities subject to GATS: No practical purpose can be served by an attempt to define "services", and the definition of trade in services should be as precise as necessary to capture all modes for the service trade (Abu-Akeel 1999, *supra* note 4, at 189).

[29] By adopting the definition in specifying the service activities subject to its discipline, GATS has failed to provide a definition of what services should mean for purposes of the agreement. Failure to address definitional matters might raise issues concerning the scope of applicability of GATS: "i) the applicability of GATS to situations where service are traded in association with trade in goods; ii) the applicability of GATS to outsourcings (externalization) of internationally traded services; and iii) the implications of the definition of trade in services on the determination of the rules of origin that are applied to international transactions involving services" (*id.*, at 189–190).

[30] GATS, *supra* note 5. Art. 1. In contrast with GATT, the definition of trade in services in GATS does not use the words "originated in" to ascribe the services to a particular country. The definition refers to the supply of services "from the territory" of one member and to the supply of services "in the territory" of one member. Nonetheless, the rules of origin are as relevant to GATS as they are to the GATT, and the use of the words "from" or "in" the territory of a member is equal to the use of the words "originating in" the territory of a member. It is inconceivable that GATS intended to consider the nationality of services as that of the country of the service supplier, which will amount to having no rule of origin at all to govern international trade in services. *See* Abu-Akeel (1999, *supra* note 4, at 208).

[31] Kennedy (1998, *supra* note 1, at 486).

[32] The definition of services was heavily negotiated, with many developing countries seeking a definition limited to cross border trade; in the end an all encompassing definition for modes of supply was arrived at. *See* Sauve (1995, pp. 125, 128).

[33] One unique to GATS, unlike GATT, is its Art. VI recognition that a lack of transparency in domestic regulatory processes may operate to inhibit access to markets – a result contrary to a Member's general obligations (Ku 1999, p. 117).

[34] Prior to the Uruguay Round, the Organization for Economic Cooperation and Development (OECD) established international frameworks (referred to as "Codes") for liberalizing trade in services. The codes were created to "...abolish...restrictions on the movement of capital" and "eliminate ... restriction on current invisible transactions .... " "Invisible transactions" are service transactions. However, the codes were limited in many ways: they only applied to OECD members, they lacked a dispute settlement provisions with binding arbitral powers; and finally they made it easy to reserve obligations on different grounds. Thus, the OECD Codes did not provide a comprehensive multilateral agreement to liberalize trade in services. *See* Sauve (1995, *supra* note 38, at 36–37).

[35] The domestic regulation of professional activities is the most pertinent example, GATS, *supra* note 5. Art. 6. 6.

most pertinent example. Regulations relating to foreign investment are directly relevant to the supply of a service through the establishment of commercial presence, while certain immigration regulations are also relevant to the supply of services through the presence of natural persons.

However, these areas of regulation are relevant to obligations under GATS only to the extent that they affect the supply of a service. GATS covers any tradable service in any sector with the exception of the air transport sector, most of which is excluded from coverage. Apart from this, the only services excluded from the coverage of the Agreement are those supplied "in the exercise of governmental authority". For a service to be so considered, it has to be supplied neither on a commercial basis, nor in competition with one or more service suppliers.[36]

Assignment

To ensure students become equipped with the capability to apply knowledge from the classroom to the field, students are, in this chapter, required to write a report, deliver a presentation and participate in a discussion on the following issues:

1. The characteristics and difficulties of regulating trade in services compared with regulating trade in goods.
2. The historical development and the importance of service trade and regulation on service trade, particularly, in consideration of the legal characteristics of GATS compared with GATT.
3. The Antigua & Barbuda vs. US-Gambling Services case focusing on the exceptionally legitimate measures for the policy objectives to protect the public order.

[36] GATS, *supra* note 5. Art. 1.

General Application

7

Learning Objectives

This chapter is to help students understand:

1. Characteristics of GATS provisions grouped into five categories (unconditional provisions, conditional provisions, permissive provisions, exception provisions and provisions for further rule-making) compared with those of GATT, viewed from the fact that liberalization process and negotiations in the service market are basically different from those in the goods market;
2. Importance of domestic regulation for trade in services compared with that for trade in goods;
3. Qualified conditions of member countries' maintenance of monopolies or exclusive rights to supply services;
4. Method of recognition granted through harmonization in international service markets among the WTO member countries;
5. Mandates to negotiate further GATS disciplines;

7.1 Introduction

GATS contains five types of provisions of general application: unconditional obligations[1]; conditional obligations[2]; permissive provisions; exception provisions; and provisions for further rule-making. Unconditional obligations apply to all

[1] Unconditional obligations include most-favored-nation treatment (Art. 2), transparency (Art. 3), rules on domestic regulation, monopolies (Art. 8), business practices (Art. 11) and increasing participation of developing countries (Art. 4).

[2] Conditional obligations consist of transparency (Art. 3), domestic regulation (Art. 6), monopolies (Art. 8) and payments and transfers (Art. 9).

DOI 10.1007/978-3-642-31143-7_7,

service sectors regardless of whether the Member has undertaken a specific commitment.[3]

Conditional obligations are general rules which bind a Member only in sectors or sub-sectors where it has undertaken a specific commitment. The difference between these conditional obligations and specific commitments inscribed in a Member's schedule is that Members cannot negotiate the extent to which the conditional obligations are applied: they apply in full to all scheduled services, whereas in the case of specific commitments a Member can, on the basis of negotiations, maintain restrictive measures and inscribe them in its schedule.[4]

Permissive provisions allow Members to deviate from the most-favored-nation principle, in order to engage in economic integration agreements and to apply bilateral recognition measures, as long as they abide by certain disciplines.[5] Exception provisions define certain circumstances in which a Member may impose a regulatory measure that is inconsistent with its obligations and commitments under the Agreement, so long as the measure is necessary to achieve one of the policy objectives defined in those provisions, such as the protection of life, health or public order.[6]

Provisions for further rule-making in areas where multilateral disciplines are lacking or need further elaboration are: Domestic Regulation, Emergency Safeguards, Government Procurement and Subsidies.[7]

While all of these provisions are important with regard to ensuring cooperation in opening service markets, certain provisions are far more important for the success of the agreement, which sets GATS apart from other agreements.[8]

---

[3] Such provisions are: Most-Favored-Nation Treatment, Transparency, Domestic Regulation, Monopolies, Business Practices and Increasing Participation of Developing Countries.

[4] Conditional obligations relate to Transparency, Domestic Regulation, Monopolies, and Payments and Transfers. The overlap between the titles of these provisions and those of the first category is due to the fact that certain Articles contain both conditional and unconditional obligations.

[5] Chapman and Tauber (1995, pp. 941–965), *cited by* Burr (1996, p. 674).

[6] Exception provisions are, for example, the protection of life, health or public order. GATS, *supra* note 5. Arts. 14, 14 *bis*.

[7] In contrast to this five-type analysis, some authors including Laurel S. Terry separate GATS into three parts of obligation. According to Laurel S. Terry, thus, for determining the effect of GATS on cross-border specified services, it is required to examine at least three different aspects of GATS: "one must i) consider the provisions that automatically apply to every country. . .; ii) determine if a country exempted itself from the most-favored nation provision in GATS . . .; iii) one must consult the Schedules of Specific Commitments. . ." (Terry 2001, pp. 999–1000).

[8] Burr (1996, *supra* note 47, at 673).

7.2 The Most-Favored-Nation Treatment

The Most-Favored-Nation principle[9] is one of the most important principles of GATS.[10] With regards to the principle, Members are required to grant services and service suppliers of any other Member the best treatment granted to services and service suppliers of any other country, whether or not the latter is a Member of the WTO. This obligation guarantees that any liberalization steps, whether negotiated bilaterally or applied unilaterally, will be extended to all Members. The principle of MFN has always been a cornerstone of the GATT trading system for goods. Although it does not, by itself, require any particular degree of market openness, it ensures fair competition among trading partners.[11]

The obligation to apply MFN treatment does not, however, prevent adjacent countries from exchanging advantages in order to facilitate exchanges of services limited to contiguous frontier zones where such services are locally produced and consumed. Nor does it prevent the participation of Members in economic integration agreements between countries.[12]

7.3 Transparency

Service activities are typically subject to heavy regulation. It would not be possible to achieve effective liberalization of trade in services without ensuring that suppliers of services can obtain the necessary information concerning all the rules which they have to comply with. For this, GATS provides publication of all

[9] Korea's financial problem in 1997 has been indicated as emerging out of a situation in which a number of highly leveraged *chaebols* become bankrupt as a result of over-investment in steel and cars, and weakened profitability with the cyclical downturn. The bankruptcies weakened the financial system with non-performing loans reaching 7.5 percent of GDP. The decline in stock prices further reduced the value of bank equity. All of these led to a sharp fall in external finance.

[10] GATS, *supra* note 5. Art. 2.

[11] In relation to MFN principle in GATS, the characteristics of GATS as the product of political considerations was indicated: "In GATS, unlike GATT's Art. I, members are permitted to schedule exemptions from MFN application. The exemptions for MFN, as well as the exemptions on specific comments, have been described as structural weakness. Many of the obligations are triggered by a shopping list approach and GATS can only be understood by reading the schedules both of commitments and exemptions.... The compromises necessary to create the agreement were driven by political considerations, not purely by technical trade issues. If the goal of GATS was to create an all-encompassing principle-based agreement, GATS might be adjudged a failure. However, if GATS is viewed as a first step towards liberalization along the lines of the 1947 GATT, then the jury is still out. ...the key policy feature of GATS is progressive liberalization, rather than a single reform, an idea enshrined in the preamble to GATS." *See* Sauve (1995, *supra* note 38, at 50–51).

[12] GATS, *supra* note 5. Art. 2.

relevant laws and regulation, enquiry points, notification obligations and protection of confidential information.[13]

Members are required to publish all measures of general application affecting the operation of the Agreement. Such publication must take place at the latest by the time a measure enters into force. Where for exceptional reasons publication is not practicable, laws and regulations shall otherwise be made publicly available.[14]

Each Member is required to establish one or more enquiry points to provide information on laws and regulations affecting trade in services. While enquiry points are expected to respond promptly to any request for information, they need not be depositories of laws and regulations.[15]

Members are required to notify the Services Council, at least once a year, of any new laws or regulations which significantly affect trade in sectors where that Member has scheduled specific commitments.[16] In introducing such regulatory changes, a Member must act consistently with its legal obligations under GATS. The notification obligation enables other Members to verify that this is the case. The transparency obligations do not override the need to protect confidential information: No Member is required to provide confidential information the disclosure of which would impede law enforcement or otherwise be contrary to the public interest or prejudice legitimate commercial interests of particular enterprises, public or private.[17]

7.4 Regional Agreement

Members are allowed to enter into regional agreements to liberalize trade in services. Such agreements should aim to facilitate trade between their parties. They must not raise the overall level of trade barriers vis-à-vis other Members of the WTO who are not parties to them. Such regional agreements are required to have substantial sectoral coverage, which would be assessed in terms of the number of sectors and volume of trade. It is also required that an agreement of this type would not exclude any of the four modes through which services may be supplied. These requirements are designed to prevent the conclusion of regional agreements with limited coverage, for example covering one or a few sectors, or exchanging preferential treatment in limited domains such as foreign direct investment.[18]

[13] GATS, *supra* note 5. Art. 3

[14] *Id.*

[15] *Id.*

[16] *Id.*

[17] GATS, *supra* note 5. Art. 3 bis.

[18] GATS, *supra* note 5. Art. 5.

Another requirement is that parties to these agreements must extend national treatment to each others' services and service suppliers.[19] A Member of the WTO who is a party to such an agreement is required to notify it promptly to the Services Council and to supply any relevant information that may be requested by the council.[20]

7.5 Domestic Regulation

Each Member is required to maintain procedures which allow service suppliers to appeal against administrative decisions. The procedures must provide for the prompt review of such decisions and, where justified, appropriate remedies. They may be judicial or administrative. If the procedures are administrative, and are not independent from the agency entrusted with the administrative decision concerned, the Member must ensure that the review is objective and impartial. This obligation applies to all sectors regardless of whether the Member concerned has undertaken a specific commitment or not.

In sectors where a Member has scheduled specific commitments, it must ensure that all laws, regulations, administrative guidelines or any other measures of general application affecting trade in services are administered in a reasonable, objective and impartial manner.[21] The obligation about domestic regulation focuses on the manner in which measures are administered and not on their substance.[22] Its main purpose is to ensure that foreign service suppliers are not discriminated against or impeded in their work by arbitrary or biased administration.[23]

Members are required, in sectors where they have scheduled specific commitments, to ensure that measures relating to qualification requirements and procedures, technical standards and licensing requirements and procedures do not constitute unnecessary barriers to trade in services. Such measures must be based on objective and transparent[24] criteria, such as competence and the ability to supply

[19] In other words, Art. V requires the elimination of substantially all measures which discriminate in favor of services and service suppliers of national origin vis-à-vis those of other parties to the agreement.

[20] GATS, *supra* note 5. Art. 5.

[21] GATS, *supra* note 5. Art. 6.

[22] The obligation on members pursuant to Art. 6 does not require that they enact or maintain reasonable, objective and impartial domestic regulations. The obligation on members to introduce and maintain only those domestic regulations that are consistent with GATS derives primarily from Art. II, Most-Favored Nation Treatment, Art. 16 Market Access, Art. 17 National Treatment, and Art. 20 Schedules of Specific Commitments (Jarreau 1999, *supra* note 4, at 66).

[23] GATS, *supra* note 5. Art. 6.1. Art. 6 is intended to prevent members from denying, nullifying, or impairing GATS benefits to other WTO members through the use of onerous domestic administrative measures. *See* (*id*).

[24] With relation to the transparency obligation of Art. 3, Art. 3 does not state where the publication is to occur or the duration of the publication, nor require to notify the WTO Secretariat or the Council on Trade in Services of these measures. And in the case of Notification of measures significantly affecting a member's scheduled commitments (Art. 3.3), GATS does not define when

the service. They must not be more burdensome than necessary to ensure the quality of the service.[25]

In the case of licensing procedures, the licensing procedures must not in themselves constitute a restriction. In determining whether a measure relating to technical standards constitutes an unnecessary barrier to trade in services, Members are required to take into account international standards of relevant international organizations[26] applied by the Member concerned. The term "relevant international organizations" is understood in GATS to refer to international bodies whose membership is open to all Members of the WTO.[27]

In professional service sectors where specific commitments are scheduled, a Member is required to establish adequate procedures to verify the competence of professionals of other Members. This obligation is meant to facilitate market access for service suppliers of Members with whom the concerned Member does not have recognition arrangements.[28]

7.6 Recognition

Members of the WTO are allowed to recognize[29] the education or experience obtained, requirements met, or certification granted in the territory of other Members.[30] Such recognition may be granted through harmonization, may be

a measure significantly affects a member's scheduled commitment. GATS also does not define "relevant measures of general application" nor is there any explanation of when a measure should be considered as "pertaining to or affecting" the operation of the Agreement, in Art. 3.1. Reference to the definition of "measure" would be recommended. GATS, *supra* note 5. Arts. 3.1, 18(a); Jarreau (1999, *supra* note 4, at 64).

[25] In the sector-specific context of GATS, this proportionability provision in GATS is roughly analogous to the provisions of the WTO TBT Agreement (Arts. 2.1–2.5), but adds a requirement for further work through the Council for Trade in Services to articulate and expand the disciplines contemplated here. Regarding this provision, three difficult issues are indicated: (i) determining who will judge whether national requirements are more burdensome than necessary and how the components of this equation will be measured; (ii) determining what goals of regulation are legitimate; (iii) these determinations do not reach the ultimate problem: how to deal with regulation necessary to achieve a legitimate goal that imposes greater costs on trade than the savings it achieves through achievement of its regulatory goal (Trachtman 1995, *supra* note 9, at 88–89).

[26] They would be GATS, *supra* note 5. Art. 6.5(b), "International bodies whose membership is open to the relevant bodies of all members of the WTO."

[27] GATS, *supra* note 5. Art. 6.5.

[28] GATS, *supra* note 5. Art. 6.6.

[29] GATS, *supra* note 5. Art. 7.1. Recognition may be granted through harmonization, may be based upon an agreement with other countries, or may be accorded autonomously, thus allowing members to treat service suppliers of other members differently depending on the level of qualifications granted in their country of origin.

[30] GATS, *supra* note 5. Art. 7. This provision is weak, for it allows a member to recognize or fail to recognize the education or professional license granted in another country based on its own subjective criteria. Just one positive section of the Article on recognition provides: "where appropriate recognition should be based on multilaterally agreed criteria ... members should work in cooperation with ... organizations ..." (Kilimnki 1994, p. 284, *cited by* Burr 1996, *supra* note 47, at 675–676).

based upon an agreement or an arrangement with other countries, or may be accorded autonomously. Thus, Members may treat service suppliers of other Member countries differently depending on the level of qualifications granted in their country of origin. However, Members are not allowed to discriminate in the application of their substantive standards[31] or criteria for authorization, licensing or certification of service suppliers.

In other words, there is a distinction between allowing service suppliers of certain Members to have access to the market through a fast procedural track on the basis of a recognition arrangement on the one hand, and applying different substantive requirements to service suppliers on the other hand. Thus, an individual who can meet the substantive standards should be allowed to qualify whatever his country of origin.[32] Moreover, Members who are parties to recognition agreements are required to afford adequate opportunity for other interested Members to negotiate their accession to such agreements or to negotiate comparable ones with them. If recognition is granted on an autonomous basis, the Member concerned must give adequate opportunity for any other Member to demonstrate that qualifications acquired in its territory should be recognized.[33]

Members are required to notify the Council for Trade in Services of their existing recognition measures and to state whether such measures are based on agreements or granted autonomously. They are also required to inform the Council for Trade in Services, as far in advance as possible, of the opening of negotiations on an agreement relating to mutual recognition in order to provide adequate opportunity to any other Member to indicate its interest in participating in the negotiations.[34]

---

[31] Thus, Art. 7 of GATS simply provides that a member may recognize the regulation of another country in satisfaction of its own regulatory requirements, which is somewhat softer than the more mandatory language of the Art. 2.7 of the TBT Agreement requiring to accept "as equivalent technical regulations of other Members even if these regulations differ from their own . . .." This framework for recognition is facilitative, not mandatory, leaving to members the decision of whether or not to recognize the regulation of another country. In this regard, this framework contains no discipline of proportionality, but simply a possibility of proportionality expressed through recognition. However, Art. 7 of GATS also contemplates that members may enter into mutual recognition agreement regarding the regulation of other parties to the agreement, which, depending on their scope and sectoral coverage, may be analogous to, or may be contained within, regional or other plurilateral integration agreement (Trachtman 1995, *supra* note 9, at 96).

[32] GATS, *supra* note 5. Art. 7.

[33] GATS, *supra* note 5. Art. 7.2.

[34] GATS, *supra* note 5. Art. 7.4.

Amazon and Apple under monopoly investigation for pricing of e-books

Lehman, Lee & Xu
China
August 4, 2010

According to foreign media, the attorney-general's office in the US state of Connecticut led by Richard Blumenthal is investigating the cooperation deals between Amazon, Apple and leading publishers, concerning possible antitrust violations. And they specifically intend to find out whether the companies are using their size in the market to prevent other retailers from offering lower-priced titles.

The primary investigation indicates that the e-book price of the Amazon, Apple, Borders Group Inc., Barnes &Noble Inc in best-sellers is identical. And the situation is seemed to be caused by the agreement they have reached, which could be "to the ultimate detriment to the consumer".

Apple, Amazon and the leading publishers have reached an agreement in Agency Pricing Model, which means the publisher can set the retail price on their own and get 70 % from the sales. While the price is set by publishers, the amount may be beyond a reasonable level and harm the consumer's right. The agency pricing model also leads to a uniform of the e-book price on all websites.

Although the Agency Pricing Model is widely criticized, some publishers think it may bring benefit to the competition in the e-book market since the model can bring profit to the e-book retailers and thus attract more corporations to begin the sale.

"The sales of e-books are experiencing an explosive increase in recent years. Publishers and book retailers in China should seize the opportunity and focus on this promising market. Governments should also notice the development and take an active attitude in the legislation of this field." suggested Edward E. Lehman, Managing Director of Lehman, Lee & Xu.

Source: Amazon and Apple under monopoly investigation for pricing of e-books. August 4, 2010. http://www.lexology.com/library/detail.aspx?g=ef6e7bae-b150-4b9d-bda7-dcbc51b5 19eb

7.7 Monopolies and Business Practices

In many instances governments regulate certain service activities by granting monopolies or exclusive rights to certain entities to supply the service. There may be different, and perfectly legitimate, motivations for such arrangements. However, services supplied by monopolies often constitute inputs to other service activities: obvious examples are telecommunications, financial services, and transport. The Member countries may maintain the monopolies or exclusive rights to supply a service, but the behavior of such service suppliers is always insured to be consistent with the general obligations and specific commitments of the Member concerned[35]:

For example, if a telecommunications monopoly allows interconnection to suppliers of value-added telecommunications, it should do so without discrimination reflected toward suppliers of other Members. Also, if the Member concerned has undertaken a national treatment commitment in value-added services, it must ensure that its telecommunications monopoly provides interconnection to service suppliers of other Members on a national treatment basis.

This requirement is not only confined to the sector in which a monopoly right has been granted. It also extends to the behavior of monopolies outside the scope of the monopoly rights if it concerns another sector in which specific commitments have been scheduled. In other words, where a monopoly supplier competes in the supply of a scheduled service outside the scope of its monopoly rights, the Member concerned must ensure that the supplier does not abuse its monopoly position to act in a manner inconsistent with such commitments.[36]

There may be certain business practices of service suppliers, other than monopolies, that may restrain competition and thereby restrict trade in services. Members are required, at the request of any other Member, to enter into consultations with a view to eliminating such practices, and in such consultations to accord full and sympathetic consideration to submissions by other Members.[37]

7.8 Safeguards, Government Procurement and Subsidies

Mandates are provided to negotiate further GATS disciplines on emergency safeguard measures,[38] government procurement[39] and subsidies,[40] respectively. They do not contain any disciplines; but only provide a mandate for further work. The Council for Trade in Services established the Working Party on GATS Rules to conduct work on these three subjects.[41]

Multilateral negotiations are required to take place on the question of emergency safeguard measures. The first objective of the negotiations is to determine whether an emergency safeguard mechanism is needed under GATS. If so, disciplines

[35] GATS, *supra* note 5. Art. 8.

[36] GATS, *supra* note 5. Art. 8.1.

[37] GATS, *supra* note 5. Art. 9.

[38] GATS, *supra* note 5. Art. 10.

[39] GATS, *supra* note 5. Art. 13.

[40] GATS, *supra* note 5. Art. 15.

[41] WTO-Trade Policy Course, *supra* note 2.

should be elaborated to provide such a mechanism on the basis of the principle of non-discrimination.[42]

Government procurement is defined as services purchased for governmental purposes and not with a view to commercial resale or to use in the supply of services for commercial sale. It also stipulates that Articles II (MFN), XVI (Market Access) and XVII (National Treatment) do not apply to government procurement. Members are required to conduct multilateral negotiations on government procurement in services under GATS.[43]

While discriminatory subsidies are subject to the disciplines of Article II (MFN) and Article XVII (National Treatment) where a specific commitment is scheduled, non-discriminatory subsidies are not subject to any disciplines under GATS. Members recognize that such subsidies may have distortive effects on trade in services. Members are called upon to enter into negotiations with a view to developing the necessary multilateral disciplines to avoid such trade-distortive effects, and to consider whether it is appropriate to apply countervailing measures. The role of subsidies in relation to advancement programs of developing countries is recognized, and it is accepted that any new disciplines must take into account the need for flexibility in this area.[44]

7.9 Restrictions to Safeguard Balance-of-Payments

Members are allowed to introduce restrictions on trade in services, as an exceptional measure and notwithstanding any commitments they have assumed, in order to safeguard their balance of payments position. This allowance can be invoked in the event of serious balance of payments problems and external financial difficulties, or if there is a threat of such problems. Such restrictions may include restrictions on payments or transfers which would otherwise be prohibited.[45]

If a Member introduces legitimately restrictions to safeguard its balance of payments, those restrictions must: not discriminate among services and service suppliers of different Members; be consistent with the Articles of Agreement of the International Monetary Fund; avoid unnecessary damage to the commercial, economic and financial interests of other Members and not exceed the level necessary to address the balance of payments situation; and be temporary and phased out progressively as the balance of payments improves.[46]

If a Member adopts restrictions to safeguard its balance of payments, it must promptly notify the restrictions to the General Council of the WTO and must

[42] GATS, *supra* note 5. Art. 10.

[43] GATA, *supra* note 5. Art. 13.

[44] GATS, *supra* note 5. Art. 15.

[45] GATS, *supra* note 5. Art. 12.

[46] GATS, *supra* note 5. Art. 12.2.

consult with the Committee on Balance-of-Payments Restrictions. The Committee will assess the balance of payments situation of the Member concerned and examine the justification for the restrictions applied. In such consultations, the Committee must accept all findings of a statistical nature and other facts presented by the IMF.[47]

7.10 Exceptions

GATS allows Members to introduce measures which would otherwise be inconsistent with their obligations under the Agreement; however, in exceptional circumstances and in order to pursue any of the policy objectives set out in the relevant provisions,[48] a Member is allowed to introduce a measure inconsistent with its obligations only if it is necessary. In legal terms, a measure would be necessary only if the policy objective in question cannot be equally served by an alternative measure which would be less trade-restrictive.[49]

Members may introduce measures necessary to protect morals or to maintain public order. Public order is defined to cover only situations where a genuine and sufficiently serious threat is posed to one of the fundamental interests of society. Members may also introduce such measures to protect human, animal or plant life or health, to prevent fraudulent and deceptive practices and to protect privacy and safety. Measures to ensure the equitable or effective imposition or collection of direct taxes, and measures taken pursuant to an agreement on the avoidance of double taxation, are also allowed.[50]

Members are allowed to take any action which they consider necessary for the protection of their essential security interests, and are not required to furnish any information the disclosure of which would be contrary to their essential security interests.[51]

Assignment

To ensure students become equipped with the capability to apply knowledge from the classroom to the field, students are, in this chapter, required to write a report, deliver a presentation and participate in a discussion on the following issue:

[47] GATS, *supra* note 5. Arts. 12.4–12.5.

[48] These provisions are Art. 14 (General Exceptions) and Art. 14 bis (Security Exceptions).

[49] These provisions are Art. 14 (General Exceptions) and Art. 14 bis (Security Exceptions).

[50] GATS, *supra* note 5. Art. 14.

[51] GATS, *supra* note 5. Art. 14 bis.

The legislative history to conclude GATS during the Uruguay Rounds, particularly, focusing on the fact that there are several provisions in GATS to be further negotiated for the complete agreement.

** In approaching this issue, students should give extra attention to the specific characteristics and difficulties in regulating trade in services compared with regulating trade in goods.

Specific Commitments and Other Provisions

8

Learning Objectives

This chapter is to help students understand:

1. Specific commitments under GATS compared with tariff binding under GATT;
2. Liberalizing method in service markets under GATS compared with that in goods markets under GATT;
3. Withdrawal or modification of specific commitments subject to compensatory adjustment;
4. Means by which member countries' governments maintain measures providing more favorable treatment to their domestic industries compared with foreign entities in the service sector – specifically those committed to being liberalized;
5. Two kinds of annexes to GATS;

8.1 Specific Commitments

Specific commitments under GATS are registered in schedules. Each Member of the WTO is required to have a schedule in which it registers its commitments[1] to provide market access[2] and national treatment[3] to services and service suppliers of

[1] GATS, *supra* note 5. Arts. 16, 17. A member is not forced to make specific commitments in a certain sector or sub-sector. However, when the member chooses to do so, general obligations like MFN obligations attach to those commitments.

[2] The purpose of Art. 16 Market Access is to eliminate measures that limit: (i) the number of service suppliers; (ii) the total value of service transactions; (iii) the total number of service operations or of people employed; (iv) the type of legal entity allowed to provide the service; and (v) the percentages of foreign capital shareholding or investment (Kraus 1994, *cited by* Ku 1999, *supra* note 30, at 118).

[3] It should be noted that the national treatment obligation of GATS applies to those sectors scheduled, and subject to exceptions set forth in the schedule, which makes it be subject to further

DOI 10.1007/978-3-642-31143-7_8, © Springer-Verlag Berlin Heidelberg 2012

other Members. When making a commitment, a Member binds the level of market access and national treatment specified in the schedule and undertakes not to impose any new measures that would restrict entry into the market or discriminate in favor of services or services suppliers of national origin.[4]

A specific commitment thus has an effect similar to a tariff binding under GATT. Commitments can only be withdrawn or modified after negotiation and agreement with other Members on a compensatory adjustment through which the modifying Member offers alternative commitments. However, new commitments and improvements to existing ones can be added at any time.[5]

A Member's schedule of commitments is inscribed with the limitations on market access and national treatment that a Member imposes on foreign service suppliers.[6] All schedules must specify: (1) terms, limitations, and conditions on market access; (2) conditions and qualifications on national treatment; (3) undertakings relating to additional commitments; (4) the time frame for implementation of commitments; and (5) the date of entry into force of commitments.[7] Measures that are inconsistent with both Article XVI (market access) and Article XVII (national treatment) are to be inscribed in the column relating to market access limitations, in which case the inscription will be considered a condition or qualification on national treatment as well.[8]

During the Uruguay Round negotiations participants agreed to follow a set of guidelines for the scheduling of specific commitments under GATS. The guidelines encouraged Members to use the SSC List developed during the Uruguay Round. This SSC List is based on the U.N. Provisional Central Products Classification

negotiations, based on the sectors included in a country's schedule, and further based on conditions or qualifications set out therein. GATS specifically provides that this obligation may be met by virtue of treatment that is different from the treatment applicable to domestic services and suppliers, which recognizes that national treatment is not necessarily identical treatment but, makes the applicable standard one of de factor rather than de jure national treatment (Trachtman 1995, *supra* note 9, at 68–69).

[4] Regarding the developing process of the Schedules of Specific Commitments, it is explained: "Because the GATS negotiation process was based on a request-offer system, countries exchanged information about their proposed Schedules of Specific Commitments.... This permitted a country to know before it finalized its own Schedule. . ., what it could expect from other countries. These Schedules were subject to fierce negotiations .... At a certain specified deadline, each country had to submit its final proposal including its Schedule of Specific Commitments" (Terry 2001, *supra* note 49, at 1004).

[5] Most countries listed their current regulations in the Schedules, the consequence of which is that the current law need not comply with those aspects of GATS that applied to "scheduled" services. Thus, this structure has the effect of requiring a country's future regulation of legal services to comply with GATS, and be no more restrictive than its current regulations, but "grandfathers" in the exiting set of regulations, which makes commentators often describe GATS as creating standstill provisions. Accord Cone (pp. 20–24, *cited by* Terry 2001, *supra* note 49, at 1004).

[6] Kennedy (1998, *supra* note 1, 490).

[7] GATS, *supra* note 5. Art. 20.1.

[8] GATS, *supra* note 5. Art. 20.2, *cited by* Kennedy (1998, *supra* note 1, 490).

("CPC") System.[9] Although the use of the SSC List is not mandatory, most Members have adopted it as the basis for scheduling their commitments.[10]

SSC list

The comprehensive list of sectors and sub-sectors covered under GATS was compiled by the WTO in July 1991, and may be subject to further modification in the light of developments in the services negotiations and ongoing work elsewhere.

The purpose of preparing a comprehensive list was to facilitate the Uruguay Round negotiations, ensuring cross-country comparability and consistency of the commitments undertaken. Although optional, most Members follow this classification, which in some sectors (maritime transport, financial services, and telecommunications) is being complemented by alternative models. The 160 sub-sectors are defined as aggregate of the more detailed categories contained in the United Nations provisional Central Product Classification (CPC).

Recourse to the CPC categories helps to improve clarity over the scope of the commitments actually undertaken; for each sector number, the CPC provides a brief description of what is actually covered.

The list may be viewed at http://www.wto.org/english/tratop_e/serv_e/serv_sectors_e.htm.

U.N. Provisional Central Products Classification (CPC) System

The Central Product Classification (CPC) constitutes a complete product classification covering goods and services. The CPC serves as an international standard for assembling and tabulating all kinds of data requiring product detail including industrial production, national accounts, service industries, domestic and foreign commodity trade, international trade in services, balance of payments, consumption and price statistics.

(continued)

[9] The Services Sectoral Classification List classifies services into the following twelve sectors (further divided into 155 sub-sectors): Business (six sub-sectors, including professional services); Communication (five sub-sectors, including telecommunication services); Construction and Related Engineering (five sub-sectors); Distribution (five sub-sectors, including wholesale, retail, and franchising); Education (five sub-sectors); Environment (four sub-sectors); Financial (three sub-sectors); Health and Social Services (four sub-sectors); Tourism and Travel (four sub-sectors); Recreational, Cultural, and Sporting (five sub-sectors); Transport (nine sub-sectors); Other Services Not Included Elsewhere.

[10] The GATS classification system has been criticized for lacking clarity. *See* Classification Called Unclear. 1997. Film Industry Urges Broader Application, Int'l Trade Rep. (BNA), 14: 585, *cited by* Kennedy (1998, *supra* note 1, 490).

The Central Product Classification (CPC) Ver.2 was completed on December 31, 2008.

You may view the CPC (Ver.2) at http://unstats.un.org/unsd/cr/registry/cpc-2.asp.

All schedules conform to a standard formula which is intended to facilitate comparative analysis. For each sector or sub-sector inscribed, the schedule must indicate, with respect to the four modes of supply set out in Articles I, paragraph 2, any limitations on market access or national treatment which are to be maintained. A commitment therefore consists of eight entries which indicate the presence or absence of market access and/or national treatment limitations with respect to each mode of supply.

The first column in the standard format contains the sector or sub-sector which is the subject of the commitment; the second column contains limitations on market access; the third column contains limitations on national treatment. In the fourth column, a Member may enter any additional commitments relating to matters which are not subject to scheduling under market access or national treatment. The terminology used in schedules has been standardized wherever possible.[11]

In nearly all schedules, commitments are divided into two sections: "horizontal" and "sector" schedules are bifurcated into cross-industry ("horizontal") commitments and industry-specific ("vertical") commitment.[12] The horizontal section contains limitations which are in effect across-the-board conditions and restrictions applicable to all industries listed in a Member's schedule.[13,14] These often refer to particular modes of supply, notably commercial presence and movement of natural persons; e.g., investment, taxation, real estate transactions, government subsidies, and the temporary entry of persons. Although GATS Article XX does not require cross-industry commitments, and although no guidelines were established for such commitments, the participants adopted this approach in the interest of avoiding excessive repetition in the industry-specific schedules.

[11] WTO-Trade Policy Course, *supra* note 2.

[12] All clauses in GATS are grouped into two clauses: for example, which the Most-Favored-Nation clause is a horizontal clause, the National Treatment clause is vertical, meaning that it is a conditional rule, the application of which depends on commitments made by each country, sector by sector (Da silve 1994, p. 137, *cited by* Cahn and Schimmel 1997, p. 299).

[13] Jarreau (1999, *supra* note 4, at 48).

[14] It is essential to review the notations in the horizontal commitments to determine a Member's intention and to fully understand the Member's scheduled commitments. Thus, Members have considerable autonomy regarding the manner in which their commitments are scheduled, particularly at this early stage in the international regulation of trade in services. Future schedules to come should become more uniform, to the advantage of all WTO Members and their service consumers and suppliers (*id*).

As a consequence, in order to determine the extent of market access and national treatment, it is necessary to consult both the cross-industry and specific-industry schedules. Horizontal commitments appear to the beginning of national schedules.[15]

Trade Policy Review of Japan including Horizontal Regulation in Services

(b) Services

78. Regarding the negotiations on services, Japan has been actively participating in the WTO services negotiations. It submitted a comprehensive negotiating proposal in December 2000 and then made additional proposals regarding MFN Exemptions, movement of natural persons, energy services and educational services. Furthermore, the disciplines in domestic regulation are also highly considered by Japan.
79. Japan is now partaking in the request-offer process and hopes that all Members, including the developing countries, will actively participate. As one of the most liberalized economies in terms of the number of the services sub-sectors, where specific commitments are made, Japan is prepared to take further steps to improve its commitment and encourages similar liberalization efforts by other WTO Members. Under such view, Japan submitted its initial requests to all the WTO Members on the 27th and 28th of June 2002. In general terms, Japan attaches great importance to the following issues.
    - elimination or alleviation of horizontal (cross-sectoral) regulations, which constitute substantial obstacles to the activities of foreign service suppliers, such as restrictions on the participation of foreign capital, nationality requirements for the staff and employees, restrictions on the acquisition of real estate, etc.
    - improved commitments of liberalization in those services sectors which serve as an infrastructure in support of various economic activities, such as telecommunication, construction, distribution, financial, transport, etc.
    - improved commitments of liberalization in those services sectors related to new information and communication technology, such as computer and related services, telecommunication, etc.
    - improved commitments of liberalization in various professional services supporting business activities, such as accounting and architectural services.

Source: Trade Policy review of Japan including Horizontal Regulation in Service. October 9, 2002. WT/TPR/G/107.

[15] Kennedy (1998, *supra* note 1, at 491).

The specific-industry commitments consist of a matrix in which commitments are made for each industry (reference by a SSC List number and letter, or by a U.N. Provisional Central Products Classification System number) under each of the four modes of supply. For each mode of supply, a Member may offer a "full commitment" (inscribed in the schedule by the word: "none," indicating no restrictions on market access or national treatment in a given sector and mode of supply) or a "partial commitment" (inscribed in the schedule by noting the specific market access or national treatment restrictions on a given sector and mode of supply).[16]

Full and partial commitments are "bound," requiring compensation to adversely affected Members in the event new restrictions are imposed or existing ones become more burdensome in the future. In the absence of a full or partial commitment, measures that restrict market access or are inconsistent with national treatment may be maintained or increased in the future. The absence of a commitment is inscribed in a Member's schedule with the world "unbound" in the given sector and mode of supply.[17]

When a Member undertakes a commitment it must indicate for each mode of supply what limitations, if any, it maintains on market access. Article XVI:2 of GATS lists six categories of restrictions which may not be adopted or maintained unless they are specified in the schedule.[18] All scheduled limitations on market access therefore must fall into one of these categories. They comprise four types of quantitative restrictions as well as limitations on foreign equity participation and on the types of legal entity permitted.

The national treatment obligation under Article XVII requires Members to accord to services and service suppliers of any Member treatment no less favorable than that it accords to services and service suppliers of national origin. A Member

[16] *Id.*

[17] In certain circumstances, the term "unbound" is followed by an asterisk to indicate that the mode of supply for the particular service sector is not technically feasible, e.g., cross-border supply of hair-dressing services is technically infeasible (*id.*, at 492).

[18] Typical kinds of numerical limitations that a member might inscribe in its schedule of commitments include the following: limitations in the form of quotas or the requirement of economic needs on the number of service suppliers or operations. Examples include a license for a new restaurant based on an economic needs test, annually established quotas for foreign medical practitioners, nationality requirements for service supplies (equivalent to zero quota), and restrictions on the amount of broadcasting time available for foreign firms; limitations in the form of quotas on the total value of service transactions or assets. For example, foreign bank subsidiaries' assets might be capped at a fixed percentage of total domestic assets of all banks; measures that restrict or require specific types of a legal entity or joint venture through which a service supplier may supply a service. Examples included a requirement that foreign companies establish subsidiaries, or that in a particular sector commercial presence take the form of a partnership; limitations on the total number of natural persons that may be employed in a particular sector; and limitations on the participation of foreign capital in terms of a maximum percentage limit on foreign shareholding or the total value of individual or aggregate foreign investment. *See* GATS Explanatory Note, para. C, *cited by* Kennedy (1998, *supra* note 1, at 489).

wishing to maintain measures providing more favorable treatment of nationals must inscribe these limitations in the third column of its schedule.[19]

If a Member decides to undertake any commitments relating to measures other than those subject to scheduling under market access or national treatment, for example, relating to qualification requirements, technical standards and licensing requirements, they should be inscribed as additional commitments in the fourth column of the schedule.[20]

8.2 Progressive Liberalization

Members are mandated to enter into successive rounds of negotiations in services with a view to achieving a progressively higher level of liberalization[21] through improved market access, better national treatment and the reduction or elimination of barriers to trade. This in-built commitment to further negotiations is recognition of the fact that the Uruguay Round and the following sectoral negotiations were only the first steps[22] in what is certain to be a long process of progressive liberalization.[23]

[19] GATS, *supra* note 5. Art. 17.

[20] GATS, *supra* note 5. Art. 18.

[21] Progressive liberalization, containing Arts. 19 through 21, was drafted with future negotiations in mind. The purposes of these articles are twofold: the first purpose, diplomatic in nature, is to provide for built-in rounds of successive negotiations with the aim of further liberalizing trade in services; the second purpose, essentially a shake-out provision, is to review how GATS works in practice, with the aim of entering into future negotiations to reconcile practice with expectations (Jarreau 1999, *supra* note 4, at 33–34).

[22] For the incomplete trade liberalization in services made in Uruguay Round, *see* Kennedy (1998, *supra* note 1, at 489). (Stating "Most market access and national treatment commitments to date are essentially standstill agreements .... However, Members commit not to impose additional or new trade restrictions in the future. Consequently, while GATS lays a foundation, broad trade liberalization in services did not take place in the Uruguay Round. With the exception of the financial services and telecommunications negotiations, . . . the most noteworthy achievement of the first round of services trade negotiations was to provide an unprecedented amount of information on barriers to services trade .... Thus, through the commitments that identify measures that are barriers to services trade, the Uruguay Round negotiators accomplished the twin goals of establishing benchmarks for future services trade negotiations and making barriers to services trade more transparent .... Because of the GATS positive list approach, however, benchmarks and transparency are non-existent if no market access commitment was made for a service sector or sub-sector. Improved commitments on trade liberalization of most service sectors must await the follow-on services negotiations . . . .".)

[23] GATS, *supra* note 5. Art. 19; For the achievement of GATS, as with GATT in 1947, creating and encouraging the process of liberalization, there are not only facilitative provisions but also provisions to prevent "backsliding". To the extent that GATS preserves the status quo, there will be a stable and predictable market for entrepreneurs and investors (Simser, 1996 *supra* note 26, at 54).

Successive rounds will take account of the national policy objectives and the level of development of individual Members.[24] It is recognized that the pace of liberalization will vary among Members and that developing countries may decide to open fewer sectors and fewer types of transactions in line with their development situation (nevertheless, remembering that the main beneficiary of liberalization will be the liberalizing country itself.)[25]

The schedules are annexed to GATS and form an integral part of it. Although a progressively higher level of liberalization is purposed to be achieved,[26] Members are under no formal obligation to undertake any given level of specific commitments. The only obligation is that a Member must have a schedule of specific commitments, however minimal the commitments contained in it are.

A Member may modify or withdraw a specific commitment at any time after three years following the entry into force of the commitment.[27] In some circumstances this period has been temporarily reduced to one year,[28] which allows a Member, pending entry into effect of the results of negotiations on safeguards, to modify or withdraw a specific commitment after a period of one year from the date on which the commitment enters into force.[29]

8.3 Institutional and Final Provisions

Each Member is required to consult on request with any other Member about any matter affecting the operation of the agreement. If such consultations produce no satisfactory solution, the Council may consult with the Members concerned. The consultation and dispute settlement provisions of the agreement do not apply to issues involving national treatment[30] arising from an international agreement between two Members relating to the avoidance of double taxation.

[24] GATS does not definitively regulate trade in services, but delegates to another WTO institution the obligation to develop a more detailed understanding of how the provisions of GATS should apply to service trade, which makes GATS be described as an example of a legislative delegation model of regulating service trade.; "... GATS itself delegates to Council for Trade in Services the obligations to establish the necessary body.... The Ministerial Conference, however, issued a Decision that directed the Council for Trade in Services to exercise this delegation by creating a Working Party on Professional Services, or WPPS, ... the Council on Trade in Services implemented this Ministerial Decision by creating the WPPS, ... Thus, in order to understand the impact of GATS ..., one must understand the structure of GATS. In addition, ... because GATS used a legislative-delegation model, one cannot fully understand the obligations imposed by GATS until one examines the post-GATS developments...." *See* Terry (2001, *supra* note 49, at 1015–1019).

[25] GATS, *supra* note 5. Art. 19.

[26] *Id.*

[27] GATS, *supra* note 5. Art. 21.

[28] GATS, *supra* note 5. Art. 10.

[29] GATS, *supra* note 5. Art. 19.

[30] GATS, *supra* note 5. Art. 22.

In other words, disagreements arising from double taxation agreements are not subject to dispute settlement in GATS.[31] The dispute settlement system of the WTO applies in full to GATS. According to the "non-violation" principle, the nullification or impairment of benefits conferred by a specific commitment, even if it is caused by a measure not in itself inconsistent with GATS, may also be referred to dispute settlement.[32]

Article XXVIII defines the following terms used in GATS: "measure"; "supply of a service"; "measures by Members affecting trade in services"; "commercial presence"; "sector"; "service of another Member"; "service supplier"; "monopoly supplier of a service"; "service consumer"; "person"; "natural person of another Member"; "juridical person"; "juridical person of another Member"; "direct taxes". It also defines the concepts of ownership, control and affiliation of a juridical person.[33]

8.4 Annexes

There are two kinds of annexes to GATS. Some have permanent validity, while others, which provide for negotiations to be conducted after the Uruguay Round, ceased to be effective once those negotiations were concluded.[34]

In the first category, which refers to those with a permanent validity, there are annexes on air transport services, movement of natural persons, MFN exemptions, telecommunications and financial services.[35]

The annex on air transport services specifies that only three activities in that sector are covered by GATS: aircraft repair and maintenance services; the selling and marketing of air transport services; computer reservation system services. Other services in the sector, including all services directly related to the carriage of passengers or freight, are excluded from the application of the Agreement. The annex on air transport services supplements this distinction with a set of definitions which clarifies the coverage of the disciplines.[36]

[31] *Id.*

[32] GATS, *supra* note 5. Art. 23.

[33] GATS, *supra* note 5. Art. 28.

[34] The provisions in the annexes to GATS are best understood as a road map of intentions rather than as a statement of commitments. In case of the financial service provisions of GATS, for example, while face-saving specific commitments provide some level of firm multilateral commitment, the main focus of the financial services provisions are the identification of areas where further liberalization is desirable (Sauve 1995, *supra* note 38, at 57–58).

[35] GATS Annex on Financial Services. The annexes to GATS defined financial services broadly to include: (i) insurance and related services, including reinsurance, retrocession, and intermediation such as brokerage and agency work; (ii) banking and other financial services, including deposit taking, lending, guarantees, leasing, certain trading activities and other forms of intermediation.

[36] GATS Annex on Air Transport Services.

The annex on movement of natural persons supplying services under the Agreement deals with the temporary movement of natural persons (as opposed to juridical persons) who supply services in the territory of another Member. It is made clear that the Agreement does not apply to measures regarding citizenship, residence or employment on a permanent basis, or to people who travel abroad looking for work. As a result, the Agreement applies only to the temporary stay in a foreign country of natural persons supplying services. The annex also states that Members are still allowed to regulate the entry of natural persons into their territory and impose border controls, provided that such measures are not applied in such a manner as to nullify or impair the benefits accruing to any Member under the terms of a specific commitment.[37]

The annex on Article II exemptions specifies the conditions under which a Member can be exempted from its obligations under Article II of GATS (MFN treatment).[38] Members may take exemptions from the MFN principle either at the time of entry into force of the Agreement or on their accession to the WTO. Except at these times, derogations[39] from the MFN principle may only be granted in the form of waivers under the WTO Agreement. All MFN exemptions are to be reviewed after five years by the Council for Trade in Services: after ten years they should in principle be terminated. Many countries have nevertheless indicated in their list of Article II exemptions that their intended duration was indefinite. The legal consequences of such an entry in the exemption list are unclear.[40]

The annex on telecommunications deals with this sector in its auxiliary role, as a support for other services activities. Access to telecommunications is in fact crucial to the commercial viability of other services. The annex requires each Member to ensure that the service suppliers of any other Member have reasonable and non-discriminatory access to public telecommunications networks and services for the

[37] GATS Annex on Movement of Natural Persons Supplying Services under the Agreement.

[38] GATS, Annex on Art. 2 Exemptions. The list of Art. 2 Exemptions are organized using five columns: (i) sector or subsector to which the exemption is applicable; (ii) description of the MFN inconsistent measure; (iii) names of the countries to which it applies; (iv) intended duration of the exemption; and (v) conditions for the exemption.

[39] Exemptions currently included in many Members' lists have durations intended to be "indefinite". Paragraph 6 of the annex does contain significant diplomatic overtones, as opposed to legal dictates, that may allow for ambiguously worded exemptions and exemptions of indefinite duration, which states that "in principle", exemptions should not exceed ten years, and establishes that they "shall be subject to negotiation in subsequent trade liberalizing rounds". The use of the term "in principle" implies that ambiguous exemptions and exemptions of extended duration may be technically permissible, though not encouraged. These ambiguous exemptions with indefinite durations do not comport with the spirit of GATS. *See* e.g. GATS, Fifth Protocol. (Dec. 3, 1997). http://www.wto.org/English/tratop_e/serv_e/5prote_e.htm. Accessed Feb. 21, 2012 *cited by* Jarreau (1999, *supra* note 4, at 49–50).

[40] GATS Annex on Art. 2 Exemptions.

supply of a service listed in its schedule. This annex also includes provisions on transparency and technical cooperation for developing countries.[41]

The annex on financial services adapts the basic provisions of GATS to the specificities of the financial sector. The annex includes a detailed set of definitions on financial services that have been used by Members in the preparation of their schedules of specific commitments in this sector. In addition to these definitions, the most important of the provisions in the annex excludes prudential measures taken by Members from the application of the basic provisions of the Agreement. Members are allowed to maintain measures which may not conform to the provisions of GATS for the protection of investors, depositors and policy holders, and for ensuring the integrity and stability of the financial system. Such measures may not be used by a Member, however, as a means of avoiding that Member's commitments or obligations under GATS.

Prudential measures falling within the scope of Articles XVI and XVII of GATS need not to be listed as limitations on market access and national treatment in a Member's schedule. Other sector-specific provisions in the annexes include a provision to protect individual customer information and other confidential or proprietary information and a paragraph on dispute settlement stating the need to secure relevant expertise on panels for disputes in the area of financial services. Finally, prudential measures may be recognized between countries, but any such recognition agreement will not fall within the coverage of Article VII (Recognition) of GATS.[42]

Three temporary annexes mandated post-Uruguay Round negotiations on financial services, basic telecommunications and maritime transport. Their most important legal effect was to extend for the duration of the negotiations the right to take MFN exemptions in these sectors. Following the conclusion of the post-Uruguay Round sectoral negotiations, all these annexes are no longer applicable.[43]

–Trade Disputes in Relation with **Regulation on Service in Trade (GATS)**

Appellate Body Report, China-Measures Affecting Trading Rights and Distribution Services for Certain Publications and Audiovisual Entertainment Products, WT/DS363/AB/R (Dec. 21, 2009).

(continued)

[41] GATS Annex on Telecommunications.

[42] GATS Annex on Financial Services.

[43] GATS Second Annex on Financial Services, Annex on Negotiations on Basic Telecommunications, and Annex on Negotiations on Maritime Transport Services.

Introduction

China and the United States each appeal certain issues of law and legal interpretations developed in the Panel Report, *China – Measures Affecting Trading Rights and Distribution Services for Certain Publications and Audiovisual Entertainment Products* (the "Panel Report"). The panel was established to consider a complaint by the United States concerning a series of Chinese measures regulating activities relating to the importation and distribution of: reading materials (for example, books, newspapers, periodicals, electronic publications); audiovisual home entertainment ("AVHE") products (for example, videocassettes, video compact discs, digital video discs ("DVDs")); sound recordings (for example, recorded audio tapes); and films for theatrical release. Further details regarding the content and the operation of the measures examined by the Panel are set out in section IV of this report.

The panel considered whether China's measures are consistent with China's trading rights commitments in paragraphs 1.2, 5.1, and 5.2 of China's Accession Protocol and in paragraphs 83(d) and 84(a) and (b) of China's Accession Working Party Report. China's trading rights commitments include an obligation to grant "all enterprises in China ... the right to trade", which means "the right to import and export goods". This obligation is subject to certain conditions, including that it is "[w]ithout prejudice to China's right to regulate trade in a manner consistent with the WTO Agreement". The panel found that provisions in China's measures that either limit importation rights to wholly state-owned enterprises regarding, or prohibit foreign-invested enterprises in China from importing, reading materials, AVHE products, sound recordings, and films, are inconsistent with China's obligation to grant the right to trade. The panel also concluded that several provisions of the Chinese measures at issue breach China's obligation to grant in a non-discretionary manner the right to trade.

The panel also considered claims of the United States concerning China's market access and national treatment obligations in Articles XVI and XVII, respectively, of GATS, as they relate to reading materials, AVHE products, and the electronic distribution of sound recordings. With respect to the distribution of reading materials, the panel found that provisions prohibiting foreign-invested enterprises in China from engaging in: the "master distribution" of books, newspapers, and periodicals; the "master wholesale" or wholesale of electronic publications; and the wholesale of imported reading materials, are each inconsistent with Article XVII of GATS. The panel also concluded that provisions imposing different registered capital and operating term requirements on foreign-invested wholesalers than on wholly Chinese-invested wholesalers are inconsistent with Article XVII of GATS.

Regarding the distribution of AVHE products, the panel found that several provisions permitting distribution by foreign-invested contractual joint ventures only when the Chinese partner olds a majority share are inconsistent with Article XVI:2(f) of GATS. With respect to certain provisions for which a violation of Article XVI of GATS had not been found, the panel concluded that these provisions nevertheless result in discrimination against foreign service providers in violation of Article XVII of GATS. Concerning the electronic distribution of sound recordings, the panel concluded that provisions of China's measures prohibiting foreign-invested enterprises from supplying this service are also inconsistent with Article XVII of GATS.

Findings and Conclusions

The Appellate Body:

finds that the panel did not err, in paragraphs 7.560 and 7.584 of the Panel Report, in finding that Article 30 of the *Film Regulation* and Article 16 of the *Film Enterprise Rule* are subject to China's trading rights commitments in paragraphs 1.2 and 5.1 of China's Accession Protocol and paragraphs 83(d) and 84(a) and (b) of China's Accession Working Party Report; and therefore

upholds the panel's conclusions, in paragraph 8.1.2(c)(ii), (iii), (vi), and (vii) of the Panel Report, that Article 30 of the *Film Regulation* and Article 16 of the *Film Enterprise Rule* are inconsistent with China's trading rights commitments in paragraphs 1.2 and 5.1 of China's Accession Protocol and paragraphs 83(d) and 84(a) and (b) of China's Accession Working Party Report;

finds that the panel did not err, in paragraphs 7.652 and 7.674 of the Panel Report, in finding that Article 5 of the *2001 Audiovisual Products Regulation* and Article 7 of the *Audiovisual Products Importation Rule* are subject to China's obligation, in paragraph 1.2 of China's Accession Protocol and paragraph 84(b) of China's Accession Working Party Report, to grant in a non-discretionary manner the right to trade; and therefore

upholds the panel's conclusions, in paragraph 8.1.2(d)(i) and (v) of the Panel Report, that Article 5 of the *2001 Audiovisual Products Regulation* and Article 7 of the *Audiovisual Products Importation Rule* are inconsistent with China's obligation, in paragraph 1.2 of China's Accession Protocol and paragraph 84(b) of China's Accession Working Party Report, to grant in a non-discretionary manner the right to trade.

The Appellate Body:

finds that the panel did not err, in paragraph 7.1265 of the Panel Report, in finding that the entry "Sound recording distribution services" in sector 2.D of China's GATS Schedule extends to the distribution of sound recordings in non-physical form, notably through electronic means; and, therefore

upholds the panel's conclusion, in paragraph 8.2.3(b)(i) of the Panel Report, that the provisions of China's measures prohibiting foreign-invested

(continued)

entities from engaging in the distribution of sound recordings in electronic form are inconsistent with Article XVII of GATS.

The Appellate Body recommends that the DSB request China to bring its measures, found in this report and in the Panel Report as modified by this report, to be inconsistent with China's Accession Protocol, China's Accession Working Party Report, GATS, and GATT 1994 into conformity with China's obligations hereunder.

Source: Appellate Body Report, China-Measures Affecting Trading Rights and Distribution Services for Certain Publications and Audiovisual Entertainment Products. December 21, 2009. WT/DS363/AB/R. http://www.worldtradelaw.net/reports/wtoab/china-publications(ab).pdf

Assignment

To ensure students become equipped with the capability to apply knowledge from the classroom to the field, students are, in this chapter, required to write a report, deliver a presentation and participate in a discussion on the following issue:

The development and promotion of liberalization in global service markets under GATS, focusing on the difference between liberalization in service markets and goods markets.

References

Articles

Abu-Akeel AK (1999) Definition of trade in services under the GATS: legal implications. GW J Int'l L & Econ 32

Burr MM (1996) Will the general agreement on trade in services result in international standards for lawyers and access to the world market? Ham line L Rev 20

Cahn S and Schimmel D (1997) The cultural exception: does it exist in GATT and GATS frameworks? how does it affect or is it affected by the agreement on TRIPS? Cardozo Arts & Ent L J 15

Chapman MJ and Tauber PJ (1995) Liberalizing international trade in legal services: a proposal for an annex on legal services under the general agreement on trade in services. Mich J Int'l L 16

Cone SM (1996) International trade in legal services: regulations of lawyers and firms in global practice. Little Brown 2:20–24

Da silve FH (1994) Les Six Points de Mons et Lear Suite, in L'Europe et les Enjeux du GATT dans le Domaine de L'Audiovisuel

Jarreau JS (1999) Interpreting the GATS and the WTO instruments relevant to the international trade of financial services: the lawyer's perspective. N C J Int'l L & Dom 25

Kennedy KC (1998) The GATT-WTO system at fifty. Wis Int'l L J 16

Kilimnki KS (1994) Lawyers abroad: new rules for practice in a global economy. Dick J Int'l L 12:284

Kraus J (1994) The GATT negotiations: a business guide to the results of the Uruguay round. International Chamber of Commerce 43

Ku R (1999) A GATT-ANALOGUE approach to analyzing the consistency of the FCC's foreign participation order with U.S. GATS MFN comments. GW J Inl't & Econ 32

Lee ES (2004) Anti-competitive practices as trade barriers used by Korea and Japan: focusing on service and investment market. Bond Law Review 16

Sauve (1995) Assessing the general agreement in trade in services: half-full or half-empty. World Trade 29

Simser J (1996) GATS and financial services: redefining borders. 3 Buff. J Int'l 33

Terry LS (2001) GATS' Applicability to transnational lawyering and its potential impact on U.S. state regulation of lawyers. Vand J Transnat'l L 34

Trachtman JP (1995) Trade in financial services under GATS, NAFTA and the EC: a regulatory jurisdiction analysis, column. J Transnat'l L 34

Appellate Body Report, EC-Regime for the Importation, Sale and Distribution of Bananas, WT/DS27/AB/R (Sep. 9, 1997).

United Nations, Vienna Convention of the Law of International Treaties, Jan. 27, Art 3.2. 1155 U.N.T.S. 331 (1980)

WTO, General Agreement on Trade in Service, Apr. 15, 1994, Marrakesh Agreement Establishing the World Trade Organization, Annex 1B, Legal Instruments-Results of the Uruguay Round, 33 I.L.M. 1125 (1994).

Part IV

Regulation on Trade-Related Intellectual Property Rights

Outline of TRIPs

9

Learning Objectives

This chapter is to help students understand:

1. The social and economic purpose for protecting intellectual property rights from the viewpoints of interest-balance between the right holders and users;
2. Main features of TRIPs compared with other multilateral agreements under the WTO, focusing on its legal structure and application;
3. Legal characteristics of TRIPs as an existing multilateral agreement plus terms of the agreement;
4. Main principles and objectives of TRIPs;
5. Domestic procedures and remedies of the member countries for the enforcement of intellectual property rights.

9.1 Introduction

Intellectual property rights are the rights given to persons to ownership over the creations derived from their minds.[1] Specifically, intellectual property rights give a creator the exclusive right over the use of his/her creation for a certain period of time.[2] Intellectual property rights are customarily divided into two main areas: (1) copyright and rights related to copyright and (2) industrial property.

The rights of authors of literary and artistic works (such as books and other writings, musical compositions, paintings, sculpture, computer programs and films) are protected by copyright. Also protected through copyright and related (sometimes referred to as "neighboring") rights are the rights of performers (e.g. actors, singers and musicians), producers of phonograms (sound recordings) and broadcasting organizations.[3]

[1] Garcia (2000, pp. 701, 707), cited by Su (2000, p. 172).

[2] See Folsom et al. (1995, pp. 758–766), cited by Su (2000, *supra* note 1, at 173).

[3] TRIPs Agreement Part II, Section 1.

E.S. Lee, *World Trade Regulation*,
DOI 10.1007/978-3-642-31143-7_9,

Industrial property can usefully be divided into two main areas. One area can be characterized as the protection of distinctive signs, in particular trademarks[4] (which distinguish the goods or services of one undertaking from those of other undertakings) and geographical indications (which identify a good as originating in a place where a given characteristic of the good is essentially attributable to its geographical origin).[5]

The protection may last indefinitely, provided the sign in question continues to be distinctive; other types of industrial property are protected primarily to stimulate innovation, design and the creation of technology.[6] These properties include inventions (protected by patents; in a number of countries, innovations that embody lesser technical progress than patentable inventions may be protected by utility models), industrial designs and trade secrets.[7] Protection is usually given for a finite term (typically 20 years in the case of patents).[8]

The main social purposes of protection of intellectual property rights[9] are: to encourage and reward creative work; to give an incentive and means to finance research and development activities for the development of new technology; to stimulate and ensure fair competition; to protect consumers; to facilitate the transfer of technology,[10] joint ventures and licensing; and to balance legitimate interests of right holders and of users.[11]

---

[4] TRIPs Agreement Part II, Section 2.

[5] TRIPs Agreement Part II, Section 3.

[6] TRIPs Agreement. Art. 7.

[7] TRIPs Agreement. Art. 12.

[8] TRIPs Agreement. Art. 33.

[9] For the origins of intellectual property rights included copyright, trademarks, trade secrets and patents, see Su (2000, *supra* note 1, at 174–177).

[10] In relation with not coping with the issue of new technology in the TRIPs Agreement, it has been criticized, by, for example, J.H. Reichman: "TRIPs was largely a backwards-looking agreement that relied on time-honored doctrinal norms that seemed well-suited to the creative productions of the Industrial Revolution. However, it did not seriously address the problems caused by the newer Technologies, especially information technologies, which fit imperfectly within the classical patent and copyright paradigms; ... There is still no consensus concerning such basic patent issues as the subject matter of protection; the novelty and non-obviousness standards of eligibility; the scope of the exclusive rights; or the exceptions that all states should be allowed to make. Even in copyright law, ..., no consensus has been reached with respect to fundamental scope of protection issues, or to the kinds of exceptions and limitations that states may freely implement" (Reichman 2000, pp. 442, 457–458).

[11] The purpose of the TRIPs Agreement should be constructed in consideration of the goal of the WTO. Regarding this point, Frederick M. Abbott indicated: "the overarching goal of the WTO is to raise world-wide standards of living .... The TRIPs Agreement was added to the GATT/WTO framework to assure that adequate protection of intellectual property rights promoted world trade ... the protection of intellectual property rights may itself be important. Nonetheless the core objectives of the WTO is to improve world-wide standards of living, and not to protect intellectual property rights" (Abbott 1998, p. 497).

Protecting your Intellectual Property

Be a stickler about contracts: Employees and contractors must agree that anything they create or enhance on your behalf is owned by your company

by Christine Comaford.

My biggest business challenge is finding a fair and equitable resolution to a business dispute with a former 'informal partner.' I say informal because she did not invest capital nor did we have a written agreement. It's complicated because she believes she is entitled to patent rights as well. My business is skyrocketing and here I am mired in a legal battle. What should I do? – Desperately Seeking a Solution Ouch.

......

Far too often I see examples of deals that haven't been adequately covered with contracts and intellectual property that hasn't been adequately protected. Cover your assets – or risk losing them.

......

In talking with my favorite intellectual property attorney, Eric Farber of Pinnacle Law Group, he stressed that entrepreneurs must know the four key types of intellectual property and they must protect them from the get-go.

Trademark. This protects a corporate identity, which is most often expressed in a logo or word mark. Start out by filing intent to use application first to reserve your mark. Then start using it pronto, as the key to trademarks is to use them in commerce, especially interstate. As you use your trademark, its value will increase, making it worthwhile to now register it. Don't spend the money until you determine that people will buy what you have and resonate with your brand. Once you register your trademark, add a "TM" next to it. When the trademark is granted, you'll change the TM to an R. The registration process can range in cost from about $3,000 to $5,000, including lawyer's fees.

Copyright. This is a tangible expression of an idea; a movie, song, book, or magazine. A "raw" work can't effectively be copyrighted. For example, a script can only be truly copyrighted once there is a tangible expression of it, so once it is used in a play or movie it has now crossed over to being tangible and can be copyrighted. The rumor that if you change every 15th word you can break a copyright is not true. It only costs about $40 to file a copyright.

Trade Secrets. These are formulas, like the Coca-Cola (KO) recipe. The best way to protect trade secrets is to secure them away. But often you can't – they are the key to your business. With our Coca-Cola example, workers have to mix the formula regularly, so the trade secret recipe cannot be kept under lock and key. A trademark protects the Coca-Cola brand, which is the vehicle that delivers the trade secret in tangible form to the market. If your trade secrets can be documented, be sure to stamp documents with the words "TRADE SECRET" if you are showing them to a business partner. How do you protect your employee from going to a competitor and sharing your trade secrets? Have them sign a proprietary information and inventions agreements.

(continued)

Patents. This is a massive area of the law. The U.S. Constitution empowers Congress to provide a patent system to secure, "for limited Times to . . .Inventors the exclusive Right to their . . . Discoveries." The patent statutes, as enacted, provide for three types of patents: utility, design, and plant. To obtain the most common type of patent, the utility patent, an invention must be new, useful, and non-obvious and fall within one or more of the categories of process, machine, manufacture, and composition of matter. In addition, the patent applicant must provide a written description of the invention, a description of how to make and use it, and disclose the "best mode" for practicing the invention. A valid and enforceable U.S. patent provides its owner with the right, among others, to exclude others from making, using, selling, or offering for sale the patented invention in the U.S. and its territories. The remedies for patent infringement can include one or more reasonable royalties, lost profits, and injunctions. Patents are pricey, but worth it. Budget $10,000 to $30,000 per patent you plan to file.

Protect your assets by having your employees, contractors, and business partners sign a proprietary information and inventions agreement. Then bring an IP-savvy attorney onto your team to ensure your assets are covered!

Source: Protecting Your Intellectual Property. May 8, 2008. http://www.businessweek.com/smallbiz/content/may2008/sb20080512_120611.htm

9.2 Main Features

While there have been elaborate systems of international institutions[12] and rules[13] to regulate internationally intellectual property and associated rights developed,[14] the TRIPs[15] component of the WTO Agreement represented a

[12] There are International institutions involved in IPRs-related work : Intellectual Property Organization (WIPO), World Bank, Food and Agriculture Organization (FAO), International Telecommunications Union (ITU), United Nations Conference on Trade and Development (UNCTAD), United Nations Development Program (UNDP), United Nations Environment Program (UNEP), and World Health Organization (WHO); limited membership or regional organizations are organization for Economic Co-operation and Development (OECD), European Patent Office (EPO), African Regional Industrial Property Organization (ARIPO), Andean Pact, APEC, European Union, Mercosur and NAFTA.

[13] Even though each of these rules has covered different types of intellectual property rights and have varied in terms of their objectives, the "ultimate goal has been movement towards internationally recognized and enforceable intellectual property rights" (Pechman 1998, pp. 180–181, cited by Su 2000, *supra* note 1, at 178).

[14] For a discussion on the benefits and criticisms of the international lawmaking for the protection of intellectual property rights, see Yu (2002, pp. 1–4).

[15] For a summary of the Uruguay Round negotiations leading to the TRIPS Agreement, see Braga (1995, pp. 381, 384); Croome (1995, pp. 251, 283); Preeg (1995, Chap. 21); Farkas (1996, p. 463); Abbott (1997, p. 661); Reichman (1993, p. 171, 1995, p. 345); Oman (1994, p. 18); Divney and Connell (1994, p. 1069); Ullrich (1995, p. 153); Doane (1994, p. 465).

revolution[16] in international property law.[17] The TRIPs Agreement introduced a brand new era that extends the global reach of IP regulation based on the concepts of protection and exclusion rather than dissemination and competition[18]: Unlike the earlier conventions, TRIPs does not merely circumscribe the range of acceptable polices governments may practice, but "obliges governments to take positive action to protect intellectual property rights."[19] The international minimum standards[20,21] of intellectual property protection set out in the TRIPs Agreement[22] determine, eventually, the level of competition for knowledge goods that are sold or licensed on the global market that emerged for the WTO Agreement.[23]

Before the Uruguay Round, there was no specific agreement relating to intellectual property rights in the framework of GATT.[24] However, the principles contained in GATT relating to measures affecting importation or exportation of goods and to the treatment of imported goods could apply, inter alia, to measures

[16] There have been serious debates between developing countries and developed countries on the issues:(i) whether GATT has competence in the full range of issues addressed by TRIPS (Hill 1990, p. 18, cited by Su 2000, *supra* note 1, at n. 189); (ii) whether the WTO should have jurisdiction over intellectual property instead of WIPO (Pechman 1998, *supra* note 13, at 183–184, cited by *id.*); (iii) the TRIPS Agreement exceeds the purpose of GATT (Doane 1994, *id*, at 472–473, cited by *id.*); (iv) developed countries prevent new technology from being transferred to the developing countries by the intellectual property protections (Aberto 1989, pp. 243, 252).

[17] Reichman (2000, *supra* note 10, at 442).

[18] For the three major problem areas in respect to the balanced approach to intellectual property protection for facilitating innovation, assuring wide dissemination of advances, and allowing cultures to continue their individual development, see Anawalt (2003, pp. 392–400).

[19] Hoekman and Kosteck (1995, p. 156), cited by Sell (2002, p. 79).

[20] For the distinctive characteristics of TRIPS in relation with the minimum standards, see Dreyfuss and Lowenfeld (1997, p. 279). "Of the TRIPS Agreement's three core commitments-national treatment, most-favored-nation treatment, and minimum standards-only the first two are obligations derived from pre-Uruguay Round versions of the General Agreement . . .. In contrast to the traditional GATT provisions, the minimum standards propounded by the TRIPS Agreement are based on the Berne and Paris Conventions, treaties that are principally aimed at promoting innovation by curbing practices deemed to constitute free riding . . ..".

[21] Regarding the controversy surrounding minimum standards in the WTO system, see Dreyfuss and Lowenfeld (1997, *id*, at 281). (Stating "... neither the DSU, nor the TRIPs ... provide guidance on how minimum standards ... rather than actual or optimal standards-will work in conjunction with an adjudicatory dispute resolution system ...")

[22] Agreement on Trade-Related Aspects of Intellectual Property Rights, April 15, 1994, Marrakesh Agreement Establishing the World Trade Organization (hereinafter WTO Agreement), Annex C, 33 I.L.M.1197 (1994) (TRIPS Agreement).

[23] Reichman (2000, *supra* note 10, at 442).

[24] GATT earlier addressed the issue of protection for intellectual property rights in 1979 during the Tokyo Round of GATT, where the member nations, however, rejected the Anti-Counterfeit Code which would have addressed trademark counterfeiting (Romano 1998, p. 562, cited by Su 2000, *supra* note 1, at 185).

taken in connection with intellectual property rights,[25] to the extent that they fell within their scope.[26] GATT[27] specially referred to intellectual property rights, permitting measures which would otherwise be inconsistent with the General Agreement to be taken to secure compliance with laws or regulations relating, inter alia, to intellectual property rights. The TRIPs Agreement reaffirms the national treatment in trade-related aspects of intellectual property rights,[28] however, the primary thrust of TRIPs is to mandate the content of intellectual property laws and to require particular enforcement mechanism.[29]

A salient feature of TRIPs is that comprehensive[30] intellectual property tight obligations are linked to membership on the worldwide trade system.[31] TRIPs is

[25] For the uneasy contrast between the vocabulary of intellectual property and the vocabulary of the GATT/WTO concerning, for example, "competitive" and "protective", see Dreyfuss and Lowenfeld (1997, *supra* note 20, at 280–281). (Stating "... They (intellectual property rights) are ... considered anti-competitive. TRIPs ... treats (them) ... as pro-competitive. ... GATT disfavors protectionism – a word the intellectual property community has long used to describe ... the copyright ... and trade secrets .... intellectual property regimes were initially to be integrated by the WIPO. The Uruguay Round succeeded where WIPO failed .... One of the reasons ... was that the architects of the TRIPs Agreement used words – and a concept of minimum standards – that allowed each state to read into the Agreement that it wished to see .... Success will depend on how will the GATT/WTO system addresses the difference between intellectual property and often trade matters.")

[26] In the evolution of international intellectual property, the first hurdle to protection was a failure to observe the rule of national treatment that has been carried over into the TRIPs Agreement. The principle requires that, with regard to the protection of intellectual property, each WTO Member shall accord to the nationals of other WTO Members treatment no less favorable than that it accords to its own nationals (Ugolini 1999, pp. 451, 452). Another hurdle to protection was to fail to observe the most-favored-nation rule that was incorporated into the TRIPs Agreement. Under the rule, WTO Member countries may not discriminate against nationals of one country and in favor of nationals of other countries, whether those other countries are WTO Members or not (Ugolini 1999, *id*).

[27] Art. XX(d) of GATT 1947 [now Art. XX(d) of GATT 1994]

[28] TRIPs Agreement, *supra* note 22. Art. 1.

[29] The enforcement or procedural requirements are set forth in Part III of TRIPS (*id.*, at Arts. 41–61, cited by Anawalt (2003, *supra* note 18, at 387).

[30] However, for the limits of a trade-based approach to intellectual property under the WTO, see Simon (1994), cited by Cahn and Schimmel (1997, pp. 306–307). "The TRIPs Agreement may have failed to cure the principal shortcoming of international intellectual property agreements. These agreements ... address only the acquisition, maintenance and enforcement of rights. They do not explicitly guarantee the right holders the ability to use or exercise their rights. ... Focusing on the most visible issue not resolved by the TRIPs Agreement, the failure of the WTO Agreement to guarantee true national treatment to copyright holders is quickly becoming an excuse for discrimination and exploitation."

[31] The Agreement maybe the most important international intellectual agreement that was signed in the twentieth century, however, also the most controversial: (i) It was the product of duress by powerful states against weak states. (ii) It is part of a hand bargain in which developing states received very few reciprocal gains. (iii) There is the criticism on the adverse consequences for developing countries of implementing the agreement (Drahos and Braithwaite 2002, p. 451): Panel #1: The World Trade Organization's Agreement on Trade-Related Aspects of Intellectual Property Rights (TRIPs) in Context: Economics, Politics, Law and Health: Intellectual Property, Corporate Strategy, Globalization: TRIPs in Context.

part of a more general movement[32] to standardize both the substance and procedure of intellectual property rights on a worldwide basis.[33] This movement represents a departure from the predominant approach prior to its enactment, namely, to leave substance and procedure primarily up to the various nations.[34]

The TRIPs Agreement as the most ambitious international intellectual property convention ever attempted,[35] sets out a comprehensive set of relatively high international minimum standards[36] of protection[37] to be provided in relation to the rights[38] and even (indirectly) unfair competition[39] by each Member.[40]

The main features of the TRIPs Agreement are as follows.

First, the TRIPs Agreement is to date the most comprehensive multilateral agreement on intellectual property.[41] The areas of intellectual property that it covers are: copyright[42] and related rights (i.e. the rights of performers, producers

---

[32] For the two main reasons to promote governments to enter the international agreements on the protection of intellectual property rights, see Su (2000, *supra* note 1, at 173).

[33] Anawalt (2003, *supra* note 18, at 387).

[34] *Id.*

[35] See Ministerial Declaration of Punta del Este Sept. 20. 1986, GATT Doc. Min. Dec. No. 86–1572, cited by Reichman (1996, p. 366).

[36] For the reason to adopt the international minimum standards in TRIPs, see Gana (1996, pp. 735, 757) "... the reason permitting individual nations to enact their own national intellectual property laws to meet the TRIPs Agreement was the problems which arose if one attempts to import intellectual property laws from a developed country to an underdeveloped country. Developing countries ... are unable to immediately align their current intellectual property laws with developed countries' intellectual property laws ...."

[37] Reichman (2000, *supra* note 10, at 443).

[38] The breadth of subject matters comprising the "intellectual property" to which minimum standards apply is unprecedented, as is the obligation of all WTO member states to guarantee that detailed enforcement procedures as specified in the TRIPs Agreement are available under their national laws (Reichman 1996, *supra* note 35, at 366–367).

[39] It was indicated: "Industrial property rights may be viewed as competitive restrictions which can actively serve the advancement of competition ..." (Lehmann 1985, pp. 525, 537, cited by Dreyfuss and Lowenfeld 1997, *supra* note 20, at n. 11).

[40] See TRIPs Agreement, *supra* note 22. Art. 2(1). (Incorporating by reference the Paris Convention, Art. 10 bis), cited by Reichman (1996, *supra* note 35, at 366–367).

[41] In regard to the term "intellectual property" referred in TRIPs Agreement, Scott Holiwick criticized seriously the TRIPs Agreement: "While the TRIPs Agreement was initially conceived to protect product counterfeiting and industrial theft, the language of the Agreement ... threatens each member nation's sovereignty and also undermines the cultural fabric of their respective societies. This is due, ..., to the entirely western definition of intellectual property ... which recognizes only private and not communal rights, and recognizes knowledge and innovation only on the basis of generating profit and not of meeting social needs. ... The split over this issue has often been characterized as arrogant, cash-rich, resource-poor northern nations attempting to solidify their economic position at the expense of native cash-poor, resource-rich southern nations." (Holwick 1999, p. 49).

[42] The Berne Convention only establishes minimum copyright terms. Thus, copyright terms can vary by nation. In the United States, copyright means an original work of authorship fixed in a tangible medium of expression, which includes literary works, musical works dramatic works, computer programs, sound recordings and sculptural works. See 17 U.S.C. 102(1995), cited by Curci (2002, p. 20).

of sound recordings and broadcasting organizations); trademarks[43] including service marks; geographical indications[44] including appellations of origin[45]; industrial designs; patents[46] including the protection of new varieties of plants; the layout-designs of integrated circuits[47,48]; and undisclosed information.[49] Including trade secrets and test data.[50]

Second, in respect of each of the intellectual property rights covered by the TRIPs Agreement, the Agreement stipulates the minimum standards of protection to be provided by each Member.[51] Each of the main elements of protection is defined, namely the subject-matter to be protected, the rights to be conferred and

---

[43] Trade mark is designed as any sign, or any combination of signs, capable of distinguishing the goods or service of one undertaking from those of other undertakings. TRIPs Agreement, *supra* note 22. Art. 15(1).

[44] Geographical indications mean indications which identify a good as originating in the territory of a Member, or a region of locality in that territory, where a given quality, reputation or other characteristic of the good is essentially attributable to its geographical origin. TRIPs Agreement, *supra* note 22. Art. 22(1).

[45] Geographical Indications by nature are agricultural. See Paris Convention, Paris Convention for the Protection of Industrial Property, Mar. 20, 1883, (Paris Convention), at Art. 1(3), cited by Land (2004, p. 1010, at n. 19).

[46] Patents are defined as any inventions, whether products or processes, in all fields of technology, provided that they are new, involve an inventive step and are capable of industrial application. See TRIPs Agreement Art. 27(1).

[47] According to Article 36 of the TRIPs Agreement, the scope of protection covers the following unlawful acts performed without the authorization of the right holder: importing, selling or any other form of distributing for commercial purposes a protected layout-design or IC incorporating a protected layout designs on an article incorporating such IC insofar as it constitutes to contain an unlawfully reproduced layout designs.

[48] Article 2 of the Treaty on Intellectual Property in Respect of Integrated Circuits of 1989 provides the following definitions: Integrated circuits means a product, in its final form or an intermediate form, in which the elements, at least one of which is an active element, and some of all of the interconnections are integrally formed in and/or on a piece of material and which is intended to perform an electronic function. Layout-design (topography) means the three-dimensional disposition, however expressed, of the elements, at least one of which is an active element, and of some or all of the interconnections of an integrated circuit, or such a three-dimensional disposition prepared for an integrated circuit intended for manufacturer, cited by Mangassarian (2001, n. 17).

[49] The characteristics of undisclosed information as the intellectual property rights was indicated: "Under the discipline of unfair competition, . . ., protection is not based on the existence of property rights. Hence, the provision of protection under such a discipline does not give rise to claims of property rights, with respect to trade secrets and data . . .. There is only possession of this information, which is not treated as property under the TRIPs Agreement. The TRIPs Agreement itself, . . ., refers to undisclosed information under control of a person, in clear contrast to the concept used in the sections relating to other categories . . ., such as trademarks or patents." (Correa 2002, 82 C).

[50] Besides these seven categories, a subject-matter category mentioned in Part II of the TRIPs Agreement (but not included within the definition of "intellectual Property") is entitled "Control of Anti-Competitive Practices in Contractual Licenses." See TRIPs Agreement *supra* note 22, Art. 40, cited by Reichman (1996, *supra* note 35, n. 12).

[51] TRIPs Agreement, *supra* note 22. Art. 1.

permissible exceptions to those rights, and the minimum duration of protection.[52] The Agreement sets these standards by requiring, first, that the substantive obligations of the main conventions of the World Intellectual Property Organization (WIPO),[53] the Paris Convention[54] and the Berne Convention[55] in their most recent versions, must be complied with.

With the exception of the provisions of the Berne Convention on moral rights, all the main substantive provisions of these conventions are incorporated by reference[56] and thus become obligations under the TRIPs Agreement between WTO Member countries. Secondly, the TRIPs Agreement adds a substantial number of additional obligations[57] on matters where the pre-existing conventions are silent or were seen as being inadequate.[58,59,60] The TRIPs Agreement is thus sometimes referred to as a "Berne and Paris-plus Agreement".[61,62]

---

[52] TRIPs Agreement, *supra* note 22. Part II, Sections 1–7.

[53] The WIPO has a special claim to a role in articulating international intellectual property norms. The Uruguay Round has also successfully produced TRIPs through the participation of the WIPO administrators in the identification of generally accepted international norms. The TRIPs Agreement itself contemplates (in Art. 68) that the TRIPs Council will consult with WIPO and "shall seek to establish... appropriate arrangement for cooperation with bodies of that organization". See TRIPs Agreement Art. 68; Dreyfuss and Lowenfeld (1997, *supra* note 20, at 275); Regarding a unified and universal system contemplated by the TRIPs Agreement, the article of the WIPO Copyright Treaty adopted December 20, 1996 is notable, which provides that: "This Treaty shall not have any connection with treaties other than Berne Convention, ..." Any attempt to insulate this new treaty from the system created by the TRIPs Agreement was indicated to be doubtful in successful enforcement, under the situation that it is believed that GATT/WTO decision makers should take developments in WIPO into account in construing the TRIPs Agreement (*id.*, n. 48).

[54] The TRIPs adopts a patent law minimum well above the previous standards of the Paris Convention, extending both subject matter covered and term of protection (Sell 2002, *supra* note 19, at 80).

[55] The TRIPs adds additional copy right protection, incorporating the Berne Convention for copyright norms (Sell 2002, *supra* note 19, at 80).

[56] TRIPs Agreement, *supra* note 22. Art. 2.1, and 9.1.

[57] The agreement adds more specific standards protecting computer programs, databases, sound recordings, and pharmaceutical and agricultural chemical companies (Otten and Wager 1996, pp. 391, 397).

[58] The TRIPs Agreement is not considered a new concept in international law; rather it supplements the existing international agreements governing the protection of intellectual property rights on a global scale (O'Sullivan 2000, pp. 1, 3, cited by Su 2000, *supra* note 1, at 186).

[59] Inadequate intellectual property protection under the existing international agreements was the main reason for the United States and other advanced countries to push for the TRIPs Agreement, and also the economic incentives were the reasons particularly behind the United States push for the Agreement (Williamson Sept. 25, 1989; Pechman 1998, *supra* note 13, at 183; cited by Su 2000, *supra* note 1, at n. 87).

[60] Seeking to provide great intellectual property protection, reduce barriers to trade and provide more effective enforcement and dispute settlement procedures (See TRIPs Agreement *supra* note 22, preamble), TRIPs was a direct response to this need to fill the gaps previous treaties left. See *id.* (a), cited by Land (2004, *supra* note 45, at 1010).

[61] TRIPs Agreement, *supra* note 22. Art. 2.2.

[62] The TRIPs Agreement was intended to conclude the era of global intellectual property administration under the auspices of the WIPO, and to initiate a new era of shared competence. Thus, in the

Third, the second main set of provisions deals with domestic procedures and remedies for the enforcement of intellectual property rights.[63] The Agreement lays down certain general principles applicable to all IPR (that is, intellectual property rights) enforcement procedures. In addition, it contains provisions on civil and administrative procedures[64] and remedies, provisional measures,[65] special requirements related to border measures[66] and criminal procedures.[67,68] These provisions specify, in a certain amount of detail, the procedures and remedies that must be available so that right holders can effectively enforce their rights.[69]

Fourth, the Agreement makes disputes between WTO Members about the respect of these obligations subject to the WTO's dispute settlement procedures.[70] Under the WTO, the failure of a country to meet its TRIPs obligations can put in jeopardy its market access rights and other benefits under the WTO.[71]

Fifth, TRIPs established broad categories of obligatory protection for intellectual property. In addition to these broad mandates it created specific obligations, sometimes in excruciating detail.[72] This switch from general to specific is seen by comparing the overarching requirement under TRIPs that member nations provide

---

new area, WIPO would step back into a secondary role, as the primary rules governing the protection of intellectual property would be promulgated at the WTO. It would serve as an intellectual property rights convention administrator, as a provider of technical assistance, and as a forum for considering secondary rules' changes (Abbott 1996, pp. 385–386).

[63] TRIPs Agreement, *supra* note 22. Part III, Section 1.

[64] TRIPs Agreement, *supra* note 22. Part III, Section 2.

[65] TRIPs Agreement, *supra* note 22. Part III, Section 3.

[66] TRIPs Agreement, *supra* note 22. Part III, Section 4.

[67] TRIPs Agreement, *supra* note 22. Part I.

[68] TRIPs Agreement, *supra* note 22. Part III, Section 5.

[69] See Cahn and Schimmel (1997, *supra* note 30). (Stating "The real question ... is whether the TRIPs Agreement confers to intellectual property right holders an affirmative right to exercise their intellectual property rights. The question should be answered in the negative .... First, the TRIPs Agreement, ..., focuses essentially on an intellectual property owner's right to authorize or prohibit the exploitation of his work. TRIPs fails to address the owner's positive right to exploit the intellectual property rights .... The TRIPs Agreement focuses on the acquisition, maintenance, and transfer of intellectual property rights, not on an author's right to exploit his work .... Second, while there is some language in the TRIPs Agreement ... that could be constructed as conflicting with a country's ability to restrain trade, that language is ambiguous, and leaves room for argument about its enforcement ...").

[70] See WTO Agreement, *supra* note 22, Annex 2: Understanding on Rules and Procedures Governing the Settlement of Disputes [hereinafter Settlement of Disputes]; TRIPs Agreement, *supra* note 22, Arts. 64, 68; see also Young (1996, p. 389); Abbott (1997); Geller (1995, p. 99), cited by Reichman (1996, *supra* note 35, at 367).

[71] It was indicated: "Three provisions, for the first time, 'make it likely that states will lodge actions against other states before duly constituted international bodies, with a view to vindicating the privately owned intellectual property rights of their citizens against unauthorized uses that occur outside the domestic territorial jurisdictions'" Reichman (1993, *supra* note 15, at 368–370).

[72] TRIPs Agreement, *supra* note 22. Part II, Section 1–7.

basic protections of copyrights, patents, and other forms of intellectual property with the specific protection prescribed for computer software.[73]

9.3 The Paris Convention

The Paris Convention for the Protection of Industrial Property[74] was concluded in 1883, and has been revised several times since then. The Convention is administered by WIPO[75] and applies to industrial property rights, including patents, trademarks, industrial designs, utility models, trade names, indications of source, appellations of origin, and the repression of unfair competition. In respect of Parts II, III and IV of the TRIPs Agreement, WTO Members are obliged to comply with Articles 1 through 12, and 19, of the latest act of the Convention, the Stockholm Act of 1967.[76]

The Convention provides that, as regards the protection of industrial property, each contracting nation must grant the same advantages to nationals of the other contracting nations as it grants to its own nationals.[77] The right of

[73] In particular, TRIPs provides that "patents shall be available for any inventions, where products or processes, in all field of technology, provided that they are new, involve an inventive step and are capable of industrial application." TRIPs Agreement at Art. 27(1). It also requires that "computer program, whether in source or object code, shall be protected as literary works under the Berne Convention." TRIPs Agreement, *supra* note 22, at Art. 10(1). With regards to computer program, TRIPs asserts that member nations "shall provide authors and their successors on title the right to authorize or to prohibit the commercial rental to the public of originals or copies of their copyright works." TRIPs Agreement, *supra* note 22, Art. 11, cited by Anawalt (2003, *supra* note 18, at 388).

[74] Mar. 20, 1883, 828 U.N.T.S. 305 revised by 21 U.S.T. 1583 July 14, 1967, Paris convention. The Convention concerns only: "patents, utility models, industrial designs, trademarks, service marks, trade names, indications of source or appellations of origin, and the repression of unfair competition" (*id.*, at Art. 1(2)). The convention applies particularly to the subject of geographical indications due to its recognition of agricultural and extractive products as a part of protected industrial property (Land 2004, *supra* note 45, at 1009–1010).

[75] Paris Convention and Berne Convention originally had their own International Bureau to carry out administrative tasks. In 1893, the bureaus overseeing the Berne Convention and the Paris Convention combined and formed an international organization called the United International Bureau for the Protection of Intellectual Property (BIRPI). As the importance of protecting property grew, BIRPI moved from Berne, Switzerland to Geneva to be closer to the United Nations. Ten years later, following the entry into force of the Convention Establishing the World Intellectual Property Organization, BIRPI became WIPO. Later, in 1974, WIPO became a specialized agency of the United Nations system of organizations. See World Intellectual Property Organization, http://www.wipo.int/aboutwipo/en/gib.htm. Accessed July 10, 2004.

[76] TRIPs Agreement, *supra* note 22. Art. 2.2.

[77] The Paris convention permits a member country to treat nationals of other member countries different from its own nationals, in regard to judicial and administrative procedure, jurisdiction, and to the designation of an address for service or the appointment of an agent. Paris convention, *supra* note 45. Art. 2(3).

priority[78] concerns patents, (as well as utility models, where they exist), industrial designs, and trademarks. On the basis of a regular first application file in one of the contracting nations, applications are made within a certain period of time[79] for protection in any of the other contracting nations. These later applications will be regarded as if they had been filed on the same day as the first application.[80]

The Convention contains a number of common rules on the protection of various areas of industrial property. For example, patents granted in different contracting nations are independent of each other.[81] The same rule applies to trademarks.[82] Where a trademark has been duly registered in the country of origin, it must, subject to certain exceptions, be accepted for filing and protected in its original form in the other contracting nations.[83] Each contracting nation must refuse the registration, and prohibit the use of a trademark which is considered to be well-known in that nation which constitutes a reproduction, imitation or translation, liable to create confusion, with a well-known trademark,[84] or which contains national emblems, official signs or hallmarks or names, abbreviations or emblems of international intergovernmental organizations that have been communicated through the International Bureau of WIPO.[85]

However, the Convention does not generally stipulate the subject-matter to be protected,[86] the rights to be conferred, the permissible exception, nor the minimum term of protection,[87] leaving these matters to each contracting nation to decide. Nor

---

[78] The Convention provides that the date of an applicant's foreign application is deemed the same as the data of the applicant's original application on the same invention, so long as the foreign application was filed before the first anniversary of the original application (Schaffter et al. 2002, p. 514).

[79] Twelve months for patents and utility models, and six months for industrial designs and trademarks.

[80] The Paris convention, *supra* note 45. Art. 4.

[81] The Paris convention, *supra* note 45. Art. 4 bis.

[82] The Paris convention, *supra* note 45. Art. 6.

[83] The Paris convention, *supra* note 45. Art. 6 quinquies.

[84] The Paris convention, *supra* note 45. Art. 6 bis.

[85] The Paris convention, *supra* note 45. Art. 6 ter.

[86] Limitations on the subject matter entitled to protection seem to provide rather coarse control over the balance between public access and private incentives. By fencing off entire fields from protection, such limitations make intellectual property law unavailable as a source of encouragement for whole industries. For this reason, the states may be generous on the question of subject matter protectability, and then safeguard the public's interest in access. For example, a country may tighten the scope of what it considers infringement – adjusting the degree of similarity for finding infringement of copyrights, and the degree of equivalence needed for finding infringement of patents (Dreyfuss and Lowenfeld 1997, *supra* note 20, at 286).

[87] Thus, for example, if a nation has no pharmaceutical R&D capability, it can decide that it is "immoral" to permit pharmaceuticals. Although as a practical matter such a law is aimed at foreigners – because no locals have pharmaceutical patents – it would be in compliance with the Paris Convention so long as it applied to the nation's citizens as well as foreigners (Schaffer et al. 2002, *supra* note 78, at 514).

does the Convention contain rules specifically on trade secrets and on layout-designs of integrated circuits. Therefore, the TRIPs Agreement adds a substantial number of additional obligations on these matters, and sets international standards of protection for trade secrets and layout-designs of integrated circuits.

9.4 Principles and Objectives

The fundamental rules on national[88] and most-favored-nation treatment[89] of foreign nationals[90] are commonly applied to all categories of intellectual property covered by the Agreement. These obligations cover not only the substantive standards of protection[91] but also matters affecting the availability, acquisition, scope maintenance and enforcement of intellectual property rights as well as those matters affecting the use of intellectual property rights specifically addressed in the Agreement.[92]

While the national treatment clause forbids discrimination between a Member's own nationals and the nationals of other Members, the most-favored-nation treatment clause forbids discrimination among the nationals of other Members. Each Member shall accord to the nationals of other Members treatment no less favorable than that it accords to its own nationals. Any advantage, favor, privilege or

[88] See TRIPs Agreement, *supra* note 22. Art. 3(1). Unlike GATT (1994) requiring each member to provide national treatment to products of the territory of any other member, the TRIPs Agreement requires that each WTO Member country provide national treatment of nationals of any other Member (*id*). The Paris Convention does not require a member country to provide national treatment in regard to judicial and administrative procedure, jurisdiction, and etc. Paris Convention, *supra* note 45. Art. 2(3). The Berne Convention, Rome Convention, or Washington convention did not directly qualify the rule of national treatment (Ugolini 1999, *supra* note 26, at n. 16).

[89] While GATT (1994) requires that most-favored-nation treatment of products originating in any other member country under Article I(1), the TRIPs Agreement requires most-favored-nation treatment of nationals of any other member country. See TRIPs Agreement, *supra* note 22. Art. 3 (1).

[90] TRIPs Agreement. Art. 3, 4, 5.

[91] Unlike the Paris Convention, the Berne Convention requires all signatory nations to enact certain minimum substantive laws, which include prohibitions against copying literary and artistic works and granting authors exclusive rights to adoptions and broadcasts of works (Schaffer et al. 2002, *supra* note 78, at 518).

[92] The TRIPs Agreement focuses on the acquisition, maintenance, and transfer of intellectual property rights and does not guarantee the author's right to exploit his work, while in the world of intellectual property rights the real question is whether the Agreement confers to intellectual property right holders an affirmative right. In this point, the TRIPs Agreement has been criticized for failing to cure the principal shortcoming of international intellectual property agreements like the Berne Convention, and it appears not to prevent restrictions on the exercise of intellectual property rights through the "agreement to disagree" (Cahn and Schimmel 1997, *supra* note 30, at 293–314); For details about "agreement to disagree" in TRIPs Agreement, see Cahn and Schimmel (1997, *id*., at 305–307).

immunity granted by a Member to the nationals of any other Member shall be accorded immediately and unconditionally to the nationals of all other Members.

The general goals of the TRIPs Agreement contained in the Preamble of the Agreement, include the reduction of distortions[93] and impediments to international trade,[94,95] promotion of effective and adequate protection of intellectual property rights, and ensuring that measures and procedures to enforce intellectual property rights do not themselves become barriers[96] to legitimate trade.[97,98]

The general goals contained in the Preamble of the Agreement should be read in conjunction with Article 7 (Objectives), according to which the protection and enforcement of intellectual property rights should contribute to the promotion of technological innovation[99] and to the transfer and dissemination of technology, to the mutual advantage of producers and users of technological knowledge and in a

---

[93] Trade distortion was interpreted by the United States as law of comparative advantage through failure to enforce intellectual property rights. However, the term was interpreted by India as foreign government intervention in the market place in the name of protecting intellectual property rights (Dreyfuss and Lowenfeld 1997, *supra* note 20, at n. 14).

[94] Of the three core commitments in the TRIPs Agreements – national treatment, most-favored-nation treatment, and minimum standards – only the first two deal with direct obstacles to trade, because they only address conditions that make it more difficult for foreigners, relative to domestic producers to extract profits. In the case of minimum standards, the absence of intellectual property protection is not a direct barrier to international trade (Dreyfuss and Lowenfeld 1997, *supra* note 20, at 276).

[95] For the empirical study on the effects of the TRIPs Agreement on international trade by Keith E. Maskus, see Maskus and Denubarti (1995, pp. 227, 229–230). (Stating that a higher level of intellectual property protection can have different effects on the imports: (i) increased intellectual property protection decreases trade through the decrease in demand for the protected goods because of the unwillingness to pay the royalty; (ii) greater intellectual property protection could increase demand for the protected product because people cannot get the product on the black market, which could increase trade.)

[96] It is indicated "In one scenario, innovations could flow more readily across state lines in the absence of intellectual property protection, and in the opposite scenario, innovations flow through investment and licensing, which is made more likely by the existence of intellectual protection in the receiving country" (Dreyfuss and Lowenfeld 1997, *supra* note 20, n. 10).

[97] TRIPs Agreement, *supra* note 22. Preamble.

[98] See Braga and Fink (1998, pp. 168–169). (Stating that, for example, developed countries wanting to export to developing countries with weak intellectual property protection infrastructure have to bear the additional transaction cost preventing local imitation of their goods. However, developed countries exporting to countries with a strong intellectual property protection infrastructure do not have to worry about this extra transaction cost. Thus an international intellectual property protection system will help diminish this transaction cost, which would promote the legitimate trade. The phrase underlined was added by the author.)

[99] As for now, it is somewhat restrictive for the protection of intellectual property rights to meet the promotion of technology innovation, for example, in the living systems like plants and micro-organisms. For the fundamental problems for patent law and its administration posed in plants and micro-organisms, for example, see Drahos and Braithwaite (2002, *supra* note 31, at 471).

manner conducive to social and economic welfare,[100,101,102] and to a balance of rights and obligations. The rights of Members are recognized to adopt measures for public health and other public interest reasons and to prevent the abuse of intellectual property rights, provided that such measures are consistent with the provisions of the TRIPs Agreement.[103]

9.5 Structure

The TRIPs Agreement is divided into three main sections-standards, enforcement, and dispute settlement: (i) Parts I and II of the TRIPs Agreement provide the substantive standards of intellectual property protection and outline the agreement's three core commitments-minimum standards, national treatment, and most-favored nation treatment; (ii) Part III and IV of the TRIPs Agreement set, forth general obligations governing the enforcement, acquisition and maintenance procedures for the protection of intellectual property rights; (iii) Part V of the TRIPs Agreement entails the detailed dispute prevention and settlement.

Assignment

To ensure students become equipped with the capability to apply knowledge from the classroom to the field, students are, in this chapter, required to write a report, deliver a presentation and participate in a discussion on the following issues:

The legislative history of concluding TRIPS during the Uruguay Rounds, compared with that of concluding other multilateral agreements under the WTO mechanism, focusing on conflicts and compromises between developed countries and developing countries.

[100] TRIPs Agreement, *supra* note 22. Art. 7.

[101] Su (2000, *supra* note 1, at 168). (Stating that depending on the characteristics of the country, TRIPs will have different welfare effects. For example, if one assumes that the country has little ability for domestic technological innovation and limited technology transfer and foreign direct investment, TRIPs would hurt the country because the country would be paying out royalties for the use of intellectual property.)

[102] Very wide interpretation of such notions as "mutual advantage" or "manner conducive to social and economic welfare" may take place (Mangassarian 2001, *supra* note 48, at 130).

[103] TRIPs Agreement, *supra* note 22. Art. 8.

Intellectual Property Rights Conferred in TRIPs 10

Learning Objectives
This chapter is to help students understand:
1. The most-favored nation and national treatment obligations under TRIPs compared with those under GATT and GATS;
2. Copyright and related right protection under TRIPs;
3. Trademark protection under TRIPs;
4. Geographical indication protection under TRIPs;
5. Industrial design protection under TRIPs;
6. Patent protection under TRIPs;
7. Layout-designs protection under TRIPs;
8. Undisclosed information protection under TRIPs.

10.1 Copyright

10.1.1 Provisions from the Berne Convention

During the Uruguay Round negotiations, it was recognized that the Berne Convention for the Protection of Literary and Artistic Works[1,2] already, for the most part, was providing adequate basic standards of copyright protection. Thus, it was agreed that the point of departure should be the existing level of protection under the Berne

[1] For the definition of literary and artistic works, see Berne Convention, *supra* note 20, at Art. 2(1). The Berne Convention leaves member countries to choose whether their national legislation shall impose such a requirement, while the domestic law like the United States law[17 U.S.C.A. § 102 (a)] requires that an artistic or literary work be fixed in a tangible medium of expression in order to be protected by copyright law. Berne Convention, *supra* note 20, Art. 2(2), Ugolini (1999), *supra* note 26, at. n. 37.

[2] Sept. 9. 1886, 828 U.N.T.S. 221 revised by multilateral copyright 25 U.S.T. 1341, July 14, 1971, Berne Convention, *supra* note 20.

E.S. Lee, *World Trade Regulation*,

DOI 10.1007/978-3-642-31143-7_10,

Convention[3]: The TRIPs Agreement requires compliance with the basic standards of the Berne Convention, and then, clarifies and adds certain specific points. The Agreement is structured along the lines of the so-called "Berne-plus" approach.

The Berne Convention for the Protection of Literary and Artistic Works is administered by WIPO.[4] With the exception of the provisions on moral rights, all the substantive provisions of the latest act of the Convention, the Paris Act of 1971, have been incorporated by reference into the TRIPs Agreement and thus become obligations under the TRIPs Agreement between TRIPs Member countries.[5] The Convention provides the basic principles, that is, national treatment, automatic protection and independence of protection, minimum standards of protection, permissible exceptions, terms of protection and so on.

The Convention provides national treatment[6]: works originating in one of the contracting States must be given the same protection in each of the other contracting States as is granted to the works of its own nationals.[7] Regarding automatic protection, protection may not be subject to any formality of registration, deposit, or the like.[8] Regarding independence of protection, enjoyment and exercise of the rights granted are independent of the existence of protection in the country of origin.[9]

---

[3] TRIPs Agreement, *supra* note 22. Part II, Section 1, Art. 9.

[4] The WIPO administers other treaties like the Rome Convention, International Convention for the Protection of Performers, Producers of Phonograms and Broadcasting Organizations; the Madrid Agreement Concerning the International Registrations of Marks; the Treaty on Intellectual Property in Respect of Integrated Circuits; the Vienna Agreement Establishing an International Classification of the Figurative Elements of Marks; and the Hague Agreement Concerning the International Deposit of Industrial Designs. See Texts of Treaties Administered by WIPO, at http://www.wipo.int/treaties/index.html. Accessed July 10, 2004.

[5] The Paris Act of 1971, of that Convention. *Supra* note 45. The point of departure is expressed in Art. 9.1 under Members are obliged to comply with the substantive provisions of the Paris Act of 1971 of the Berne Convention, i.e. Arts. 1 through 21 of the Berne Convention (1971) and the Appendix thereto. However, Members do not have rights or obligations under the TRIPS Agreement in respect of the rights conferred under Art. 6bis of that Convention, i.e. the moral rights (the claim to authorship and to object to any derogatory action in relation to a work, which would be prejudicial to the author's honour or reputation), or of the rights derived therefrom.

[6] The Convention, for example, permits member countries to treat the works of authors who are nationals of nonmember countries no less favorably than they treat their own nationals when those nonmember countries fail to adequately protect the works of authors who are nationals of a member country. See Berne Convention, *supra* note 20, at. 6(1).

[7] Berne Convention, *supra* note 20. Art. 5(1).

[8] Berne Convention, *supra* note 20. Art. 5(2). Universal Copyright Convention permits a member country to require formalities for protection of works first published outside of its territory or in another member country. "Formality" is only the symbol along with the copyright owner's name, and the date of first publication born in the work. See Universal Copyright Convention, Sept. 6, 1952, 6 U.S.T. 2731, 216 U.N.T.S. 134, revised by 25 U.S.T. 1341, 943 U.N.T.S. 178, July 24, 1971.

[9] Berne Convention, *supra* note 20. Art. 5(2)

With regard to minimum standards of protection, exclusive rights are granted to authors,[10] and artists' resale right, the so-called "droit de suite", concerning original works of art and original manuscripts, is optional.[11] With regard to permissible exceptions, the Convention provides for the possibility of using protected works in particular cases without having to obtain the authorization of the right holder, and without having to pay any remuneration for such use.[12]

The Convention provides the possibility of compulsory licenses for the right of broadcasting, and of communication to the public by wire, by rebroadcasting or by loudspeaker or any other analogous instrument of the broadcast of the work,[13] and for the right of recording of musical works.[14] The term of protection shall be the life of the author and 50 years after his death.[15] For photographic works and works of applied art, the minimum term of protection is 25 years from the making of the work.

Generally speaking, as with the Paris Convention, the Berne Convention leaves the means of enforcement entirely to the national laws.[16] It states that "apart from the provisions of this Convention, the extent of protection, as well as the means of redress, are accorded exclusively to the laws of the country where protection is aimed".[17] Berne does provide for one mandatory procedure, the seizure of infringing copies; however, that remedy shall: take place in accordance with the legislation of each country.[18]

Chinese Film Group files first civil copyright lawsuit

Aug 12, 2010
Written by Jared Moya

The China Film Copyright Protection Association (CFCPA) says it's targeting 365pub.com and Cnnip.com and several Internet cafes for the facilitation of copyright infringement.

(continued)

---

[10] These rights include the right of translation Art. 8, the right of reproduction Art. 9, the right of public performance and of communication to the public of a performance (Art. 11), the right of broadcasting, and of communication to the public by wire, by rebroadcasting or by loudspeaker or any other analogous instrument of the broadcast of the work (Art. 11bis) , the right of public recitation (Art. 11ter) , the right of adaptation, arrangement and other alteration (Art. 12), and the right of making the cinematographic adaptation and reproduction of a work (Art. 14).

[11] Berne Convention, *supra* note 20. Art. 14 ter.

[12] Such exceptions include reproduction in certain special cases (Art. 9(2)), quotations and use of works by way of illustration for teaching purposes (Art. 10), reproduction of newspaper or similar articles and use of works for the purpose of reporting current events (Art. 10 bis), and ephemeral recordings (Art. 11 bis(3)).

[13] Berne Convention, *supra* note 20. Art. 11 bis(2).

[14] Berne Convention, *supra* note 20. Art. 3(1).

[15] Berne Convention, *supra* note 20. Art. 7.

[16] See generally Berne Convention, *supra* note 20.

[17] Berne Convention, *supra* note 20. Art. 5(2), cited by Anawalt (2003, *supra* note 18, at 386).

[18] Berne Convention, *supra* note 20. Art. 16(3), cited by Anawalt (2003, *id.*, at 386–387).

The CFCPA held a press conference recently to announce that had filed its first ever civil copyright lawsuit since it morphed from a simple trade association to a copyright management group back in 2008.

It said it had filed a complaint of copyright infringement against 365pub.com, Cnnip.com, in addition to several unnamed Internet cafes, and is seeking an end to the infringement, a public apology, and, of course monetary damages

"The copyrights of pirated films belong to CFCPA members who have authorized us to manage them," said Zhu Yongde, Chairman of the CFCPA.

He said that the way the scheme worked is that 365pub and Cnnip would distribute copyrighted films to Internet cafes like those mentioned in the suit, and would then collect user fees for the privilege.

"Playing pirated films on the Internet for just three days probably lost us 100 million yuan at the box office," said An Xiaofen, producer of the popular Chinese action film Ip Man 2, one of the movies observed being pirated en masse.

Xiaofen estimates that he lost perhaps as much as 100 million yuan ($15 million USD) being that the number of illegal downloads has surpassed some 10 million, and at least one third of pirates usually otherwise buy a legal copy of the DVD.

The CFCPA estimates that 96 % of the movies available on the Internet in China are pirated, and that only 10 % of those in theaters actually make a profit.

Part of the problem, the CFCPA says, is that infringers are usually only fined well below the maximum of 500,000 yuan ($74,000 USD), and in some cases pay copyright holders as little as a few hundred yuan (100 yuan = $15 USD).

Stay tuned.

Source: Chinese Film Group Files First Civil Copyright Lawsuit. 12 August 2010 http://www.zeropaid.com/news/90256/chinese-film-group-files-first-civil-copyright-lawsuit/

10.1.2 Berne-Plus Provisions

In addition to incorporating the substantive provisions of the Berne Convention, the TRIPs Agreement contains the following clarifications and additional obligations.[19] With regard to expression/idea dichotomy, TRIPs Agreement confirms that

[19] TRIPs Agreement, *supra* note 22. Part III, Section 1, Art. 41.

copyright protection shall extend to expressions and not to ideas, procedures, and methods of operation or mathematical concepts as such.[20]

With regard to computer programs,[21] it is provided that computer programs, whether in source or object code, shall be protected as literary works under the Berne Convention (1971).[22] This provision confirms that computer programs must be protected under copyright and that those provisions of the Berne Convention that apply to literary works shall be applied also to them.[23]

It confirms further, that the form in which a program is, whether in source or object code, does not affect the protection. The obligation to protect computer programs as literary works means, for example, that only those limitations that are applicable to literary works may be applied to computer programs.[24] It also confirms that the general term of protection of 50 years applies to computer programs.[25]

With regard to compilations of data, it is clarified that databases and other compilations of data or other material shall be protected as such under copyright even where the databases include data that as such are not protected under copyright.[26] Databases are eligible for copyright protection provided that they by reason of the selection or arrangement of their contents constitute intellectual creations. The provision also confirms that databases have to be protected regardless of which form they are in, i.e., whether in machine-readable or other form. Furthermore, the provision clarifies that such protection shall not extend to the data or material itself,

---

[20] TRIPs Agreement, *supra* note 22. Art. 9.2.

[21] In the United States, software means "a set of computer program, procedures, and possibly associated documentation concerned with the operation of a data processing system, e.g. complies, library, routines, manuals, circuit diagrams". United States Copyright Office, Library of congress, compendium of Copyright Office Practices, 1984, para 32, cited by Mangassarian (2001, *supra* note 48, at 137). Some writers distinguish between programs (the specific executable code models) and software (the complete set of programs plus documentation) (Reed 1996, cited by Magassarian 2001, *id.*, at 136), and other use the term "software" interchangeably for both of these elements otherwise it could create a lot of complication in practice (Mangassarian 2001, *id*). However, generally speaking, the term "software" has much more broader connotations than "program", *id.*

[22] TRIPs Agreement, *supra* note 22. Art. 10.1.

[23] The scope of copyright protection for computer program and databases varies by nation. For review of some of the key differences between the Japanese approach to copyright protection and the American approach, see Karjala and Sugiyama (1988, p. 613), cited by Curci (2002, *supra* note 42, at n. 33).

[24] For the computer programs as the deeply controversial subject matter, and the legal control of software presenting perplexing problems for courts and legislatures, see Anawalt (2003, *supra* note 18, at 388–389). (Stating "computer programs lie an abounding between information and function . . .", "what monopoly control should be granted works whose function depends on the configuration and use of information? . . .").

[25] Possible shorter terms applicable to photographic works and works of applied art may not be applied.

[26] TRIPs Agreement, *supra* note 22. Art. 10.2.

and that it shall be without prejudice to any copyright subsisting in the data or material itself.[27]

With regard to term of protection, the term of protection shall be the life of the author and 50 years after his death.[28] It is further provided that whenever the term of protection of work, other than a photographic work or a work of applied art, is calculated on a basis other than the life of a natural person, such term shall be no less than 50 years from the making of the work, 50 years from the end of the calendar year of making.[29]

With regard to limitations and exceptions, Members are required to confine limitations or exceptions to exclusive rights to certain special cases which do not conflict with a normal exploitation of the work and do not unreasonably prejudice the legitimate interests of the right holder.[30] This is a horizontal provision that applies to all limitations and exceptions permitted under the provisions of the Berne Convention and the Appendix thereto as incorporated into the TRIPs Agreement. The application of these limitations is permitted also under the TRIPs Agreement, but they must be applied in a manner that does not prejudice the legitimate interests of the right holder.

10.1.3 Related Rights

Related rights protected by TRIPs include the right of performers, producers of phonograms and broadcasting organization.[31] Performers shall have the possibility of preventing the unauthorized fixation of their performance on a phonogram (e.g. the recording of a live musical performance).[32] The fixation right covers only aural not audiovisual fixations. Performers must also be in a position to prevent the reproduction of such fixations. They shall also have the possibility of preventing the unauthorized broadcasting by wireless means and the communication to the public of their live performance.[33]

Regarding the protection of phonograms, Members have to grant producers of phonograms an exclusive reproduction right.[34] In addition to this, they have to grant an exclusive rental right at least to producers of phonograms.[35] The provisions on

[27] *Id.*

[28] Berne Convention, *supra* note 20. Art. 7.(1) as incorporated into the TRIPs Agreement

[29] TRIPs Agreement, *supra* note 22. Art. 12.

[30] TRIPs Agreement, *supra* note 22. Art. 13.

[31] TRIPs Agreement, *supra* note 22. Art. 14.

[32] TRIPs Agreement, *supra* note 22. Art. 14.1.

[33] *Id.*

[34] TRIPs Agreement, *supra* note 22. Art. 14.2.

[35] TRIPs Agreement, *supra* note 22. Art. 14.4.

rental rights apply also to any other right holders in phonograms as determined in national law.[36]

Broadcasting organizations shall have the right to prohibit unauthorized fixation, the reproduction of fixations, and the rebroadcasting by wireless means of broadcasts, as well as the communication to the public of their television broadcasts.[37] The term of protection is at least 50 years for performers and producers of phonograms, and 20 years for broadcasting organizations.[38] Any Member may, in relation to the protection of performers, producers of phonograms and broadcasting organizations, provide for conditions, limitations, exceptions and reservations to the extent permitted by the Rome Convention.[39]

VFM wins match broadcast rights

2010/8/11

Viet Nam Football Media (VFM) has officially announced their attainment of commercial and TV rights to air football matches on Bong Da TV and sport events on VCTV3 in co-operation with the Viet Nam Cable Television (VCTV).

VFM, which became operational in 2009, also announced that VCTV3 would change its name to The Thao TV.

These two channels will be the only stations in the country licensed to broadcast sport news and events live every day. They also have the right to broadcast matches from the leading football tournaments such as Premier League, Ligue 1, Bundesliga, V-Leauge and the top tennis tournaments year-round.

Ha Noi T&T voted top team

Ha Noi T&T were voted the best football team in July, while the team's manager Phan Thanh Hung was voted as the best coach.

Timothy from Ha Noi Hoa Phat was voted as the best player after scoring seven goals in July.

The capital won two matches, drew two and lost one last month. The team is on track to take the V-League title with 45 points after 24 rounds. The tournament only has two more rounds to go and will conclude on August 22.

This is the second time that T&T grabbed two titles in one month.

(continued)

[36] It is not subject to the impairment test as in respect of cinematographic works. However, it is limited by a so-called grandfathering clause, according to which a Member, which on April 15, 1994 (the date of the signature of the Marrakesh Agreement) had in force a system of equitable remuneration of right holders in respect of the rental of phonograms, may maintain such system provided that the commercial rental of phonograms is not giving rise to the material impairment of the exclusive rights of reproduction of right holders.

[37] TRIPs Agreement, *supra* note 22. Art. 14.4.

[38] TRIPs Agreement, *supra* note 22. Art. 14.5.

[39] TRIPs Agreement, *supra* note 22. Art. 14.6.

Nation wins golds at karate champs

Viet Nam won two gold medals at the AKF Junior and Cadet Karate Championship in Hong Kong last week.

Tran Hoang Yen Phuong and Nguyen Van Su won golds in the junior female 53 kg and junior male 68 kg categories, respectively.

It is the first time Su has won international honours. Phuong on the other hand won a bronze medal at the World Women's Karate Cup in Paris in June.

Viet Nam's Tang Thi Hoa also won a gold medal in the women's 59 kg category and two bronzes in the cadets' events.

Viet Nam finished the tournament, which ended on Sunday, in fourth place, behind Iran, Japan and Kazakhstan. – VNS

Source: VFM wins match broadcast rights 11 August 2012. http://vietnamnews.vnagency.com.vn/Sports/202399/VFM-wins-match-broadcast-rights.html

10.2 Trademark

10.2.1 Introduction

Any sign, or any combination of signs, capable of distinguishing the goods and services of one undertaking from those of other undertakings, must be eligible for registration as a trademark, provided that it is visually perceptible.[40] Such signs, in particular words including personal names, letters, numerals, figurative elements and combinations of colors as well as any combination of such signs, shall be eligible for registration as trademarks. Where signs are not inherently capable of distinguishing the relevant goods or services, Member countries are allowed to require, as an additional condition for eligibility for registration as a trademark, that distinctiveness has been acquired through use.[41]

Members are free to determine whether to allow the registration of signs those are not visually perceptible (e.g. sound or smell marks). Members may make register ability depend on use. Service marks are required to be protected in the same way as marks distinguishing goods.[42]

Skype told by EU that "Sky" is trademarked

Posted on 11 August 2010
by Sylvie Barak.

[40] TRIPs Agreement, *supra* note 22. Art. 15.

[41] TRIPs Agreement, *supra* note 22. Art. 15.1, and 15.4.

[42] See e.g. TRIPs Agreement, *supra* note 22. Art. 16.2, and 62.3.

The Sky seems to be falling for VoIP firm Skype, with British Sky Broadcasting (BSkyB) seeming to win a trademark dispute which effectively pulls the "Sky" out from under Skype's feet.

BSkyB has long maintained its customers are often "confused" by the similar name and logos of the firms. Who said too much TV didn't frazzle the mind?

Sadly for Skype, however, the firm's recent IPO filing brought to light the fact Europe has returned a "negative first instance decision" on the trademark dispute between the two firms, in BSkyB's favor, which means the Sky really does belong to Rupert Murdoch, although naturally Skype will be appealing.

Should the firm lose the appeal, it will have to either change its brand name or pay BSkyB a license fee to continue using its name and logo.

BSkyB has picked on Skype ever since Murdoch tried and failed to buy the firm back in early 2006, and has been trying to block Skype trademark applications ever since. Skype has had to fight the same type of trademark battles in Switzerland, Turkey and Brazil, but has thus far managed to defend itself.

"We regard our brand as one of our most valuable assets," Skype said in a statement, adding that should it lose the dispute, it could have serious implications for the firm. "The unlicensed use of our brand by third parties could harm our reputation, cause confusion among our users, and severely undermine the value of our brand in the marketplace".

"We intend to appeal this decision by submitting a notice of appeal to the OHIM Board of Appeal, and if necessary to the General Court at the Court of Justice of the European Community," the firm says.

Why Skype has been singled out for special attention is a little strange, especially considering the UK's IPO database contains over 500 trademarks with the word "Sky" in them.

Of course, all that's left now is for Skype to look, er, heavenward and pray that it doesn't find itself called "pe" anytime soon.

Source: Skype told by EU that "Sky" is trademarked. Sylvie Barak. 11 August 2010. http://unplugged.rcrwireless.com/index.php/20100811/news/2675/skype-told-by-eu-that-sky-is-trademarked/

10.2.2 Rights Conferred in Respect of Trademark and of Well-Known Mark

The owner of a registered trademark must be granted the exclusive right to prevent all third parties not having the owner's consent from using in the course of trade for goods or services signs which are identical or similar to those in respect of which the trademark is registered, where such use would result in a likelihood of confusion. In case of the use of an identical sign for identical goods or services, a likelihood of confusion must be presumed.[43]

With regard to well-known marks, which supplement the protection required by Article 6bis of the Paris Convention, as incorporated by reference into the Members are obliged to refuse or to cancel the registration, and to prohibit the use of mark conflicting with a mark which is well known. Protection must extend to these goods or services, provided that the use of the trademark would indicate a connection between those goods or services and the owner of the registered trademark, and the interests of the owner are likely to be damaged by such use.[44]

Members may provide limited exceptions to the rights conferred by a trademark, such as fair use of descriptive terms, provided that such exceptions take account of the legitimate interests of the owner of the trademark and of third parties.[45] Initial registration and each renewal of registration of a trademark shall be for a term of no less than seven years. The registration of a trademark shall be renewable indefinitely.[46]

Cancellation of a mark on the grounds of non-use cannot take place before three years of uninterrupted non-use has elapsed unless valid reasons based on the existence of obstacles to such use are shown by the trademark owner. Circumstances arising independently of the will of the owner of the trademark, such as import restrictions or other governmental restrictions, shall be recognized as valid reasons of non-use.[47] Use of a trademark by another person, when subject to the control of its owner, must be recognized as use of the trademark for the purpose of maintaining the registration.[48] It is further required that use of the trademark in the course of trade shall not be unjustifiably encumbered by special requirements, such as use with another trademark, use in a special form, or use in a manner detrimental to its capability to distinguish the goods or services.[49]

United States-Section 211 Omnibus Appropriations Act of 1998[50]

Introduction and Background Information

This dispute centers on the protection of trademarks. In an act of agreement between the European Communities and the United States that the legal interpretation of the Panel Report, United – Section 211 Omnibus

[43] TRIPs Agreement, *supra* note 22. Art. 16.1.

[44] TRIPs Agreement, *supra* note 22. Art. 16.3.

[45] TRIPs Agreement, *supra* note 22. Art. 17.

[46] TRIPs Agreement, Art. 18.

[47] TRIPs Agreement, *supra* note 22. Art. 17.1.

[48] TRIPs Agreement, *supra* note 22. Art. 19.2.

[49] TRIPs Agreement, *supra* note 22. Art. 20.

[50] Appellate Body Report. Jan. 2, 2002. United States-Section 211 Omnibus Appropriations Act of 1998. WT/DS176/AB/R. (U.S.-Section 211 AB Report).

Appropriations Act of 1998 needed to be reexamined albeit for different reasons, both the European Communities and that United States appealed the Report. The Panel Report in question was generated from the Panel establish in September of 2000 to evaluate a complaint by the European Communities about Section 211 of the United States Omnibus Appropriations Act of 1998 ("Section 211").[51] The European Communities found Section 211 to be inconsistent with the Agreement on Trade-Related Aspects of Intellectual Property Rights (the "*TRIPs Agreement*"),[52] when consider along with provisions in the Paris Convention[53] for the protection of Industrial Property which had been amended in 1967 by the Stockholm Act (the "Paris Convention (1967)").[54]

Section 211 gathers a set group of trademarks, commercial names, trade names, mainly those connected to the confiscation by the Cuban Government on or after 1 January 1959. Section 211 relies heavily on the definition of a "designated national" which means "a national of any foreign country who is a successor-in-interest to a designated national" under Section 515.305 of Title 31, Code of Federal Regulations ("CFR"). Since the term "confiscated" is set up to single out designated nationals affected by the Cuban Assets Control Regulations (the "CACR") enacted in July 1963, the original documentation was mainly concerned with Cuba. According to United States law, any and all property transactions involving Cuban nationals require a license from the OFAC.[55]

Before Section 211 came into effect, most situations involving the registration and renewal of trademarks formerly owned by Cuban nationals were handled under Section 515.527 of Title 31 CFR.[56] Six months after the beginning of Section 211, the CACR were amended to prohibit the registration and renewal of trademarks and trade names connected to confiscated businesses or businesses assets without the consent of the original owner or the successor-in-interest.[57] When Section 211 and CACR are considered together, a set category of trademarks and trade names become problematic. This group of trademarks and trade names would have been protected under trademark and trade name law in the United States except for the combination of these two acts.[58]

(continued)

[51] Omnibus Consolidated and Emergency Supplemental Appropriations Act, 1999, section 211, Pub. L. No. 105–277, 112 Stat. 2681–2688 (1998) (Omnibus Appropriations Act).

[52] TRIPS Agreement, *supra* note 22.

[53] Paris Convention, *supra* note 45.

[54] U.S.-Section 211 AB Report, *supra* note 153, para. 1.

[55] *Id.* para. 4.

[56] *Id.* para. 6.

[57] *Id.* para. 7.

[58] *Id.* para. 8.

The Panel found that trade names are not within the realm of intellectual property covered by the TRIPs Agreement and limited its review to an exploration of Section 211 in connection to trademarks. The Panel recommended to the Dispute Settlement Body (the "DSB") that the United States would do well to make its measures conform to its obligations under the TRIPs Agreement.[59]

Agreements and sections in question:

Rationale and Holdings

Article 6quinquies of the Paris Convention (1967)

The Appellate Body agrees that Section 211(a)(1) deals with the ownership of a particular set of trademarks and the obligation of countries under the Paris Union, Article 6quinquies A(1) does not pertain to ownership but for protecting the trademark registered in the country of origin.[60] Consequently the Panel's finding in paragraph 8.89[61] of the Panel Report that Section 211 (a)(1) is not inconsistent with Article 2.1 of the TRIPs Agreement when viewed with Article 6quinquies A(1) of the Paris Convention (1967).[62]

Article 2 of the Paris Convention (1967) and Article 3 of the TRIPs Agreement

Under the topic of national treatment, the European Union would like to see Section 211(a)(2) and (b) as declared to be violating the TRIPs Agreement on the grounds that it treats non-United States nationals less favorably than United States nationals as successors-in-interest and as bona fide successors-in-interest to original owners, and the original owners.[63] The Panel found that Section 211(b) applied to successors-in-interests from all origins, not excluding United States nationals, and therefore, does not dis-

[59] *Id.* para. 11.

[60] *Id.* para. 147.

[61] Panel Report, United States-Section 211 Omnibus Appropriations Act of 1998, WT/DS176/R, para. 8.89 (Aug. 6, 2001) (U.S.-Section 211 Panel Report) (stating that "We conclude that Art. 6quinquies A(1) addresses the form of the trademark and therefore find that Section 211(a)(1) is not inconsistent with Art. 6quinquies A(1) of the Paris Convention (1967) as incorporated into the TRIPS Agreement by means of a reference in its Art. 2.1.").

[62] U.S.-Section 211 AB Report, *supra* note 153, para. 148.

[63] *Id.* para. 244.

criminate.[64] The United States believes that its doctrine of not recognizing the property of foreign confiscations should protect it. This should not be applied to trademarks within the United States, even if those trademarks are connected to Cuba.[65] Consequently, the Appellate Body finds that Section 211(a)(2) and (b) are inconsistent with the Paris Convention (1967) in regards to the national treatment obligation of the United States.[66]

Article 4 of the TRIPs Agreement

Along with concerns of the treatment of foreign nationals, the obligation of the most-favored-nation is seen as threatened by this piece of United States legislation.[67] While the United States argues that discrimination does not exist because Cuban nationals would not be able to export materials in the first place, this reasoning does not account for what happens to Cuban national in different locales than Cuba and as such, this constitutes discrimination.[68] The Appellate Body reverses the Panel's findings in paragraphs 8.148[69] and 8.175[70] of the Panel Report and determines that Section 211(a)(2) as well as Section 211(b) are inconsistent with Article 4 of the TRIPs Agreement.[71]

Commentary

The Appellate Body carefully stepped through politics to find a line it would like to continue in the future. The Appellate Body came to the decision that trademark law belonged in the arena of national law rather than international law. Since national law determines trademark ownership, and not Article

(continued)

[64] *Id.* para. 271.

[65] *Id.* para. 295.

[66] *Id.* para. 296.

[67] *Id.* para. 297.

[68] *Id.* para. 317.

[69] U.S.-Section 211 Panel Report, *supra* note 153, para. 8.148. (Stating that "Based on the foregoing reasons, we conclude that Section 211(a)(2) does not deny Cuban nationals any advantage, favor, privilege or immunity that it accords to other foreign nationals. We therefore find that Section 211(a)(2) is not inconsistent with Art. 4 of the TRIPs Agreement").

[70] U.S.-Section 211 Panel Report, *supra* note 153, para. 8.175. (Stating that "The United States argues that Section 211(b) does not grant an "advantage, favor, privilege, or immunity" to non-Cuban nationals that they do not grant to Cuban nationals. The United States contends that neither one nor the other can enforce a trademark based on a foreign confiscation. The United States further argues that US courts will not enforce or recognize an asserted rights to trademarks used in connection with confiscated assets by any successor-in-interest, whether Cuban or not.").

[71] U.S.-Section 211 AB Report, *supra* note 164, para. 319.

6quinquies of the Paris Convention (1967) or the TRIPs Agreement, Section 211 is not inconsistent with these pieces of legislation. The question of trademarks and under what circumstances do other countries have the right to deny trademark protection has both been protected and given a loophole that will create future problems. If trademark protection belongs in national law courts, then the WTO has inadvertently given the Member Countries more power to deny trademark protection.[72] The Appellate Body avoided making any comment on the specific relationship between the United States and Cuba in regards to most-favored nation status, trade names, and Section 211. This move was apparently supported by both the United States and the European Community. The Appellate Body may also have found it most prudent to avoid reopening a can of worms as long as possible. However, the Appellate Body did comment all WTO Members.[73]

Source: United States-Section 211 Omnibus Appropriations Act of 1998.

10.2.3 Geographical Indications

Geographical indications are defined, for the purposes of the Agreement, as indications which identify a good as originating in the territory of a Member, or a region or locality in that territory, where a given quality, reputation or other characteristic of the good is essentially attributable to its geographical origin.[74] Thus, this definition specifies that the quality, reputation of other characteristics or a good can each be a sufficient basis for eligibility as a geographical indication, where they are essentially attributable to the geographical origin of the good.

Interested parties must have legal means to prevent use of indications which misleads the public as to the geographical origin of the good, and use which constitutes an act of unfair competition.[75] The registration of a trademark which uses a geographical indication in a way that misleads the public as to the true place of origin must be refused or invalidated ex officio if the legislation so permits or at the request of an interested party.[76]

---

[72] Bhala and Gantz (2003, p. 217).

[73] Editorial Staff of International Legal Materials. 2002. International Law In Brief: Judicial and Related Documents. Am. Soc'y Int'l L. Mar. http://www.asil.org/ilib/ilib0503.htm#j4. Accessed Feb. 22, 2012.

[74] TRIPs Agreement, *supra* note 22. Art. 22.1.

[75] TRIPs Agreement, *supra* note 22. Art. 22.2.

[76] TRIPs Agreement, *supra* note 22. Art. 22.3.

Why Parma ham stands in way of trade talks

Published On Mon Jul 19 2010
By Michael Geist
Internet Law Columnist

Canada is currently negotiating two major international trade agreements whose success may ultimately depend on the level of protection provided to Parma ham. While it may seem hard to believe, the Canada – European Union Comprehensive Economic and Trade Agreement (CETA) and the Anti-Counterfeiting Trade Agreement (ACTA) are both facing increasing opposition based on European demands to expand protection for "geographical indications."

Geographical indications (GI) are signs used on goods – frequently food, wine, or spirits – that have a specific geographical origin and are said to possess qualities, reputation or characteristics that are essentially attributable to that place of origin. Given the quality associated with the product, proponents of GI protection argue that it is needed to avoid consumer confusion as well as to protect legitimate producers.

Europe has the most extensive geographical indication protections in the world. These include Protected Designation of Origin (PDO), which covers agricultural products produced, processed and prepared in a given geographical area using recognized know-how; Protected Geographical Indication (PGI), which covers agricultural products linked to the geographical area; and Traditional Specialty Guaranteed (TSG), which highlights traditional character, either in the composition or means of production.

The net effect of the European system is that hundreds of items enjoy special legal protection. In fact, the system is so extensive that the Canadian Association of Importers and Exporters have expressed concern that CETA could lead to new restrictions on the use of words such as "pizza" or "feta."

The GI protection under European law frequently clashes with the fact that for many consumers the GI has ceased to be associated with a particular geographic region and is instead viewed as a generic term for a particular type of product.

For example, many consumers might not associate champagne wines with a specific region in France, but rather to a particular kind of white wine. Similarly, the term "cologne," which is widely used to refer to perfumed fragrances, actually has its origins in the German city of Cologne.

Canadian courts have grappled with a number of geographical indications cases in the past, including an attempt by the Italian authority that regulates "Parma" for cured ham to stop Maple Leaf Meats from using the Parma trademark for some its meat products. The court sided with the Canadian producer, ruling that consumers would not associate its meat with products originating in Parma, Italy.

(continued)

Over the past two decades, Canada has made significant changes to its own geographical indications system. These include taking many popular terms – including Chablis, Champagne, Port, Bordeaux, Burgundy, Medoc, Grappa, Schnapps and Sambuca – off a generic list so that they could enjoy new geographical indication protection.

The irony with the Europe's zeal to protect geographical indications within trade agreements is that effect may be to stifle trade, by stopping foreign competitors from marketing similar products using names that are understood by consumers as generic descriptions.

The latest round of CETA negotiations took place last week in Brussels, with the GI issue (along with protections for industrial designs that cover the fashion industry) a top priority for the European delegation. The Canadian government unsurprisingly faces some opposition to the demands from domestic producers.

Similarly, the ACTA negotiations, which have become increasingly acrimonious, have hit a major roadblock with the Europeans demanding extensive new enforcement powers – including criminal and civil penalties – for GI violations. The U.S. and Canada have been resisting the demand, leading Karel de Gucht, a European Commissioner, to warn last week that this was a "red line" issue that could cause the EU to rethink the merits of the entire treaty.

Source: Why Parma ham stands in way of trade talks. Michael Geist. Jul. 19, 2010. http://www.thestar.com/article/836492–geist-why-parma-ham-stands-in-way-of-trade-talks

Interested parties must have the legal means to prevent the use of a geographical indication identifying wines for wines not originating in the place indicated by the geographical indication.[77] This applies even where the public is not being misled, there is no unfair competition and the true origin of the good is indicated or the geographical indication is accompanied by expressions such as "kind", "type", "style", "imitation" or the like.[78]

Similar protection must be given to geographical indications identifying spirits when used on spirits. Protection against registration of a trademark must be provided accordingly.[79] A number of exceptions to the protection of geographical

[77] TRIPs Agreement, *supra* note 22. Art. 23.

[78] TRIPs Agreement, *supra* note 22. Art. 23.1.

[79] TRIPs Agreement, *supra* note 22. Art. 23.2.

indications are provided, which are of particular relevance in respect of the additional protection for geographical indications for wines and spirits.[80]

Georgian Wines to receive protected Geographical Indication in EU

Civil Georgia, Tbilisi / 29 Jul.'10 / 13:50
EU and Georgia will give a preliminary endorsement to an agreement on the protection of their respective geographical indications on July 29.

Text of the agreement will be initialed by Georgian Deputy Foreign Minister Davit Jalagania and Nicolas Verlet, director of international affairs at the European Commission's Directorate General for Agriculture.

On the initial stage 18 Georgian wines will be given protected geographical indication in EU, including Khvanchkara, Kindzmarauli, Saperavi, Mukuzani and Tvishi.

"Georgia is the first among the EU Neighborhood Countries to take this important step forward in promoting and protecting the quality of the agricultural production. The objective of the Agreement was to reduce misuses and abuses of the names of products," EU delegation in Georgia said

Source: Georgian Wines to Receive Protected Geographical Indication in EU. Civil Georgia, Tbilisi. 29 July 2010. http://www.civil.ge/eng/article.php?id=22557

10.3 Industrial Design

Members are obliged to provide for the protection of independently created industrial designs that are new or original.[81] Members may provide that designs are not new or original if they do not significantly differ from known designs or combinations of known design features. Members may provide that such protection shall not extend to designs dictated essentially by technical or functional considerations.[82]

Regarding the textile designs, a special provision is provided to take into account the short life cycle and sheer number of new designs in the textile sector:

[80] For example, Members may allow continued and similar use of a particular geographical indication of another Member identifying wines or spirits in connection with goods or services by any of its nationals or domiciliaries who have used that indication in a continued manner with regard to the same or related gods or services in the territory of that member either goods faith preceding that date Art. 24.4

[81] TRIPs Agreement, *supra* note 22. Art. 25.1.

[82] *Id.*

requirements for securing protection of such designs, in particular in regard to any cost, examination or publication, must not unreasonably impair the opportunity to seek and obtain such protection. Members are free to meet this obligation through industrial design law or through copyright law.[83]

Members are required to grant the owner of a protected industrial design the right to prevent third parties not having the owner's consent form from making, selling or importing articles bearing or embodying a design which is a copy, or substantially a copy, or the protected design, when such acts are undertaken for commercial purposes.[84]

Members are allowed to provide limited exceptions to the protection of industrial designs, provided that such exceptions do not unreasonably conflict with the normal exploitation of protected industrial designs and do not unreasonably prejudice the legitimate interests of the owner of the protected design, taking account of the legitimate interests of third parties.[85] The duration of protection available shall amount to at least 10 years.[86] The wording "amount to" allows the term to be divided into, for example, two periods of five years.

Style means business

Thursday, August 12, 2010

Stakeholders in the fashion industry should remain focused and not become distracted by the beautiful clothes, glamorous models, exotic atmosphere, of the industry if they want to be successful.

Carl Francis, permanent secretary in the Ministry of Trade and Industry advised this at the opening of the Making Style Gala Fashion Collections 2010, on Saturday at the Hyatt Regency, Wrightson Road, Port-of-Spain.

"Practitioners who wish to succeed must follow sound business and corporate practices and the industry itself must be competitive and relevant in a demanding global environment. Our country is blessed with abundant creativity and artistic talent, much of which has been expressed at a global level."

"When combined with the proper infrastructure, these elements form the core of what is required for a successful creative industry," he said.

Francis said fashion is a manufacturing and service business just like any other.

"While the process of designing is a creative activity, true success lies in producing quality goods and services which meet customer needs," he said.

……

[83] TRIPs Agreement, *supra* note 22. Art. 25.2.

[84] TRIPs Agreement, *supra* note 22. Art. 26.1.

[85] TRIPs Agreement, *supra* note 22. Art. 26.2.

[86] TRIPs Agreement, *supra* note 22. Art. 26.3.

"The Academy's programs are structured to ensure that the next generation of fashion designers graduate with high levels of technical expertise business savvy and knowledge of the global fashion industry in order for them to be able to compete successfully," Francis said.

......

"This sector has strong export capabilities especially in clothing, textiles, jewelry and cosmetics. There are also strong synergies with other aspects of the creative industries, for example, costuming and design and the areas of film and music," he said.

"We see niche market opportunities for fashion products in textile design, customized tailoring for men and women, high-end fashion merchandise, resort wear collections, accessories design and manufacture of handbags, swimsuits, belts and jewelry, for example. The potential exists to create a viable sustainable fashion industry with global potential."

......

"Expand and increase your borders beyond the region, even if it means exploring previously unknown territory. The Economic Partnership Agreement concluded with the European Union is an excellent example of an opportunity waiting to be grasped by the local fashion industry. Your technique and your standards must however be up to par," he said.

Source: Style means business. August 12, 2010. http://www.newsday.co.tt/businessday/0,125658.html

10.4 Patents

10.4.1 Introduction

Member countries are required to make patents available for inventions, whether products or processes, in all fields of technology without discrimination, subject to the normal tests of novelty, inventiveness and industrial applicability. It is also required that patents be available and patent rights enjoyable without discrimination as to the place of invention and whether products are imported or locally produced.[87]

There are three permissible exceptions to the basic rule on patentability;

One is for inventions contrary to public order or morality; this explicitly includes inventions dangerous to humans, animals or plant life or health or seriously prejudicial to the environment. This is subject to the condition that the commercial exploitation of the invention must also be prevented and that this prevention must

[87] TRIPs Agreement, *supra* note 22. Art. 27.1.

be necessary for the protection of ordure public or morality[88]; The second exception is that Members may exclude from patentability diagnostic, therapeutic and surgical methods for the treatment of humans or animals[89]; The third is that Members may exclude plants and animals other than micro-organisms and essentially biological processes for the production of plants or animals other than non-biological and microbiological processes. However, any country excluding plant varieties from patent protection must provide an effective sui generis system of protection.[90]

10.4.2 Patent Rights Conferred in TRIPs

Patent rights conferred in the TRIPs Agreement are grouped into product patent and process patent. Where the subject-matter of a patent is a product, the exclusive rights conferred will prevent others from the acts of: making, using, offering for sale, selling, or importing for these purposes that product.[91] Where the subject-matter of a patent is a process, the exclusive rights conferred will prevent others from the act of using the process, and from the acts of: using, offering for sale, selling, or importing for these purposes at least the product obtained directly by that process.[92]

Patent owners shall also have the right to assign, or transfer by succession, the patent and to conclude licensing contracts.[93,94] Members may provide limited exceptions to the exclusive rights conferred by a patent, provided that such exceptions do not unreasonably conflict with a normal exploitation of the patent

[88] TRIPs Agreement, *supra* note 22. Art. 27.2.

[89] TRIPs Agreement, *supra* note 22. Art. 27.3(a).

[90] An acceptable sui generis system of protection for plant varieties would be one that is consistent with the International Convention for the Protection of New Varieties of plants. As part of the TRIPs Agreement's built in agenda, Members also agree to review patent protection for plants and animals in 1998. See TRIPs Agreement, Art. 27.3(b), cited by Kennedy (1998, p. 479).

[91] In respect of the exclusive rights conferred by the copyrights or patent rights, their matter of parallel import is controversial among the member countries. For the parallel imports under the TRIPs Agreement, see Dreyfuss and Lowenfeld (1997, *supra* note 20, n. 12). (Stating "Negotiations over the issue of parallel imports have broken down over the TRIPs Agreement .... Doctrines that deem authorized sales in one trading region to exhaust intellectual property interests in other regions have the advantage of facilitating the movement of goods. This, an exhaustion doctrine would be in the spirit of the reminder of the free trade provisions of the GATT. However, these doctrines, ..., limit right holder's ability to extract maximum profits .... Thus, exhaustion doctrines discourage innovation and are somewhat contrary to the spirits of TRIPs. Exhaustion, then, is one issue that could have forced the grafters of TRIPs to consider the inconsistency between free trade and intellectual property protection. Instead, they provided in Art. 6 that 'nothing in this Agreement shall be used to address the issue of the exhaustion of intellectual property rights'").

[92] TRIPs Agreement, *supra* note 22. Art. 28.1.

[93] TRIPs Agreement, *supra* note 22. Art. 28.2.

[94] TRIPs Agreement, *supra* note 22. Art. 28.

and do not unreasonably prejudice the legitimate interest of the patent owner, taking account of the legitimate interests of third parties.[95] The term of protection available shall not end before the expiration of a period of 20 years from the filing date.[96]

Members shall require that an applicant for a patent shall disclose the invention in a manner sufficiently clear and complete for the invention to be carried out by a person skilled in the art and may require the applicant to indicate the best mode for carrying out the invention known to the inventor at the filing date or, where priority is claimed, at the priority date of the application.[97]

India wins Patent Dispute against China for Flu Medicine

Indo-Asian News Service
New Delhi, August 06, 2010

India has won a crucial patent dispute against China for treating influenza and epidemic fever through medicinal formulations using 'pudina' (mint) and 'kalamegha' (andrographis), the Lok Sabha was informed on Friday. Minister of State for Health and Family Welfare S Gandhiselvan said Chinese pharmaceutical company Livzon Pharmaceutical Group Inc, Guangdong, had filed a patent application with the European Patent Office (EPO).

The minister, in a written reply, said China, in its patent application, claimed to have traditional medicine composition for treatment of avian influenza, as well as its method for preparation and application. It was filed in January 2007.

He said officials at EPO, after examining the application, conveyed their intention to grant the patent to the Chinese company.

But April 27, this year, the Department of Ayurveda, Yoga and Naturopathy, Unani, Siddha and Homoeopathy (AYUSH) found in its digital library that they had references from Ayurveda and Unani books about the use of pudina and kalamegha being used to treat influenza and epidemic fever.

"Traditional Knowledge Digital Library (TKDL) jointly set up by AYUSH and CSIR made a submission to EPO on the basis of available prior art references from Ayurveda and Unani text books the details of four medicinal formulations where pudina and kalamegha have been used for the treatment of influenza, epidemic fever," Gandhiselvan said.

In their application, they also stated that the uses of these products have been known for hundreds of years in the Ayurveda and Unani systems of medicine.

"A team of examiners in EPO considered the evidences on pre-existing knowledge of Ayurveda and Unani," he added.

(continued)

[95] TRIPs Agreement, *supra* note 22. Art. 30.

[96] TRIPs Agreement, *supra* note 22. Art. 33.

[97] TRIPs Agreement, *supra* note 22. Art. 29.1.

On June 10 this year, the patent office decided to cancel their earlier intention of granting patent to the Chinese firm.

"The EPO thus upheld the Indian claim that the medicinal properties of pudina and kalamegha were known to Indian traditional medical system in particular for treatment of influenza and epidemic fever," he added.

Source: India wins patent dispute against China for flu medicine. August 6, 2010. http://www.hindustantimes.com/India-wins-patent-dispute-against-China-for-flu-medicine/Article1-583231.aspx

10.4.3 Compulsory Licensing

In order to shield patent owners from excessive government encroachment on their exclusive rights,[98] Article 31 of the TRIPs Agreement tightly regulates any compulsory license system (euphemistically referred to in the Agreement as "other use without authorization of the right holder") that is used by a Member to force a patent owner to license a government entity or a third party designated by the Member.[99]

Allowed compulsory licensing and government's use without the authorization of the right holder are made subject to conditions[100] aimed at protecting the legitimate interests of the right holder. Patent rights are required to be enjoyable without discrimination as to the field of technology, and whether products are imported or locally produced.[101] An application to use the subject-matter of a patent must be considered on its individual merits.[102]

For the obtainment of compulsory license, as a general rule, an unsuccessful attempt must be made first to obtain a voluntary license on reasonable commercial terms and conditions within a reasonable period.[103] The scope and duration of such use without the authorization of the right holder must be limited to the purpose for

[98] Circumstances in which a compulsory license may be authorized in countries with such measures include situations where the owner fails to work the invention within a certain period of time after receiving a patent, or to prevent or remedy other anti-competitive practices that might result or have resulted from the exercise of the exclusive patent rights by the owner (Kennedy 1998, *supra* note 193, at 480).

[99] Kennedy (1998), *supra* note 193, at 480.

[100] TRIPs Agreement, *supra* note 22. Art. 31.

[101] TRIPs Agreement, *supra* note 22. Art. 27.1.

[102] TRIPs Agreement, *supra* note 22. Art. 31(a).

[103] This requirement may be waived by a Member in cases of national emergency, circumstance of extreme urgency, or public non-commercial use. See TRIPs Agreement, our. 31(b).

which it was authorized.[104] Any authorization to use the subject-matter of a patent must be non-exclusive.[105] Any such use shall be authorized predominantly for the supply of the domestic market of the Member authorizing such use.[106]

The right holder must be paid adequate remuneration in the circumstances of each case, taking into account the economic value of the license.[107] The legal validity of any decision relating to the authorization to the remuneration shall be subject to judicial review or other independent review by a higher authority within the Member.[108] The requirements concerning the need to attempt first to negotiate a voluntary license, the limitation of the authorization to use for the supply of the domestic market predominantly,[109] and the amount of remuneration are relaxed where a compulsory license is granted to remedy a practice determined after judicial or administrative process to be anti-competitive.[110]

Roche has denied the contact with the MHWFA regarding the compulsory licensing of Tamiflu

2009/08/27, 14:39:09 Healthkoreanews admin@hkn24.com

A senior official of Roche, a multinational pharmaceutical company, said that Roche has not been in contact with South Korean government concerning the compulsory licensing of Roche's Tamiflu.

Urs H. Flueckiger, Roche Korea's president said in his e-mail interview with Health Korea news on 26 August, "Roche hasn't got in contact with the Korean Ministry for Health, Welfare and Family Affairs(MHWFA) regarding the compulsory licensing of Tamiflu and has no plan to communicate with the South Korean government, even in the future."

He also said, "Roche's annual production capacity of Tamiflu of 400 million treatments couldn't be enough to cover the population of the whole world. But we have enough Tamiflu to supply to South Korea. It is going to be supplied to South Korean government on time."

Those remarks could be interpreted as a kind of Roche's rejection of South Korean government's demand, if any, for additional purchase of Tamiflu.

(continued)

[104] In the case of semiconductor technology such use may be authorized only for public non-commercial use or to remedy a practice determined after judicial or administrative process to be anti-competitive. See TRIPs Agreement, *supra* note 22. Art. 31(c).

[105] *Id.*

[106] In the case of a customs union such as the EU it is open question whether the relevant market is the entire territory of the customs union or the territory of on individual member-state.

[107] The need to correct any anti-competitive practices may be taken into account in determining the amount of the remuneration. See TRIPs Agreement, *supra* note 22. Art. 31(g).

[108] TRIPs Agreement, *supra* note 22. Art. 31(h).

[109] TRIPs Agreement, *supra* note 22. Art. 31(f).

[110] TRIPs Agreement, *supra* note 22. Art. 31(c).

Source: Roche has denied the contact with the MHWFA regarding the compulsory licensing of Tamiflu. Aug. 27, 2009. http://www.hkn24.com/news/articleView.html?idxno=31764

10.5 Layout-Designs

Member countries are required to protect the layout-designs of integrated circuits in accordance with the provisions of the IPIC Treaty (the Treaty on Intellectual Property in Respect of Integrated Circuits), negotiated under the auspices of WIPO in 1989.[111] These provisions deal with, inter alia, the definitions of "integrated circuit" and "layout-design (topography)", requirements for protection, exclusive rights, and limitations.

An "integrated circuit" means a product, in its final form or an intermediate form, in which the elements, at least one of which is an active element, and some or all of the interconnections are integrally formed in and/or on a piece of material and which is intended to perform an electronic function.[112] A "layout-design (topography)" is defined as the three-dimensional disposition, however expressed, of the elements, at least one of which is an active element, and of some or all of the interconnections of an integrated circuit, or such a three-dimensional disposition prepared for an integrated circuit intended for manufacture.[113]

The obligation to protect layout-designs applies to such layout-designs that are original in the sense that they are the result of their creators' own intellectual effort and are not commonplace among creators of layout-designs and manufacturers of integrated circuits at the time of their creation.[114] The exclusive rights include the right of reproduction and the right of importation, sale and other distribution for commercial purposes.[115]

The conditions in the case of compulsory licensing of patents[116] apply mutatis mutandis to compulsory or non-voluntary licensing of a layout-design or to its use by or for the government without the authorization of the right holder, instead of the provisions of the IPIC Treaty on compulsory licensing.[117] In the case of semi-conductor technology, compulsory use may be authorized for public non-

[111] TRIPs Agreement, *supra* note 22. Art. 35.

[112] Treaty on Intellectual property in respect of Integrated Circuits. Art. 2–7.

[113] *Id.* Art. 12, and 16.3.

[114] TRIPs Agreement, *supra* note 22. Art. 35.

[115] TRIPs Agreement, *supra* note 22. Art. 36.

[116] TRIPs Agreement, *supra* note 22. Art. 31.

[117] TRIPs Agreement, *supra* note 22. Art. 37.2.

commercial use or to remedy a practice determined after judicial or administrative process to be anti-competitive.[118]

Huawei accused of stealing Trade Secrets by Motorola

2010/07/23
Ananth Krishnan

The Chinese company describes the accusations as 'groundless.'

Chinese telecom giant Huawei, under the scanner in India for security reasons, has been accused by American mobile phone company Motorola of stealing trade secrets.

The American firm on Friday filed a lawsuit against the Chinese company, charging that it had obtained confidential information from its former employees. Huawei on Thursday denied the claims, describing the accusations as "groundless." The claims come amid an already-raging debate over Chinese telecom companies' overseas ventures.

The Indian government has restricted imports of equipment from Chinese telecom firms, including Huawei, citing the possibility of embedded malware in equipment. Huawei and other Chinese firms have, however, strongly refuted the claims, saying there has been no evidence, so far, of any problems with their equipment.

Motorola has now accused Huawei, which has been trying to enter the U.S. market, of stealing trade secrets, and then selling equipment built using confidential information. Motorola had earlier accused another U.S.-based firm, Lemko, of stealing information from its former employees. But in a lawsuit filed on Friday, the American company for the first time named Huawei in the case, accusing Lemko of passing information on to the Chinese firm.

Huawei, has, however, denied any relationship with Lemko, besides supplying some equipment. "Huawei will vigorously defend itself against baseless allegations," the firm said in a statement, Agence France-Presse reported.

"As an active and significant player in global standards-setting bodies, Huawei has great respect for the rights of intellectual property holders, and will with equal vigour protect its own hard-earned intellectual property rights."

Media reports in the U.S. said Motorola had earlier refrained from naming Huawei in the case because it considered selling its networks business to the Chinese firm. But after the deal went to Siemens, it changed tack. Huawei has earlier faced charges from another U.S. technology company, Cisco, for stealing software.

(continued)

[118] TRIPs Agreement, *supra* note 22. Art. 31(c).

The charges were, however, dropped when Huawei reportedly altered some of its products.

Source: Huawei accused of stealing trade secrets by Motorola. Ananth Krishnan. 23 July 2010. http://www.thehindu.com/business/companies/article528771.ece

10.6 Undisclosed Information

The TRIPs Agreement requires undisclosed information – trade secrets or know-how – which has not been covered in multilateral treaties[119] to benefit from protection.[120] The protection must apply to information that constitutes a secret[121] that has commercial value because it is secret and that has been subject to reasonable steps to keep it secret.[122]

The Agreement does not require undisclosed information to be treated as a form of property, but it does require that a person lawfully in control of such information must have the possibility of preventing it from being disclosed to, acquired by, or used by others without his or her consent in a manner contrary to honest commercial practices.[123] "Manner contrary to honest commercial practices" includes breach of contract, breach of confidence and inducement to breach, as well as the acquisition of undisclosed information by third parties who knew, or were grossly negligent in failing to know, that such practices were involved in the acquisition.[124]

The Agreement also contains provisions on undisclosed test data and other data whose submission is required by governments as a condition of approving the marketing of pharmaceutical or agricultural chemical products which use new chemical entities. In such a situation the Member government concerned must protect the data against unfair commercial use. In addition, Members must protect such data against disclosure, except where necessary to protect the public, or unless steps are taken to ensure that the data are protected against unfair commercial use.[125]

---

[119] Anawalt (2003), *supra* note 18, at 389.

[120] TRIPs Agreement, *supra* note 22. Art. 39.

[121] For the controversial aspects of protection of undisclosed information, see Anawalt (2003, *supra* note 18, at 389) (stating "identification of . . . 'trade secret' presents a very difficult problem . . ., trade secret claims are simply over-exaggerated").

[122] TRIPs Agreement, *supra* note 22. Art. 39.2.

[123] *Id.*

[124] TRIPs Agreement, *supra* note 22. Art. 39.2.10.

[125] TRIPs Agreement, *supra* note 22. Art. 39.3.

10.7 Anti-competitive Practices

It is recognized that some licensing practices or conditions pertaining to intellectual property rights which restrain competition may have adverse effects on trade and may impede the transfer and dissemination of technology.[126] Member countries may adopt, consistently with other provisions of the Agreement, appropriate measures to prevent or control practices in the licensing of intellectual property rights which are abusive and anti-competitive.[127]

The Agreement provides for a mechanism whereby a country seeking to take action against such practices involving the companies of another Member country can enter into consultations with that other Member and exchange publicly available non-confidential information of relevance to the matter in question and other information available to that Member, subject to domestic law and to the conclusion of mutually satisfactory agreements concerning the safeguarding of its confidentiality by the requesting Member.[128] Similarly, a country whose companies are subject to such action in another Member can enter into consultations with that Member.[129]

FTC launches probe on patent abuses

Large companies with widespread technologies will be targeted

August 10, 2010

Korea's antitrust body has launched an extensive investigation into possible patent-related abuses by 40 domestic and 19 foreign IT companies, the government said yesterday.

"With the increase in patent conflicts in the IT world, there are growing concerns about patent abuse," the Fair Trade Commission (FTC) said in a statement yesterday. "In the IT industry, patents are often more critical than in other sectors and can determine whether a company fails of succeeds."

This marks the largest investigation into such matters undertaken in Korea, officials said.

The probe will cover IT companies specializing in semiconductors, computers and mobile telecommunications products. The investigation is expected to last six to eight weeks.

"Companies with market dominance and widespread technologies that have become industry standards will be targeted," said Kim Jun-beom, director of the FTC's market supervision team. "Foreign companies that have a large influence on the domestic market also will be targeted."

(continued)

---

[126] TRIPs Agreement, *supra* note 22. Art. 40.1.

[127] TRIPs Agreement, *supra* note 22. Art. 40.2.

[128] TRIPs Agreement, *supra* note 22. Art. 40.3.

[129] TRIPs Agreement, *supra* note 22. Art. 40.4.

Though Kim did not identify the companies that will be investigated, some experts say the probe will likely cover large Korean firms such as Samsung Electronics, LG Electronics and Hynix Semiconductor.

The FTC started the investigation last Friday, questioning local and foreign firms. The agency will follow up with companies that it suspects violated patent laws and regulations.

The investigation comes amid growing tension between the government and large corporations. The current administration has criticized conglomerates over several issues as of late, including alleged unfair practices toward smaller companies.

"Local small and midsize enterprises have suffered considerable damage from patent-related abuses by large domestic and foreign companies," Kim said.

The government said some large firms have forced licensees to purchase goods and technologies unrelated to the patents licensed and coerced their partners not to trade with competitors.

Other concerns revolve around large companies charging unreasonably high royalties for the use of their patents.

Source: FTC launches probe on patent abuses. August 10, 2010. http://joongangdaily.joins.com/article/view.asp?aid=2924404

Assignment

To ensure students become equipped with the capability to apply knowledge from the classroom to the field, students are, in this chapter, required to write a report, deliver a presentation and participate in a discussion on the following issues:

1. The recent world-wide developments of protecting geographical indications among the Member countries under the WTO mechanism.
2. The legislative history of the TRIPs' provisions in relation to geographical indications focusing on the conflicts and compromises between the European countries and the United States.
3. The WTO Member countries' domestic protection of the undisclosed information under the TRIPs.

Enforcement 11

Learning Objectives

This chapter is to help students understand:

1. Basic objectives of the provisions on enforcing protection of intellectual property rights under TRIPs;
2. Civil and administrative measures required to be available in respect of any activity infringing intellectual property rights covered in TRIPs;
3. Provisional measures to permit effective action against infringements and to include expeditious remedies under TRIPs;
4. Necessity to enforce the border measures for the proper protection of intellectual property rights;
5. Criminal procedures applied in cases of willful trade mark counterfeiting or copyright piracy on a commercial scale.

11.1 Coverage

TRIPs Agreement requires Member countries to create comprehensive and detailed enforcement mechanisms.[1] Procedural requirements cut even more deeply into national legal systems than substantial requirements because they dictate how a nation is courts and administration bodies shall behave.[2] The provisions[3] on enforcement have two basic objectives: one is to ensure that effective means of enforcement are available to right holders; the second is to ensure that enforcement

[1] Anawalt (2003, *supra* note 18, at 390).

[2] *Id.*

[3] These provisions are divided into five sections. The first section lays down general obligations that all enforcement procedures must meet. These are notably aimed at ensuring that they are effective and that certain basic principles of due process are met. The following sections deal with civil and administrative procedures and remedies, provisional measures, special requirements related to border measures and criminal procedures.

DOI 10.1007/978-3-642-31143-7_11,

procedures are applied in such a manner as to avoid the creation of barriers to legitimate trade and to provide for safeguards against their abuse.[4]

The Agreement makes a distinction between infringing activity in general, in respect of which civil judicial procedures and remedies must be available,[5] and counterfeiting and piracy[6] – the more blatant and egregious forms of infringing activity – in respect of which additional procedures and remedies must also be provided, namely border measures and criminal procedures. [7] For this purpose, counterfeit goods are in essence defined as goods involving slavish copying of trademarks, and pirated goods as goods which violate a reproduction right under copyright or a related right.[8]

11.2 General Obligations

Enforcement procedures must be such as to permit effective action[9] against any act of infringement of intellectual property rights, and the remedies available must be expeditious in order to prevent infringements and must constitute a deterrent to further infringements. On the other hand, enforcement procedures must be applied in such a manner as to avoid the creation of barriers to legitimate trade[10] and to provide for safeguards against their abuse.[11]

---

[4] TRIPs Agreement, *supra* note 22. Part III, Section 1, Art. 41.1.

[5] TRIPs Agreement, *supra* note 22. Part III, Section 2, 3.

[6] TRIPs Agreement, *supra* note 22. Part III, Section 3.

[7] In regard to such a distinction, the concept of minimum standards requires careful consideration in treating with the controversy regarding intellectual property issues between states: "Where consensus among nations is clean, as it is with respect to counterfeiting and piracy, best rules have emerged .... Where consensus has not emerged, however, minimum standards represent an agreement to disagree on the optimal level of protection. Imposing a level of protection that was not bargained for ... may, ..., promote trade and enrich current rights holders, but it may also work hardship on individual states. ... most worrisome was that high standards of protection could raise the costs of innovation and impede the creation of new knowledge" (Dreyfuss and Lowenfeld 1997, *supra* note 20, at 296).

[8] TRIPs Agreement, *supra* note 22. Art. 51. 14.

[9] TRIPs was the first WTO agreement to impose positive obligations on WTO signatories to adopt the new law; previously, WTO agreements had relied on negative prohibitions, not affirmative obligations (Schaffer et al. 1971, *supra* note 78, at 519).

[10] Regarding a country's ability to restrain trade, some provisions in the TRIPs Agreement and in the Berne Convention are assessed to be ambiguous. Such an example could be shown in the Art. 13 of the TRIPs Agreement providing, in regard to the copyright, that "members shall confine limitations or exceptions to exclusive rights to certain special cases which do not conflict with a normal exploitation of the work and do not unreasonably prejudice the legitimate interests of the right holder" (Cahn and Schimmel 1997, *supra* note 30, at 306).

[11] The TRIPs Agreement explicitly permits members to adopt appropriate measures to control abuse of intellectual property rights, TRIPs Agreement, *supra* note 22. Arts. 8(2), 40(2); and provides certain guidelines as to the form that those measures might take, TRIPs Agreement, *supra*

The following provisions are general principles to guarantee due process: enforcement procedures must be fair and equitable, and they may not be unnecessarily complicated or costly, or entail unreasonable time-limits or unwarranted delays. Decisions on the merits of a case shall preferably be in writing and reasoned, and they shall be made available at least to the parties to the proceeding without undue delay.[12] Decisions on the merits of a case shall be based only on evidence in respect of which parties were offered the opportunity to be heard.[13] The parties to a proceeding shall have an opportunity for review by judicial authority of final administrative decisions and of at least the legal aspects of initial judicial decisions on the merits of the case.[14] However, there is no obligation to provide an opportunity for review of acquittals in criminal cases.[15]

The provisions on enforcement do not create any obligation to put in place a judicial system for the enforcement of intellectual property rights distinct from that for the enforcement of law in general, nor does it affect the capacity of Members to enforce their law in general.[16] In addition, it is stated that nothing in these provisions creates any obligation with respect to the distribution of resources as between enforcement of intellectual property rights and the enforcement of law in general. However, a number of countries have found it helpful to establish special enforcement units that pool together required experience needed to effectively fight against counterfeiting and piracy. Moreover, some countries have centralized certain types of intellectual property issues in one or a limited number of courts in order to ensure the availability of necessary expertise.

---

note 22. Arts. 31, 40. Intellectual property law holds always risk-abuse of the market power created by exclusivity, which is generally sought to be controlled through the concept of intellectual property misuse and through invocation of competition or antitrust laws. The negotiators of the Uruguay Round, however, did not place competition law on their agenda except some statements adopted in the biennial meeting of the WTO at ministerial level (Dreyfuss and Lowenfeld 1997, *supra* note 20, at 286); See Abbott (1996, *supra* note 62, at 400); For example, Ministerial Conference in Singapore in 1996 agreed to establish a working group to study issue relating to the interaction between trade and competition policy.

WTO/Singapore Ministerial 1996_Ministerial Declaration. http://www.wto.org/english/thewto_e/minist_e/min96_e/wtodec_e.htm. Accessed Oct. 19, 2012. And Doha Declaration in 2001 instructed working group to focus on clarifying: "... and provision on "hardcore" cartels ...; ways of handling voluntary cooperation on competition policy among WTO member governments; support for progressive reinforcement of competition institution ..." WTO/Doha declaration. http://www.wto.org/english/tratop_e/dda_e/dohaexplained_e.htm. Accessed Oct. 19, 2012.

[12] TRIPs Agreement, *supra* note 22. Art. 41.2.

[13] TRIPs Agreement, *supra* note 22. Art. 41.3.

[14] This is subject to judicial provisions in a Members law concerning the importance of a case.

[15] TRIPs Agreement, *supra* note 22. Art. 41.4.

[16] TRIPs Agreement, *supra* note 22. Art. 41.5.

Another sign of a rough economy: Even cheaper knockoffs

By STEPHANIE CLIFFORD. August 6, 2010, 10:31 am

In this economy, even counterfeiters are trading down.

After years of knocking off luxury products like $2,800 Louis Vuitton handbags, criminals are discovering there is money to be made in faking the more ordinary—like $295 Kooba bags and $140 Ugg boots. In California, the authorities recently seized a shipment of counterfeit Angel Soft toilet paper.

The shift in the counterfeiting industry, which costs American businesses an estimated $200 billion a year, plays to recession-weary customers looking for downmarket deals, the authorities say. And it has been fueled in part by factories sitting idle in China. Almost 80 percent of the seized counterfeit goods in the United States last year were produced in China, where the downturn in legitimate exports during the recession left many factories looking for goods—in some cases, any goods—to produce.

"If there is demand, there will be supply," said John Spink, associate director of the Anti-Counterfeiting and Product Protection Program at Michigan State University. In China, he said, "It's all of a sudden them saying, 'We have low capacity. What can we make?'"

The answer is increasingly knockoffs of lesser-known brands, which are easy to sell on the Internet, can be priced higher than obvious fakes, and avoid the aggressive programs by the big luxury brands to protect their labels, retail companies and customs enforcement officials say.

The results: Faux Samantha Thavasa bags for $113 and Ed Hardy hoodie sweatshirts for $82.50. And, bizarrely, imitations that are more expensive than the real ones: In 2007, Anya Hind march sold canvas totes that said "I'm Not a Plastic Bag" for $15. Now fakes are available on the Web for $99.

"If it's making money over here in the U.S., it's going to be reverse-engineered or made overseas," said Jonathan Erece, a trade enforcement coordinator for U.S. Customs and Border Protection in Long Beach, Calif. "It's like a cat-and-mouse game."

……

The counterfeiters are also lifting photos and text from legitimate websites, further fooling some shoppers.

"The consumer is blind as to the source of the product," said Leah Evert-Burks, director of brand protection for Ugg Australia's parent company, the Deckers Outdoor Corporation. "Counterfeit websites go up pretty easily, and counterfeiters will copy our stock photos, the text of our website, so it will look and feel like" the company site, she said.

While all of it is illegal, the authorities do not publish statistics on what brands' products are being counterfeited. But designers and trade experts said the down-market trend in counterfeiting became more noticeable over the last year, as counterfeiters got more inventive. The field is big: The total value of counterfeit goods seized by U.S. customs officials increased by more than 25 percent each year from 2005 to 2008, using the government's fiscal calendar. In fiscal 2009, as imports overall dropped by 25 percent, the value of counterfeit products seized dropped by only 4 percent to $260.7 million.

The official statistics capture only a piece of the problem, companies and experts say, because so many counterfeiters market directly to customers on the Internet and many of those sales go undetected by the authorities.

"Online is much harder" to patrol and enforce, said Todd Kahn, general counsel for Coach, the handbag and accessories company.

That is particularly true for smaller brands, as Anna Corinna Sellinger, co-founder and creative director of the New York clothing and accessories company Foley & Corinna, learned.

A couple of years ago, she began checking out which Foley & Corinna items were selling on eBay. Her city tote, which now retails for $485, was a popular item, but on some listings "there was something off—it's a color I never did, or a leather I never did," she said.

As other sites proliferated, and Corinna Sellinger noticed more and more Internet fakes, she stopped looking altogether.

……

Source: Another sign of a rough economy: Even cheaper knockoffs. Stephanie Clifford. 6 August 2010. http://www.mb.com.ph/articles/270958/another-sign-a-rough-economy-even-cheaper-knockoffs

DTI on anti-piracy campaign

Aug 12, 2010 5:26 PM | By Sapa

The department of trade and industry said it will launch an anti-piracy campaign next month to protect artists' copyright to their work and a commission to investigate wrongdoing by royalty collecting societies. Deputy Minister Thandi Tobias-Pokolo said the commission will be headed by a judge, but declined to give further information on its composition, powers or life span.

She said both the campaign and the commission were a response to complaints from artists about piracy, incorrect distribution of royalties and a lack of government support. Problems surrounding royalties were "blamed as a cause leading to artists dying poor," she told a media briefing in Cape Town. Tobias-Pokolo said the campaign would also serve to educate artists to protect their rights and not to sign these away for "20 or 40 years" and then take the law into their own hands by confiscating counterfeit products from street vendors.

(continued)

> "We want to avoid artists taking the law into their own hands and losing."
> She said five government departments would be involved in the campaign, including the police and communications, which will be asked to look into artists' complaints of not being paid their dues by the SABC.
>
> Source: DTI on anti-piracy campaign. Aug. 12, 2010. http://www.timeslive.co.za/entertainment/article599120.ece/DTI-on-anti-piracy-campaign

11.3 Civil and Administrative Measures

Civil judicial procedures are required to be available in respect of any activity infringing intellectual property rights covered by the Agreement. With regard to due process, defendants are entitled to written notice which is timely and contains sufficient details of the claims. Parties must be allowed to be represented by independent legal counsel, and procedures may not impose overly burdensome requirements concerning mandatory personal appearances.[17] All parties are entitled to substantiate their claims and to present all relevant evidence, while confidential information must be identified and protected.

Regarding rules on evidence, in a situation where evidence that is likely to be important for one party is in the possession of the opposing party, the court must be empowered, provided that certain conditions are met, to order the latter party to produce that evidence. In addition, courts may be authorized to make their decisions on the basis of information presented to them, if a party refuses without good reason access to evidence that is in his or her possession, subject to providing the parties an opportunity to be heard.[18]

It is provided on injunctions, damages and other remedies.

Regarding injunctions, the courts are required to be empowered to order injunctions, i.e. to order a party to desist from infringements, including the possibility to prevent imported infringing goods from entering into domestic distribution channels,[19] except the case where a person has acted in good faith.[20]

Regarding damages, the courts are required to be empowered to order an infringer, at least if he or she acted in bad faith, to pay the right holder adequate damages.[21] They must also be authorized to order the infringer to pay the right

[17] TRIPs Agreement, *supra* note 22. Art. 42.

[18] TRIPs Agreement, *supra* note 22. Art. 43.

[19] TRIPS Agreement, *supra* note 22. Art. 50(1). This article obliges states to allow local judiciaries to order "provisional measures" even without a prior hearing of the alleged infringers, but there is no firm obligation to exercise this power in practice. Moreover, judicial application of the "irreparable harm" test frequently results in the denial of preliminary injunctions even in developed countries, which further weakens the thrust of these provisions. See (*id.* Art. 50(2)).

[20] TRIPs Agreement, *supra* note 22. Art. 44.

[21] TRIPs Agreement, *supra* note 22. Art. 45.1.

holder's expenses. These expenses may include appropriate attorney's fees. In appropriate cases, the courts may be authorized to order recovery of profits and/or payment of pre-established damages even where the infringer acted in good faith.[22]

Regarding other remedies,[23] in order to create an effective deterrent to infringement, it is required that the judicial authorities must have the authority to order infringing goods to be disposed of outside the channels of commerce, or, where constitutionally possible, destroyed.[24] Similarly, it must be possible to dispose of materials and instruments predominantly used in the production of the infringing goods. In considering such requests, the courts must take into account proportionality between the seriousness of the infringement and the remedies ordered as well as the interests of third parties. In respect of counterfeit trademark goods, it is clarified that the simple removal of the trademark unlawfully affixed shall not be sufficient, other than in exceptional cases, to permit release of the goods into the channels of commerce.[25]

Judicial authorities may be authorized to order the infringer to inform the right holder of the identity of third persons involved in the production and distribution of the infringing goods or services and of their channels of distribution.[26] This option is aimed at assisting the right holders to find the source of infringing goods and to take appropriate action against other persons in the distribution channels. This provision must be applied in a way that is in proportion to the seriousness of the infringement.

Certain safeguards are provisioned against abuse of enforcement procedures. It is required that the judicial authorities must have the authority to order the applicant who has abused enforcement procedures to pay an adequate compensation to the defendant who has been wrongfully enjoined or restrained to cover both the injury suffered and expenses. Such expenses may include appropriate attorney's fees.[27] Public authorities and officials are exempted from liability to appropriate remedial measures only where actions are taken or intended in good faith in the course of the administration of that law.[28]

---

[22] TRIPs Agreement, *supra* note 22. Art. 45.2.

[23] *Id.* Art. 44. Regarding remedies in general, the TRIPS provisions require that states empower local judicial authorities to order compensatory damages, expenses, and attorney's fees and, in "appropriate cases," lost profits or liquidated damages (*id.* Art. 45). Courts must likewise have authority to impound or destroy infringing goods or equipment likely to contribute to the production of infringing goods, and they must not normally release counterfeit trademarked goods into the stream of commerce even after removal of the offending marks. See (*id.* Art. 46) (disallowing compensation for such acts). However, the local authorities may require claimant to indemnify parties who are wrongly or abusively subjected to any of the procedures mentioned above (*id.* Art. 48, cited by Reichman 2000, *supra* note 35, fn. 28).

[24] TRIPs Agreement, *supra* note 22. Art. 46.

[25] *Id.*

[26] TRIPs Agreement, *supra* note 22. Art. 47.

[27] TRIPs Agreement, *supra* note 22. Art. 48.

[28] *Id.*

US Report on protection of Intellectual Property Rights in Asia

Russia will remain on the Priority Watch List in 2010. While Russia has made some progress over the past several years in improving IPR protection and enforcement, concerns remain, particularly with respect to Russia's continued failure to implement fully its commitments in the November 2006 Bilateral Agreement on Protection and Enforcement of Intellectual Property Rights ("IPR Bilateral Agreement").

In the IPR Bilateral Agreement, Russia committed to fight optical disc and Internet piracy, enact legislation to protect against unfair commercial use of undisclosed test or other data generated to obtain marketing approval for pharmaceutical products, deter piracy and counterfeiting through enhanced criminal penalties, strengthen border enforcement, and conform its laws to international IPR norms. Russia's continued delays in fully implementing this Agreement are particularly troubling, since, with respect to several of the obligations, the IPR Bilateral Agreement established an agreed-upon deadline of June 1, 2007. While the amendments to the Civil Code and Customs Code have been introduced into the Duma they have not yet become law. Amendments to the Law on Medicines were enacted in 2010; they did not implement the provisions of the IPR Bilateral Agreement on protection of pharmaceutical test data.

The United States urges Russia to strengthen its enforcement efforts against piracy and counterfeiting, which remain major concerns. The U.S. copyright industries report significant losses due to copyright infringement, especially through online piracy, which has continued to grow. Despite the closing of some illegal websites offering pirated music, many more have sprung up in their place. In 2009, Russian law enforcement agencies conducted raids on optical disc production facilities suspected of engaging in pirate activities; however, many surprise raids are minimally effective because the date and time of pending raids is often leaked to the optical disc plant in advance. While the level of cooperation among Russian agencies in optical disc raids is increasing, the quality of raids, and the level of police expertise, is uneven nationwide. A number of factors limit the effectiveness of raids, including the monetary damages threshold required to initiate criminal actions, and the general reluctance of prosecutors to initiate criminal cases in the field of IPR, even when there is evidence of a violation of criminal code provisions.

……

Source: US Report on protection of Intellectual Property Rights in Asia. United States Trade Representative, Special 301 Report 2010. at 23–24

11.4 Provisional Measures

Regarding prompt and effective provisional measures, enforcement procedures are required to permit effective action against infringements and to include expeditious remedies.[29] As these judicial procedures may take a fair amount of time, it is necessary for the judicial authorities to have the authority to order prompt and effective provisional measures in order to stop an alleged infringement immediately.[30] Regarding provisional measures, it requires each country to ensure that its judicial authorities have the authority to order prompt and effective provisional measures.[31] Such measures must be available in respect of any intellectual property right.[32]

Provisional measures have to be available in two situations: One is where they are needed to prevent an infringement from occurring and to prevent infringing goods from entering into the channels of commerce.[33] This includes preventing imported infringing goods from being dispersed into domestic distribution channels immediately after customs clearance; the other situation is where such measures are needed to preserve relevant evidence in regard to the alleged infringement.[34]

Effective use of provisional measures may require that action be taken without giving prior notice to the other side. Therefore, the judicial authorities must have the authority to adopt provisional measures inaudita altera parte, i.e. without prior hearing of the other side, where appropriate, in particular where any delay is likely to cause irreparable harm to the right holder, or where there is a demonstrable risk of evidence being destroyed.[35] Where provisional measures have been adopted inaudita altera parte, the parties affected must be given notice, without delay after the execution of the measures at the latest. The defendant has a right to review with a view to deciding, within a reasonable period after the notification of the measures, whether these measures shall be modified, revoked or confirmed.[36]

Regarding safeguard against abuse the provisions on provisional measures contain certain safeguards against abuse of such measures. The judicial authority may require the applicant to provide a security or equivalent assurance sufficient to protect the defendant and to prevent abuse.[37] Provisional measures shall, upon request by the defendant, be revoked or otherwise cease to have effect, if the applicant fails to initiate proceedings leading to a decision on the merits of the

---

[29] TRIPs Agreement, *supra* note 22. Art. 41.1.

[30] TRIPs Agreement, *supra* note 22. Art. 41.2.

[31] TRIPs Agreement, *supra* note 22. Art. 50.

[32] TRIPs Agreement, *supra* note 22. Art. 50.1

[33] TRIPs Agreement, *supra* note 22. Art. 44(1).

[34] TRIPs Agreement, *supra* note 22. Art. 50(1).

[35] TRIPs Agreement, *supra* note 22. Art. 50.2.

[36] TRIPs Agreement, *supra* note 22. Art. 50.4.

[37] TRIPs Agreement, *supra* note 22. Art. 50.3.

case within a reasonable period to be determined by the judicial authority ordering the measures.[38]

11.5 Border Measures

The emphasis in the enforcement part of the TRIPs Agreement is on internal enforcement mechanisms, which, if effective, would enable infringing activity to be stopped at source, the point of production. Where possible, this is both a more effective way of enforcing IPRs and less liable to give rise to risks of discrimination against imports than special border measures. However, the Agreement recognizes that such enforcement at source will not always be possible and that in any event not all countries are WTO Members, and therefore bound by the TRIPs Agreement.

Members are required by provisional measures to adopt administrative or judicial procedures which afford, rights-holders the opportunity to stop the importation of infringing goods at the border through customs action.[39] The special requirements related to border measures are provided.[40] Thus, the imposition of order controls against imports of counterfeit goods operates as "a safety net in the event that enforcement at the source has not taken place".[41]

The goods subject to border enforcement procedures must include at least counterfeit trademark and pirated copyright goods that are being presented for importation,[42] leaving flexibility to Member governments on whether to include imports of goods which involve other infringements of IPRs.[43,44] Under these provisions, rights holders may take legal action to compel the domestic customs authorities to suspend the release of imported goods into free circulation whenever the complainants have valid grounds for suspecting that the items in question are "counterfeit trademark or pirated copyright goods."[45]

---

[38] TRIPs Agreement, *supra* note 22. Art. 50.6.

[39] TRIPs Agreement, *supra* note 22. Part III, Section 3.

[40] TRIPs Agreement, *supra* note 22. Part III, Section 4.

[41] Reichman (1997, p. 343).

[42] TRIPs Agreement, *supra* note 22. Art. 51, For this purpose, "counterfeit trade mark goods" are defined as goods or packaging that bear unauthorized trademarks identical or similar to registered marks for such goods; and "pirated copyright goods" are defined as "unauthorized direct copies of protected Article the making of which would have infringed either copyright law or related rights laws in the country of importation"(*id.*, Art. 51, n. 14). The seizure provisions would thus apply to sound recordings protected only under a neighboring rights law, as well as to more traditional literary and artistic works (*id.*; see also *id.*, Arts. 12, 14; Reichman 1997, *supra* note 15, at 368–370). (discussing coverage of neighboring rights in TRIPS Agreement)

[43] TRIPs Agreement, *supra* note 22. Art. 51.

[44] This provision is one example of international minimum standards of protection to be provided in TRIPs Agreement.

[45] TRIPS Agreement, *supra* note 22. Art.51. For this purpose, "counterfeit trademark goods" are defined as goods or packaging that bear unauthorized trademarks identical or similar to registered

The basic procedure enables a right holder who believes that the prohibited importation may occur to "file an application in writing with a competent authority, providing adequate prima facie evidence and a sufficiently detailed description of the goods."[46] This border measures mechanism could become the most promising feature of the TRIPs enforcement exercise, provided that states implement them in a genuinely nondiscriminatory fashion and do not erect disguised barriers to trade.[47]

Trademark's Customs Recordal is applicable now in Sudan

KHARTOUM - Abu-Ghazaleh Intellectual Property (AGIP) announced in a press release that the record for trademarks is now applicable at the Directorate General of Customs in Sudan.

In accordance with Article 22 of the Regulation of Procedure of the Customs Borders Measures for the Protection of Intellectual Property Rights, the rights owner may deposit with the Customs Directorate the documents proving his/her ownership of the said rights in order to protect them at the Customs stations for fee to be specified by the financial regulations, however well-known trademarks will be automatically protected.

The Customs Directorate will prepare a register with serial numbers of the applications including the addresses of the owners of the IP rights and their legal representatives and issue a circular of the registered applications to all customs stations.

Moreover, if the IPRs owner has sufficient evidence of the process of importing goods that constitute an infringement to his/her own rights, the owner may submit an application to the Customs Directorate for suspension of Customs clearance procedure, enclosing the following documents:

1. A copy of the registration certificate approved by the concerned authorities.
2. A copy of the Power of Attorney if the applicant is recipient agent.
3. An illustrative picture of the counterfeit good/s.
4. An illustrative picture of the original product/s.
5. A copy of the original product model and the counterfeit one.

(continued)

marks for such goods; and "pirated copyright goods" are defined as "unauthorized direct copies of protected Article the making of which would have infringed either copyright law or related rights laws in the country of importation" (*id.*, Art. 51 n. 14). The seizure provisions would thus apply to sound recordings protected only under a neighboring rights law as well as to more traditional literary and artistic works (*id.*; see also *id.*, Arts. 12, 14; Reichman 1997, *supra* note 15, at 342).

[46] Otten and Wager (1996, *supra* note 57, at 405–406). Remedies may include destruction or disposal in a manner that avoids harm to the right holder; and the re-exportation of counterfeit goods is prohibited in principle. See TRIPS Agreement, *supra* note 1, art. 59; Otten and Wager (1996, *id.*, at 406).

[47] See, e.g., Kastenmeier and Beier (1989, pp. 285–298); Reichman (1989, pp. 829–839). (Discussing Anti-Counterfeiting Code first proposed, but not adopted, toward the end of the Tokyo Round of GATT negotiations) cited by Reichman (1989), *supra* note 15, at 342.

The Sudanese Directorate General of Customs has not yet specified official fees for trademark's record.

Source: Trademark's Customs Recordal Is Applicable Now in Sudan. Aug. 10, 2010. http://www.ag-ip-news.com/GetArticle.asp?Art_ID=8411&lang=en

Members are also free to determine whether to apply these procedures to parallel imports: It is understood that there shall be no obligation to apply such procedures to imports of goods put on the market in another country by or with the consent of the right holder.[48] Members may exclude from the application of these procedures de minims imports, i.e. small quantities of goods of a non-commercial nature contained in travelers' personal luggage or sent in small consignments.[49] Members are free to decide whether to apply corresponding procedures to the suspension by customs authorities of infringing goods destined for exportation from their territories, or to goods in transit.[50]

Regarding competent authority, the basic mechanism required by the Agreement is that each Member must designate a "competent authority" for the efficient enforcement of border measures, which could be administrative or judicial in nature, to which applications by right holders for customs action shall be lodged.[51] The right holder lodging an application to the competent authority shall be required to provide adequate evidence of a prima facie infringement of his IPR and to supply a sufficiently detailed description of the goods to make them readily recognizable by the customs authorities.

The competent authorities shall then inform the applicant whether the application has been accepted and, if so, for what period, and give the necessary directions to customs officers.[52] After this, it is the responsibility of the applicant to initiate proceedings leading to a decision on the merits of the case. The Agreement requires a system to be put in place under which action will be taken on the basis of an application from a right holder, but leaves it to determine whether they require competent authorities to act upon their own initiative.

Regarding safeguards against abuse, the provisions on border measures require the taking of what are essentially provisional measures against imports of infringing goods. The competent authority may require the applicant to provide a security or equivalent assurance sufficient to protect the defendant and the competent

[48] TRIPs Agreement, *supra* note 22. Art. 51, Footnote 13.

[49] TRIPs Agreement, *supra* note 22. Art. 50.

[50] TRIPs Agreement, *supra* note 22. Art. 51.

[51] *Id.*

[52] TRIPs Agreement, *supra* note 22. Art. 52.

[53] TRIPs Agreement, *supra* note 22. Art. 53.1.

[54] TRIPs Agreement, *supra* note 22. Art. 54.

authorities and to prevent abuse. However, such security or equivalent assurance may not be such as to unreasonably deter recourse to these procedures.[53] The importer and the applicant must be promptly notified of the detention of goods,[54] and if the right holder fails to initiate proceedings leading to a decision on the merits of a case within ten working days, the goods shall normally be released.[55] Where goods involve the alleged infringement of industrial designs, patents, layout-designs or undisclosed information, the importer must be entitled to obtain their release on the posting of a security sufficient to protect the right holder from any infringement, even if proceedings leading to the decision on the merits have been initiated.[56]

Once judicial proceedings on the merits of a case have been initiated, the judicial authority may continue the suspension of the release of goods in accordance with a provisional judicial measure. The applicant may be required to pay appropriate compensation to persons whose interests have been adversely affected by the wrongful detention of goods or through detention of goods released pursuant to the failure of the applicant to initiate in time proceedings leading to a decision on the merits of the case.[57]

In regard to remedies, the competent authorities must have the power to order the destruction or disposal outside the channels of commerce of infringing goods in such a manner as to avoid any harm to the right holder. In regard to counterfeit trademark goods, the authorities may not allow the re-exportation of the infringing goods in an unaltered state or subject them to a different customs procedure, other than in exceptional circumstances. These remedies are without prejudice to other rights of action open to the right holder, such as to obtain damages through civil litigation, and are also subject to the right of the defendant to seek review by a judicial authority.[58]

Officials incinerate fake drugs

Tuesday, August 10, 2010

Kim Yuthana and Tep Nimol

A police officer inspects a pile of counterfeit pharmaceuticals yesterday before officials destroyed the haul by setting it on fire. Police yesterday destroyed about 19 tons of fake pharmaceutical drugs confiscated from city pharmacies and drug smugglers, officials said. Mok Chito, director of the Interior Ministry's criminal police, said expired drugs and chemical-laced

(continued)

---

[53] TRIPs Agreement, *supra* note 22. Art. 53.1.

[54] TRIPs Agreement, *supra* note 22. Art. 54.

[55] TRIPs Agreement, *supra* note 22. Art. 55.

[56] TRIPs Agreement, *supra* note 22. Art.53.2.

[57] TRIPs Agreement, *supra* note 22. Art.56.

[58] TRIPs Agreement, *supra* note 22. Art.59.

foods were also burned during a blaze at the Choeung Ek dumpsite yesterday morning.

"These fake drugs are very dangerous to people's health if they are circulated at markets," he said. "We have collected them since March this year in order to burn them."

He said most of the drugs had been smuggled into Cambodia from China and called for all users of medicines to be careful. The destruction of the drugs came as Ke Kim Yan, chairman of the National Authority for Combating Drugs, led a 22-member delegation to Vietnam in an effort to strengthen the cooperation between the two countries' anti-drug authorities.

"The official visit ... was made in an attempt to strengthen bilateral cooperation on the issue of illegal drugs, and to exchange experience between the two countries," said Neak Yuthea, director of the ministry's Department of Legislation, Education and Rehabilitation.

Figures released by the NACD last week showed that the number of drug users in the Kingdom had fallen to 5,700 this year, representing a drop of 300 users from 2009 figures.

Neak Yuthea said the dip was the result of the migration of some drug users, coupled with a growing awareness of the dangers of illegal drug use.

Source: Officials incinerate fake drugs. Kim Yuthana, and Tep Nimol. August 10, 2010. http://www.phnompenhpost.com/index.php/2010081041123/National-news/officials-incinerate-fake-drugs.html

11.6 Criminal Procedures

Criminal procedures should be applied at least in cases of willful trademark counterfeiting or copyright piracy on a commercial scale.[59] The Agreement leaves it to Members to decide whether to provide for criminal procedures and penalties to be applied in other cases of infringement of intellectual property rights, in particular where they are committed willfully and on a commercial scale.[60]

Sanctions must include imprisonment and/or monetary fines sufficient to provide a deterrent, consistent with the level of penalties applied for crimes of a corresponding gravity. Criminal remedies in appropriate cases must also include seizure, forfeiture and destruction of the infringing goods and of materials and instruments used to produce them.[61]

Conclusively speaking, the enforcement provisions of the TRIPs Agreement have been drafted in terms of broad legal standards rather than as narrow rules.

[59] TRIPs Agreement, *supra* note 22. Art.61.

[60] *Id.*

[61] *Id.*

Their very ambiguity, which some have criticized,[62] allows either the Council for TRIPs or duly appointed dispute-settlement panels to take local circumstances and diverse legal philosophies into account when seeking to mediate actual or potential conflicts between states.[63] Under the broad safeguard provisions of article 41(5), moreover, disgruntled foreign rights holders cannot complain about levels of judicial or administrative inefficiency deriving primarily from the poorer countries' lack of resources unless they can also muster convincing evidence of discrimination.[64]

Counterfeiting and Piracy against which Criminal Procedures are applied

Counterfeiting has evolved in recent years from a localized industry concentrated on copying high-end designer goods to a sophisticated global business involving the mass production and sale of a vast array of fake goods, including items such as counterfeit medicines, health care products, food and beverages, automobile and airplane parts, toothpaste, shampoos, razors, electronics, batteries, chemicals, and sporting goods.

Counterfeiting and piracy affects the profits of legitimate producers and impacts consumers whose lives and safety are at risk when they purchase fake goods. It also damages the economies of the countries in which it occurs by decreasing tax revenue and deterring investment. Counterfeiters and pirates generally pay no taxes or duties, and they often disregard basic standards for worker health and safety and product quality and performance.

……

Stronger and more effective criminal and border enforcement is required to stop the manufacture, import, export, transit, and distribution of pirated and counterfeit goods. Through bilateral consultations, FTAs, and international organizations, USTR (that is, the Office of the United States Trade Representative) is working to ensure that penalties have deterrent effects, and that penalties include significant monetary fines and meaningful sentences of imprisonment. Additionally, important elements of a deterrent enforcement

(continued)

[62] See, e.g., Dreier (1996, pp. 259–261, 272–273).(Criticizing preference for flexible standards over formal rules in general and the watered down language of art. 41(1) which was changed from a requirement to "provide effective procedures" to that of providing procedures that "permit effective action" in particular), cited by Reichman (1997, *supra* note 15, at 344).

[63] See Otten and Wager (1996, *supra* note 57, at 403). ("These provisions aim to recognize basic differences between national legal system, while being sufficiently precise to provide for effective enforcement action as well as safeguards against abuse in the use of enforcement procedures."); see also Gana (1996, *supra* note 36, at 770–771).(stressing alien and conflicting values of some developing countries in regard to enforcement procedures) cited by Reichman (*supra* note 15, at 344).

[64] See TRIPS Agreement, *supra* note 22. Art. 41(5), cited by Reichman (*id*).

system include requirements that pirated and counterfeit goods – as well as materials and implements used for their production – are seized and destroyed.

The manufacture and distribution of pharmaceutical products bearing counterfeit trademarks is a growing problem that has important consequences for consumer health and safety. Such trademark counterfeiting is one dimension of the larger problem of substandard medicines. The United States notes its particular concern with the proliferation of the manufacture, sale, and distribution of counterfeit pharmaceuticals in countries such as Brazil, China, India, Indonesia, and Russia.

Source: Counterfeiting and Piracy against which criminal procedures are applied. United States Trade Representative, 2010 Special 301 Report, pp.9 ~ 11

11.7 Institutional Provisions

11.7.1 Council for TRIPs

The Council for TRIPs, open to all Members of the WTO, is the body responsible for the administration of the Agreement and in particular for monitoring the operation of the Agreement. One of the key mechanisms for monitoring is the examination of each Member's national implementing legislation by the other Members. Members are required to notify the laws and regulations made effective by that Member pertaining to the subject-matter of the Agreement to the Council for TRIPs, in order to assist the Council in its review of the operation of the Agreement.[65]

The WTO constitutes a forum for further negotiations aimed at enhanced commitments in the area of intellectual property, as in other areas covered by the WTO Agreement. Certain specific areas of further work are called for in the text of the TRIPs Agreement. These areas include: the negotiation of a multilateral system of notification and registration for geographical indications for wines[66]; the review, after four years, of the option to exclude from patentability certain plant and animal inventions[67]; and the examination of the applicability to TRIPs of non-violation complaints under the dispute settlement process.

[65] TRIPs Agreement, *supra* note 22. Art. 63.2.

[66] TRIPs Agreement, *supra* note 22. Art. 23.

[67] TRIPs Agreement, *supra* note 22. Art. 27.3(b).

11.7.2 Notification

The TRIPs Agreement obliges the WTO Members to make certain notification to the Council for TRIPs.[68] These notifications facilitate the Council's work of monitoring the operation of the Agreement and promote the transparency of Members' policies on intellectual property protection. In addition, Members wishing to avail themselves of certain flexibility provided in the Agreement that relate to the substantive obligations have to notify the Council.[69]

Members are required to notify the laws and regulations on the subject-matter of the Agreement (the availability, scope, acquisition, enforcement and prevention of the abuse of intellectual property rights) by which they give effect to the Agreement's provisions.[70] Laws and regulations should be notified promptly as of the time that the corresponding substantive TRIPs obligation starts to apply. Given the difficulty of examining legislation relevant to many of the enforcement obligations in the TRIPs Agreement, Members have undertaken, in addition to notifying legislative texts, to provide information on how they are meeting these obligations by responding to a checklist of questions.

Members are allowed to avail themselves of certain options in regard to the definition of beneficiary persons and national treatment, provided that notifications are made to the Council for TRIPs.[71] Members are required to establish and notify contact points in their administrations for the purposes of cooperation with each other aimed at the elimination of trade in infringing goods.[72]

---

[68] TRIPs Agreement, *supra* note 22. Art.63.2.

[69] International trade rules are usually enforced under either centralized or decentralized models. See Fried, (1994, p. 20) (contrasting decentralized model of the North American Free Trade Agreement (NAFTA) and the U.S.-Canada Free Trade Agreement (FTA), which rely on the judicial systems of member states, with centralized model of the European Union, which relies increasingly on a new, supra-national enforcement structure). The TRIPS component of the WTO Agreement combines features of both approaches. As explained in the text, it relies primarily on the decentralized legal and administrative machinery of the member states' domestic laws, which must implement the minimum standards governing enforcement of international intellectual property rights prescribed by part III of the TRIPS Agreement ("Enforcement of Intellectual Property Rights"). At the same time, the Council for TRIPS monitors compliance at the international level and provides an open forum for persuasion and mediation that falls short of formal litigation between states. See TRIPS Agreement, *supra* note 22, Arts. 63(2), 68 (empowering Council for TRIPS to monitor compliance with both enforcement procedures and substantive standards of protection); Otten and Wager (1996, *supra* note 57, at 409–411) (stressing Council for TRIPS' role in monitoring implementation and compliance as a defining characteristic of the trade-based approach); see also Dreyfuss and Lowenfeld (1997, *supra* note 20, at 284–285). (Stressing rule of periodic reviews by Council for TRIPS as substituting for unilateral policy review by trade ministries of developed countries).

[70] TRIPs Agreement, *supra* note 22. Art. 63.2.

[71] TRIPs Agreement, *supra* note 22. Art. 1.3, and 3.1.

[72] TRIPs Agreement, *supra* note 22. Art. 69.

WTO Dispute Settlements in relation with Intellectual Property Rights

In April 2007, the United States requested WTO dispute settlement consultations with China over deficiencies in China's legal regime for protecting and enforcing copyrights and trademarks on a wide range of products. After those consultations failed to resolve the matter, the United States requested the establishment of a WTO panel. A WTO panel was established to examine this. The WTO Dispute Settlement Body ("DSB") adopted a panel report ruling in favor of the United States that found (1) China's denial of copyright protection to works that do not meet China's content review standards is impermissible under the TRIPs Agreement; and (2) China's Customs rules cannot allow seized counterfeit goods to be publicly auctioned after only removing the infringing mark. With respect to the third claim concerning China's thresholds for criminal prosecution and conviction of counterfeiting and piracy, while the United States prevailed on the interpretation of the important legal standards in Article 61 of the TRIPs Agreement, including the finding that criminal enforcement measures must reflect and respond to the realities of the commercial marketplace, the panel found that it needed additional evidence before it could uphold the overall U.S. claim that China's criminal thresholds are too high. China notified the DSB that China intended to implement the recommendations and rulings of the DSB in this dispute, and stated it would need a reasonable period of time for implementation. On June 29, 2009, the United States and China notified the DSB that they had agreed on a one-year period of time for implementation. The United States is working with China on its implementation of the DSB recommendations and rulings in this dispute.

Following the 1999 Special 301 review, the United States initiated dispute settlement consultations concerning the European Union's (EU) regulation on food-related geographical indications (GIs), which appeared to discriminate against foreign products and persons – notably by requiring that EU trading partners adopt an "EU-style" system of GI protection – and appeared to provide insufficient protections to trademark owners. The DSB adopted a panel report ruling in favor of the United States that the EU GI regulation is inconsistent with the EU's obligations under the TRIPs Agreement and the General Agreement on Tariffs and Trade 1994. On March 31, 2006, the EU published a revised GI Regulation that is intended to comply with the DSB recommendations and rulings. There remain some concerns, however, with respect to this revised GI Regulation, which the United States has asked the EU to address, and the United States intends to continue monitoring this situation.

Source: WTO Dispute Settlements in relation with Intellectual Property Rights United States Trade Representative 2010 Special 301 Report. pp. 16–17

11.7.3 Cooperation with WIPO

To facilitate the implementation of the TRIPs Agreement, the WTO concluded with WIPO an agreement on cooperation between the two organizations. As explicitly set out in the Preamble to the TRIPs Agreement, the WTO aims to establish a mutually supportive relationship with WIPO. The Agreement provides for cooperation in three main areas, namely notification of, access to and translation of national laws and regulations; implementation of procedures for the protection of national emblems; and technical cooperation.

The cooperation agreement provides that the International Bureau of WIPO and the WTO Secretariat shall enhance cooperation in their legal-technical assistance and technical cooperation activities relating to the TRIPs Agreement for developing countries, so as to maximize the usefulness of those activities and ensure their mutually supportive nature. The assistance they make available to the members of their own organization will be made available also to the members of the other organization. The General Assembly of WIPO has also agreed that the International Bureau should make arrangements so as to be able to respond to requests from developing countries for WIPO legal and technical assistance relating to the TRIPs Agreement, and that it should expand the coverage of the TRIPs Agreement in existing WIPO development cooperation activities.

Assignment

To ensure students become equipped with the capability to apply knowledge from the classroom to the field, students are, in this chapter, required to write a report, deliver a presentation and participate in a discussion on the following issues:

1. Improper enforcement of the protection of intellectual property rights in Member countries which would be in breach of the TRIPs Agreement, considering the Estimates of the Trade Barriers of the US Counterpart Countries presented by the US International Trade Representative.
2. US, Australia vs. EC-Geographic Indication case focusing on the availability of protection and improper enforcement of IPR protection.

References

Abbott FM (1996) The new global technology regime: the WTO TRIPs agreement and global economic development. Chicago-Kent Law Rev 72

Abbott FM (1997) WTO dispute settlement and the agreement on trade-related aspects of intellectual property rights, in international trade law and the GATT-WTO dispute settlement system. Kluwer Law International

Abbott FM (1997) The future of the multilateral trading system in the context of TRIPS. Hastings Int'l Comp Law Rev 20

Abbott FM (1998) The enduring enigma of TRIPs: a challenge for the world economic system. J Int'l Econ Law
Aberto C (1989) The economics of intellectual property rights and the GATT: a view from the south. Vanderbilt J Transnat'l Law 22
Anawalt HC (2003) International intellectual property, progress, and the rule of law. Santa Clara Computer & High Tech Law J 19
Bhala R, Gantz DA (2003) Intellectual property and trademarks rights. Arizona J Int'l Comp Law 20
Braga CAP (1995) Trade-related intellectual property issue: the Uruguay round agreement and its economic implications, in the Uruguay round and the developing countries
Braga CAP and Fink C (1998) The relationship between intellectual property rights and foreign direct investment. Duke J Comp & Int'l Law 9
Cahn S, Schimmel D (1997) The cultural exception: does it exist in GATT and GATS frameworks? how does it affect or is it affected by the agreement on TRIPs? Cardozo Arts & Ent Law J 15
Correa CM (2002) Public health and international laws: unfair competition under the TRIPs greement: protection of data submitted for the registration of pharmaceuticals. Chicago J Int'l Law
Croome J (1995) Reshaping the world trading system: a history of the Uruguay round. The World Trade Organization, Geneva, p. 130
Curci FX (2002) Symposium: transnational business law in the twenty-first century: protecting your intellectual property rights overseas. Transnat'l Law 15
Divney JA, Connell GJ (1994) Intellectual property provisions of the GATT. University of Colorado Law Rev 23
Doane ML (1994) TRIPS and international intellectual property protection in an age of advancing technology. American University J Int'l Law & Policy 9
Drahos P, Braithwaite J (2002) Proceedings of the 2002 conference access to medicines in the developing world: international facilitation or hindrance? Wisconsin Int'l Law J 20
Dreier T (1996) TRIPS and the enforcement of intellectual property rights, in from GATT to TRIPS-the agreement on trade-related aspects of intellectual property rights. In: Beier F-K and Schricker G (eds.) John Wiley & Sons Ltd.
Dreyfuss RC, Lowenfeld AF (1997) Two achievement of the Uruguay round: putting TRIPs and dispute settlement together. Virginia J Int'l Law 37
Farkas LP (1996) Trade-related aspects of intellectual property, in world trade organization, the multilateral framework for the 21st century and U.S. implementing legislation. In: Stewart TP (ed) ABA Section of International Law and Practice
Folsom RH et al. (1995) International business transactions, Sweet & Maxwell
Fried JT (1994) Two paradigms for the rule of international trade las. United States Law J 39
Gana R (1996) Prospects for developing countries under the TRIPs agreement. Vanderbilt J Transnat'l Law 29
Garcia G (2000) Economic development and the course of intellectual property protection in Mexico. Int'l Law J 27
Geller PE (1995) Intellectual property in the global marketplace: impact of TRIPs dispute settlement? Int'l Law 29
Hill E (1990) U.S. addresses contentious issues in negotiation on trade-related aspects of intellectual property rights. Business America 18
Hoekman B, Kosteck M (1995) The political economy of the world trading system: from GATT to WTO. Oxford University Press, Oxford
Holwick S (1999) Trade and the environment: developing nations and the agreement on trade-related aspects of intellectual property rights. Colorado J Int'l: Environ Law & Policy
Karjala D, Sugiyama K (1988) Fundamental concept of Japanese and American copyright law. America J Comp Law 36

Kastenmeier RW, Beier D (1989) International trade and intellectual property: promise, risks and reality. Vanderbilt J Transnat'l Law 22
Kennedy KC (1998)The GATT-WTO system at fifty. Wisconsin Int'l Law J 16
Land JN (2004) Intellectual property protection as viewed through the European community's treatment of geographical indications: what lessons can TRIPs learn? Cardozo J Int'l & Comp Law 11
Lehmann M (1985) The theory of property rights and the protection of rev. Indus. Property & Copyright Law
Mangassarian E (2001) Technological trends and the changing face of international intellectual property law. Int'l Legal Perspectives 11
Maskus KE, Denubarti M (1995) How trade-related are intellectual property rights? J Int'l Econ 39
Ugolini MA (1999) Gray-market goods under the agreement on trade-related aspects of intellectual property rights. Transnat'l Law 12
O'Sullivan MJ (2000) International copyright: protection for copyright holders in the Internet age. N.Y. Int'l Law Rev 13
Oman R (1994) Intellectual property after the Uruguay round. J Copyright Soc U.S.A. 42
Otten A, Wager H (1996) Compliance with TRIPs: the emerging world view. Vanderbilt J Transnat'l Law 29
Pechman RJ (1998) Seeking multilateral protection for intellectual property: the United States "TRIPs" over special Global Trade 7, p. 301
Preeg EH (1995) Trades in a brave new world; the Uruguay round and the future of the international trading system. International trade regulation. University of Chicago Press
Reed C (2012) Computer law, 7th edn. Universal Law Publishing Co.
Reichman JH (1989) Intellectual property in international trade: opportunities and risks of a GATT connection. Vanderbilt J Transnat'l Law 22
Reichman JH (1993) The TRIPS component of the GATT's Uruguay round; competitive prospects for intellectual property owners in an integrated world market. Fordham Intellectual Property, Media Ent Law J 4
Reichman JH (1995) Universal minimum standards of intellectual property protection under the TRIPS component of the WTO agreement. Int'l Law 29
Reichman JH (1996) Compliance with the TRIPs agreement: introduction to scholorly debate. Vanderbilt J Transnat'l Law 29
Reichman JH (1997) Symposium: intellectual property law in the international marketplace: trade-related aspects of intellectual property rights. Virginia J Int'l Law 37
Reichman JH (2000) The TRIPs agreement comes of age: conflict or cooperation with the developing countries? Int'l Law 32
Romano F (1998) Global trademark and copyright 1998: protecting intellectual property rights in the international marketplace. International Conventions and Treaties
Schaffter R, Earle B, Agusti F (2002) International business law and its environment. Thomson/Western
Sell SK (2002) Industry strategies for intellectual property and trade: the quest for TRIPs, and post-TRIPs strategies. Cardozo J Int'l Comp Law 10
Simon E (1994) The integration of intellectual property and trade policy. ALAI
Su E (2000) The winners and the losers: the agreement on trade-related aspects of intellectual property rights and its effects on developing countries. J Int'l Law 23
Ullrich H (1995) TRIPS; adequate protection, inadequate trade, adequate competition policy. Pacific Rim Law & Policy J 4
Williamson D (1989) Addressing inadequate intellectual property protection in the Uruguay round. Business America 4
Young MK (1996) Dispute resolution in the Uruguay round: lawyers triumph over diplomats. Int'l Law 29
Yu PK (2002) Symposium: world trade intellectual property and the global elites: international lawmaking in the new millennium: an introduction. Int'l & Comp Law 10

Appellate Body Report, United States-Section 211 Omnibus Appropriations Act of 1998, WT/DS176/AB/R, (Jan. 2, 2002)

Panel Report, United States-Section 211 Omnibus Appropriations Act of 1998, WT/DS176/R, (Aug. 6, 2001)

Universal Copyright Convention, Sept. 6, 1952, 6 U.S.T. 2731, 216 U.N.T.S. 134, revised by 25 U.S.T. 1341, 943 U.N.T.S. 178, July 24, 1971.

WTO, Agreement on Trade – Related Aspects of Intellectual Property Rights, April 15, 1994, Marrakesh Agreement Establishing the World Trade Organization, Annex C, Legal Instruments-Results of the Uruguay Round, Vol. 33, I.L.M. (1994)

Part V

Regulation on Trade Disputes and Further Issues

12 Regulation on Trade Dispute

Learning Objectives

This chapter is to help students understand:

1. The purpose and function of the trade policy review mechanism compared with specific obligations under multilateral trade agreements;
2. Relation between the trade policy review mechanism and dispute settlement mechanism;
3. Features of dispute settlement understandings as the quasi-judicial nature;
4. Main principles of the dispute settlement understanding dealing with disputable issues among Member countries;
5. Two-tier mechanism of the WTO dispute settlement mechanism;
6. Features of arbitrations under the WTO dispute settlement mechanism compared with general commercial arbitration;
7. Panels' rights to seek information and technical advice from experts.

12.1 Introduction

12.1.1 Trade Policy Review

The Trade Policy Review Mechanism (TPRM) was introduced into GATT in 1989 following the Mid-Term Review of the Uruguay Round. The mechanism was confirmed as an integral part of the WTO in Annex 3 of the Marrakesh Agreement Establishing the World Trade Organization.[1]

The purpose of the TPRM is to "contribute to improved adherence by all Members to rules, disciplines and commitments made under Multilateral Trade Agreements and, where applicable, Plurilateral Trade Agreements, and hence to the

[1] Before 1995, trade policy reviews were restricted to trade in goods. In conformity with WTO rules, since 1 January 1995 reviews have also covered new areas like trade in services and intellectual property rights.

E.S. Lee, *World Trade Regulation*,
DOI 10.1007/978-3-642-31143-7_12, © Springer-Verlag Berlin Heidelberg 2012

smoother functioning of the multilateral trading system, by achieving greater transparency in, and understanding of, the trade policies and practices of Members". The review covers the full range of individual Members' trade policies and practices and their impact on the functioning of the multilateral trading system. It is not confined to a consideration of the trade policies from the point of view of consistency with the WTO rules. The purpose is to enable a collective appreciation and evaluation of these policies and practices. It is not meant to serve as a basis for enforcement of specific obligations or to impose new commitments.

The TPRM seeks to achieve its objectives by conducting reviews, over time, of all the WTO Members. Through such reviews, Members undertake the regular collective appreciation of the trade policies and practices of trading partners. Also examined are the impact on the multilateral trading system of such policies and practices. The reviews are set against the background of each country's wider economic and developmental needs, policies, objectives, and of its external economic environment.

With relation to scope of reviews, reviews in the TPRM seek to show the extent to which individual trading entities follow basic WTO principles concerning: transparency of trade policies; non-discrimination in treatment of trading partners; whether their policies contribute to trade liberalization; the degree of stability and predictability in trade policies; the pattern of protection and the extent to which tariffs only are used as measures of protection in trade in goods; restrictions used in trade in services; the record of adherence to the multilateral trading system, including the dispute settlement.

Regarding the relation between TPRM and dispute settlement, the TPRM is an exercise on transparency and understanding based on economic principles and the broad objectives of the WTO. Thus, the trade policy reviews: are not intended to be assessments of how well individual Members are adhering to particular WTO rules; cannot serve as a basis for dispute settlement procedures, and may not impose new policy obligations on the Members under review.

12.1.2 TPRM in Practice

12.1.2.1 General

The TPRM is the only WTO forum where all aspects of trade policies come under discussion by the whole membership. The Mechanism constitutes an objective, independent evaluation and "external audit" of the trade and economic situation of Members. The TPRM offers a forum where policies can be explained and discussed, where information can be sought and concerns can be expressed on a non-confrontational and non-legalistic basis.

The TPRM has increased transparency in the trade policies and practices of GATT and WTO Members. The TPRM process has frequently illuminated areas of WTO obligations which may have received insufficient attention to date and thus helped to ensure that these are addressed. The Mechanism's spotlight has effectively focused on all the main players in the WTO trading system and has illuminated the most significant trends.

The TPRM has stimulated the internal evaluation of trade policies in Member countries, particularly in developing countries. The review process strengthens the hands of domestic agencies promoting liberalization, supports trade reforms and, thus, helps individual Members to become better WTO citizens. The more than 80 reviews conducted have highlighted interlink ages between trade and internal economic reform, the inter-sectored effects of protection (and liberalization), and their implications for the multilateral system. Many reviews have also illustrated the importance of "new" issues such as the relationship between trade and competition policy, and the trade impact of investment measures.

12.1.2.2 Frequency of Reviews

The frequency of reviews of a Member is related to its weight in the multilateral trading system, as defined by the Member's share of world trade in goods and services. On this basis, Members are reviewed under one of three different cycles: every two years for the four largest trading entities, counting the European Communities as one; every four years for the next sixteen Members; every six years for other Members, with provision for a longer interval for the least-developed countries.

The frequency of review for individual Members, based on trade flows in October 1995, is as follows (listed in descending order of trade): two-year cycle: the European Communities, the United States, Japan and Canada; four-year cycle: Hong Kong; China; Korea; Singapore; Switzerland; Mexico; Australia; Malaysia; Thailand; Norway; Indonesia; Brazil; Turkey; South Africa; Israel; India and United Arab Emirates; six-year cycle: all other WTO Member (most developing and transition economies, including the least-developed countries for which a longer cycle may also be used).

Principles used to establish the schedule of second and subsequent reviews include: reviews are set counting from the date of the previous review meeting; the cycle of reviews is applied with a general flexibility of up to six months; and for the four largest trading entities, every second review has an interim character.

Variations in trade in goods and services flows may alter the ranking of Members and thus their review cycles, for example as a result of changes in commodity prices. Although in practice this has not affected the review cycles of Members, countries in the lowest ranking of the four-year cycle may well change in the future.

12.1.3 Review

The Secretariat report focuses on the trade policies and practices of the Member under review, seen, to the extent necessary, in the context of the evolution of overall macro-economic and structural policies in a representative period up to the present date. The aims and structure of the report are essentially the same for all Members, variations reflecting the Members' frequency of review and economic characteristics.

Most secretariat reports are prepared following a format containing "Summary Observations" and four chapters: (i) The economic environment (covering major features of the economy, recent economic performance, trade patterns in goods and services, evolution of foreign investment, and trade-related aspects of the foreign exchange regime); (ii) Institutional aspects of trade and investment policy-making, including participation in multilateral and regional agreements, and trade disputes and consultations; (iii) Trade policies and practices by measure (covering all types of measures directly affecting imports, exports, trade in services, and production and trade in goods); (iv) Trade policies and practices by sector (agriculture/forestry/fisheries, mining, industry and services).

The Secretariat Report is based on official information and comments provided by the authorities, complemented by material from other sources deemed appropriate by the Secretariat.

All chapters of the Secretariat report are checked for factual accuracy with the Member concerned, although the Secretariat retains final responsibility for their contents. The "Summary Observations" (which are in effect the Secretariat's conclusions on the trade policies being reviewed) are not shown to the country under review until the report is ready to be issued to all Members. Reports by Members under review take the form of policy statements. Policy statements aim to outline the objectives and main directions of trade policies, in a forward-looking perspective.

A statement may also contain a succinct presentation of recent trends and problems, including those encountered in foreign markets. Statements are typically between 10 and 30 pages. The actual form and length are in the last instance determined by the Member under review.

A TPRM review consists of several steps whose timing is agreed between the Secretariat and the country under review. Particularly critical is the agreed date for the review meeting, as that largely determines the timing of other steps, given the time required to complete various tasks and the rules of procedure agreed by the WTO Members. The following general sequence may be identified: collation of information; visit to the capital; final preparation of documents; review meeting organized and conducted; and publication of documents.

The Secretariat prepares a detailed country questionnaire, drawn up according to the planned structure of the report. The national authorities of the Member under review are sent the questionnaire and have some four weeks to prepare and provide replies, including government publications and other official data on core issues. For some reports, a second questionnaire is sent before the visit to the capital as a follow-up to the government's replies to the first questionnaire.

A Secretariat team undertakes a visit of one week to ten days to the country under review for discussions with government ministries and other relevant agencies. The team generally consists of two or three staff members of the Trade Policy Review Division. Discussions usually take place on the basis of the questionnaire(s) sent in advance. Alternatively, a preliminary draft of the Secretariat report may form the basis for discussions.

During the visit, the Secretariat's team often consults not only with government agencies, but also with private enterprise (Chambers of Manufacturers, Commerce, etc.) and research institutes. The Secretariat drafts its report, progressively submitting all chapters for verification (alternatively, this may be done before the visit to the capital). National authorities have some two weeks to verify the Secretariat drafts and furnish comments on them.

The Secretariat incorporates the government's comments and finalizes its draft. The Secretariat report and the government's policy statement are sent for translation into other WTO official languages four weeks before they are circulated. The Secretariat report and the policy statement are reproduced and circulated four weeks before the review meeting.

12.2 Dispute Settlement

12.2.1 Introduction

12.2.1.1 Purpose

The dispute settlement system of the WTO is a central element[2] in providing security and predictability[3] to the multilateral trading system resulting from the Uruguay Round.[4] Its aim is to secure a positive solution to a dispute.[5] The purpose of the WTO Understanding on Rules and Procedures Governing the Settlement of Disputes (DSU) is to provide for an efficient, dependable and rule-oriented system to resolve,[6] within a multilateral framework,[7] disputes arising in relation to the

[2] The dispute settlement mechanism contained in the understanding on Rules and Procedures Governing the settlement of Dispute has been evaluated to be the central pillar of and the "most individual contribution" to the WTO multilateral trading system. See Albren (1996, pp. 85, 106), cited by Chua (1998, p. 171).

[3] For the certainty and predictability to the multilateral trading system with regard to the objective of the WTO Agreement from the viewpoint of the previous decisions of the GATT/WTO panels, see Chua (1998, *id.*, at 172–173). (Stating "... If the WTO Agreement is interpreted in on ad hoe way, without regard to previous decisions, uncertainty will arise as to whether government policies are inconsistent with the WTO Agreement ....")

[4] Dispute Settlement Understanding Art. 3.2. (DSU).

[5] DSU, *id.* Art. 3.7.

[6] The DSU does not simply codify the dispute settlement procedures under the General Agreement on Tariffs and Trade regime, but represents a significant shift to a rule-based model of dispute settlement (Chua 1998, *supra* note 2, at 171).

[7] In a flank attack on unilateral actions taken by the United States under Section 301 of the Trade of 1974, see 19 U.S.C. §2411, cited by Kennedy (1998, p. 516); DSU, *supra* note 4. Art. 23, Strengthening the Multilateral System, flatly prohibits Members from making unilateral determinations on the following matters: (1) whether an Uruguay Round agreement has been violated, (2) whether another Member has failed to implement a DSB recommendation within a reasonable period of time, or (3) whether the level of suspension of concessions is appropriate. The DSU is the exclusive mechanism for resolving these issues, absent the mutual agreement of the disputing Members (Kennedy 1998, *id.*, at 516–517).

application of the Marrakesh Agreement Establishing the World Trade Organization. Throughout this description, the Marrakesh Agreement Establishing the World Trade Organization, including its annexes, will be referred to as the "WTO Agreement", whereas the agreements composing it will be referred to as the "WTO agreements".

The WTO dispute settlement system favors mutually agreed solutions consistent with the WTO agreements, and parties are encouraged to develop mutually satisfactory solutions, even when the matter is before a panel.[8] The WTO dispute settlement mechanism is a rule-oriented system[9] where recommendations and rulings must aim at achieving a satisfactory settlement in accordance with the right and obligations of the Members under the WTO Agreement.[10] As a result, all solutions to matters formally placed under the consultation and dispute settlement provisions of the WTO agreements, including arbitration awards, must be consistent with those agreements and must not nullify and impair benefits accruing to any Member under those agreements.[11]

If it is not possible to reach a mutually agreed solution, the first objective of the dispute settlement system is normally to secure the withdrawal of the measures concerned if they are found to be inconsistent with the WTO Agreement.[12] The prompt settlement of situations in which a Member considers that benefits accruing to it directly or indirectly under the WTO Agreement are being impaired by measures taken by another member is essential to: the effective functioning of the WTO; and the maintenance of a proper balance between the rights and obligations of its Members.[13] Efficiency is achieved through detailed procedural provisions, including provisions which allow a party to move forward with the case even in the absence of agreement of the other party.[14]

---

[8] DSU, *supra* note 4. Art. 11.

[9] For the criticism and reform proposals for the current rule-oriented approach of the DSU, see Specht (1998, pp. 90–91). "One criticism is that the process is too secret and should be more open. The confidentiality of the proceedings is not favored by 'many groups whose interests are immediately and directly affected by . . . decisions' of the DSB, particularly regarding decisions involving environmental matters. A second major criticism targets the lack of DSU provisions prescribing qualifications for appeals to the Appellate Body. Without a mechanism in place to discourage frivolous appeals, the appellate Body would be overloaded thus delaying the adoption of the reports. Therefore, a minimum threshold for appeals to the Appellate Body should be established. Another objection concerns the system of sanctions. It is questionable to what extent compliance with the panel and Appellate Body rulings and recommendations can be enforced. Termination of infringing measures is, of course, more desirable than retaliation. Furthermore, the retaliatory measures only work effectively when member states of similar economic power are involved. In order to effectively render a claim of a small and poorer country against a large and wealthier country, it has been suggested that the WTO itself should be authorized to bring complaints and enforce them."

[10] DSU, *supra* note 4. Art. 3.4.

[11] DSU, *supra* note 4. Art. 3.5.

[12] DSU, *supra* note 4. Art. 3.7.

[13] DSU, *supra* note 4. Art. 3.3.

[14] DSU, *supra* note 4. Art. 4.3 or 6.1.

The procedures for dispute settlement which are laid down in the DSU have many features which make it quasi-judicial in nature. First, there is assured access to these procedures. Second, there is near automaticity in decision-making in all key issues related to settlement of individual disputes. Third, firm time limits are stipulated for each stage of the process. And finally, there is provision for appellate review.

Appeals' trends under the WTO

Under Rule 20(1) of the *Working Procedures*, an appeal is commenced by giving notice in writing to the DSB and filing a Notice of Appeal with the Appellate Body Secretariat. Rule 23(1) of the *Working Procedures* allows a party to the dispute other than the initial appellant to join the appeal, or appeal on the basis of other alleged errors, by filing a Notice of Other Appeal within 12 days of the filing of the Notice of Appeal.

Figure 12.1 shows the ratio of appeals dealing with original disputes to appeals dealing with complaints brought pursuant to Article 21.5 of the DSU.

Figure 12.2 shows the percentage of panel reports appealed by year of adoption since 1996. No panel reports were appealed in 1995. The overall average of panel reports that have been appealed from 1995 to 2009 is 68 percent.

Figure 12.3 shows the number of times specific WTO agreements have been addressed in the 100 Appellate Body reports circulated from 1996 through 2009.

Source: World Trade. February 17, 2010.WT/AB/13. http://www.wto.org/english/tratop_e/dispu_e/ab_annual_report09_e.doc.

12.2.1.2 Principles

The DSU promotes the use of a multilateral system of dispute settlement in place of unilateralism[15] in the resolution of trade conflicts.[16] This multilateral system is based on the principles for the management of disputes developed under Articles XXII and XXIII of GATT 1947, as further elaborated and modified by the DSU.[17] The WTO dispute settlement provisions are composed of a set of internationally agreed rules to which the WTO Members must have recourse where they seek redress of the effects of measures of other WTO Members under the WTO

[15] For the unilateralism under the WTO dispute settlement procedures, see Leebron (1995, pp. 14–16). "One of the important issues raised in the Uruguay Round negotiations was unilateralism, ... understood to mean actions by the United States under Section 301 ... as well as the related 'Super 301' and 'Special 301'. ... Although these provisions ... limit particular use of section 301, there is nothing in section 301 itself that would require action in violation of Art. 23 of the Dispute Settlement Understanding. ..."

[16] DSU, *supra* note 4. Art. 23.1.

[17] *Id.*

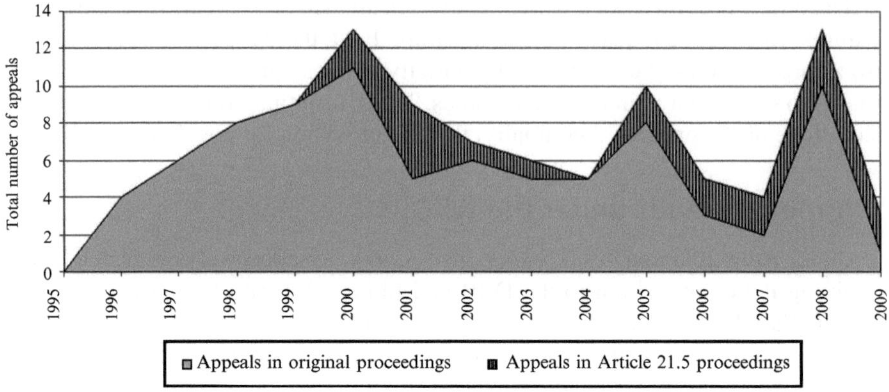

Fig. 12.1 Appeals in original proceedings and Article 21.5 proceedings 1995–2009

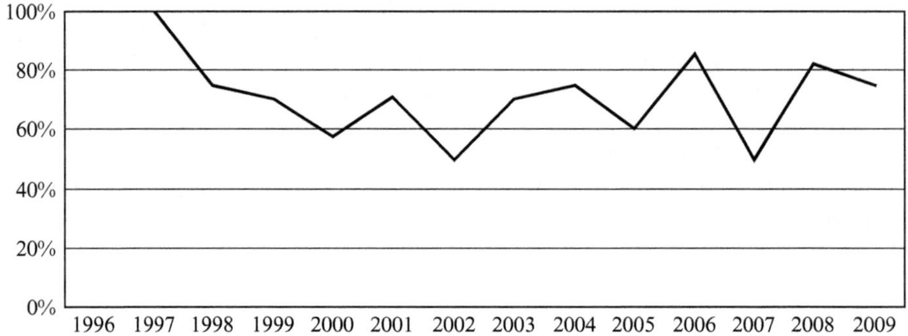

Fig. 12.2 Percentage of panel reports appealed 1996–2009 *. (* Figure 12.2 is based on year of adoption by the DSB, which may not necessarily coincide with the year in which a panel report was circulated or appealed.)

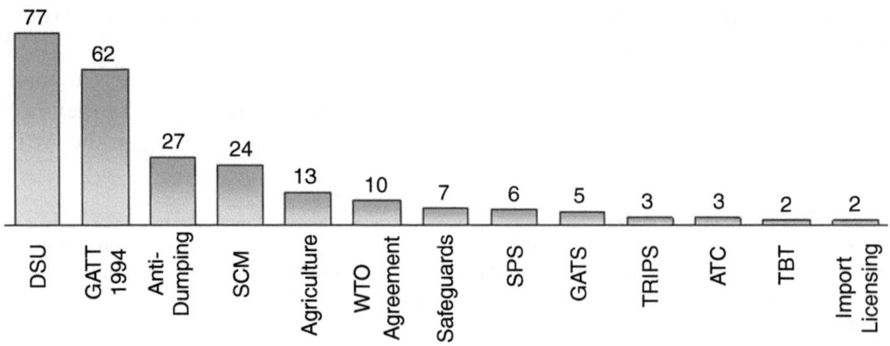

Fig. 12.3 WTO agreements addressed in appeals 1996–2009. Source: World Trade, Feb. 17, 2012. WT/AB/13

agreements,[18] i.e. when they allege: (i) a violation of obligations or other nullification or impairment of benefits under the agreements; or (ii) an impediment to the attainment of any objective of the agreements.[19]

When a Member seeks redress of the effects of measures of other Members under the WTO Agreement, it must not determine that any of the situations under (i) or (ii) above exists except through recourse to dispute settlement in accordance with the rules and procedures of the DSU. It must make any such determination consistent with the findings contained in the panel or Appellate Body report adopted by the DSB or in an arbitration award rendered under the DSU.[20] It has also to respect the relevant procedures under the DSU with respect to the implementation of recommendations and rulings and suspension of concessions or other obligations.[21]

Subject to certain conditions and exceptions, the DSU is applicable in a uniform manner to disputes under all of the WTO Agreements. The rules and procedures under the DSU apply to all disputes brought pursuant to the consultation and dispute settlement provisions of the WTO agreements listed in Appendix 1 DSU, subject to such special or additional rules and procedures on dispute settlement contained in the specified covered agreements.[22] To the extent that there is a difference between the rules and procedures of the DSU and the special and additional rules and procedures, the latter prevails.[23]

12.2.1.3 Functions

The WTO dispute settlement system serves to preserve the rights and obligations of Members under the WTO Agreement and to clarify the existing provisions of the WTO Agreement in accordance with customary rules of interpretation[24,25] of public

[18] *Id.*

[19] DSU, *supra* note 4. Art. 23.2(a).

[20] DSU, *supra* note 4. Art. 23.2(a).

[21] DSU, *supra* note 4. Art. 23.2(b), (c).

[22] DSU, *supra* note 4. Art. 1.2 and Appendix 2.

[23] DSU, *supra* note 4. Art. 1.2.

[24] For the interpretation of WTO Agreements vis-à-vis construction rules, see Trachman (1999, pp. 339–340).

[25] For the Dispute Settlement Understanding Standards Interpretation of WTO Agreement, see Rogers and Whitlock (2002, pp. 483–484). "DSU Article 3(2) requires that Panels apply 'customary rules of interpretation of public international law' in interpreting WTO provisions. In case after case, the Appellate Body has interpreted this language to imply the application of the principles embodied in the Vienna Convention on the Law of Treaties' ('Vienna Convention') Art. 31, n. 90 which sets forth the default rules of interpretation, and Art. 32, which sets forth the supplementary rules of interpretation. In the WTO Appellate Body Report on Alcoholic Beverages, the Appellate Body commented on the relationship between the Vienna Convention and the meaning of any given WTO provision by saying: The provision of the treaty art to be their ordinary meaning in their context. The object and purpose of the treaty are also to be takes into account in determining the meaning of its provisions. (Where treaty language would permit two interpretations equally, the interpretation more consistent with the treaty's object and purpose should be adopted). . . . Interpretation must give meaning and effect to all the terms of the treaty. An interpreter is not free to

international law.[26] This is without prejudice to the rights of Members to seek authoritative interpretation of provisions of a WTO agreement through decision-making under the WTO Agreement,[27] or, where applicable, a plurilateral trade agreement.[28] Recommendations and rulings under the WTO dispute settlement system cannot add to or diminish the rights and obligations provided in the WTO agreements.[29]

The concept of nullification or impairment of benefits is central to dispute settlement in the WTO.[30] In case of violation of an agreement, nullification or impairment is presumed to exist. This means that there is normally a presumption that a breach of the rules has an adverse impact on other WTO Members. In such a case, it will be up to the Member against which the complaint is brought to rebut the charge.[31]

In the absence of a violation by another WTO Member, i.e. in a situation of "non-violation nullification or impairment"[32] or as a result of any other situation,[33] no presumption applies and the complaining party bears the burden of proof of establishing the existence of a nullification or impairment.[34,35] The

adopt a reading that would result in reducing whole clauses or paragraphs of a treaty to redundancy or inutility. The Appellate Body's view of how to interpret WTO agreements is important background to a discussion of the consistency of a WTO Member's national regulatory scheme with that Member's WTO obligations."

[26] DSU, *supra* note 4. Art. 3.2.

[27] See: Art. IX: 2 Marrakesh Agreement Establishing World Trade Organization

[28] DSU, *supra* note 4. Art. 3.9.

[29] DSU, *supra* note 4. Art. 3.2 and 19.2.

[30] GATT 1994 Art. XXIII: 1.

[31] DSU, *supra* note 4. Art. 3.8.

[32] GATT 1994 Art. XXIII: 1(b).

[33] GATT 1994 Art. XXIII: 1(c).

[34] The non-violation concept was succinctly framed by the WTO Appellate Body in its India-Mailbox decision, referring to the cause of action as it was understood in the context of the General Agreement on Tariffs and Trade (GATT) 1947 and as it is understood in the context of GATT 1994: In the absence of substantive legal rules in many areas relating to international trade, the "non-violation" provision of Art. XXIII:1(b) was aimed at preventing contracting parties from using non-tariff barriers or other policy measures to negate the benefits of negotiated tariff concessions. Under Art. XXIII:1(b) of the GATT 1994, a Member can bring a "non-violation" complaint when the negotiated balance of concessions between Members is upset by the application of a measure, whether or not this measure is inconsistent with the provision of the covered agreement. The ultimate goal is not the withdrawal of the measure concerned, but rather achieving a mutually satisfactory adjustment, usually by means of compensation. See India-Patent Protection for Pharmaceutical Chemical Products, Report of the appellate Body para. 41, WTO Doc. WT/DS50/AB/R (Dec. 19, 1997), available in 1997 WL78/259, at 11, cited by Abbott (2000, p. 173).

[35] There is a close correlation between the concept of non-violation nullification or impairment and the concept of the good faith execution of treaty obligations. The Vienna Convention on the Law of Treaties, which essentially codifies the customary international law applicable to treaties, establishes a requirement that treaties be executed in good faith. The good faith execution of a treaty inherently demands that a party not take actions that undermine the performance of the treaty that is, that a party to a treaty not seek to defeat the object and purpose of a treaty by actions

DSU develops the rules applicable to situations where either of the two latter situations are invoked.[36] An example of a report based on a finding of "non-violation nullification or impairment" is the report of the panel on EEC – Payments and Subsidies Paid to Processors and Producers of Oilseeds and Related Animal-Feed Proteins, which dealt with a US claim that the EC had impaired its zero tariff binding on oilseeds by providing domestic subsidies to the EC oilseed industry.

With respect to the WTO agreements falling under Annex 1A of the WTO Agreement (trade in goods), the complainant generally has to demonstrate that benefits accruing to it under a WTO agreement have been nullified or impaired.[37] With regard to Annex 1B (trade in services), the failure by any Member to carry out its obligations or specific commitments under GATS gives another Member the right to have recourse to the DSU.[38] Nullification or impairment of a benefit which could be reasonably expected to accrue to a Member under a specific commitment can be alleged in the absence of a conflict with the provisions of GATS.[39]

Finally, the provisions of Articles XXII and XXIII of GATT 1994 as elaborated and applied by the DSU are applicable to consultations and dispute settlement under the Agreement on Trade-Related Aspects of Intellectual Property Rights. However, during a period of 5 years from the entry into force of the WTO Agreement, Members do not have the right to allege nullification or impairment in cases where a measure adopted by a Member does not conflict with that Member's obligations under the WTO Agreement[40] or in any other situation except a violation of the WTO Agreement.[41,42]

12.2.1.4 Two-Tier Mechanism

The WTO dispute settlement mechanism provides for three main ways of resolving disputes: (i) bilateral consultations; (ii) good offices, conciliation and mediation;

inconsistent with law object and purpose, even if those actions might not be specifically precluded by the terms of the treaty. Treaty law requires such a good faith doctrine since it is practicable for parties to specify every possible step that parties should avoid. The concept of non-violation nullification or impairment in the GATT/WTO context may be viewed substantially as a way of restating the good faith requirement. That is, WTO Members should not seek to undermine the value of concessions they have granted in trade negotiations by taking steps that, while not specifically precluded by the WTO Agreement, nevertheless are inconsistent with allowing the concessions to be used by their intended beneficiaries. Viewed in this way, at least some non-violation causes of action could quite properly be reframed as cause of action demanding good faith execution of WTO obligations (Abbott 2000, *id.*, at 177–178).

[36] DSU, *supra* note 4. Art. 26.

[37] GATT 1994 Art. XXIII: 1.

[38] GATS Art. XXIII: 1.

[39] GATS Art. XXIII: 3.

[40] GATT 1994 Art. XXIII: 1(b).

[41] GATT 1994 Art. XXIII: 1(c).

[42] TRIPs Agreement. Art. 64.

and (iii) adjudication, including arbitration. With the exception of arbitration, adjudication cannot be requested until consultations have taken place or unsuccessful attempts to consult have been made. The DSU contains rules and procedures to be followed by the WTO Members for both consultations and adjudications.

The DSU favors solutions mutually acceptable to the parties to the dispute, provided that they are consistent with the WTO Agreements.[43] Mutually agreed solutions to matters formally placed under the consultation and dispute settlement provisions of the covered agreements must be notified to the DSB and the relevant Councils and Committees, where any Member may raise any point relating thereto.[44]

For an example of notified solution, see Korea – Measures Affecting the Shelf-Life of Products, where the parties notified a mutually acceptable solution to the DSB. Consultations are subject to the provisions of Article 4 DSU and the individual WTO agreements. Their objective is to allow parties to obtain satisfactory adjustment of the matter before resorting to further actions.[45]

Each Member undertakes to accord sympathetic consideration to, and afford adequate opportunity for consultation regarding, any representation made by another Member concerning measures affecting the operation of any WTO agreement.[46] Consultations have a number of functions. They allow parties to clarify the facts of the matter, thus dispelling misunderstandings as to the actual nature of the measure at issue.[47] They may allow parties to find a mutually satisfactory solution, and, if no solution is found at that stage, permit them to take stock of the issues which were not solved through consultations.[48] Article 5 of the DSU provides for good offices, conciliation and mediation to be undertaken voluntarily if the parties to the dispute agree.[49] Good offices, conciliation and mediation may begin at any time and be terminated at any time.[50] If the parties so agree, these procedures may continue while the panel process proceeds.[51]

Adjudication under the DSU can be by a panel[52] or an arbitrator.[53] Panel reports may be subject to an appeal to the Appellate Body.[54] Panel and Appellate Body reports have to, where applicable, contain the recommendation that a measure

[43] DSU, *supra* note 4. Art. 3.7.

[44] DSU, *supra* note 4. Art. 3.6.

[45] DSU, *supra* note 4. Art. 4.5.

[46] DSU, *supra* note 4. Art. 4.2.

[47] DSU, *supra* note 4. Art. 11.

[48] *Id.*

[49] DSU, *supra* note 4. Art. 5.1.

[50] DSU, *supra* note 4. Art. 5.3.

[51] DSU, *supra* note 4. Art. 5.5.

[52] DSU, *supra* note 4. Art. 6 to 16.

[53] DSU, *supra* note 4. Art. 15.

[54] DSU, *supra* note 4. Art. 17.

which was found inconsistent with the WTO agreement be brought into conformity with that agreement. Panel and Appellate Body reports may suggest ways in which the Member concerned could implement the recommendations.[55]

Dispute Settlement without recourse to Panels and the Appellate Body

Mediation, conciliation and good offices

The DSU provides for good offices, conciliation and mediation on a voluntary basis if the parties to the dispute agree (Article 5.1 of the DSU). Good offices normally consist primarily of providing logistical support to help the parties negotiate in a productive atmosphere. Conciliation additionally involves the direct participation of an outside person in the discussions and negotiations between the parties. In a mediation process, the mediator does not only participate in and contribute to the discussions and negotiations, but may also propose a solution to the parties. The parties would not be obliged to accept this proposal.

Good offices, conciliation and mediation may begin at any time (Article 5.3 of the DSU), but not prior to a request for consultations because that request is necessary to trigger the application of the procedures of the DSU, including Article 5 (Article 1.1 of the DSU). For example, the parties can enter into these procedures during their consultations. If this happens within 60 days after the date of the request for consultations, the complainant must not request a panel before this 60-day period has expired, unless the parties jointly consider that the good offices, conciliation or mediation process has failed to settle the dispute (Article 5.4 of the DSU). However, these procedures can be terminated at any time (Article 5.3 of the DSU). If the parties so agree, these procedures may continue while the panel proceeds with an examination of the matter (Article 5.5 of the DSU).

The proceedings of good offices, conciliation and mediation are strictly confidential, and do not diminish the position of either party in any following dispute settlement procedure (Article 5.2 of the DSU).

Unlike panel and Appellate Body proceedings, the process of good offices, conciliation or mediation should not result in legal conclusions, but assist in reaching a mutually agreed solution. The Director-General may involve Secretariat staff to support the process, but these staff members must be insulated from subsequent dispute settlement procedures (i.e. at the panel stage). A request to the Director-General must also identify whether it is for good offices, conciliation and/or mediation, even though the Director-General's role may change during the Article 5 procedure.

The DSU specifically foresees good offices, conciliation and mediation for disputes involving a least-developed country Member. Where the consultations have not resulted in a satisfactory solution and the least-

(continued)

[55] DSU, *supra* note 4. Art. 19.

developed country Member so requests, the Director-General or the Chairman of the DSB must offer their good offices, conciliation and mediation. Here as well, the aim is to assist the parties to settle the dispute before the establishment of a panel (Article 24.2 of the DSU).

Source: Dispute Settlement System Training Module: Chapter 8. http://www.wto.org/english/tratop_e/dispu_e/disp_settlement_cbt_e/c8s1p2_e.htm

12.2.1.5 Coverage

The DSU is, in principle, applicable to disputes under any of the WTO agreements,[56] taken individually or in combination.[57] The list of the agreements to which the DSU applies is contained in Appendix 1 DSU. They are referred to as the "covered agreements" in the DSU.[58] The DSU is applicable to the resolution of disputes under the Marrakesh Agreement Establishing the World Trade Organization, as well as all the agreements annexed thereto subject, for some of them, to special or additional rules and procedures contained in Appendix 2 DSU. Many matters brought before the DSB include alleged violations of more than one covered agreement. In European Communities – Regime for the Importation, Sale and Distribution of Bananas, for instance, the matter included alleged violations of GATT 1994, the Import Licensing Agreement, the Agreement on Agriculture, the TRIMs Agreement and GATS.

The covered agreements include the plurilateral trade agreements contained in Annex 4 of the WTO Agreement. However, the applicability of the DSU to the plurilateral trade agreements is subject to the adoption of a decision by the parties to each of these agreements setting out the terms for the application of the Understanding to the individual agreement, including any special and additional rules or procedures. Such a decision was taken by the Committee of the Agreement on Government Procurement. No such decision has been adopted by the Committee on Trade in Civil Aircraft.

[56] For the covered agreements as the unique law applicable in WTO dispute resolution, see Trachman (1999, *supra* note 24, at 343). (Stating "... while Panel and the Appellate Body are only permitted to apply WTO law, they refer to non-WTO international law in two types of cases. First, ... they refer to customary rules of interpretation of international law. This does not appear to include substantive non-WTO international law. While Art. 31(3)(c) of the Vienna Convention, which is taken as reflective of customary rules of interpretation, refers to applicable international law, it does so only to indicate what materials texts. ... Second, substantive non-WTO international law may be incorporated by reference in WTO law, either by treaty language may be such as the references in TRIPS to intellectual property treaties. ...")

[57] DSU, *supra* note 4. Art. 1.1 .

[58] *Id.*

12.2.2 Institutional Provisions

12.2.2.1 Introduction

The operation of the WTO dispute settlement process involves the Dispute Settlement Body, the panels and the Appellate Body, the parties and the WTO Secretariat. The General Council discharges its responsibilities with respect to dispute settlement through the Dispute Settlement Body which is composed of representatives of all of the WTO Members.

Panels and the Appellate Body are the entities in charge of adjudicating disputes. The former are composed of experts selected on an ad hoc basis. The latter is a permanent group of seven experts in trade issues and trade law in charge of reviewing the legal aspects of the reports issued by panels.[59] Any WTO Member may have recourse to the WTO dispute settlement mechanism or be subject to dispute settlement.[60]

The WTO Secretariat is responsible for the administrative aspects of dispute settlement, as well as for assisting panels on the legal and procedural aspects of the matters dealt with.[61]

12.2.2.2 Dispute Settlement Body

The general rule is for the DSB to take decisions by consensus, as is the case for all decision-making in the WTO. It is deemed to have decided by consensus on a matter submitted for its consideration, if no WTO Member, present at the meeting of the DSB when the decision is taken, formally objects to the proposed decisions.[62] However, a radically different procedure is followed in decision-making at four key stages in the dispute settlement process: establishment of panel, adoption of panel and Appellate Body reports and authorization for retaliation.

At these stages the decision is taken to accept the request or adopt the report unless there is a consensus against it. The rule of negative consensus on these matters makes decision-making quasi-automatic. This contrasts sharply with the situation that prevailed under GATT 1947, when reports of panels could only be adopted on the basis of consensus. Unlike under GATT 1947, the DSU provides no opportunity for blockage in decision-making.

The DSB meets as often as necessary to adhere to the time frames provided for in the DSU. All Members are entitled to participate in meetings of the DSB. However, when the DSB administers the dispute settlement provisions of a Plurilateral Trade Agreement, only Members that are parties to that Agreement may participate in decisions or actions taken by the DSB with respect to disputes under the Agreement.[63]

[59] DSU, *supra* note 4. Art. 11, and 17.

[60] DSU, *supra* note 4. Art. 1.

[61] DSU, *supra* note 4. Art. 27,1.

[62] DSU, *supra* note 4. Art. 2.4, Footnote 1.

[63] DSU, *supra* note 4. Art. 2.1.

In a dispute settlement procedure involving a least-developed country Member, when a satisfactory solution has not been found during consultations, the Chairman of the DSB must, upon request by a least-developed country Member, offer his or her good offices, conciliation or mediation with a view to assisting the parties to settle the dispute, before a request for a panel is made.[64] In providing such assistance the Chairman of the DSB may consult any source which he or she deems appropriate.

12.2.2.3 Panels

Where the Members concerned cannot find a mutually agreed solution through consultations, the DSB must, at the request of a party to the dispute, establish a panel of three to five independent trade experts appointed on an ad hoc basis. The panel must review the factual and legal aspects of the case and submit a report to the DSB.[65] It must make an objective assessment of the matter before it, including an objective assessment of the facts of the case and the applicability, of and the conformity of challenged measures with, the relevant covered agreements, and make such findings as will assist the DSB in making its rulings or recommendations.[66]

Panels are to be composed of well-qualified, governmental and/or non-governmental individuals, including persons who have served on or presented a case to a panel; or have served as a representative of a Member or of a contracting party to GATT 1947 or as a representative to the Council or Committee to any covered agreement or its predecessor (Kennedy or Tokyo Round) agreement; or have served in the Secretariat; or have taught or published on international trade law or policy; or have served as a senior trade policy official of a WTO Member.[67]

Selection of panelists is made with a view to ensuring the independence of panel members, a sufficiently diverse background and a wide spectrum of experience.[68] Citizens of the WTO Members whose governments are parties to the dispute or third parties as defined in the DSU may not serve on a panel concerned with that dispute, unless the parties to the dispute agree otherwise.[69] Panelists may be selected from an indicative list maintained by the Secretariat. The WTO Members may periodically suggest names to be added to the list upon approval by the DSB.[70] When a dispute is between a developing country Member and a developed country Member, the developing country Member may request that the panel include at least one panelist from a developing country Member.[71]

---

[64] DSU, *supra* note 4. Art. 24.2.

[65] DSU, *supra* note 4. Art. 12.7.

[66] DSU, *supra* note 4. Art. 11.

[67] DSU, *supra* note 4. Art. 8.1.

[68] DSU, *supra* note 4. Art. 8.2.

[69] DSU, *supra* note 4. Art. 8.3.

[70] DSU, *supra* note 4. Art. 8.4.

[71] DSU, *supra* note 4. Art. 8.10.

Panelists are proposed by the Secretariat to the parties to the dispute, who may oppose nominations only for compelling reasons.[72] Panelists are normally appointed by agreement of the parties. Where there is no agreement within 20 days after the date of establishment of the panel, the composition of the panel will, at the request of either party, be determined by the Director-General of the WTO, in consultation with the Chairman of the DSB and the Chairman of the relevant Council or Committee.[73] Once appointed, panelists serve in their individual capacities, not as government representatives or as representatives of any organization.[74] They are also subject to the Rules of Conduct for the Understanding on Rules and Procedures Governing the Settlement of Disputes (see: Rules of Conduct).

12.2.2.4 Appellate Body

If a party files an appeal against the report of the panel, the Appellate Body shall review the legal issues addressed by the panel and confirm or modify its findings.[75] In Brazil – Measures Affecting Desiccated Coconut, the Appellate Body upheld both the findings and legal interpretations of the panel. In contrast, in Japan – Taxes on Alcoholic Beverages, the Appellate Body affirmed the panel's conclusions but pointed out several areas where it considered the panel had erred in its legal reasoning.

Persons serving on the Appellate Body serve on divisions in rotation.[76] The DSB is responsible for appointing Appellate Body members.[77] The Appellate Body must be composed of persons of recognized authority, with demonstrated experience in law, international trade and the subject matter of the WTO Agreements generally.[78] The Appellate Body membership must be broadly representative of membership of the WTO.[79]

[72] DSU, *supra* note 4. Art. 8.6.

[73] DSU, *supra* note 4. Art. 8.7.

[74] DSU, *supra* note 4. Art. 8.9.

[75] DSU, *supra* note 4. Art. 17.6.

[76] DSU, *supra* note 4. Art. 17.1.

[77] DSU, *supra* note 4. Art. 17.2.

[78] DSU, *supra* note 4. Art. 17.3. 33 I.L.M. at 1236. After extended conflict over the geographical composition of the group, the initial members of the Appellate Body have been designated. The seven individuals who were appointed are: James Bacchus, a former U.S. Congressman and former Special Assistant to the United States Trade Representative; Christopher Beeby, a trade diplomat and former Ambassador from New Zealand; Klaus-Dieter Ehlermann, a German trade lawter and professor of international economic law; Florentino Feliciano, a Filipino Supreme Court Justice and former trade lawyer; Mitsuo Matsushita, a Japanese professor of international economic law with ties to the Japanese Ministry of Finance and Ministry of International Trade and Industry; Julio Lacarte Muro, a Uruguayan trade diplomat and participant in all eight GATT negotiation rounds; and Said el-Naggar, and Egyptian professor of economics. Biographical Notes on Members of World Trade Organization Appeals Body, (July–Dec.) Daily Rep. For Executives (BNA) No. 230, at M-1 (Nov. 30, 1995).

[79] DSU, *supra* note 4. Art. 17.3.

Each of the seven experts on the Appellate Body is appointed for a four-year term which is renewable once.[80] Three of them (called a Division) serve on any one case. The Appellate Body determines its own rules of procedure, that is, Working Procedures for Appellate Review.[81] An Appellate Body Secretariat provides assistance and administrative support to the Appellate Body.[82]

12.2.2.5 Arbitration

Arbitration may be resorted to by parties to a dispute, through mutual agreement.[83] The DSU does not contain detailed procedures regarding resort to arbitration, selection and operation of arbitrators or arbitrating entities. Parties to the dispute are free to apply the rules and procedures they deem appropriate through mutual agreement. Articles 21 and 22 DSU apply mutatis mutandis to arbitral awards.[84]

Arbitration may also be used to establish the "reasonable period of time" for implementation of DSB recommendations and rulings[85] and may be resorted to by a party subject to suspension of concessions or other obligations if it objects to the level of suspension proposed or claims that the principles and procedures to be followed by a complaining party suspending concessions or other obligations were not respected by that party.[86] In Japan – Taxes on Alcoholic Beverages, the United States applied for binding arbitration to determine the reasonable period of time for implementation by Japan of the recommendations of the Appellate Body. The Arbitrator found the reasonable period for implementation to be 15 months.[87]

12.2.2.6 Interested Parties

Only WTO Members can take part in dispute settlement under the WTO. The WTO dispute settlement is not open to the WTO observers, other international organizations, non-governmental organizations, local governments or private persons.

More than one Member may request the establishment of a panel related to the same matter, in which case a single panel may be established to examine these

[80] DSU, *supra* note 4. Art. 17.2.

[81] The Working Procedures appellate Review provide, inter alia, for the following: every effort will be made to take decisions by consensus; to ensure consistency and coherence in decision-making, the appellate Body members will convene on a regular basis to discuss matters of policy, practice, and procedure; the three-remedy division responsible for deciding an appeal will exchange view with other members before the division finalizes its reports; and uniform procedural rules govern filing and service of documents, exparte communications, notice of appeal, the contents of written submissions, and transmittal of the record. See Working Procedures for Appellate Review. 1997. WT/AB/WP/3, cited by Kennedy (1998, *supra* note 7, at 514).

[82] DSU, *supra* note 4. Art. 17.7.

[83] DSU, *supra* note 4. Art. 25.

[84] DSU, *supra* note 4. Art. 25.4.

[85] DSU, *supra* note 4. Art. 21.3(c).

[86] DSU, *supra* note 4. Art. 22.6.

[87] DSU, *supra* note 4. Art. 21.4.

complaints.[88] In United States-Import Prohibition of certain Shrimp and Shrimp Products, the DSB decided to establish one single panel, despite the separate request made by India once a panel had already been established at the request of the other Members. If more than one panel is established to examine complaints related to the same subject matter, the same persons are required, to the greatest extent possible, to serve as panelists on each of the separate panels and the timetable for the cases is to be harmonized.[89] In European Communities – Measures Affecting Meat and Meat products (Hormones), for instance, the complaint of Canada and that of the United States were reviewed by two separate panels composed of the same individuals.

Under certain conditions, parties which did not request consultations in the first place may request to be joined in consultations. If a Member other than the consulting Members considers that it has a substantial trade interest in provisioned consultations,[90] it may notify the consulting Members and the DSB of its desire to be joined in the consultations. Such a notification has to be submitted within 10 days after the circulation of the original request for consultations.[91] If the consulting Member to whom the request for consultation was addressed agrees that the claim of substantial interest is well founded, the requesting Member joins the consultations.[92] The DSB must be informed accordingly. If the request is not accepted, the Member concerned is free to request separate consultations.[93] Requests to be joined in consultations are found in almost all cases submitted to the DSB.

Complainant and respondent Members are the main parties to the disputes. Third parties also have an opportunity to be heard by panels and to make written submissions, provided they have a substantial interest in the matter before the panel and they have notified their interest to the DSB.[94] If a third party considers that a measure already the subject of a panel nullifies or impairs benefits accruing to it under any covered agreement, it may make its own request for the establishment of a panel. The original panel will be assigned the new dispute wherever possible.[95]

12.2.2.7 Experts

Panels have the right to seek information and technical advice from any individuals or bodies which they deem appropriate. They may seek information from any

---

[88] DSU, *supra* note 4. Art. 9.1.

[89] DSU, *supra* note 4. Art. 9.3.

[90] Art. XXII:1, GATT 1994; Art. XXII:1, GATS; other corresponding provisions of other covered agreements

[91] DSU, *supra* note 4. Art. 4.11.

[92] *Id.*

[93] *Id.*

[94] DSU, *supra* note 4. Art. 10.2.

[95] DSU, *supra* note 4. Art. 10.4.

relevant source.[96] However, before seeking information and technical advice from any individual or body within the jurisdiction of a Member, the panel must inform that Member.[97]

Panels may consult experts to obtain their opinion on certain aspects of the matter before them.[98] Regarding expert review group, with respect to a factual issue concerning a scientific or other technical matter raised by a party to a dispute, panels may request an advisory report in writing from an expert review group.[99] Expert review groups are under the panels' authority and report to the panel.[100] Their terms of reference and detailed working procedures are decided by the panel.[101] Final reports of expert review groups are issued to the parties to the dispute when submitted to the panel. Reports have only an advisory value.[102]

Participation in expert review groups is restricted to persons of professional standing and experience in the field in question.[103] Citizens of parties to the dispute cannot serve on an expert review group without the joint agreement of the parties to the dispute, except in exceptional circumstances when the panel considers that the need for specialized scientific expertise cannot be fulfilled otherwise. Government officials of parties to the dispute may not serve on an expert review group. Members of expert review groups serve in their individual capacities and not as government representatives, nor as representatives of any organization. Governments or organizations therefore must not give them instructions with regard to matters before an expert review group.[104]

12.2.2.8 Secretariat

1. Director-General

   The Director-General of the WTO may, acting in an ex officio capacity, offer good offices, conciliation or mediation with a view to assisting Members to settle a dispute.[105] Such an offer may normally be made during the consultation

[96] DSU, *supra* note 4. Art. 13.1.

[97] *Id.*

[98] Provisions in the covered agreements pursuant to which panels may have the possibility or the obligation to seek opinions of experts are the following: Art. 11.2 Agreement on the Application of Sanitary and Phytosanitary Measures; Art. 14.2 and 3, Annex 2 Agreement on Technical Barriers to Trade; Art. 19.3 and 4, Annex 2 Agreement on Implementation of Art. VII of the General Agreement on Tariffs and Trade 1994; Arts. 4.5, 24.3 Agreement on Subsidies and Countervailing Measures (SCM Agreement).

[99] DSU, *supra* note 4. Art. 13.2.

[100] DSU, *supra* note 4. Appendix 4.

[101] DSU, *supra* note 4. Appendix 4.1

[102] DSU, *supra* note 4. Appendix 4.6.

[103] DSU, *supra* note 4. Appendix 4.2.

[104] DSU, *supra* note 4. Appendix 4.3.

[105] DSU, *supra* note 4. Art. 5.6.

period, but good offices, conciliation or mediation[106] may, with the agreement of the parties to the dispute, continue while the panel process proceeds.[107]

In a dispute settlement procedure involving a least-developed country Member, when a satisfactory solution has not been found during consultations, the Director-General will, upon request by a least-developed country Member, offer his or her good offices, conciliation or mediation in order to help the parties to the dispute, before a request for a panel is made.[108] In providing such help, the Director-General may consult any source which he or she considers appropriate.[109]

The Director-General may also be requested, in certain circumstances, to appoint panel members. This is the case where, within 20 days after the date of the establishment of a panel, there has been no agreement among the parties on the composition of the panel.[110] The Director-General can act only at the request of either party in the dispute. The Director-General must determine the composition of the panel in consultation with the Chairman of the DSB and the Chairmen of the relevant Councils or Committees, after consulting the parties to the dispute.[111] He or she must appoint the panelists whom he or she considers most appropriate in accordance with the DSU and any other special or additional rules or procedures of the covered agreement(s) concerned in the dispute.

The Director-General may appoint an arbitrator[112] in cases where it is necessary to determine the reasonable period of time for implementation[113] or where a suspension of concessions or other obligations has been authorized by the DSB and the Member concerned objects to the level of suspension proposed, or claims that the principles and procedures to be followed when considering what concessions or other obligations to suspend were not respected.[114] The appointment of an arbitrator by the Director-General is an alternative to arbitration by the original panel.[115] which shall carry it out if its members are

---

[106] For the non-application of DSU of Art. 5 providing for good offices, conciliation, or mediation, see Porges (2003, pp. 164–165). "... There has been no mediation to date within a dispute. The only known mediation to date ... occurred instead of dispute settlement proceedings. The mediation successfully settled the differences between the parties...."

[107] DSU, *supra* note 4. Art. 5.5.

[108] DSU, *supra* note 4. Art. 24.2.

[109] For an example under GATT 1947, see: Japan – Measures Affecting the World Market for Copper Ores and Concentrates – Good Offices Report by the Director-General (BISD 36 S/199).

[110] DSU, *supra* note 4. Art. 8.7.

[111] *Id.*

[112] The arbitrator is not authorized to reconsider the merits of a case. Moreover, for example, with regard to the suspension remedy itself an arbitrator has only a limited function: to "determine whether the level of such suspension is equivalent to the level of nullification or impairment". DSU, *supra* note 4. Art. 22, para. 7. Cited by Reitz (1996, pp. 592–539).

[113] DSU, *supra* note 4. Art. 21.3(c).

[114] DSU, *supra* note 4. Art. 22.6.

[115] It arbitration is ordered, the DSB refers the question of the appropriate level of suspension back to the original panel if its members are still available; otherwise the DSB refers the matter to on

available.[116] The Director-General may appoint as arbitrator an individual or a group.

2. Secretariat Staff
The Secretariat staff ensures the administrative support of the DSB.[117] The Secretariat also assists Members in respect of dispute settlement at their request.[118] The Secretariat is to provide additional legal advice and assistance in respect of dispute settlement to developing country Members. To this end, the Secretariat is required to make available a qualified legal expert from the WTO technical cooperation services to any developing country Member which so requests. The appointed expert will assist the developing country Member. However, the expert must do so in such a way that the continued impartiality of the Secretariat is respected.[119]

   The Secretariat assists panels, especially on the legal, historical and procedural aspects of the matters dealt with by the panels, but also with respect to secretarial and technical support.[120] The Secretariat staff assisting a panel is usually composed of a secretary to the panel and a legal officer.

12.2.3 Procedures

12.2.3.1 Rules of Conduct

Under the DSU, the "players" in a dispute settlement process are subject to certain rules aimed at ensuring due process and unbiased recommendations and rulings. For instance, there must not be any ex parte communications with the panel or Appellate Body members concerning matters under consideration by the panel or the Appellate Body.[121] Rules of Conduct for the Understanding on Rules and Procedures Governing the Settlement of Disputes are applicable to panel members, Appellate Body members, experts assisting panels, arbitrators, Secretariat staff and members of the Textile Monitoring Body, referred to as "covered persons".

---

arbitrator or group of arbitrators appointed by the Director-General. DSU, *supra* note 4. Art. 22.6, cited by Reitz (1996, *supra* note 112, at 592–539). Thus although styled as "arbitration" the process may actually be second phase of the panel proceeding that led to the finding of a violation in the first instance (Reitz 1996, *id*).

[116] The Understanding does not specify what is meant by members being "available". The situation of some, but not all members of the original panel being available can be expected arise. The Director-General might appoint as arbitrator the member or members of the original panel who are available, or replace a missing panel member, or designate a new person or group. The Understanding appears to leave this in the discretion of the Director-General (Reitz 1996, *supra* note 112, fn. 175).

[117] DSU, *supra* note 4. Art. 27.1.

[118] DSU, *supra* note 4. Art. 27.2.

[119] *Id.*

[120] DSU, *supra* note 4. Art. 27.1.

[121] DSU, *supra* note 4. Art. 18.1.

Under the Rules of Conduct, covered persons are required to be independent and impartial, to avoid direct or indirect conflicts of interest, and to respect the confidentiality of proceedings of bodies pursuant to the dispute settlement mechanism, in order to ensure that the integrity and impartiality of that mechanism is maintained. In particular the covered persons are required to disclose the existence or development of any interest, relationship or matter that he or she could reasonably be expected to know and that is likely to affect, or give rise to justifiable doubts as to that person's independence or impartiality. Such disclosure has to include information on financial, professional and other active interest as well as considered statements of public opinion and employment or family interests.

12.2.3.2 Consultation

In the DSU, Members affirm their resolve to strengthen and improve the effectiveness of the consultation procedures.[122] As part of this resolve, they undertake to accord sympathetic consideration to, and afford adequate opportunity for, consultations regarding any representation made by another Member concerning measures affecting the operation of any WTO Agreement taken within the territory of the original Member.[123] Requests for consultations[124] must be notified to the DSB,[125] but the consultations themselves remain confidential.[126] Mutually agreed solutions to matters formally raised under the consultation provisions of the covered agreements must be notified to the DSB and the relevant councils and committees, where any Member may raise any point relating to them.[127]

There are rules for normal consultations and for consultations on urgent matters. Before initiating consultations, a Member must exercise its judgment as to whether such an action would be fruitful, the aim of the dispute settlement mechanism being to secure a positive solution to the dispute.[128] The Member to which a normal request for consultation is made is required, unless otherwise mutually agreed, to reply to the request within 10 days after the date of its receipt and to enter into consultations in good faith within a period of no more than 30 days after the date of

[122] DSU, *supra* note 4. Art. 4.1.

[123] DSU, *supra* note 4. Art. 4.2, and footnote 3 to Art. 4.3.

[124] For the bilateral vs. plurilateral consultation under the GATT Art. XXIII and GATT Art. XXIII, see Porges (2003, *supra* note 106, at 157–160). (Stating "... The procedural choice between Art. XXIII and Art. XXII as a vehicle provides an opportunity to signal a desire to talk settlement, or instead, to enhance the leverage of a single disputant by soliciting attendance by others who are supportive and to build coalitions. An Art. XXII consultation provides a stage on which to pillory a Member with an unpopular measure ... In theory, disputes where the consultations are solely conducted under Art. XXII should be less likely to settle ... they do find that involvement of multiple complaints, ..., reduces the likelihood that the defending party will make concessions").

[125] DSU, *supra* note 4. Art. 4.4.

[126] DSU, *supra* note 4. Art. 4.6.

[127] DSU, *supra* note 4. Art. 3.6.

[128] DSU, *supra* note 4. Art. 3.7.

receipt, with a view to reaching a mutually satisfactory solution.[129] If the requested Member does not do so, the Member that requested consultations may proceed directly to request the establishment of a panel.[130]

In cases of urgency, including those which concern perishable goods, Members must enter into consultations within a period of no more than 10 days after the date of receipt of the request. If the consultations fail to settle the dispute within a period of 20 days after the date of receipt of the request, the complaining party may request the establishment of a panel.[131] Under the DSU, a third party requesting to join consultations must have a substantial trade interest. Moreover, such a third party may participate at the consultation stage only if consultations were requested duly[132] and if the Member to which the request is made agrees that the third party has a substantial trade interest.

12.2.3.3 Panels

If the consultations have failed to settle a dispute within 60 days after the date of receipt of the request for consultations, the complaining party may request the establishment of a panel. An earlier request for a panel is permitted if the consulting parties jointly consider that consultations have failed to settle the dispute.[133] A request for the establishment of a panel must be made in writing. It must indicate whether consultations were held, identify the specific measures at issue and provide a brief summary of the legal basis of the complaint sufficient to present the problem clearly.[134]

The panel will be established at the latest at the DSB meeting following that at which the request first appears as an item on the agenda of the DSB, unless the complaining party no longer requests it or the DSB decides by consensus at that meeting not to establish a panel.[135] If the complaining party so requests, a special meeting of the DSB must be convened for the purpose of establishing the panel within 15 days of the request, provided that at least 10 days' advance notice is given.[136]

[129] Art. II of the DSU provides that panels should consult regularly with the parties to the dispute and give them adequate opportunity to develop a mutually satisfactory solution, and some GATT panel reports in the 1972–1984 period recorded activity by the panel encouraging settlement negotiations. Cited by Porges (2003, *supra* note 106, at 167). However, it was indicated to be on trace in any WTO panel report of any conciliation or mediation activity by a WTO panel proceeding ID.

[130] DSU, *supra* note 4. Art. 4.3.

[131] DSU, *supra* note 4. Art. 4.8.

[132] See Art. XXII:1, GATT 1994; Art. XXII:1, GATS; other corresponding provisions of the covered agreements.

[133] DSU, *supra* note 4. Art. 4.7.

[134] DSU, *supra* note 4. Art. 6.2.

[135] DSU, *supra* note 4. Art. 6.1.

[136] DSU, *supra* note 4. Footnote 5 to Art. 6.1.

A panel is considered to be properly constituted after the terms of reference[137] have been agreed upon and the panelists have been selected.[138] Panels usually have standard terms of reference, unless the parties to the dispute agree otherwise within 20 days from the establishment of the panel.[139] In Brazil – Measures Affecting Desiccated Coconut, special terms of reference were agreed upon by the parties. The practice of the WTO has been to refer, in the standard terms of reference, to the document in which the complaining party (parties) has (have) requested the establishment of the panel, and to leave it to the panel to decide on any jurisdictional issue as well as whether sufficient consultations took place on the measure for which a panel is requested. If other than standard terms of reference are agreed upon, any Member may raise any point relating thereto in the DSB.[140] This provision is indicative of the multilateral character of the DSU dispute settlement process.

The composition of the panel[141] takes place once the panel has been established by the DSB. Potential candidates must meet certain requirements in terms of qualifications. Panels are composed of three panelists unless the parties to the dispute agree, within 10 days from the establishment of the panel, to a panel composed of five panelists.[142] The Secretariat proposes nominations for the panel to the parties to the dispute. The parties to the dispute must not oppose nominations except for compelling reasons.[143]

An indicative list has been established, containing the names of governmental and non-governmental persons, from which panelists may be drawn.[144] Citizens of a party or a third party to a dispute may not serve as panelists, without the agreement of the parties.[145] When a dispute is between a developing country Member and a developed country Member the panel shall, if the developing country Member so requests, include at least one panelist from a developing country Member.[146]

If there is no agreement on the composition of the panel within 20 days after the date of its establishment, either party may request the Director-General to determine the composition of the panel by appointing panelists, in consultation with the Chairman of the DSB and the Chairman of the relevant Council or Committee.[147] The Chairman of the DSB shall inform the Members of the composition of the panel thus formed no later than 10 days after the date the Chairman receives such a request.[148]

---

[137] DSU, *supra* note 4. Art. 7.

[138] DSU, *supra* note 4. Art. 8.

[139] DSU, *supra* note 4. Art. 7.1.

[140] DSU, *supra* note 4. Art. 7.3.

[141] DSU, *supra* note 4. Art. 8.

[142] DSU, *supra* note 4. Art. 8.5.

[143] DSU, *supra* note 4. Art. 8.6.

[144] DSU, *supra* note 4. Art. 8.4.

[145] DSU, *supra* note 4. Art. 8.3.

[146] DSU, *supra* note 4. Art. 8.10.

[147] DSU, *supra* note 4. Art. 8.7.

[148] United States - The Cuban Liberty and Democratic Solidarity Act, WT/DS 38 (Mar. 31, 1998).

Where more than one Member requests the establishment of a panel related to the same matter, the DSB should, whenever feasible, establish a single panel to examine these complaints taking into account the rights of all Members concerned.[149] If more than one panel is established, to the greatest extent possible the same persons are required to serve as panelists on each of the separate panels.[150]

Terms of Reference

A panel's terms of reference are important for two reasons. First, terms of reference fulfill an important due process objective — they give the parties and third parties sufficient information concerning the claims at issue in the dispute in order to allow them an opportunity to respond to the complainant's case. Second, they establish the jurisdiction of the panel by defining the precise claims at issue in the dispute. The followings are the illustrated cases in relation with terms of reference.

T.6.1.2 Brazil — Desiccated Coconut, p. 22, DSR 1997:I, p. 167 at 186 (WT/DS22/AB/R)

… the "matter" referred to a panel for consideration consists of the specific claims stated by the parties to the dispute in the relevant documents specified in the terms of reference. We agree with the approach taken in previous adopted panel reports that a matter, which includes the claims composing that matter, does not fall within a panel's terms of reference unless the claims are identified in the documents referred to or contained in the terms of reference.

T.6.2.6 India — Patents (US), paras. 89–90 (WT/DS50/AB/R)

… a claim must be included in the request for establishment of a panel in order to come within a panel's terms of reference in a given case. …

… the convenient phrase, "including but not necessarily limited to", is simply not adequate to "identify the specific measures at issue and provide a brief summary of the legal basis of the complaint sufficient to present the problem clearly" as required by Article 6.2 of the DSU. If this phrase incorporates Article 63, what Article of the TRIPs Agreement does it not incorporate? Therefore, this phrase is not sufficient to bring a claim relating to Article 63 within the terms of reference of the Panel.

Source: Terms of Reference of Panels. http://www.wto.org/english/tratop_e/dispu_e/repertory_e/t6_e.htm

[149] Shrimp United States - Import Prohibition of certain Shrimp and Shrimp Products, complaint by India, Malaysia, Pakistan and Thailand, WT/DS 58 (Oct. 12, 1998).

[150] DSU, *supra* note 4. Art. 9.3.

12.2.3.4 Panel Process

During an initial "organizational" meeting, the panel, guided by the suggested timetable in Appendix 3 DSU, determines its calendar of work in consultation with the parties.[151] Parties exchange written submissions and the panel convenes at least two hearings where parties are entitled to present their views orally and the panel may ask clarifications and questions.[152] Panels have the right to ask written questions. Third parties with a substantial interest in the matter before the panel, and who have notified their interest to the DSB, are to be granted an opportunity to be heard by the panel and make written submissions.[153] Generally, parties exchange sequentially, within two months from the composition of the panel, a first set of written submissions in which the complaining party presents the arguments in support of its claim(s), and the respondent party presents the arguments for refusing to accept the claims of the complaining party (parties). The third parties receive these submissions.[154]

Within two weeks of the exchange of submissions, the panel holds its first meeting with the parties during which parties plead their case and are invited to respond to questions from the panel and from the other parties in order to clarify all the legal and factual issues. During this first meeting, a session for the third parties is held during which they are invited to submit their arguments to the panel. Within four weeks after the first panel meeting, parties exchange written rebuttals and the panel holds a second substantive meeting with the parties. Once written submissions have been received and the parties and third parties have been heard, the panel issues the draft descriptive part of its panel report for comments in writing by the parties.[155] In accordance with the proposed timetable in Appendix 3 DSU, parties are invited to make comments on the draft descriptive part within two weeks.

Two to four weeks after the receipt of comments on the descriptive part, the panel issues its interim report containing the revised descriptive part and the findings of the report. Parties are again invited to make comments and may request an interim review meeting of the panel to further argue specific points raised with

[151] DSU, *supra* note 4. Art. 12.3.

[152] For the dark sides of the legalization of the panel process which taken the form, for example, of a dramatic increase in procedural claims and objections raised by disputing parties, as well as in the number of pages spent by panels on procedural issues, under the WTO mechanism, see Pauwelyn (2003, pp. 126–129). "First, the legalization has focused almost exclusively on the panel and appellate Body Process ... with the risk of 'too much law' in that process, the fact remains ... there is 'not enough law' ... The second ... it sometimes risks going too far, especially when it is viewed in the context of state-to-state legislation... The combined result of these two flaws ... is that the WTO has been faced with a number of disputes that have remained unresolved even after they went through the entire WTO litigation process...".

[153] DSU, *supra* note 4. Art. 10.2.

[154] DSU, *supra* note 4. Art. 10.3.

[155] DSU, *supra* note 4. Art. 15.1.

respect to the interim report. This is the interim review stage.[156] The final report must contain a reference to all the arguments raised by the parties during the interim review stage.[157]

Finally, the panel issues its final report to the parties within two weeks following the interim review meeting and circulates it to all members three weeks after issuance.

12.2.3.5 Time Periods

As a general rule, panels are required to issue the final report to the parties within six months from the date when the composition and the terms of reference of the panel have been agreed upon. In cases of urgency, the panel is to aim to issue its report to the parties to the dispute within three months from its constitution.[158] When the panel considers that it cannot issue its report within six months or three months in case of urgency, it must inform the DSB in writing of the reasons for the delay and provide an estimate of the period within which it will issue its report. In any case, the examination is to be completed within nine months of the establishment of the panel.[159] Panels may suspend their work at the request of the complaining party for a period not exceeding 12 months.

12.2.3.6 Specific Timetables Under SCM Agreement

Accelerated procedures with shorter time periods apply under the Agreement on Subsidies on Countervailing Measures, with respect to dispute settlement on prohibited subsidies and actionable subsidies. Regarding prohibited subsidies, if consultations have not led to a mutually agreed solution within 30 days,[160] any party to the consultation may refer the matter to the DSB for immediate establishment of a panel, unless the DSB decides by consensus not to establish a panel. The panel must submit its report within 90 days of the date of its composition and establishment[161] and the DSB must adopt the report within 30 days of its circulation to all Members, unless it decides by consensus not to adopt it or unless one of the parties notifies the DSB of its decision to appeal.[162] Otherwise, for the purpose of dispute settlement in relation to prohibited subsidies, time periods applicable under the DSU for the conduct of such disputes shall be half those set out in the DSU.[163]

Dispute settlement with respect to actionable subsidies is also subject to some specific deadlines. For instance, composition and terms of reference of the panel

[156] DSU, *supra* note 4. Art. 15.

[157] DSU, *supra* note 4. Art. 15.3.

[158] DSU, *supra* note 4. Art. 12.8.

[159] DSU, *supra* note 4. Art. 12.9.

[160] SCM Agreement, *supra* note 98. Art. 4.4.

[161] SCM Agreement, *supra* note 98. Art. 4.6.

[162] SCM Agreement, *supra* note 98. Art. 4.8.

[163] SCM Agreement, *supra* note 98. Art. 4.12.

must be established within 15 days from the date the panel is established[164] and the panel must circulate its report to all Members within 120 days of the date of its composition and the establishment of its terms of reference.[165] The DSB must adopt the report within 30 days of its circulation to all Members, unless it decides by consensus not to adopt it or unless one of the parties notifies the DSB of its decision to appeal.[166] Other specific deadlines apply to the work of the Appellate Body and the adoption of its report,[167] as well as for the time period beyond which the DSB must authorize the complaining Member to take countermeasures.[168]

In cases of multiple complainants where more than one panel is established, the timetable for the process before each panel must be harmonized.[169] Where a single panel is established, it must organize its examination and present its findings to the DSB in such a manner that the rights which the parties to the dispute would have enjoyed had separate panels examined the complaints are in no way impaired. If one of the parties requests, the panel must submit separate reports on the dispute concerned. The written submissions by each of the complainants must be made available to the other complainants, and each complainant has the right to be present when any one of the other complainants presents its views to the panel.[170]

12.2.3.7 Appeal Process

The Appellate Body is responsible for hearing appeals from panel decisions.[171] Only parties to the dispute, not third parties, may appeal a panel report. Third parties which have notified the DSB of a substantial interest in the matter before the panel, may make written submissions to, and be given an opportunity to be heard by, the Appellate Body.[172]

Appeals are limited to issues of law covered in the panel report and legal interpretations developed by the panel.[173] The Appellate Body must address, but also limit its review to, each of the issues of law covered by the panel report and the legal interpretations developed by the panel which were appealed during the appellate proceeding.[174] The Appellate Body may uphold, modify or reverse the legal findings and conclusions of the panel.[175] The Appellate Body shall

[164] SCM Agreement, *supra* note 98. Art. 7.4.
[165] SCM Agreement, *supra* note 98. Art. 7.5.
[166] SCM Agreement, *supra* note 98. Art. 7.6.
[167] SCM Agreement, *supra* note 98. Art. 7.7.
[168] SCM Agreement, *supra* note 98. Art. 7.9.
[169] DSU, *supra* note 4. Art. 9.3.
[170] DSU, *supra* note 4. Art. 9.2.
[171] DSU, *supra* note 4. Art. 17.
[172] DSU, *supra* note 4. Art. 17.4.
[173] DSU, *supra* note 4. Art. 17.6.
[174] DSU, *supra* note 4. Art. 17.6 and 12.
[175] DSU, *supra* note 4. Art. 17.13.

generally complete its review process within 60 days. In no case shall it exceed 90 days.[176]

12.2.3.8 Deliberation and Decision-Making

Panel deliberations are confidential.[177] Reports of panels are drafted without the presence of the parties to the dispute, in the light of the information provided and the statements made.[178] The opinions expressed in the panel report by individual panelists are anonymous.[179] Before the entry into force of the WTO, a few panel reports included dissenting opinions.[180]

The proceedings of the Appellate Body are confidential. Reports of the Appellate Body are drafted without the presence of the parties to the dispute and in the light of the information provided and the statements made.[181] The opinions expressed in the Appellate Body report by individuals serving on the Appellate Body are anonymous.[182] To date, there have not been any dissenting opinions, and the Rules of Procedure of the Appellate Body envisage that members of the Appellate Body shall make every effort to take their decisions by consensus. Where, nevertheless, a decision cannot be arrived at by consensus, the matter at issue has to be decided by majority vote.

12.2.3.9 Content of Reports

Panel reports have two main parts: the "descriptive part" and the "findings". The descriptive part is usually composed of an introduction, factual aspects, claims of the parties (also sometimes called "Findings Requested"), submission(s) of the third party or parties, main arguments of the parties and specific arguments raised during the interim review stage.[183] The "findings" part is composed of the findings as such

---

[176] DSU, *supra* note 4. Art. 17.5.

[177] DSU, *supra* note 4. Art. 14.1.

[178] DSU, *supra* note 4. Art. 14.2.

[179] DSU, *supra* note 4. Art. 14.3.

[180] See: e.g. EEC – Program of Minimum Import Prices, License and Surety Deposits for Certain Processed Fruits and Vegetables (BISD 25 S/68).

[181] DSU, *supra* note 4. Art. 17.10.

[182] DSU, *supra* note 4. Art. 17.11.

[183] For the lack of a satisfactory method for resolving issues of that raised in disputes before panels, see Reitz (1996, *supra* note 112, at 602–603). (Stating "the system has lacked and continues to lack a satisfactory method for resolving issues of fact that arise in disputes before panels. Some controversies are framed in terms of the facial validity of trade measures in dispute, but inevitably controversies take the form of considering the effects of trade measures in dispute, and sometimes take the form of considering the purposes of the measures. Questions of effect and purpose are issues of fact, for which rules of evidence, burden of proof, and so forth must be created. Panels and the Appellate Body will be forced to develop methods for dealing with disputes that turn on questions of fact. They will be aided to some extent by the power, under GATT 1994, to refer some issues to groups of experts, or in the case of remedies, to an arbitrator. However, that will be only a partial solution to the broader problem and, even where referrals are made, the

and the conclusions and recommendations. An Appellate Body report has a somewhat different structure: it is generally composed of an introduction including some factual aspects, a part on the issues raised in the appeal, and the discussion of these issues, and the findings and conclusions and recommendations.

Where a panel or the Appellate Body concludes that a measure is inconsistent with a covered agreement, it must recommend that the Member concerned bring the measure into conformity[184] with that agreement. In addition to its recommendations, the panel or Appellate Body may suggest ways in which the Member concerned could implement the recommendations.[185] Recommendations or rulings[186] made by the Dispute Settlement Body shall be aimed at achieving a satisfactory settlement of the matter in accordance with the rights and obligations under this understanding and under the covered agreement.[187]

12.2.3.10 Adoption

Regarding adoption of panel reports, within 60 days after the date of circulation of a panel report to the Members, the report must be adopted at a DSB meeting unless a party to the dispute formally notifies the DSB of its decision to appeal or the DSB decides by consensus not to adopt the report.[188] If a party has notified its decision to appeal, the report by the panel cannot be considered for adoption by the DSB until after completion of the appeal.[189] This adoption procedure is without prejudice to

---

Appellate Body and panels will face questions concerning how the experts or arbitrator determined the facts in controversy.")

[184] For the reasons for preferring the compliance remedy under the WTO dispute resolution system, see Reitz (1996, *supra* note 112, at 589). (Stating "There are several obvious reasons for preferring the compliance remedy. It restores the equilibrium of the international economic order under the terms of the prior agreements of the parties concerned. Once the offending measure how been terminated or corrected, a good relationship among the disputants should also be restored. Other remedies may have secondary consequences that con not be offset easily and that may linger well beyond the appropriate time. One weakness in a pure compliance remedy, however, is that the aggrieved party many have suffered injury during the period of violation for which no restitution or damages are imposed on the offending party. Unfortunately, a compliance-centered remedial system does not deal effectively with such matters").

[185] DSU, *supra* note 4. Art. 19.1.

[186] For the paradoxical terms of "recommendations or rulings", see Reitz (1996, *supra* note 112, at 596). (Stating "'recommendations or rulings' is drawn directly from the awkward phrasing of GATT Art. XXIII. This phrase seems paradoxical. In the normal meaning of words, recommendations can be accepted or rejected as the parties see fist while rulings are meant to be definitive. Either conciliation or adjudication can lead to a 'satisfactory settlement' if that phrase is construed broadly. Reference to 'rights and obligations' is more aligned with rulings than to recommendations.")

[187] DSU, *supra* note 4. Art. 3.4.

[188] This virtually automatic adoption panel reports led the parties to introduce an additional layer of possible review through the establishment of a standing Appellate Body (Leebron 1995, *supra* note 15, at 15).

[189] DSU, *supra* note 4. Art. 16.4.

the right of Members to express their views on a panel report.[190] If a meeting of the DSB is not scheduled during this period, such a meeting of the DSB must be held to discuss and adopt the report.[191]

Regarding adoption of Appellate Body Reports, an Appellate Body Report must be adopted by the DSB and unconditionally accepted by the parties to the dispute unless the DSB decides by consensus not to adopt the Appellate Body report within 30 days following its circulation to Members. This adoption procedure is without prejudice to the right of Members to express their views on an Appellate Body report. If a meeting of the DSB is not scheduled during this period, such a meeting must be held to discuss and adopt the report.[192] A practice has developed whereby the Appellate Body report and the related panel report, as modified by the Appellate Body report, are adopted by the DSB at the same time.

12.2.4 Voluntary Implementation

In the WTO, there is no independent policing body responsible for enforcing the recommendations of panels and the Appellate Body. The DSB states that prompt compliance with the recommendations or rulings of the DSB is essential in order to ensure the effective resolution of disputes.[193] The DSB, composed of all the WTO Members, supervises the implementation of panel and Appellate Body reports.

The surveillance and implementation procedures require that: at a DSB meeting held within 30 days after the adoption of the report(s), the losing party must state its intentions in respect of implementation of the recommendations adopted.[194] If it is impracticable to comply immediately, the party will be granted a reasonable period of time. This reasonable period of time: (i) may be the period of time proposed by the Member concerned with the approval of the DSB[195]; or (ii) may be agreed upon by the parties within 45 days after the adoption of the report[196]; or (iii) may be determined by arbitration within 90 days after the adoption of the report.[197]

When the reasonable period of time is arbitrated, a guideline for the arbitrator is that the reasonable period of time to implement panel or Appellate Body

[190] *Id.*

[191] DSU, *supra* note 4. Footnote 7 to Art. 16.4.

[192] DSU, *supra* note 4. Art. 17.14, and Footnote 8 to Art. 17.14.

[193] DSU, *supra* note 4. Art. 21.1.

[194] DSU, *supra* note 4. Art. 21.3.

[195] DSU, *supra* note 4. Art. 21.3(a).

[196] DSU, *supra* note 4. Art. 21.3(b).

[197] DSU, *supra* note 4. Art. 21.3(c).

recommendations should not exceed 15 months from the date of adoption of a panel or Appellate Body report.[198] However, that time may be shorter or longer, depending upon the particular circumstances.[199]

The period from the date of establishment of a panel by the DSB until the date of determination of the reasonable period of time is also not to exceed 15 months unless the parties to the dispute agree otherwise. Where either the panel or the Appellate Body has acted to extend the period of time for their consideration of a case, the additional time taken shall be added to the 15-month period; however, unless the parties to the dispute agree that there are exceptional circumstances, the total time is not to exceed 18 months.[200] If there is disagreement as to the consistency with the WTO Agreement of measures taken to comply with DSB recommendations, a party may have recourse to dispute settlement procedures, referring the matter to the initial panel wherever possible for expedited adjudication.[201]

12.2.5 Non-compliance

In cases of non-compliance parties may agree to compensation.[202] In the absence of such agreement the prevailing Member may retaliate,[203] but only after obtaining the prior authorization of the DSB. If the WTO Member concerned fails within the reasonable period of time to bring the measure found to be inconsistent with

[198] In Japan – Taxes on Alcoholic Beverages (WT/DS11), the arbitrator found 15 months to be the reasonable period for implementation of the recommendations.

[199] DSU, *supra* note 4. Art. 21.3.

[200] DSU, *supra* note 4. Art. 21.4.

[201] DSU, *supra* note 4. Art. 21.5.

[202] The Understanding obligates a prevailing party to propose suspensions in the same sector as that in which the violation was found. Thus, if the violation concerned goods, the retaliation remedy should, if practicable and effective, apply to goods. Otherwise, the prevailing party may seek to suspend concessions or obligations in other sectors under the same agreement. If that is not practicable and, effective, and if "the circumstances are serious enough," the suspension may apply to concessions or obligations under another covered agreement. DSU, *supra* note 4. Art. 22, para. 3(0), cited by Reitz (1996, *supra* note 112, fn. 176).

[203] The integrated dispute settlement under WTO mechanism allows for the possibility of the prevailing party suspending concessions under one agreement when another party has nullified or impaired its rights under a different agreement (Leebron 1995, *supra* note 15, at 16). This allowance is to "spread the leverage", that is, more countries will have the potential to suspend concessions of substantial interest to their trading partiers, which is different from that under the GATT system. Under the GATT system, a country with very limited imports of goods from another GATT party to which it exports goods had virtually no means to insist that country honor its GATT commitments (Leebron 1995, *id*).

the covered agreement into compliance in accordance with the recommendations, that Member must, if so requested, enter into negotiations[204] with a view to agreeing on mutually acceptable compensation.[205]

The DSU provides that compensation or retaliation are only temporary measures available in the event that the recommendations and rulings are not implemented within a reasonable period of time. DSU authorization for retaliatory measures, that is, suspension of concessions,[206] will be granted within 30 days from the expiration of the "reasonable period of time" unless arbitration by the original panel is requested in respect of the Level of suspension proposed.[207]

---

[204] Negotiations over compensation are likely to take place without formal participation of the panel, the DSB, or any other GATT entity, but the Direction-General or others in the WTO Secretariat's office may assist in certain individual controversies (Reitz 1996, *supra* note 112, at 590).

[205] For the complicated aspects of compensation, see Kennedy (1998, *supra* note 7, at 515–516). (Stating "Compensation might restore the overall balance of trade liberalization that existed to the dispute if, for example, the offending Member offers to reduce tariffs on products of export interest to the complaining Member. However, any compensation agreement in the form of improved market access for the complaining Member's goods must be 'consistent with the covered agreements,' that is, it must be instituted on an MFN basis, thereby generalizing the benefit of the compensation to all WTO Members. This requirement could complicate compensation negotiations.")

[206] Regarding the suspension of concessions, the general principle is that the complaining Member fist should seek to suspend concessions with respect to the same sector in which the violation occurred, i.e., cross-sector retaliation is discouraged. For example, with respect to a trade-in-goods violation, a suspension of concessions may take place with regard to goods generally. If GATS has been violated, then the suspension should focus on the principal service sector affected (there are eleven, including, for example, telecommunication and financial services) If the TRIPS Agreement has been violated, then the suspension should focus on the specific intellectual property right that was violated (e.g., patent, trademark, copyright). DSU Art. 22.3(f), cited by Kennedy (1998, *supra* note 7, at 516). If a sector-specific suspension is not practicable or effective, then the suspension may be in other sectors under the same agreement (e.g., suspension of telecommunication trade benefits in retaliation for a financial services violation). If such retaliation is not practicable or effective, or the circumstances are serious enough, then suspension under another agreement may be authorized. DSU, *supra* note 4. Art. 22.3, cited by Kennedy (1998, *id*). The level of the suspension is to e equivalent to the level of the nullification or impairment. If the Member concerned objects to the proposed level of suspension or to cross-sector retaliation, the matter is to be referred to binding arbitration which is to be completed within 60 days. DSU, *supra* note 4. Art. 22.3, cited by Kennedy (1998, *id*).

[207] DSU, *supra* note 4. Art. 22(6), The arbitrator may only examine whether the level of the retaliatory measures is equivalent to the level of nullification or impairment caused by the condemned measure and whether such measures are permitted under the covered agreement. The DSB will authorization to retaliate in accordance with the arbitrator's decision unless there is a consensus against it. DSU, *supra* note 4. Art. 22(7). This procedure was applied for the first time in the European Communities-Regime for the Importation, Sales and Distribution of Bananas. Distribution of Bananas, Decision by Arbitrators, WT/DS27/ARB/ECU (Mar, 24, 2000) European Communities-Regime for Importation, Sales and ("Banana Dispute"), where the arbitrator reduced the level of suspension sought by the United States against the EU from US$520,000,000 to US$191,400,000. This level was determined by the arbitrators to be the level

The full implementation of the recommendation to bring a measure into conformity with the covered agreements remains the preferred outcome.[208] The matter is retained on the agenda of the DSB until the issue is resolved. However, in the case of a non-violation complaint, there is no obligation to withdraw the measure found to be nullifying or impairing the benefit under, or impeding the objections of the relevant covered agreements. In such cases the parties to the dispute have to make mutually satisfactory adjustments and compensation may be a part of such adjustment.

12.2.6 Surveillance

Surveillance by the DSB is an important feature of the dispute settlement mechanism of the WTO. Good-faith compliance by the Member, surveillance and authorization of retaliatory measures are the only instruments available to the WTO to secure the implementation of panel and Appellate Body recommendations.[209]

Assignment

To ensure students become equipped with the capability to apply knowledge from the classroom to the field, students are, in this chapter, required to write a report, deliver a presentation and participate in a discussion on the following issues:

---

of nullification suffered by the United States and was approved by the DSB. Similarly, in European Communities-Measures Concerning Meat Products (Hormones), European Communities-Measures Concerning Meat and Meat Products (Hormones), WT/DS26, the EU offered compensation in view of the likelihood that it would not be able to comply with the recommendations and rulings of the DSB by the deadline. Canada and the united States, however, requested authorization for the suspension of concessions in the amount of US$202,000,000 and CAN$75,000,000, respectively. At the EU's request, the level of suspension was referred to the original Panel for arbitration. The arbitrators determined the level of nullification suffered by the United States to be equal to US$116,800,000 and that of Canada to be equal to CAN$11,300,000. Cited by Clough (2000, pp. 262–323).

[208] See DSU, *supra* note 4. Art. 22.1. For more detailed, see Kennedy (1998, *supra* note 7, at 515). (Stating "By removing the offending measure, trade liberalization is promoted and trade equilibrium restored. In terms of a complete remedy, however, the aggrieved Member is not necessarily made whole solely by the removal of the offending measure. The specific remedy of removing the offending measure may not compensate the complaining Member for any trade losses it may have suffered as a result of the responding Member's violation. However, in cases involving, for example, as improper assessment of ordinary customs duties, antidumping duties, or countervailing duties, refund procedures exist under national law.")

[209] For the proposals towards both more effective sanctions and positive incentives to achieve implementation, see Pauwelyn (2003, *supra* note 152, at 136–137). (Stating "the role of the DSB as a multilateral compliance body should be enhanced. . . . Obtaining compliance with WTO rules should not be a burden borne only by the complaint. In order to get a more active DSB its decision making rule of positive consensus ought then be changed to, for example, three-fourths majority. In some cases . . . , in order to end a dispute, a waiver may be needed . . .").

1. The historical experience of the Member countries' use of dispute settlement procedures since the WTO launched in 1995.
2. The US-Section 301 case focusing on the violation of the WTO Agreement by the legislations themselves, which are not in compliance with the WTO provisions.

Further Issues 13

Learning Objectives

This chapter is to help students understand:

1. Conflicts and harmonization between the rules of the multilateral trading system and policies to protect the environment;
2. Main reasons of the WTO mechanism's failure to provide complete provisions to cover the environment;
3. The WTO's competence for policy coordination in the environmental area;
4. Anti-competitive practices as trade barriers;
5. International efforts to regulate anti-competitive practices;

13.1 Trade and Environments

13.1.1 Introduction

During the past roughly 20 years since the WTO was established, for the purpose of sustainable development[1] and promotion of free trade, a variety of issues have attracted the Members' interests. Among those, the relationship between trade and environment has constantly drawn their attention and has challenged the principles and institutions of the international trade order. Along with this problem, the WTO has difficulty in interpreting whether a series of unilateral trade measures of one Member country are appropriate under a multilateral trading system aiming at

[1] Faced with a chronical wave of criticism over the GATT's promotion of trade liberalization at the expense of environmental merits, see Generally Esty (1993, pp. 52–54); McDonald (1993, pp. 397, 405, n. 32), cited by Ni (2004, pp. 111, 115). The WTO incorporated environmental concerns into its system (Ni 2004, *id.*): the Preamble to the Marrakesh Agreement not only addressed the significance of free trade and market access, but also highlighted the value of sustainable development (Ni 2004, *id*).

E.S. Lee, *World Trade Regulation*,
DOI 10.1007/978-3-642-31143-7_13,

preserving the environment or are abused to protect the Member country's domestic market.

Traditionally, there have been two possible routes in the WTO to tackle the trade and environment issues, that is, through the negotiation and consensus among the WTO Members and recourse through the dispute settlement procedures. Besides the latter recourse with some progressive efficiency in dealing with this issue, even though the WTO has coped with this problem through ministerial conferences and tried to harmonize between trade and the environment by founding the Committee on Trade and Environment (CTE),[2] the WTO has been unable to give any resolute attitude for diverse pending issues concerning environmental trade measures and has failed to launch a new round of trade-environment negotiations.

Considering the gradual environmental aggravation and serious pollution across the planet, it is required to harmonize the environmental preservation through, for instance, the proper utilization of trade-related environmental measures with the principle of free trade under the WTO as soon as possible. If environmental problems, in particular, are not handled timely, it will cost an excessive amount of money and time to restore the environment. The fact that unresolved environmental problems can use up all the profits from the WTO's free trade urges us to build the system to impose timely and efficiently trade measures related to environment.

The purpose of this article is to seek harmonized resolutions of trade and environmental conflicts within the WTO agreements, considering the practical difficulty of relating legally the multilateral environmental agreements (MEAs) with the WTO provisions. These resolutions are discussed under the presumption that environmental issues in the WTO are better served under a "one-pillar" concept with the WTO as a sole column rather than a "two-pillar" idea with the WTO and a created world environment organization.[3] This article focuses on finding the most economical and efficient way to meet the fierce clash of interests among the WTO Member countries as well as to establish universal and valid standards.

13.1.2 Trade and Environmental Conflicts Under GATT/WTO

13.1.2.1 Main Issues on Trade and Environmental Conflicts

Since the early 1970s, as worries about how economic growth affects social development and the environment[4] emerged and the Group on Environmental

[2] Decision on Trade and Environment. Apr. 15, 1994. Legal Instruments–Results of the Uruguay Round, Ministerial Decisions (adopted by the Trade Negotiations Committee, 1994), 33 I.L.M. 1267 called for the establishment of a Committee on Trade and Environment.

[3] For the details about the "one-pillar" concept and the "two-pillar" idea, see Calderin (2002, pp. 35, 43–57).

[4] Regarding, for example, the three categories of environmental harm from trade, that is, physical harm, physical harm through the market, and economic harm through the market, see Calderin (2002, *id.*, at 49–57).

Measures and International Trade[5] was established in the General Agreement on Tariffs and Trade[6] (GATT) the Bureau,[7] in order to review the impact of trade on the environment,[8] held discussions[9] over trade and the environment,[10] especially on efficient interaction between trade liberalization and the environment, have been seriously debated.[11] At the Uruguay Round, even though there was not sufficient discussion on performance to address environmental concerns, new sources were introduced which admit initiating the matters related to the environmental preservation and sustainable development[12] before the multilateral negotiations.[13]

Pursuant to a Ministerial Declaration annexed to the Marrakesh Agreement establishing the WTO in 1994, the CTE,[14] a non-negotiating body for exploring

---

[5] This was the first institutional framework within the GATT to address the environmental issue since the creation of GATT in 1947. WTO Secretariat, Symposium. Mar. 15–16, 1999. High Level Symposium on Trade and Environment Background Document. WTO Trade and Environment Division, para. 2. http://www.wto.org/english/tratop_e/envir_e/tr_envbadoc.htm. Accessed Feb. 22, 2012.

[6] General Agreement on Tariffs and Trade, Arts. I, III, Oct. 30, 1947. Stat. A-11, 55 U.N.T.S. 61: 194. [hereinafter GATT]. The GATT parties adopted GATT again, with minor changes, as part of the agreement creating the WTO. Marrakesh Agreement Establishing the World Trade Organization. Apr. 15, 1994. I.L.M. 33: 1144. [hereinafter WTO Agreement]. When it is necessary to distinguish the two, they are called "GATT 1947" and "GATT 1994." WTO Agreement, Art. II:4.

[7] When environmental concerns became domestic and international policy issues in the 1970s, they were not addressed within GATT, but through the UN system. In participation of the 1972 UN Conference on the Human Environment, GATT members agreed to form the EMIT Working Group (Shaffer 2001, pp. 1, 17).

[8] WTO Secretariat, *supra* note 214, paras. 2, 6, 7.

[9] During the discussions, environmentalists portrayed the world trade system as "GATTzilla," while trade advocates predicted a period of veiled trade restrictions and "green" protectionism that threatened to revert the international community back to the chaos that embroiled the 1930s (Gaines 2001, pp. 739, 752).

[10] The United States and EC, not wanting challenges by environmentalists to jeopardize the conclusion of the Uruguay Round, attempted to defuse these challenges to trade policy by supporting the formation within GATT of the EMIT Working Group, followed by the creation of a formal Committee within the new and expanded WTO structure, the CTE (Shaffer 2001, *supra* note 216, at 20).

[11] Environment Backgrounder of WTO Secretariat. Feb. 2004. Trade and Environment at the WTO: background document. http://www.wto.org/english/tratop_e/envir_e/envir_backgrnd_e/contents_e.htm. Accessed Feb. 23, 2012.

[12] WTO Agreement, *supra* note 215. Preamble. (Stating "the optimal use of the world's resources in accordance with the objective of sustainable development, seeking . . . to protect and preserve the environment . . ..").

[13] For the failures to amend GATT to address environmental concerns during the Uruguay Round (Knox 2004, pp. 1, 14–19).

[14] Shaffer (2001, *supra* note 216, at 20).

the environmental implications of trade,[15] was established[16] and has handled issues related to trade and environmental problems[17] so far.[18] The CTE has tried to come up with various plans including stretching Article XX of GATT or revising it in order to adapt the trade measures in compliance with the environmental purposes of MEAs at the WTO.[19]

The proposals made in the CTE[20] could be grouped into two areas: (i) a legal framework to clarify the relationship between the WTO and MEAs with specific reference to the exception provisions in Article XX of; (ii) some making environment-related results in some or all of the TBT, SPS, TRIPs, Agricultural Agreements, and General Agreements on Trade in Services (GATS), which others feel confident that environmental concerns have been sufficiently dealt with already in these agreements.[21]

In seeking efficient methods to harmonize trade liberalization ideals surrounding environmental protection, Members are limited by the fact that every tool should meet the principle of the WTO: enhancing a multilateral cooperative system that pursues trade liberalization.[22] Particularly, environmental trade measures based on

---

[15] It extended observer status to the United Nations, the United Nations Conference on Trade and Development (UNCTAD), the World Bank, the International Monetary Fund (IMF), the United Nations Environment Program (UNEP), the United Nations Development Program (UNDP), the Commission for Sustainable Development (CSD), the Food and Agricultural Organization (FAO), the International Trade Center (ITC), the Organization for Economic Cooperation Development (OECD), and the European Free Trade Association (EFTA). WTO Secretariat, *supra* note 214, paras. 43–44.

[16] Shaffer (2001, *supra* note 216, at 17).

[17] For the limited performance of the CTE to conclude the detailed resolution of trade and environment conflicts, see Shaffer (2001, *supra* note 216, at 1–93). (Examining how the WTO has addressed trade and environment issues through a specialized CTE, and treats the CTE as a site to assess central concerns of governance in a globalizing economy).

[18] Shaffer (2001, *supra* note 216, at 1–93).

[19] Outside of the WTO, the Organization for Economic Cooperation and Development studied issues viewed as germane to the trade versus environment debate through a series of meetings of an ad hoc group called the Joint Session of Trade and Environment Expert (Gaines 2001, *supra* note 218, at 753, *cited by* Rietvelt 2005, pp. 473, 490). In addition, academic studies and conferences addressing trade and the environment proliferated (Gaines 2001, *id.*, at 753–754).

[20] With relation to the CTE proposals' dependence, in the US-Shrimp case which was the first major trade-environment dispute following the CTE 1996 Report, the claimants, the respondent and third-party participants each supported their positions by citing different paragraphs from the Report. *See* Panel Report. May 15, 1998. United States-Import Prohibition of Certain Shrimp and Shrimp Products, paras. 4.1–4.73. WT/DS58/R. [hereinafter US-Shrimp Panel Report], *cited by* Shaffer (2001, *supra* note 216, at 38), as well as the dispute settlement panel and the Appellate Body cited the Report. *See* US-Shrimp Panel Report, *id.*, paras. 7.50, 9.1 *cited by* Shaffer (2001, *id*).

[21] Shaw and Schwartz (2002, pp. 129, 133).

[22] For the state of play in the CTE, see Shaw and Schwartz (2002, *id.*, at 129–144). (Discussing on: (i) The WTO-MEAs relationship; (ii) Subsidy Reform; (iii) TRIPs and biodiversity; (iv) Precaution; (v) GMOs and biosafety).

non-product-related process or production (PPMs) – and issues of paramount importance to environmental measures which may discriminate on the basis of the processes behind products – are inherently difficult to legitimate under the WTO rules.[23] The legitimacy of measures based upon PPMs underlying the environmental regime is easily contradictory to the non-discrimination principle embedded in the multilateral trading system.[24]

Under the current WTO system under which Member governments, in most dispute cases, have had no option but to resort to the dispute settlement process of the GATT/WTO, the final decision of the Appellate Body in the US-Shrimp case[25] may predict more or less optimistically the practical possibility that there would be no policy contradiction "between upholding and safeguarding an open, non-discriminatory and equitable multilateral trading system on the one hand, and acting for the protection of the environment and the promotion of sustainable development[26] on the other."[27]

13.1.2.2 Environmental Measures Under the WTO

1. Environmental Measures under GATT Provisions

Since GATT primarily is aimed at removing trade restrictions, the legality of environmental trade restrictions imposed by Member governments or MEAs[28] under GATT should be recognized according to the requirements of GATT

[23] Shaw and Schwartz (2002, *id.*, at 147). (Stating "Many countries including developing countries consider that allowing WTO Members to discriminate against products based on non-product-related PPMs is a fundamental and impermissible alteration of the present balance of rights and obligations of Members under the WTO Agreement.")

[24] Shaw and Schwartz (2002, *id.*, at 132).

[25] Appellate Body Report. Oct. 12, 1998. United States-Import Prohibition of Certain Shrimp and Shrimp Products, WT/DS58/AB/R. (US-Shrimp AB Report). (Concerning a ban on importation of certain shrimp and shrimp products imposed by the US).

[26] For the definition of the term "sustainable development," *See* Calderin (2002, *supra* note 212, at 45, n. 64).

[27] Bree (1998, 99, 102) Art. XX GATT-Quo Vadis?, *cited by* Rietvelt (2005, *supra* note 228, at 490).

[28] There are approximately 240 multilateral environmental agreements (MEAs), out of which about 20 include provisions that can affect trade. For further information, see WTO Secretariat. 25 Apr. 2003. Matrix on Trade Measures Pursuant to Selected MEAs. WT/CTE/W/160/Rev.2, TN/TE/S/5. Among the trade-related MEAs, there are Montreal Protocol on Substances that Deplete the Ozon Layer. Sept. 16, 1987. 1522 U.N.T.S. 3. *reprinted in* 26 I.L.M. 1541 (Nov. 1987) (entered into force Jan. 1, 1989) [hereinafter Montreal Protocol], stipulating that the production and consumption of compounds that deplete ozone in the stratosphere-chlorofluorocarbons (CFCs) are to be phased out, Convention on International Trade in Endangered Species of Wild Fauna and Flora. Mar. 3, 1973. 27 U.S.T. 1087, 933 U.N.T.S. 243 (CITES), regulating the trade of wild animals and plants written in the list of annexes across the borders among members and non-members, Basel Convention on the Control of Transboundary Movements of Hazardous Waste and their Disposal. Mar. 22, 1989. 28 I.L.M 657, prohibiting hazardous wastes or other wastes to be exported to a non-Party or to be imported from a non-Party, and etc., which regulate trade in a variety of methods to protect environment.

provisions. Possibly the most conflicting regulations in interpreting and adopting environmental trade measures among GATT provisions[29] are the so-called "three pillars"[30] of GATT[31]: (i) general most-favored-nation treatment requiring that a country treat all contracting parties alike for the purpose of any "advantage, favor, privilege or immunity"[32]; (ii) national treatment on internal taxation and regulation prohibiting a contracting party from imposing regulations or taxes in a way "so as to afford protection" against import competition[33]; (iii) general elimination of quantitative restrictions prohibiting quantitative restrictions on imports of a particular type or from a specific country or on the exportation or sale for export of any product destined for a particular country[34] and so on.[35]

While trade-related environmental measures accepted by governments or environmental agreements can be an efficient means in implementing environmental policy, under GATT principles of nondiscrimination,[36] these measures may be at risk of being ruled GATT-inconsistent[37] and, thus, no longer acceptable under GATT/WTO system.[38] They are significantly against the most-favored-nations principle.[39] For example, all kinds of products containing chlorofluoro carbons are banned from trade under the Montreal Protocol[40] even though they are interpreted as like products under GATT standards. Exports of hazardous and other wastes to nonparties are also prohibited under the Basel Convention, which is in violation of GATT Article XI prohibition[41] against quantitative restrictions on imports and exports.[42]

---

[29] For the conflicts between GATT and domestic environmental laws, see Knox (2004, *supra* note 222, at 5–10).

[30] Some commentators have enumerated a fourth central obligation: the elimination on, or abstention from, the use of non-tariff, trade distorting measures, *See* Anderson (1993, pp. 751, 756); Jackson (1992, pp. 1227, 1232), cited by Hudnall (1996, pp. 175, 183).

[31] Some commentators also have suggested that Art. XXI (Exception for Security Interest) may be useful in an environmental context. *See* Anderson (1993, *id.*, *cited by* Hudnall 1996, *id.*, at 183). Although this article will briefly address this provision, no nation has ever relied on the Art. XXI to justify an environmental measure (*id*).

[32] GATT 1994, *supra* note 215. Art. I (General Most-Favored-Nation Treatment).

[33] GATT 1994, *supra* note 215. Art. III (National Treatment on Internal Taxation and Regulation).

[34] GATT 1994, *supra* note 215. Art. XX (General Exceptions).

[35] Meier (1997, pp. 241); Knox (2004, *supra* note 222, at 4–5).

[36] GATT 1994, *supra* note 215. Arts. I, III.

[37] For the more details, see Knox (2004, *supra* note 222, at 11–13).

[38] Hudnall (1996, *supra* note 239, at 204).

[39] GATT 1994, *supra* note 215. Art. I.

[40] Montreal Protocol, *supra* note 237, at 1541.

[41] Although Art. XI. 2 provides for certain exceptions to the general prohibition against such restrictions, hazardous wastes are unlikely to fall into the categories of "products essential to the exporting contracting parties" or products which are in "temporary surplus" (Hudnall 1996, *supra* note 239, at 205).

[42] Baker (1993, pp. 437, 444).

Considering the fact that the trade-related environmental measures, particularly under MEAs, would likely be inconsistent with nondiscrimination principles,[43] or prohibitions quantity restrictions,[44] Article XX exceptional provisions are necessary to protect the trade measures for environmental protection from potential conflicts with GATT provisions.[45] Under GATT, when trade-related[46] measures for environmental protection are against one of the above principles or provisions, the legitimacy of the measures should be secured from exceptional provisions in GATT.[47]

GATT exceptional provisions[48] represent an attempt to strike a balance between permitting the regulation of trade to promote non-commercial goals in certain recognized areas, such as health and environment, while also policing these regulations to ensure they are not applied in ways that restrict trade beyond what is necessary to promote such goals.[49] According to the exception provisions of GATT, Members should meet both individual requirements and two conditions imposed by the chapeau of Article XX requiring nations under the equal condition that there should not be any arbitrary or unjustifiable discrimination and disguised restriction to trade.[50]

In order for trade-related measures for environmental protection to have legitimacy, first of all, the measures should fall within the scope of Article XX.[51] Many of the challenged measures[52] brought under GATT/WTO Dispute Settlement Procedures that were found inconsistent with GATT/WTO rules, in fact, satisfied this scope-related requirement under Article XX.[53]

---

[43] GATT 1947, *supra* note 215. Arts. I, III.

[44] GATT 1947, *supra* note 215. Art. XI.

[45] Knox (2004, *supra* note 222, at 12).

[46] For the "trade" vs. "trade-relate" relating to TRIPs, for instance, see Thomas (2002, pp. 791, 792). "[A]lthough intellectual property rights can be traded in licensing and other rights-transfer agreements, neither intellectual property rights nor intellectual property need be traded for TRIPs to apply. Rather, the larger premise of TRIPs is that intellectual property rights are affected by trade . . . ."

[47] GATT 1994, *supra* note 215. Art. XX.

[48] For the roots of the language of Art. XX of GATT 1994, see Reif and Eckert (2004, pp. 657, 680–681).

[49] Reif and Eckert (2004, *id.*, at 679–680).

[50] These are softened National Treatment and Most-Favored-Nation Treatment (Jackson 1992, *supra* note 239, at 1240).

[51] This requirement is often referred to as the "policy test" Yavitz (2001–2002, pp. 203, 215).

[52] Those measures were measure to reduce cigarette use in Thailand-Cigarettes. Report of the Panel. 1990. Thailand-Restrictions on Importation of and Internal Taxes on Cigarettes, para. 72, (Nov. 7, 1990), GATT B.I.S.D. (37th Supp.) at 200. (Thailand-Cigarettes), protection of dolphin life in Tuna in US-Tuna(EEC). Report of the Panel. 1994. United States-Restrictions on Imports of Tuna(EEC), GATT Doc. DS29/R (June 16, 1994) [US-Tuna(EEC)] and protection of turtles in US-Shrimp.

[53] Emslie (2005, pp. 485, 514).

The measures should also be proven to have met either the requirement "necessary to protect human, animal or plant life or the health"[54] or the requirement "relating to the conservation of exhaustible[55] natural resources[56] if such measures are made effective in conjunction with restrictions on domestic production or consumption."[57] This necessary requirement[58] prohibits a Member from adopting a measure that is inconsistent with any other GATT/WTO provision if any alternative, which is not inconsistent with other GATT/WTO provisions, can reasonably be employed by such Member.[59] However, this necessary test is not whether the "policy underlying the measure" is necessary but, rather, whether the "measure" is necessary to achieve the stated policy objective.[60]

Additionally, these measures should not bring any arbitrary or unjustifiable discrimination nor be a disguised restriction,[61] which is often referred to as the "chapeau" requirement.[62] Article XX thus offers general exceptions from

[54] GATT 1994, *supra* note 215. Art. XX(b). For the construction of this provision in the least inconsistent to GATT, *See* Thailand-Cigarettes, *supra* note 261, para. 72; Panel Report. Jan. 29, 1996. United States-Standards for Reformulated and Conventional Gasoline, para. 6.20, WT/DS2/R. (US-Gasoline Panel Report).

[55] Referring to the textual interpretation of Art. XX in finding that the term "exhaustible" does not exclude "renewable" resources like living animals, the Appellate Body in US-Shrimp noted that the treaty must be read "in the light of contemporary concerns of the community of nations about the protection and conservation of the environment." US-Shrimp AB Report, *supra* note 234, para. 128, *cited by* Rietvelt (2005, *supra* note 228, at 485, n. 73).

[56] This is, so called, the "necessary requirement" or "nexus requirement." For the term "nexus requirement" which is arguably more appropriate in avoiding any confusion, see Philip Bentley (2000, pp. 107, 112), cited by Emslie (2005, *supra* note 262, at 512 n. 147). ("Although Art. XX(b) and (d) require that the measure be necessary for the goal sought, Art. XX(g) does not require the restrictive measure to be necessary to the objective of protecting the exhaustible natural resource; instead, it only require that it 'relate' to the objective . . . ."). However this difference may not have a significant impact, "presumably because any measure that limits depletion of a natural resource is justified *per se*" and "arguably" would meet a necessary requirement in any event (*id*).

[57] GATT 1947, *supra* note 215. Art. XX(g). According to this provision, measures' main purpose should be protection. Report of the Panel. 1988. Canada-Measures Affecting Exports of Unprocessed Herring and Salmon (Mar. 22, 1988) GATT B.I.S.D. (35th Supp.) at 98. (Canada-Herring and Salmon).

[58] For the major cases applying the necessary requirement, see Thailand-Cigarettes, *supra* note 261; Report of the Panel. 1991. United States-Restrictions on Imports of Tuna (Mexico) (circulated Sep. 3, 1991), GATT B.I.S.D. (39th Supp.) at 155. [US-Tuna(Mexico)]; and Appellate Body Report. Apr. 5, 2001. European Communities-Measures Affecting Asbestos and Asbestos-Containing Products. WT/DS135/AB/R. (EC-Asbestos AB Report).

[59] Thailand-Cigarettes, *supra* note 261, para. 74, *cited by* Emslie (2005, *supra* note 262, at 514–515).

[60] Yavitz (2001–2002, *supra* note 260, at 215).

[61] GATT 1994, *supra* note 215. Chapeau of Art. XX.

[62] US-Shrimp AB Report which made the most detailed consideration of the meaning of the chapeau. US-Shrimp AB Report, *supra* note 234, paras. 150–151.

international trade obligations for trade measures employed in the pursuit of certain specified goals or purposes including environment protection.[63]

With respect to the applicability of the trade-related environmental measures, particularly, under the MEAs even under GATT system prior to the WTO system, applying Article XX(b) and (g) would seemingly not be difficult, since each of the MEAs represents the collective judgment of many governments that restricting trade in specified ways is necessary under the Article XX(b), and since trade measures relate to the conservation of exhaustible natural resources as long as they meet the requirements under the Article XX (g).[64]

Since the MEAs are all open to every country and apply their trade restrictions only to countries whose behavior does not conform to the norms in the agreements, MEAs' measures would also seem to meet the requirement in the chapeau of Article XX.[65]

2. Environmental Measures under Other WTO Agreements

One outcome of the Uruguay Round is raising various environment-related issues in the preamble[66] and expanding the application of the regulations related to environmental protection which would impede the flow of international trade.[67] Even though it has historically been understood that preambles of international agreements do not create enforceable measures,[68] the WTO can be defined as an environmental organization[69] considering the fact that the preamble defines the organization and states its purpose.[70] As such, its continued existence depends on its ability to advocate for environmental protection and preservation, which will lead to a level of sustainable development.[71]

---

[63] Gaines (2001, p. 740).

[64] Knox (2004, *supra* note 222, at 12).

[65] Knox (2004, *supra* note 222). Even GATT legal experts consulted during the drafting of CITIES and Montreal Convention had said that the trade restrictions in those agreements would fall within Art. XX (*id*).

[66] Environmental issues in the WTO preamble are: (i) "allowing for the optimal use of the world's resources"; (ii) "in accordance with the objective of sustainable development"; (iii) "seeking both to protect and preserve the environment." For more details, see Calderin (2002, *supra* note 212, at 43–57).

[67] For the WTO having an environmental heart, see Calderin (2002, *supra* note 212, at 43–57). ("Its (WTO's) main purpose is to expand the production and exchange of goods and services between its Members .... WTO must do all that is possible to ensure its continued existence defending itself from dangers that threatens its existence. Examples of such dangers are environmental degradation and over-exploitation of world resources... Hence, the preamble ... includes language that calls for the protection and preservation of the world's environment and resources ....").

[68] Calderin (2002, *supra* note 212, at 47).

[69] *Id.*

[70] *Id.*

[71] *Id.*, at 48

There are two WTO environment-related agreements which regulate the issues pertaining to human, animal and plant life and health, and environment. One is the Agreement on Technical Barriers to Trade [hereinafter TBT Agreement][72] and the other is the Agreement on the Application of Sanitary and Phytosanitary Measures (SPS Agreement).[73]

The SPS Agreement addresses measures taken to protect humans, animals and plants from certain risks to life and health,[74] including risks arising from additives, contaminants or toxins in foods.[75] As such, the SPS Agreement offers all qualified sanitary and phytosanitary measures, the definition of which comprises and exceeds measures that protect human, animal, and plant life and health.[76] Under the agreement, Member countries are required to base their sanitary and phytosanitary measures upon international standards, guidelines or recommendation, however, Member countries may maintain a higher level[77] of the measures than the measures based on the relevant international standards, if there is a scientific justification.[78]

The SPS Agreement[79] states Members' right to implement sanitary and phytosanitary measures based on both scientific justification[80] and risk assessment.[81] Each Member country should meet two conditions: One is that Members must not cause any unfair discrimination, nor disguised restriction in determining the level of protection.[82] The second condition involves establishing or maintaining sanitary or phytosanitary measures to achieve the appropriate level of sanitary or

[72] Agreement on Technical Barriers to Trade. Apr. 15, 1994. Marrakesh Agreement Establishing the World Trade Organization, Annex 1A, Legal Instruments-Results of the Uruguay Round, 33 I.L.M. 1125. (TBT Agreement).

[73] Agreement on the Application of Sanitary and Phytosanitary Measures. Apr. 15, 1994. Marrakesh Agreement Establishing the World Trade Organization. Annex 1A. Legal Instruments-Results of the Uruguay Round. 33 I.L.M. 1125. (SPS Agreement).

[74] For insufficiency of the SPS Agreement to cover health or environmental risks, see Charnovitz (2000, pp. 271, 276–277). (Stating, for example, protection against (real or imagined) human health risks from bioengineered processed products is apparently not covered by the SPS because genetic modification is not listed in the SPS categories, even though the applicability of the SPS to genetic modification products is remaining as complex).

[75] SPS Agreement, *supra* note 282. Annex A.

[76] Meier (1997, *supra* note 244, at 275–276).

[77] "The SPS Agreement and the TBT Agreement do not clearly recognize a right to establish SPS measures and technical regulations respectively providing a lower level of protection than would be afforded by a measure conforming to international standards or guidance, which may represent an implicit requirement for WTO to conform their measures to international standards, unless they wish to impose more protective requirements" (Ferris and Zhang 2002, pp. 429, 453).

[78] SPS Agreement, *supra* note 282. Arts. 3.1, 3.3.

[79] SPS Agreement, *supra* note 282. Arts. 2, 3, 5 and etc.

[80] SPS Agreement, *supra* note 282. Art. 3.3.

[81] SPS Agreement, *supra* note 282. Art. 5.3.

[82] SPS Agreement, *supra* note 282. Art. 5.5.

phytosanitary protection using or selecting alternatives that have the same effects on protection and also are considerably less trade-restrictive.[83]

This trade-restrictive condition of the SPS Agreement shows two different aspects from that of the TBT Agreement: (i) Members shall ensure that restrictive measures should not be more trade-restrictive than required to achieve their appropriate level of sanitary or phytosanitary protection.[84] For being violated for this condition, the alternative must be "significantly," not just marginally, less trade restrictive[85]; (ii) the measures should have feasibility technically and economically.[86]

The TBT Agreement addresses all voluntary and mandatory standards for products, other than any that qualify as sanitary and phytosanitary measures under the SPS Agreement,[87] which indirectly impact free trade through the measures, including technical regulations for the protection of human health or safety, animal or plant life or health, or the environment.[88] Those measures or regulation should be subject to the principles of the national treatment and the most-favored-nation treatment, and should not be more trade-restrictive than necessary to fulfill a legitimate objective,[89] taking into account the risks non-fulfillment would create.[90]

These two agreements recognize the rights of the WTO Members to establish national requirements that are more stringent than international standards, even though the level of "legitimate" purposes to be accepted is different between two agreements,[91] provided that such requirements conform to the WTO rules that protect against unnecessary, unjustified, arbitrary and disguised discrimination towards products of other WTO Members.[92] The WTO rules do not expressly

[83] SPS Agreement, *supra* note 282. Art. 5.6 n. 3.

[84] SPS Agreement, *supra* note 282. Art. 5.6 n. 3; Charnovitz (1994, pp. 1, 11).

[85] Meier (1997, *supra* note 244, at 279).

[86] Meier (1997, *supra* note 244, at 279).

[87] TBT Agreement, *supra* note 281. Art. 1.5.

[88] TBT Agreement, *supra* note 281. Art. 2.2.

[89] For the interpretation of this prohibition to be environmentally friendly, see Calderin (2002, *supra* note 212, at 57). ("[S]ince it pressures Members to find legitimate environmental reasons for its standards, rather than simply disguising its protectionist measures in the clothing of environmentalism. . . . [I]t entices governments that are interested in erecting barriers to trade, to invest in research to find environmental justification for the measures . . . .").

[90] TBT Agreement, *supra* note 281. Arts. 2.1–2.2.

[91] Under the SPS Agreement, for a higher level of protection to be imposed, the member should essentially prove the necessity of the measure by way of a scientific risk assessment, SPS Agreement, *supra* note 282. Art. 5.1; under the TBT Agreement, higher level of protection than that established by other Members may be imposed where the measure represents the appropriate level of protection, TBT Agreement, *supra* note 281. Art. 2.4.

[92] Ferris and Zhang (2002, *supra* note 286, at 452).

encourage the application of more stringent standards, but rather the harmonization of standards.[93]

SPS and TBT Agreements which are legally self-sufficient substantial provisions[94] come closer to the intention of environmental protection than other WTO Agreements.[95] These two agreements could be more actively used for environmental protection because Member countries could introduce or maintain trade-restrictive environmental measures even though the measures are not in compliance with other WTO agreements.

Whether SPS and TBT Agreements are to be applied to trade-related measures for environmental protection ahead of the exceptional provisions in GATT should be seen in the future in more dispute cases: With respect to the cases of TBT, the Agreement is arguably more generous than Article XX in allowing exceptions to GATT, and purports to supersede Article XX in cases of conflict.[96]

In the US-Gasoline case,[97] it was claimed that the U.S. provisions of controlling gasoline were against the precepts of the TBT Agreement [98]; however, the panel withheld its judgment on this point.[99] Reflecting the panel's conclusion with reservation, it is uncertain that this provision can be applied for environmental issues. The panel expressed its opinion in this case that the U.S. provisions of gasoline are in breach of the GATT provisions[100] and that the US regulations do not have to be debated whether they are not in compliance with the provisions of the TBT Agreement.[101]

As such, by failing to consider the TBT Agreement,[102] even though the Appellate Body implied either that the TBT Agreement does not supersede Article XX in cases of conflict or that the Agreement has a scope as narrow or narrower than Article XX,[103] the case, arguably, indicates that TBT Agreement actually imposes

[93] For more detailed discussions, see Ferris and Zhang (2002, *supra* note 286, at 452–453).

[94] Panel Report. Aug. 18, 1997. European Communities-Measures Concerning Meat and Meat Products (Hormones), paras. 8.31–8.42. WT/DS26/R/USA. (EC-Hormones(US) Panel Report).

[95] For the conflicts between domestic environmental laws and SPS/TBT Agreement, see Knox (2004, *supra* note 222, at 19–24).

[96] Meier (1997, *supra* note 244, at 279).

[97] US-Gasoline Panel Report, *supra* note 263.

[98] TBT Agreement, *supra* note 281. Art. 2 ("Preparation, Adoption and Application of Technical Regulations by Central Government Bodies").

[99] US-Gasoline Panel Report, *supra* note 263, para. 6.4.

[100] GATT 1994, *supra* note 215. Arts. III, V & XX(b), (d) & (g).

[101] US-Gasoline Panel Report, *supra* note 263, para. 8.1.

[102] The Panel in the case did not treat with the TBT Agreement, because it was found to be unnecessary to consider the TBT Agreement by the reason that the US Regulation at issue was not qualified for an exception under Art. XX. US-Gasoline Panel Report, *supra* note 263, para. 6.43.

[103] Meier (1997, *supra* note 244, at 279).

additional requirements on top of the general GATT rules, "the interpretative provision" notwithstanding, and that it may defeat an Article XX defense.[104]

In EC-Asbestos, even though the Appellate Body declined to analyze the applicability of the TBT Agreement,[105] the Body noted that the TBT Agreement being a "specialized legal regime" that "applies solely to a limited class of measures,"[106] imposes obligations that "seem to be different from, and additional to, the obligations imposed on Members under GATT 1994."[107]

With respect to the cases of SPS, the Agreement, offering an exception for all qualified sanitary and phytosanitary measures, might allow national environmental measures that a GATT/WTO panel previously would have rejected. As for now, in EC-Hormones,[108] EC-Asbestos,[109] and Japan-Agricultural Products,[110] Appellate Body recognized the WTO Members' right to determine their own level of health protection. Apart from the above two agreements, WTO environment-related provisions include a number of trade regulations such as WTO Agricultural Agreement[111] and WTO Agreement on Subsidies and Countervailing Measures[112] which defines non-actionable assistance and subsidy in relation to the environment.[113]

The WTO Trade-Related Aspects of Intellectual Property Rights [hereinafter TRIPs][114] also excludes necessary inventions from patents or prohibits them from being used for business in order to protect human, animal, plant life or health and

---

[104] *Id.*

[105] The Panel decided that the French Decree did not meet the definition of "technical regulation" under the TBT Agreement. Panel Report. Sep. 18, 2000. European Communities-Measures Affecting Asbestos-Containing Products. WT/DS135/R. (EC-Asbestos Panel Report)

[106] EC-Asbestos AB Report, *supra* note 267, para. 80.

[107] *Id. cited by* Bhala and Gantz (2002, pp. 457, 511).

[108] Appellate Body Report. 16 January 1998. EC Measures Concerning Meat and Meat Products (Hormones). WT/DS48/AB/R. (EC-Hormones AB Report), para. 177.

[109] EC-Asbestos AB Report, *supra* note 267, para. 168.

[110] Appellate Body Report. Feb. 22, 1999. Japan-Measures Affecting Agricultural Products. WT/DS76/AB/R. (Japan-Agricultural Products AB Report), paras. 95–101.

[111] Agreement on Agriculture annex 2. Apr. 15, 1994. Marrakesh Agreement Establishing the World Trade Organization, Annex 1A, Legal Instruments-Results of the Uruguay Round, 33 I.L. M. 1125. (Agriculture Agreement).

[112] Agreement on Subsidies and Countervailing Measures art. 8. Apr. 15, 1994. Marrakesh Agreement Establishing the World Trade Organization, Annex 1A, Legal Instruments-Results of the Uruguay Round, 33 I.L.M. 1125. (SCM Agreement).

[113] The assistance "(i) is a one-time non-recurring measure; and (ii) is limited to 20 percent of the cost of adaptation; and (iii) does not cover the cost of replacing and operating the assisted investment, which must be fully borne by firms; and (iv) is directly linked to and proportionate to a firm's planned reduction of nuisances and pollution, and does not cover any manufacturing cost savings which may be achieved; and (v) is available to all firms which can adopt the new equipment and/or production processes." SCM Agreement, *id.*, art. 8.2(c).

[114] Agreement on Trade-Related Aspects of Intellectual Property Rights arts. 27.2–27.3 & etc., Apr. 15, 1994, Marrakesh Agreement Establishing the World Trade Organization, Annex 1 C, Legal Instruments-Results of the Uruguay Round, 33 I.L.M. 1125. (TRIPs Agreement).

environment. The TRIPs Agreement thus allows Members to prevent them from obtaining patents that may endanger their ecological survival.[115] Moreover, by excluding certain inventions and process from being patentable, the Member countries are ensuring that they will not need to pay a foreign entity for the right to use domestic natural resources that may be essential to protect human, animal, or plant life or health.[116]

General Agreement on Trade in Services[117] provides that as long as such measures do not constitute a means of arbitrary or unjustifiable discrimination between countries, or a disguised restriction on trade in services, any necessary measures may be imposed to protect human, animal or plant life or health. Such respective provisions of various agreements dealing with environmental issues are directed broadly through the preamble of the WTO Agreement which addresses sustainable development.[118]

13.1.3 Judicial Interpretation on Environmental Measures Under GATT/WTO System

13.1.3.1 Judicial Interpretation Under GATT Mechanism

1. General

Out of several panel procedures[119] that have been carried out under GATT mechanisms related to environment-protecting measures or human-health measures, only three panels were settled and adopted by GATT signatories. Most disputes under GATT were mainly about the general elimination of quantitative

---

[115] Calderin (2002, *supra* note 212, at 56).

[116] *Id.*

[117] General Agreement on Trade in Services art. XIV, Apr. 15, 1994, Marrakesh Agreement Establishing the World Trade Organization, Annex 1B, Legal Instruments-Results of the Uruguay Round, 33 I.L.M. 1125. (GATS).

[118] For a view to regard the sustainable development in the Preamble as the customary international law, *see*, e.g., Dailey (2000, pp. 331, 347–348), cited by Rietvelt (2005, *supra* note 228, at 497, n. 144) ("[I]n the last twenty years, the principle of sustainable development has become accepted as a rule of customary international law .... The multilateral consensus supporting the rule of sustainable development has been broad and consistent for the last twenty years. The state practice and opinio juris supporting the principle of sustainable development are sufficiently strong to create an international legal obligation on the part of nations to exploit their resources in a manner that is sustainable ....").

[119] Report of the Panel. Feb. 22, 1982. United States-Prohibition of Imports of Tuna and Tuna Products from Canada. GATT B.I.S.D. (29th Supp.), at 91. (US-Canadian Tuna); Canada-Herring and Salmon. Report of the Panel adopted on 22 March 1988. Canada Measures Affecting Exports of Unprocessed Herring and Salmon. L/6268-35 S/98; Thailand-Cigarettes, *supra* note 261; *US*-Tuna(Mexico). Report of the Panel. 15 Sep. 2011. United States Measures concerning the Importation, Marketing and Sale of ATuna and Tuna Products. WT/DS381/R; US-Tuna(EEC), *supra* note 261; Report of the Panel. Oct. 11, 1994. United States-Taxes on Automobiles. DS31/R. (US-Automobile).

restrictions, national treatment on internal taxation and regulation, and general exceptions.[120]

Regarding general elimination of quantitative restrictions, almost all cases,[121] apart from US-Automobiles,[122] were brought based on violation of provisions against quantitative restrictions[123] and panels concluded that the provisions were violated. In US-Canadian Tuna[124] and Thailand-Cigarettes,[125] panels came to the conclusion that import-banning measures of importing countries could not fulfill the provisions[126] permitting exception in importing agricultural produces. In the case of Canada-Salmon and Herring,[127] panel decided that exception clauses permitting restriction for standards, and etc.[128] were not satisfied.[129]

Several cases[130] were also regarding national treatment on internal taxation and regulation. In the case of Thailand-Cigarettes,[131] the Panel concluded that imposition of internal tax on the imported cigarettes was consistent with the national treatment required in the Article III.2[132] of GATT. In the cases of US-Tuna (Mexico) and US-Tuna (EEC), it was disputed whether the US import prohibition on tuna was in compliance with the national treatment on the domestic regulations[133] in Article III.4[134] of GATT.

The panel of US-Tuna (EEC) concluded that the United States import prohibitions on tuna and tuna products were not legitimated under the national treatment principle because the distinction from fishing customs and method of

[120] For environmental disputes in GATT. http://www.worldtradelaw.net/reports/wtopanels/wtopanels.asp. Accessed 24 Feb. 2012.

[121] US-Canadian Tuna, *supra* note 328; Canada-Herring and Salmon, *supra* note 328; Thailand-Cigarettes, *supra* note 261; US-Tuna(Mexico), *supra* note 328; US-Tuna(EEC), *supra* note 261; US-Automobiles, *supra* note 328.

[122] US-Automobiles, *supra* note 328.

[123] GATT 1947, *supra* note 215. Art. XI.1.

[124] US-Canadian Tuna, *supra* note 328, para. 4.6.

[125] Thailand-Cigarettes, *supra* note 261, para. 70.

[126] GATT 1947, *supra* note 215. Art. XI.2(c).

[127] Canada-Herring and Salmon, *supra* note 328.

[128] GATT 1947, *supra* note 215. Art. XI.2(b).

[129] Canada-Herring and Salmon, *supra* note 328, para. 4.2.

[130] They are Thailand-Cigarettes, *supra* note 261; US-Tuna(Mexico), *supra* note 328; US-Tuna (EEC), *supra* note 261, and US-Automobile, *supra* note 328.

[131] Thailand-Cigarettes, *supra* note 261, paras. 84–85.

[132] GATT 1947, *supra* note 215. Art. III.2.

[133] Although quantitative restriction against imports is banned under Art. XI.1 of GATT, in case the measure doesn't violate the principle of most-favored-nation treatment nor national treatment on internal taxation and regulation, and according to Art. III.4, foreign goods are not discriminated from domestic like goods, national measures can be imposed on the importing goods.

[134] GATT 1947, *supra* note 215. Art. III (National Treatment on Internal Taxation and Regulation).

tuna-capture does not affect on the unique feature of tuna and tuna products.[135] The implication of the panel's interpretation of GATT provisions was that any law restricting imports on the basis of their non-product-related process or production method[136] would necessarily violate the national treaty[137] and provisions on anti-dumping and countervailing duties[138] unless the PPM affected the physical characteristics of the product.[139]

In the case of US-Automobiles, the panel found that both impositions of the luxury tax and the gas guzzler tax were consistent with national treatment in Article III.2[140] of GATT due to imposing the same conditional tax on like products.[141] The panel, however, found the US regulation to be inconsistent with domestic regulations provisioned in Article III.4[142] of GATT, as the separate foreign fleet accounting discriminated against foreign cars and the fleet averaging differentiated between imported and domestic cars on the basis of factors relating to control or ownership of producers or importers (i.e. based on origin), rather than on the basis of factors directly related to the products as such.[143]

2. General Exceptions

Reviewing the application of general exceptions of GATT,[144] panels have not often quoted Article XX (b) allowing restricted measures necessary to protect human, animal or plant life or health, (g) relating to the conservation of exhaustible natural resources,[145] and provisions of the chapeau of Article XX, but also there have never been trade measures justified with those provisions. With this, the interpretation[146]

---

[135] US-Tuna (EEC), *supra* note 261, para. 5.8.

[136] For the seemingly proper right of the member countries to decide whether it participates in the trade of products made by the inefficient use of resources in relation with Art. XX(e), see Calderin (2002, *supra* note 212, at 60–62).

[137] GATT 1947, *supra* note 215. Art. III.

[138] GATT 1947, *supra* note 215. Arts. XI.2(c), VI.

[139] Knox (2004, *supra* note 222, at 8).

[140] GATT 1947, *supra* note 215. Art. III.2

[141] US-Automobiles, *supra* note 328, paras. 5.43, 6.1(a)–(b).

[142] GATT 1947, *supra* note 215. Art. III.4

[143] US-Automobiles, *supra* note 328, paras. 5.55, 6.1(c).

[144] GATT 1947, *supra* note 215. Art. XX. ("Subject to the requirement that such measures are not applied in a manner which would constitute a means of arbitrary or unjustifiable discrimination between countries where the same conditions prevail, or a disguised restriction on international trade, nothing in this Agreement shall be construed to prevent the adoption or enforcement by any contracting party of measures: . . . (*b*) necessary to protect human, animal or plant life or health; . . . (*g*) relating to the conservation of exhaustible natural resources if such measures are made effective in conjunction with restrictions on domestic production or consumption; . . . .").

[145] The invocation of an Art. XX (b) human health exception has never been successful because most measures fail the "necessary" test, while the exhaustible resource exception has accepted twice (Yavitz 2002, pp. 43, 49 (footnotes omitted)).

[146] For the definition of the term "interpretation" in comparison with the term "construction", see Trachtman (1999, pp. 333, 339). ("[I]n Anglo-American parlance, interpretation refers to the

of Article XX of GATT, the environmental provision, is arguably slanted to the viewpoint of free trade, and thus is accused of its negativity toward environmental protection.[147]

In the case of Canada-Salmon and Herring,[148] with relation to analyzing Article XX(g), the panel recognized that salmon and herring stocks are "exhaustible natural resources"[149] but held that the Canadian law was not "related to" the conservation of salmon and herring nor was it "in conjunction with" restrictions on domestic production or consumption.[150]

Analyzing the phrases "relating to" and "in conjunction with" in subparagraph (g), the panel held: the term "relating to" means that a measure must be "primarily aimed at the conservation of exhaustible natural resource"[151]; the term "in conjunction with" in Article XX(g) is to be interpreted in a way that ensures that the scope of possible actions under that provision corresponds to purpose of the GATT provisions concerned[152]; a trade measure could, therefore, be considered to be made effective "in conjunction with" production restrictions only if it was primarily aimed at rendering effective these restrictions.[153]

Having interpreted the terms "relating to" and "in conjunction with" to mean "primarily aimed at," the panel concluded that it was not necessary to analyze the Canadian law at issue either under the requirements of the Article XX chapeau or in relation to the overall purpose and aim of Article XX.[154]

---

determination of the meaning of words, contained in a contract, statute or treaty, while construction refers to the determination of the intent of the parties in connection with a matter not specifically addressed in the text of the document. While the distinction may be a matter of degree, construction raises greater questions of legitimacy, of fidelity to the intent of the parties and – in statutory or treaty contents – of democracy."); For the adoption of the concept of the interpretation and construction involved by the WTO dispute resolution process, see Trachtman (1999, *id.*, at 340) ("The WTO dispute resolution process often involves interpretation: … Some dispute resolution proceedings involve construction… . [C]onstruction decisions are those involving non-violation nullification or impairment … . [R]ecent WTO jurisprudence has seemingly rejected construction … . However, construction occurs where concepts that are intended are implicit in the text though they are not expressly articulated … .").

[147] Hudnall (1996, *supra* note 239, at 197).

[148] Canada-Herring and Salmon, *supra* note 328.

[149] *Id.* para. 4.4.

[150] *Id.* para. 4.4.

[151] *Id.* para. 4.6.

[152] *Id.*

[153] *Id.*

[154] Ala'i (1999, pp. 1129, 1140).

The US-Tuna (Canada)[155] panel, adopting the reasoning[156] of the panel in the Canada Herring and Salmon case,[157] concluded that, because Article XX(g) was intended to allow contracting parties to take trade measures primarily aimed at restricting production or consumption only within their jurisdiction,[158] the US actions were deemed impermissible because they were focused not on domestic but on extraterritorial tuna production.[159] Such decisions have, even though they have never been adopted, shed useful light on the failures of the GATT structure to properly address environmental concerns in the context of trade liberalization.[160]

In the case of Thailand-Cigarettes, the panel concluded that the import restrictions were not "necessary" within the meaning of Article XX (b), because Thailand prohibited the importation of cigarettes and other tobacco preparations, but authorized the sale of domestic cigarettes, finding that a measure is not "necessary" unless there is no available "alternative measures which could reasonably be expected to employ and which is not inconsistent with other GATT provisions."[161] In this case, the "necessary" test was construed to require that a country seeking to justify a trade-restrictive environmental measure show that there exists no other less GATT-inconsistent means of attaining that environmental objective.[162]

As such, the panel limited the basis of its decision to the interpretation of the word "necessary" in subparagraph (b), using by analogy the interpretation of the word "necessary" in subparagraph (d).[163] Furthermore, there was no discussion by the panel of the requirements of the Article XX chapeau to determine whether the measures at issue resulted in "arbitrary or unjustified discrimination," or were an attempt at "disguised restriction" or protectionism.[164]

---

155 US- Canadian Tuna, *supra* note 328.

156 The Canada Herring and Salmon panel determined that a measure could be considered to have been taken "in conjunction with" restrictions on production only "if it was primarily aimed at rendering effective these restrictions." Canada-Herring and Salmon, *supra* note 328, para. 4.6.

157 Because the principle of stare decisis does not apply within the two systems, the Panels and the Appellate Body frequently refer to prior precedents for guidance in settling disputes. Japan-Alcoholic Beverages AB Report, *supra* note 198, *cited by* Stewart and Johanson (2003, pp. 1, 27).

158 For the panel's use of the word "extrajurisdictional" rather "extraterritorial" without any definition of an extrajurisdictional offense, see Charnovitz (1993, pp. 475, 496–497); see also Esty (1993, *supra* note 210, at 105, n. 5).

159 Hudnall (1996, *supra* note 239, at 197).

160 *Id.*

161 Cheyne (1992, pp. 14, 17, nn. 46–47, *cited by* Hudnall 1996, *supra* note 239, at 188).

162 Esty (1993, *supra* note 210, at 48, n. 15).

163 GATT 1947, *supra* note 215. Art. XX (d), *cited by* Ala'i (1999, *supra* note 363, at 1144).

164 Ala'i (1999, *supra* note 363, at 1144).

In the cases of US-Tuna (Mexico)[165] and US-Tuna (EEC),[166] concerning the issue of US measure, the panel concluded that the US import prohibition to pursue its dolphin protection objectives for environmental policies was not justified by the exceptions in Article XX (b), (d), or (g) regarding measures to secure compliance with laws or regulations,[167] finding that: justification under the "necessary" standard "required a showing by the party invoking the Article XX exception . . . that it had exhausted all options reasonably available to it to pursue its . . . protection objectives through measures consistent with the General Agreement, in particular, through the negotiation[168] of international cooperative arrangements[.]"[169]

This language both ignored efforts the US government had made to negotiate agreements on dolphin conservation and appeared to extend the "least GATT-inconsistent" interpretation of "necessary" to all of the Article XX categories.[170] The panel interpreted the word "necessary" as used in subparagraph (b)[171] to mean that the measure must not only be the least-GATT-inconsistent measure,[172] but that the United States must have imposed the measure after it had exhausted all other options.[173] The panel rejected the United States' Article XX (g) argument based on the failure of the measure at issue to satisfy the "primarily aimed at" requirement of that subparagraph, which had been previously interpreted in the cases including Thailand-Cigarettes.[174]

[165] US-Tuna (Mexico), *supra* note 267.

[166] After Mexico failed to pursue adoption of the Tuna-dolphin report, the EC and Netherlands brought another claim to GATT dispute resolution, challenging not only the direct ban on tuna that had been the subject of the first US-Tuna case, but also a secondary ban imposed by the MMPA on imports of tuna from "intermediary" nation that could not prove they had not imported tuna subject to the direct ban, US-Tuna (EEC), *supra* note 261, paras. 4.1–4.7; however, the second US-Tuna closely followed the reasoning of the first report in concluding that the import restrictions were inconsistent with Art. XI and that Art. XX could not justify the law (Knox 2004, *supra* note 222, at 15).

[167] US-Tuna (Mexico), *supra* note 267, para. 7.1; US-Tuna (ECC), *supra* note 261, para. 6.1.

[168] "[The US-Tuna] decision's preference for multilateral solutions over unilaterally imposed trade-related measures has either influenced or been incorporated into subsequent international instruments" (Ni 2004, *supra* note 1, at 115). For example, "Principle 12 of the 1992 Rio Declaration demanded mutual support between trade and environmental regimes" (*id.*).

[169] US-Tuna (Mexico), *supra* note 267, para. 5.28.

[170] Knox (2004, *supra* note 222, at 10).

[171] "The Panel of US-Tuna (EEC) articulated the test of Art. XX (b) most completely, even though it is still less detailed than the tests that have been applied under Art. XX (g): (i) national measure to protect human, animal, or plant life or health (policy test), (ii) necessary requirements, (iii) requirements by the chapeau of Art. XX, (iv) consideration of alternative GATT-consistent measures" (Meier 1997, *supra* note 244, at 280).

[172] US-Tuna (Mexico), *supra* note 167, para. 5.28.

[173] *Id.* para. 5.33, *cited by* Ala'i (1999, *supra* note 363, at 1148).

[174] Ala'i (1999, *id.*).

The panel, while applying a three-step analysis in analyzing Article XX (g),[175] applied the interpretation of prior panel in Canada-Salmon and Herring by concluding that "relating to" and "in conjunction with" are interpreted to mean "primarily aimed at."[176] It is unprecedented that the panel rejected to extend an exception to allow a trade measure aimed at forcing other countries to change their policies "including policies to protect living things,"[177] evaluating the impact of such a measure on the "objectives of the General Agreement."[178]

Even though the results of the two US-Tuna cases, in which the trade-environment conflict first came to a head, were never adopted by GATT Council, the cases received widespread attention and caused many, particularly, environmentalists to view GATT in a very unfavorable light.[179] However, US-Tuna (EEC) was the first case to recognize explicitly the importance of the environment and to refer to the "objective of sustainable development,"[180] which foreshadowed a new era under the WTO establishing with dual objectives,[181] that is, free trade and the objective of sustainable development.[182]

In the case of US-Automobiles, the panel concluded that the Corporate Average Fuel Economy regulation cannot be justified by Article XX (g) or (d) of GATT given it chooses the separate foreign fleet accounting.

Reviewing the above cases, in Canadian Salmon-herring, Thailand-Cigarettes, and US-Tuna (Mexico), the panels based their decisions on narrow interpretations of the words "necessary," "related to," and "in conjunction with" in subparagraphs (b), (d), and (g) of Article XX.[183] Particularly, there has been no discussion in any of those decisions about the goals and policies that the Article XX exceptions

[175] For the more details, *see* Ala'i (1999, *id.*, at 1151).

[176] US-Tuna (EEC), *supra* note 261, para. 5.22, *cited by* Ala'i (1999, *id.*, at 1152).

[177] US-Tuna (EEC), *id.* para. 5.38, *cited by* Ala'i (1999, *id.*, at 1153).

[178] US-Tuna (EEC), *id.* para. 5.38, *cited by* Ala'i (1999, *id.*).

[179] Emslie (2005, *supra* note 262, at 511–512); For more details, see Howse (2002, pp. 91, 493–494, *cited by* Rietvelt 2005, *supra* note 228, at 483 n. 68). ("Before the US-Tuna rulings, the prevailing view was that Art. XX of the GATT decided any conflicts between free-trade rule and environmental norms in favor of the latter. The US-Tuna panels tried to switch the preference in favor of the latter. Worse still, they approached the question solely from the perspective of effects on liberalized trade. Traditionally, the GATT demonstrated respect for regulatory diversity and progressive government. But after US-Tuna, environmentalists – and others with concerns about how the trading system balances competing values – saw the GATT as a regime dedicated to the triumph of free trade over all other human concerns.").

[180] US-Tuna (EEC), *supra* note 261, para. 5.42.

[181] "The WTO [purports to have] a commitment to an open, non-discriminatory and equitable multilateral trading system on the one hand, and to protection of the environment, and promotion of sustainable development on the other." Quoting Preamble of the (Marrakesh) Ministerial Decision on Trade and Environment, Apr. 15, 1994, GATT/MTN. TNC/MIN (94) /1/Rev.1, *cited by* Rietvelt (2005, *supra* note 228, at 498).

[182] Ala'i (1999, *supra* note 363, at 1153).

[183] Ala'i (1999, *id.*, at 1154).

generally seek to promote and protect within the multilateral trading system,[184] except in US-Tuna (EEC), where the panel refers to the "objectives of the General Agreement," the importance of "sustainable development," and the "environment."[185]

Under Article XX (b), (d), and (g), the standards deciding justification would be "the least-restrictive means test."[186] It was commented that such a strict interpretation set a "high hurdle for environmental policies" because a policy approach to intrude less on trade is always conceivable and therefore in some sense available.[187] Thus, under the (pre-WTO) GATT mechanism, the trade-related measure for environmental protection has had difficulties in securing recognition with its legitimacy.[188]

It also seems difficult to induce case law on interpretation of trade measures related to environmental protection from the conclusions of panels under the GATT mechanism. Upon review of the trade disputes related to environmental measures under GATT, interpretations of Article XX (b), (d), (g) and the chapeau will be found to be incoherent and unpredictable. Even though there does not seem to be a problem in terms that panels of GATT do not have to follow the principle of *stare decisis*,[189] it will be a crucial issue from the viewpoint of legal stability and predictability in the application of law.

13.1.3.2 Judicial Interpretation Under the WTO Mechanism

1. General

Since the WTO was launched, several cases including US-Gasoline,[190] US-Shrimp and EC-Asbestos[191] handled by the dispute settlement procedures focused mainly on general exceptions, the most-favored nation treatment, national treatment, the TBT Agreement and the SPS Agreement. Comparing jurisprudence of the WTO about these cases with that of GATT, the Dispute Settlement Body at the WTO is more positive about legitimating trade-related measures for environmental protection through the judicial interpretation of general exceptions than GATT.

---

[184] *Id.*

[185] US-Tuna (EEC), *supra* note 261, para. 5.38.

[186] Trebilcock and Howse (1999).

[187] Esty (1993, *supra* note 210, at 48).

[188] Trebilcock and Howse (1999, *supra* note 395, at 338). ("There have, however, been comments that those definitions do not seem to pose an insurmountable threat to environmental measures: For example, even in the context of the US-Tuna case, the United States arguably had exhausted available alternative measures by pursuing the tuna problem with Mexico in the context of both bilateral and regional negotiations.") Hudnall (1996, *supra* note 239, at 188).

[189] For the issue of *stare decisis* in the current WTO dispute settlement process, see Blackmore (2004, pp. 487, 487–519). (Overviewing the issue of stare decisis in the current WTO dispute settlement process and proposing the way to institute *stare decisis* within the process).

[190] Appellate Body Report. Apr. 29, 1996. United States-Standards for Reformulated and Conventional Gasoline, WT/DS2/AB/R. (US-Gasoline AB Report).

[191] EC-Asbestos AB Report, *supra* note 267.

For instance, in the case of US-Shrimp and EC-Asbestos, the Appellate Body made it clear that interpretation and application of the Article XX is necessary to settle disputes regarding trade-related environmental measures until the new measures from the Environmental Committee are made,[192] and applying the exemption in a way that has renewed both debate and controversy surrounding the relationship between trade and environment.[193]

2. US-Gasoline

The main issue of the case of US-Gasoline was whether the US gasoline regulation violated Article I, Article III, and Article XX of GATT 1994 and Article II of the TBT Agreement.[194] The Appellate Body, applying a "two-tier approach,"[195] concluded that US measures were found to satisfy Article XX(g), but to violate Article XX[196] because the method of making its standards of gasoline rule did not meet the requirements of the chapeau of the Article XX,[197] which ensures that exceptions in GATT Article XX are not abused or misused,[198] that is, the measure is not a "disguised restriction on international trade."[199]

In the process,[200] the Appellate Body cleared away two obstacles to using Article XX(g) that dated back to the US-Tuna report[201]: (i) the least GATT-inconsistent

[192] US-Shrimp AB Report, *supra* note 234, para. 155.

[193] *Id.* para. 118. (Quoting the US-Gasoline AB Report, *supra* note 193, at 22).

[194] TBT Agreement, *supra* note 281. Art. 2 (Preparation, Adoption and Application of Technical Regulations by Central Government Bodies).

[195] The Appellate Body in its analysis of this case created a two-tier (prong) test in identifying whether a measure complies with Art. XX. "First, the Appellate Body evaluates if a measure fulfills the requirements of any of the subparagraphs, that is, evaluates the baseline establishment rule under the requirements of subparagraph (g) of Art. XX. If a measure complies with any of the subparagraphs, the Appellate Body then examines if the manner in which the measure is applied complies with the chapeau of Art. XX." US-Gasoline AB Report, *supra* note 399, at 22, *cited by* Calderin (2002, *supra* note 212, at 54, n. 99).

[196] With respect to the Art. XX defense, the panel had concluded that "i) the U.S. rule could not be justified under Art. XX (b) as 'necessary to protect human ... health' because the rule had at its disposal other means less inconsistent with GATT to accomplish the same health and environmental goals, and ii) the EPA rule could not be justified under Art. XX (g) as 'relating to' the conservation of 'exhaustible natural resources' since affording treatment to imports in accordance with Art. III:4 would not necessarily prevent the attainment of the desired level of conservation of fair quality under the rule." US-Gasoline Panel Report, *supra* note 263, paras. 6.26, 6.28, 6.40, *cited by* Choinski (2002, pp. 569, 590).

[197] US-Gasoline AB Report *supra* note 399, at 26–27.

[198] *Id.*, at 22.

[199] *Id.*, at 20.

[200] The test that the Panel and the Appellate Body have applied when considering Art. XX(g) in US-Gasoline can be consolidated: "i) definition of petroleum as natural resources, ii) measure's aim, iii) national measure's effect in conjunction with restrictions on domestic production or consumption, iv) requirements by the chapeau of Art. XX v) jurisdictional requirements, vi) consideration of alternative course of action, vii) resolution by international agreement" (Meier 1997, *supra* note 244, at 280–281).

[201] US-Tuna (Mexico), *supra* note 267, para. 7.1; US-Tuna (EEC), *supra* note 261, paras. 6.1, 5.28.

test could not be imported into Article XX(g)[202]; (ii) Article XX(g) language "in conjunction with restrictions on domestic production or consumption" could not be interpreted to be "primarily aimed at" making the domestic restrictions effective.[203] Instead, the language required only "even-handedness in the imposition of restrictions, in the name of conservation, upon the production or consumption of exhaustible natural resources."[204]

Regarding "relating to," the Appellate Body interpreted the term as requiring a "substantial relationship" of the measure and the conservation of resources and did not overload it with the consideration of the objectives of GATT,[205] which was regarded as a step towards a more environmentally friendly reading of Article XX (g).[206] As such, the Appellate Body stated that Article XX (g) requires "even-handiness" and not "identity of treatment," and so long as domestic restrictions were also subject to equivalent restrictions, then the requirements of subparagraph (g) as indicated by the words "in conjunction with" were satisfied.[207] This was a significant departure from prior panel decisions under the GATT mechanism and is a signal that the Appellate Body does not intend to continue on the "narrow interpretative path" of prior panels with regard to Article XX (g).[208]

The Appellate Body then turned to the interpretation of the Article XX chapeau and stated that while the requirements of the subparagraph (g) were applicable to the measure itself, that is, the "baseline establishment rule," the chapeau "by its express terms" addresses "the manner in which that measure is applied,"[209] expanding the scope of Article XX by holding that the Vienna Convention[210] requires that each Article XX subparagraph impose a different burden based on the different words in the statute,[211] and each subparagraph must be interpreted specifically based on the specific facts of each case.[212]

---

[202] US-Gasoline AB Report, *supra* note 399, at 15–16.

[203] *Id.*, at 19–20.

[204] *Id.*, at 19–21, *cited by* Knox (2004, *supra* note 222, at 33).

[205] *Id.*, at 19, *cited by* Bree (1998, *supra* note 236, at 113).

[206] Hunter et al. (1996); Foster (1997–98, pp. 393, 430, *cited by* Bree 1998, *supra* note 236, at 113).

[207] US-Gasoline AB Report, *supra* note 399, at 20–21, *cited by* Ala'i (1999, *supra* note 363, at 1159).

[208] Ala'i (1999, *id.*, at 1158–1159).

[209] US-Gasoline AB Report, *supra* note 399, at 22, *cited by* Ala'i (1999, *id.*, at 1159).

[210] For the critics to the excessive reliance upon the Vienna Convention in interpretation from the viewpoint of interpretative approach of international treaty, see Knox (2004, *supra* note 222, at 47–74). (Stating that a greater reliance upon Art. 31(3) of the Vienna Convention instead of an ad hoc assortment of interpretive tools including the Appellate Body's adoption in Shrimp-Turtle would not provide indisputable measures to every issue).

[211] US-Gasoline AB Report, *supra* note 399, at 17, *cited by* Ala'i (1999, *supra* note 363, at 1160).

[212] US-Gasoline AB Report, *id.*, *cited by* Ala'i (1999, *id.*, at 1160).

Interpreting the term "a disguised restriction on international trade,"[213] the Appellate Body noted that the same considerations evaluated under the tests for "arbitrary and unjustifiable discrimination"[214] should also be considered when determining whether a measure amounts to a "disguised restrictions," but that the main focus for the latter test should be evaluating whether the measure represents "abuse or illegitimate use" of the Article XX exceptions.[215]

Interpreting the Article XX's chapeau, the Appellate Body, incorporating a "balancing test" to balance Article XX interests with the trade liberalization goals of GATT 1994 in each case that comes before it,[216] which has been followed by the later cases,[217] noted that the United States had not tried to cooperate with concerned countries to address the administrative problems and that it appeared to have disregarded the potential financial burdens on foreign refiners.[218] It further pointed out that if Article XX exceptions are not to be abused or misused, the measures falling within the particular exceptions must be applied reasonably, with due regard both to the legal duties and rights of the parties concerned.[219]

Although the Appellate Body ruled against regulations whose aim was environmental protection and preservation,[220] the decision was estimated to be environmentally conscious and to imply that the desired goal of the WTO was to protect

---

[213] The Appellate Body found that the U.S. regulations constituted a disguised restriction on international trade because the United States had not shown any attempt to mitigate such discrimination or alleviate the costs imposed by the regulations on foreign gasoline producers as it had for domestic producers. US-Gasoline AB Report, *supra* note 399, at 28, *cited by* Reif and Eckert (2004, *supra* note 257, at 697).

[214] The Appellate Body, in making the "unjustifiable discrimination" determination, underscored the fact that the United States had "more than one alternative course of action available ... in promulgating regulations implementing the CAA" that were less inconsistent with GATT. US-Gasoline AB Report, *supra* note 399, para. 4.10, *cited by* Choinski (2002, *supra* note 405, at 591–592). Had it chosen such alternative courses, the United States could have avoided subjecting imported gasoline to the discriminatory treatment that resulted from the imposition of more exacting statutory baselines (Choinski 2002, *id.*, at 592).

[215] US-Gasoline AB report, *supra* note 399, at 25, *cited by* Reif and Eckert (2004, *supra* note 257, at 697).

[216] Ala'i (1999, *supra* note 363, at 1162).

[217] *See*, for example, US-Shrimp AB Report, *supra* note 234, para. 15.6; Panel Report. June 15, 2001. United States-Import Prohibition of Certain Shrimp and Shrimp Products-Recourse to Art. 21.5 of DSU by Malaysia, para. 156, WT/DS58/RW. (US-Shrimp (21.5) Panel Report).

[218] The U.S. government had argued on appeal that allowing individual baselines for foreign refiners would have caused administrative difficulties and that imposing a uniform statutory baseline on all domestic refiners would have required to bear large financial burdens. US-Gasoline AB Report, *supra* note 399, at 25.

[219] *Id.*

[220] *Id.*, at 29–30.

and preserve the environment[221] in an open, equitable and nondiscriminatory fashion if possible.[222]

3. US-Shrimp

Like the previous US-Tuna disputes under GATT system, the main battlefield in the US-Shrimp cases rested on the interpretation of GATT Article XX, focusing on the environmental exceptions in paragraphs (b), (g), and its chapeau,[223] and on whether there was a geographic or jurisdictional limitation on paragraph (b) and (g), or whether a Member could invoke those exceptions to protect environmental interests beyond its territory.[224] Even though the panel in US-Tuna (Mexico) used the drafting history to decide that nothing had changed in the last decades,[225] the Appellate Body[226] explicitly acknowledged the need to "broaden the scope of the environmental exception" due to raising international concerns about the environment.[227] Particularly, the report not only acknowledged the "principle of sustainable development" as "generally accepted" but also "fundamentally based a part of its analysis on this principle."[228]

In the case that marks perhaps "one of the most complicated and convoluted legal analysis ever rendered,"[229] the Appellate Body, applying "customary rules of interpretation of international law,"[230] and then a two-tier analysis[231] to Article XX as in US-Gasoline,[232] held that analysis of an Article XX exception should initially begin with the specific exception claimed, and that the chapeau addresses only the application of a measure[233] that has been determined to fall within a specific exception.[234]

---

[221] The Appellate Body pointed out that in the preamble to the WTO Agreement and in the Decision on Trade and Environment, there is specific acknowledgement to be found about the importance of coordinating policies on trade and the environment. *Id.*

[222] Calderin (2002, *supra* note 212, at 54).

[223] US-Shrimp AB Report, *supra* note 234, paras. 111–188, *cited by* Ni (2004, *supra* note 210, at 116).

[224] US-Shrimp Panel Report, *supra* note 229, paras. 3.183–3.234, *cited by* Ni (2004, *id*).

[225] US-Tuna (Mexico), *supra* note 267, para. 5.26 (concerning the question whether the protecting of extra jurisdictional living beings can be justified by Art. XX (b)), *cited by* Bree (1998, *supra* note 236, at 109).

[226] US-Shrimp AB Report, *supra* note 234, para. 98.

[227] Bree (1998, *supra* note 236, at 109).

[228] *Id.*

[229] Rietvelt (2005, *supra* note 228, at 474).

[230] US-Shrimp AB Report, *supra* note 234, para. 114.

[231] This sequential analysis reflects the "fundamental structure and logic of Art. XX, because the measure must first meet the specific requirements of a given exception before it is examined under the broad standards of the Chapeau"(Rogers and Whitlock 2002, *supra* note 25, at 486–487).

[232] US-Gasoline AB Report, *supra* note 399, at 22.

[233] In contrast to the Panel's "chapeau-down" approach, the Appellate Body established this proper sequence for carrying out an analysis under Art. XX (Rietvelt 2005, *supra* note 228, at 484).

[234] Knox (2004, *supra* note 222, at 34).

The Appellate Body concluded: The United States' measure[235] to protect sea turtles serves an environmental objective that is recognized as legitimate under paragraph (g) of the Article XX of GATT 1994.[236] In its consideration of whether turtles were covered by the exception for "natural resources" in Article XX (g), the Appellate Body found that the meaning of the words in the exception is not "'static'[237] ... but is rather 'by definition, evolutionary'",[238] as in the Canadian Salmon-Herring case.[239]

However, in the Canadian Salmon-Herring, the panel needed to note only that the "United States agreed that salmon and herring were exhaustible natural resources," and the two US-Tuna panel reports did not spend a single word on that problem, therefore, the US-Shrimp Appellate Body report was the first to thoroughly address whether "living resources" fall under the definition of "exhaustible natural resources."[240]

Agreeing that Section 609 was a measure "relating to" the conservation of exhaustible natural resources,[241] the Appellate Body concluded that the statute came within the exception in Article XX (g) despite the fact that Section 609 called for a unilateral ban on imports on the United States.[242] These types of attempts to influence production and process methods outside the jurisdiction of the importing country have been anathema to many in the GATT community, and some have since expressed "alarm that the Appellate Body decision apparently allows the use of these process standards."[243]

Regarding the term "relating to," the Appellate Body, overruling the US-Tuna Report,[244] interpreted the term similarly to how it had in the US-Gasoline dispute,[245] which fulfills the "self-imposed requirements of treaty interpretation," as it

---

[235] Departments of Commerce, Justice, and State, the Judiciary, and Related Agencies Appropriations Act of 1990. Pub. L. 101–162, Title VI, §609, Nov. 21, 1989, 103, Stat. 1037 (codified at 16 U.S.C. 1037).

[236] The Appellate Body sought guidance from other external international instruments other than WTO Agreements such as the 1982 Convention on the Law of the Sea, the Convention on Biological Diversity, and the Resolution on Assistance to Developing Countries, which was adopted in conjunction with the Convention on the Conservation of Migratory Species of Wild Animals, in attempting to define the term "natural resources." US-Shrimp AB Report, *supra* note 234, paras. 129–130, *cited by* Stewart and Johanson (2003, *supra* note 366, at 34).

[237] In the past, the panels have accepted dolphins, clean air, and petroleum as exhaustible natural resources (Meier 1997, *supra* note 244, at 280–281).

[238] Reif and Eckert (2004, *supra* note 257, at 685 (footnotes omitted)).

[239] Canada-Herring and Salmon, *supra* note 328, para. 4.4.

[240] Bree (1998, *supra* note 236, at 106–107 (footnotes omitted)).

[241] US-Shrimp AB Report, *supra* note 234, para. 145, *cited by* Chang (2005, pp. 25, 35).

[242] Chang 2005, *id.*, at 35.

[243] *Id.*

[244] US-Shrimp AB Report, *supra* note 234, para. 118.

[245] Bree (1998, *supra* note 236, at 113).

reflects the ordinary meaning of the terms, to read in their context, and in the light of the object and purpose of GATT.[246]

Analyzing the last clause of Article XX (g), which requires that the measures at issue "are made effective in conjunction with restrictions on domestic production and consumption," the Appellate Body, noting that the US legislation imposed similar restrictions both on US shrimp trawl vessels and shrimp importers,[247] concluded: it was "in principle, ... an even-handed measure."[248] As such, the interpretation of Article XX (g) has been consistent with the Appellate Body Report in the US-Gasoline case, but has incorporated "new perspectives that are consistent with and can be related to principles of international environmental law."[249]

This measure, however, has been enforced by the United States in a manner which constitutes arbitrary and unjustifiable discrimination between Members of the WTO, contrary to the requirements of the chapeau of Article XX: because in relation with the manner of implementation of the law it is "more concerned with effectively influencing the WTO Members to adopt essentially the same comprehensive regulatory regime as that applied by the United States to its domestic shrimp trawlers"[250] and, more importantly, because the United States failed to engage in international negotiations[251] with shrimp exporting countries before[252] imposing the embargo.[253]

Examining the US measures first with regard to the prohibition against unjustifiable or arbitrary discrimination,[254] in interpretation of the Article XX chapeau, the Appellate Body declared that it was enough that the measure be held inconsistent with Article XX because Section 609[255] constituted both unjustifiable and arbitrary

---

[246] *Id.*, at 114.

[247] *Id.*, at 115.

[248] US-Shrimp AB Report, *supra* note 234, para. 144; Bree (1998, *id.*, at 115).

[249] Bree (1998, *supra* note 236, at 115).

[250] US-Shrimp AB Report, *supra* note 234, at 165.

[251] "Thus, the Appellate Body incorporated this mandate into the Shrimp case by equating the failure of the United States to pursue negotiations with Asian nations with arbitrary and unjustifiable discrimination" (Ni 2004, *supra* note 210, at 112).

[252] For the interpretation issue of the term "before" herewith, in US-Shrimp (21.5) Panel Report and US-Shrimp (21.5) AB Report (Appellate Body Report. Oct. 22, 2001. United States-Import Prohibition of Certain Shrimp and Shrimp Products-Recourse to Art. 21.5 of DSU by Malaysia. WT/DS58/AB/RW. (US-Shrimp (21.5) AB Report)), See Ni (2004, *supra* note 210, at 123–129). (Stating that the Panel declined to confirm the superiority of multilateral approaches over unilateral means, instead of clarifying the legal implications of the term "before," and the Appellate Body did not expressively deal with this critical issue in its review).

[253] US-Shrimp AB Report, *supra* note 234, paras. 166–172.

[254] *Id.* para. 160.

[255] Department of Commerce, Justice and State, the Judiciary, and Related Agencies Appropriations Act, 1990, Pub. L. No. 101–162, 103 Stat. 988 (1989) (codified at 16 U.S.C. § 1537 (1994)). This provision banned the importation into the United States of shrimp harvested with technology that could adversely affect certain sea turtles, with the provided exemptions for

discrimination,[256] without specifically addressing the issue of whether the statute, in fact, constituted a "disguised restriction on international trade."[257] This reasoning of the decision was in compliance with reasoning in the Appellate Body Report in the US-Gasoline case, [258] and has been followed by EC-Asbestos.[259]

In the process, the Appellate Body, noting that the discrimination in Article XX is different in its nature and quality from the discrimination in the treatment of products in the meaning of Article I, III, XI,[260] as already held in the case of US-Gasoline, looked at the actual application of the US import ban and concluded that the "cumulative effect" of the differences[261] in the means of application of Section 609 constituted an "unjustifiable discrimination."[262] The Appellate Body based its finding of arbitrary discrimination on two points, which made it significantly briefer than cases concerning unjustifiable discrimination[263]: (i) the rigidity and inflexibility of the certification process and (ii) the lack of transparency,[264] predictability, and thus, due process and basic fairness in the certification process.[265]

While, in general, the parties to the US-Shrimp dispute, the WTO, and environmental groups agree that the chapeau is designed to prevent the abuse of Article XX exceptions, the exact meaning and application of the dual requirements is debated

---

imports from nations that were certified to have a regulatory program and average rates of incidental turtle takings comparable to those of the United States and for nations where particular fishing environment did not pose a threat to sea turtles (*Id. cited by* Reif and Eckert 2004, *supra* note 257, at 683).

256 Dailey (2000, *supra* note 327, at 374), *cited by* Rietvelt (2005, *supra* note 228, at 488).

257 Dailey (2000, *id*).

258 EC-Hormones AB Report, *supra* note 317, para. 239.

259 Rief and Eckert (2004, *supra* note 257, at 696).

260 US-Shrimp AB Report, *supra* note 234, para. 142, *cited by* Bree (1998, *supra* note 236, at 120–121).

261 The Appellate Body criticized the following features of the US measures in its actual application: "i) coercing other members to adopt essentially the same regulatory program; ii) failing to engage in serious multilateral negotiations with the objective of concluding bi-or multilateral agreements for the protection of sea turtles; ii a) the United States concluded one regional agreement, but did not negotiate with other countries; iii) countries desiring certification under Section 609 were treated differently" Bree (1998, *supra* note 236, at 121).

262 US-Shrimp AB Report, *supra* note 234, para. 176, *cited by* Bree (1998, *supra* note 236, at 120–121).

263 Bree (1998, *supra* note 236, at 127).

264 It was indicated to be noteworthy that the lack of transparency was one of the complaints concerning the WTO dispute settlement procedure Bree (1998, *supra* note 236, at 127 n. 171).

265 US-Shrimp AB Report, *supra* note 234, paras. 177–184, *cited by* Bree (1998, *supra* note 236, at 127).

seriously[266] due to its ambiguous language.[267] The Appellate Body read the chapeau as giving it broad powers[268] to strike a "balance" or draw a "line of equilibrium,"[269] between the environmental interests protected by the exceptions in Article XX and the trade interests promoted by the "substantive" provisions of GATT,[270] that is, "between the right of a Member to invoke an exception under Article XX and the duty of that same Member to respect the treaty rights of other Members."[271] While this "balancing test" resembles those proposed by some environmental critics, it suffers from the "unpredictability"[272] inherent in all balancing tests.[273]

The decision has also an important meaning as the first GATT/WTO case to deal with the issue of nongovernmental amicus submission[274] in dispute settlement proceedings.[275] The Appellate Body held that the NGO's amicus briefs were

---

[266] Bree (1998, *supra* note 236, at 106).

[267] SPS Agreement, *supra* note 282. Art. 5.5, provides more clearly than the GATT provisions: "[M]embers shall avoid arbitrary or unjustifiable distinctions in the levels it considers to be appropriate in different situations, if such distinctions result in discrimination or a disguised restriction on international trade[.]" EC-Hormones Panel interpreted this provision in line with the standards of the chapeau of Art. XX of the GATT 1994 quoting the Appellate Body Report in the US-Gasoline. EC-Hormones (US) Panel Report, *supra* note 303, paras. 8.215–8.216.

Against this interpretation by the Panel, the Appellate Body, considering that there are structural differences between the standards of Art. 5.5 of the SPS Agreement (*id.*, para. 239), found that the question whether arbitrary or unjustifiable differences or distinctions in levels of protections established by a Member do in fact result in discrimination or a disguised restriction in international trade should be solved in the circumstance of each individual case (*id.*, para. 240).

[268] Regarding interpretation of the chapeau of Art. XX in US-Shrimp, Rief and Eckert criticized: "the Appellate Body's finding that ... illustrates the wide latitude for panel or Appellate Body interpretation of provisions like Art. XX. This holding opens the door to the potential creation of a costly and lengthy administrative hurdle that lacks any basis in the language of Art. XX .... [T]he Appellate Body's interpretation of the opening paragraph of Art. XX has provided dispute settlement panel with increased discretion to uphold or strike down legitimate health and safety regulations depending primarily on a particular panel's view of the facts and circumstances of a case" (Reif and Eckert 2004, *supra* note 257, at 693–694).

[269] For the flexible location of the line of equilibrium, *see* US-Shrimp AB Report, *supra* note 234, para 159. (Ruling "[t]he location of the line of equilibrium, as expressed in the chapeau, is not fixed and unchanging; the line moves as the kind and the shape of the measures at stake vary as the facts making up specific cases differ"); see also US-Shrimp (21.5) Panel Report, *supra* note 426, para. 5.51 (ruling "the position of the line itself depends on the type of measure imposed and on the particular circumstance of this case").

[270] Knox (2004, *supra* note 222, at 37).

[271] US-Shrimp AB Report, *supra* note 234, para. 15.6, *cited by* Rietvelt (2005, *supra* note 228, at 486).

[272] Rief and Eckert (2004, *supra* note 257, at 693–694).

[273] Knox (2004, *supra* note 222, at 37).

[274] The Center for Marine Conservation (CMC) and the Center for International Environmental Law ("CIEL") jointly submitted an amicus brief while the World Wide Fund for Nature (WFN) filed an independent amicus brief. *See* US-Shrimp Panel Report, *supra* note 229, para. 3.129.

[275] *Id.* para. 3.129.

acceptable in panel proceedings,[276] stating that "those briefs formed part of the appellant's submission, and observed that it is for a participant in an appeal to determine for itself what to include in its submission,"[277] which was followed in other later cases.[278]

Regarding the jurisdiction problem,[279] although it left open the possibility that Article XX(g) has a jurisdictional limitation[280] it would be easier to meet than that[281] imposed by the US-Tuna panels.[282] The US-Shrimp dispute seemed to make it clear that MEA-mandated trade restrictions against MEA parties would satisfy the chapeau, since in such cases the parties themselves would have demarcated their own "line of equilibrium" between trade and environmental concerns,[283] even though it has sometimes been estimated to remain doubtful that other trade restrictions, especially if aimed at an extrajurisdictional resource, would survive the chapeau.[284]

The Appellate Body, with regard to the trade measures based on PPMs, reversing the legal interpretation of the panel,[285] concluded that Members may restrict

---

[276] US-Shrimp AB Report, *supra* note 234, para. 187.

[277] *Id.* para. 81.

[278] The cases are Thailand-H Beams, US-Shrimp (21.5-Malaysia), *See* Appellate Body Report. Sep. 26, 2002. European Communities-Trade Description of Sardines, para. 156 nn. 56–57. WT/DS231/AB/R. (EC-Sardines AB Report), EC-Asbestos, US-Lead and Bismuth II (Bhala and Gantz 2002, *supra* note 316, at 269).

[279] In US-Tuna (Mexico), relying on the reasoning of the Canadian Salmon-Herring Report (Canadian Herring and Salmon, *supra* note 328, para. 4.6), the Panel held that extraterritorial enforcement of any regulation is contrary to GATT policies, US-Tuna(Mexico), *supra* note 267, *cited by* Rietvelt (2005, *supra* note 228, at 483, n. 68). In US-Tuna (EEC), the Panel backed off from its somewhat rigid stance, however, by reopening the possibility that countries may enforce environmental regulation abroad, but only if doing so will not infringe upon the sovereignty of other member countries (Rietvelt 2005, *supra* note 228, at 483, n. 68).

[280] The Appellate Body, avoiding dealing with the jurisdiction of extraterritorial application of environmental trade measures by the United States, see US-Shrimp AB Report, *supra* note 234, para. 133, considered the trade ban on shrimp product to be a measure in compliance with the provisions of Art. XX(g) (*id.*, Paras. 125–145).

[281] US-Tuna (EEC) Panel Report, *supra* note 261, para. 5.28; US-Tuna (Mexico) Panel Report, *supra* note 267, para. 5.28.

[282] Knox (2004, *supra* note 222, at 35).

[283] For the primary reliance of the Appellate Body on an extratextual principle to read the chapeau, see Knox (2004, *supra* note 222, at 56). (Stating that the Appellate Body, making little or no effort to find the ordinary meaning of "arbitrary or unjustifiable discrimination" and "disguised restriction on international trade," read the chapeau as giving it broad powers to strike a balance or find a "line of equilibrium" between trade and environmental interests).

[284] Knox (2004, *supra* note 222, at 38–39); Rietvelt (2005, *supra* note 228, at 489). ("[T]he arguments of earlier cases condemning unilateral measures under Art. XX seem to have merely transferred bases from the interpretation of the exceptions to the interpretations of the chapeau . . . .").

[285] The panel examined the U.S. measure under the Section 609 with regard to the chapeau of Art. XX, which prohibits application of measures that would constitute "arbitrary or unjustifiable

imports based on the method of production (that is, the method of shrimp harvest), which can be justified with the Article XX provided that it is not implemented in an arbitrary or discriminatory manner.[286]

Ultimately, while the Appellate Body concluded that the US import ban was not justified under GATT Article XX,[287] it nonetheless applied Article XX "in a manner more accommodating to US trade restrictions than earlier GATT reports."[288] The US-Shrimp appellate decision strengthens the right of the state to adopt conservation measures by a "liberal interpretation of exhaustible natural resources,"[289] indicating that "unilateralism may, in fact, be a common aspect and application of Article XX (g) justifiable measures,"[290] even though the practical application of such an assertion is open for debate.[291]

The Appellate Body also called for multilateral solutions to respond to concern over endangered sea turtles, which has led the WTO panels to have repeatedly referred to the need to pursue multilateral solutions to environmental problems,[292] by citing to the Inter-American Convention for the Protection and Conservation of

---

discrimination between countries where the same conditions prevail," and finally found that Section 609 did indeed violate the chapeau of Art. XX, and therefore found no need to address whether the measure fell under any of the exceptions. *See* Rietvelt (2005, *supra* note 228, at 482).

[286] Against this decision, complaint, Thailand, criticized highly that the right to discriminate based on "like product" had not been accepted in the WTO mechanism and that the Appellate Body, on its own initiative, had altered the balance of rights and obligations under the WTO Agreement. WTO Dispute Settlement Body. Dec. 14, 1998. Minutes of Meeting, held in the centre William Rappard on Nov. 6, 1998, WTO Doc. WT/DSB/M/50.

[287] Shaffer (2001, *supra* note 216, at 39).

[288] The Appellate Body found that Art. XX must be read "in light of contemporary concerns of the community of nations about the protection and conservation of the environment." US-Shrimp AB Report, *supra* note 234, para. 129.

[289] Rietvelt (2005, *supra* note 228, at 488).

[290] US-Shrimp AB Report, *supra* note 234, at 121, *cited by* Rietvelt (2005, *supra* note 228, at 488).

[291] Rietvelt (2005, *supra* note 228, at 489).

[292] With regard to the preference for multilateralism in the WTO to deal with environmental issues, it is arguably problematic for the Appellate Body to recommend a multilateral approach when trade-related measures in an MEA could be challenged under the DSU. The preference for multilateral solutions in the WTO, however, has been arguably weakened by the Appellate Body's implicit nod of acceptance for multilateral trade measures outside of MEA. *See* Shaw and Schwartz (2002, *supra* note 230, at 145). However, the Appellate Body's eagerness to adopt international environmental rules would be consistent with the provisions on treaty interpretation in the Understanding on Rules and Procedures Governing the Settlement of Dispute that require taking into account customary norms of international law, *see* Understanding on Rules and Procedures Governing the Settlement of Disputes. Apr. 15, 1994. Marrakesh Agreement Establishing the World Trade Organization, Annex 2. Legal Instruments-Results of the Uruguay Round. 33 I.L.M. 1125. (DSU), *cited by* Ni (2004, *supra* note 210, at 120), as stipulated in the Vienna Convention on the Law of the Treaties. May 23, 1969. Vienna Convention on the Law of Treaties Arts. 31–32, 1155 U.N.T.S. 331, 340. (Vienna Convention), *cited by* Ni (2004, *id.*, at 120).

Sea Turtles.[293] As such, the Appellate Body recognizes the "growing importance of the environment, sustainable development, and Article XX within the WTO system."[294]

4. US-Shrimp (21.5)

With regard to the US implementation of the Appellate Body's decision, the panel ruled that the United States, in revising the guidelines implementing Section 609,[295] had addressed the concerns set out by the Appellate Body,[296] and reaffirmed that: the optional way for the parties to this dispute to contribute effectively to the protection of sea turtles[297] in a manner consistent with WTO objectives,[298] including sustainable development, would be to reach cooperative agreements[299] on integrated conservation strategies.

Regarding the cooperative agreements, the panel and the Appellate Body upheld the Appellate Body decision[300] in US-Shrimp that the U.S. government could impose the restrictions only after it made serious efforts in good faith[301] to negotiate an agreement on sea turtle conservation with all interested parties, not that it could impose the restrictions after an agreement was concluded.[302] After reviewing US efforts to reach an agreement, the panel concluded that the United States was in

---

[293] This is a multi-national convention negotiated by the United States with some of the affected countries for the protection and conservation of sea turtles. Inter-American Convention for the Protection and Convention of Sea Turtles, opened for signature Dec. 1, 1996, 37 I.L.M. 1246 (1996).

[294] Ala'i (1999, *supra* note 363, at 1169).

[295] For the consideration of Section 609 as a "carrot" and a "stick" that would together serve to extend sea turtle protection beyond the limited confines of U.S. waters and its exclusive economic zone, see Rietvelt (2005, *supra* note 228, at 479–480).

[296] US-Shrimp AB Report, *supra* note 234, para. 98.

[297] For the sea turtles and shrimp trawling as the most wasteful commercial fishery in the world from the viewpoint of environmentalist, see Rietvelt (2005, *supra* note 228, at 476–478).

[298] "Both to protect and preserve the environment and to enhance the means for doing so in a manner consistent with their respective needs and concerns at different levels of economic development." WTO Agreement preamble.

[299] The implementation panel interpreted that because the United States had an obligation to negotiate, but not necessarily, at this stage, an obligation to reach an international agreement. US-Shrimp(21.5) Panel Report, *supra* note 426, para. 5.67, and thus the United States had to make "serious good faith efforts" to negotiate an international agreement (*id.*, para. 5.86).

[300] For the different interpretation with regard to this point, see Ni (2004, *supra* note 210, at 130). (Stating "the US-Shrimp Decision was contextually interpreted to be unclear whether the Appellate Body intended to require the conclusion of an international agreement in order for the U.S. import ban to be valid, or whether the United States was merely obliged to make good faith efforts to negotiate with the complaining Members.").

[301] For the significance of good faith, *see* US-Shrimp (21.5) Panel Report, *supra* note 426, para. 5.60 (stating "[T]he notion of good faith ... implies a continuity of efforts which ... is the only way to address successfully the issue of conservation and protection of sea turtles through multilateral negotiations ... even though the Appellate Body only refers to 'serious efforts', the notion of good faith efforts implies ... .").

[302] Knox (2004, *supra* note 222, at 39).

compliance with this requirement,[303] because the United States had entered into a binding agreement with Latin American countries even though it had failed to reach such an agreement with Malaysia.[304]

As such, the Appellate Body read the chapeau in consistence with the spirit of many of the environmental critics' proposals[305] by allowing the chapeau to justify unilateral measures – even a unilateral measure identical in many respects to the law that led to the US-Tuna decisions – as long as they are applied flexibly and in connection with good-faith[306] efforts to reach a multilateral agreement.[307] The agreements cover, *inter alia*, the design, implementation and use of "turtle excluder devices" while taking into account the specific conditions in the different geographical areas concerned.[308]

Surrounding the US-Shrimp case, some WTO Members were afraid of the potential abuse of unilateral measures in the name of environmental protection.[309] In order to clarify the relationship between the WTO and MEAs as well as to prevent abuse, two suggestions were made: (i) to amend Article XX to accommodate the use of trade measures pursuant to MEAs; or (ii) to make additional interpretations or understandings of Article XX.[310] These were suggested on the

[303] US-Shrimp (21.5) Panel Report, *supra* note 426, para. 5. 87.

[304] *Id.* para. 5.72–5.86.

[305] Knox (2004, *supra* note 222, at 41).

[306] Malaysia, meanwhile, took the position that once it was in the process of negotiating with the United States, the United States should drop its ban on the importation of shrimp from Malaysia. The United States was of the view that it was negotiating in good faith and was entitled to maintain its ban until the negotiations resulted in an agreement. A WTO panel and the Appellate Body ruled against Malaysia. *See* US-Shrimp (21.5) AB Report, *supra* note 461, at 49–51, *cited by* Cone (2003, pp. 245, 248–249). On the basis of the panel and Appellate Body reports, it was considered fair to state that, in the guise of raising procedural points under the relevant WTO agreements and rules, Malaysia was simply re-itigating the WTO decision calling for negotiations between Malaysia and the United States (Cone 2003, *id.*).

[307] Knox (2004, *supra* note 222, at 41).

[308] US-Shrimp (21.5) Panel Report, *supra* note 426, paras. 7.1–7.2.

[309] *See*, for example, Oxley (Feb. 2002), *cited by* Rietvelt (2005, *supra* note 228, at 493). (Stating that the international trade community protests the Shrimp/Turtle holding in the sense that it leaves the door cracked open for countries to unilaterally impose extraterritorial trade restrictions based on individual, domestic agendas-perhaps more importantly-without necessitating changes to the WTO rules); For additional arguments of what Oxley views as dangerous precedents made by the Appellate Body, see *id.*, at 4, *cited by* Rietvelt (2005, *id.*, at 493, n. 129) (listing: Art. XX(g) can have extraterritorial reach; A trade restriction can be imposed on a product if its processing method has negative environmental consequences; International declarations and conventions, regardless of their status, create legitimate grounds to trigger the use of the exceptions under Art. XX; Non-trade elements of the Preamble, e.g., "sustainable development," now diminish the standing of the international trade responsibilities of the WTO as its primary purpose).

[310] Swiss Proposals to Clarify the WTO-MEA Relationship Based on the Principles of Mutual Supportiveness and Deference. WTO Committee on Trade and Environment. 19 October, 2000. Clarification of the Relationship between the WTO and Multilateral Environmental Agreements. WTO Doc. WT/CTE/W/168; WTO Committee on Trade and Environment. 8 June, 2000. The Relationship Between the Provisions of the Multilateral Trading System and Multilateral Environmental Agreements(MEAs), WTO Doc. WT/CTE/W/139.

presumed basis of "*persona non grata* of unilateral measures in the multilateral trade system," when the legitimate measures based on MEAs are acceptable under the WTO and the relationship between the WTO and MEAs is clarified, which will lead trade toward a multilateral system.[311]

5. EC-Asbestos

The case of EC-Asbestos,[312] "furthering the interpretation of the WTO rules of importance to the trade and environment debate,"[313] attracted attention because the Appellate Body accepted a French import ban as legitimate under Article XX(b) on the grounds that it was a "necessary"[314] measure to achieve the legitimate goal of protecting human life and health, meeting the requirements of the chapeau of Article XX.[315] With relation to the "necessary" test, the Appellate Body, referring approvingly to a GATT panel's decision in Thailand-Cigarettes,[316] stated that whether another WTO-consistent measure is "reasonably available" involves a "weighing and balancing process" that includes a consideration of "the extent to which the alternative measure contributes to the realization of the end pursued."[317] The Appellate Body found that there were no fewer trade restrictive measures available that would achieve the same end as the import ban and, as a result, the measure was necessary under paragraph (b).[318]

From an environmental viewpoint, this decision is seen as proof of the more positive attitude of the Appellate Body toward the environment considering its inclusion of environmental measures.[319] This is in spite of the Appellate Body's conclusion of the "least GATT-inconsistent" gloss,[320] such as the US-Tuna

---

[311] With these suggestions, there would be serious debates surrounding the issues about what criteria should be used to define a MEA and whether it is the role of the WTO to decide these criteria. *See* Shaw and Schwartz (2002, *supra* note 230, at 149).

[312] EC-Asbestos AB Report, *supra* note 267, paras. 101–103.

[313] Shaw and Schwartz (2002, *supra* note 230, at 150).

[314] The Appellate Body read Art. XX(b) to incorporate a least GATT-inconsistent requirement that, without GATT-consistent measure, the party should use that which entails "the least degree of inconsistency with other GATT provisions." EC-Asbestos AB Report, *supra* note 267, para. 171.

[315] For the criticism against this part of the decision by the panel from the view point of judicial economy, *See* Bhala and Gantz (2002, *supra* note 316, at 517). ("[O]nce the Appellate Body determined that . . . were not 'like product', there was no violation . . ., and thus no absolute need to resort to the exception in Art. XX. Arguably, the Art. XX issue became moot. Nor would the Appellate Body's normal appreciation for 'judicial economy' seem to support the need for this portion of the decision.").

[316] Thailand-Cigarettes, *supra* note 261, para. 75.

[317] EC-Asbestos AB Report, *supra* note 267, para. 172, *cited by* Reif and Eckert (2004, *supra* note 257, at 689).

[318] EC-Asbestos AB Report, *supra* note 267, para. 175, *cited by* Reif and Eckert (2004, *supra* note 257).

[319] Bhala and Gantz (2002, *supra* note 316).

[320] US-Tuna (EEC), *supra* note 261, para. 4.12; US-Tuna (Mexico), *supra* note 267, para. 4.4.

panels.[321] This finding was also read to be a signal to the WTO to recognize that human health[322] is superior to exhaustible natural resources, which could be signaled by the Appellate Body's stating "'[t]he more vital or important [the] common interest or values pursued, the easier it would be to accept as 'necessary' measures designed to achieve those ends."[323]

Another notable point of view expressed by the Appellate Body is the arguably expanded test for physical characteristics to include toxicity in analyzing the "likeness" of a product in Article III of GATT 1994. The Appellate Body, holding that the panel should not have excluded "the health risks associated with chrysotile asbestos fibers from its examination of the physical properties of that product,"[324] decided that carcinogenesis and toxicity are major characteristics of chrysotile asbestos fibers in defining "physical properties" of products that are likely to influence the competitive relationship between products in the marketplace.[325] The Appellate Body reversed the conclusion of the panel that asbestos fibers and cement-based products and the products used in France as its substitute were "like products."[326]

The Appellate Body initially pointing out that the panel did not analyze the element of risk when comparing "like products,"[327] utilized the same test as the panel, the "market-based approach" to likeness with criteria of "physical properties, end-uses, consumers' tastes and habits, and tariff classification,"[328] but did not agree with the manner in which the panel applied the test[329]: The only similarities the Appellate Body found were a few isolated circumstances in which the end-uses for the products were same.[330] The Appellate Body commented that the analysis of end-uses and consumers' tastes and habits are particularly important under Article III considering the provision's concerns with competitive relationship in the marketplace.[331]

---

[321] EC-Asbestos AB Report, *supra* note 267, para. 171, *cited by* Knox (2004, *supra* note 222, at 31–32).

[322] The EC-Asbestos was the first case out of the GATT/WTO cases to accept the member countries' measure to protect human health, since measures to protect human health in the Thailand-Cigarettes, however, the measure was not accepted under Art. XX(b). *See* Thailand-Cigarettes, *supra* note 261, paras. 63, 75–77, 81.

[323] WTO Appellate Body Report on Korea-Measures Affecting Imports of Fresh, Chilled and Frozen Beef, WTO Doc. WT/DS161/AB/R, WT/DS169/AB/R, para. 172 (Jan. 10, 2001).

[324] EC-Asbestos AB Report, *supra* note 267, para. 116.

[325] *Id.* para. 114.

[326] *Id.* paras. 125–126, 132.

[327] EC-Asbestos AB Report, *supra* note 267, para. 85.

[328] *Id.* para. 110.

[329] EC-Asbestos AB Report, *supra* note 267, *cited by* Yavitz (2001–2002, *supra* note 354, at 59).

[330] EC-Asbestos AB Report, *supra* note 267, para. 125, *cited by* Yavitz (2001–2002, *supra* note 354, at 61).

[331] EC-Asbestos AB Report, *supra* note 267, para. 117, *cited by* Yavitz (2001–2002, *supra* note 354, at 60).

The matter has also taken on significance in that it was the first case[332] which enabled the WTO Dispute Settlement Body to go through TBT Agreement: The Appellate Body reached the conclusion that the French Decree is a technical regulation under the TBT Agreement,[333] because; the banning decree at issues, which on the face of it was not a technical regulation, was the document that laid down the characteristics of products containing asbestos fibers as well as applicable administrative provisions.[334] The analysis and application of the TBT Agreement in interpreting "like products" would be one of the main subjects on trade and environmental issues in the WTO world.[335]

Regarding the minimum standards of the TBT and SPS Agreements, the Appellate Body, affirming the EC-Hormones[336] Appellate Body's positive decision for the "autonomous right"[337] of the WTO Members to determine their own level of protection of health,[338] emphasized the WTO Members' own rights.[339] The Appellate Body, recognizing that scientific opinions can differ,[340] noted that parties need

[332] This case regarding the TBT Agreement was accepted by European Communities-Trade Description of Sardines: The Appellate Body noted that EC-Asbestos established three criteria for a document to be a technical regulation; "i) The document must apply to an identifiable products. ii) The document must lay down characteristics of the product. iii) Compliance with the product characteristics must be mandatory." *See* EC-Sardines AB Report, *supra* note 487; Panel Report. May 29, 2002. European Communities-Trade Description of Sardines. WT/DS231/R. (EC-Sardines Panel Report). The Appellate Body, relying on EC-Asbestos, noted that "a product does not necessarily have to be mentioned explicitly in a document for that product to be an identifiable product. Identifiable does not mean expressly identified." *See* EC-Sardines Panel Report, *id.*, para. 7.41. The Appellate Body, furthermore, noted that, based on EC-Asbestos, "product characteristics include not only 'features and qualities intrinsic to the product,' but also those that are related to it, such as 'means of identification'" (Bhala and Gantz 2002, *supra* note 281, at 273).

[333] EC-Asbestos AB Report, *supra* note 267, para. 75.

[334] Shaw and Schwartz (2002, *supra* note 230, at 151).

[335] *Id.*, at 150.

[336] EC-Hormones AB Report, *supra* note 317.

[337] This right comes from one of three substantive principles which the Appellate Body in EC-Hormones, EC-Asbestos, and US-Shrimp looked beyond the text before it to cite, that is, "i) each WTO member has the right to determine its own level of protection of health and safety; ii) natural resources are generally understood to include living natural resources; and iii) international environment measures should normally be based on multilateral agreement." For more details, see Knox (2004, *supra* note 222, at 52–59).

[338] EC-Hormones AB Report, *supra* note 317, para. 177.

[339] *Id.* para. 168.

[340] The Appellate Body in EC-Hormones and Australia Salmon stated that an adequate assessment did not have to make a monolithic finding and could be presented both a mainstream and a divergent scientific view. *See* EC-Hormones AB Report, *supra* note 317, paras. 187, 194; Australia Measures Affecting Importation of Salmon. Report of the Appellate Body. 20 Oct. 1998. WT/DS18/AB.R., (Australia-Salmon AB Report), paras. 123–124.

not only adopt measures consistent with the mainstream view in the scientific community.[341]

With respect to the preliminary procedural matter, the Appellate Body, on the basis of Article 16 (1) of the Working Procedures for Appellate Review,[342] issued instructions to non-party participants in the proceeding as to how they might apply for leave to file written briefs,[343] which went well beyond the limited approval given to NGO briefs in the course of US-Shrimp.[344] Even though the Appellate Body generated great controversy[345] by choosing not to review amici curiae briefs in making its decision after developing elaborate procedures,[346] for those concerned with the uneasy relationship between trade and the environment under the WTO, this is a case of some importance.[347]

This case was also the first case for the Appellate Body to examine the scope of Article XXIII:1(b) of GATT, that is, the non-violation provision, where the Appellate Body, holding that, since Article XXIII:1(b) uses the term "any" measures, health measures are among those which may establish a cause of action under the provision,[348] rejected the EC's assertion there may be no nullification or impairment where GATT Article XX exceptions related to "health objectives" are operable.[349]

6. Other Cases

There have been four dispute cases reviewed by the Appellate Body under the SPS agreement which are likely to be influential to trade and environment conflicts:

In EC-Hormones, the Appellate Body found that the EC measure to ban the sale of meat from cattle treated with hormones violated the SPS Agreement because it was not based on a risk assessment[350]; In Australia-Salmon, the Appellate Body found that Australia's import prohibition on fresh, chilled and frozen salmon to prevent fish-bone diseases from spreading into Australia's environment and

[341] Knox (2004, *supra* note 222, at 43).

[342] Art. 16 (1) provides: "[W]here a procedural question arises ... a division may adopt an appropriate procedure ... provided that it is not inconsistent with the DSU ... ."

[343] For more detailed information, see Additional Procedure Adopted Under Rule 16 (1) of the Working Procedures for Appellate Review. Nov. 8, 2000. WT/DS135/9.

[344] US-Shrimp AB Report, *supra* note 234, paras. 50–52.

[345] Against this unusual action by the Appellate Body, the General Council instructed the Appellate Body to act "with extreme prudence" regarding the acceptance of briefs from non-governmental organizations, *See* WTO Members Warn Appellate Body on Amicus Procedures, Inside U.S. Trade, Dec. 1, 2000 (electronic edition) 1, *cited by* Bhala and Gantz (2002, *supra* note 316, at 510), while the Appellate Body's denial of leave to all 11 NGOs that complied with its procedural requirements sparked a wave of protest by NGOs (Yavitz 2001–2002, *supra* note 354, at 56–57).

[346] Yavitz (2001–2002, *supra* note 354, at 56 (footnotes omitted)).

[347] Bhala and Gantz (2002, *supra* note 316).

[348] EC-Asbestos AB Report, *supra* note 267, para. 188.

[349] Bhala and Gantz (2002, *supra* note 316, at 515).

[350] EC-Hormones AB Report, *supra* note 317, para. 253

affecting its fishing industry violated the SPS Agreement, because it was not based on a proper risk assessment, constituted a disguised restriction on trade, and was more trade restrictive than necessary[351]; In Japan- Agricultural Products,[352] the Appellate Body concluded that the Japanese measure violated the SPS Agreement because it was not based on an adequate risk assessment, was maintained without sufficient scientific evidence, and because the regulations did not comply with the SPS Agreement's transparency requirements[353];

In Japan-Importation of Apples,[354] the Appellate Body found that Japan's phytosanitary measure at issue was maintained "without sufficient scientific evidence" and that was not imposed in respect of a situation "where relevant scientific evidence is insufficient."[355]

Regarding the "science requirement"[356] that the sanitary and phytosanitary measure should be based on scientific principle,[357] the Appellate Body in Japan-Agricultural Products interpreted that the provision required that there should be a rational or objective relationship between the SPS measure and the scientific evidence.[358] The Panel and Appellate Body concluded that Article 2.2 was being violated because Japan could not show that the quarantine and fumigation used for one variety of fruit or nut would be inadequate for other varieties.[359]

[351] Australia-Salmon AB Report, *supra* note 549, para. 279.

[352] The dispute was about the Japanese regulation that required exporters of fruits and nuts to submit to an extensive testing process on each new variety of fruit or nut intended to be shipped to Japan. Japan-Agricultural Products AB Report, *supra* note 319, para. 2

[353] *Id.* para. 143

[354] The dispute was concerning whether Japanese phytosanitary measures on imported U.S. apples are inconsistent with its obligation under the SPS Agreement, GATT 1994, and the Agreement on Agriculture. Appellate Body Report. Nov. 26, 2003. Japan-Measures Affecting the Importation of Apples, paras. 1–4. WT/DS245/AB/R. (Japan-Importation of Apples AB Report).

[355] *Id.* para. 243.

[356] For purposes of analysis, the provisions of the SPS Agreement can be broken down into nine key disciplines (Charnovitz 2000, *supra* note 283, at 278–290): (i) "science requirement" (SPS Agreement art. 2.2); (ii) "requirement for a risk assessment" (SPS Agreement art. 5.1); (iii) "requirement for national regulatory consistency" (SPS Agreement art. 5.5); (iv) "the least trade restrictiveness requirement" (SPS Agreement art. 5.6); (v) "discipline to forbid arbitrary or unjustifiable discrimination" (SPS Agreement art. 2.3); (vi) "requirement to use international standards" (SPS Agreement art. 3.1); (vii) "discipline involving the recognition of equivalence" (SPS Agreement art. 4.1); (viii) "discipline regarding approval and inspection procedures" (SPS Agreement art. 8); (ix) "precautionary principle in relation with provisional measures" (SPS Agreement art. 5.7). SPS Agreement, *supra* note 282.

[357] SPS Agreement, *supra* note 282. Art. 2.2.

[358] Japan-Agricultural Products AB Report, *supra* note 563, para. 24

[359] *Id.* para. 84; Panel Report. Oct. 27, 1998. Japan-Measures Affecting Agricultural Products, paras. 8, 26–27. WT/DS76/R. (Japan-Agricultural Products Panel Report).

Regarding the requirement for a "risk assessment,"[360] the requirement that the sanitary and phytosanitary measures should be based on[361] the risk assessment[362] has proven to be of central importance in enforcing the SPS Agreement, which has often been litigated in SPS-related WTO disputes[363] and consequently "resulting in a small body of case law."[364] The Appellate Body found that a risk assessment must find evidence of an ascertainable risk,[365] stating it will not be sufficient for governments to impose regulations simply on the basis of the theoretical risk that underlines all scientific uncertainty.[366]

In Australia-Salmon, the Appellate Body agreed that lending too much weight to "unknown and uncertain elements" in risk assessment is not proper under the SPS Agreement,[367] even though there is not any criterion on the magnitude of risk to maintain acceptable risk assessment.[368]

Regarding "the least trade restrictiveness requirement" that "sanitary and phytosanitary measures should not be more trade-restrictive than required to achieve their appropriate level of protection,"[369] the Appellate Body interpreted Article 5.6: "i) government are obligated to determine and reveal their chosen level of protection to the WTO panels so that SPS rules can be applied[370]; ii) in analyzing an alternative measure, panels will consider whether it matches the intended level of protection, not the actual level of protection achieved by the SPS measure that is

---

[360] For the definition of the term "risk assessment," *see* SPS Agreement, *supra* note 282. Annex A.4.

[361] The Appellate Body in EC-Hormones interpreting "based on" as a "substantive requirement" (EC-Hormones AB Report, *supra* note 317, para. 193), stated that the risk assessment had to "sufficiently warrant," "sufficiently support," "reasonably warrant," "reasonably support," or "rationally support" using the health measure, and that these must be an "objective relationship" or a "rational relationship" between the risk and the measure (Charnovitz 2000, *supra* note 283, at 281–282).

[362] SPS Agreement, *supra* note 282. Art. 5.1.

[363] EC-Hormones AB Report, *supra* note 317, paras. 178–209; Australia-Salmon AB Report, *supra* note 549, paras. 112–138; Japan-Agricultural Products AB Report, *supra* note 563, paras. 109–114.

[364] Charnovitz (2000, *supra* note 283, at 279)

[365] EC-Hormones AB Report, *supra* note 317, para. 187; Australia-Salmon AB Report, *supra* note 549, para. 125, *cited by* Charnovitz (2000, *supra* note 283, at 280).

[366] EC-Hormones AB Report, *supra* note 317, para. 186, *cited by* Charnovitz (2000, *supra* note 283, at 280).

[367] Australia-Salmon AB Report, *supra* note 549, para. 129.

[368] *Id.* para. 124; EC-Hormones AB Report, *supra* note 317, para. 186.

[369] SPS Agreement, *supra* note 282. Art. 5.6.

[370] Australia-Salmon AB Report, *supra* note 549, para. 206, *cited by* Charnovitz (2000, *supra* note 283, at 285).

the target of the WTO lawsuit[371]; iii) the complaining country must show that the alternative measure exists."[372]

With relation to the requirement to use international standards, by conforming to the international standard, a government's measure would be presumed to be complied with SPS rules, which would be rebuttable, however.[373] If a government chooses to pursue a level of health protection higher than the international standard, then it must meet all other requirements imposed by the SPS Agreement.[374]

Regarding "provisional measures," Article 5.7 of the SPS Agreement[375] states that, where relevant scientific evidence is insufficient, a government may "provisionally adopt sanitary or phytosanitary measures on the basis of available pertinent information,"[376] which provides a good window for introducing the so-called "precautionary principle."[377] The Japan-Agricultural Products was the first case to deal with the Article 5.7,[378] where Japan argued that "varietal testing could be considered a provisional measure,"[379] against which the Appellate Body stated that Japan had not obtained information for an objective assessment as to whether fruit varieties manifest dissimilar quarantine effects.[380]

In EC-Hormones, the EC chose to invoke 5.1 instead of 5.7, by calling attention to the "precautionary principle,"[381] which characterized as a "rule of customary international law,"[382] against which the panel[383] and the Appellate Body[384] stated and confirmed that even if it was part of customary international law, the

---

[371] Japan-Agricultural products AB Report, *supra* note 319, paras. 197–200, *cited by* Charnovitz (2000, *supra* note 283, at 285).

[372] Japan-Agricultural products AB Report, *supra* note 319, paras. 126, 130, *cited by* Charnovitz (2000, *supra* note 283, at 285).

[373] Charnovitz (2000, *supra* note 283, at 286).

[374] SPS Agreement, *supra* note 282. Art. 3.3.

[375] For the comment on the Art. 5.7 as insufficient provisions, see Charnovitz (2000, *supra* note 283, at 292) ("[P]recautionary principle should be written into the Article . . . word 'provisionally' is . . . objected to . . . some business groups and developing country . . . view Art. 5.7 as a potential loophole that allows trade restrictions lacking a scientific basis") (footnotes omitted).

[376] SPS Agreement, *supra* note 282. Art. 5.7.

[377] Charnovitz (2000, *supra* note 283, at 288).

[378] *Id.*

[379] Japan-Agricultural Products Panel Report, *supra* note 568, paras. 4.187–4.188.

[380] Japan-Agricultural Products Panel Report, *id.*, paras. 4.48–4.60; Japan-Agricultural Products AB Report, *supra* note 319, paras. 92–94, *cited by* Charnovitz (2000, *supra* note 283, at 289).

[381] The Rio Declaration of 1992 was evaluated to make the most well-known formulation of the "precautionary approach": "Where there are threats of serious or irreversible damage, lack of full scientific certainty shall not be used as a reason for postponing cost-effective measures to prevent environmental degradations" (Charnovitz 2000, *supra* note 283, at 293).

[382] Charnovitz (2000, *supra* note 283, at 289).

[383] EC-Hormones (US) Panel Report, *supra* note 303, para. 8.157.

[384] EC-Hormones AB Report, *supra* note 317, paras. 123–125.

precautionary principle would not override Article 5.1, particularly since the precautionary principle had been incorporated into Article 5.7.[385]

The SPS Agreement, as well as TBT Agreement, coming closer to the intention of environmental protection than other WTO agreements, could be more actively used for environmental protection and might allow national environmental measures[386] that GATT/WTO Dispute Settlement Body previously would have rejected, because Member countries could introduce or maintain trade-restrictive environmental measures as their positive rights, not as mere passive exceptions like in GATT, even though the measures are not in compliance with other WTO agreements. As for now, in EC-Hormones,[387] EC-Asbestos,[388] and Japan-Agricultural Products,[389] Appellate Body recognized the WTO Members' positive right to determine their own level of health protection.

13.1.4 The WTO's Shift to More Environmentally Friendly Approaches

A careful look at the disputes under the WTO provisions shows that the WTO has substantially been developing interpretative principles for accommodating both trade and environmental concerns: A series of rulings by the WTO Dispute Settlement Body has established the "principle that trade rules do not stand in the way of legitimate environmental regulation."[390]

The Appellate Body in US-Gasoline, the first case under the WTO mechanism, ruled that US restrictions on importing gasoline from Member countries cannot be justified.[391] Even though environmentalists have charged that the WTO infringed the US right to protect the environment, the Appellate Body concluded that the US regulations for the conservation of exhaustible natural resources were themselves legitimate[392] under Article XX of GATT.[393] The Appellate Body merely did not acknowledge the US procedural provisions which were against the principle of

[385] For some additional observations about the precautionary principle offered by the Appellate Body, see Charnovitz (2000, *supra* note 283, at 289–290).

[386] For the conflicts between domestic environmental laws and TBT/SPS Agreement, see Knox (2004, *supra* note 222, at 19–24).

[387] EC-Hormones AB Report, *supra* note 317, para. 177.

[388] EC-Asbestos AB Report, *supra* note 267, para. 168.

[389] Japan-Agricultural Products AB Reports, *supra* note 319, para. 95–101.

[390] About fixing this kind of principles in the WTO system, environmentalists say that "although we lost in combats, we won the war" (Weinstein and Charnovitz 2001, pp. 147, 151).

[391] US-Gasoline AB Report, *supra* note 399, at 26–27.

[392] For the favorable comment on this decision to affirm the U.S. right to protect the environment as a significant finding by the USTR, *see* Dispute Settlements in the WTO: Hearing before the Subcommand. 2000. Int'l trade on the S. Common Fin., 106th Cong. 6. (Testimony of Ambassador Charlene Barshefsky, U.S. Trade Reprehensive).

[393] US-Gasoline Panel Report, *supra* note 263, para. 5.1.

national treatment by requiring stricter standards for foreign refiners than domestic ones.[394] The Appellate Body did not single-handedly damage the US right to protect environment.

The next case was US-Shrimp, in which the WTO panel[395] and Appellate Body concluded that the US measure based on the harvest devices not designed to protect endangered sea turtles was not justified under the WTO provisions.[396] The Appellate Body turned its serious attention to the ordinary meaning of the language in GATT Article XX[397] and concluded that the US regulation itself serves an environmental objective that is recognized as legitimate,[398] however, like in the US-Gasoline case, its enforcement constituted a means of arbitrary or unjustifiable discrimination between countries.[399]

The conclusion of the US-Shrimp case revealed that import banning against a certain country is permissible even when it is for protecting exhaustible natural resources out of its territories. Accordingly, in both US-Gasoline and US-Shrimp, the Appellate Body upheld the validity of the measures in question,[400] while striking down the manner in which the measures were implemented.[401] Furthermore, both Appellate Bodies reiterated that Members have a right to take measures to protect the environment.[402]

---

[394] The Appellate Body's following conclusions are particularly of symbolic significance from the viewpoints of the environmental protection under the WTO: "WTO Members have a large measure of autonomy to determine their own policies on the environment, their environmental objectives and the environmental legislation they enact and implement. So far as concerns the WTO, that autonomy is circumscribed only by the need to respect the requirements of the General Agreement and the other covered agreements." US-Gasoline AB Report, *supra* note 399, at 19, *cited by* Rietvelt (2005, *supra* note 228, at 483).

[395] US-Shrimp Panel Report, *supra* note 229, para. 7.62.

[396] US-Shrimp AB Report, *supra* note 234, para. 187.

[397] The Appellate Body, particularly, criticized the panel for failing to examine the ordinary meaning of the words of Art. XX. US-Shrimp AB Report, *supra* note 234, para. 115.

[398] This decision made compliance with the ruling relatively easier for the United States: "The United States did not have to repeal or amend the law. Rather ... the United States could channel its resources into resolving the dispute in a way consistent with the goals of the statute and the WTO decision ... the Department of State revised its guidelines for implementing section 609 to increase the transparency and predictability of decision making .... In addition ... attempted to launch multilateral negotiation on a sea turtle conservation ...." (Reif and Eckert 2004, *supra* note 257, at 684).

[399] US-Shrimp AB Report, *supra* note 234, para. 186.

[400] For the criticism against this view in relation with US-Shrimp, however, *see* Rietvelt (2005, *supra* note 228, at 489). ("Yet the mere possibility that unilateral trade measures may be allowed in the future has the international trade community up in arms. However, it is important to note most analyses of the Shrimp/Turtle decision come from journals and publications not-so-coincidentally entitled with such names as 'Journal of Environmental Law' and 'Environmental Law Reporter'").

[401] Calderin (2002, *supra* note 212, at 55).

[402] *Id.*

This attitude of the WTO toward the environment protection is considered to "have moved away from the mercantilist ethos," which has dominated the GATT era, offering a broader interpretation of the goals of the WTO, and have reconstructed "the normative hierarchy of the WTO by creating parity between the environmental exceptions included in Article XX and the substantive obligations of GATT" (e.g., Articles I and III).[403]

This is considered so even though the Appellate Body has been criticized to "ignore the principle of sustainable development[404] focusing on the perceived incorrect interpretation and application of GATT Article XX and its exceptions,"[405] or to "give little ground for hope that the WTO will tolerate any real-world unilateral use of trade leverage in furtherance of environmental protection objectives reaching beyond national boundaries."[406] As such, the US-Shrimp Appellate Body report would be evaluated to "lead the WTO dispute settlement bodies to keep an open mind towards all kinds of global problems, and not view the problems from the trade perspective."[407]

The fact that the Appellate Body objected only to the procedural aspect in the US-Gasoline and the US-Shrimp cases and found that the Article XX (g) exception was flexibly applicable provides an increased opportunity for future panels and the Appellate Body to use the "discretion embedded in the Article XX (g) exception" to advance the shaping functions reflected in that provision.[408]

There was an epochal conclusion in the EC-Asbestos case, where the WTO Appellate Body supported the French measure that prohibits the importing of goods containing ingredients harmful to human health from Canada. Although the Appellate Body in EC-Asbestos has not directly addressed the problem inherent to the US-Tuna holding that products cannot be differentiated solely on the basis of their PPM,[409] it has rejected an attempt by a WTO panel to narrow the scope of likeness

---

403 Perez (2005, pp. 735, 755).

404 For an example of critical comments on the decision relating to this principle from the viewpoint of environmentalism, see Rietvelt (2005, *supra* note 228, at 473–499). (Stating that in the Appellate Body's US-Shrimp decision the application of sustainable development as a legal concept was conveniently ignored and such oversights have evidenced the need for a more neutral forum and arbiter of international trade-environment issues).

405 Rietvelt (2005, *supra* note 228, at 497), indicated: "The guidelines for interpreting treaties are given in the Vienna Convention on the Law of Treaties Art. 31(1) stipulates that '[a] treaty shall be interpreted in good faith in accordance with the ordinary meaning to be given to the terms of the treaty in their context and in the light of its object and purpose.' The Convention later specifies the need that the treaty be interpreted as a whole, 'including its preamble and annexes.' Therefore, in seeking to understand and apply the meaning of a GATT provision, for example, it may not be enough to look only to the text of the particular provision." (footnotes omitted).

406 Gaines (2001, *supra* note 272, at 743–744), *cited by* Chang (2005, *supra* note 450, at 34).

407 Bree (1998, *supra* note 236, at 129).

408 Reif and Eckert (2004, *supra* note 257, at 686).

409 US-Tuna (Mexico), *supra* note 267, para. 3.16.

far more drastically than the US-Tuna panels,[410] and moreover, it has completely revitalized Article XX.[411]

Such an attitude of the Appellate Body is in harmony with the moderate environmentalists to have proposed broadening the scope of likeness and revitalizing the environmental exceptions in Article XX,[412] and is different from the panel's decisions in the two US-Tuna cases. The GATT panels in US-Tuna cases determined that US restrictions on imports of canned tuna from nations that did not enforce dolphin-safe fishing methods could not be justified under GATT on environmental grounds because it was against the principle of non-discrimination.[413] These cases are regarded to be representatives of the apparent "penchant of GATT panel to interpret GATT in a manner to discourage the use of unilateral environmental measures" even to accomplish multilateral goals.[414]

As such, the Appellate Body took an opportunity to further calm the environmental community by confirming the applicability of the human health exception,[415] which succeeded from the Appellate Body's decision in US-Shrimp to hold that the US regulation was a measure "relating to" the conservation of an exhaustible natural resource within the meaning of Article XX (g) exception.[416]

It was also the notable case in which the WTO took steps to rule on the SPS and TBT Agreements,[417] as well as considering the definition of the term "like product," and treated with the "concept of precaution"[418] under the WTO rules.[419] In relation to the SPS[420] and TBT Agreements, the Appellate Body concluded, on the basis of the Body's reasoning with the minimum standards of the SPS Agreement in EC-Hormones,[421] that the TBT Agreement requires its parties to use relevant international standards "as a basis for" these domestic TBT measures except

[410] *Id.* para. 3.50.

[411] Knox (2004, *supra* note 222, at 30).

[412] *Id.*

[413] Meier (1997, *supra* note 244, at 241).

[414] Hudnall (1996, *supra* note 239, at 202).

[415] Bhala and Gantz (2002, *supra* note 316, at 517).

[416] US-Shrimp AB Report, *supra* note 234, para. 141 (stating that this step to rule on the TBT Agreement should provide sufficient impetus for Member States to pay closer attention to this agreement).

[417] Shaw and Schwartz (2002, *supra* note 230, art. 151).

[418] For the definition of precaution, see Shaw and Schwartz (2002, *supra* note 230, at 140) ("Defined as taking precautionary measures when there is insufficient scientific proof, yet ... could lead to irreversible damage or risk ...."); and for the concept of precaution, in particular, incorporated in the SPS Agreement and TBT Agreement, see Shaw and Schwartz (2002, *id.*, at 142).

[419] Shaw and Schwartz (2002, *supra* note 230, at 150–151).

[420] For the cases on SPS Agreement, *see* Japan-Importation of Apples AB Report, *supra* note 563; EC-Asbestos AB Report, *supra* note 267; Japan-Agricultural Products AB Report, *supra* note 319; EC-Hormones AB Report, *supra* note 317; Australia-Salmon AB Report, *supra* note 549.

[421] EC-Hormones AB Report, *supra* note 317, para. 177.

when the international standards "would be ineffective or inappropriate means for the fulfillment of the legitimate objectives pursued."[422]

With regard to the requirement that SPS or TBT measures must not be any more trade restrictive than necessary to fulfill a legitimate objective[423] (in the TBT Agreement), or not more trade restrictive than required to achieve the appropriate level of sanitary or phytosanitary protection[424] (in the SPS Agreement), in the case of Australia-Salmon,[425] the Appellate Body said that a measure will fail this requirement in the SPS Agreement only if there is a reasonably available alternative that is "significantly less trade restrictive" and that "achieves the Member's appropriate level of sanitary or phytosanitary protection,"[426] which is obviously similar to the Panel decision's interpretation of GATT Article XX(b) in the EC-Asbestos.[427]

The Appellate Body so far has adopted the interpretations of the SPS and TBT Agreements that mirror several moderate proposals made by environmental critics: that "every party has the right to adopt a standard with a higher level of protection than the international standard"; that "SPS measures with higher levels of protection need not be in accord with the 'majority' scientific view"; and that "a substantial burden of proof is on the party challenging the SPS and TBT measure even if the measure exceeds the international standard."[428]

Even though there has been criticism of the WTO from the environmental viewpoint, the organization has tried to respect Members' environmental policies and measures to protect their environments provided that the measures are legitimate and justifiable under the WTO provisions. In opposition to the other WTO organization's record of ineffective dealings concerning trade and environmental conflicts, the Appellate Body has consistently tried to confirm its position as the environmentalist of the WTO.

13.1.5 Effective Nexus Between Trade and Environment

The seeming conflict between the promotion of free trade and the protection of the environment should be harmonized in order to cope with environmental issues

[422] TBT Agreement, *supra* note 281. Art. 2.4.

[423] TBT Agreement, *supra* note 281. Art. 2.2.

[424] SPS Agreement, *supra* note 282. Art. 5.6.

[425] Australia-Salmon AB Report, *supra* note 549, para. 194.

[426] *Id.* (citing SPS Agreement, *supra* note 282. Art. 5.6), *cited by* Knox (2004, *supra* note 222, at 44 n. 180).

[427] EC-Asbestos Panel Report, *supra* note 314, para 8.177, *cited by* Knox (2004, *supra* note 222, at 44 n. 180).

[428] Knox (2004, *supra* note 222, at 45).

effectively.[429] Giving priority to free trade and restricting trade measures related to environment excessively will accelerate the exhaustion of resources and damage on environment. On the other hand, if environmental protection were placed ahead of free trade and excessive import restrictions were accepted, the result would impose such a high level of international standards on developing countries that it would detract those countries' economic development efforts. The concept of international trade is not complete without taking into consideration its environmental issues[430] and the long-term positive effects of sustainable development on the international trade and human beings' welfare level in the end.

For harmonizing these two issues, policies should be sought, which promote the free trade that eliminates trade barriers and, simultaneously protect the environment and human, animal and plant life needed to achieve sustainable development. Reviewing disputes relating to these two seemingly conflicting issues, simultaneous harmonization between free trade and protecting the environment could substantially be carried out by a proper interpretation of the Article XX of GATT 1994. Considering the fact that the WTO Dispute Settlement Body [hereinafter DSB] has interpreted the trade-related environmental measures more positively and actively, and acknowledged the legitimacy of substantial regulation for environmental protection consistently, particularly when compared to the panels under the GATT system, the WTO seems well-positioned to interlace those two issues smoothly.

In spite of such endeavors and performances made through the DSB at the WTO, however, free trade supporters including developing nations and

[429] The proposed effective methods of nexus between trade and environment, suggesting to choose understandings or guidelines of relationships between the WTO and MEAs or approaches to modify the regulations of the WTO, as in general exceptions of Art. XX, up to now are: "i) the 'status quo' approach seeks to address the WTO-MEA relationship in various ways while not amending the GATT/WTO. This approach is based on the premise that the WTO already has sufficient scope to accommodate the use of trade-related measures pursuant to MEAs; that only a small number of MEAs contain trade measures; and that thus far there has not been any dispute about trade measures under MEA. (Submitted by India, Hong Kong, and Egypt in 1996); ii) the 'waiver' approach is that WTO Members collectively decide to authorize Members to derogate from their delegation for a limited period of time. (Submitted by Hong Kong in 1996) This approach is very accessible to the Members because waivers do not need to be ratified by each WTO Member; iii) the 'clarification of WTO rules' approach is to adopt an Understanding or Guidelines on the WTO-MEA relationship or to amend WTO rules, specifically the general exceptions in Art. XX. (Submitted by European Communities, Switzerland, and Japan); iv) the 'approach to clarifying the WTO-MEA relationship along the lines of cooperation' is to clarify the relationship through an interpretative decision based on the general approach of mutual supportiveness and deference without amendments of WTO rules. (Submitted by Switzerland)" (Shaw and Schwarz 2002, *supra* note 230, at 134–137). Besides, the United States has long been a strong advocate of WTO action on harmful fisheries subsidies to address the harmonization between the trade and the environment and sustainable development. For the details, see Mattice (2004, pp. 573, 573–585).

[430] Calderin (2002, *supra* note 212, at 36).

environmentalists[431] do not seem satisfied with the efforts of the WTO. Environmentalists indicate the following reasons for criticizing the WTO: (i) it is not easy to pass the two-tier test[432] to apply the exceptions of Article XX of GATT, and (ii) GATT's Article XX does not specify expressively exceptional measures for environmental protection.

Developing nations, on the contrary, are already worrying about potential abuse of trade measures based on environmental protection, even though, the WTO just recently began to manage to affirm the legitimacy of environmental trade measures through the judicial interpretation of the provisions concerned.

13.1.5.1 Modification and Creation of the WTO Provisions

In order to address more specifically the criticism from both free trade supporters and environmentalists on how to harmonize trade and environmental measures, the listed exceptions of the Article XX of GATT would be better served by implementing independent measures for protecting the environment.[433] After that, the new environmental agreement can be separated from the WTO or attached to the WTO Agreements as an annex,[434] which will provide a way to accept trade measures under the WTO that is lawfully legitimated under the independent or annexed stand-alone approved environmental agreement.[435]

---

[431] For the north–south challenge in linking trade and environmental standards, see Thomas (2002, *supra* note 255, at 818–819). ("While economic consequences are at the nub of developing-country government opposition, they alone do not explain it. The special bitterness often present in such objections derives from a widely held belief that the attempt to include ... environment standards is no more than rank protectionism thinly disguised ....").

[432] For example, the Appellate Body's test for discrimination under the chapeau of Art. XX has been criticized by one former USTR official who calls the provision "a proverbial 'eye of the needle' through which hardly any national environmental measure will be able to pass" (Gaines 2001, *supra* note 272, 773, *cited by* Reif and Eckert 2004, *supra* note 257, at 693).

[433] There is an opinion that Art. 20(k) can be created to regulate environmental measures independently, which can lead the measure to be used with flexibility. *See* Nissen (1997, pp. 901, 925–928).

[434] The official position of the WTO is that environmental issues fall outside of its jurisdiction as a body concerned with trade. For example, the WTO stated that other agencies specialized in environmental issues are better qualified to undertake those issues, because the WTO is only competent to deal with trade. World Trade Organization, trading into the future 46 (2nd ed. Mar. 2001). http://www.wto.org/english/res_e/doload_e/tif.pdf, Accessed Feb. 24, 2012, *cited by* Thomas (2002, *supra* note 255, at 792).

[435] For policies called 'Making clean the provisions of the WTO' related to efficient linkage trade with environment, *see* Nissen (1997, *supra* note 642, at 911–928); WTO CTE. Oct. 19, 2000. Resolving the Relationship between WTO Rules and Multilateral Environmental Agreement, submission by the European Community. WTO Doc. WT/CTE/W/170; WTO CTE. Oct. 19, 2000. Clarification of the Relationship between the WTO and Multilateral Environmental Agreements, submission by Switzerland, WTO Doc. WT/CTE/W/168; WTO CTE. June 12, 1996. Submission by Korea on Item 1, WTO CTE. May 30, 1996. The Relationship between Trade Measures Pursuant to MEAs and the WTO Agreement, Proposal by Japan. WTO Doc. WT/CTE/W/31; and WTO CTE. Feb. 19, 1996. Submission by the European Community on Item 1.

The deliberated agreement on these basic requirements includes all MEAs confirmed by member's mutual consent, and could suggest clarified standards about the trade-related environmental measures and policies to the Members. Thus, it is the ideal approach for the proper environmental protection under the WTO mechanism to conclude the independent and self-sufficient environmental agreement, whether it is placed within WTO or out of it. However, considering the intense conflicts of interest and disputes between Member countries, it will be difficult to make it sooner rather than later[436]:

In the first place, when trade-related environmental measures are independently listed into Article XX as exceptions, there may be contradictory concerns about uncertainty and abuse surrounding the enforcement of the measures. Developed countries that advocate the trade-related environmental measures would consider it a repeat mistake of the current GATT/WTO system to link trade measures with environmental problems. In other words, Members complain it is very hard to overcome difficulties such as setting up the standards for complying with the "necessary" conditions or "chapeau" requirements in applying Article XX's exceptions. On the other hand, from the viewpoint of developing countries with negative attitudes against trade-related environmental measures, under the multilateral free trade system, it could provide a discretionary chance that the respective trade restrictions of Member countries possibly constitute a non-tariff barrier.

With relation to making the independent or annexed environmental agreement, the complications and difficulties to induce agreements among the Member countries have been evidenced through the legislative history of the Uruguay Rounds and ministerial conferences under the WTO. Considering the critical gap in viewpoints between the free traders and the environmentalists, it will take substantial time to build a consensus about the agreement.

As an alternative, the following supplementary suggestions shall reflect reality and facility. To reduce the concerns about uncertainty and abuse argued respectively by each side simultaneously, it is suggested that the exceptions of Article XX (b) should add trade-related measures for environmental protection and the Agreement on Trade-Related Environmental Measures should be newly established,

[436] Regarding the provision alteration, Professor Jackson has skeptical about the methods (Jackson 1992, *supra* note 239, 1227). On the contrary, it was emphasized that it is the best way to amend the provisions of the WTO (Nissen 1997, *supra* note 642).

through which environment-related measures could be smoothly inserted into the multilateral trade mechanism at the WTO.[437]

In this way, as environmental measures are not included in additional provisions of Article XX independently [i.e. like (k)], but included in clause (b) in parallel with other existing measures, as differently from the advanced countries' concerns, satisfying the requirements would be easier than GATT/WTO have ever experienced, and, by including environmental measures expressively into exceptions, a satisfying requirement could be more easily developed.

As for now, without environmental measures being listed separately as exceptions, since the environmental measure has to meet narrowly and limitedly the conditions of (b) or (g), the WTO DSB cannot help being strict in enforcing the requirements concerning this measure. Under such a mechanism, it would be more difficult to cope with the newly-emerging delicate environmental issues, not to speak of the currently contradictory matters.

In the case that environmental measures are listed in Article XX independently [i.e. (k)], the requirements of those measures to be legitimate should be newly interpreted through dispute settlement procedures.[438] This case contrasts with the case of inclusion of environmental measures in clause (b) where the degree and contents of "necessary" condition and "chapeau" requirements required under Article XX are interpreted according to those that have already been established through the judicial interpretations under the WTO. Particularly, considering the signal of the WTO to regard human health as superior to the exhaustible natural resources which can be read in the EC-Asbestos,[439] adding up the environmental measures in Article XX (b) would seemingly make it easier for the DSB to accept those measures than in Article XX (g).

When an environmental trade measure is provisioned in Article XX (b) parallel with other measures, developing countries concerned about abuse will be relieved: While adding this measure as an independent term [i.e. (k)] to Article XX would

---

[437] Similarly, Chantal Thomas suggested as follows: "Art. XX (b) could be amended to read 'necessary to protect human, animal or plant life or health in accordance with principles recognized in the multilateral environmental agreements listed in the annex hereto' and GATT Art. XX (g) could be amended to read 'relating to the conservation of exhaustible natural resources in accordance with principles recognized in the multilateral environmental agreements listed in the annex hereto []' ...." (*See* Thomas 2002, *supra* note 255, at 813). However, this approach is different from the approach suggested in this paper from the fact that the annex would then choose and list any multilateral environmental agreements established out of WTO mechanism that WTO Members felt that had attained a sufficient level of legitimacy to warrant their specific recognition.

[438] US-Gasoline AB Report, *supra* note 399, at 17. (Stating "applying the basic principle of interpretation ... are to be given their ordinary meaning ... the Panel Report failed to take adequate account of the words actually used by Art. XX in its several paragraphs ... 'necessary' in paragraphs (a), (b) and (d); 'essential' in paragraph (j); 'relating to' in paragraph (c), (e) and (g); 'for the protection of' in paragraph (f); 'in pursuance of' in paragraph (h); and 'involving' in paragraph (i)"). This reasoning has been adapted by US-Shrimp. *See* US-Shrimp AB Report, *supra* note 234, at 120.

[439] EC-Asbestos AB Report, *supra* note 267, para. 172.

mean that the legitimacy of environmental measures be interpreted more widely, including it in (b) implies securing the same level of legitimacy of environmental measures to the level for protecting humans, animals or plants health and life which already has been accepted without much controversy under the past GATT system.[440]

Additionally, including the environmental measures expressly in clause (b) parallel with other existing measures would reduce or eliminate the contentious debate having surrounded whether or not the principle of sustainable development has risen to the level of customary international law in interpretation of the environmental measures under the WTO provisions.[441]

Regarding the Agreement on Trade-Related Environmental Measures, to prevent conflicts with both parties' interests in accepting the independent environmental measures into WTO, the measures complying with measures' standards provisioned in the Agreement should be confirmed with their legitimacy under the WTO provisions.[442] Such standards will enable DSB of the WTO to solve the difficulty in deciding criteria when DSB judges the legitimacy of measures relating to MEAs. Consideration should properly be paid in establishing basic criteria: The basic criteria should not be hard for Members to satisfy, and the criteria chosen and adopted by the Agreement should not be taken advantage of by Member countries as disguised restrictions under the system, particularly, due to ambiguous provisions of the WTO.

Throughout the legislative history of GATT/WTO agreements, there have often been the "creative ambiguities" as the legacy of compromises and the result of negotiated outcomes[443] with regard to the complex issues. In the case of these ambiguities, however, the dispute settlement mechanism has to be utilized again to

---

[440] Thailand-Cigarettes, *supra* note 261, paras. 63, 75–77, 81; Bhala and Gantz (2002, *supra* note 316, at 515).

[441] For the debate on this point raised in relation with the US-Shrimp decision, see Rietvelt (2005, *supra* note 228, at 496–498).

[442] For the suggestions that the GATT be amended to extend the exemptions of Art. XX to include trade provisions of MEAs, *see* WTO CTE. June 25, 1999. Communication from the Secretariat for the Vienna Convention and the Montreal Protocol, UNCEP, WTO Doc. WT/CTE/W/115; WTO CTE. Feb. 19, 1996. Submission by the European Community on Item 1. For the similar exemptions that can be provided through Art. XXV waiver clause on a case by case basis, see WTO CTE. June 25, 1999. Communication from the Secretariat for the Vienna Convention and the Montreal Protocol, UNEP, WTO Doc. WT/CTE/W/115.

[443] Shaw and Schwartz (2002, *supra* note 230, at 151).

clarify or modify the WTO rights or obligations, which will weaken the legal certainty or predictability under the WTO system.[444]

With respect to the plausible contents of the agreement, which might be a core of this suggestion, it would be acceptable if the levels of trade measures and main contents of the agreement are as same as those of the TBT Agreement and the SPS Agreement.[445] It is meaningful that the level of trade measures and main contents of the agreement would be decided in congruence with those under the TBT and SPS Agreements considering the harmonized approach of both agreements employed in dealing with linkages between free trade objectives and legitimate regulatory objectives such as human health protection:

Given that the main purpose of these two agreements is avoiding the possibility of Member countries' (including developed countries) abuse of non-tariff barriers by applying Article XX, this level of Agreement on Trade-Related Measures will convince the developing countries that this agreement would block the chance of abusing environmental measures which have allegedly occurred even under the current Article XX (b) or (g) of GATT; Given both agreements emphasize that Members have the "right" to protect human health or the environment[446] instead of dealing with those legitimate regulatory concerns as mere marginalized "exceptions," which is a distinctive feature vis-à-vis GATT,[447] a higher level of legitimate regulatory protection of the environment would be secured under the proposed mechanism.

The basic obligations imposed by this agreement require that trade-related environmental measures should be based on scientific principles[448] and satisfy

---

[444] The WTO has strengthened a dispute settlement mechanism for the legal certainty or predictability, *see* WTO Dispute Settlement Body. Dec. 11, 1996. Rules of Conduct for the Understanding on Rules and Procedures Governing the Settlement of Disputes. WTO Doc. WT/DSB/RC/1, preamble, *cited by* Tanaka (2003, pp. 113, 145), entailing "multilateral quasi-judicial proceedings," which seeks the efficient resolution of conflicts between national trade policies (*see* DSU, *supra* note 4, arts. 3.3, 12.8, *cited by* Tanaka 2003, *id.*, at 145), and articulation of rules and principles governing multilateral trade relations. *See* Carmody (1997, pp. 615, 618–619, *cited by* Tanaka 2003, *id.*, at 145–146).

[445] An amendment to the SPS Agreement was suggested by Chantal Thomas, which sets forth conditions under which WTO Members can administer health and safety regulations affecting trade flows: "[h]ave the right to take sanitary and phytosanitary measures in accordance with the preconditionary principle [or approach] ... in Art. 2(1)." *See* Thomas (2002, *supra* note 255, at 814).

[446] For instance, SPS Art. 2 provisions that Members have the right to take sanitary measures necessary for the protection of human health ("... for the protection of human, animal or plant life or health, of the environment ... ." SPS Agreement, *supra* note 282. Art. 2), while the TBT Preamble recognizes that no country should be prevented from taking measures. ("Recognizing that no country should be prevented from taking measures necessary to ... for the protection of human, animal or plant life or health ... ." TBT Agreement preamble).

[447] For more details, *see* Cho (2005, pp. 625, 660–665).

[448] SPS Agreement, *supra* note 282. Art. 5.

international standards.[449] The Agreement on Trade-Related Environmental Measures can accept the established international standards adopted by several principal environmental agreements just as the TBT[450] and SPS[451] Agreements encourage Members to follow other externally established standards, guidelines, recommendations and harmonization[452]: i.e. in case of the SPS Agreement, the following external agreements are accepted; Codex Alimentarius, Office International des Epizootics(OIE), and the International Plant Protection Convention.[453] Each Member, provided that there are appropriate reasons, can maintain even stricter environmental restrictions than international standards.[454]

When there are different levels of environmental restrictions between importing countries and exporting countries, the principle of equivalence can be adopted when the exporter's level could be substantially matched with the importer's level through the utilization of an objective environmental assessment, in order to make environmental restrictions objective.[455]

Establishing or amending domestic standards of environmental restrictions, a Member country should legitimize several facts: i.e. (i) Members should report the establishing or amending domestic standards of environmental restrictions to the newly established Environmental Commission at the WTO and other Members concerned to attain their transparency[456]; (ii) Disputes related to environmental measures should observe the procedures of Dispute Settlement Body of the WTO,[457] and the panels or the Appellate Body should systematically be able to get advisory report from Expert Review Group like in the case of SPS Agreement,[458] or TBT Agreement.[459]

---

[449] SPS Agreement, *supra* note 282. Art. 3.

[450] TBT Agreement, *supra* note 281. Art. 4.1.

[451] SPS Agreement, *supra* note 282. Art. 3.

[452] This deference to certain international standards explicitly has been suggested as one of the accommodation models between the WTO and other regimes, that is, comity, choice of forum or choice of law, preemption, and deference: "The WTO uses a deference model for some . . . (IMF) decisions . . . SPS defers to certain international standards explicitly . . . WTO language . . . 'sustainable development' implicitly defers to environmental norms. . .. AB . . . deferred to . . . (CITES) . . . DSU provisions allow WTO panels to seek the advice of experts . . . commentators have suggested that 'environmental experts could be allowed to sit on GATT Panels dealing with trade and environmental disputes'"(Kelley 2006, pp. 79, 92–102 (footnotes omitted)).

[453] SPS Agreement, *supra* note 282. Art. 3.4.

[454] SPS Agreement, *supra* note 282. Art. 3.3.

[455] SPS Agreement, *supra* note 282. Art. 4.

[456] SPS Agreement, *supra* note 282. Art. 7.

[457] SPS Agreement, *supra* note 282. Art. 11.1.

[458] SPS Agreement, *supra* note 282. Art. 11.2.

[459] TBT Agreement, *supra* note 281. Art. 14.2; Besides, there are two other agreements providing advisory report, that is, Agreement on Implementation of Art. VII of the General Agreement on Tariffs and Trade 1994 arts. 18, 19, Apr. 15, 1994, Marrakesh Agreement Establishing the World Trade Organization, Annex 1A, Legal Instruments-Results of the Uruguay Round. 1994. 33 I.L.M.

For developing countries: through advice, credits, donations and grants, technologies of environmental protection and measurement are offered[460]; to give export chances to developing countries, a reservation period shall be given to them about interested items[461]; in accordance with agreements, all or parts of obligation can be forborne for some period.[462]

With this amended provision in Article XX, legal stability and expectance can be enhanced in applying trade-related environmental measures by approving them expressly as one of the listed exceptions of GATT. Furthermore, by including trade-related environmental measures explicitly into the WTO mechanism, environmental measures can be under watch and restraint by the WTO, which will help prevent, in advance, Members' trade-related measures from being shown up as non-tariff barriers until the free-trade objective is fulfilled under the WTO.

In case of establishing agreements, of course, a scientific environmental protection policy should be developed and improved because trade measures for environmental protection are to be strictly regulated under the WTO. It is also essential that environmental policies should be established and managed with harmonization to cope with the environmental issues which are the global common challenges.

This approach would thus be more realistic than previously discussed approaches because it can reduce and accommodate the interests conflicts between developed countries listed by environmentalists and developing countries worried about the abuse of trade-related environmental measures.[463]

13.1.5.2 Redefinition of Like Product

One of the most controversial issues in interpreting products under GATT in linking trade with environmental policies is defining what a "like product." is[464] The difficulty in defining like products[465] related to environmental issues is whether

1125, (Customs Valuation Agreement) and Agreement on Subsidies and Countervailing Measures art. 24, Apr. 15, 1994, Marrakesh Agreement Establishing the World Trade Organization, Annex 1A, Legal Instruments-Results of the Uruguay Round. 1994. 33 I.L.M. 1125, (Subsidies and Countervailing Measures Agreement).

[460] TBT Agreement, *supra* note 281. Art. 12; SPS Agreement, *supra* note 282. Art. 10.

[461] SPS Agreement, *supra* note 281. Art. 10.3.

[462] SPS Agreement, *supra* note 281. Art. 10.2.

[463] This approach would also be such considering the fact: "the inclusion of affirmative environmental standards into the WTO mechanism has been negatively evaluated, particularly, among the developing countries, because it would in effect be the result of a shift in institutional strategy from a 'soft law' to a 'hard law' approach." *See* Thomas (2002, *supra* note 255, at 812).

[464] Trebilcock and Howse (1999, *supra* note 395, at 397).

[465] For the GATT/WTO disputes on the term "like products," particularly, with respect to the Art. III of the GATT, see Appellate Body Report. Oct. 4, 1996. Japan-Taxes on Alcoholic Beverages. WT/DS8/AB/R, WT/DS10/AB/R, WT/DS11/AB/R, (Art. III:2 of the GATT 1994); Appellate Body Report. July 30, 1997. Canada-Certain Measures Concerning Periodicals, WT/DS31/AB/R, (Art. III:2 and Art. III:4 of the GATT 1994); Panel Report, July 2, 1998. Indonesia-Certain Measures Affecting the Automobiles Industry, WT/DS54/R, WT/DS55/R, WT/DS59/R, WT/DS64/R, (Art. I:1 and III:2 of the GATT 1994); EC-Asbestos AB Report, *supra* note 267, (Art. III:4 of the GATT 1994).

the product that is made by methods that harm the environment and another product that damages the environment less can be treated as like products, although the final physical characteristics are same.

If each nation treats these products differently and each nation imposes differential tariffs in accordance with the level of environmental pollution or imposes tariff to internalize environmental cost caused by producing process, there will be no problems from an environmental viewpoint.[466] On the other hand, if these products are treated as like products, imposing tariffs such as differentiated tariff and environmental cost can possibly violate "the most-favored nation principle."[467]

The biggest difference in interpreting the term "like product" between the WTO and MEAs would be whether the process and production methods shall be taken into account or not in defining it. The provisions in the WTO Agreement have treated a product as a like product if it has identically physical characteristics, despite adopting different PPMs.[468] Lots of provisions in MEAs which emphasize environmental protection take approaches that focus on PPMs[469] rather than physical characteristics in defining a "like product."[470]

Trade restrictions, in particular, by adopting PPMs in interpreting "like products," can cause serious troubles in keeping pace with provisions of the WTO Agreement because trade restrictions would be imposed even though the physical characteristics are identical when the adopted PPMs are different.[471] Although has no definite provisions of "like product,"[472] common views made through the decisions of US-Tuna cases show that "like products" are decided by "physical characteristics, the characteristics of ingredients, final usage purpose, habits of customers, not by PPMs."[473] The panel thus interpreted "like product" under Article III according to the rule of the "product-process distinction"[474] and

[466] Jackson et al. (1995, pp. 44–45).

[467] Walker (1993, pp. 44–45).

[468] For the rule to interpret "like products" under Art. III, see Hudec (1998, pp. 619, 624). "The only kind of product distinction that can be recognized under Art. III is a distinction based on the qualities of the product themselves or the characteristics that govern product qualities. Product distinctions based on characteristics of the production process or of the producer that are not determinants of product characteristics are viewed as illegitimate."

[469] For the concept of PPMs in the world of the WTO/GATT from the viewpoints of the environmentalism, *see* Calderin (2002, *supra* note 212, at 61–62). ("[P]PMs are not a new concept to the world of the WTO/GATT. Art. XX, subparagraph(e) allows countries to apply measures that prohibit or restrict the importation of products of prison labor. Prison labor is a PPM . . . like in the example of tuna, the product made from prison labor is not different than the same type of product made by wage-earner . . ..") .

[470] *See*, for example, Montreal Protocol, *supra* note 237, at 1541.

[471] *Id.*

[472] Jackson (1969, p. 258).

[473] US-Tuna (Mexico), *supra* note 267, para. 7.1; US-Tuna (EEC), *supra* note 261, para. 5.8.

[474] The panel concluded that, by using the method of catching tuna as a basis for differential treatment of imports, the U.S. measures attempted to regulate the method of catching tuna rather

concluded that the United States violated its national treatment obligations under Article III because imported tuna was the same product as domestic tuna but was treated less favorably.[475]

The panel in US-Automobiles, finding the US standard[476] to be based on factors relating to the control or ownership of producers/importers to cars as products,[477] concluded that differential treatment of products under the US measure was not permitted under Article III:4.[478] The panel, employing the "aim and effects approach,"[479] found that the distinction made under the gas guzzler tax pursued the legitimate objective of concerning fossil fuels,[480] in respect to the US gas guzzler tax on designated automobiles according to their fuel efficiency.[481] The case poses an important question on how to reach on acceptable discussion under Article III when the disproportionate effect on foreign goods is inherent in the nature of the regulation.[482]

In order to balance the value of free-trade and environmental protection, the value of environmental protection, which has been evaluated rather poorly, should be advanced by defining the term of "like products" more obviously; i.e. the definition of "like products" should be shifted from the way of emphasizing physical characteristics into the way of emphasizing functional characteristics. The term of "functional characteristics" should be defined prudently, and, in particular, the function in relation with socio-economic aspects should be considered. Such a shift of the way of defining "like products" not only strengthens the relationship between trade and environment efficiently, but also is expected to help take the measure for animal or plant health and safety legally related to the TBT

than the product and were not justified under GATT. US-Tuna(Mexico), *supra* note 267, paras. 5.14–5.15; Three years later, a new GATT panel in US-Tuna (EEC) made same conclusion. *See* US-Tuna (EEC), *supra* note 261, para. 5.15.

475 US-Tuna (EEC), *supra* note 261, paras. 5.8–5.16.

476 US-Automobiles, *supra* note 328, para. 5.39.

477 *Id.* paras. 5.53–5.55.

478 *Id.* para. 5.54.

479 The US-Beverages (Report of the Panel, June 19, 1992. United States-Measures Affecting Alcoholic and Malt Beverages. GATT B.I.S.D. (39th Supp.) at 206 (US-Beverages)) was the first case to suggest the aim and effects test advocating that the issue presented by Art. III should not be the matter of distinguishing the determinants of product characteristics and the aspects of the production process, but rather deciding the policy purposes behind the product – process distinction rule. *See* Snape and Lefkovitz (1994, pp. 777, 796); Hudec (1998, *supra* note 677, at 626); Howse and Regan (2000, pp. 249, 11: 268, *cited by* Mungkalarungsi (2002, pp. 361, 375). The panel stated that the distinction in various U.S. laws between low-alcohol and high-alcohol beer was made for purposes of protecting social welfare, and that such product distinction did not create adverse conditions of competition for Canadian brewers because Canadian brewers produced both types of beer (Hudec 1998, *id.*, at 627; Petersmann 1993, pp. 43, 64, *cited by* Mungkalarungsi 2002, *id.*, at 375).

480 Mungkalarungsi (2002, *id.*, at 378).

481 US-Automobiles, *supra* note 328.

482 Hudec (1998, *supra* note 677, at 629).

Agreement and SPS Agreement which are parallel with the above proposed Agreements on Trade-Related Environmental Measures.

Such the signs of redefinition of "like products" could be found in the decision of the Appellate Body at the WTO, even though, under the current trade regulations, it is difficult to take trade restrictions on the base of PPMs that are not connected to the characteristics of product: Under the GATT mechanism, the panel of US-Tuna (Mexico) showed definite attitudes that trade measures based on PPMs could not be justified under the GATT provisions.[483] According to the panel, by using the method of catching tuna as a basis for differential treatment of imports, the US measures attempted to regulate the method of catching tuna rather than the product and were not justified under GATT.[484] Similar rationale can be seen in subsequent dispute settlement decisions under GATT.[485]

Under the WTO mechanism, however, the Appellate Body in US-Shrimp decided that trade restrictions against the products including environmentally non-sustainable production process and methods could be acceptable by defining "like products" in a narrower sense[486] than before.[487] It is also very significant to environmentalism[488] that Appellate Body took into account its process and ingredients in defining "like products"[489] in EC-Asbestos.[490] In defining "like products," using a "market-based approach," the Appellate Body examined physical properties, end users and tariff classification,[491] and reasoned that the health risk should be included in the analysis of "physical properties," as well as with respect to "consumer taste."[492] As such, under the WTO mechanism, the Appellate Body in the above two cases, differing from the decision of US-Gasoline,[493] began to take

[483] US-Tuna (Mexico), *supra* note 267, para. 3.16.

[484] *Id.* paras. 5.14–5.15.

[485] For the same conclusion on the same facts in US-Tuna (EEC) *supra* note 267, para. 5.15.

[486] US-Shrimp AB Report, *supra* note 234, para. 93.

[487] US-Tuna (Mexico), *supra* note 267, para. 3.50.

[488] Bhala and Gantz (2002, *supra* note 316, at 516), (stating "While one can argue the practical desirability of the Panel's relegation of health concerns to Art. XX (b), confining the 'like product' analysis under Art. III:4 to commercial and trade considerations, the environmental community should be buoyed by this aspect of the Appellate Body's determination.").

[489] There are two different views about the Appellate Body decision on this point: (i) "The analysis in Asbestos would allow governments to differentiate among products based on their PPMs as long as the differentiation does not result in less favorable treatment." *See* Howse and Tuerk (2001, pp. 283, 297–298); (ii) "[A]ny optimism that future WTO panels will tolerate origin-neutral PPMs in the context of Art. III would be unfounded." *See* Charnovitz (2002, pp. 59, 92).

[490] EC-Asbestos AB Report, *supra* note 267, para. 48.

[491] *Id.* para. 59.

[492] *Id.* para. 61.

[493] The panel stated that the wording of Art. III:4 does not allow less favorable treatment to depend on the characteristics of the producer and the nature of data held by them because the treatment of the imported and domestic goods concerned should be assured on the objective basis of their likeness as products and should not be exposed to a highly subjective and variable treatment according to extraneous factors. *See* US-Gasoline Panel Report, *supra* note 263, paras. 6.11–6.13.

into account environmental consideration in determining even though it is still unclear whether the Appellate Body takes into account the environmental concerns arising solely from the PPMs of a product in determining the likeness of a product.[494]

Even though the WTO does not, and should not, have the capacity to dictate adequate PPMs to its Members,[495] the WTO Members should have increased sovereignty to analyze the production methods of goods that they import, as long as the analysis and resulting measures do not constitute arbitrary and unjustifiable discrimination.[496] Thus each Member should be able to decide whether it wishes to participate in the trade of products made by the inefficient use of resources.[497] By doing so, the WTO structure would help promote sustainable development and the optimal use of the world's resources.[498] Increasing such sovereignty under the WTO is in line with the balanced approach which has been encouraged by the WTO Appellate Body since the US-Gasoline.[499]

If the Members of the WTO and MEAs have conflicts due to the ambiguous terms like "like products," these kinds of problems should be settled by DSB at the WTO, provided that the parties are the Members of the WTO.[500] Considering the potential advent of diverse environmental changes, such ambiguous terms would fairly be difficult to clarify solely through the jurisdictional interpretation by the DSB.

In order to harmonize the trade and environmental policies without friction, every endeavor should be made to stipulate the definition or range of the ambiguous terms. Redefining the conception of "like product" will contribute to connecting trade and environment together by amending of the WTO provisions as well as annexing of the environmental agreement discussed above.

13.1.6 Conclusion

Two ways to solve the disputes in relation to disharmony between trade and environmental policies can be outlined: (i) after occurrence of dispute, its main issue can be brought to the DSB and settled (ex post approach)[501]; (ii) before occurrence of disputes, potentially conflicting provisions and measures can be

---

[494] Knox (2004, *supra* note 222, at 30).

[495] Calderin (2002, *supra* note 212, at 61).

[496] *Id.*

[497] *Id.*

[498] *Id.*, at 62.

[499] US-Gasoline AB Report, *supra* note 399, at 28–29; US-Shrimp AB Report, *supra* note 234, para. 170.

[500] DSU, *supra* note 4. Art. 1 (Coverage and Application).

[501] For the three effects of the judicial resolution of legal conflicts between trade and environment, see Knox (2004, *supra* note 222, at 74–78).

solved politically through mutual agreements and consensus among the Members (ex ante approach).[502] Surrounding the two ways, even though it could be argued that the judicial effort to devise a politically acceptable resolution of trade and environment conflicts may have seemed doubtable, or even quixotic, without the political resolution, governments have consistently accepted most elements of the judicial resolution. The above analysis shows that the ex post approach should be pursued parallel to an ex ante approach for the actual harmonization of trade and environment conflicts.

Summarizing the cases dealt in the dispute settlement procedures of GATT, the justification of trade measures aiming at environmental protection had been strictly interpreted. Consequently, GATT/ WTO mechanism has been accused of being negative about environmental protection. Fortunately, however, since the launch of the WTO, trade measures for environmental protection in several cases have been justified in accordance with the judicial interpretation on the Article XX of GATT. This progressive interpretation on the provisions is meaningful considering the fact that it offered the driving force to revolutionize the nature of the dispute on trade and environment. Such an interpretation is substantially evaluated to improve the value of the sustainable development and environmental protection.

However, if the criterion of connecting trade with environment is not established and main issues are solved just by interpreting the existing provisions, it can threaten the certainty and predictability in applying law when new environmental issues such as biological diversity, GMOs, or sustainable management of resources are raised. It is essential, therefore, that the definite standard of connection of trade regulation with environmental regulation, most of all, should be established. Apparently, up to now, the strategies under the WTO system to linking the environmental issues with trade have tended to avoid friction of Members' interests and facilitate the harmonious approaches in lessons of GATT/WTO mechanism's failure to solve this problem due to Members' contradictory interests. The following are explanations for why the suggestions in this article may be the most appropriate in dealing with trade and environment issue as compared with those of the past.

Today, an important and urgent problem which faces the world is to protect the global environment, at least, at the same level as that of human, animal or plant health and life provided in exceptions of Article XX of GATT1994. There cannot be any differentiation which is more important between human beings, animals or plants health and life, and environmental protection, thus, they equally need an urgent resolution, that is, mutual equity is needed in dealing with these issues. The measures to protect animal and plant health or lives without environmental protection would be only a short-term ad hoc device.

Under the WTO mechanism, which has been equipped with judicially higher stability and predictability than under GATT for the past 12 years, there have not

[502] About this opinion, for example, Dr. Sylvia Ostry has mentioned that WTO system is unable to be altered only by lawsuits and political method should be chosen as a preferred choice. WTO Secretariat. 2000. *supra* note 214, Trade, Development and the Environment. 46.

been any fatal errors or criticisms against the WTO related to animal or plant health or life in the process of fulfilling the WTO agreements including the TBT and SPS Agreements, and of settling disputes. As above, establishing a comprehensive environmental agreement at the same level as the TBT and SPS Agreements and inserting environmental measures into exceptions of Article XX of GATT will, at least, at the same level as the current protection of human beings, animals and plants health, meet the problems of the legitimacy and block the chance of abuse of trade measures in pursuit of environmental protection with balance.

Another appropriateness of this proposal is that it will relieve the disapproval against establishing new environmental provisions at the WTO, especially that of developing countries. Considering the fact that the SPS Agreement has been established and enforced without any fatal problems, even though developing countries expressed their complaints during the SPS Agreement negotiations of the Uruguay Round, developing countries do not have to worry about the newly established agreements and provisions which are quite similar to the SPS Agreement in their purpose and the level of contents. Export-oriented developing countries will be the most benefited by concluding this kind of agreement. Customers in developed countries will make demands on regulations that will force developing countries to lose trade when their relaxed environmental standards do not meet the requirements of the developed countries.

In conclusion, the approaches above are attractive to both developed countries and developing ones. For developed countries, legitimacy and predictability can be improved in applying these measures. For developing countries, which have chronically worried about abusing trade measures related to environment, the Trade-Related Agreement on Environment can function as a safety valve to block the chance of abuse.

To allow more widely the usage of trade measures aiming at environmental protection through the amendment and creation of the WTO provisions, consensus and mutual agreement among Members should, first of all, be brought to the table based on learning from the experience of Uruguay Round negotiations. In order to achieve this goal, the participation of all Members of the WTO including developing countries is necessary, and financial and technical support for nations which do not have sufficient capacities to deal with environmental affairs should be considered.

13.2 Trade and Anti-competitive Practices

13.2.1 Anti-competitive Practices as Trade Barriers

An important goal of international trade organizations like the World Trade Organization (the WTO) is to remove trade barriers among frontiers in order to secure fair and free opportunities of competition for the Member countries. However, unfair and anti-competitive practices by private firms in the domestic markets can be manipulated to provide a further means of protection in addition to trade barriers at the frontiers. As the major frontier barriers to international trade among the

Member countries have been reduced through multilateral negotiations under the GATT/WTO system there has been an increasing world-wide interest in other types of anti-competitive practices.

Many approaches have been made bilaterally, plurilaterally and multilaterally to regulate and eliminate unfair and anti-competitive practices as trade barriers. Herewith, trade barrier means any kind of entry barrier to an importing countries' domestic market which impedes the complete national treatment. One approach is to harmonize the conflicts between the trade policies and the competition policies, which have recently received rising interest worldwide.[503]

Entry barriers to the domestic market of importing countries are primarily the matter of competition policy which is under the control of domestic competition authorities. However, it can also be understood to be a matter of trade policy from the viewpoint of the exporting countries' trade authorities. In principle, the basic purpose of trade policies and competition policies is the same, that is, the improvement of economic efficiency and the consumer's welfare-level.[504] Thus two policies share the common objectives through non-discriminatory, transparent, rules-based regimes.

However, in the course of the enforcement of the two policies, conflicts can occur when different policies with conflicting priorities are imposed.[505] Traditional discussions have focused on evaluating the effect of trade policy on domestic competition policy. As the trade barriers among major countries have been substantially removed, international trade institutes such as the WTO and Organization for Economic Cooperation and Development (OECD) have recently been concentrating on the effect of domestic competition policy on trade policy.[506]

The main purpose of the international discussions on the effect of competition policy on international trade[507] is to reduce the disparity between individual countries' markets, and to secure a fair and free domestic market structure for

[503] Over the last half-century, the Members of the GATT/ WTO have accomplished much in the way of trade liberalization; however, they have not changed the relationship between trade laws and competition laws in a global economy (Stewart 1999, p. 736).

[504] Kennedy (2001, p. 585).

[505] The different objectives of the trade laws and the competition laws in the United States, for example, have been indicated: "While the antitrust laws are intended to protect competition and, thereby, consumers, the trade laws are intended to protect and enhance the positions of U.S. competitors whether in the U.S. market or in foreign markets" Barringer (1998, p. 462); "Some market access problems are specific to particular competitors, and others reflect more general distortions of competition. Competition law can address the latter group, but remembering that it 'prefects competition, not competitors' it may not always be an appropriate vehicle" (Wood 1995, cited by *id.*, at 462. n. 17).

[506] Young (2001, p. 756).

[507] As now, it might be difficult to ascertain whether in fact anti-competitive business practices have to any significant extent replaced formal barriers to trade as impediments to market access. Indeed, there is no mechanism for even beginning to explore this question much less resolving the problem if such practices actually have a significant impact on trade (Barringer 1998, *supra* note 714, at 477).

access to the domestic market under the precondition that the trade barriers between the frontiers should be eliminated completely.[508] In the absence of effective competition law to regulate private anti-competitive practices[509] in the domestic markets, the gains from liberalized trade may be undermined, and conversely, the absence of trade and investment liberalization defers or prevents access to pro-competitive foreign goods.

It is unrealistic to treat international trade policies and competition policies separately, and indeed, there are many examples of how these two policy issues intersect, overlap, or are affected reciprocally.[510] Thus, anti-competitive practices have been highlighted as one kind of trade barrier is, which could, if not regulated appropriately, interrupt access to the domestic market of imported goods for foreign exporters.[511]

13.2.2 International Efforts to Regulate Anti-competitive Practices

Since the international attempt to establish international rule to regulate restrictive business practices[512] through the Havana Charter for the International Trade Organization[513] in 1948 failed, efforts have been made in vain to create an international

[508] In connection with an agreement on competition policy, the arguments run that harmonization of national anti-trust laws would have at least salutary benefits: "i) a WTO competition policy agreement that harmonized national laws would provide a more predictable legal environment. ii) WTO-centered dispute settlement would reduce duplication of enforcement efforts by national enforcement authorities. iii) harmonization under WTO auspices would avoid conflicting jurisdictional disputes and potential conflicting decisions by national enforcement authorities" (Kennedy 2001, *supra* note 713, at 586).

[509] The best method for removing these private barriers would be through aggressive enforcement of competition laws. Thus, competition policy directed at private anti-competitive practices is a natural complement to a set of international rules regulating government barriers to market access (*id.*, at 587).

[510] OECD, Complementarities between Trade and Competition Policies, COM/TD/DAFFE/CLP (98)98/FINAL, 4–9(1999).

[511] The most visible and well documented instance of a cross border dispute regarding alleged restrictive business practices affecting trade would be the film dispute between the U.S. and Japan [Section 304 Determinations: Barriers to Access to the Japanese Market for Consumer Photographic Film and Paper, 61 Fed. Reg. 30, 929 (June 18, 1996)] (Barringer 1998, *supra* note 714, at 460).

[512] In an era of globalizing national economies, international enterprises could operate in "a twilight zone" or "no man's land" without being affected by national competition causes. In such situations, extraterritorial application of national competition laws might be attempted, which, however, is often ineffective and creates conflicts among nations. That is part of the background for international cooperation in the competition policy being called for among the national authorities (Matsushita 1999, p. 250).

[513] Jackson et al. (1995, *supra* note 675, at 1092–1094).

consensus on the regulation of anti-competitive business practices.[514] Hereafter, discussions are made on how international trade-related institutes have attempted to harmonize the individual countries' competition policies for establishing common regulation rule.

First, there has been the International Trade Organization's (ITO) plan to regulate restrictive business practices.[515] The ITO suggested regulations would have forced Members to prevent business practices hampering international trade which restrained competition, limited access to markets or fostered monopolistic control, whichever were harmful to the expansion of production or trade.[516] The ITO charter would have also made provision for consultation procedures for cases where Member countries permitted a restrictive business practice, and it also would have stipulated procedures for the ITO to investigate complaints raised by one party.[517]

Even though the ITO provisions were not written into the General Agreement,[518] efforts to conclude an agreement on restrictive business practices have continuously appeared.[519] However, they concluded that it would have been unrealistic to draw up a multilateral agreement to control international restrictive business practices,

[514] The alleged facts and related business practices at issue in the film dispute between the U.S. and Japan and the underlying disagreements as to the competitive effects of practices alleged, are assessed to raise serious doubts about the ability of the world trading community to harmonize competition policy rules among countries (Barringer 1998, *supra* note 714, at 460–461).

[515] Jackson et al. (1995, *supra* note 675, at 1092).

[516] ITO Charter, Art. 46(1), The kinds of practices that would have been subject to ITO investigation were: "fixing prices, terms or conditions ...; excluding enterprises from, or allocating or dividing, any territorial market ... or allocating customers, or fixing sales quotas ...; discriminating against particular enterprises; limiting production or fixing production quotas; preventing by agreement the development or application of technology or invention ...; and extending the use of intellectual property rights to matters which are not within the scope of such grants, ..." *id.*, Art. 46 (3), cited by Jackson et al. (1995, *supra* note 675 at 1092).

[517] *Id.*, Arts. 47–48, cited by *id.*

[518] However, there are those that view some GATT provisions as bearing directly or indirectly, on business practices. See, for example, OECD, Competition Elements in International Trade Agreements: A Post-Uruguay Round Overview of WTO Agreements. COM/TD/DAFFE/CLP (98)26/FINAL, 5–12(1999). Jackson (2000, p. 240).

[519] There have been discussions about a WTO Agreement on Competition designed to deal with market access problems caused by anti-competitive practices. So far, it has been suggested that a WTO Agreement on Competition could be limited to a Ministerial Declaration to facilitate the application of Art. XXIII: 1(b) "Private anticompetitive practices can nullify and impair concession. The failure of a member to apply its national competition law to a private anticompetitive practice that has the effect of nullifying or impairing a concession is a valid basis for complaint under Art. XXIII: 1(b). Such a failure will be construed as an 'application' of a measure, as called for by Art. XXIII: 1(b)." Hindly, Competition Law and the WTO: Alternative Structures for Agreement in Fair Trade and Harmonization: Prerequisite for Free Trade, cited by Bellis (2000, pp. 365–366).

except for consultations to attempt to resolve allegations of restrictive business practices affecting trade.[520,521] Since the implementation of the WTO mechanism,[522] renewed interest has arisen in this matter[523] and has made it try to treat the relationship between trade and competition policy.[524]

Second, there have been OECD guidelines for multinational enterprises. The OECD guidelines[525] were intended to be recommendations to multinational enterprises operating in Member countries' territories, the observance of which was voluntary and not legally binding.[526] Since the guidelines were suggested in 1976, several attempts to establish international rules to regulate the anti-competitive practices have not yet been realized.[527] However, OECD Member

[520] The Decision of the Contracting Parties on Restrictive Business Practices, 1960 O.J.(L1015). That was the only effort of the GATT to address cartels and their effect on trade prior to the establishment of the working group in 1996 to treat with trade and competition policy (Barringer 1998, *supra* note 714, at 463, n. 22).

[521] Under the 1960 GATT decision on restrictive business practices, in the 1996 Japan-Film case the United States requested consultations with Japan, but failed (Southwick 2000, p. 964).

[522] Even though the WTO mechanism moves the GATT system from a soft law to a hard law, there are important gaps in the WTO rule system. One of the gaps is the absence of minimum rules on the maintenance of competitive domestic markets. (Underlining has been added by the author.) (Abbott 1999, p. 185).

[523] Bellis (2002, *supra* note 728, at 361).

[524] Ministerial Conference in Singapore in 1996 agreed to establish a working group to study issues relating to the interaction between trade and competition policy. WTO/Singapore Ministerial 1996 – Ministerial Declaration, http://www.wto.org/english/thewto_e/minist_e/min96_e/wtodec_e.htm. Accessed Oct. 19, 2012. And Doha Declaration in 2001, instructed working group to focus on clarifying: core principles including transparency, non-discrimination and procedural fairness, and provision on "hardcore" cartels (i.e. cartels that are formally set up); ways of handling voluntary cooperation on competition policy among WTO member governments; support for progressive reinforcement of competition institution in developing countries through capacity building. WTO/Doha declaration, http://www.wto.org/english/tratop_e/dda_e/dohaexplained_e.htm. Accessed Oct. 19, 2012.

[525] OECD, International Investment and Multinational Enterprises [rev. ed. (1979)], as amended, OECD, International Investment and Multinational Enterprises: The 1984 Review of the 1976 Declaration and Decisions, 9 (1984), cited by Jackson et al. (1995, *supra* note 675, at 1094).

[526] According to the 1976 OECD Guidelines on Multinational Enterprises regarding competition practices, enterprises should do as follows: "i) refrain from abusing a dominant position; ii) should not restrict purchasers, … to resell, …; iii) refrain from participating in … strengthening the restrictive effects… cartels or restrictive agreements which are competition – restrictive…; and iv) be ready to consult and co-operate with competent authorities of countries concerned." cited by *id.*

[527] There has continuously been a series of Council Recommendations, Committee Reports and Working Party reports addressing issues of competition policy as it affects trade since 1976.

countries have recently become interested in the international regulation of these practices.[528]

Third, there were efforts by the United Nations to regulate restrictive business practices.

After UNCTAD extended initial consideration to the matter of restrictive business practices in the 1970s, in 1980, the United Nation Conference on Restrictive Business Practices adopted a code of conduct,[529] which is generally accepted as being the most detailed international agreement on the issue. According to the code, independent enterprises should refrain from certain practices which limit market access or otherwise unduly restrain competition[530] and refrain from abusing their dominant economic position through certain practices.[531] However, the code does not seem to have had much effect to date compared with the other attempts made by the UN to regulate business behavior.[532]

Fourth, a draft of the international antitrust code was put forward.[533] A group composed mainly of antitrust experts, and scholars from Germany, the United States, Japan, Switzerland and Poland proposed the Draft International Antitrust Code[534] in 1993. The draft code required a minimum standard for national antitrust

---

[528] See the various documents issued by the Joint Group on Trade and Competition such as Complementary between Trade and Competition Policies COM/TD/DAFFE/CLP(98)98/FINAL (1999).

[529] Set of Multilaterally Agreed Equitable Principles and Rules (herein after Principles and Rules), U.N.Doc. TD/RBP/10(1980), cited by Jackson et al. (1995, *supra* note 675, at 1095).

[530] Such practices included: "i) agreements fixing prices; ii) collusive tendering; iii) market or customer allocation arrangements; iv) sales and production allocation; v) collective action to enforce arrangements; vi) concerted refusal of supplies to potential importers; and vii) collective denial of access to an arrangement or association." Principles and Rules, *id.*, D.3. cited by Jackson et al. (1995, *supra* note 675, at 1095–1096).

[531] Such acts included: " i) predatory behavior towards competitors; ii) discriminatory pricing or terms or conditions . . .; iii) mergers, takeovers, joint ventures . . .; iv) fixing the reselling prices in importing countries; v) restrictions on the importation ; and vi) when not for ensuring the achievement of legitimate business purpose: i) partial or complete refusals to deal; ii) making the supply . . . dependent upon the acceptance of unfair terms; iii) imposing restrictions; iv) making the supply . . . dependent upon the tied purchase." Principles and Rules, *id.*, at D. 4, *cited by* Jackson et al. (1995, *supra* note 675, at 1096).

[532] *Id.*, at 1097.

[533] This draft was different from the above three attempts in character from the viewpoint that the draft was not the multilateral type but the plurilateral one. This is not as comprehensive as a multilateral arrangement currently, however, plurilateral arrangement might be more feasible than a multilateral agreement in the competition law area (Matsushita 1999, *supra* note 721, at 249, 250–251).

[534] The "Draft International Antitrust Code as a GATT-MTO-Plurilateral Trade Agreement" and accompanying commentary were reprinted in BNA Antitrust & Trade Reg. Reb., vol. 64, no. 1628 (August 19, 1993). See Petersmann (Dec. 1993, p. 35, cited by Jackson et al. 1995, *supra* note 675, at 1097).

laws.[535] The draft code divided 'business restraints' into two groups: horizontal and vertical.[536]

It also made provisions for the control of abuse of a dominant position which adversely affects competition in any market.[537] The International Antitrust Authority was scheduled to be established to implement the code.[538] An International Antitrust Panel was also to be created and to be operated like the GATT dispute settlement panel.[539] The code would seem to be too specific, however, if it is developed into international rules to regulate the anti-competitive practices in the future, it will be more effective than past proposals.[540,541]

While those multilateral or plurilateral attempts have been failed,[542] the problem of the anti-competitive practices has been raised in recent years in another GATT/WTO contexts[543]. There has also been general consensus that the interface between

[535] The Draft stipulated four principles: "i) establishment of national laws to solve international competition problems; ii) national treatment; iii) establishment of minimum standards for antitrust rules and; iv) establishment of an international authority to settle disputes over antitrust issues." cited by Jackson et al. (1995, *supra* note 675, at 1097).

[536] Regarding the shapes of the horizontal and vertical restricts, see the Draft, Arts. 4–5. Cited by *id.*, at 1097–1098

[537] These include: limiting production, markets or technical development to the prejudice of consumers, applying dissimilar conditions which place other trading parties at a competitive disadvantage and making the conclusion of contracts subject to acceptance of supplementary obligations. Draft, Art. 14. cited by *id.*, at 1099

[538] *Id.*

[539] *Id.*, at 1097–1100.

[540] Besides the above multilateral and plurilateral attempts, there have been bilateral attempts to regulate anti-competitive practices. There are a number of bilateral agreements on competition policy, which, currently, may be only possible form of agreement (Matsushita 1999, *supra* note 721, at 251).

[541] Work by the OECD's Joint Group on Trade and Competition has identified five international options to improve the coherence between trade and competition policies: enhanced voluntary convergence; enhanced bilateral co-operation between competition authorities; regional agreements containing competition policy provision; plurilateral competition policy agreements; and multilateral competition policy agreement. OECD, International Options to Improve the Coherence between Trade and Competition Policies, COM/TD/DAFFE/CLP(99)102/FINAL,2(2000).

[542] According to the record to date on reaching agreements restricting anti-competitive practices and market structures, for example, in Japan, using GATT/WTO mechanisms has been completely unsuccessful: besides the film case (see *supra* note 10), the EC raised in 1983 a complaint under Art. XXIII : I(c) of the GATT alleging that the "difficulty of penetrating the Japanese market" resulted from keiretsu structures, lost distribution systems, restrictive regulations for the introduction of new products or prices, and "less visible barriers, but failed" (Southwick 2000, *supra* note 730, at 963–964).

[543] At least, three WTO agreements speak directly to the issue of restrictive business practices: "i) Art. 9 of the Agreement on Trade-Related Investment Measures (TRIMs Agreement) directs . . . to consider whether the TRIMs Agreement should be complemented with provisions on investment and competition policy; ii) Arts. 8, 31 and 40 of the Agreement on the Trade-Related Aspects of Intellectual Property Rights (TRIPS Agreement) address issues of anticompetitive practices . . .;

trade and competition policies has become more important due to the ongoing process of economic globalization.[544,545] Besides the international attempts to treat with this matter,[546] many developed countries have regulated various kinds of anti-competitive practices through the expansion and application of the concept of "fair trade" provided in international or individual domestic trade laws, along with the extraterritorial application of their domestic competition laws.[547]

For example, according to Section 301(d) of the Trade Act of 1974,[548,549] toleration by the government of systematic anti-competitive activities by/among private firms that have the effect of restricting access of the imported goods to the domestic market may be regarded as 'unreasonable' acts.[550] The concept of reasonable or fair trade practice, which exceeds the scope of the tariff or non-tariff

iii) Arts. VIII and IX of the General Agreement on Trade in Services (GATS) prohibit monopoly service suppliers from discriminating . . . and obligate WTO Members to enter into consultations . . . on restrictive business practices of service suppliers" (Kennedy 2001, *supra* note 713, at 602–603).

[544] OECD, International Options to Improve the Coherence between Trade and Competition Policies, COM/DAFFE/CLP(99)102/FINAL,2(2000).

[545] Besides the economic globalization, this consensus was triggered by other factors, such as trends toward regional integration, the rebirth of capitalism in Eastern Europe, the Latin American economic reforms, the creation of WTO, the new legal instruments for dealing with regulatory reform in open economics, and the growing number of competition case involving more than one country (Kennedy 2001, *supra* note 713, at 587).

[546] Trade disputes on the anti-competitive practices might in theory be resolved under a non-violation nullification or impairment action in the WTO Dispute Settlement Understanding, however, the lack of clarity of the WTO System in applying the non-violation rules makes such solutions problematic on all sides (Abbott 1999, *supra* note 731, at 185).

[547] For the cases relating to extraterritorial enforcement of the U.S. Antitrust Laws, see Jackson et al. (1995, *supra* note 675, at 1078–1089).

[548] 19 U.S.C.A §2411(d) Section 301 gives the United States President a broad authority to take all appropriate steps within his power to obtain the elimination of a transgression, if he determines that a foreign country has committed any one of several transgressions: " i) maintaining unjustifiable or unreasonable trade barriers. . .; ii) imposing discriminatory or other unjustifiable or unreasonable burdens or restrictions . . .; iii) granting export subsidies . . .; iv) imposing unjustifiable or unreasonable restrictions" (Swan 1990, p. 48).

[549] The aggressive resent-oriented approach under Section 301 of the Trade Act of 1974 was evaluated to be in sharp contrast to the cautious approach of cooperation, consensus building and the development of procedural mechanisms to address cross border competition issues advocated by the official U.S. policy (Barringer 1998, *supra* note 714, at 460).

[550] Folsom and Gordon (1996, p. 536).

barriers at the frontiers has become the widely and strictly accepted basis of securing fair competition in the domestic market for foreign companies.[551]

Assignment

To ensure students become equipped with the capability to apply knowledge from the classroom to the field, students are, in this chapter, required to write a report, deliver a presentation and participate in a discussion on the following issues:

1. The conflicts and harmonization between free trade promotion and environmental protection focusing on the sanitary and phytosanitary measures under the WTO mechanism.

References

Additional Procedure Adopted Under Rule 16 (1) of the Working Procedures for Appellate Review. Nov. 8, 2000. WT/DS135/9.

Biographical Notes on Members of World Trade Organization Appeals Body, Daily Rep. For Executives (BNA) No. 230, 1995.

Departments of Commerce, Justice, and State, the Judiciary, and Related Agencies Appropriations Act of 1990. Pub. L. 101–162, Title VI, §609, Nov. 21, 1989, 103, Stat. 1037 (codified at 16 U.S.C. 1037).

Department of Commerce, Justice and State, the Judiciary, and Related Agencies Appropriations Act, 1990, Pub. L. No. 101–162, 103 Stat. 988 (1989) (codified at 16 U.S.C. § 1537 (1994)).

OECD, Complementarities between Trade and Competition Policies, COM/TD/DAFFE/CLP(98) 98/FINAL, 4–9(1999).

OECD, International Options to Improve the Coherence between Trade and Competition Policies, COM/DAFFE/CLP(99)102/FINAL, 2000.

United Nations, Vienna Convention on the Law of the Treaties. May 23, 1969, Vienna Convention on the Law of Treaties, 1155 U.N.T.S. 331, 340 (1969).

WTO Secretariat, Report on the WTO's high-level symposium on trade and development, International Institute for Sustainable Development, (Mar. 17–18, 1999).

WTO, Decision on Trade and Environment. Apr. 15, 1994. Legal Instruments – Results of the Uruguay Round, Ministerial Decisions, 33 I.L.M. 1267.

WTO Secretariat. Matrix on Trade Measures Pursuant to Selected MEAs. WT/CTE/W/160/Rev.2, TN/TE/S/5. Among the trade-related MEAs, there are Montreal Protocol on Substances that Deplete the Ozon Layer. Sept. 16, 1987. 1522 U.N.T.S. 3. (Apr. 25, 2003).

WTO, Understanding on Rules and Procedures Governing the Settlement of Disputes, Apr. 15, 1994, Marrakesh Agreement Establishing the World Trade Organization, Annex 2. Legal Instruments-Results of the Uruguay Round. 33 I.L.M. 1125 (1994).

[551] Possible options for solving cases involving such anti-competitive practices, for example, in the United States are: "i) proceed under Section 301; ii) bring an anti-trust action in a United States court . . .; iii) seek dispute resolution procedures under WTO; or iv) urge "positive comity" on the foreign enforcement agencies. . . to fully enforce their competition cases . . ." (Ehrenhaft and Holdo Sept. 1995). (file-Lex).

WTO Committee on Trade and Environment, Clarification of the Relationship between the WTO and Multilateral Environmental Agreements, WT/CTE/W/168 (Oct. 19, 2000).
WTO Committee on Trade and Environment, The Relationship Between the Provisions of the Multilateral Trading System and Multilateral Environmental Agreements (MEAs), WT/CTE/W/139. (June 8, 2000).
WTO Committee on Trade and Environment, Resolving the Relationship between WTO Rules and Multilateral Environmental Agreement, WT/CTE/W/170 (Oct. 19, 2000).
WTO CTE. Oct. 19, 2000. Clarification of the Relationship between the WTO and Multilateral Environmental Agreements, submission by Switzerland, WTO Doc. WT/CTE/W/168; WTO CTE. June 12, 1996.
WTO CTE. May 30, 1996. The Relationship between Trade Measures Pursuant to MEAs and the WTO Agreement, Proposal by Japan. WTO Doc. WT/CTE/W/31; and WTO CTE. Feb. 19, 1996.
WTO CTE. June 25, 1999. Communication from the Secretariat for the Vienna Convention and the Montreal Protocol, UNCEP, WTO Doc. WT/CTE/W/115; WTO CTE. Feb. 19, 1996.
WTO CTE. June 25, 1999. Communication from the Secretariat for the Vienna Convention and the Montreal Protocol, UNEP, WTO Doc. WT/CTE/W/115.
World Trade Organization, trading into the future 46 (2nd ed. Mar. 2001). http://www.wto.org/english/res_e/doload_e/tif.pdf, Accessed 24 Feb. 2012, *cited by* Thomas, *supra* note 255.

Book

Esty DC (1993) Greeting the GATT: trade, environment and the future. Oxford University Press
Folsom RH, Gordon MW (1996) International business transactions. University of California Publishing
Howse R, Tuerk E (2001) The EU and the WTO: legal and constitutional issues. Hart Publishing
Jackson JH (June 1969) World trade and the law of GATT. Lexis Law Pub
Jackson JH (2000) The world trading system 240
Jackson JH, Davey WJ, Sykes Jr. AO (1995) Legal problem of international economic relations: cases, materials and text, 3rd edn. West Publishing
Trebilcock MJ, Howse R (1999) The regulation of international trade, 2nd edn. Routledge
Walker SL (1993) Environmental protection versus trade liberalization, finding the balance: an examination of the legality of environmental regulation under international trade law regimes. Faculties Universitaires Saint-Louis

Article

Abbott FM (1999) Prevention and settlement of economic disputes between Japan and the United States. Arizona J Int'l Comparative Law 16
Abbott FM (2000) Report: TRIPs in Seattle: the not-so-surprising failure and the future of the TRIPs agenda. Berkeley J Int'l Law 18
Ala'i P (1999) Free trade or sustainable development? An analysis of the WTO appellate body's shift to a more balanced approach to trade liberalizations. American University Int'l Law Rev 14
Albren B (1996) The continued need for a narrowly-tailored, rule-based dispute resolution mechanism in future free trade agreement. Suffolk Transnat'l Law J 20
Anderson B (1993) Unilateral trade measures and environmental protection policy. Temple Law Rev 66
Baker B (1993) Protection, not protectionism: multilateral environmental agreements and the GATT. Vanderbilt J Transnat'l Law 26

Barringer WH (1998) Competition policy and cross border dispute resolution: lessons learned from the U.S. – JAPAN film dispute. George Mason Law Rev 6
Bellis J-F (2000) Anti-competitive practices and the WTO: the elusive search for new world trade rules. New Directions Int'l Economic Law
Bhala R, Gantz DA (2002) WTO case review 2001. Arizona J Int'l and Comparative Law 19
Blackmore DT (2004) Eradicating the long standing existence of a no-precedent rule in international trade law-looking toward stare decisions in WTO dispute settlement. North Carolina J Int'l Law Commercial Regulation 29
Bree A (1998) The environmental exception after the shrimp/turtle appellate body report. Dick J Int'l Law 17
Calderin CA (2002) The emergence of a responsible green World Trade Organization: why creating a world environment organization would hinder this goal. U. C. Davis J Int'l Law Policy 8
Carmody C (1997) Of substantial interest: third parties under GATT. Michigan J Int'l Law 18
Chang HF (2005) Environmental trade measures, the shrimp-turtle rulings, and the ordinary meaning of the text of the GATT. Chap Law Rev 8
Charnovitz S (1993) The environment vs. trade rules: defogging the debate. Environmental Law 23
Charnovitz (1994) The North American free trade agreement. Law Pol'y Int'l Bus 26
Charnovitz S (2000) The supervision of health and biosafety regulation by world trade rules. Tulane Environ Law J 13
Charnovitz (2002) The law of environmental "PPMs" in the WTO: debunking the myth of illegality. Yale J Int'l Law 27
Cheyne I (1992) Environmental treaties and the GATT. Rev European Community Int'l Environ Law 1
Cho S (2005) Linkage of free trade and social regulation: moving beyond the entropic dilemma. Chicago J Int'l Law 5
Choinski AS (2002) Symposium, anatomy of a controversy: the balance of political forces behind implementation of the WTO's gasoline decision. Law Policy Int'l Bus 33
Chua ATL (1998) Precedent and principles of WTO panel jurisprudence. Berkeley J Int'l Law 16
Clough CM (2000) The WTO dispute settlement system-a practitioner perspective. Fordham Int'l Law J 24
Cone SM (2003) The environment and the World Trade Organization. New York Law School J Int'l Comparative Law 22
Dailey V (2000) Sustainable development: reevaluating the trade vs. turtles conflict at the WTO. J Transnat'l Law Policy 9
Ehrenhaft PE, Holdo A (1995) Corporate Counsel committee briefing on international antitrust and U.S.–Japan relations. The American Soc Int'l Law Newsletter
Emslie JJ (2005) Labeling programs as a reasonably available least restrictive trade measure under Article XX's nexus requirement. Brok J Int'l Law 30
Ferris Jr. RJ, Zhang H (2002) The challenges of reforming an environmental legal culture: assessing the status quo and looking at post-WTO admission challenges for the People's Republic of China. Georgetown Int'l Environ Law Rev 14
Foster ME (1997–98) Trade and environment: making room for environmental trade measures within the GATT. Southern California Law Rev 71
Gaines S (2001) The WTO's reading of the GATT Article XX chapeau: a disguised restriction on environmental measures. University of Pennsylvania J Int'l Economic Law 22
Howse R (2002) The appellate body rulings in the shrimp/turtle case: a new legal baseline for the trade and environment debate. Columbia J Environ Law 27
Howse R, Regan D (2000) The product/process distinction-an illusory basis for disciplining 'Unilateralism' in trade policy. European J Int'l Law 11
Hudec RE (1998) GATT/WTO constraints on national regulation: requiem for an "Aim and Effects" test. Int'l Law 32

Hudnall S (1996) Towards a greener international trade system: multilateral environmental agreements and the World Trade Organization. Columbia J Law Social Problems 29
Hunter et al. (1996) International environmental law and policy
Jackson JH (1992) Symposium, environmental quality and free trade: interdependent goals or world trade rules and environmental policies: congruence or conflict. Washington and Lee Law Rev 49
Kelley CR (2006) Power, linkage and accommodation: the WTO as an international actor and its influence on other actors and regimes. Berkeley J Int'l Law 24
Kennedy KC (1998) The GATT-WTO system at fifty. Wisconsin Int'l Law J 16
Kennedy KC (2001) Global trade issues in the new millennium: foreign direct investment and competition policy at World Trade Organization. George Washington Int'l Law Rev 33
Knox JH (2004) The judicial resolution of conflicts between trade and the environment. Harvard Environ Law Rev 28
Leebron D (1995) An overview of the Uruguay round results. Columbia J Transnat'l Law 34
Matsushita M (1999) Prevention and settlement of economic disputes between Japan and the United States. Arizona J Int'l Comparative Law 16
Mattice AL (2004) The fisheries subsidies negotiations in the World Trade Organization: a "Win-Win-Win" for trade, the environment and sustainable development. Golden Gate University Law Rev 34
McDonald J (1993) Greening the GATT: harmonizing free trade and environmental protection in the new world order. Environ Law 23
Meier M (1997) GATT, WTO, and the environment: to what extent do GATT/WTO rules permit member nations to protect the environment when doing so adversely affects trade? Colorado J Int'l Environ Law Policy 8
Mungkalarungsi T (2002) The Trade and environment debate. Tulane J Int'l Comparative Law 10
Ni K-J (2004) Redefinition and elaboration of an obligation to pursue international negotiations for solving global environmental problems in light of the WTO shrimp/turtle compliance adjudication between Malaysia and the United States. Minnesota J Global Trade 14
Nissen JL (1997) Achieving a balance between trade and the environment: the need to amend the WTO/GATT to include multilateral environmental agreement. Law Policy Int'l Bus 28
Oxley A (Feb. 2002) Implications of the decisions in the WTO shrimp turtle dispute. Int'l Trade Strategies Ltd.
Pauwelyn J (2003) The limits of litigation: "Americanization" and negotiation in the settlement of WTO Dispute. Ohio Saint J Dispute Resolution 19
Perez O (2005) Multiple regimes, issue linkage, and international cooperation: exploring the role of the WTO. University of Pennsylvania J Int'l Economic Law 26
Petersmann E-U (1993) International trade law and international environment law: prevention and settlement of international environmental disputes in GATT. J World Trade 27
Petersmann E-U (Dec. 1993) International competition rules for the GATT-MTO world trade and legal system. J World Trade 27
Philip Bentley QC (2000) A re-assessment of Article XX, paragraphs (B) and (G) of GATT 1994 in the light of growing consumer and environmental concern about biotechnology. Fordham Int'l Law J 24
Porges A (2003) Settling WTO disputes: what do litigation models tell us? Ohio Saint J Dispute Resolution 19
Reif TM, Eckert J (2004) Courage you can't understand: how to achieve the right balance between shaping and policing commerce in disputes before the World Trade Organization. Columbia J Transnat'l Law 42
Reitz C (1996) Enforcement of the General Agreement on Tariffs and Trade. University of Pennsylvania J Int'l Economic Law 17
Rietvelt M (2005) Multilateral failure: a comprehensive analysis of the shrimp/turtle decision. Indiana Int'l Comparative Law Rev 15

Rogers JW, Whitlock JP (2002) Is section 337 consistent with the GATT and the TRIPs agreement? American University Int'l Law Rev 17
Shaffer GC (2001) The World Trade Organization under challenge: democracy and the law and politics of the WTO's treatment of trade and environment matters. Harvard Environ Law Rev 25
Shaw S, Schwartz R (2002) Trade and environment in the WTO: state of play. J World Trade 36
Snape WJ, Lefkovitz NB (1994) Greening the GATT: setting the agenda/greening the GATT within the existing framework – Searching for GATT's environmental Miranda: are "Process Standards" getting "Due Process?" Cornell Int'l Law J 27
Specht D (1998) The dispute settlement systems of WTO and NAFTA-analysis and comparison. Georgia J Int'l Comparative Law 27
Stewart TP (1999) U.S.–JAPAN economic disputes: the role of antidumping and countervailing duty laws. Arizona J Int'l Comparative Law 16
Stewart TP, Johanson DS (2003) A nexus of trade and the environment: the relationship between the Cartagena Protocol on biosafety and the SPS agreement of the World Trade Organization. Colorado J Int'l Environ Law Policy 14
Southwick JD (2000) Operation of the WTO agreements in the context of global commerce and competition. Investment and Labor Market, Law Policy Int'l Bus 31
Swan AC (1990) Prevention and settlement of economic disputes between Japan and the United States. Arizona J Int'l Comparative Law 16
Tanaka M (2003) Bridging the GAP between northern NGOS and southern sovereigns in the trade-environment debate: the pursuit of democratic dispute settlements in the WTO under the Rio Principles. Ecology Law Quarterly 30
Thomas C (2002) Trade-related labor and environment agreement? J Int'l Economic Law 5
Trachman JP (1999) The domain of WTO dispute resolution. Harvard Int'l Law J 40
Weinstein MM, Charnovitz S (2001) The greening of the WTO. Foreign Affairs 80
Wood DP (1995) Antitrust: a remedy for trade barriers? The Asian. Law Program, Japan Information Access Project
Young MK (2001) Global trade issues in the new millennium: lessons from the battle fronts: U.S. – Japan trade wars and their impact on the multilateral trading system. George Washington Int'l Law Rev 33
Yavitz L (2001–2002) The WTO and the environment: the shrimp case that created a new world order. J Natural Resour Environ Law 16
Yavitz L (2002) The World Trade Organization appellate body report, European communities – measures affecting asbestos asbestos-containing products, WT/DS135/AB/R. Minn J Global Trade 11

WTO Dispute Settlement Report

Panel Report, Thailand-Restrictions on Importation of and Internal Taxes on Cigarettes, (Nov. 7, 1990).
Panel Report, Indonesia-Certain Measures Affecting the Automobiles Industry, WT/DS54/R, WT/DS55/R, WT/DS59/R, WT/DS64/R (July 2, 1998).
Panel Report, United States-Import Prohibition of Certain Shrimp and Shrimp Products, WT/DS58/R. (May 15, 1998).
Panel Report, United States-Standards for Reformulated and Conventional Gasoline, WT/DS2/R (Jan. 29, 1996).
Panel Report, European Communities-Measures Concerning Meat and Meat Products (Hormones), WT/DS26/R/USA (Aug. 18, 1997).
Panel Report, European Communities-Measures Affecting Asbestos-Containing Products, WT/DS135/R (Sep. 18, 2000).
Panel Report, United States-Taxes on Automobiles, DS31/R (Oct. 11, 1994).

Panel Report, United States Measures concerning the Importation, Marketing and Sale of A Tuna and Tuna Products, WT/DS381/R (Sep. 15, 2011).
Panel Report, United States-Import Prohibition of Certain Shrimp and Shrimp Products-Recourse to Article 21.5 of DSU by Malaysia, WT/DS58/RW (June 15, 2001).
Panel Report, Japan-Measures Affecting Agricultural Products, WT/DS76/R. (Oct. 27, 1998).
Panel Report, European Communities-Trade Description of Sardines, WT/DS231/R (May 29, 2002).
Panel Report, United States-Restrictions on Imports of Tuna (EEC), DS29/R (June 16, 1994).
Panel Report, United States-Prohibition of Imports of Tuna and Tuna Products from Canada, GT/DS21/R - 39 S/155 (Sep. 3, 1991).
Panel Report, Canada Measures Affecting Exports of Unprocessed Herring and Salmon, L/6268-35 S/98 (Mar. 22, 1988).
Panel Report, Measures affecting meat and meat products (Hormones), WT/DS26, (July 26, 1999)
Panel Report, Canada-Measures Affecting Exports of Unprocessed Herring and Salmon, (Mar. 22, 1988)
Panel Report, United States-Restrictions on Imports of Tuna (Mexico), (Sep. 3, 1991)
Panel Report, United States-Measures Affecting Alcoholic and Malt Beverages, (June 19, 1992)
Appellate Body Report, Appellate Body Report on Korea-Measures Affecting Imports of Fresh, Chilled and Frozen Beef, WT/DS161/AB/R, WT/DS169/AB/R, (Jan. 10, 2001)
Appellate Body Report, India-Patent Protection for Pharmaceutical Chemical Products, WT/DS50/AB/R (Dec. 19, 1997)
Appellate Body Report, United States-Import Prohibition of Certain Shrimp and Shrimp Products, WT/DS58/AB/R (Oct. 12, 1998).
Appellate Body Report, European Communities-Measures Affecting Asbestos and Asbestos-Containing Products, WT/DS135/AB/R (Apr. 5, 2001)
Appellate Body Report, Japan-Measures Affecting Agricultural Products, WT/DS76/AB/R (Feb. 22, 1999).
Appellate Body Report, EC Measures Concerning Meat and Meat Products (Hormones), WT/DS48/AB/R (Jan. 16. 1998).
Appellate Body Report, United States-Standards for Reformulated and Conventional Gasoline, WT/DS2/AB/R (Apr. 29, 1996).
Appellate Body Report, Australia Measures Affecting Importation of Salmon, WT/DS18/AB.R (Oct. 20, 1998).
Appellate Body Report, Japan-Measures Affecting the Importation of Apples, WT/DS245/AB/R (Nov. 26, 2003).
Appellate Body Report, Japan-Taxes on Alcoholic Beverages, WT/DS8/AB/R, WT/DS10/AB/R, WT/DS11/AB/R (Oct. 4, 1996).
Appellate Body Report, Canada-Certain Measures Concerning Periodicals, WT/DS31/AB/R (July 30, 1997).
Appellate Body Report, United States-Import Prohibition of Certain Shrimp and Shrimp Products-Recourse to Article 21.5 of DSU by Malaysia, WT/DS58/AB/RW (Oct. 22, 2001).
Appellate Body Report, European Communities-Trade Description of Sardines, WT/DS231/AB/R, (Sep. 26, 2002).
WTO, European Communities – Regime for the Importation, Sale and Distribution of Bananas – Recourse to Arbitration by the European Communities under Article 22.6 of the DSU, WT/DS27/ARB/ECU (Mar. 24, 2000).

WTO Agreement

WTO, Agreement on Implementation of Article VII of the General Agreement on Tariffs and Trade 1994, Apr. 15, Marrakesh Agreement Establishing the World Trade Organization, Annex 1A, Legal Instruments-Results of the Uruguay Round, 33 I.L.M. 1125 (1994)

WTO, Agreement on Subsidies and Countervailing Measures, Apr. 15, 1994, Marrakesh Agreement Establishing the World Trade Organization, Annex 1A, Legal Instruments-Results of the Uruguay Round, 33 I.L.M. 1125 (1994)

WTO, Agreement on Trade-Related Aspects of Intellectual Property Rights arts. 27.2-27.3 & etc., Apr. 15, 1994, Marrakesh Agreement Establishing the World Trade Organization, Annex 1 C, Legal Instruments-Results of the Uruguay Round, 33 I.L.M. 1125. (1994)

WTO, Agreement on Agriculture, Apr. 15, 1994, Marrakesh Agreement Establishing the World Trade Organization, Annex 1A, Legal Instruments-Results of the Uruguay Round, 33 I.L.M. 1125 (1994).

WTO, Agreement on Technical Barriers to Trade, Apr. 15, 1994, Marrakesh Agreement Establishing the World Trade Organization, Annex 1A, Legal Instruments-Results of the Uruguay Round, 33 I.L.M. 1125 (1994).

WTO, Agreement on the Application of Sanitary and Phytosanitary Measures, Apr. 15, 1994, Marrakesh Agreement Establishing the World Trade Organization, Annex 1A, Legal Instruments-Results of the Uruguay Round, 33 I.L.M. 1125 (1994)

WTO, Agreement on Subsidies and Countervailing Measures, Apr. 15, 1994, Marrakesh Agreement Establishing the World Trade Organization, Annex 1A, Legal Instruments-Results of the Uruguay Round, 33 I.L.M. 1125 (1994).

WTO, General Agreement on Trade in Services, Apr. 15, 1994, Marrakesh Agreement Establishing the World Trade Organization, Annex 1B, Legal Instruments-Results of the Uruguay Round, 33 I.L.M. 1125. (1994)

WTO, Marrakesh Agreement Establishing the World Trade Organization, Apr. 15, 1994, Legal Instruments- Results of the Uruguay Round, I.L.M. 33: 1144 (1994).

Index

E.S. Lee, *World Trade Regulation*,
DOI 10.1007/978-3-642-31143-7, © Springer-Verlag Berlin Heidelberg 2012

MIX
Papier aus verantwortungsvollen Quellen
Paper from responsible sources
FSC® C105338

If you have any concerns about our products,
you can contact us on
ProductSafety@springernature.com

In case Publisher is established outside the EU,
the EU authorized representative is:
Springer Nature Customer Service Center GmbH
Europaplatz 3, 69115 Heidelberg, Germany

Printed by Libri Plureos GmbH
in Hamburg, Germany